READINGS
IN
PSYCHOLOGY:
UNDERSTANDING
HUMAN
BEHAVIOR

READINGS IN PSYCHOLOGY: UNDERSTANDING HUMAN BEHAVIOR

SECOND EDITION

JAMES A. DYAL

Professor of Psychology
Texas Christian University

McGRAW-HILL BOOK COMPANY

New York   St. Louis   San Francisco
Toronto   London   Sydney

READINGS IN PSYCHOLOGY: UNDERSTANDING HUMAN BEHAVIOR

TO MY WIFE
EARLENE
AND TO
JACK AND MARK

PREFACE

To the Professor:

Like most teachers of the introductory course in psychology you have probably occasionally felt that your course would have more impact if the students had access to original papers representative of our psychological literature. Many of you have taken time to survey portions of the literature, obtain reprints of selected articles, and place them on reserve in the library. Even at best you probably found that this procedure was time-consuming and left something to be desired in terms of actual availability of the articles to your students. An alternative approach is to make use of one of the several good anthologies of readings now available. None of these books include all of the selections which you would have chosen had you edited the book. Nevertheless, it is hoped that the scope of the present book is sufficiently broad that you will have little difficulty finding important and readable selections in each chapter.

The basic purpose of this revision of *Readings in Psychology* is essentially the same as that of the first edition: to provide for students of introductory psychology a group of articles which will be representative of the major problems and approaches to the study of behavior. This revision holds to the previously specified objectives of facilitating the teaching of the methods of experimental and clinical psychology, communicating through primary sources some of the basic knowledge which has been derived through the application of these methods and modifying student attitudes regarding the nature of man in general and themselves in particular. Of necessity, the book is broad in scope with regard to both technical content and type of presentation. It reflects a range of philosophical approaches from radical Behaviorism to Existentialism. The articles present points of view which should be relevant to the interests of a variety of undergraduate liberal arts majors, e.g., biology, chemistry, political science, economics, sociology, philosophy, religion, and, of course, psychology.

Biological, psychological and sociocultural factors are presented in each content chapter. It is felt that this approach makes sense to the student and also continually reminds him of the breadth of concern and variety of approaches inherent in contemporary psychology. Although an attempt was made to avoid articles which were primarily applied in nature, a number of articles which indicate how general psychological principles can be applied to everyday behavior have been included.

The three major objectives of the book are to facilitate the teaching of the methods of experimental and clinical psychology, the *communication of knowledge* which has been derived by the use of these methods, and the *modification of student attitudes* regarding the nature of man in general and themselves in particular. The articles also seem to fall into three categories which to some degree correspond to the objectives. About one fourth of the articles consists of *reports of single experiments*. These selections serve to illustrate the methods of psychological experimentation and to communicate certain psychological generalizations. Another fourth of the readings represents *summaries of research programs* of outstanding experimental psychologists. In addition to presenting more information than the single experiments, these articles emphasize the great contributions made by long term experimental programs which extensively explore a particular problem area. Examples of this type of paper are Miller's "Recent Studies of Conflict and Drugs" and Harlow's "The Nature of Love." The remaining half of the book is devoted to *psychological essays or commentaries*. These are primarily designed to introduce the student to characteristic problems of psychology and to state a point of view.

Some of them are theoretical papers which add to the student's knowledge or help him to reorganize knowledge that he already has, e.g., Sargent's "Reaction to Frustration—A Critique and Hypothesis." Many of the readings of this type represent less scientifically developed areas of psychology such as personality dynamics and motivation and serve primarily to modify the student's attitudes regarding the nature of man and himself. Examples of this type of article are Horney's "Culture and Neurosis" and Rogers' "Becoming a Person."

I have been most gratified by the positive reception which was accorded the first edition. I am grateful for the thoughtful comments and ratings of the selections made by colleagues and students from many colleges and universities throughout the country. Although several of these raters suggested that relatively few changes should be made in the revision, I felt that by retaining about half of the articles in the first edition and adding more current material a stronger text could be created. As a result, 45 percent of the selections from the first edition have been dropped and new articles substituted. Furthermore, in order to give the book both greater breadth and depth, twenty additional articles have been added. Half of these form a new chapter entitled "Cogent Commentaries." It is expected that these articles will lend themselves especially well to the stimulation of classroom discussion.

There are, of course, many ways in which a book of readings can profitably enrich the introductory course. I would like to suggest one possible procedure which has worked well for several users of this text. The material in the *basic* textbook is presented during the first 75 to 80 percent of the course. Then the last 20 to 25 percent of the course is concentrated on reading and discussing the readings. Students seemingly derive more from the readings in this way because they are better prepared to read them knowledgeably after covering most of the content of the usual introductory course. This procedure can also be profitably modified by integrating some of the selected readings into the course during the concentration on the basic text.

The bulk of the credit for this book is due to the authors of the articles themselves. The future generations of psychologists who are now in their embryonic stage of development in our courses in Introductory Psychology will do well to emulate their careful experimentations and perceptive interpretations of behavior. The authors and publishers were most generous in granting permission to reproduce their articles. Specific credits are given at the beginning of each selection. It should also be noted that although some of the articles are abridged, the specific points of abridgment are not indicated in order to avoid interference with smooth communication. I am grateful for the secretarial aid provided by Miss Carolyn Castleberry, Miss Frankie Denton and Miss K'lee Hetherington.

JAMES A. DYAL

CONTENTS

Preface, v

Sociocultural Factors

CHAPTER 4   EMOTION AND BEHAVIOR, 109

Biological Factors

Psychological Factors

Sociocultural Factors

CHAPTER 5   FRUSTRATION AND CONFLICT, 137

Biological Factors

Psychological Factors

Sociocultural Factors

CHAPTER 6   PERCEPTION AND BEHAVIOR, 160

Biological Factors

Psychological Factors

Sociocultural Factors

CHAPTER 7 LEARNING AND MEMORY, 190

Biological Factors

Psychological Factors

Sociocultural Factors

CHAPTER 8 THINKING, REASONING, AND PROBLEM SOLVING, 242

Biological Factors

Psychological Factors

Sociocultural Factors

CHAPTER 9 INTELLIGENCE, 266

Biological Factors

Sociocultural Factors

CHAPTER 13 BEHAVIOR DISORDERS, 388

Biological Factors

Psychological Factors

Sociocultural Factors

CHAPTER 14 COGENT COMMENTARIES, 417

HISTORY
AND
METHOD
IN
PSYCHOLOGY

1

At the present time perhaps the most succinct and generally accepted definition of psychology is that it is the "science of behavior." However, this has not always been the case. As recently as 100 years ago psychology was not scientific or very much concerned about behavior. Like all sciences, psychology has emerged from the "mother of knowledge"—philosophy. Philosophers have been concerned about psychological topics for thousands of years, but their basic method of arriving at knowledge has been to "reason out" the answers, an approach known as *rationalism*. The generalizations thus obtained could not be called scientific, since science always involves the addition of controlled observation to the process of reasoning.

One of the primary thrusts toward making psychology into an independent, empirically based science was led by the German psychologist Wilhelm Wundt. In 1874, he published his masterpiece, *Physiological Psychology*, the avowed purpose of which was to "present to the public . . . an attempt to mark out a new domain of science." And in 1879 he established at the University of Leipzig the first formal experimental psychology laboratory. One of Wundt's outstanding pupils was E. B. Titchener, who brought Wundtian psychology to America. During the decades immediately preceding and following 1900, American psychology was completely dominated by the Titchenerian Structuralist school. *Structuralism* held that the task of psychology was to analyze complex states of consciousness into their basic, irreducible elements through the method of introspection (see Selection 1). Thus psychology was conceived of as that science which analyzes mental contents in a manner analogous to the way in which chemistry analyzes physical properties. It is perhaps a tribute to the scholarly productivity of Wundt and the militant dedication of Titchener that three major schools of psychology had their initial impetuses as revolts against Structuralism. These schools are *Functionalism*, *Behaviorism*, and *Gestalt psychology*.

In America the most influential contemporary of Wundt was William James. James was very much opposed to the Structuralist view that psychology should analyze experience into elementary sensation. He viewed consciousness as more analogous to a stream of experience in which the "self" provided continuity and relations among the conscious elements. As a philosopher-psychologist, James was concerned that psychology not be prematurely narrowed to include only those events which could be investigated in an experimental laboratory. The contrast in orientation between Titchener and James is nicely stated by Heidbreder as follows: "Whereas Titchener was intent chiefly on making the new psychology a science, James was more concerned that the new sciences be psychology."[1] James strongly influenced the thinking of another philosopher-psychologist, John Dewey, and together they provided the major intellectual heritage for the Functionalist school. Their philosophy came to be known as Pragmatism, and it greatly influenced their views of the task and method of psychology. The term "pragmatism" itself points up the emphasis of the entire approach. It derives from the Greek word "prágma," meaning action. James's psychology was a psychology of action. He criticized the older rational psychologies for concentrating on the inner faculties of man, such as reasoning and

[1] E. Heidbreder, *Seven Psychologies*, Century Company, New York: 1933, p. 152.

imagining, without considering how these activities are modified by the environment in which the individual exists. The Functionalists conceived of man's mind or states of consciousness as conditioned by his adaptation to his environment. To use James's words, ". . . mental life is primarily teleological"; that is, both mind and body were conceived to be products of evolution, their primary purpose being to aid in man's survival. Thus, we can see the great influence which Charles Darwin's theory of evolution has had on psychology.

James's psychology was influenced not only by the fact that he was a philosophical pragmatist, but also by the fact that he was trained originally as a physician. He proposed that "all mental states . . . are followed by bodily activity of some sort." It was the task of psychology to determine the physiological correlates of mental processes. Thus, in summary, the Functionalist school conceived the subject matter of psychology to be states of consciousness which were modified by man's environment and which served to facilitate his future adaptation. The method of psychology was both introspection and experimentation by an outside observer.

Around 1912 a major revolution took place in psychology with the advent of Behaviorism. This radical position was proposed most vigorously by John B. Watson. He maintained that as long as psychology conceived its subject matter to be states of consciousness which were to be analyzed by the subjective process of introspection, it would never become an objective science. He proposed that psychology should do away with the concept of mind and concentrate on controlled observation of behavior. Internal processes, such as thinking, could not be studied directly by psychology but could only be inferred from responses of the individual, for example, verbal reports. Watsonian Behaviorism sought to establish functional relationships between the stimuli impinging on the organism and the responses made by the organism. He says, "The interest of the behaviorist in man's doings is more than the interest of the spectator—he wants to control man's reactions as physical scientists want to control and manipulate other natural phenomena. It is the business of behavioristic psychology to be able to predict and control human activity. To do this it must gather scientific data by experimental methods. Only then can the trained behaviorist predict, given the stimulus, what reaction will take place; or, given the reaction, state what the stimulation or stimulus is that has caused the reaction."[2] The basic arguments advanced by Watson against the older Structuralist and Functionalist psychologies are presented in Selection 3. In addition, some of the implications of the Behaviorist platform with respect to "societal engineering" are suggested.

It was also in 1912 that the Gestalt rebellion against Wundt's elementism was definitely formulated as a school by three psychologists in Frankfort, Germany. They were Max Wertheimer, Kurt Koffka, and Wolfgang Kohler. They maintained that the Structuralist analysis of experience into sensory elements missed the most important fact of experience, namely, that it was organized into meaningful wholes. Although the Gestaltists preferred to define psychology as the science of behavior, they were disenchanted with the emphasis on molecular behavior which characterized American behaviorism. Furthermore, they were quite willing to use introspection as an observational technique to discover meaningful organization of molar behavior. In Selection 4, Koffka distinguishes between molar and molecular behavior, and then relates molar behavior to both geographic and behavioral environments, to conscious experience, and to underlying physiological processes. This totality is designated as the psychophysical field, and the task of psychology is to understand how molar behavior is determined by this field.

---

[2] John B. Watson, *Behaviorism*, W. W. Norton & Company, Inc., New York, 1924, p. 11

Our conception of the nature of man at mid-twentieth century has been most strongly influenced by two intellectual giants, neither of whom was a psychologist. We have already seen how Charles Darwin's views on adaptation directly influenced the Functionalist school. It should be apparent that his more general influence on man's conception of his own place in nature extends far beyond his direct effect on psychology. Another ubiquitous theme in our contemporary intellectual climate is *psychoanalysis*, a view of man which was formulated and effectively propounded by Sigmund Freud. In Selection 5, Freud discusses his two most important concepts regarding the dynamics of behavior: namely, that the vast bulk of the determinants of our behavior are unconscious and that sexual impulses play an especially important role in motivation and personality dynamics.

The first five readings introduce you to some of the major concepts of five of the major schools of psychology as stated in the writings of their chief proponents. The next three selections discuss several aspects of scientific methodology as it applies to psychology. Selection 6 is taken from a book by Dr. Arthur J. Bachrach in which he presents a more extended discussion of psychological research.[3] Bachrach proposes that the two primary goals of any science are the *understanding* and *control* of its subject matter. In addition, he suggests description and prediction as important subgoals. Description, prediction, and understanding would appear to be attained by *descriptive* sciences such as astronomy and portions of geology, biology, and psychology. The *experimental* sciences such as physics and chemistry and portions of geology, biology, and psychology are able, in addition, to control their subject matter. After stating the goals of science, Bachrach goes on to show how observation becomes refined into experimentation, which leads us to lawful relationships and prediction and control of future events. Since the entire process is dependent on the adequacy with which we can measure our independent and dependent variables, Bachrach concludes with a discussion of some fundamental types of measuring scales.

In his article on "Psychology as a Science" (Selection 7), Professor Gregory A. Kimble points out that, like other sciences, the task of psychology is to establish scientific laws. He notes two general types of laws which are formulated by psychologists: those which state a relationship to exist between two responses, R-R laws, and those which state a stimulus-response relationship, S-R laws. He suggests that the latter laws are preferable in that the conditions under which they are obtained offer the possibility of more precise control of extraneous variables. Although Dr. Kimble's views are definitely in the tradition of Behaviorism, they should be thought of as Neobehavioristic. As we have seen, Watson felt that through complete control of the external stimulus he would be able to perfectly predict the response. Neobehaviorists have liberalized the strict S-R formulation to include the organism as a critical source of variables which influence response. However, since we cannot observe directly the processes within the organism, they must be inferred from the relationships which obtain between stimulus and response. We thus construct ideas or concepts which will help us to explain the observed relationships. These constructs vary considerably in the degree to which they include physiological terms in their definition. Some concepts, such as anger, are inferred from physiological measures and overt responses. Other constructs which are attributed to the organism have little physiological reference, for example, the concept of attitude. But regardless of which of these types of intervening variables we use, their meaning depends on the operations which we perform to demonstrate their effect on behavior. Thus, an

[3] A. J. Bachrach, *Psychological Research: An Introduction*, 2d ed., Random House, Inc., New York, 1965.

operational definition of a construct such as anger is a statement of those observations which are necessary before we will infer that a person is in a state of being angry.

Selections 6 and 7 have emphasized, respectively, the role of observations and the role of constructs and laws in scientific methodology. Selection 8 by Dr. Ray Hyman is concerned with the role of theory in psychological science. The force of the discussion is to demonstrate how psychological concepts ". . . and the systematic context of these concepts—can provide limitations and constraints on acceptable methodology." He examines the procedures of three different psychologists as they attempt to make sense out of their experimental observations. (Remember: understanding as a goal of science.) Hyman distinguishes between formal theory and informal theory as methods of organizing past observations and guiding new observations. The two extreme positions on the formal-informal continuum are represented by the interpretations of Clark Hull and B. F. Skinner, respectively. In the formal procedure Hull formulates a set of behavior postulates (induced in part from previous research) and then makes deductions from these postulates regarding the outcomes of future experiments. Skinner, on the other hand, tries to stay quite empirically oriented without reliance on formal theoretical constructs. He is especially opposed to attempts to interpret behavior on the basis of physiological mechanisms. Hebb occupies a somewhat intermediate position on the formal-informal theory dimension, but both Hull and Skinner make use of physiological concepts in coming to understand behavior. Hebb, on the other hand, is a physiological theorizer who constructs a view of how the central nervous system must function in order to account for certain phenomena of perception, learning, and motivation.

In concluding our overview of these three readings on methodology, perhaps it should be pointed out that each of the three authors represents a particular theoretical bias. Bachrach's paper (Selection 6) may be fairly represented as positively inclined toward Skinner's orientation; Kimble's (Selection 7) views are certainly consistent with the more formal Hullian approach; and Hyman tends to take a somewhat middle-of-the-road view, although he certainly is generally critical of Skinner's radical empiricism. Such differences in approach to theory are probably typical of all sciences, and such diversity within psychology is to be encouraged rather than condemned since it permits us to "cast a broader net" in our search for understanding of human behavior.

As may be seen by a brief glance at the table of contents, each of the subject-matter chapters in this book is organized in such a way that biological, psychological, and sociocultural factors relating to that particular topic are discussed. This organization highlights the fact that psychology is concerned with the determinants of behavior from the biochemical level through the cultural level. The importance of interaction between biological and social sciences for the understanding of human behavior is emphasized in Selection 9 by Marston Bates, a zoologist.

Selection **1** | MIND,
CONSCIOUSNESS
AND THE METHOD
OF PSYCHOLOGY*

EDWARD B. TITCHENER
Cornell University

We have defined mind as the sum-total of human experience considered as dependent upon the experiencing person. We have said, further, that the phrase "experiencing person" means the living body, the organised individual; and we have hinted that, for psychological purposes, the living body may be reduced to the nervous system and its attachments. Mind thus becomes the sum-total of human experience considered as dependent upon a nervous system. And since human experience is always process, occurrence, and the dependent aspect of human experience is its mental aspect, we may say, more shortly, that mind is the sum-total of mental processes. All these words are significant. "Sum-total" implies that we are concerned with the whole world of experience, not with a limited portion of it; "mental" implies that we are concerned with experience under its dependent aspect, as conditioned by a nervous system; and "processes" implies that our subject-matter is a stream, a perpetual flux, and not a collection of unchanging objects.

Consciousness, as reference to any dictionary will show, is a term that has many meanings. Here it is, perhaps, enough to distinguish two principal uses of the word.

In its first sense, consciousness means the mind's awareness of its own processes. Just as, from the common-sense point of view, mind is that inner self which thinks, remembers, chooses, reasons, directs the movements of the body, so is consciousness the inner knowledge of this thought and government. You are conscious of the correctness of your answer to an examination question, of the awkwardness of your movements, of the purity of your motives. Consciousness is thus something more than mind; it is "the perception of what

passes in a man's own mind"; it is "the immediate knowledge which the mind has of its sensations and thoughts."

In its second sense, consciousness is identified with mind, and "conscious" with "mental." So long as mental processes are going on, consciousness is present; as soon as mental processes are in abeyance, unconsciousness sets in.

The first of these definitions we must reject. It is not only unnecessary, but it is also misleading, to speak of consciousness as the mind's awareness of itself. The usage is unnecessary, because, as we shall see later, this awareness is a matter of observation of the same general kind as observation of the external world; it is misleading, because it suggests that mind is a personal being, instead of a stream of processes. We shall therefore take mind and consciousness to mean the same thing. But as we have the two different words, and it is convenient to make some distinction between them, we shall speak of mind when we mean the sum-total of mental processes occurring in the life-time of an individual, and we shall speak of consciousness when we mean the sum-total of mental processes occurring *now*, at any given "present" time. Consciousness will thus be a section, a division, of the mind-stream.

THE METHOD OF PSYCHOLOGY

Scientific method may be summed up in the single word "observation"; the only way to work in science is to observe those phenomena which form the subject-matter of science. And observation implies two things: attention to the phenomena, and record of the phenomena; that is, clear and vivid experience, and an account of the experience in words or formulas.

In order to secure clear experience and accurate report, science has recourse to experiment. An experiment is an observation that can be repeated, isolated and varied. The more frequently you can *repeat* an observation, the more likely are you to see clearly what is there and to describe accurately what you have seen. The more strictly you can *isolate* an observation, the easier does your task of observation become, and the less danger is there of your being led astray by irrelevant circumstances, or

* Abridged from Edward Bradford Tichener, *A Text-book of Psychology,* The Macmillan Company, New York, 1911, pp. 15–20. Reprinted by permission of the Estate of E. B. Titchener.

of placing emphasis on the wrong point. The more widely you can *vary* an observation, the more clearly will the uniformity of experience stand out, and the better is your chance of discovering laws. All experimental appliances, all laboratories and instruments, are provided and devised with this one end in view: that the student shall be able to repeat, isolate and vary his observations.—

The method of psychology, then, is observation. To distinguish it from the observation of physical science, which is inspection, a looking-at, psychological observation has been termed introspection, a looking-within. But this difference of name must not blind us to the essential likeness of the methods.

Selection **2** | THE DEFINITION
OF PSYCHOLOGY*

WILLIAM JAMES
Harvard University

The definition of Psychology may be best given in the words of Professor Ladd, as the *description and explanation of states of consciousness as such.* By states of consciousness are meant such things as sensations, desires, emotions, cognitions, reasonings, decisions, volitions and the like. Their "explanation" must of course include the study of their causes, conditions, and immediate consequences, so far as these can be ascertained.

Psychology is to be treated as a natural science in this book. This requires a word of commentary. Most thinkers have a faith that at bottom there is but one Science of all things, and that until all is known, no one thing can be completely known. Such a science if realized, would be Philosophy. Meanwhile it is far from being realized; and instead of it, we have a lot of beginnings of knowledge made in different places, and kept separate from each other merely for practical convenience' sake, until with later growth they may run into one body of Truth. These provisional beginnings of learning we call "the Sciences" in the plural.

* Abridged from William James, *Psychology*, Henry Holt and Company, Inc., New York, 1892, pp. 1–8. Reprinted by permission of the publisher.

In order not to be unwieldy, every such science has to stick to its own arbitrarily-selected problems, and to ignore all others. Every science thus accepts certain data unquestioningly, leaving it to the other parts of Philosophy to scrutinize their significance and truth. All the natural sciences, for example, in spite of the fact that farther reflection leads to Idealism, assume that a world of matter exists altogether independently of the perceiving mind. Mechanical Science assumes this matter to have "mass" and to exert "force," defining these terms merely phenomenally, and not troubling itself about certain unintelligibilities which they present on nearer reflection. Motion similarly is assumed by mechanical science to exist independently of the mind, in spite of the difficulties involved in the assumption. So Physics assumes atoms, action at a distance, etc., uncritically; Chemistry uncritically adopts all the data of Physics; and Physiology adopts those of Chemistry. Psychology as a natural science deals with things in the same partial and provisional way. In addition to the "material world" with all its determinations, which the other sciences of nature assume, she assumes additional data peculiarly her own, and leaves it to more developed parts of Philosophy to test their ulterior significance and truth. These data are—

1. *Thoughts and feelings*, or whatever other names transitory *states of consciousness* may be known by.
2. *Knowledge*, by these states of consciousness, of other things. These things may be material objects and events, or other states of mind. The material objects may be either near or distant in time and space, and the states of mind may be those of other people, or of the thinker himself at some other time.

All mental states (no matter what their character as regards utility may be) are followed by bodily activity of some sort. They lead to inconspicuous changes in breathing, circulation, general muscular tension, and glandular or other visceral activity, even if they do not lead to conspicuous movements of the muscles of voluntary life. Not only certain particular states of mind, then (such as those called volitions, for example) but states of mind as such, *all* states of mind, even mere thoughts and feelings, are *motor* in their consequences. This will be made manifest in detail as our study advances. Meanwhile let it be set down as one of the fundamental facts of the science with which we are engaged.

It was said above that the "conditions" of states of consciousness must be studied. The immediate condition of a state of consciousness is an activity of some sort in the cerebral hemispheres. This proposition is supported by so many pathological facts, and laid by physiologists at the base of so many of their reasonings, that to the medically educated mind it seems almost axiomatic. It would be hard, however, to give any short and peremptory proof of the unconditional dependence of mental action upon neural change. That a general and usual amount of dependence exists cannot possibly be ignored.

This conception is the "working hypothesis" which underlies all the "physiological psychology" of recent years, and it will be the working hypothesis of this book. Taken thus absolutely, it may possibly be too sweeping a statement of what in reality is only a partial truth. But the only way to make sure of its unsatisfactoriness is to apply it seriously to every possible case that can turn up. To work an hypothesis "for all it is worth" is the real, and often the only, way to prove its insufficiency. I shall therefore assume without scruple at the outset that the uniform correlation of brain-states with mind-states is a law of nature.

Selection **3** | WHAT IS BEHAVIORISM?*

JOHN B. WATSON
Johns Hopkins University

THE OLD AND NEW PSYCHOLOGY CONTRASTED

Before beginning our study of "behaviorism" or "behavioristic" psychology, it will be worth our while to take a few minutes to look at the

* From John B. Watson, *Behaviorism*, 1st ed., W. W. Norton & Company, Inc., New York, 1924, pp. 3–7. Copyright 1924, 1925 by The People's Institute Publishing Company, Inc.; 1930, rev. ed., W. W. Norton & Company, Inc.; 1952, 1953, by John B. Watson. Reprinted by permission of W. W. Norton & Company, Inc., New York.

conventional school of psychology that flourished before the advent of behaviorism in 1912—and that still flourishes. Indeed we should point out at once that behaviorism has not as yet by any means replaced the older psychology—called *introspective psychology*—of James, Wundt, Külpe, Titchener, Angell, Judd, and McDougall. Possibly the easiest way to bring out the contrast between the old psychology and the new is to say that all schools of psychology except that of behaviorism claim that *"consciousness" is the subject matter of psychology.* Behaviorism on the contrary, holds that the subject matter of human psychology is the *behavior or activities of the human being.* Behaviorism claims that "consciousness" is neither a definable nor a usable concept; that it is merely another word for the "soul" of more ancient times. The old psychology is thus dominated by a kind of subtle religious philosophy.

An examination of consciousness

From the time of Wundt on, consciousness becomes the keynote of psychology. It is the keynote of all psychologies today except behaviorism. It is a plain assumption just as unprovable, just as unapproachable, as the old concept of the soul. And to the behaviorist the two terms are essentially identical, so far as concerns their metaphysical implications.

To show how unscientific is the concept, look for a moment at William James' definition of psychology. "Psychology is the description and explanation of states of consciousness as such." Starting with a definition which *assumes* what he starts out to prove, he escapes his difficulty by an *argumentum ad hominem.* Consciousness—Oh, yes, everybody must know what this "consciousness" is. When we have a sensation of red, a perception, a thought, when we *will* to do something, or when we *purpose* to do something, or when we *desire* to do something, we are being *conscious.* All other introspectionists are equally illogical. In other words, they do not tell us what consciousness is, but merely begin to put things into it by assumption; and then when they come to analyze consciousness, naturally they find in it just what they put into it. Consequently, in the analyses of consciousness made by certain of the psychologists you find such elements as *sensations* and their ghosts, the *images*. With others you find not only sensations, but so-called *affective elements;* in still others you find such elements as *will*—the so-called conative element in consciousness. With some psychologists you find many hundreds of sensations of a certain type; others maintain that only a few of that type exist. And so it goes. Literally hundreds of thousands of printed pages have been published on the minute analysis of this intangible something called "consciousness." And how do we begin work upon it? Not by analyzing it as we would a chemical compound, or the way a plant grows. No, those things are material things. This thing we call consciousness can be analyzed only by *introspection*—a looking in on what goes on inside of us.

As a result of this major assumption that there is such a thing as consciousness and that we can analyze it by introspection, we find as many analyses as there are individual psychologists. There is no way of experimentally attacking and solving psychological problems and standardizing methods.

The advent of the behaviorists

In 1912 the behaviorists reached the conclusion that they could no longer be content to work with intangibles and unapproachables. They decided either to give up psychology or else to make it a natural science. They saw their brother-scientists making progress in medicine, in chemistry, in physics. Every new discovery in those fields was of prime importance; every new element isolated in one laboratory could be isolated in some other laboratory; each new element was immediately taken up in the warp and woof of science as a whole. May I call your attention to the wireless, to radium, to insulin, to thyroxin, and hundreds of others? Elements so isolated and methods so formulated immediately began to function in human achievement.

In his first efforts to get uniformity in subject matter and in methods the behaviorist began his own formulation of the problem of psychology by sweeping aside all mediaeval conceptions. He dropped from his scientific vocabulary all subjective terms such as sensa-

tion, perception, image, desire, purpose, and even thinking and emotion as they were subjectively defined.

The behaviorist's platform

The behaviorist asks: Why don't we make what we can *observe* the real field of psychology? Let us limit ourselves to things that can be observed, and formulate laws concerning only those things. Now what can we observe? Well, we can observe *behavior—what the organism does or says.* And let me make this fundamental point at once: that *saying* is doing—that is, *behaving.* Speaking overtly or to ourselves (thinking) is just as objective a type of behavior as baseball.

The rule, or measuring rod, which the behaviorist puts in front of him always is: Can I describe this bit of behavior I see in terms of "stimulus and response"? By stimulus we mean any object in the general environment or any change in the tissues themselves due to the physiological condition of the animal, such as the change we get when we keep an animal from sex activity, when we keep it from feeding, when we keep it from building a nest. By response we mean anything the animal does—such as turning towards or away from a light, jumping at a sound, and more highly organized activities such as building a skyscraper, drawing plans, having babies, writing books, and the like.

At this point let me diverge to emphasize the fact that almost from infancy society begins to prescribe behavior. A Chinese baby must use chop sticks, eat rice, wear certain kinds of clothes, grow a queue, learn to speak Chinese, sit in a certain kind of way, worship his ancestors, and the like. The American baby must use a fork, learn quickly to form habits of personal cleanliness, wear certain kinds of clothes, learn reading, writing and arithmetic, become monogamous, worship the Christian God, go to church and, yes, even to speak upon a public platform. It is presumably not the function of the behaviorist to discuss whether these things which society prescribes serve as a help or a hindrance to the growth or adjustment of an individual. The behaviorist is working under the mandates of society and consequently it does come within his province to say to society: "If you decide that the human organism should behave in this way, you must arrange situations of such and such kinds." I would like to point out here that some time we will have a behavioristic ethics, experimental in type, which will tell us whether it is advisable from the standpoint of present and future adjustments of the individual to have one wife or many wives; to have capital punishment or punishment of any kind; whether prohibition or no prohibition; easy divorces or no divorces; whether many of our other prescribed courses of conduct make for adjustment of the individual or the contrary, such for example as having a family life or even knowing our own fathers and mothers.

Selection **4** | PRINCIPLES OF GESTALT PSYCHOLOGY*

KURT KOFFKA
Smith College

Three different definitions of our subject matter can be discriminated: Psychology as the science of consciousness, of mind, and of behaviour. Although psychology was reared as the science of consciousness or mind, we shall choose behaviour as our keystone. That does not mean that I regard the old definitions as completely wrong—it would be strange indeed if a science had developed on entirely wrong assumptions—but it means that if we start with behaviour it is easier to find a place for consciousness and mind than it is to find a place for behaviour if we start with mind or consciousness.

The swing from consciousness to behaviour is largely due to the work of American psychology, although, as far as I know, William McDougall was actually the first to define psychology in terms of behaviour. But what he meant by behaviour was something different from and much more inclusive than what is meant by the American school which takes its

name from this term. Since their usage of the term is restricted and implies a *theory* of behaviour we must return to McDougall's usage, which is purely descriptive and therefore does not prejudge in favour of any theory.

MOLAR AND MOLECULAR BEHAVIOUR

The difference between McDougall's and the behaviourists' meaning of behaviour has been very appropriately described by Tolman as the difference between behaviour as a molar and a molecular phenomenon. Without going into a detailed exposition at this moment I will give a few examples to bring this difference home. A molar behaviour is: the student's attendance at class, the lecturer's delivery, the pilot's navigation, the excitement of the spectators at a football game, Mr. Babbitt's flirtation, Galileo's work which revolutionized science, the hunting of the hound and the running of the hare, the biting of the fish and the stalking of the tiger, in short, all those countless occurrences in our everyday world which the layman calls behaviour. Molecular behaviour, on the other hand, is something very different: the process which starts with an excitation on the sensory surface of an animal, is conducted by nerve fibres to nerve centres, switched over to new, efferent nerves, and ends in a muscle contraction or a gland secretion. Now the ordinary man, probably more than 99% of the population of the earth, knows nothing about the latter, whereas everyone knows the former; on the other hand, those who know anything about physiology will have to admit that molar behaviour always implies muscle contractions which in their turn set our limbs into motion and are activated by nervous impulses. It is very easy to pass from a statement like this to another: molar behaviour is a secondary phenomenon; it is but the last outwardly observable result of a great number of physiological processes; these are the primary events; these form continuous causal sequences; and, therefore, these alone can form the subject matter of a science. Therefore, for behaviourism molar behaviour supplies no more than the problems, the solutions must always be given in terms of molecular behaviour, so that the finished system of psychology will contain only molecular data, the molar ones having been completely eliminated. We are not yet concerned with the particular mode in which behaviourism tried to carry through its programme, but we may emphasize two aspects of its doctrine: (1) It attributes reality to parts, denying it to the wholes which these parts compose: the molar has to be resolved into the molecular; (2) as a result of this, psychology would forever remain exposed to the criticism of the Moral Sciences which we have discussed at the end of the first chapter. Meaning and significance could have no possible place in such a molecular system; Caesar's crossing the Rubicon: certain stimulus-response situations; Luther at Worms: so many others; Shakespeare writing "Hamlet"; Beethoven composing the Ninth Symphony; an Egyptian sculptor carving the bust of Nephretete, would all be reduced to the stimulus-response schema. What then holds our interest in these occurrences? If they are nothing but combinations of *one* type of events, stimulus-response sequences, why do we not take as much interest in the sequence of numbers that come out as winners on the roulette table, why do we not pore over a list of all the bridge hands that have ever been dealt? The behaviourist will explain this by saying that the sequence of stimulus-response situations in most of us has been such that now we react positively to Shakespeare and Beethoven, and negatively to statistics of rouge et noir. At this the historian would throw up his hands in despair, and would continue his work confirmed in the conviction that psychology, whatever else it might be, is perfectly useless for his purposes, and the behaviourist would let the historian continue writing his fiction, equally convinced that his was the only truth.

Clearly such a state of affairs is highly unsatisfactory to anyone who is not a sceptic by nature or profession. What can he do to satisfy the just claims of the two opposing factions, to prevent the disruption of knowledge into a number of incoherent sciences? If psychology is to be the science of behaviour, must it not have a real place for Caesar, Shakespeare, Beethoven, a place which gives to the behaviour of these men the same *outstanding* and *distinctive* position in his system which they enjoy in the estimation of the ordinary educated person and the historian? It is clear that such an aim cannot be achieved if psychology begins and ends with molecular behaviour. Let us try molar behaviour instead. Perhaps it will be possible to find a place for molecular behaviour in a system that begins and ends with molar.

MOLAR BEHAVIOUR AND ITS ENVIRONMENT

What is the most general statement we can make about molar behaviour? That it takes place in an environment, whereas molecular behaviour takes place within the organism and is only initiated by environmental factors, called the stimuli. Molar behaviour of the type we have chosen for our examples occurs in an external setting: the student's class performance occurs in the classroom in which the lecturer holds forth; conversely, the lecturer behaves in a room filled with students who at least understand his language, if nothing else; Mr. Babbitt flirts in a very definite *social* environment, to say nothing about the partner necessary for this accomplishment; the hound and the hare both run through the field, and for each of them the other is the outstanding object of the environment. All this sounds obvious and banal. But it is not quite as trivial as it appears at first sight. For in reality there are, in all of the cases just mentioned, two very different environments to be distinguished from each other, and the question has to be raised: In which of them has molar behaviour taken place? Let us illustrate our proposition by an example taken from a German legend.

The geographical and the behavioural environment On a winter evening amidst a driving snowstorm a man on horseback arrived at an inn, happy to have reached a shelter after hours of riding over the wind-swept plain on which the blanket of snow had covered all paths and landmarks. The landlord who came to the door viewed the stranger with surprise and asked him whence he came. The man pointed in the direction straight away from the inn, whereupon the landlord, in a tone of awe and wonder, said: "Do you know that you have ridden across the Lake of Constance?" At which the rider dropped stone dead at his feet.

In what environment, then, did the behaviour of the stranger take place? The Lake of Constance. Certainly, because it is a true proposition that he rode across it. And yet, this is not the whole truth, for the fact that there was a frozen lake and not ordinary solid ground did not affect his behaviour in the slightest. It is interesting for the geographer that this behaviour took place in this particular locality, but not for the psychologist as the student of behaviour; because the behaviour would have been just the same had the man ridden across a barren plain. But the psychologist knows something more: since the man died from sheer fright after having learned what he had "really" done, the psychologist must conclude that had the stranger known before, his riding behaviour would have been very different from what it actually was. Therefore the psychologist will have to say: There is a second sense to the word environment according to which our horseman did not ride across the lake at all, but across an ordinary snow-swept plain. His behaviour was a riding-over-a-plain, but not a riding-over-a-lake.

What is true of the man who rode across the Lake of Constance is true of every behaviour. Does the rat run in the maze *the experimenter* has set up? According to the meaning of the word "in," yes and no. Let us therefore distinguish between a *geographical* and a *behavioural* environment. Do we all live in the same town? Yes, when we mean the geographical, no, when we mean the behavioural "in."

Granted, then, that our theory will be a molar theory, nevertheless it is a purely physiological theory, even though mental facts, facts of direct experience, are used in its construction. Does that not reveal a materialistic bias, does it not imply a valuation with regard to reality in which the physical ranks higher than the mental? Is this theory not, after all, a posthumous child of materialism? Let me quote a very impressive paragraph from Wertheimer: "When one goes to the root of one's aversion to materialism and mechanism, does one then find the *material properties* of the elements which these systems combine? Frankly speaking, there are psychological theories and many psychological textbooks which treat consistently of elements of *consciousness* and are nevertheless more materialistic, barren, lacking in meaning and significance than a living tree which possibly possesses nothing of consciousness. It cannot matter of what material the particles of the universe consist, what matters is the kind of whole, the significance of the whole."

Thus the alleged materialistic bias of our theory disappears. A physiological theory which allows to physiological processes more than mere summative combination of excitations is less materialistic than a psychological theory which allows only sensations and blind associative bonds between them. But we can say even a little more. Is our theory really *purely* physiological? Would it not mean an abandonment of fact if it were? For the physiological processes which we construct as the correlates of consciousness are known to us in the first place through their conscious aspect. To treat them as though they were purely physiological, without this conscious aspect, would be to neglect one of their outstanding characteristics. True enough, this conscious side of the processes does not enter into our causal explanations, but it has to be recognized as a fact nevertheless. And that leads to the conclusion that it is of the warp and woof of certain events in nature that they "reveal themselves," that they are accompanied by consciousness. Why they are so, and what special characteristics a process must have in order to be so, these are questions that cannot now be answered, and perhaps may never be. But if we accept our conclusion, consciousness can no longer be regarded as a mere epiphenomenon, a mere luxury, which might just as well be absent. For in an aspect which we do not know, these processes would be different, were they not accompanied by consciousness.

And this leads us to our last point. What about the consciousness of animals? That the behaviour of animals is molar and not molecular is a fact. Animal and human behaviour belong together; they are not totally different. On the other hand, we can never observe their behavioural environment, their consciousness. But the same is true with regard to any behavioural environment except our own. Directly, I can only know my own consciousness, you yours, yet nobody thinks of claiming a unique position for himself in the universe. Therefore the assumption of animal consciousness is nothing essentially new. However, if we do assume it, we are still faced with the problem, when shall we attribute consciousness to animals, when not? Is there, e.g., a definite point in the phylogenetic series where consciousness emerges? If so, where is it? Is an amoeba conscious? If not, a crab, a spider, a fish, a chick, a cat, a monkey, an anthropoid ape? Let us frankly admit that there is no answer to this question. Since we do not know what properties make a physiological process the correlate of a conscious one, we have absolutely no criterion by which we can decide with certainty whether any behaviour is conscious behaviour or not. All attempts to establish such criteria have begged the question by assuming a necessary relation between certain types of behaviour and consciousness. But in our system this whole problem is of no importance. Have we not learned from Wertheimer that there are much more essential characteristics of behaviour than whether it is conscious or merely physiological? Molar behaviour will be a field process; by studying the behaviour we can draw conclusions with regard to the field in which it occurs; we can make molar physiological theories. Because of our isomorphism we can even go a step further; we can describe this field in behavioural rather than physiological terms. This is very useful, because we have a behavioural terminology for such field descriptions, but not a physiological one. When I said previously that a chimpanzee used a "stool," I employed behavioural terminology. How could I, at the present state of science, have used a physiological one? And yet I need not mean more by this terminology than a description of the physiological field, leaving it entirely outside the scope of science, whether a behavioural field corresponded to it or not. Thus we are even less anthropomorphic than we appeared in our last discussion of the problem. There we claimed that the assumption of a behavioural environment was not anthropomorphism; now we are willing to give up even the behavioural environment, substituting for it a physiological field, the properties of which can best be described in behavioural terms. Thus the issue between us and the behaviourists with regard to animal psychology is not conscious behaviour vs. purely physiological behaviour, but physiological behaviour of the *field* type vs. physiological behaviour of the mechanical connection type. This issue can and must be decided on the plane of pure science, and the decision cannot fail to affect the wider issues which distinguish gestalt theory and behaviourism.

One last remark in this connection: we said that physiological processes that are accompanied by consciousness must in some unknown aspect differ from physiological processes which have no such accompaniment. We must add that in other relevant aspects they must be alike. For they are all field processes. Our whole solution of the mind-body problem would help us nought if we restricted the field concept to conscious physiological processes. But we do not. We view these as part events in a much wider field event and thereby avoid the argument against the behavioural field as a fundamental category which we have termed the insufficiency of the behavioural field. Let us introduce for future use the term "psychophysical field," indicating by this term both its physiological nature and its relation to direct experience.

THE TASK OF OUR PSYCHOLOGY

And now we can formulate the task of our psychology: it is *the study of behaviour in its causal connection with the psychophysical field.* This general programme must be made more concrete. Anticipating, we can say that the psychophysical field is organized. First of all it shows the polarity of the Ego and the environment, and secondly each of these two polar parts has its own structure. Thus the environment is neither a mosaic of sensations nor a "blooming, buzzing confusion," nor a blurred and vague total unit; rather does it consist of a definite number of separate objects and events, which, as separate objects and events, are products of organization. Likewise, the Ego is neither a point nor a sum or mosaic of drives or instincts. To describe it adequately we shall have to introduce the concept of personality with all its enormous complexity. Therefore if we want to study behaviour as an event in the psychophysical field, we must take the following steps:

1. We must study the organization of the environmental field, and that means (a) we must find out the forces which organize it into separate objects and events, (b) the forces which exist between these different objects and events; and (c) how these forces produce the environmental

field as we know it in our behavioural environment.

2. We must investigate how such forces can influence movements of the body.

3. We must study the Ego as one of the main field parts.

4. We must show that the forces which connect the Ego with the other field parts are of the same nature as those between different parts of the environmental field, and how they produce behaviour in all its forms.

5. We must not forget that our psycho-physical field exists within a real organism which in its turn exists in a geographical environment. In this way the questions of true cognition and adequate or adapted behaviour will also enter our programme.

Selection 5 | TWO PROPOSITIONS OF PSYCHOANALYSIS*

SIGMUND FREUD
Vienna

There are two tenets of psycho-analysis which offend the whole world and excite its resentment; the one conflicts with intellectual, the other with moral and aesthetic prejudices. Let us not underestimate these prejudices; they are powerful things, residues of valuable, even necessary, stages in human evolution. They are maintained by emotional forces, and the fight against them is a hard one.

The first of these displeasing propositions of psycho-analysis is this: that mental processes are essentially unconscious, and that those which are conscious are merely isolated acts and parts of the whole psychic entity. Now I must ask you to remember that, on the contrary, we are accustomed to identify the mental with the conscious. Consciousness appears to us as positively the characteristic that defines mental life, and we regard psychology as the study of the content of consciousness. This even appears so evident that any contradiction of it seems obvious nonsense to us, and yet it is impossible for psycho-analysis to avoid this contradiction, or to accept the identity between the conscious and the psychic. The psycho-analytical definition of the mind is that it comprises processes of the nature of feeling, thinking, and wishing, and it maintains that there are such things as unconscious thinking and unconscious wishing. But in doing so psycho-analysis has forfeited at the outset the sympathy of the sober and scientifically minded, and incurred the suspicion of being a fantastic cult occupied with dark and unfathomable mysteries.[1] You yourselves must find it difficult to understand why I should stigmatize an abstract proposition, such as "The psychic is the conscious," as a prejudice; nor can you guess yet what evolutionary process could have led to the denial of the unconscious, if it does indeed exist, nor what advantage could have been achieved by this denial. It seems like an empty wrangle over words to argue whether mental life is to be regarded as co-extensive with consciousness or whether it may be said to stretch beyond this limit, and yet I can assure you that the acceptance of unconscious mental processes represents a decisive step towards a new orientation in the world and in science.

As little can you suspect how close is the connection between this first bold step on the part of psycho-analysis and the second to which I am now coming. For this next proposition, which we put forward as one of the discoveries of psycho-analysis, consists in the assertion that impulses, which can only be described as sexual in both the narrower and the wider sense, play a peculiarly large part, never before sufficiently appreciated, in the causation of nervous and mental disorders. Nay, more, that these sexual impulses have contributed invaluably to the highest cultural, artistic, and social achievements of the human mind.

In my opinion, it is the aversion from this conclusion of psycho-analytic investigation that is the most significant source of the opposition it has encountered. Are you curious to know

[1] Literally: "that wishes to build in the dark and fish in murky waters."—Tr.

how we ourselves account for this? We believe that civilization has been built up, under the pressure of the struggle for existence, by sacrifices in gratification of the primitive impulses, and that it is to a great extent for ever being re-created, as each individual, successively joining the community, repeats the sacrifice of his instinctive pleasures for the common good. The sexual are amongst the most important of the instinctive forces thus utilized: they are in this way sublimated, that is to say, their energy is turned aside from its sexual goal and diverted towards other ends, no longer sexual and socially more valuable. But the structure thus built up is insecure, for the sexual impulses are with difficulty controlled; in each individual who takes up his part in the work of civilization there is a danger that a rebellion of the sexual impulses may occur, against this diversion of their energy. Society can conceive of no more powerful menace to its culture than would arise from the liberation of the sexual impulses and a return of them to their original goal. Therefore society dislikes this sensitive place in its development being touched upon; that the power of the sexual instinct should be recognized, and the significance of the individual's sexual life revealed, is very far from its interests; with a view to discipline it has rather taken the course of diverting attention away from this whole field. For this reason, the revelations of psycho-analysis are not tolerated by it, and it would greatly prefer to brand them as aesthetically offensive, morally reprehensible, or dangerous. But since such objections are not valid arguments against conclusions which claim to represent the objective results of scientific investigation, the opposition must be translated into intellectual terms before it can be expressed. It is a characteristic of human nature to be inclined to regard anything which is disagreeable as untrue, and then without much difficulty to find arguments against it. So society pronounces the unacceptable to be untrue, disputes the results of psychoanalysis with logical and concrete arguments, arising, however, in affective sources, and clings to them with all the strength of prejudice against every attempt at refutation.

But we, on the other hand, claim to have yielded to no tendency in propounding this objectionable theory. Our intention has been solely to give recognition to the facts as we found them in the course of painstaking researches. And we now claim the right to reject unconditionally any such introduction of practical considerations into the field of scientific investigation, even before we have determined whether the apprehension which attempts to force these considerations upon us is justified or not.

These, now, are some of the difficulties which confront you at the outset when you begin to take an interest in psycho-analysis. It is probably more than enough for a beginning. If you can overcome their discouraging effect, we will proceed further.

Selection **6** | CHARACTERISTICS AND GOALS OF SCIENCE*

ARTHUR J. BACHRACH
Arizona State University

Some important characteristics of science   I have already noted that science is a mixture of doubt and certainty. I think the good scientist is arrogantly humble. This isn't just a play on words; I think he should be arrogant in method and humble in his belief in his knowledge. To me, as a psychologist, this is particularly applicable. There is so much we do not know as yet in the study of behavior that a proper humility is essential, but this should never lead us to accept unscientific explanations of behavior (such as "human nature") which conflict with a forthright scientific method. It is better, as Skinner has suggested to remain without an answer than to accept an inadequate one. This is a major characteristic of science, the ability to wait for an answer combined with a continuing search for an explanation and a rejection of premature explanation. Skinner has also suggested other characteristics of science, among these the following: science is a set of attitudes, "it is a disposition to deal with the facts rather than with what someone has said about them." Science rejects its own

* Abridged from Arthur J. Bachrach, *Psychological Research: An Introduction*, 2d ed., Random House, Inc., New York, 1965, chap. 2, pp. 27–52.

authorities when their statements conflict with the observations of natural events. *Data prevail, not men.*

Science, Skinner observes, "is a willingness to accept facts even when they are opposed to wishes." Science places a high premium on honesty and incidents of altering data to fit in with one's pet theory are unusual. But even accepting the honesty of an investigator, no one who is firmly committed to a point of view relishes seeing it demolished. If his own data succeed in destroying treasured beliefs, the scientist accepts the facts, even though it involves the loss of an old friend, a bosom theory. The moral here is clear: don't get involved with proving anything, let the data guide you. As Skinner says, "Experiments do not always come out as one expects, but the facts must stand and the expectations fall. The subject matter, not the scientist knows best."[1]

Skinner has also noted that science is more than a set of attitudes, it is also "a search for order, for uniformities, for lawful relations among the events in nature." It begins with a single, carefully observed event and proceeds eventually to the formulation of a general law.

The goals of science Ultimately, no matter what the scientific disciplines, the goal of science is the understanding and control of its subject matter. It may be easier to accept the understanding part of that pair because there are sciences that presently have no control of their subject matter as, for example, the disciplines of astronomy or geology. Astronomy has a highly developed body of knowledge allowing astronomers to describe and predict with high accuracy the movements of stars, for example, or the appearance of a comet. Mark Twain's Connecticut Yankee might have startled and impressed King Arthur's court by predicting an eclipse, but this is now accepted as a commonplace type of prediction. With these skills of prediction and description, astronomy still has no way of controlling celestial events;

[1] "In the nineteenth century the famous French mathematician Lagrange once appeared before a learned society to explain a proof he had worked out for a previously unsolved problem. No sooner had he started to read his paper than he suddenly stopped talking, frowned, then folded his papers and remarked, 'Gentlemen, I must think further about this.' " This is the self-correcting scientist. We probably could do very nicely with more paper-folders.

therefore, it may be said that astronomy is a descriptive science. It may further be said that astronomy will be a "pure" science when it does gain control over eclipses and comets; but this is somewhat tangential, although in recent years an experimental geology has been developed, moving the descriptive science of geology closer to an experimental one.

I have brought into the goal of science two other aspects related to the goals of *understanding* and *control*—these are *description* and *prediction,* and the first of these is description. For underlying every science is observation and measurement, providing a description of events and a way of quantifying them so that experimental manipulation may be achieved. It might be said that the two critical foundations of science are observation and experiment and that measurement provides a meaningful way in which events and their manipulation may be ordered. The ultimate goal in science is, of course, an ordering of facts into general, consistent laws from which predictions may be made, but it inevitably starts with observation. I would like to discuss observation and experiment briefly, then the use of measurement and finally, the ordering of observation and experimental facts into general laws.

Observation and experiment Science is always a balance of observation and experiment, for observation is the empirical gathering of facts and experiment is the active reasoning about these facts and the manipulation of them for further knowledge. It also involves further observation under the controlled experimental condition. It has been said by students of science that Descartes and Bacon represent opposites in an approach to scientific activity. Descartes did all his work in bed while Bacon is said to have died at the age of 65 from a cold which he contracted while he was experimenting in a snow drift. For Descartes, it was possible to obtain the two elements of fact and reason—which are crucial in science—without experimentation, yet this is generally not the way science advances. Reason is extended in experimentation but is rooted in observation.

Bronowski has observed that science is a way of describing reality and "is therefore limited by limits of observation, and it asserts nothing which is outside of observation. Anything else is not science—it is scholastics." Here Bronowski is invoking the image of scholasticism, the philosophy of Medieval Western Europe which was essentially anti-empirical and certainly anti-experimental in the modern sense. But when he says that science is limited by limits of observation, he is stating one of the boundaries of scientific methodology. When he says that science asserts nothing that is outside of observation, he is again stating a basic tenet of scientific method. The observable is the very keystone of science. Einstein suggested that the fundamental unit in physics was *event—signal—observer*. By this he meant that when an event occurs it presents some outward manifestation and requires an observer to record it. Certainly this triad of event—signal—observer is basic to sciences other than physics, and it is the responsibility of the scientist, no matter what discipline he works in, carefully to observe the signal which represents the event and accurately to record it. It is for this reason that instrumentation develops. It has been said that man is between an atom and a star and has developed the microscope and the telescope to extend his views in both directions. The main purposes that an instrument serves are to provide accurate observation to eliminate observer bias and to extend and quantify the observations of the human researcher.

Now there are certainly problems in observation and in any discussion of the observer. It is important to refer to Heisenberg, a German physicist who, in 1927, stated the Principle of Uncertainty (or Indeterminancy), which held that it was not possible to determine at the same time both the position and speed of an electron. The observer must observe one or the other event. If he chooses to observe the position of the electron with complete accuracy, then he must relinquish an accurate evaluation of its speed and, conversely, if he wishes to study the velocity, he cannot observe its position with accuracy. The Principle of Uncertainty has come to mean that to study an event the observer must interfere with its natural course. As a result, the scientist cannot have all the relevant information he requires at the same time. This, of course, has been taken into account in research and is really at the basis of repeated experiments in which different variables are studied in isolation. In psy-

chology, the Principle of Uncertainty has been invoked in discussions of such things as introspection, because it is not truly possible to look at oneself with clarity.

To return to Bronowski's statement that anything outside observation is not science, I would like to elaborate on this from my own point of view to say that one of the critical requirements of observation is that it be replicable, i.e., reported by others who also are able to see and record it. This is what is meant by a data language in science. A simple example would be a physicist's pointer readings, where one observer can report an alteration in the pointer on a meter and have this observation repeated by others. The more accurate the measurement, the closer the replication of observation can be. One of the basic problems in psychology has been the lack of a universal data language to which observations may be related and in which observations may be expressed. It is obviously different, for instance, to talk about a disordered personality and a deflection in a needle of three degrees. The margin of error in the former description is great, while in the latter it is minimal. Psychology's need for a data language to sharpen observation has been considered by Greenspoon and [by] Davis, both of whom suggest physical referents for psychological observation and description.

I suggest, then, that if the observation is not clear or replicable within the limits of observation defined, then it is not liable to scientific study. It may become so in the future when instrumentation enlarges the ability to measure and observe, but this in no way changes the criterion for scientific boundaries. As we saw in discussing characteristics of science, it is better to wait for an answer than to create an inadequate one.

There are many areas of study which may be approached experimentally, using all the sophisticated statistical and design techniques available to science, yet still remain outside the realm of scientific investigation. One of these, singled out because it illustrates many of the things I wish to bring out, is the area of parapsychology, the study of paranormal events, such as telepathy and extrasensory perception (ESP). There is no doubt that there are investigators in parapsychology who are diligent, industrious and creative. At the moment, however, despite the use of scientific tools such as experimental design and statistical proof, there are factors which place parapsychology beyond science. One of these is the problem of observer replicability. For example, the failure of one investigator to achieve results with a particular experimental subject while another investigator apparently gets good results in terms of high scoring on extrasensory perception tasks, has been explained as a problem in attitude. An experimenter who is hostile to the hypothesis of extrasensory perception will not get good results, while a sympathetic experimenter will. The assumption (as yet unproved) is that these attitudes in some way affect the mental activity of the subject.

Even though it may sound unnecessarily restrictive, it must be said that the data of parapsychology cannot be admitted as scientific data until the observations are consistent from experimenter to experimenter under specified conditions and with control of the variables. This does not condemn such data to a limbo from which they cannot return. It simply means that Bronowski's observation about the nonscientific character of events outside of observation must be kept in view in evaluating such research, even though the experiments are carefully conceived and executed.

Parapsychology is not alone in suffering from the problem of observer replication. Many areas of psychology labor under this handicap, largely, as I have said, because there is no clear data language which would allow for (or create) observer agreement. So parapsychology gets different results from subjects under different experimental conditions and with different experimenters. This variability of performance, while regrettable, is not unusual. What seems to exclude parapsychology from the body of science is its initial assumption of *paranormal* events, illustrated in the word *extrasensory* perception. The initial assumption is that the data of parapsychology start outside normal events, and investigation has always been directed by this assumption. Science starts with the basic statement that events in nature (including behavior) are ordered and lawful and that the goal of a scientist is the search for order and similarity.

The major difficulty posed by parapsychology is its acceptance of a dualistic position, which separates it completely from the natural sciences. I have no intention of getting involved in a rehash of the mind-body problem at this point—the book is too short for that—but I will state that psychology, as a science, must accept the monistic position of science and reject the temptation to deal with mental events as though they existed separately from physical ones. The main reason for this is simply that this position has proved successful in other sciences and fits into the search for order and uniformity basic to scientific methodology. To establish a second realm of the mental confounds the science. The argument that there are obviously mental events—such as thought processes and dreams—again confounds the issue, because the study of these events must proceed along lines established in science.

Reason from experiment: toward order and law The first step in scientific method, then, is observation or the empirical gathering of facts. But facts themselves are not enough. They are merely the first step. As I have mentioned, ordering through reasoned activity is essential to the achievement of the ultimate goals of science. Science is by no means merely a collection of isolated facts, no matter how accurately they have been observed and recorded. It is the search for consistency or order within the facts which characterizes the scientific method.[2] To record X and Y and Z accurately is indeed the critical first step, but science eventually has to describe the similarities existing among variables and their functional relationship. As Bronowski has observed ". . . the truth of science is not truth to fact, which can never be more than approximate, but the truth of the laws which we see within the facts."

The scientist moves from the careful observation of events to a search for order, for consistencies and uniformities, for functional, lawful relationships among the events which he has studied. Beginning with a single isolated

[2] In 1848, Renan wrote in *L'Avenir de la Science (The Future of Science)*: "All the special sciences start by the affirmation of unity, and only begin to distinguish when analysis has revealed numerous differences where before had been visible nothing but uniformity. Read the Scottish psychologists, and you will find at each page that the primary rule of the philosophical method is to maintain distinct that which is distinct, not to anticipate facts by a hurried reduction to unity, not to recoil before the multiplicity of causes."

event, he attempts to find more and more information which will relate events in some meaningful and consistent order. He requires uniformity of events. Bronowski elsewhere has said:

We cannot define truth in science until we move from fact to law. And within the body of laws in turn, what impresses us as truth is the orderly coherence of the pieces. They fit together like the characters in a great novel, or like the words in a poem. Indeed, we should keep that last analogy by us always. For science is language and, like a language, it defines its parts by the way they make up a meaning. Every word in the sentence has some uncertainty of definition, and yet the sentence defines its own meaning and that of its words conclusively. It is the eternal unity and coherence of science which give it truth, and which make it a better system of prediction than any less orderly language.

In this sense, science becomes a language, as Bronowski has suggested, for describing nature. It begins with a statement of faith and assumption that the world is orderly, that the events in the world are lawful and understandable. This is no less true of psychology and the study of behavior than it is of the study of physics or chemistry. A psychologist cannot function effectively as a scientist unless he accepts the assumption that behavior is lawful and understandable, recognizing also the somewhat chilling fact that the scientific goal is control of behavior. Later on, when we talk about ethical considerations in research, we will discuss some of the problems of ethics in the control of behavior. At the moment I need only observe that psychology, as a scientific discipline, accepts the general tenet of the lawfulness and uniformity of natural events, a tenet which every other science has discovered to be a critical foundation.

And so observation has taken us to experimentation and experimentation has taken us to the search for order and uniformity upon which we may base laws. Sidman has offered an interesting account of a personal experience which illustrates the importance of uniformities in scientific methodology. He writes:

As a young graduate student . . . I felt that my work had to be different, that it had to produce something new that would startle the world. Along

these lines I once wrote a paper, describing some of my work in which I emphasized how different my experiments were from anything else that had ever been done. One of my teachers, W. N. Schoenfeld, agreed that the data were very interesting. But he went on to add that I had written the paper from a peculiar point of view. I had emphasized the *differences* between my work and everyone else's. But science does not ordinarily advance that way. It is the job of science to find orderly relations among phenomena, not differences. It would have been more useful if I could have pointed out the similarities between my work and previous experiments.

This does not mean, by any stretch of the imagination, that scientists are attempting to conform. Nor are they merely trying to repeat the experiments of others, or question experimental data which others may have achieved. Far from it. It means simply that the more we can develop likenesses and orderly relationships among events, the closer we are to effective prediction and control of our science. When we discover, for example, the likenesses which exist between the baccillus, the virus and the crystal, or the functional similarities which may exist between the cell and the organism and society, we move closer to effective prediction.

Prediction from observation and experiment I have noted that science is a technique for ordering events into lawful relationships, and that the goal of science is prediction and control based on such lawfulness. A law, as it is usually described, is a collection of facts grouped into a consistent body of knowledge, from which it is possible to make predictions. But it is obvious that no prediction is completely certain because it is not possible to know all the variables operating in a particular situation. All we ask of a prediction is that it be based on a lawful ordering of events and that it forecast, as accurately as possible, what will happen in a future event within a range of uncertainty.

This introduces the basic concept of probability, which is fundamental to scientific method. We talk about the probabilities of an event occurring. We are, in a sense, giving odds, saying the chances are that if X is manipulated in a certain fashion, Y will change in a certain way. Experimentation is clearly a method for increasing the likelihood of the prediction being correct.

So far I have touched upon the elements of *observation, experiment,* and *prediction* as they relate to scientific method and the ultimate goals of understanding, prediction and control. But I have not spent much time on the problem of control itself. It should be apparent that once we are able successfully to predict events, we have achieved a degree of control over them. I'll be coming back to this later on in discussing experimental manipulation. At the moment, I would like to go back to the other basic element in the beginnings of a science, the one which, coupled with observation, underlies all science, descriptive or experimental. This is the question of measurement. *Measurement in science.* In discussing the question of description in scientific methodology, I have used a number of examples covering such differing events as a virus, a fly and a dog. There are, to be sure, different levels of description in science ranging from description of cellular activity in a human to this same human courting his girl friend. The narrower the focus of activity, the easier it is to measure. For example, a scientist might be infinitely more accurate in describing electrical activity occurring in a person's cell membrane than he would be in describing dating behavior. There are enormously complicated problem areas, such as tensions that lead to war and racial and religious prejudice, which we have been relatively unable to solve. We have not been able to solve them in large measure because they cannot be effectively described. In viewing such significant problem areas, I agree with Underwood who observed: "I would defend the proposition that research in psychology necessarily involves measurement, and that the rapidity with which research will embrace . . . significant behaviors depends upon our ability to break them down into relevant parts which can be measured." One cannot, for example, measure prejudice, which is only a general term for a large number of activities. However, one can begin to break prejudice down into its relevant parts by cataloguing the number of hotels and restaurants in a particular community that refuse to admit members of a minority group. This is only a small beginning of measurement to be sure, but none the less it is a beginning.

The two basic questions in measurement are (1) does the phenomenon exist? and (2) if it exists, to what extent does it exist? As these questions are posed in scientific terms, the first is a nominal type of measurement. As the term nominal suggests, this is a naming operation which simply differentiates one event from another. It is a frequent basis of measurement description. For example, classification of flowers or birds is a nominal operation. But let's see where this might lead.

To take another illustration, numbering prisoners in a penitentiary is nominal. This basic classification may be sufficient for the needs of the prison authorities, but it is possible that they may wish to separate the prisoners into groups based on an estimate of the severity of the crime for which they were imprisoned. Assuming that forgery is a less serious crime than murder, Prisoner No. 400–097 (a forger) is placed in a different cell block from Prisoner No. 400–789 (a murderer). The numbers differentiate the two on a nominal scale, the separation in terms of severity of crime differentiates them on an *ordinal* scale. It is apparent that an ordinal scale, such as a rating of severity of criminal acts, can be highly subjective. Suppose it were possible to work out an exact scale of severity so that the interval murder $\leftrightarrow$ forgery was equal in severity to the interval forgery $\leftrightarrow$ shoplifting. In terms of increasing seriousness of crime the ordinal scale would read: shoplifting—forgery—murder. If such a scale worked, it might be used by a judge in determining sentences, or by a parole board in assessing release of prisoners. When an ordinal scale is divided into equal steps or gradations of such changes in intensity, it is referred to as an *equal interval* scale. A final development in scaling would be one in which it were possible to establish an absolute zero point on the scale. An equal interval scale with an absolute zero point is called a *ratio* scale.

At this point I would like to express an opinion that may well meet with some disagreement. I would say that ultimately all measurements must have some physical referent. There are phenomena which are called subjective, but if they cannot eventually lead to measurement, they cannot be considered as scientific data. This is not making a shrine out of the methods or techniques used by physics and the other sciences, but indicates that until subjective phenomena are rendered measurable and quantifiable, they can yield little meaningful information. I believe that research problems such as those of anxiety and emotion, which have always been matters of concern for psychologists, may be most fruitful when approached in terms of physiological change and a measurement of such physiological change.

There have been many definitions of emotion. But the one factor common to all of these definitions is some change in the activity of the autonomic nervous system, a physiological event which is subject to measurement. In recent years, covert behavior—which has often been referred to as unconscious and presumably not subject to experimental investigation—has been studied in a careful and ingenious fashion by Hefferline and his colleagues. There is clear indication of the possibility of measuring minute behavioral events with physiological recordings.

It has always been true that the information available to a scientist is largely dependent upon the refinement of his instruments. Each year, as finer and finer instruments are made available to the researcher, more and more information previously considered subjective comes under the scrutiny of the experimental investigation.

REFERENCES

Bronowski, Jacob, *The Common Sense of Science.* Cambridge: Harvard University Press, 1953.

Feigl, Herbert, Operationism and Scientific Method. *Psychological Review,* 52: 250–259, 1945.

Sidman, Murray, *Tactics of Scientific Research.* New York: Basic Books, 1960.

Selection **7** | PSYCHOLOGY AS A SCIENCE*

GREGORY A. KIMBLE
Duke University

The approach I would like to take to this discussion of psychology as a science is simply that, whether or not such is generally the case

* From Gregory A. Kimble, "Psychology as a Science." *Scientific Monthly,* 77: 156–160, 1953. Reprinted by permission of the publisher.

now, it is possible to approach the problems of psychology scientifically. Furthermore, it seems to me that about our only hope in this task lies in making use of the things that the philosophers of science are able to tell us. I have, therefore, tried to decide just what lessons these philosophers can teach us and how they can be applied to psychology. My sincere hope is that the summary of my thinking on the topic which I am about to present does not do the philosophers too great an injustice, or, if it does, that they can at least be philosophical about it.

Let us begin by stating the subject matter with which psychology deals. The standard definition of psychology is that it is *the science of behavior.* This definition probably needs clarification. On the one hand it covers less than you may have expected. On the other, it covers too much. Note first that the definition says nothing about mind, or experience, or consciousness. This is not merely an attempt to finesse the problems raised by these three terms. If they are to be used at all in a science of psychology, they will have to be introduced in a way to be described later. A second point is that the behavior with which the psychologist deals tends to be limited to its grosser aspects. Where internal physiological processes are a part of psychology, they are conceived as aids to conceptualization rather than as a part of its basic subject matter. I shall return more than once to the question of the relationship between psychology and physiology; let us turn now to a discussion of the use of the term, "science" in the expression, "science of behavior."

The word, science, refers to the attempt that people called scientists make to bring order into the world of observable events. Scientists are, of course, not the only ones trying to bring order into the world. Others are the theologians, some literary people, and the philosophers. The scientific way of approaching the task differs from these latter ways, chiefly in terms of its initial data. All science begins with the sensory experience of a perceiving scientist. These sensory experiences, which are private and not a part of science, give rise to its initial data, that is, to a publicly observable *report* of such experiences. In this sense, psychology is exactly like any other science. The report with which psychologists are provided may be about rats running a maze, physiological processes, test results, or even the scientist's own introspection. But the element of all of this that is useful is the report that is open to public inspection.

The particular task which the psychologist has taken for himself is that of trying to make some sense of behavior. But we have just seen that, as scientists, psychologists must concern themselves with events that are publicly observable and, therefore, verifiable. This restriction on the activities of psychologists raises a question: Just what kinds of observations can they make on behavior that are of this sort? The answer to this question comes in two parts. First, psychologists have found (just as other scientists in other fields have found) that human behavior is so complicated that it is impossible even to talk about all of the activity of an individual at any one time. So, in practice, they restrict their observation to limited portions of behavior called responses. Second, even responses cannot, without the aid of photographic assistance, be recorded in detail. So, their reports of behavior typically deal with some abstracted characteristic like the speed or the magnitude of the response.

Having stated the general manner in which the psychologist views behavior, a word must now be said about a primary assumption, which is that these various aspects of behavior are related to events in the person's past and present environment. Although the collection of variables in this category might better be called antecedent and attendant circumstances, the psychological convention is to call them stimuli. When the psychologist speaks of stimuli he usually is referring more or less broadly to events or changes in events in the environment. So far as these stimulus variables are concerned, they are so numerous that no attempt to enumerate them here is possible. A few examples will have to do. In the field of learning, for one example, the efficiency of a learned reaction is known to depend in a regular fashion upon the number and spacing of practice trials, upon the amount of reward the subject is given for making the response, and upon many other variables. In vision, what a person sees (really what he *says* he sees) is known to depend upon the area of the visual stimulus,

upon its brightness, upon the duration of its presentation in the visual field, and so on. One thing that should be noticed about these particular examples of environmental events is that they are quantifiable in terms of some standard physical measuring scale. Not all variables with which psychologists have to deal are yet subject to measurement in any very respectable sense of the word. For the kind of information that is needed to build a science of psychology, however, quantification of these independent variables is a necessity of which psychology is acutely aware.

The final task in the development of a behavior science is simply that of stating the relationships that exist among the variables that have been isolated. What psychologists are after is a set of laws of the general type: $R = f(S)$, where R is some aspect of a response, S is a stimulus event and f represents the functional relationship. These are what I will call S-R laws. It should, of course, be realized that the formula, $R = f(S)$, is highly schematized. Behavior is seldom predictable from knowledge of a single S-variable. The S in this equation stands for an indefinite number of antecedent conditions which in actual practice will have to be discovered along with their relevance to behavior.

Because of this complexity in the determination of behavior, the S-R laws have turned out to be very difficult to discover. Where this has happened, psychologists have sometimes had more success using a different approach, in an attempt to discover the relationships that exist among *response* variables. As a convenient example of this, one may take the very important work of the clinical psychologists and the psychological testers. They almost never deal with the S-R type of relationship at all. Instead they use what are sometimes called R-R laws. The distinction between these two types of relationship is shown in the following example. There is some rather good evidence to suggest that an individual who is frustrated in his various strivings develops a tendency toward aggressive behavior. For purposes of exposition, it can be assumed that this is a well-established relationship. On this basis, if one knew that an individual had been frustrated many times in his efforts to achieve important goals, it could be predicted that he would show aggressive behavior. In this case, an *S-R* law would be used to make the prediction. The determining *S*-variable is the frequent blocking of goal-directed behavior, and the dependent response variable is the aggressive behavior. If it were known that aggressive behavior in some form always occurs as a consequence of frustration and that it never occurs in the absence of frustration, there would be some point in saying that aggression occurs *because* of frustration. Furthermore, given a control over the person's environment and a knowledge of the *S-R* law, the amount of his aggressive behavior could be controlled.

A clinical psychologist, on the other hand, might give this same person a psychological test and come out with the statement that he has strong aggressive tendencies and may be expected to show a great deal of hostile behavior on many occasions. This prediction (which would be as correct as the other one) would be made in terms of a different kind of law. What the clinician has done is to observe a small segment of the individual's behavior in a controlled situation called a test, and, from his behavior in this situation, to make a prediction about other behavior. His prediction is made in terms of an $R_2 = f(R_1)$ kind of relationship, in which R_2 is the predicted aggressive behavior, R_1 is the predicted-from-test behavior, and the function is a correlation coefficient. These *R-R* laws are diagnostic laws, and carry no implications of causality. (The statement that the person tested is aggressive because the clinician has given him a test is obviously absurd, at least until such a time as the clinician's services are more expensive and, therefore, more frustrating than they are now.) Furthermore, the *R-R* laws provide no control over behavior in the absence of further information of the *S-R* type.

The commodities in which the psychologist deals are, then, two types of relationship which I have called *S-R* and *R-R* laws. The precise statement of a large number of such laws would be extremely valuable, but it would not make psychology a high-order science. What would still be needed would be the collection of the *S-R* and *R-R* relationships into some more orderly or integrated kind of formulation. In actual practice, it has been found useful to

attempt the formulation without the comprehensive set of empirical laws it is hoped eventually to integrate. Such attempts at formalization are called systematic psychology or psychological theory.

The form that psychological theorizing has taken has been toward the development of intervening state variables which are considered as standing between *S* and *R* or between R_1 and R_2, depending upon the kind of relationship. The intervening states that have been postulated have been of two general sorts, physiological states and hypothetical constructs. If we consider first the type of intervening variable used by the more physiologically minded psychologists, the paradigm in terms of which they attempt to explain behavior may be expressed in the following way: *S-O-R*. Stimulation according to this scheme is thought of as producing some physiological or organic change in the individual. And this physiological change, in turn, is thought of as being responsible for whatever behavior is being observed. Such psychologists investigate the relationships between neural, glandular, circulatory, and muscular events, on the one hand, and behavioral events on the other.

Another large group of psychologists make use of the hypothetical construct type of intervening variable in their explanation of behavior. The paradigm, in terms of which such psychologists work, is the following: *S-H-R*. Antecedent stimulus conditions are thought of as defining a hypothetical intervening state in terms of which responses are predicted. Examples of such hypothetical constructs in fairly general use are: habit, motivation, fatigue, attitude, symbolic processes, and the like. About these hypothetical constructs, there are a number of things that need to be said. The first of these is that there is no reason in the world to assume that they *must* have any actual existence inside the organism or anywhere else. Some of them, at least, are analogous to the physicists' concept of velocity which derives its meaning from its definition: $V = S/T$. The physicists do not spend much time worrying about what or where velocity really is. Psychologists, on the other hand, spend a good bit of time looking for the neurophysiological events which they think *have* to exist and to correspond to their concepts, however imperfect. What is worse, they spend even more time speculating about them. There are just two comments that I wish to make about this. One is that, although all behavior probably has its neurophysiological aspects, mere speculation about them is a fruitless procedure. The other is that, although physiological *information* may someday turn out to be useful for psychology, there is nothing in the program of psychology which makes such information indispensable. For all practical purposes, it is possible to construct a science of psychology in which the organism is considered as empty. For my own part, I can conceive of a psychology based on stimulus and response events entirely, one in which the existence of the organism is a completely unimportant fact. The scientific account will, after all, deal with behavior in the abstract. Such a science no more needs to refer to the organism than the science of gravitation needs to refer to stones or to the Leaning Tower of Pisa.

Whether the constructs that are introduced between stimuli and responses are physiological or purely hypothetical, they have to meet certain criteria to be acceptable. The most important of these criteria can be summed up in one word: *meaningfulness.* Intervening variables must be meaningful in two ways. The first is what has been called *operational meaning.* The meaningfulness of a concept in this sense depends upon the adequacy of its definition. A concept may be said to be adequately defined providing there exists a set of defining statements for it which lead eventually to phenomena in the sensory experience of the scientist, and providing further that these statements are such that any properly qualified and equipped person can put them to a test. This requirement is no more than a particular application of the more general criterion of public observability.

Concepts for which no such definition is *possible* are of no use to science. This is not, however, to say that concepts which have never been adequately defined never will be. They may or may not be. Concepts such as mind, consciousness, and experience are in the class of intervening variables for which no satisfactory operational definition exists. This is

in part because of the complexity of the phenomena involved, and in part because of their inherent privacy. But this state of affairs does not demand the conclusion that respectable definition is impossible.

On the other hand, an operational definition of these terms (assuming it is achieved) does not guarantee their utility. The second kind of meaningfulness remains to be demonstrated. This point can be made clear with the aid of an illustration. I can define a construct as follows: Kappa (for Kimble) = the square root of the number of hairs on my head divided by my diastolic blood pressure minus the length of my great toe. This concept, Kappa, although its operational definition is impeccable, has not been used much in psychology because, so far as we know, it has no meaningful relationship to any of the events with which psychologists are supposed to be dealing. In this second sense, a concept is meaningful if it is related to behavior, or aids in its prediction.

Just as there are two major kinds of laws with which the psychologist deals, there are two kinds of operations in terms of which a concept may acquire operational meaning. The first of these is by definition in terms of antecedent stimulus conditions. The second is by an inference from behavior. To illustrate, let us consider a case in which both types of definition have been used and return to the example of aggression. It has already been pointed out that predictions of aggressive behavior might be made either from a knowledge of an individual's history of frustration or from his behavior on a test. Using exactly the same evidence, there can be developed two different definitions of the concept aggression. In terms of antecedent conditions, aggression can be defined as a positive function of the number of frustrations a person has experienced. In terms of behavior, it can be said that a person is aggressive if his pattern of test responses is so and so. The one thing we cannot say is that we now have two different definitions of the "same thing." Different definitions define different concepts. In psychology, especially, there is the need to be cautioned against the tendency to treat things as identical just because they have the same name. Whether the frustration-produced aggression has anything to do with the test-defined aggression is an empirical question which can be decided by research.

As I see it, just one final point needs to be made with respect to the science of psychology as it is developing. It must be presented as a sort of confession. Not all psychologists agree with the analytical, behavioristic (what James would have called "tough-minded") sort of analysis I have been presenting of the field. In psychology, we hear a great deal about "the total situation," "the whole child," "the whole personality," and "global intelligence." Psychologists who use these expressions object to the type of account I have given, chiefly because of the analytical approach which it implies. This cold analysis, they say, is wrong because it fails to capture the warmth and vitality of human behavior as we know it in our common-sense, firsthand experience. Unfortunately for common sense, that is how it is with science. Common sense tells us that the world is flat; science says that it is round. Our firsthand experience tells us that the sun moves slowly around us; science says that we are moving around the sun, and at a breakneck speed. Direct observation tells us that the chairs in which we are sitting are solid; science says that they are mostly empty space. The mere fact that some line of scientific argument produces a description of the world that fails to correspond to our naive experience of it is no obstacle to that argument. And if there are aspects of behavior that cannot be handled in the way I have been describing, I know of no way of finding this out without giving it a try.

At a somewhat different level, the opponents of behavioristic psychology sometimes object that the analysis of behavior destroys its essentially continuous or integrated character, and robs it of its wholeness. They now propose what they call a field theoretical approach to human behavior and very bitterly deplore what they call the *mechanism* of the sort of argument I have been expounding. They say that their new field theories stand to the more orthodox psychology as does the theory of relativity to Newtonian mechanics. The adequacy of this analogy, of course, depends upon some understanding of what the term, "field," means in physics. It seems to have been used in two rather different ways. Basically, by a "field,"

the physicist means a system of interrelated variables that differs from other systems of physics partly in the kind of calculus which expresses the interdependencies. Unfortunately, the mathematics are difficult, even for a physicist. So, for their nonmathematical brethren, the theoretical physicists have constructed models (as, for example, the Rutherford-Bohr atom) in an attempt to convey what is involved in their equations. Since the so-called field theories in psychology consist of anthropomorphic models in this second sense, it seems to me that they cannot be called field theories in the sense that the theoretical physicist uses the expression. On the other hand, if one wished to consider as field theories approaches to psychology that come closer to the actual mathematical statement of the interdependencies involved, then the very people who bear the stigma, "mechanistic," would have to qualify as the greatest field theorists of them all. Finally, it must be pointed out that science is concerned with the regularities in the world; that is, with events that repeat themselves. Whole situations do not repeat themselves, at least not very often. Analysis of the elements common to somewhat different situations will be absolutely essential in order to achieve a science of psychology.

This, then, is what the science of psychology, as it begins to be rather definitely defined, is like. It is concerned with the prediction of behavior either in terms of other behavior or else in terms of antecedent stimulus conditions. Its proponents are trying to develop a consistent body of scientific knowledge expressed in terms of whatever lawful relationships may be found to exist among these variables. Because of the tremendous complexity of this task, it has been necessary to use concepts that are considered formally as intervening between stimuli and responses in one case and between predicted responses and predicted-from responses in another. Furthermore, different psychologists develop different kinds of concepts. Some use mechanistic ones, some use field theoretical ones, others think physiologically. Which of these approaches is the best cannot be decided on the basis of *type* of concept. What really counts is the extent to which these concepts aid in the primary task of psychology—the understanding of behavior.

Selection **8** | THE NATURE OF
PSYCHOLOGICAL
INQUIRY*

RAY HYMAN
University of Oregon

METHOD AND CONTENT IN INQUIRY

"The idea is a seed; the method is the earth
furnishing the conditions in which it may develop, flourish and give the best fruit according
to its nature. But as only what has been sown
in the ground will ever grow in it, so nothing
will be developed by the experimental method
except the ideas submitted to it. The method
itself gives birth to nothing." (Claude Bernard,
1865.)

Psychological inquiry consists of a number
of different kinds of activity. One is the formulation and selection of problems for investigation; it is this activity that gives an investigator
his creative role. A second type is the making
of observations and the collecting of facts that
are relevant to a problem; this endeavor lends
support to the popular stereotype of the scientist as a technician who mixes chemicals in
test tubes, bombards elements in cyclotrons,
and reads pointers on dials. A third is the
processing and analysis of the facts; this
fosters the picture of the scientist as a fellow
who juggles numbers, fits equations, and draws
graphs. A fourth is that of explaining or "making sense" out of the data; this gives the investigator the role of theoretician and thinker.
A fifth involves communicating or reporting
conclusions to colleagues; it is this activity,
more than any other, that gives the scientist
his reputation for being obscure and difficult to
understand.

These steps characterize inquiry in other
sciences as well as psychology. What distinguishes psychological inquiry from physical inquiry or biological inquiry are not the kinds
of activity as such, but the subject matter—
what the inquiry is about. The particular subject matter is what you study in psychology
courses—courses that go under such names

as learning, sensation, perception, motivation
and emotion, socialization, thinking and problem-solving personality, and intelligence.

That we can and do talk about method and
content separately does not mean that these
aspects of psychology can be dealt with separately in research. In fact, as we shall note
later on, when a psychologist studies a subject
matter without careful consideration of how his
methods interact with his concepts, he frequently ends up with meaningless or ambiguous outcomes. Conversely, some psychologists
become so attached to particular methods that
they allow them to dictate the matter of their
investigations. Either extreme, of course, results in wasteful research.

Before we elaborate further on the intimate
connection between method and content, we
should spell out the sense in which we employ
the term "content." Any particular inquiry
deals directly with unique and concrete events.
A psychologist, for example, may turn on a
1000-cycle tone for five seconds before he applies a shock to the foot of a dog. Or he may
have a judge sort out a series of colors according to his preferences. Each of these situations
is unique and quite complex. The dog may be
a mongrel, picked up from the streets, with an
unknown history. He may whine, bare his teeth,
wag his tail, attempt to scratch a flea, or engage in a number of other movements while
the tone is sounding. The experimenter who
turns on the tone may be thinking about a
quarrel he had with his wife. The judge who is
sorting the colors might be recently divorced,
suffering from a slight attack of asthma, and
participating in the experiment to get his mind
off his troubles. All these details, and the
many, many more that are connected with the
particular events that the psychologist observes, do *not* form the content of psychological
inquiries.

Scientific inquiry is not about particular
events. Instead, in any inquiry an investigator
selects from particular events only certain aspects which are treated as instances of more
general, repeatable events. The pairing of a
tone with a shock is taken as an example of
what is called "avoidance conditioning." After
a number of pairings of the tone with the
shock, the dog will learn to lift his leg at the
sound of the tone and thereby avoid the shock.

* Ray Hyman, *The Nature of Psychological Inquiry.*
© 1964. Reprinted by permission of Prentice-Hall,
Inc., Englewood Cliffs, N. J.

This relationship between the tone and the leg response is considered an example of a "conditioned reflex"—and it is assumed that this "conditioned reflex" can be established with other animals in other situations. In other words, the psychological inquiry is about something that can be repeatedly observed—a concept and a relationship among concepts. The particular event—this particular mongrel dog in the laboratory on that particular day—can never be witnessed again. But, on the assumption that he is dealing with a "law of nature," the psychologist hopes that the event—pairing a conditioned stimulus with an unconditioned stimulus with the resulting new connection between stimulus and response—is repeatable.

The interaction of subject and method

Psychological inquiry, like all scientific inquiry, then, is about concepts and their interrelationships. Entire "schools" within psychology can be identified in terms of the kinds of concepts they include and exclude from the scope of psychology. When Wilhelm Wundt founded the first laboratory of experimental psychology in 1879, he defined psychology as the study of the elements of conscious experience. The primary elements of consciousness, for him, were "pure" sensations. To study these primary contents of consciousness, he put adult human beings through extensive training in attending to and reporting only pure sensations—patches of light, odors, sounds—sensations stripped of their interpretation. Later researchers called this brand of psychology "structuralism" and its chief methodological tool was termed "introspection." In addition to Wundt's laboratory at Leipzig, the chief centers of structural psychology were at the University of Würzburg in Germany and at Cornell University in the United States.

Some 30 years after Wundt began psychology as a separate form of inquiry, dissatisfaction with his form of psychology led to new "schools." John B. Watson, in the United States, proposed behaviorism as an alternative to structural psychology. From then on, in his militant program, psychology was to be a natural science. It would not deal with subjective, private experience. Instead, it would focus

only on what could be observed as organisms went about solving problems, mastering mazes, reacting to stimulation. What could be observed was behavior—which was made up of such things as glandular and muscular responses to external stimulation.

As psychological history, the preceding two paragraphs are oversimplified and highly inadequate. But they will serve our purpose of indicating the close relationship between subject matter and method. Structural psychology was more than just an emphasis on a particular kind of concept or content—it also implied a particular method for collecting and evaluating data. And this method, introspection, limited psychological inquiry to adult human beings who were willing to go through the lengthy training necessary to learn how to observe their own sensory life. When structuralism was abandoned, the grounds, to a large extent, were methodological. The major technique, introspection, could not produce results that could be obtained in other laboratories. In America Edward B. Titchener could not observe the new conscious elements that the psychologists at Würzburg in Germany had discovered. A bitter controversy erupted. Eventually psychologists abandoned both structuralism as a subject matter and introspectionism as a method.

Watson, too, founded his behaviorism on a method—objective observation of behavior. His "school" ruled out subjective methods such as introspectionism on the grounds that they were unreliable. Psychology as a science had to be based on what could be observed and agreed on by different viewers. Even while he was ruling out certain kinds of data and methods, however, Watson extended the scope of psychological inquiry to include children, illiterates, and animals. In fact, the method of behaviorism could be applied to any creature that could move or "behave" in an observable way in response to external stimulation.

Conceptual systems as guides to inquiry

These brief comments on structural and behavioral psychologies reveal how the content of an inquiry—its concepts and the systematic context of these concepts—can provide limitations and constraints on acceptable methodology. No inquiry, as we shall see, arises in a vacuum. The psychologist who conducts research begins with some sort of a conceptual system—however vague and ill formed—and ends up with a clearer and better formed conceptual system. It may be helpful to use the analogy of a "mental map" to describe this system. The map, always incomplete and inaccurate, nevertheless provides a rough guide on what to explore and where to point. It helps to provide a *conceptual focus* for the inquiry.

The reverse relationship can also hold. Quite frequently a new method, usually developed in another field, will open up new subject matters for inquiry. Developments in brain surgery, electronics, and miniaturization of electrodes, for example, have recently opened up areas of research into brain mechanisms that were inaccessible to psychological inquiry only a few years ago. Similar impetus for psychological inquiry has come from developments in pharmacology, zoology, mathematics, and statistics. Within the field of psychology itself, important breakthroughs and changes in subject matter have followed the development of techniques for scaling responses, measuring attitudes, measuring meaning, and so on.

Although this reciprocal relationship between content and method exists, it is not perfect. Methods can survive long after the conceptual system that gave rise to them has been rejected or discredited. Such is the case with G. T. Fechner's psychophysical methods for measuring sensory thresholds—these methods are still employed today but within a conceptual framework different from that of their origin. Likewise, conceptual systems can survive inadequate methods—psychologists are still trying to study the mechanisms of thinking but have abandoned the original approach to this task by way of classical introspection.

That methods can be separated from their original subject matter represents a mixed blessing. On the one hand, it is clear that the application of methods developed for one purpose to new subject matters often results in new and creative breakthroughs. This happened in psychology, for example, when Louis L. Thurstone, bored with studying judgments of weight substituted more interesting stimuli in their place as a way of teaching the psycho-

physical methods. The result was a whole new field of attitude measurement and scaling that has played a significant role in the development of social psychology as an empirical science.

Unfortunately, the separation of method from content often seems to result in trivial or misleading research. Psychologists frequently seize on a new method without adequately understanding its limitations and the assumptions on which it is based. In employing methods they do not fully understand, investigators often wind up in the ludicrous position of using a technique which assumes a type of relationship that the investigators' theoretical models deny. Some investigators, for example, apply the method of factor analysis, which assumes that individual traits combine additively, to a psychoanalytical theory which clearly implies that traits combine in a nonadditive manner.

In sum, then, the point we want to make is that all psychological inquiry is guided by a conceptual system. This conceptual system—including subject matter, preconceptions, concepts, values, restrictions—serves as a basis for organizing experiments, selecting facts, analyzing data, and interpreting results. Because the conceptual framework limits what the experimenter sees and deals with, it serves both to facilitate and to hinder the development of psychological knowledge. On the one hand, it serves as the necessary background against which to give new facts significance as well as being the basis for determining the relevance of issues. On the other hand, it can also result in failure to see important facts, in missed discoveries, and in the inability to adjust to new facts. The importance of the conceptual system goes beyond its relationship to a particular methodology. The conceptual focus is also what gives unity and coherence to the different activities that form the complex process of psychological inquiry.

Formal versus informal approaches

Psychologists differ greatly among themselves concerning the applicability of formal theory to research on animal and human behavior. At one extreme was the late psychologist Clark Hull, who devoted much of his career to developing a rigorous, formal, deductive theory for all of human behavior. In reply to the question of whether psychology is ready for such a rigorous theory, Hull had this to say[1]

No doubt many will feel that such standards of scientific theory may be suitable for theoretical physics, but that they are quite impossible in psychology, at least for the present. To take such a view is equivalent to holding that we can have no genuinely scientific theory in psychology. This is indeed conceivable, but if so we ought not to pretend to have theories at all. There are signs that the beginnings of a genuinely scientific theory of mammalian behavior are already on their way.

At the other extreme we find B. F. Skinner, who believes that at psychology's present stage of development the attempt to provide formal theories is premature. Indeed, he feels that formal theories can retard the development of psychological research. In an article written 15 years after Hull saw the "beginnings of a genuinely scientific theory" of behavior, Skinner raised two arguments against the use of theory in psychology.[2] First, Skinner believes that an emphasis on formalization may seduce us into forgetting our primary task of accounting for

behavior in its relation to certain manipulable variables; [instead,] we are likely to close our eyes to it and to use the theory to give us answers in place of the answers we might find through further study. It might be argued that the principal function of learning theory to date has been, not to suggest appropriate research, but to create a false sense of security, an unwarranted satisfaction with the *status quo.*

Skinner's second argument is that

research designed with respect to theory is also likely to be wasteful. That a theory generates research does not prove its value unless the research is valuable. Much useless experimentation results from theories, and much energy and skill are absorbed by them. Most theories are eventually over-

thrown, and the greater part of the associated research is discarded.

Skinner on superstitious behavior

Because it is easy to misinterpret what Skinner means by "theory," we shall begin our illustrations of how interpretation enters into psychological research by describing one of Skinner's own studies. We shall then follow the analysis of Skinner's approach to investigating and reporting on psychological phenomena with an extensive analysis of two other examples. By making such a detailed comparison, we not only should be in a better position to see how three outstanding psychologists approach the investigation and explanation of behavior from different viewpoints, but we should also be in a better position to sense the role that interpretation and explanation plays in all research.

In 1948 Skinner reported some interesting observations on what he referred to as "superstition" in the pigeon.[3] He introduced the study by "hypothesizing" that: "Whenever we present a state of affairs which is known to be reinforcing at a given drive, we must suppose that conditioning takes place, even though we have paid no attention to the behavior of the organism in making the presentation." To illustrate this generalization, he described the following experiment. A pigeon, which is kept in a hungry state by being maintained at 75 per cent of its normal body weight, is placed in a special cage for a few minutes each day. A mechanism presents food to the bird at regular intervals *"with no reference whatsoever to the bird's behavior."* Since the pigeon is hungry and since food, under these conditions, is a "reinforcer," we can expect, along with Skinner, that whatever the pigeon happens to be doing at the time the food is presented should be reinforced, or strengthened. In Skinner's "explanatory system," this means that the behavior occurring at the time the pigeon is given food will more likely occur again.

And that is exactly what did happen. At least it did in six out of the eight pigeons who were observed in this situation. One pigeon happened to be turning in a counterclockwise

[1] C. L. Hull. Conflicting psychologies of learning—a way out. *Psychol. Rev.,* 1935, **42,** 491–516.
[2] B. F. Skinner. Are theories of learning necessary? *Psychol. Rev.,* 1950, **57,** 193–216.

[3] B. F. Skinner. "Superstition" in the pigeon. *J. exp. Psychol.,* 1948, **38,** 168–72.

rotation when the food came. With repeated presentations of the food, this pattern of behavior developed into a conditioned response. Between reinforcements the pigeon would perform this counterclockwise "dance" two or three times until the food was presented again. Another bird developed "a 'tossing' response, as if placing its head beneath an invisible bar and lifting it repeatedly." The other birds who showed conditioning developed equally arbitrary patterns of behavior.

Skinner's explanation of this behavior is fairly straightforward.

The bird happens to be executing some response [i.e., activity] as the hopper (which presents the food) appears; as a result it tends to repeat this response. If the interval before the next presentation is not so great that extinction takes place, a second "contingency" is probable. This strengthens the response still further and subsequent reinforcement becomes more probable. It is true that some responses go unreinforced and some reinforcements appear when the response has not just been made, but the net result is the development of a considerable state of strength.

Drawing on his previous experience with this kind of conditioning as well as additional observations made in the present situation, Skinner adds further explanations and makes some concrete predictions about what would happen, say, if the interval between arbitrary reinforcements were lengthened or shortened. One generalization (which other more theoretically minded psychologists would call a testable hypothesis) is that, as the interval between food presentations is made shorter, conditioning should be speedier and more obvious. One basis for this "deduction" is that, as time passes after reinforcement, a pigeon is more and more likely to drift into other behavior; it would therefore be less likely to be repeating its first response when the food comes a second time. A related reason is that as the time interval increases the pigeon is also less likely to be in the same part of the cage the second time the food is presented. If the time interval between reinforcements becomes very short, Skinner even predicts what the nature of the conditioned response will be. "In the limiting case of a very brief interval the behavior to be expected would be holding the

head toward the opening through which the magazine [food dispenser] has disappeared."

Skinner is able to make further speculations concerning what would happen under different levels of drive, under gradually increasing intervals between reinforcements, and with the termination of reinforcements. In these latter cases, he is able to describe further observations that support his generalizations.

Although Skinner avoids setting down his results in the guise of a formal theory, he does not hesitate, after a fashion, to use his highly controlled experiment on pigeons to suggest possible "explanations" of supersition as it occurs at the human level under nonlaboratory conditions. In his own words:

The experiment might be said to demonstrate supersition. The bird behaves as if there were a causal relation between its behavior and the presentation of food, although such a relation is lacking. There are many analogies in human behavior. Rituals for changing one's luck at cards are good examples. A few accidental connections between a ritual and favorable consequences suffice to set up and maintain the behavior in spite of many unreinforced instances. The bowler who has released a ball down the alley but continues to behave as it he were controlling it by twisting and turning his arm and shoulder is another case in point. These behaviors have, of course, no real effect upon one's luck or upon a ball half way down an alley, just as in the present case the food would appear as often if the pigeon did nothing—or, more strictly speaking, did something else.

We can now better grasp what Skinner means when he takes a stand against theories. Skinner obviously *does* theorize in some meanings of that term. He generalizes beyond his immediate results. He makes predictions on the basis of these generalizations. He states his expectations concerning what would happen if the interval were shortened, if drive were increased, if different intervals were employed on the same bird, and so on. These predictions or expectations can be checked by gathering further data. When the new data conflict with his expectations, he revises these expectations and changes his generalizations. Because he deliberately avoids stating and testing formal hypotheses, Skinner may achieve greater flexibility in adapting his expectations and observations to immediate feedback from each new item of information. On the other hand, Skinner's failure to formalize his system makes it difficult, if not impossible, for him to convey to his readers the actual basis for his generalizations and the reasons for his choice of one variable rather than another in making new observations.

Skinner also does not hesitate to employ his results to help us "understand" behavior of human beings in more complex situations. He employs his pigeon experiment as a model for certain kinds of human rituals and superstitions. The actual testing of this application of the model is impossible within Skinner's framework.

Yet it is clear that Skinner is against the use of models in psychological inquiry when they are employed in another form. He has been consistently against attempts by other psychologists to "explain" behavior of organisms in neurological terms. In fact, the kind of theory that Skinner is against is the kind that uses theoretical terms, such as "synapses," "neurones," or "connections"—terms that are on a conceptual level different from the observed behavior for which the experimenter wants to account.

So here is one approach to the interpretation of data. Skinner is unwilling to jump from the pigeon's food-oriented behavior to the pigeon's brain, but, within his system, he is willing to jump from the pigeon's behavior to the superstitious rituals of people in card games and at the bowling alley.

Hebb on the conceptual nervous system

Our third case history represents, more than does the previous one, the kind of theorizing that Professor Skinner claims can lead to wasteful and valueless research. Skinner especially questions the appropriateness of theories that refer to events taking place in what he calls "the conceptual nervous system." Such events are taking place at a different level and within a different conceptual framework from those that the psychologist is trying to predict. In Skinner's view such conceptual constructs represent unnecessary middlemen. Almost as if in direct reply to Skinner, the psychologist Hebb entitled one of his addresses "Drives and

the C. N. S. (Conceptual Nervous System)."[4] In this address, Hebb shows how his own conceptions of motivation have gradually been changed both in conformity with experimental evidence and in terms of new conceptions of the nervous system. Hebb's theorizing employs what psychologists call hypothetical constructs —theoretical entities that presumably could refer to actual and observable structures. Hebb's theoretical terms are constructs like synaptic knobs, cell assemblies, and phase sequences, all of which might plausibly turn out to have real physiological counterparts. Using such terms, Hebb has constructed a theory[5] that has been extremely productive in new research in both the physiology and the psychology of learning and motivation.

Our analysis of the development of Hebb's ideas on motivation will reveal how an interpretative approach condemned by Skinner can profitably serve as a model for continually adjusting our ideas about one domain of behavior.

By the time that an objective, behavioristic psychology began to attack the problem of why animals behave as they do, it was natural to emulate the approach of physics and chemistry and seek for the causes of action outside of the object rather than inside of it. Consequently, in the prevailing doctrine of motivation in American psychology up until the 1930's, an animal or human being was regarded as passive unless acted upon by external forces. The analogy, almost certainly influenced by the Industrial Revolution, was that an organism is like a machine that operates only when it is supplied with power from a separate source. These sources of power or "drive" were held to be the so-called primary drives of hunger, sex, thirst, pain, and mothering. Other instigations to behavior such as seeking status, power, money and the like were seen as deriving by association from these more fundamental drives.

As Hebb points out, this conception of motivation was supported in the minds of psychologists by their conception of the nervous system as being inert unless activated from the outside. The early studies of nerve fibers,

[4] D. O. Hebb. *Psychol. Rev.*, 1955, **62**, 243–254.
[5] D. O. Hebb. *Organization of Behavior*. New York: Wiley, 1949.

for example, indicated that they are inert until set off from the outside. This overly simple notion of motivation has persisted to the present day within psychology, Hebb implies, because many psychologists, even those who openly repudiate using the nervous system as a model, actually are still influenced by this outdated conception of the nervous system. It is not the attempt to use the nervous system as a model that interferes with contemporary theorizing, but the use of the wrong model—a model that has been abandoned by neurologists.

Even from the start, this stimulus-response conception of external drive was confronted with obvious difficulties. Animals were active when none of the primary drives seemed to be acting. They appeared to learn things about their environment and to seek and explore new situations even when they were not hungry or thirsty. The advocates of the predominant stimulus-response concept, however, handled these apparent exceptions in one of two ways. Some added the concept of acquired, or learned, drives to supplement the inborn, or primary, drives; some admitted the existence of additional basic motives such as activity and exploratory drives.

Here we come across an interesting illustration of how explanatory systems are "saved" or retained in the face of contradictory or challenging data. Unlike the stereotype that many textbooks convey, a scientist does not eagerly or willingly change his explanatory conceptions in the face of contradictory evidence. He attempts to salvage his theory by at least three expedients.

In the first place, he will try to deny that the apparent exceptions are really exceptions at all. When animals seem to learn in the absence of a primary drive, the results are inconclusive because it is difficult, if not impossible, to be really sure that all of the animals' primary needs for sex, food, water, and avoidance of pain are really at zero-level.

In the second place, the theorist may add supplementary principles or hypotheses to his original system. Thus, the advocate of classical drive theory can admit the existence of an exploratory drive to account for an animal's learning in a new situation and thereby save the rest of the system as well as the notion of external causes. Or he can add the idea of

learned, or acquired, drives and so explain an animal's willingess to run a maze for novel stimulation as a secondary drive that derives its force from previous association of novel stimuli with obtaining food.

A third expedient is for the investigator to confine himself to types of inquiry or phenomena that best fit his conception. Hebb cites a number of easily accessible phenomena that, in retrospect, were well known and embarrassing to the dominant drive-conception during the first half of the twentieth century. He suggests that "we may overlook the rather large number of forms of behavior in which motivation cannot be reduced to biological drive plus learning. Such behavior is most evident in higher species, and may be forgotten by those who work only with the rat or with restricted segments of the behavior of dog or cat."

But despite the confinement of many psychologists to specific observational conditions, information began accumulating from a variety of sources until psychology as a whole was forced to come to grips with these apparent exceptions to the classical concept of drive. By the time of World War II, and thereafter, more and more psychologists were willing to admit the existence of a class of exploratory-activity drives. For Hebb, at least, this attempt to save motivational theory by simply appending more and more drives was dissatisfying. "We must not multiply drives beyond reason, and at this point one asks whether there is no alternative to the theory in this form."

The alternative that Hebb adopted was based on a newer conception of the central nervous system that developed around 1930. The nerve cell, it seems, actually is not physiologically inert when it is not being stimulated externally. It is active on its own account and can discharge without stimulation. "The nervous system is alive, and living things by their nature are active." In his new theory, Hebb gradually saw that the problem was not to account for the energizing of behavior but rather for its direction. In the earlier view, hunger was seen as a drive that arouses an animal to action. In the newer version, the animal is already active. Hunger is no longer a drive; it does not prod the animal into action. Instead it is a cue that guides or directs the animal's behavior into one kind of activity rather than another. If the rat is hungry his activity will be focused on food-getting. If he is not hungry he will be just as active, but he will focus on some other kind of activity.

Here we see how rephrasing a question, or refocusing our interest, can be a turning point both for theorizing and for guiding further research. Hebb, at that point in his development, held that the human brain is "built to be active, and that as long as it is supplied with adequate nutrition [it] will continue to be active. Brain activity is what determines behavior, and so the only behavioral problem becomes that of accounting for *inactivity*."

This new conceptual framework appeared to account for a lot of behavior that previously did not fit into motivational theory. It made sense for example, out of the data Hebb had obtained in an earlier experiment. In this experiment all the students in a large school were told that they no longer were required to work unless they wanted to. If they made noise and interrupted other children at work, their "punishment" would be to be sent outside to play; the reward for being good was to do more work. "In these circumstances, *all* of the pupils discovered within a day or two that, within limits, they preferred work to no work (and incidentally learned more arithmetic and so forth than in previous years)."

Effects of sensory deprivation on Hebb's theory
Although this new viewpoint toward motivation helped to tie together more data about human behavior, some new experimental evidence soon convinced Hebb that he should revise his conception of motivation once again. The key experiment that raised the doubts in Hebb's mind was conducted by three psychologists in his department at McGill University.[6] In this experiment, a student was paid to lie on a bed in a small room for 24 hours a day, with time out for eating and going to the toilet. Each subject wore translucent goggles, gloves and cardboard cuffs, and every effort was made to prevent auditory or other sensory stimulation. In other words, within the limits of feasibility and ordinary comfort, the experimenters attempted to create a situation where each subject could spend a long period of time with no

[6] W. H. Bexton, W. Heron, and T. H. Scott. Effects of decreased variation in the sensory environment. *Canad. J. Psychol.*, 1954, **8**, 70–76.

sensory input. Although the students were paid 20 dollars a day, which was double what they could earn on other jobs, and although they were encouraged to remain in the experiment as long as they wanted, very few subjects were willing to remain in this condition for more than a few days. The experiment soon became a classic and opened up a whole new line of research on the topic of sensory deprivation.

For Hebb, the experiment was a fatal blow to his theory of motivation. Although the subjects were well paid and were asked essentially to do nothing, they enjoyed the experiment only for from four to eight hours. Beyond this limit, they became increasingly restless, developed a strong need for stimulation, showed signs of disorganization, and revealed other symptoms of psychological impairment. Hebb asked himself:

If the thought process is internally organized and motivated, why should it break down in conditions of perceptual isolation, unless emotional disturbance intervenes? . . . The subjects were reasonably well adjusted, happy, and able to think coherently for the first four or five hours of the experiment; why, according, to my theory, should this not continue, and why should the organization of behavior not be promptly restored with restoration of the normal environment?

In an effort to find answers to his questions, Hebb once again turned to the latest findings of brain physiology to see if they could offer him some clues.

One important clue was the discovery in the brain stem of an "arousal system." During the first half of this century, the classical conception was developed that sensory input from the receptors—such as eye, ear, nose, and touch receptors—made its way by relatively efficient and direct sensory pathways to the sensory areas of the cortex. The new conception suggests that sensory input actually travels to the cortex by two different pathways. One pathway is the classical one leading to the sensory cortex. This route is efficient and leads to relatively localized stimulation of parts of the brain. The second route for the incoming sensory input is by way of the arousal system in the brain stem. The incoming stimulation to the brain stem results in a diffuse, nonspecific stimulation of the cortex. Whereas the stimulation coming to the cortex by the main sensory pathways provides the organism with specific, qualitative information, the stimulation that reaches the cortex through the second, non-specific pathway does not provide information. Rather it serves to tone up the cortex, to arouse it, to alert it for action. In fact, in experiments where this second pathway is surgically blocked, the animal becomes permanently inert and enters a coma.

Hebb conceptualizes these new findings in terms of their implication for psychology by suggesting that "we can now distinguish two quite different effects of a sensory event. One is the *cue function*, guiding behavior; the other, less obvious but no less important, is the *arousal* or *vigilance function*. Without a foundation of arousal, the cue function cannot exist." Hebb sees the arousal function as the equivalent of the energizing function of drive in the earlier stimulus-response formulations. So, in a sense, both empirical findings from psychological research and the newer physiological evidence of an arousal system bring Hebb back to the earlier conception of drive as an energizer of behavior. The newer conception, however, is a much more sophisticated version of the earlier theory of external motivation. It incorporates the stimulus-response model; but it also includes many phenomena that could not be handled by the earlier model. The new theory suggests that drive, or motivation, can either facilitate or impair performance. Low motivation results in poor performance; high motivation also can result in poor performance. This suggests that there is an optimal level of motivation for different types of tasks. For well-practiced and simple tasks, the higher the drive the better the performance. For example, if we are studying speed of running away from a noxious stimulus, then we would expect the speed to increase with the degree of painfulness of the stimulus. Even with such a straightforward task, however, if the arousal becomes extreme, paralysis induced by fear can result. On the other hand, if we are observing a more delicate task such as threading a needle, even a moderate amount of arousal might impair performance.

An even more interesting implication of this conception is the so-called discrepancy hypothesis. This hypothesis suggests that for any situation, an organism is motivated to seek an optimal amount of stimulation or arousal. If the incoming stimulation follows a pattern of complete expectation it does not serve to arouse or stimulate the individual. Hebb and others, for example, have used such a notion to explain why so-called popular music does not remain popular for very long. With repetition it no longer produces novel or unexpected stimulation. On the other hand, if the incoming stimulation is too chaotic and novel, then it will result in a level of activation beyond the optimal. This is why, for example, a modern composition in music, reaching the ears for the first time of one used to music of the Romantic period, can sound repulsive and annoying. The new conception suggests that individuals will constantly seek some deviation from what they are used to, but will avoid too much deviation.

With this new conception, Hebb feels that drive theory can now account, for the first time, for such things as the positive attraction that risk-taking and thrill-seeking seem to have for human beings. "This taste for excitement *must* not be forgotten when we are dealing with human motivation. It appears that, up to a certain point, threat and puzzle have positive motivating value, beyond that point negative value."

Of course, the new conception raises many problems. It, too, has inconsistencies and apparent contradictions to resolve. But its value lies in its ability to tie together phenomena that fitted into the older conceptions along with phenomena that did not fit so well. Moreover, the conception suggests a series of new empirical observations that can be made to clarify it as well as to test its implications. Already, a wide variety of experimentation owes its instigation to this new conception of the role of drive and cue in motivation. But this is the way explanation "works" within the process of inquiry.

The value of theories

Although Skinner feels that his approach is more likely to lead to valuable research, and that approaches such as Hebb's will lead to wasteful and useless research, Skinner has avoided the obviously sticky issue of specifying how we decide whether research is valuable or not. But we probably would have little or no dissent among most psychologists if we said that research generated by both Skinner's approach and Hebb's theory have contributed significantly to the advance of modern psychological inquiry. Skinner argues, as we saw, that "Most theories are eventually overthrown, and the greater part of the associated research is discarded." The evidence, at least as put together by historians of science in other scientific fields, seems to contradict Skinner's contention. Most theories are eventually overthrown, as Skinner maintains, but some of the research which they generated often survives and becomes incorporated and reinterpreted within succeeding theories. Following are some obvious examples. The Copernican system did not discard the data of Ptolemy, but merely rearranged them. Tycho Brahe's hybrid compromise between Copernicus and Ptolemy was overthrown by Kepler, but in so doing, Kepler retained and used all of Brahe's carefully collected data. The phlogiston theory of combustion, among other things, led to the discovery of oxygen. When Lavoisier overthrew it, he did not discard the various experimental data which it had generated; he incorporated all of them within the new system.

Although the scientific history of psychology is rather short, there is no reason to doubt the value and usefulness of much data that was collected under what we now consider faulty or discarded theories.

Whatever makes research valuable, whatever makes the difference between inquiries that succeed and those that fail, it seems clear that the essential ingredient does not reside in the nature of the explanatory system that guides the researcher in his inquiry and in his interpretations of the results.

Selection **9** | MAN IN NATURE*

MARSTON BATES
University of Michigan

Psychology and anthropology are the social sciences most clearly related to biology. Both, in fact, include large areas of knowledge that could be regarded as purely biological. Comparative psychology deals with the behavior of animals—or may even be extended to include

* Marston Bates, *Man in Nature*, 2d ed. © 1964. Reprinted by permission of Prentice-Hall, Inc., Englewood Cliffs, N.J.

plant behavior. Experimental psychology always includes much biological material, even when the experiments involve human subjects and are aimed at solving human problems. Physical anthropology is also largely a biological science, and covers genetics, human physical types, and racial diversity, and fossils of men or man-like animals. Physical anthropology, therefore, is that part of the science concerned with man as an animal; the other parts of anthropology concentrate more on man as a bearer of culture.

The distinctions among social psychology, social anthropology, and sociology are far from clear-cut. Differences in points of view, methods, and problems dealt with are most easily explained in terms of the historical development of the different sciences. Psychology, traditionally, has been concerned with the behavior of men as individuals. Anthropology started as the study of exotic people, strange tribes with strange ways, and, through its branch of archaeology, also encompassed the prehistoric past. Sociology, in its beginnings, investigated the institutions of Western civilization, things like class structure, urbanization, religious and educational institutions. These distinctions have long been blurred, but they are still discernible.

Since sociology has been mainly focused on the institutions of civilization, it has had less direct contact with biology than its sister sciences. Yet a prime interest of sociology is the study of human populations, which forms the subject of the special science of *demography*. The study of human populations and the study of the populations of other organisms have much in common, and the two subjects have become closely related. It is interesting that the vocabulary and concepts used in population study were for the most part first developed by demographers, and subsequently applied to organisms other than man.

Sociology has also directed its attention to the environmental relations of men and human institutions, and has developed a special field called human ecology. The relations between human and other kinds of ecology, however, have not been carefully worked out, and there is considerable disagreement about the meaning of the term. Human ecology, however defined, is close to human geography, which is generally considered to be another social science. Economics, curiously, has the same Greek root as ecology (*oikos*, meaning household), and phrases like "the economy of nature" and "the ecology of man" illustrate how easily the two words may be interchanged. But as the sciences are practiced in our universities, there is little connection between ecology and economics.

BIOLOGICAL AND SOCIAL SCIENCES

The relationship between the biological and social sciences begins with the problem of the biological roots of cultural phenomena. We are here concerned with the differences between man-as-an-animal and man-as-a-bearer-of-culture. One extreme view holds that human behavior is culturally determined and that man's animal background is irrelevant and meaningless. The other extreme considers that since man so obviously is an animal, everything about him must have a biological explanation.

The truth probably lies somewhere in between. Man has retained his animal constitution which forms, however distantly, a background for his actions; but his actions are more than those of just an animal. Nutrition and reproduction, for instance, are universal biological drives found in all organisms. Yet food behavior and sexual behavior in man cannot be understood in purely biological terms. What one eats, when one eats, how one eats, whom one eats with vary greatly from culture to culture and are clearly learned patterns of behavior. Hunger, however, still has a physiological basis; digestion is still a chemical process, even though this does not explain why, among some peoples, ants are highly prized food while, among others, the idea of eating ants is horrifying. The hunger drive may be thwarted by fasting for cultural reasons, and sometimes men will die rather than eat food they believe unfit.

Sex similarly is channeled by custom and by culture among all known peoples. There are always rules about who may marry whom, and there is always a taboo against incest—though what is considered to be incest may vary tremendously. Man is extraordinary among animals in having a continuous sexuality; he is also extraordinary in suppressing that sexuality in cults of chastity. The immense variety of forms of individual or institutional sexual behavior of different peoples can hardly be explained biologically, but underneath there is a biological drive which is related to the biological drive in all forms of sexual reproduction. But how, with all of this complexity, do we find the biological basis? How do we determine what is innate, instinctive, "natural" for man?

The concept of evolution teaches us that the cultural grew out of the biological just as, at another level, the living grew out of the inorganic. Life started, somehow, as a development from inorganic processes; and culture started, somehow, from biological origins. But once culture started, once man started transmitting learned behavior from generation to generation, human behavior began to take on special aspects.

Every man is the consequence of his two inheritances. We can call one somatic and the other extrasomatic. The somatic inheritance is biological, and depends on genes and chromosomes; the extrasomatic is cultural, and depends on symbolic forms of communication. We can find all sorts of analogies between the two systems. The symbol systems on which tradition depends compare with the genetic systems on which biological inheritance depends. Cultural traits are adaptive, in many ways, as are biological traits, and the various kinds of adaptations can be studied. The diffusion of cultural traits can be traced and we see blending or hybridization—and conflict—in cultures. But it is dangerous to forget that we are dealing with two very different systems. That the two often show analogies does not mean that they are the same thing. We can learn much about each of the systems, however, by studying the analogies—if we are careful—and it is unfortunate that the two systems are generally studies by quite different people, working in different scientific worlds.

If we look at the man-and-culture relationship from the point of view of organism and environment, we are confronted with this question: Is culture an attribute of the human organism, or is it part of the human environment? The ways of answering this can serve as a somewhat oversimplified distinction between the psychological and anthropological views of man. Psychologists tend to consider culture as a part of the environment: they concentrate on the reactions of the individual to his culture, how he copes with it or fails, how he becomes adjusted or frustrated. The anthropologist, on the other hand, tends to regard culture as a part of the man: When he studies Dyaks in Borneo or Hopi in the United States and describes their ways of life, he is analyzing the adjustments of man and culture to the environment.

For the biologist, culture must at times be viewed as part of the man, at other times as part of the environment. We must always be aware that we are dealing with the man-culture-environment complex. When we study man's ecological relationships, it is generally man and culture versus the environment that interests us. The ecological character of a man in the Congo, for instance, depends on whether he is a food-gathering pygmy, an agricultural Bantu, or an industrialized Belgian.

On the other hand, when we study man's physiology, it is more useful to treat culture as a part of the environment. If we are interested in the heat relations of the human animal, for example, his clothing and housing and his work habits become environmental effects. Cultural influences are so pervasive that the study of human biology, or man's uncultured physiology, is made very difficult. Temperature relations, nutritional needs, sexual behavior, excretory functions, all the basic physiological processes, may be influenced in many subtle ways by cultural factors. This fact sometimes disrupts cross-cultural medical work. Treatment effective in the United States or Europe may not necessarily be equally applicable in China or tropical Africa. The effect of chemicals on pathogens remains the same, but the human factor, the human reaction, may vary greatly.

But what are the peculiar characteristics of man? What do all men share that other animals do not have? We might try to sort out these qualities, lumping what may be trivial with what may be important, under the headings of physical, behavioral, and cultural characteristics.

Physical characteristics

Man's most striking anatomical characteristics stem from his upright posture and bipedal locomotion. The habit of walking on the hind legs, which leaves the hands and arms—the forelegs—free at all times for manipulating or carrying objects, involves numerous anatomical changes. Man's legs, unlike those of the great apes and most other primates, are much longer than the arms, and there are many alterations in the pelvic region, especially the ilium. Man's foot, with the great toe in line with the other toes and with the high arch, is quite different from the foot of apes; it is well adapted to walking or running, but not much good for grasping branches. The head is poised on the spinal column so that man looks forward when standing upright.

Man has a very large brain compared with those of apes and other mammals. The cranial capacity of modern man is 1200–1500 cc, as against the 350–450 cc of the chimpanzee, and brain size undoubtedly affects intelligence and the ability to learn. Many other characteristics of the head are peculiarly human: the comparatively vertical face, the great reduction in the projection of the jaws, the distinct chin, the prominent nose with its elongated tip, the outwardly rolled mucous membrane of the lips, the rolled margin of the ears. And then of course there is the peculiar distribution of hair, or lack of hair. Mostly we can only guess about the significance of these differences.

Man also differs markedly from the apes in having greatly reduced canine teeth, no more prominent than the premolars and incisors on either side. Since the time of Darwin, scientists have thought that the reduction of the canine teeth might be related to tool using: that man with a club did not need his teeth for offense or defense; or, contrariwise that lacking large canines, man needed a club.

Behavioral characteristics

Man is unique among the primates in being a predatory, carnivorous animal. To be sure, many groups of modern men are primarily or exclusively vegetarian, but only because they are able to prepare seeds, tubers, and other vegetative materials by cooking with fire. Without fire man's vegetable diet would be limited to fruits, nuts, and similar special plant products. On the other hand, man can digest all kinds of meat—molluscs, insects, fish, and meat from fellow mammals—without cooking.

Even if we did not have the evidence of the fossil record, we could deduce that man became a hunter before he had learned to master fire.

Man is also a highly social animal, and he is understandable only in terms of his social relationships. Man, as a solitary individual, is basically helpless, despite his vaunted intelligence. If we try to visualize the life of the human animal in the Old Stone Age, we realize that only cooperating groups could catch needed animal food or ward off enemies such as the big cats.

Many kinds of animals show social behavior in the sense that different individuals of the same species act cooperatively for special or varied purposes. The most elaborate societies, aside from the human species, are those of the insects. But insect societies are quite different from those of vertebrates, in that they are based primarily on purely instinctive behavior; and even though a particular termite, ant, or bee colony may be composed of many thousands of individuals, they are all members of a single family, consisting of a mother (the queen) and her multitudinous offspring. Comparisons between insect societies and vertebrate societies are only analogies; the sometimes striking similarities are the consequence of quite different evolutionary histories.

There is a wide variety of social behavior in different vertebrates, as is reflected in the words we use for group labels: school, herd, flock, pack, and so forth. The study and analysis of such social interaction constitute a rapidly growing field of biological research.[1]

Man is a mammal and we can best understand the development of human social behavior by looking at comparable behavior in other mammals. There are three basic classes of individuals within any mammal species: males, females, and young. If we consider social behavior to be a continuing interaction among individuals of a species, we thus have six major kinds of interactions: male-female, female-young, young-young, female-female, male-male, and male-young. With mammals, female-young interaction is universal and inevitable, since the young are dependent on the mother until weaned. There must also be at least periodic male-female interaction, since fertilization is internal. Young-young interaction is almost equally inevitable, since several young are born at a time with most mammals, and where birth is single, a new infant is generally born before the previous one has become completely independent.

In many mammals, a single male may be associated with several females and with their young, forming a polygynous family. The rarest form of association involves several males, females, and young, and in it all six types of possible cooperative interaction must occur if the group is to function smoothly. This sort of social grouping, which occurs in a few mammal groups, including the canines (dogs, wolves, etc.) and the primates, is especially interesting in its bearing on the origins of human behavior. It is difficult to imagine how the complications of language communication could have developed except within fairly large cooperating bands, bands larger than the nuclear family. This intragroup cooperation and communication surely form the essence of purely human behavior.

Man has another even more unusual behavioral characteristic: the long period from birth to sexual maturity. The human infant is completely dependent on adults for from 6 to 8 years, the ape infant for perhaps 2 years, most monkeys for only 1 year. Man reaches puberty at about 14 years and full adult powers at about 20; the corresponding figures for the great apes are about 8 and 12. Mammals other than primates generally show even more rapid developmental rates. This slow human development, taking place within a social group, provides the behavioral basis for culture, for during the long period, the adults can teach and the young can learn. The extrasomatic inheritance of culture requires both transmitting and receiving mechanisms, teaching and learning; the study of these is the crux of a large part of the science of psychology.

Cultural characteristics

Man may be defined facetiously as a "featherless biped." But when we try to formulate a scientific definition, we tend to use cultural rather than physical or behavioral terms. We say that man is peculiar because he has lan-

---

[1] See in this series, V. G. Dethier and E. Stellar, *Animal Behavior*, 2nd ed., p. 106ff. (Englewood Cliffs, N.J.: Prentice-Hall, 1964).

guage—has developed symbols that make abstract thought possible—or because he makes tools, or because he uses fire.

Human language is in some ways similar to, but in other ways vastly different from, other kinds of animal communication. We simply have no idea about its evolutionary history, though many people have speculated about its possible origins. There is, for instance, the "bow-wow" theory, that language started from attempts to imitate animal sounds. Or the "ding-dong" theory, that it arose from natural sound-producing responses. Or the "pooh-pooh" theory, that it began with violent outcries or exclamations.

We have no way of knowing whether the kinds of men represented by the earliest fossils could talk or not. The languages of living men all seem to be about equally complex, equally remote from the signal cries of apes, monkeys, or other animals. Some living peoples, such as the Australian aborigines, have simple material cultures; others, Europeans, for instance, have complex cultures; but we cannot show any relation between the evolution of material culture and the evolution of language. There are thousands of kinds of languages spoken in the world today, and the linguistic experts can trace trends of orderly change within them. Yet none of these throw light on the origin or evolution of language, only on its change and diversification.

Language does not leave fossils, at least not until it has become written. We do find fossil tools, however, which give us clues to the evolution of culture. Tool-using is not unique to man; some insects and vertebrates also have this ability. Tool-making is not unique either, since some monkeys and apes may break off branches to use as sticks. Man's uniqueness is in *the making of tools in accord with a predetermined plan or pattern.* Stones that were obviously shaped for some particular purpose by chipping occur in deposits that date from early in the Pleistocene period. Animals with this essential human characteristic, then, have been around for several hundred thousand years.

The use of fire is more difficult to determine than the habit of shaping tools. There is clear evidence of hearths in the caves at Choukoutien, where Peking man was found, that are thought to date from about the middle of the Pleistocene. But it is more convenient to use tools, rather than fire or language, for drawing the line between man and not-man.

CAPABILITY AND ACHIEVEMENT

When we look about us, the difference between man and other animals seems enormous. Man, with his culture, has spread all over the world, has learned to adapt to the most diverse climates and habitats. He has drastically altered the landscape of large parts of the earth. The canyons of Manhattan may be trivial when compared with the Grand Canyon of the Colorado, but the canyons of Manhattan still are awe-inspiring, and they were built by the efforts of a quite puny animal in a very few years. They are products of the human mind, a mind that seems very different from anything else we can find in nature.

We tend, as scientists, philosophers, or artists, to be impressed with this achievement when we look at man. Because of this, we tend to look at man himself as something quite different from anything else in the system of nature. Certainly biology becomes hopelessly inadequate when we set out to study the human achievement. But, as Harry Harlow has pointed out:[2] "The probability that a relatively small intellectual gain by man over the anthropoid apes would make possible the development of symbolic language and also culture is given small consideration. It is a common error to fail to differentiate between capability and achievement. Thus, the fledgling swallow a few days before it can fly differs little in anatomical and physiological capacity from the swallow capable of sustained flight, but from the point of view of achievement the two are separated by what appears to be an abysmal gulf."

[2] The evolution of learning, in *Behavior and Evolution*, Anne Roe and G. G. Simpson, eds., p. 278. (New Haven: Yale University Press, 1958.)

THE DEVELOPMENT OF BEHAVIOR | 2

In a very real sense, a complete understanding of the development of behavior necessarily would entail consideration of all the facets of behavior which are discussed throughout the remainder of this book. However, because we cannot conveniently consider everything at once, we leave the elaboration of more specific aspects of functioning to the relevant chapters. In this chapter we examine some of the kinds of evidence which support the general psychological principle that the structure and behavior of the organism depend on a continual interaction of hereditary mechanisms with environmental factors.

BIOLOGICAL FACTORS

With regard to the biological development of the organism, this principle implies that no anatomical structure can be said to be determined exclusively by gene structure. On the contrary, biological structure is determined by the biochemical composition of the genes in interaction with the surrounding intracellular and extracellular biochemical environment. Although it is generally conceded that hereditary and environmental factors interact, in determining behavioral development Dr. Anne Anastasi points out in Selection 10 that it is important to ask the further question of how this interaction takes place. She suggests that the action of heredity in determinants upon behavior is always indirect since no psychological trait is determined by heredity per se. However, hereditary factors can be ordered in terms of degree of indirectness. An example of a hereditary factor which is quite indirect in its effect is social stereotypes associated with particular physiques. The behavioral characteristics of mental defects caused by faulty gene structure (e.g., phenylpyruvic amentia) are considerably more direct. Anastasi notes that, as the more indirectly a hereditary factor affects behavior, the greater is the diversity of possible behavioral outcomes. Anastasi distinguishes between organic and behavioral types of environmental factors and orders these on a continuum of breadth of influence. In conclusion, she examines seven different research approaches to answer the question "How?"

PSYCHOLOGICAL FACTORS

Although the old adage that "you can't teach an old dog new tricks" is a gross oversimplification, it does appear that there are certain times in the development of higher animals which are critical for the development of certain types of behavior. In Selection 11, Dr. J. P. Scott reviews extensive evidence for the existence of critical-period phenomena in the areas of learning, infantile stimulation, and social relationships. He also considers some mechanisms which might provide the basis for these critical periods. Among the possible psychological mechanisms which might be involved are levels of emotional arousal, ability to be fear conditioned, ability to perform certain social behavior patterns, and appropriately developed sensory and motor capacities. Scott's views suggest the general principle that biological and psychological systems become organized as quickly as the capacity is available for such organization. If a "normal" environmental support is present, the organism becomes organized in a way which is typical for the species and thus generally adaptive. If normal environmental experiences are absent or if quite abnormal experiences are provided, the effects may be irreversible.[1]

SOCIOCULTURAL FACTORS

Further support for the above principle is provided by a series of experiments from Dr. Harry Harlow's laboratory. In earlier research (Selection 20) Harlow had shown that the "love" of an infant monkey for his mother surrogate was more dependent on tactual factors involved in "contact comfort" than on the satisfaction of the hunger drive. Harlow has continued to work on the variables which influence the development of heterosexual affectional systems. He and his wife report on some of this research in Selection 12. They found that if animals were subjected to total social deprivation during the first two years of life, the capacity for normal social interactions as adults was obliterated or at least greatly reduced. Another group of animals was raised, at least during the first six months, without physical contact with other monkeys, although some of them had contact with cloth or wire mother surrogates. As adults many of these animals showed abnormal behavior patterns, including staring and rocking movements and self-injurious behavior. Furthermore, the attempts to breed these animals ended in utter failure. Lack of contact with real mothers and with peers during early life resulted in gross distortions of social and sexual behavior as adults. That the infant-infant contact is important is illustrated by the fact that if babies who were raised on cloth surrogate mothers were given twenty minutes per day in an enriched environment in which they could play with their peers, they developed normally, both socially and sexually. It would appear that, in monkeys and men, peer-group contacts are important for developing appropriate sex-role behavior.

In Selection 13, Dr. Ruth Benedict, a cultural anthropologist, examines several types of role conflicts which are dictated by the child's biology but which may be ameliorated to a greater or lesser degree by his culture. Her paper thus emphasizes the interaction of biological, psychological, and cultural determinants of behavior by illustrating the wide range of "adjustments which are possible within a universally given, but not so drastic, set of physiological facts."

[1] The interested student should be aware of a reply to Scott's article: T. C. Schnerla and Jay S. Rosenblatt, "Critical Periods in the Development of Behavior," *Science*, 139:1110–1116, March, 1963.

Selection **10** | HEREDITY, ENVIRONMENT, AND THE QUESTION "HOW?"*

ANNE ANASTASI
Fordham University

Two or three decades ago, the so-called heredity-environment question was the center of lively controversy. Today, on the other hand, many psychologists look upon it as a dead issue. It is now generally conceded that both hereditary and environmental factors enter into all behavior. The reacting organism is a product of its genes and its past environment, while present environment provides the immediate stimulus for current behavior. To be sure, it can be argued that, although a given trait may result from the combined influence of hereditary and environmental factors, a specific difference in this trait between individuals or between groups may be traceable to either hereditary or environmental factors alone. The design of most traditional investigations undertaken to identify such factors, however, has been such as to yield inconclusive answers. The same set of data has frequently led to opposite conclusions in the hands of psychologists with different orientations.

Nor have efforts to determine the proportional contribution of hereditary and environmental factors to observed individual differences in given traits met with any greater success. Apart from difficulties in controlling conditions, such investigations have usually been based upon the implicit assumption that hereditary and environmental factors combine in an additive fashion. Both geneticists and psychologists have repeatedly demonstrated, however, that a more tenable hypothesis is that of interaction (*15, 22, 28, 40*). In other words, the nature and extent of the influence of each type of factor depend upon the contribution of the other. Thus the proportional contribution of heredity to the variance of a given trait, rather than being a constant, will vary under different environmental conditions. Similarly, under dif-

ferent hereditary conditions, the relative contribution of environment will differ. Studies designed to estimate the proportional contribution of heredity and environment, however, have rarely included measures of such interaction. The only possible conclusion from such research would thus seem to be that both heredity and environment contribute to all behavior traits and that the extent of their respective contributions cannot be specified for any trait. Small wonder that some psychologists regard the heredity-environment question as unworthy of further consideration!

But is this really all we can find out about the operation of heredity and environment in the etiology of behavior? Perhaps we have simply been asking the wrong questions. The traditional questions about heredity and environment may be intrinsically unanswerable. Psychologists began by asking *which* type of factor, hereditary or environmental, is responsible for individual differences in a given trait. Later, they tried to discover *how much* of the variance was attributable to heredity and how much to environment. It is the primary contention of this paper that a more fruitful approach is to be found in the question *"How?"* There is still much to be learned about the specific *modus operandi* of hereditary and environmental factors in the development of behavioral differences. And there are several current lines of research which offer promising techniques for answering the question "How?"

VARIETY OF INTERACTION MECHANISMS

Hereditary factors

If we examine some of the specific ways in which hereditary factors may influence behavior, we cannot fail but be impressed by their wide diversity. At one extreme, we find such conditions as phenylpyruvic amentia and amaurotic idiocy. In these cases, certain essential physical prerequisites for normal intellectual development are lacking as a result of hereditary metabolic disorders. The individual will be mentally defective, regardless of the type of environmental conditions under which he is reared.

A somewhat different situation is illustrated by hereditary deafness, which may lead to

* From Anne Anastasi, "Heredity, Environment, and the Question 'How?,' " *Psychological Review*, 65: 197–208, 1958. Copyright 1958 by the American Psychological Association and reproduced by permission.

intellectual retardation through interference with normal social interaction, language development, and schooling. In such a case, however, the hereditary handicap can be offset by appropriate adaptations of training procedures. It has been said, in fact, that the degree of intellectual backwardness of the deaf is an index of the state of development of special instructional facilities. As the latter improve, the intellectual retardation associated with deafness is correspondingly reduced.

A third example is provided by inherited susceptibility to certain physical diseases, with consequent protracted ill health. If environmental conditions are such that illness does in fact develop, a number of different behavioral effects may follow. Intellectually, the individual may be handicapped by his inability to attend school regularly. On the other hand, depending upon age of onset, home conditions, parental status, and similar factors, poor health may have the effect of concentrating the individual's energies upon intellectual pursuits. The curtailment of participation in athletics and social functions may serve to strengthen interest in reading and other sedentary activities. Concomitant circumstances would also determine the influence of such illness upon personality development. And it is well known that the latter effects could run the gamut from a deepening of human sympathy to psychiatric breakdown.

Finally, heredity may influence behavior through the mechanism of social stereotypes. A wide variety of inherited physical characteristics have served as visible cues for identifying such stereotypes. These cues thus lead to behavioral restrictions or opportunities and—at a more subtle level—to social attitudes and expectancies. All of these influences eventually leave their mark upon his abilities and inabilities, his emotional reactions, goals, ambitions, and outlook on life.

The genticist Dobzhansky illustrates this type of mechanism by means of a dramatic hypothetical situation. He points out that if there were a culture in which the carriers of blood group AB were considered aristocrats, and those of blood group O laborers, then the blood-group genes would become important hereditary determiners of behavior (*12*, p. 147). Obviously the association between blood group and behavior would be specific to that culture.

But such specificity is an essential property of the causal mechanism under consideration.

More realistic examples are not hard to find. The most familiar instances occur in connection with constitutional types, sex, and race. Sex and skin pigmentation obviously depend upon heredity. General body build is strongly influenced by hereditary components, although also susceptible to environmental modification. That all these physical characteristics may exert a pronounced effect upon behavior within a given culture is well known. It is equally apparent, of course, that in different cultures the behavioral correlates of such hereditary physical traits may be quite unlike. A specific physical cue may be completely unrelated to individual differences in psychological traits in one culture, while closely correlated with them in another. Or it may be associated with totally dissimilar behavior characteristics in two different cultures.

It might be objected that some of the illustrations which have been cited do not properly exemplify the operation of hereditary mechanisms in behavior development since hereditary factors enter only indirectly into the behavior in question. Closer examination, however, shows this distinction to be untenable. First it may be noted that the influence of heredity upon behavior is always indirect. No psychological trait is ever inherited as such. All we can ever say directly from behavioral observations is that a given trait shows evidence of being influenced by certain "inheritable unknowns." This merely defines a problem for genetic research; it does not provide a causal explanation. Unlike the blood groups, which are close to the level of primary gene products, psychological traits are related to genes by highly indirect and devious routes. Even the mental deficiency associated with phenylketonuria is several steps removed from the chemically defective genes that represent its hereditary basis. Moreover, hereditary influences cannot be dichotomized into the more direct and the less direct. Rather do they represent a whole "continuum of indirectness," along which are found all degrees of remoteness of causal links. The examples already cited illustrate a few of the points on this continuum.

It should be noted that as we proceed along the continuum of indirectness, the range of variation of possible outcomes of hereditary factors expands rapidly. At each step in the causal chain, there is fresh opportunity for interaction with other hereditary factors as well as with environmental factors. And since each interaction in turn determines the direction of subsequent interactions, there is an ever-widening network of possible outcomes. If we visualize a simple sequential grid with only two alternatives at each point, it is obvious that there are two possible outcomes in the one-stage situation, four outcomes at the second stage, eight at the third, and so on in geometric progression. The actual situation is undoubtedly much more complex, since there will usually be more than two alternatives at any one point.

In the case of the blood groups, the relation to specific genes is so close that no other concomitant hereditary or environmental conditions can alter the outcome. If the organism survives at all, it will have the blood group determined by its genes. Among psychological traits, on the other hand, some variation in outcome is always possible as a result of concurrent circumstances. Even in cases of plenylketonuria, intellectual development will exhibit some relationship with the type of care and training available to the individual. That behavioral outcomes show progressive diversification as we proceed along the continuum of indirectness is brought out by the other examples which were cited. Chronic illness *can* lead to scholarly renown or to intellectual immaturity; a mesomorphic physique *can* be a contributing factor in juvenile delinquency or in the attainment of a college presidency! Published data on Sheldon somatotypes provide some support for both of the latter outcomes.

Parenthetically, it may be noted that geneticists have sometimes used the term "norm of reaction" to designate the range of variation of possible outcomes of gene properties (cf. *13*, p. 161). Thus heredity sets the "norm" or limits within which environmental differences determine the eventual outcome. In the case of some traits, such as blood groups or eye color, this norm is much narrower than in the case of other traits. Owing to the rather different psychological connotations of both the words "norm" and "reaction," however, it seems less confusing to speak of the "range of variation" in this context.

A large portion of the continuum of hereditary influences which we have described coincides with the domain of somatopsychological relations, as defined by Barker et al. (6). Under this heading, Barker includes "variations in physique that affect the psychological situation of a person by influencing the effectiveness of his body as a tool for actions or by serving as a stimulus to himself or others" (*6*, p. 1). Relatively direct neurological influences on behavior, which have been the traditional concern of physiological psychology, are excluded from this definition, Barker being primarily concerned with what he calls the "social psychology of physique." Of the examples cited in the present paper, deafness, severe illness, and the physical characteristics associated with social stereotypes would meet the specifications of somatopsychological factors.

The somatic factors to which Barker refers, however, are not limited to those of hereditary origin. Bodily conditions attributable to environmental causes operate in the same sorts of somatopsychological relations as those traceable to heredity. In fact, heredity-environment distinctions play a minor part in Barker's approach.

Environmental factors

Organic   Turning now to an analysis of the role of environmental factors in behavior, we find the same etiological mechanisms which were observed in the case of hereditary factors. First, however, we must differentiate between two classes of environmental influences: (a) those producing organic effects which may in turn influence behavior and (b) those serving as direct stimuli for psychological reactions. The former may be illustrated by food intake or by exposure to bacterial infection; the latter, by tribal initiation ceremonies or by a course in algebra. There are no completely satisfactory names by which to designate these two classes of influences. In an earlier paper by Anastasi and Foley (4), the terms "structural" and "functional" were employed. However, "organic" and "behavioral" have the advantage of greater familiarity in this context and may be less open to misinterpretation. Accordingly, these terms will be used in the present paper.

Like hereditary factors, environmental influences of an organic nature can also be ordered along a continuum of indirectness with regard to their relation to behavior. This continuum closely parallels that of hereditary factors. One end is typified by such conditions as mental deficiency resulting from cerebral birth injury or from prenatal nutritional inadequacies. A more indirect etiological mechanism is illustrated by severe motor disorder—as in certain cases of cerebral palsy—*without* accompanying injury to higher neurological centers. In such instances, intellectual retardation may occur as an indirect result of the motor handicap, through the curtailment of educational and social activities. Obviously this causal mechanism corresponds closely to that of hereditary deafness cited earlier in the paper.

Finally, we may consider an environmental parallel to the previously discussed social stereotypes which were mediated by hereditary physical cues. Let us suppose that a young woman with mousy brown hair becomes transformed into a dazzling golden blonde through environmental techniques currently available in our culture. It is highly probable that this metamorphosis will alter, not only the reactions of her associates toward her, but also her own self-concept and subsequent behavior. The effects could range all the way from a rise in social poise to a drop in clerical accuracy!

Among the examples of environmentally determined organic influences which have been described, all but the first two fit Barker's definition of somatopsychological factors. With the exception of birth injuries and nutritional deficiencies, all fall within the social psychology of physique. Nevertheless, the individual factors exhibit wide diversity in their specific modus operandi—a diversity which has important practical as well as theoretical implications.

Behavioral The second major class of environmental factors—the behavioral as contrasted to the organic—are by definition direct influences. The immediate effect of such environmental factors is always a behavioral change. To be sure, some of the initial behavioral effects may themselves indirectly affect the individual's later behavior. But this relationship can perhaps be best conceptualized in terms of breadth and permanence of effects. Thus it could be said that we are now dealing, not with

a continuum of indirectness, as in the case of hereditary and organic-environmental factors, but rather with a continuum of breadth.

Social class membership may serve as an illustration of a relatively broad, pervasive, and enduring environmental factor. Its influence upon behavior development may operate through many channels. Thus social level may determine the range and nature of intellectual stimulation provided by home and community through books, music, art, play activities, and the like. Even more far-reaching may be the effects upon interests and motivation, as illustrated by the desire to perform abstract intellectual tasks, to surpass others in competitive situations, to succeed in school, or to gain social approval. Emotional and social traits may likewise be influenced by the nature of interpersonal relations characterizing homes at different socioeconomic levels. Somewhat more restricted in scope than social class, although still exerting a relatively broad influence, is amount of formal schooling which the individual is able to obtain.

A factor which may be wide or narrow in its effects, depending upon concomitant circumstances, is language handicap. Thus the bilingualism of an adult who moves to a foreign country with inadequate mastery of the new language represents a relatively limited handicap which can be readily overcome in most cases. At most, the difficulty is one of communication. On the other hand, some kinds of bilingualism in childhood may exert a retarding influence upon intellectual development and may, under certain conditions, affect personality development adversely (2, 5, 10). A common pattern is that the child speaks one language at home and another in school, so that his knowledge of each language is limited to certain types of situations. Inadequate facility with the language of the school interferes with the acquisition of basic concepts, intellectual skills, and information. The frustration engendered by scholastic difficulties may in turn lead to discouragement and general dislike of school. Such reactions can be found, for example, among a number of Puerto Rican children in New York City schools (3). In the case of certain groups, moreover, the child's foreign language background may be perceived by himself and his associates as a symbol of minority group status and may thereby augment any emotional maladjustment arising from such status (34).

A highly restricted environmental influence is to be found in the opportunity to acquire specific items of information occurring in a particular intelligence test. The fact that such opportunities may vary with culture, social class, or individual experiential background is at the basis of the test user's concern with the problem of coaching and with "culture-free" or "culture-fair" tests (cf. 1, 2). If the advantage or disadvantage which such experiential differences confer upon certain individuals is strictly confined to performance on the given test, it will obviously reduce the validity of the test and should be eliminated.

In this connection, however, it is essential to know the breadth of the environmental influence in question. A fallacy inherent in many attempts to develop culture-fair tests is that the breadth of cultural differentials is not taken into account. Failure to consider breadth of effect likewise characterizes certain discussions of coaching. If, in coaching a student for a college admission test, we can improve his knowledge of verbal concepts and his reading comprehension, he will be better equipped to succeed in college courses. His performance level will thus be raised, not only on the test, but also on the criterion which the test is intended to predict. To try to devise a test which is not susceptible to such coaching would merely reduce the effectiveness of the test. Similarly, efforts to rule out cultural differentials from test items so as to make them equally "fair" to subjects in different social classes or in different cultures may merely limit the usefulness of the test, since the same cultural differentials may operate within the broader area of behavior which the test is designed to sample.

METHODOLOGICAL APPROACHES

The examples considered so far should suffice to highlight the wide variety of ways in which hereditary and environmental factors may interact in the course of behavior development. There is clearly a need for identifying explicitly the etiological mechanism whereby any given hereditary or environmental condition ultimately leads to a behavioral characteristic—in other words, the "how" of heredity and environment. Accordingly, we may now take a quick look at some promising methodological approaches to the question "how."

Within the past decade, an increasing number of studies have been designed to trace the connection between specific factors in the hereditary backgrounds or in the reactional biographies of individuals and their observed behavioral characteristics. There has been a definite shift away from the predominantly descriptive and correlational approach of the earlier decades toward more deliberate attempts to verify explanatory hypotheses. Similarly, the cataloguing of group differences in psychological traits has been giving way gradually to research on *changes* in group characteristics following altered conditions.

Among recent methodological developments, we have chosen seven as being particularly relevant to the analysis of etiological mechanisms. The first represents an extension of selective breeding investigations to permit the identification of specific hereditary conditions underlying the observed behavioral differences. When early selective breeding investigations such as those of Tryon (36) on rats indicated that "maze learning ability" was inherited, we were still a long way from knowing what was actually being transmitted by the genes. It was obviously not "maze learning ability" as such. Twenty—or even ten—years ago, some psychologists would have suggested that it was probably general intelligence. And a few might even have drawn a parallel with the inheritance of human intelligence.

But today investigators have been asking: Just what makes one group of rats learn mazes more quickly than the other? Is it differences in motivation, emotionality, speed of running, general activity level? If so, are these behavioral characteristics in turn dependent upon group differences in glandular development, body weight, brain size, biochemical factors, or some other organic conditions? A number of recent and ongoing investigations indicate that attempts are being made to trace, at least part of the way, the steps whereby certain chemical properties of the genes may ultimately lead to specified behavior characteristics.

An example of such a study is provided by Searle's (31) follow-up of Tryon's research. Working with the strains of maze-bright and maze-dull rats developed by Tryon, Searle demonstrated that the two strains differed in a number of emotional and motivational factors, rather than in ability. Thus the strain differences were traced one step further, although many links still remain to be found between maze learning and genes. A promising methodological development within the same general area is to be found in the recent research of Hirsch and Tryon (18). Utilizing a specially devised technique for measuring individual differences in behavior among lower organisms, these investigators launched a series of studies on selective breeding for behavioral characteristics in the fruit fly, *Drosophila*. Such research can capitalize on the mass of available genetic knowledge regarding the morphology of *Drosophila*, as well as on other advantages of using such an organism in genetic studies.

Further evidence of current interest in the specific hereditary factors which influence behavior is to be found in an extensive research program in progress at the Jackson Memorial Laboratory, under the direction of Scott and Fuller (30). In general, the project is concerned with the behavioral characteristics of various breeds and cross-breeds of dogs. Analyses of some of the data gathered to date again suggest that "differences in performance are produced by differences in emotional, motivational, and peripheral processes, and that genetically caused differences in central processes may be either slight or nonexistent" (29, p. 225). In other parts of the same project, breed differences in physiological characteristics, which may in turn be related to behavioral differences, have been established.

A second line of attack is the exploration of possible relationships between behavioral characteristics and physiological variables which may in turn be traceable to hereditary factors. Research on EEG, autonomic balance, metabolic processes, and biochemical factors illustrates this approach. A lucid demonstration of the process of tracing a psychological condition to genetic factors is provided by the identification and subsequent investigation of phenylpyruvic amentia. In this case, the causal chain from defective gene, through metabolic disorder and consequent cerebral malfunctioning, to feeblemindedness and other overt symptoms can be described step by step (cf. *32; 33*, pp. 389–391). Also relevant are the recent

researches on neurological and biochemical correlates of schizophrenia (9). Owing to inadequate methodological controls, however, most of the findings of the latter studies must be regarded as tentative (19).

Prenatal environmental factors provide a third avenue of fruitful investigation. Especially noteworthy is the recent work of Pasamanick and his associates (27), which demonstrated a tie-up between socioeconomic level, complications of pregnancy and parturition, and psychological disorders of the offspring. In a series of studies on large samples of whites and Negroes in Baltimore, these investigators showed that various prenatal and paranatal disorders are significantly related to the occurrence of mental defect and psychiatric disorders in the child. An important source of such irregularities in the process of childbearing and birth is to be found in deficiencies of maternal diet and in other conditions associated with low socioeconomic status. An analysis of the data did in fact reveal a much higher frequency of all such medical complications in lower than in higher socioeconomic levels, and a higher frequency among Negroes than among whites.

Direct evidence of the influence of prenatal nutritional factors upon subsequent intellectual development is to be found in a recent, well controlled experiment by Harrell et al. (16). The subjects were pregnant women in low-income groups whose normal diets were generally quite deficient. A dietary supplement was administered to some of these women during pregnancy and lactation, while an equated control group received placebos. When tested at the ages of three and four years, the offspring of the experimental group obtained a significantly higher mean IQ than did the offspring of the controls.

Mention should also be made of animal experiments on the effects of such factors as prenatal radiation and neonatal asphyxia upon cerebral anomalies as well as upon subsequent behavior development. These experimental studies merge imperceptibly into the fourth approach to be considered, namely, the investigation of the influence of early experience upon the eventual behavioral characteristics of animals. Research in this area has been accumulating at a rapid rate. In 1954, Beach and Jaynes (8) surveyed this literature for the *Psy-*

chological *Bulletin,* listing over 130 references. Several new studies have appeared since that date (e.g., *14, 21, 24, 25, 35*). The variety of factors covered ranges from the type and quantity of available food to the extent of contact with human culture. A large number of experiments have been concerned with various forms of sensory deprivation and with diminished opportunities for motor exercise. Effects have been observed in many kinds of animals and in almost all aspects of behavior, including perceptual responses, motor activity, learning, emotionality, and social reactions.

In their review, Beach and Jaynes pointed out that research in this area has been stimulated by at least four distinct theoretical interests. Some studies were motivated by the traditional concern with the relative contribution of maturation and learning to behavior development. Others were designed in an effort to test certain psychoanalytic theories regarding infantile experiences, as illustrated by studies which limited the feeding responses of young animals. A third relevant influence is to be found in the work of the European biologist Lorenz (*23*) on early social stimulation of birds, and in particular on the special type of learning for which the term "imprinting" has been coined. A relatively large number of recent studies have centered around Hebb's (*17*) theory regarding the importance of early perceptual experiences upon subsequent performance in learning situations. All this research represents a rapidly growing and promising attack on the modus operandi of specific environmental factors.

The human counterpart of these animal studies may be found in the comparative investigation of child-rearing practices in different cultures and subcultures. This represents the fifth approach in our list. An outstanding example of such a study is that by Whiting and Child (*38*), published in 1953. Utilizing data on 75 primitive societies from the Cross-Cultural Files of the Yale Institute of Human Relations, these investigators set out to test a number of hypotheses regarding the relationships between child-rearing practices and personality development. This analysis was followed up by field observations in five cultures, the results of which have not yet been reported (cf. *37*).

Within our own culture, similar surveys have been concerned with the diverse psychological environments provided by different social classes (*11*). Of particular interest are the study by Williams and Scott (*39*) on the association between socioeconomic level, permissiveness, and motor development among Negro children, and the exploratory research by Milner (*26*) on the relationship between reading readiness in first-grade children and patterns of parent-child interaction. Milner found that upon school entrance the lower-class child seems to lack chiefly two advantages enjoyed by the middle-class child. The first is described as "a warm positive family atmosphere or adult-relationship pattern which is more and more being recognized as a motivational prerequisite of any kind of adult-controlled learning." The lower-class children in Milner's study perceived adults as predominantly hostile. The second advantage is an extensive opportunity to interact verbally with adults in the family. The latter point is illustrated by parental attitudes toward mealtime conversation, lower-class parents tending to inhibit and discourage such conversation, while middle-class parents encourage it.

Most traditional studies on child-rearing practices have been designed in terms of a psychoanalytic orientation. There is need for more data pertaining to other types of hypotheses. Findings such as those of Milner on opportunities for verbalization and the resulting effects upon reading readiness represent a step in this direction. Another possible source of future data is the application of the intensive observational techniques of psychological ecology developed by Barker and Wright (*7*) to widely diverse socioeconomic groups.

A sixth major approach involves research on the previously cited somatopsychological relationships (*6*). To date, little direct information is available on the precise operation of this class of factors in psychological development. The multiplicity of ways in which physical traits—whether hereditary or environmental in origin—may influence behavior thus offers a relatively unexplored field for future study.

The seventh and final approach to be considered represents an adaptation of traditional twin studies. From the standpoint of the question "How?" there is need for closer coordination between the usual data on twin resemblance and observations of the family interactions of twins. Available data already suggests, for example, that closeness of contact and extent of environmental similarity are greater in the case of monozygotic than in the case of dizygotic twins (cf. *2*). Information on the social reactions of twins toward each other and the specialization of roles is likewise of interest (*2*). Especially useful would be longitudinal studies of twins, beginning in early infancy and following the subjects through school age. The operation of differential environmental pressures, the development of specialized roles, and other environmental influences could thus be more clearly identified and correlated with intellectual and personality changes in the growing twins.

Parenthetically, I should like to add a remark about the traditional applications of the twin method, in which persons in different degrees of hereditary and environmental relationships to each other are simply compared for behavioral similarity. In these studies, attention has been focused principally upon the amount of resemblance of monozygotic as contrasted to dizygotic twins. Yet such a comparison is particularly difficult to interpret because of the many subtle differences in the environmental situations of the two types of twins. A more fruitful comparison would seem to be that between dizygotic twins and siblings, for whom the hereditary similarity is known to be the same.

In Kallmann's monumental research on psychiatric disorders among twins (*20*), for example, one of the most convincing bits of evidence for the operation of hereditary factors in schizophrenia is the fact that the degrees of concordance for dizygotic twins and for siblings were practically identical. In contrast, it will be recalled that in intelligence test scores dizygotic twins resemble each other much more closely than do siblings—a finding which reveals the influence of environmental factors in intellectual development.

of indirectness." The more indirect their connection with behavior, the wider will be the range of variation of possible outcomes. One extreme of the continuum of indirectness may be illustrated by brain damage leading to mental deficiency; the other extreme, by physical characteristics associated with social stereotypes. Examples of factors falling at intermediate points include deafness, physical diseases, and motor disorders. Those environmental factors which act directly upon behavior can be ordered along a continuum of breadth or permanence of effect, as exemplified by social class membership, amount of formal schooling, language handicap, and familiarity with specific test items.

Several current lines of research offer promising techniques for exploring the modus operandi of hereditary and environmental factors. Outstanding among them are investigations of: (a) hereditary conditions which underlie behavioral differences between selectively bred groups of animals; (b) relations between physiological variables and individual differences in behavior, especially in the case of pathological deviation; (c) role of prenatal physiological factors in behavior development; (d) influence of early experience upon eventual behavioral characteristics; (e) cultural differences in child-rearing practices in relation to intellectual and emotional development; (f) mechanisms of somatopsychological relationships; and (g) psychological development of twins from infancy to maturity, together with observations of their social environment. Such approaches are extremely varied with regard to subjects employed, nature of psychological functions studied, and specific experimental procedures followed. But it is just such heterogeneity of methodology that is demanded by the wide diversity of ways in which hereditary and environmental factors interact in behavior development.

SUMMARY

The heredity-environment problem is still very much alive. Its viability is assured by the gradual replacement of the questions, "Which one?" and "How much?" by the more basic and appropriate question, "How?" Hereditary influences—as well as environmental factors of an organic nature—vary along a "continuum

REFERENCES

1. Anastasi, Anne. *Psychological testing.* New York: Macmillan, 1954.
2. Anastasi, Anne. *Differential psychology.* (3rd ed.) New York: Macmillan, 1958.
3. Anastasi, Anne, & Cordova, F. A. Some effects of bilingualism upon the intelligence test performance of Puerto Rican children in

New York City, *J. Educ. Psychol.*, 1953, **44**, 1–19.

4. Anastasi, Anne, & Foley, J. P., Jr. A proposed reorientation in the heredity-environment controversy. *Psychol. Rev.*, 1948, **55**, 239–249.

5. Arsenian, B. Bilingualism in the postwar world. *Psychol. Bull.*, 1945, **42**, 65–86.

6. Barker, R. G., Wright, Beatrice A., Myerson, L., & Gonick, Mollie R. Adjustment to physical handicap and illness: a survey of the social psychology of physique and disability. *Soc. Sci. Res. Coun. Bull.*, 1953, No. 55 (rev.).

7. Barker, R. G., & Wright, H. F. *Midwest and its children: the psychological ecology of an American town.* Evanston, Ill.: Row, Peterson, 1955.

8. Beach, F. A., & Jaynes, J. Effects of early experience upon the behavior of animals. *Psychol. Bull.*, 1954, **51**, 239–263.

9. Brackbill, G. A. Studies of brain dysfunction in Schizophrenia. *Psychol. Bull.*, 1956, **53**, 210–226.

10. Darcy, Natalie T. A review of the literature on the effects of bilingualism upon the measurement of intelligence. *J. genet. Psychol.*, 1953, **82**, 21–57.

11. Davis, A., & Havighurst, R. J. Social class and color differences in child rearing. *Amer. sociol. Rev.*, 1946, **11**, 698–710.

12. Dobzhansky, T. The genetic nature of differences among men. In S. Pearsons (Ed.) *Evolutionary thought in America.* New Haven: Yale University Press, 1950. Pp. 86–155.

13. Dobzhansky, T. Heredity, environment, and evolution. *Science*, 1950, **111**, 161–166.

14. Forgus, R. H. The effect of early perceptual learning on the behavorial organization of adult rats. *J. comp. physiol. Psychol.*, 1954, **47**, 331–336.

15. Haldane, J. B. S. *Heredity and politics.* New York: Norton, 1938.

16. Harrell, Ruth F., Woodyard, Ella, & Gates, A. I. *The effect of mothers' diets on the intelligence of the offspring.* New York: Bur. Publ. Teach. Coll., Columbia Univer., 1955.

17. Hebb, D. O. *The organization of behavior.* New York: Wiley, 1949.

18. Hirsch, J. & Tryon, R. C. Mass screening and reliable individual measurement in the experimental behavior genetics of lower organisms. *Phychol. Bull.*, 1956, **124**, 429–430.

19. Horwitt, M. K. Facts and artifact in the biology of schizophrenia. *Science*, 1956, **53**, 429–430.

20. Kallman, F. J. *Heredity in health and mental disorder; principles of psychiatric genetics* in the light of comparative twin studies. New York: Norton, 1953.

21. King, J. A., & Gurney, Nancy L. Effect of early social experience on adult aggressive behavior in C57BL10 mice. *J. comp. Physiol. Psychol.*, 1954, **47**, 326–330.

22. Loevinger, Jane. On the proportional contributions of differences in nature and in nurture to differences in intelligence. *Psychol. Bull.*, 1943, **40**, 725–756.

23. Lorenz, K. Der Kumpan in der Umwelt des Vogels, Der Artgenosse als auslosendes Moment sozialer Verhaltungsweisen. *J. 3 Orn., Lpz.*, 1935, **83**, 137–213; 289–413.

24. Luchins, A. S., & Forgus, R. H. The effect of differential postweaning environment on the rigidity of an animal's behavior. *J. genet. Psychol.*, 1955, **86**, 51–58.

25. Melzack, R. The genesis of emotional behavior: an experimental study of the dog. *J. comp. physiol. Psychol.*, 1954, **47**, 166–168.

26. Milner, Esther A. A study of the relationships between reading readiness in grade one school children and patterns of parent-child interaction. *Child Develpm.*, 1951, **22**, 95–112.

27. Pasamanick, B., Knobloch, Hilda, & Lilienfeld, A. M. Socioeconomic status and some precursors of neuropsychiatric disorder. *Amer. J. Orthopsychiat.*, 1956, **26**, 594–601.

28. Schwesinger, Gladys C. *Heredity and environment.* New York: Macmillan, 1933.

29. Scott, J. P., & Charles, Margaret S. Some problems of heredity and social behavior. *J. genet. Psychol.*, 1953, **48**, 209–230.

30. Scott, J. P., & Fuller, J. L. Research on genetics and social behavior at the Roscoe B. Jackson Memorial Laboratory, 1946–1951—a progress report. *J. Hered*, 1951, **42**, 191–197.

31. Searle, L. V. The organization of hereditary maze-brightness and maze-dullness. *Genet. psychol. Monogr.*, 1949, **39**, 279–325.

32. Snyder, L. H. The genetic approach to human individuality. *Sci. Mon., N.Y.*, 1949, **68**, 165–171.

33. Snyder, L. H., & David, P. R. *The principles of heredity.* (5th ed.) Boston: Heath, 1957.

34. Spoerl, Dorothy T. Bilinguality and emotional adjustment. *J. abnorm. soc. Psychol.*, 1943, **38**, 37–57.

35. Thompson, W. R., & Melzack, R. Early environment. *Sci. Amer.*, 1956, **194** (1), 38–42.

36. Tryon, R. C. Genetic differences in maze-learning ability in rats. *Yearb. nat. Soc. Stud. Educ.*, 1940, **39**, Part I, 111–119.

37. Whiting, J. W. M. *et al.* Field guide for a study of socialization in five societies. Cam-

bridge, Mass.: Harvard Univ., 1954 (mimeo.).

38. Whiting, J. W. M., & Child, I. L. *Child training and personality: a cross-cultural study.* New Haven: Yale University Press, 1953.

39. Williams, Judith R., & Scott, R. B. Growth and development of Negro infants: IV. Motor development and its relationship to child rearing practices in two groups of Negro infants. *Child Develpm.*, 1953, **24**, 103–121.

40. Woodworth, R. S. Heredity and environment: a critical survey of recently published material on twins and foster children. *Soc. Sci. Res. Coun. Bull.*, 1941, No. 47.

Selection **11** | CRITICAL PERIODS IN BEHAVIORAL DEVELOPMENT*

J. P. SCOTT
*Roscoe B. Jackson
Memorial Laboratory,
Bar Harbor, Maine*

A number of years ago I was given a female lamb taken from its mother at birth. My wife and I raised it on the bottle for the first 10 days of life and then placed it out in the pasture with a small flock of domestic sheep. As might have been expected from folklore, the lamb became attached to people and followed the persons who fed it. More surprisingly, the lamb remained independent of the rest of the flock when we restored it to the pasture. Three years later it was still following an independent grazing pattern. In addition, when it was mated and had lambs of its own it became a very indifferent mother, allowing its offspring to nurse but showing no concern when the lamb moved away with the other members of the flock.

Since following the flock is such a universal characteristic of normal sheep, I was impressed by the extensive and permanent modification of this behavior that resulted from a brief early experience. The results suggested that

* Abridged from J. P. Scott, "Critical Periods in Behavioral Development, *Science,* 138: 949–958, 1962. Reprinted by permission of the author and the publisher.

Freud was right concerning the importance of early experience, and pointed toward the existence of critical periods in behavioral development. As I soon discovered, there is considerable evidence that a critical period for determining early social relationships is a widespread phenomenon in vertebrates; such a critical period had long been known in ants.

Freud had attempted to explain the origin of neuroses in human patients as the result of early experience and had implied that certain periods in the life of an infant are times of particular sensitivity. In 1935, Lorenz emphasized the importance of critical periods for the formation of primary social bonds (imprinting) in birds, remarking on their similarity to critical periods in the development of the embryo, and McGraw soon afterward pointed out the existence of critical periods for optimal learning of motor skills in the human infant.

Since then, the phenomenon of critical periods has excited the imagination of a large group of experimenters interested in human and animal development. In describing this fast-moving scientific field, I shall point out some of the most significant current developments.

To begin with, three major kinds of critical-period phenomena have been discovered. These involve optimal periods for learning, for infantile stimulation, and for the formation of basic social relationships. The last of these has been established as a widespread phenomenon in the animal kingdom and consequently receives major attention in this article.

PROCESS OF PRIMARY SOCIALIZATION

Since one of the first acts of a young mammal is to nurse, and since food rewards are known to modify the behavior of adult animals, it once seemed logical to suppose that the process of forming a social attachment begins with food rewards and develops as an acquired drive. However, the experimental evidence does not support this extreme viewpoint. Brodbeck reared a group of puppies during the critical period of socialization, feeding half of them by hand and the other half by machine, but giving all of them the same degree of human contact. He found that the two sets of puppies became equally attached to people. This result was later confirmed by Stanley and his co-workers, who found that the only difference in response between the machine-fed and the hand-fed puppies was that the latter yelped more when they saw the experimenter. Elliot and King fed all their puppies by hand but overfed one group and underfed another. The hungry puppies became more rapidly attached to the handlers. We can conclude that, in the dog, food rewards per se are not necessary for the process of socialization, but that hunger will speed it up.

Fisher reared fox terrier puppies in isolation boxes through the entire socialization period. The puppies were fed mechanically (thus, food was entirely eliminated as a factor in the experiment), but they were removed from the boxes for regular contacts with the experimenter. One group of puppies was always rewarded by kind social treatment. A second group was sometimes rewarded and sometimes punished, but in a purely random way. Still a third group was always punished for any positive approach to the experimenter. The puppies that were both rewarded and punished showed most attraction and dependency behavior with respect to the experimenter, and the puppies that were always punished showed the least. After the treatment was discontinued, all the puppies began coming toward the experimenter, and the differences rapidly disappeared. This leads to the surprising conclusion that the process of socialization is not inhibited by punishment and may even be speeded up by it.

The results of these experiments on dogs agree with evidence from other species. While they were going on, Harlow was performing his famous experiments with rhesus monkeys isolated at birth and supplied with dummy "mothers." When given the choice between a comfortable cloth-covered mother without a nipple and an uncomfortable mother made of wire screening but equipped with a functional nursing bottle, the young rhesus monkeys definitely preferred the cloth-covered models from which they had received no food rewards. Harlow concluded that the acquired-drive theory of the origin of social attachment could be discarded.

Later, Igel and Calvin performed a similar but more elaborate experiment with puppies. These animals had more opportunity to choose,

being provided with four kinds of mother models: comfortable and uncomfortable, each type with and without nipples. Like rhesus monkeys, the puppies preferred the comfortable "mother" but usually chose one with a nipple. Thus, it appears that food rewards do contribute something to the social relationship, although they do not form its prime basis.

Since then Harlow has raised to maturity the monkeys raised on dummy mothers, has mated them, and has observed their behavior toward their own young. They become uniformly poor mothers, neglecting their offspring and often punishing them when they cry. In spite of such rejection, the young rhesus infants desperately crawl toward their mothers and give every evidence of becoming attached to them, although perhaps not as strongly as in the normal relationship. Here again punishment does not inhibit the formation of a social bond.

The hypothesis that the primary social bond originates through food rewards had already been shown to be invalid in the precocial birds, many of which form attachments prior to the time when they begin to feed. Lorenz was the first to point out the significance of this phenomenon, which he called "imprinting." He also stated that it differed from conditioning, primarily in that it was very rapid and apparently irreversible. However, rapid formation and great persistence are also characteristic of many conditioned responses and other learned behavior. Fabricius pointed out that no sharp line can be drawn between imprinting and conditioning, and Collias concluded that imprinting is a form of learned behavior that is self-reinforcing.

The process of imprinting in young ducklings and chicks has since been experimentally analyzed in much detail, with results that invariably confirm the conclusion that it takes place without any obvious external rewards or reinforcement. Hess found that if he caused young ducklings to follow a model over varying distances or over hurdles, the ducklings which had to make the greater effort became more strongly imprinted. He also found that the drug meprobamate and its congener carisoprodol, which are muscle relaxants as well as tranquilizers, greatly reduce imprinting if given during the critical period. James found that chicks would become attached to an object illuminated by a flickering light, even though they were not allowed to follow, and Gray later showed that they will become attached to a motionless object illuminated by a steady light and viewed from an isolation box. It is therefore apparent that chicks can become imprinted without following, although muscular tension may still be important.

We may conclude that these young birds become attached to any object to which they are long exposed during the critical period, even when their contact is only visual. We may also conclude that the speed of formation of a social bond is dependent upon the degree of emotional arousal, irrespective of the nature of that arousal. Whether attachment is the result of the emotion itself or of the reduction of emotion as the chick or duckling approaches the model is still a matter of conjecture.

TIMING MECHANISMS

The basic timing mechanisms for developmental periods are obviously the biological processes of growth and differentiation, usually called maturation. For various reasons, these are not precisely correlated with age from birth or hatching. For example, birds often retain newly formed eggs in their bodies overnight, thus incubating them for several hours before laying. By chilling duck eggs just before placing them in an incubator (thus killing all embryos except those in the earliest stages of development) Gottlieb was able to time the age of ducklings from the onset of incubation rather than from hatching and found that variation in the timing for the critical period was much reduced. No such exact timing studies have been made in mammals, but I have estimated that there is at least a week's variation in development among puppies at 3 weeks of age, and the variation among human infants must be considerably greater.

Another approach to the problem is to try to identify the actual mechanisms which open and close a period. Since an important part of forming a primary social relationship appears to be emotional arousal while the young animal is in contact with another, it is obvious that the critical period for socialization could be timed by the appearance of behavioral mechanisms which maintain or prevent contact, and this indeed is the case. There are demon-

strable positive mechanisms, varying from species to species, which bring young animals close to other members of their kind: the clinging response of young rhesus monkeys; the following response of chicks, ducklings, and lambs and other herd animals; the social investigation, tail wagging, and playful fighting of puppies; and the visual investigation and smiling of the human infant. These are, of course, accompanied by interacting responses from adult and immature members of the species: holding and clasping by primate mothers, brooding of mother hens and other birds, calling by mother sheep, investigation and play on the part of other young puppies, and the various supporting and nurturing activities of human mothers.

If contact and emotional arousal result in social attachment, there must be negative mechanisms which prevent such attachment once the critical period is past. Perhaps the most widespread of these is the development of a fear response which causes the young animal to immediately leave the vicinity of a stranger and hence avoid contact. This developing fear response is found in young chicks, ducklings, dogs (2), rhesus monkeys, and in many other birds and mammals. Even in children there is a period between the ages of 5 and 12 months in which there is a mounting fear of strangers, sometimes called "8-months anxiety." As already pointed out, there is a time in development when certain fear responses actually facilitate imprinting, but, as they grow stronger, the escape reaction follows so quickly that it prevents contact altogether. Another sort of negative mechanism is the rejection of strange young by adult sheep, goats, and many other herd animals. In these species the mothers become strongly attached to the young within a few hours after birth and refuse to accept strangers thereafter. This indicates that the rapid formation of emotional bonds is not limited to young animals.

These timing mechanisms all depend primarily on the development of social behavior patterns, but both sensory and motor development can also influence timing. For example, a very immature animal cannot maintain contact by following, and in slowly developing altricial birds such as jackdaws and doves, the period of imprinting comes much later than it does in the precocial species. In the human

ant the process of socialization begins be-
e the adult motor patterns develop, but con-
t is maintained by visual exploration and by
smiling response to human faces. Thus,
erstanding the process of socialization and
iming mechanisms in any particular species
lires a systematic study of the development
he various capacities which affect the time
nset and the duration of the critical period.
se include sensory, motor, and learning
acities as well as the ability to perform
intial patterns of social behavior.

he fact that emotional arousal is so
ngly connected with the process of primary
alization suggests that the capacity to
luce emotional reactions may also govern
time of onset of a critical period. Figure 4
amarizes the results of a study of emotional
velopment in the dog during the critical
riod. If puppies are kept in large fields,
otally isolated from people, fear and escape
responses toward human beings very nearly
reach a maximum by the time the puppies are
14 weeks old—a finding that fixes the upper
limit of the period of socialization. On the
other hand, the peak of the emotional response
to isolation in a strange place occurs when
puppies are approximately 6 to 7 weeks old,
as does the peak of the heart-rate response to
handling. At this age, such emotional arousal
actually contributes to the strength of the
social bond. Fuller was unable to condition the
heart-rate response consistently until puppies
were 5 weeks old. This indicates that one of
the factors that brings the critical period to a
close may be the developing ability of the
young puppy to associate fear responses with
particular stimuli.

All this suggests that if the development of
the escape response to strangers could be held
in check, the critical period might be extended
indefinitely. Raising puppies in small isolation
boxes during the critical period inhibits the
development of the escape response, but they
still show obvious signs of fear when they are
first removed from their cages. Fuller reports
some success in socializing these older pups
by overcoming their fear responses, either by
careful handling or through the use of tranquilizing drugs.

Fear responses thus have the dual effect of
facilitating the formation of the social bond
during the critical period (along with other

emotions) and of bringing the period to a
close. This is understandable because the type
of fear which terminates the critical period is a
developing fear of strange animals. In the early
part of the critical period the escape reaction is
either lacking or is momentary and weak. At
the close of the period it is strong enough to
prevent contact altogether.

FORMATION OF AFFECTIONAL
BONDS IN ADULT LIFE

Until recently, most investigators have concentrated their attention on the critical period
for primary socialization or imprinting and few
have gone on to study similar phenomena in
later development. This field of investigation
is just beginning to open up, though many
related facts have long been known. For example, many birds form strong pair bonds
which are maintained as long as both members survive. In studying the development of
various types of social bonds in different
species of ducks, Schutz finds that, while attachments to particular individuals may be
formed in the early critical period from 12 to 17
hours after hatching, the critical period for
the attachment to the species may not come
until sometime later, in some cases as late as
30 days after hatching, and the attachment to
a particular member of the opposite sex, or the
pair bond, does not come until the age of 5
months or so. Schutz also finds that female
mallards cannot be sexually imprinted with
respect to other species but always mate with
other mallards no matter what their earliest
experience has been. A similar phenomenon is
reported by Warriner, who finds that male
pigeons prefer to mate with birds whose color
is similar to that of the parents who reared
them, whether of the same or another color
from themselves, but females show no preference.

Certain species of mammals, such as foxes,
form long-lasting mating bonds. It is possible
that the violence of the sexual emotions contributes to the formation of the adult bond,
just as other sorts of emotional arousal are
important to the primary socialization of the
infant. Klopfer has suggested that the rapid
formation of the social bond in a mother goat
toward her kid is the result of the high degree

of emotional arousal which accompanies the birth of the offspring.

In short, it seems likely that the formation of a social attachment through contact and emotional arousal is a process that may take place throughout life, and that although it may take place more slowly outside of certain critical periods, the capacity for such an attachment is never completely lost.

At this point it may be remarked that, in attempting to analyze the development of affection and social bonds objectively, scientists have often tried to simplify the problem by postulating various unitary, unromantic, and sometimes unesthetic explanations. One of these was the "acquired drive" hypothesis—that children love you because you feed them. Taking a more moderate view Harlow has emphasized "contact comfort" as a major variable —that the young monkey begins to love its mother because she feels warm and comfortable—but that a number of other factors are involved. As this article indicates, evidence is accumulating that there is a much less specific, although equally unromantic, general mechanism involved—that given any kind of emotional arousal a young animal will become attached to any individual or object with which it is in contact for a sufficiently long time. The necessary arousal would, of course, include various specific kinds of emotions associated with food rewards and contact comfort.

It should not be surprising that many kinds of emotional reactions contribute to a social relationship. The surprising thing is that emotions which we normally consider aversive should produce the same effect as those which appear to be rewarding. This apparent paradox is partially resolved by evidence that the positive effect of unpleasant emotions is normally limited to early infancy by the development of escape reactions.

Nevertheless, this concept leads to the somewhat alarming conclusion that an animal (and perhaps a person) of any age, exposed to certain individuals or physical surroundings for any length of time, will inevitably become attached to them, the rapidity of the process being governed by the degree of emotional arousal associated with them. I need not dwell on the consequences for human behavior, if this conclusion should apply to our species as well as to other animals, except to point out that it provides an explanation of certain well-known clinical observations such as the development by neglected children of strong affection for cruel and abusive parents, and the various peculiar affectional relationships that develop between prisoners and jailors, slaves and masters, and so on. Perhaps the general adaptive nature of this mechanism is that since the survival of any member of a highly social species depends upon the rapid development of social relationships, a mechanism has evolved which makes it almost impossible to inhibit the formation of social bonds.

CRITICAL PERIODS OF LEARNING

Unlike the process of socialization, the phenomenon of critical periods of learning was first noticed in children rather than in lower animals. McGraw's famous experiment with the twins Johnny and Jimmy was a deliberate attempt to modify behavioral development by giving one of a pair of identical twins special early training. The result varied according to the activity involved. The onset of walking, for example, was not affected by previous practice or help. Other activities, however, could be greatly speeded up—notably roller skating, in which the favored twin became adept almost as soon as he could walk. In other activities performance was actually made worse by early practice, simply because of the formation of unskillful habits. McGraw concluded that there are critical periods for learning which vary from activity to activity; for each kind of coordinated muscular activity there is an optimum period for rapid and skillful learning.

In addition to these studies on motor learning there are many experiments demonstrating the existence of critical periods for the learning of social behavior patterns. It has long been known that many kinds of birds do not develop the characteristic songs of their species if they are reared apart from their own kind. More recently, Thorpe discovered a critical period for this effect in the chaffinch. If isolated at 3 or 4 days of age, a young male chaffinch produces an incomplete song, but if he hears adults singing, as a fledgling 2 or 3 weeks old or in early juvenile life before he sings himself, he will the next year produce the song characteristic of the species, even if he has been kept in isolation. In nature, the fine details of the song are added at the time of competition over territory, within a period of 2 or 3 weeks, when the bird is about a year old. At this time it learns the songs of two or three of its neighbors, and never learns any others in subsequent years. The critical period for song learning is thus a relatively long one, but it is definitely over by the time the bird is a year old. There is no obvious explanation for its ending at this particular time, but it is possible that learning a complete song pattern in some way interferes with further learning.

King and Gurney found that adult mice reared in groups during youth fought more readily than animals isolated at 20 days of age. Later experiments showed that most of the effect was produced in a 10-day period just after weaning, and that similar experience as adults produced little or no effect. Thus, there appears to be a critical period for learning to fight through social experience, and this experience need be no more than contact through a wire. In this case the effect is probably produced by association with other mice before the fear response has been completely developed. Similarly, Fisher and Fuller inhibited the development of attacking behavior in fox terriers by raising them in isolation through the critical period for socialization. The animals would fight back somewhat ineffectually if attacked, but did not initiate conflicts. Tinbergen found a critical period in dogs for learning territorial boundaries, coinciding with sexual maturity.

The results of corresponding experiments on sexual behavior vary from species to species. In mice, rearing in isolation produced no effects. Beach found that male rats reared with either females or males were actually slower to respond to sexual behavior than isolated males, and he suggested that habits of playful fighting established by the group-reared animals interfered with sexual behavior later on. In guinea pigs, contact with other young animals improves sexual performance.

On the other hand, young chimpanzees reared apart from their kind can only be mated with experienced animals. Harlow discovered that his rhesus infants reared on dummy mothers did not develop normal patterns of sexual behavior, and he was able to obtain matings only by exposing females to experienced males. Normal behavior can be developed by allowing 20-minute daily play periods with other young monkeys, but if rhesus infants are reared apart from all other monkeys beyond the period when they spontaneously play with their fellows, patterns of both sexual and maternal behavior fail to develop normally. These results suggest that play has an important role in developing adult patterns of social behavior in these primates, and that the decline of play behavior sets the upper limit of the critical period during which normal adult behavior may be developed.

It is difficult to find a common factor in these critical periods for learning. In some species, such as rats, mice, dogs, and sheep, certain critical periods for learning coincide with the period for primary socialization and seem to be similarly brought to a close by the development of fear reactions. Other critical periods, in chaffinches and dogs, coincide with the formation of adult mating bonds. However, the critical period for sexual learning in the rhesus monkey comes later than that for primary socialization, as do critical periods for various kinds of learning in human beings.

Part of this apparent inconsistency arises from our ignorance regarding timing mechanisms. One such mechanism must be the development of learning capacities, and we have evidence in dogs, rhesus monkeys, and human infants that learning capacities change during development, sometimes in a stepwise fashion. One element in these capacities is the ability to learn things which facilitate subsequent learning.

CRITICAL PERIODS FOR EARLY STIMULATION

Experiments to determine the effects of early stimulation have been mainly performed on infant mice and rats, which are usually weaned at about 21 days at the earliest, and have been concerned with the effect of stimulation during this pre-weaning period. All investigators beginning with Levine and Schaefer, agree that rats handled during the first week or 10 days of life have a lessened tendency to urinate and defecate in a strange "open field" situation, learn avoidance behavior more readily, and survive longer when deprived of food and water. In short, early stimulation produces an animal that is less timorous, learns more quickly, and is more vigorous. Levine found that the effect could be obtained by a variety of stimuli, including electric shock and mechanical shaking as well as handling. This ruled out learned behavior as an explanation of the effect, and Levine, Alpert, and Lewis discovered that animals handled in the early period showed a much earlier maturation of the adrenocortical response to stress. Levine interpreted these results as indicating that the laboratory environment did not provide sufficient stimulation for the proper development of the hormonal systems of the animals. This interpretation is in agreement with Richter's finding that laboratory rats are quite deficient in adrenocortical response as compared with the wild variety.

Denenberg takes a somewhat different approach, pointing out that there should be optimal levels of stimulation, so that either very weak or very strong stimulation would produce poor results.

Analyzing the effect on avoidance learning, Denenberg and his associates found that both unhandled controls and rats handled for the first 20 days performed poorly, the former because they were too emotional and the latter because they were too calm to react quickly. An intermediate amount of emotional response produces the best learning, and this can be produced by handling only in the first 10 days of life; handling during the second 10 days has a lesser effect. No handling produces too much emotionality, and handling for 20 days results in too little. Irrespective of the effect on learning, the data lead to the important conclusion that emotional stimulation during a critical period early in life can lead to the reduction of emotional responses in later life.

More precisely, there appear to be two critical periods revealed by research on early stimulation of rats, one based on a physiological process (the development of the adrenal cortical stress mechanism) and extending to 16 days of age at the latest, the other based on a psychological process (the reduction of fear through familiarity), beginning about 17 days when the eyes first open and extending to 30 days. The effects of handling during these two periods are additive, and many experiments based on arbitrary time rather than developmental periods undoubtedly include both.

The deleterious effects of excessive stimulation in the life of the infant may also be interpreted as a traumatic emotional experience. Bowlby, in studying a group of juvenile thieves, found that a large proportion of them had been separated from their mothers in early infancy, and he postulated that this traumatic emotional experience had affected their later behavior. Since this conclusion was based on retrospective information, he and his co-workers have since studied the primary symptoms of separation and have described in detail the emotional reactions of infants sent to hospitals, and thus separated from their mothers. Schaffer found a difference in reaction to separation before 7 months and separation afterward. Both sets of infants were disturbed, but they were disturbed in different ways. Infants show increasingly severe emotional reactions to adoption from 3 through 12 months of age. It seems logical to place the beginning of the critical period for maximum emotional disturbance at approximately 7 months—at the end of the critical period for primary socialization, which Gray places at approximately 6 weeks to 6 months. Infants whose social relationships have been thoroughly established and whose fear responses toward strangers have been fully developed are much more likely to be upset by changes than infants in which these relationships and responses have not yet been developed.

However, not all apparently "traumatic" early experiences have such a lasting effect. Experimental work shows that young animals have a considerable capacity to recover from unpleasant emotions experienced in a limited period in early life, and that what is traumatic in one species may not be in another. While young rats become calmer after infantile stimulation, young mice subjected to excessive auditory stimulation later become more emotional. At this point it is appropriate to point out that critical periods are not necessarily involved in every kind of early experience. Raising young chimpanzees in the dark produces degeneration of the retina, but this is a long and gradual process.

Another approach to the problem is to stimulate emotional responses in mothers and observe the effect on the offspring. Thompson and other authors have shown that the offspring of rats made fearful while pregnant are more likely to be overemotional in the open-field situation than the offspring of animals not so stimulated. Since any direct influence of maternal behavior was ruled out by cross-fostering experiments, it seems likely that the result is produced by modification of the adrenocortical stress mechanism—in this case, by secretion of maternal hormones acting on the embryo rather than by stimulation after birth of the young animal itself. No precise critical period for the effect has been established, but it is probably confined to the latter part of pregnancy. Similar effects have been obtained in mice, and if such effects can be demonstrated in other mammals, the implications for prenatal care in human beings are obvious.

It is interesting to note that, whereas shocking the mother both before and after parturition has the effect of increasing emotional responses in the young, the emotional responses of young rats are *decreased* when the treatment is applied directly to them. The explanation of this contradiction must await direct experiments on the endocrine system.

GENERAL THEORY OF CRITICAL PERIODS

There are at least two ways in which experience during critical periods may act on behavioral development. The critical period for primary socialization constitutes a turning point. Experience during a short period early in life determines which shall be the close relatives of the young animal, and this, in turn, leads the animal to develop in one of two directions—the normal one, in which it becomes attached to and mates with a member of its own species, or an abnormal one, in which it becomes attached to a different species, with consequent disrupting effects upon sexual and other social relationships with members of its own kind.

The concept of a turning point applies equally well to most examples of critical periods for learning. Up to a certain point in development a chaffinch can learn several varieties of song, but once it has learned one of them it no longer has a choice. Similarly, the human infant can learn either sex role up to a certain age, but once it has learned one or

the other, changing over becomes increasingly difficult. What is learned at particular points limits and interferes with subsequent learning, and Schneirla and Rosenblatt have suggested that there are critical stages of learning—that what has been learned at a particular time in development may be critical for whatever follows.

A second sort of action during a critical period consists of a nonspecific stimulus producing an irrevocable result, not modifiable in subsequent development. Thus, almost any sort of stimulus has the effect of modifying the development of the endocrine stress mechanism of young rats in early infancy.

Is there any underlying common principle? Each of these effects has its counterpart in embryonic development. Up to a certain point a cell taken from an amphibian embryo and transplanted to a new location will develop in accordance with its new environment. Beyond this turning point it develops in accordance with its previous location. Some cells retain a degree of lability, but none retain the breadth of choice they had before. Similarly, specific injuries produced by nonspecific causes are also found in embryonic development: damage to an embryonic optic vesicle results in a defective eye, no matter what sort of chemical produces the injury. It is obvious that the similarity between this case and the critical period for early stimulation can be accounted for by the single common process of growth, occurring relatively late in development in the case of the endocrine stress mechanism and much earlier in the development of the eye. The effects are nonspecific because of the fact that growth can be modified in only very limited ways, by being either slowed down or speeded up.

Both growth and behavioral differentiation are based on organizing processes. This suggests a general principle of organization: that once a system becomes organized, whether it is the cells of the embryo that are multiplying and differentiating or the behavior patterns of a young animal that are becoming organized through learning, it becomes progressively more difficult to reorganize the system. That is, organization inhibits reorganization. Further, organization can be strongly modified only when active processes of organization are going on, and this accounts for critical periods of development.

CONCLUSION

The concept of critical periods is a highly important one for human and animal welfare. Once the dangers and potential benefits for each period of life are known, it should be possible to avoid the former and take advantage of the latter.

The discovery of critical periods immediately focuses attention on the developmental processes which cause them. As these processes become understood, it is increasingly possible to deliberately modify critical periods and their results. For example, since the development of fear responses limits the period of primary socialization, we can deliberately extend the period by reducing fear reactions, either by psychological methods or by the use of tranquilizing drugs. Or, if it seems desirable, we can increase the degree of dependency of a child or pet animal by purposely increasing his emotional reactions during the critical period. Again, if infantile stimulation is desirable, parents can be taught to provide it in appropriate amounts at the proper time.

Some data suggest that for each behavioral and physiological phenomenon there is a different critical period in development. If this were literally true, the process of development, complicated by individual variability, would be so complex that the concept of critical periods would serve little useful purpose. Some sort of order can be obtained by dealing with different classes of behavioral phenomena. For example, it can be stated that the period in life in which each new social relationship is initiated is a critical one for the determination of that relationship. Furthermore, there is evidence that critical-period effects are more common early in life than they are later on, and that the critical period for primary socialization is also critical for other effects, such as the attachment to particular places, and many overlap with a critical period for the formation of basic food habits.

We may expect to find that the periods in which actual physiological damage through environmental stimulation is possible will turn out to be similarly specific and concentrated in early life.

A great deal of needed information regarding the optimum periods for acquiring motor and intellectual skills is still lacking. These skills are based not merely on age but on the relative rate of maturation of various organs. Any attempt to teach a child or animal at too early a period of development may result in his learning bad habits, or simply in his learning "not to learn," either of which results may greatly handicap him in later life. In the long run, this line of experimental work should lead to greater realization of the capacities possessed by human beings, both through avoidance of damaging experiences and through correction of damage from unavoidable accidents.

Selection **12** | THE EFFECT OF REARING CONDITIONS ON BEHAVIOR*

HARRY F. HARLOW
MARGARET K. HARLOW
University of Wisconsin

A wealth of clinical evidence shows that human children who have never had adequate maternal care or who have been separated from adequate maternal care within some critical stage, suffer disturbance and delay or even irreparable damage in terms of subsequent personal-social development. The importance of maternal ministrations in the child's development is further supported by many clinical investigations and by some limited experimental data.

Personality malfunctions that have been attributed to maternal inadequacy include such syndromes as marasmus, hospitalism, infantile autism, feeble-mindedness, inadequate maternal responsiveness, and deviant or depressed heterosexuality. If these disorders are the results of maternal inadequacy, only research with human subjects can establish the conditions and kinds of maternal behavior that produce them. Unfortunately, experiments crit-

* H. F. Harlow and M. K. Harlow, "The Effect of Rearing Conditions on Behavior," *Bulletin of the Menninger Clinic,* **26,** 213–224, 1962.

ical to the resolution of these problems cannot be done with human subjects. We cannot rear babies in illuminated black boxes during the first half-year, year, or two years of their lives. We cannot have mothers rear their children in isolation from other children and from adults for the first two, four, or eight years. We dare not have human children reared with either no mothers or inadequate mothers while providing them with maximal opportunity to interact with age-mates, either identically reared or differentially reared. Yet these are the kinds of experiments which are required if we are to assess the effects of maternal variables unconfounded with other experiential variables on the child's personal-social development.

Most clinical investigations have given primary attention to the effects of maternal privation, defined as absence or inadequacy of maternal responsiveness, or to maternal deprivation, defined as infant separation after the infant has established profound, or at least adequate, maternal attachments. Relatively little attention has been given to the effects of the absence or inadequacy of opportunity for the child to interact with other children and to form adequate affectional patterns with and for them. We know that it is important for the child to form effective infant-mother affectional patterns, but it also is likely that he must form effective child-child affectional patterns if he is to attain normal personal-social, sexual, and parental patterns. Obviously these affectional systems are not independent. It is possible, but by no means a certainty, that at the human level, normal child-child affection requires previous affectional bonds between mother or mother-figure and child. It is certain that the mother plays an important role in the formation of peer affections by providing for and encouraging associations between infants or children, or by preventing or discouraging such associations. Human mothers may also markedly influence the nature and course of child-child relationships.

Psychoanalytic theory, which looks for temporal reduction and temporal primacy, will ascribe primary importance to the earliest causes and conditions whether or not these are of greatest importance. Initial traumas have a false clarity as causative agents since they are not confounded by preceding events, whereas the role of all subsequent events is confounded

by the role of these events operating during previous experience. Yet primacy in time need not, and often should not, be equated with primacy in importance.

EFFECTS OF TOTAL SOCIAL DEPRIVATION ON MONKEYS

Six years ago we took two newborn rhesus monkeys, one male and one female, and subjected them to total social deprivation for the first two years of life. Each was placed in a solid, illuminated cage such that it never saw any other animal—monkey or human—even though it was tested for food responsiveness and learning by remote-control techniques. During isolation these monkeys adapted to solid food slowly and learned with great difficulty, but they were found to have normal weight and good coats when removed—there were no signs of marasmus. At the conclusion of the two years' isolation, they were tested for social responsiveness to each other and to normal monkeys smaller and younger than themselves. They did not respond to each other and either froze or huddled in a corner when abused by the younger animals. Placed together in a cage in a room with many caged monkeys, they showed withdrawal from this new external world, and in the more than two years they lived together, they remained abnormally frightened, showed minimal interaction, and engaged in no sex activities. In follow-up social tests at four years of age with smaller and weaker monkeys, they made no effort to defend themselves except for one brief episode with one of the pair, after which it curled into a ball and passively accepted abuse. The potential for social behaviors in these animals had apparently been obliterated.

EFFECTS OF EARLY PARTIAL SOCIAL DEPRIVATION

We have data on various groups of monkeys raised from the day of their birth without their mothers and without any monkey companionship at least through the first half-year. One group of 56, now ranging in age from five to eight years, was raised in individual bare wire cages where they could see and hear other

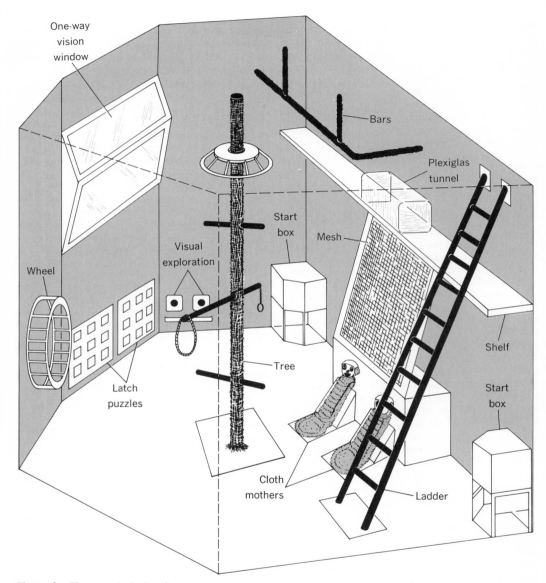

Figure 1 Playroom test situation.

monkeys, but not touch them. A group of four was similarly housed for up to five years, but had access to a single wire surrogate[1] during

the first half-year of life. A third group of over 100 monkeys was raised identically except for access to a cloth surrogate[2] or to both a cloth surrogate and a wire surrogate during at least

[1] A wire surrogate mother is a bare, welded wire cylindrical form surmounted by a wooden head with a crude face and supported semiupright in a wooden frame. (See Fig. 1, page 126).

[2] A cloth surrogate differs from the wire surrogate in that the wire cylinder is cushioned with a sheathing of terry cloth.

six months of the first year.[3] Approximately half of these animals have been housed after six months or one year of age with another monkey of like age and like or unlike sex for part or all the time since.

Although there may be differences in the personal-social behaviors of the monkeys comprising these groups, we cannot be sure at the present time, and for this reason we group them together. Many members of all three groups have developed what appear to be abnormal behaviors, including sitting and staring fixedly into space, repetitive stereotyped circling movements about the cage, clasping the head in the hands and arms while engaging in rocking, autistic-type movements, and intrapunitive responses of grasping a foot, hand, arm, or leg and chewing or tearing at it with the teeth to the point of injury.

The sex behavior of the six oldest wire-cage-raised monkeys was first measured by Mason[4] in 1960 and compared with that of rhesus monkeys of equal age which had lived in the wild during most of the first year of life. All the wild-raised monkeys, male and female, showed normal sex behavior, characterized in the male by dorsoventral mounting, clasping the legs of the female by the feet, and holding the buttocks by the hands. The females in turn sexually presented themselves by elevating their buttocks and tails, lowering their heads, and frequently looking backward without threatening. No laboratory-raised male or female showed normal sex behavior. Attempted mounting by the male was random in regard to body part, and the most frequent pattern was grasping a side of the female's body and thrusting laterally. The female's patterns were totally disordered and often involved sitting down and staring aimlessly into space. Although none of these animals was sexually mature, heterosexual positioning in both male and female normally develops during the second year.

We have subsequently tested many wire-cage- and surrogate-mother-raised males and females with experienced breeding females and

experienced breeding males, respectively, in a large 8-foot by 8-foot by 8-foot room especially designed for breeding studies. All the males have continued to show the disorganized and inappropriately oriented sexual responsiveness which we have already described, and no male has ever appropriately mounted our experienced and cooperative breeding-stock females, let alone achieved intromission.

With a single exception we have never seen normal, appropriate sexual posturing in our wire-cage- or surrogate-raised females. The females do not approach the males, nor do they groom or present. One cloth-surrogate-raised female was not impregnated throughout six mating sessions, and during this time she began to respond positively and appropriately to the males and eventually developed a normal, full-blown pattern of sexual presentation and sexual posturing during copulation.

EFFECTS OF MATERNAL CONDITIONS

Direct comparison of the effects of being raised by real monkey mothers and cloth surrogate mothers on subsequent personal-social development has been measured by the use of our playpen test situation. In two playpen situations babies were housed with their real mothers, and in a third setup the babies were housed with cloth mothers. The playpen, whose floor plan is given in Figure 2, consists of large living cages each housing a mother and an infant and adjoining a compartment of the playpen. A small opening in each living cage restrains the mother, but gives the infant continuous access to the adjoining playpen compartment. During two daily test sessions, each an hour in length, the screens between playpen compartments were raised, permitting the infant monkeys to interact as pairs during the first six months and as both pairs and groups of four during the second six months. Two experimenters independently observed and recorded the behavior exhibited during test sessions.

The infants raised by real monkey mothers were more socially responsive to each other than were the infants raised by the cloth surrogates. They showed a wider range of facial expressions, and, probably of paramount importance, they developed simple interactive

[3] Harlow, H. F.: The Nature of Love. *Amer. Psychologist* **13**: 673–685, 1958.

Harlow, H. F.: Love in Infant Monkeys. *Sci. Amer.* **200**:68–74, 1959.

[4] Mason, W. A.: The Effects of Social Restriction on the Behavior of Rhesus Monkeys: I. Free Social Behavior. *J. Comp. Physiol. Psychol.* **53**:582–589, 1960.

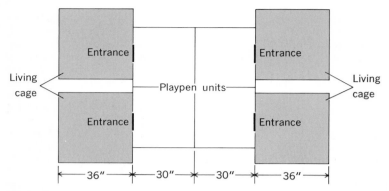

Figure 2 Playpen test situation.

play patterns earlier than the surrogate-raised monkeys and achieved a level of complex play patterns not achieved by the surrogate-raised monkeys during an 18-month test period.

All the male, mother-raised infants have at one time or another responded sexually toward the mother with pelvic thrusting and in at least two cases by dorsoventral mounting. In three cases pelvic thrusting to a female was observed before 50 days of age and in a fourth case, before 100 days of age. Only two (one male and one female) cloth-surrogate-raised monkeys were observed to show pelvic thrusting to the surrogate, and this occurred initially at approximately 100 days of age. Frequency of this sexual play was much higher toward real mothers than toward surrogates. In both situations maximal frequency occurred at about five months and then declined, apparently being superseded by thrusting directed toward other infants.

Surrogate babies and mothered babies showed no significant differences in first-observed, infant-directed thrusting, but the actual mean score of the surrogate group was lower. The frequency of sexual play was higher for the real-mothered babies than for the surrogate babies. Finally, seven of eight mother-raised monkeys showed appropriate adult-form sex behaviors during the first 18 months, including ankle clasp by the males, whereas adult-oriented sex behavior was not observed in the cloth-surrogate-raised babies.

There is every reason to believe that normal mothering facilitates the development of heterosexual behavior in rhesus monkeys. This may be in part the result of direct contacts with the

mother growing out of the intimate bonds between mother and child. One must not, however, underestimate the importance of the role which the real mother apparently plays, indirect though it is, in stimulating the infants to associate with other infants. This is accomplished from the third month on by discouraging the infant from constant clinging as it matures. From time to time the mother restrains the infant's approaches or cuffs it if it nips her or pulls her hair. The chastised infant seeks the companionship of other babies until the storm subsides—the other mothers by this time generally reject all but their own babies—and in the infant-infant interchanges, strong affectional bonds develop along with behaviors, sexual and nonsexual, appropriate to the sexes.

In the present study, as in all ordinary human situations, there is confounding in the roles played by the mother-infant affectional systems and the infant-infant and peer-peer affectional systems in determining later behavior.

It is obvious that we must not underestimate the importance and role of the infant-infant affectional system as a determiner of adolescent and adult adjustments. It is more than possible that this system is essential if the animal is to respond positively to sheer physical contact with a peer, and it is through the operation of this system, probably both in monkey and man, that sexual roles become identified and, usually, acceptable.

The role of the mother in the formation of the adult personality is obviously important, but the exact mechanics are open for experimentation. The most tender and intimate associations occur at a stage in which the monkey infant and human infant can to a considerable extent be molded. Monkey and human mother both have the obligation of gradually dissolving the intense physical bonds which characterize the early mother-child relationship. For the monkey mother it is easy and natural—when the infant becomes mature enough and strong enough to become bothersome, she rejects or punishes it and the baby retreats for a time. Subsequently, she welcomes the baby back. Independence is gradually established. For the human mother, with her more complicated motivational systems and her complex culture, it may be difficult to achieve this gradual separation. The overprotective mother is a well-known clinical extreme in the human problem of weaning the infant and child emotionally. Probably the surrogate monkey mother is a parallel of the overprotective human mother, failing usually to equal the normal mother in rearing socially and sexually adjusted monkeys because, at least in part, she is ever available to provide comfort and security. She never discourages contact and thereby never encourages independence in her infant and affectional relationships with other infants and children. The normal state of complete dependency necessary in early infancy is prolonged until it hinders normal personal-social development.

As we have already pointed out, four of our laboratory-raised females never had real mothers of their own, one being raised in a bare wire cage and three with cloth surrogates. The first week after the birth of the baby to the wire-cage-raised female, the mother sat fixedly at one side of the cage staring into space, almost unaware of her infant or of human beings, even when they barked at and threatened the baby. There was no sign of maternal responses, and when the infant approached and attempted contact, the mother rebuffed it, often with vigor, as shown in Figure 3.

The next two unmothered mothers constantly rebuffed the approaches of their infants, but, in addition, frequently engaged in cruel and unprovoked attacks. They struck and beat their babies, mouthed them roughly, and pushed their faces into the wire-mesh floor. These attacks seemed to be exaggerated in the presence of human beings, and for this reason all formal testing was abandoned for three

Figure 3 Typical behavior of unmothered mother toward her infant. Mother is looking upward while crushing her baby against the cage floor.

days for the third unmothered mother because we feared for the life of the infant. The fourth unmothered mother ignored and rejected her infant but did not exhibit excessive cruelty.

In strong contrast to the frailty of the maternal affectional system was the vigor and persistence of the infants' bondage to the mother—time after time, hour after hour, the infants returned, contacted, and clasped the mother in spite of being hit, kicked, and scraped unceremoniously off the mother's body, as shown in Figure 4. The physical punishment which these infants took or sought for the privilege of brief contact even to the back or side of the mother's body testified to the fact that, even in infants, attachment to the mother may be prepotent over pain and suffering. One could not help but be reminded of children, removed from indifferent or cruel, indigent, and alcoholic parents, whose primary insistent wish is to return home.

The degree to which monkey data are generalizable to the human being will remain an unsolved dilemma. Nevertheless, we are so struck by the many apparent analogies that we are tempted to say the monkey experiments give us faith in the human clinical observations.

Infants raised by live mothers were more advanced in social and sexual behavior than infants raised by surrogate mothers in a controlled playpen situation. The mother's role is not entirely clear, however, because in a more stimulating playroom situation, surrogate-mothered babies have shown normal social and sexual behavior.

Over all, it appears that the longer and the more complete the social deprivation, the more devastating are the behavioral effects. Further research is needed to evaluate the relative contributions of live mothers and infant companions to later adjustment.

Figure 4 Typical clinging response of infant illustrating mother's vigorous rejection.

Selection **13** | CONTINUITIES AND DISCONTINUITIES IN CULTURAL CONDITIONING*

RUTH BENEDICT
Columbia University

SUMMARY

Infant rhesus monkeys have been reared starting on the first day of life in a variety of situations, including total isolation; partial isolation either in individual bare wire cages in a colony room for two years or longer, or in individual wire cages with access to one or two mother surrogates for at least the first six months and in situations with real or surrogate mothers plus contact with other infants for the first year or two of life.

Total isolation for two years resulted in failure to display social or sexual behavior in the next two years, spent in a joint living cage. Results on six months of such isolation are still being gathered and suggest severe, but not complete, social deficits. Only mild effects have been observed thus far in monkeys isolated through the first 80 days of life.

Partial isolation has produced behavioral aberrations in many monkeys and sexual inadequacy in all males and in all but one female. Four females were impregnated, in spite of inadequate posturing, and proved to be completely inadequate mothers.

All cultures must deal in one way or another with the cycle of growth from infancy to adulthood. Nature has posed the situation dramatically: on the one hand, the new born baby, physiologically vulnerable, unable to fend for itself, or to participate of its own initiative in the life of the group, and, on the other, the adult man or woman. Every man who rounds out his human potentialities must have been a son first and a father later, and the two roles are physiologically in great contrast; he must first have been dependent upon others for his very existence, and later he must provide such security for others. This discontinuity in the life cycle is a fact of nature and is inescapable. Facts of nature, however, in any discussion of human problems, are ordinarily read off not at their bare minimal but surrounded by all the local accretions of behavior to which the stu-

* From Ruth Benedict, "Continuities and Discontinuities in Cultural Conditionng," *Psychiatry*, 1:161–167, 1938. Copyrght held by The William Alanson White Psychiatric Foundation, Inc. Reprinted by special permission of The William Alanson White Psychiatric Foundation, Inc.

dent of human affairs has become accustomed in his own culture. For that reason, it is illuminating to examine comparative material from other societies in order to get a wider perspective on our own special accretions. The anthropologist's role is not to question the facts of nature, but to insist upon the interposition of a middle term between "nature" and "human behavior"; his role is to analyze that term, to document local man-made doctorings of nature, and to insist that these doctorings should not be read off in any one culture as nature itself. Although it is a fact of nature that the child becomes a man, the way in which this transition is effected varies from one society to another, and no one of these particular cultural bridges should be regarded as the "natural" path to maturity.

From a comparative point of view, our culture goes to great extremes in emphasizing contrasts between the child and the adult. The child is sexless, the adult estimates his virility by his sexual activities; the child must be protected from the ugly facts of life, the adult must meet them without psychic catastrophe; the child must obey, the adult must command this obedience. These are all dogmas of our culture, dogmas which, in spite of the facts of nature, other cultures commonly do not share. In spite of the physiological contrasts between child and adult, these are cultural accretions.

The major discontinuity in the life cycle is of course that the child who is at one point a son must later be a father. These roles in our society are strongly differentiated; a good son is tractable, and does not assume adult responsibilities; a good father provides for his children and should not allow his authority to be flouted. In addition, the child must be sexless so far as his family is concerned, whereas the father's sexual role is primary in the family. The individual in one role must revise his behavior from almost all points of view when he assumes the second role.

I shall select for discussion three such contrasts that occur in our culture between the individual's role as child and as father: (1) responsible-non-responsible status role; (2) dominance-submission; (3) contrasted sexual role. It is largely upon our cultural commitments to these three contrasts that the discontinuity in the life cycle of an individual in our culture depends.

RESPONSIBLE–NON-RESPONSIBLE STATUS ROLE

The techniques adopted by societies which achieve continuity during the life cycle in this sphere in no way differ from those we employ in our uniform conditioning to three meals a day. They are merely applied to other areas of life. We think of the child as wanting to play and the adult as having to work, but in many societies the mother takes the baby daily in her shawl or carrying net to the garden or to gather roots, and adult labor is seen even in infancy from the pleasant security of its position in close contact with its mother. When the child can run about, it accompanies its parents still, doing tasks which are essential and yet suited to its powers, and its dichotomy between work and play is not different from that its parents recognize, namely the distinction between the busy day and the free evening. The tasks it is asked to perform are graded to its powers, and its elders wait quietly by, not offering to do the task in the child's place. Everyone who is familiar with such societies has been struck by the contrast with our child training. Dr. Ruth Underhill tells me of sitting with a group of Papago elders in Arizona when the man of the house turned to his little three-year-old granddaughter and asked her to close the door. The door was heavy and hard to shut. The child tried, but it did not move. Several times the grandfather repeated: "Yes, close the door." No one jumped to the child's assistance. No one took the responsibility away from her. On the other hand there was no impatience, for after all the child was small. They sat gravely waiting till the child succeeded and her grandfather gravely thanked her. It was assumed that the task would not be asked of her unless she could perform it, and, having been asked, the responsibility was hers alone just as if she were a grown woman.

The essential point of such child training is that the child is from infancy continuously conditioned to responsible social participation, while at the same time the tasks that are expected of it are adapted to its capacity. The contrast with our society is very great. A child does not make any labor contribution to our industrial society except as it competes against an adult; its work is not measured against its own strength and skill but against high-geared industrial requirements. Even when we praise a child's achievement in the home, we are outraged if such praise is interpreted as being of the same order as praise of adults. The child is praised because the parent feels well disposed, regardless of whether the task is well done by adult standards, and the child acquires no sensible standard by which to measure its achievement. The gravity of a Cheyenne Indian family ceremoniously making a feast out of the little boy's first snowbird is at the furthest remove from our behavior. At birth the little boy was presented with a toy bow, and from the time he could run about serviceable bows suited to his stature were specially made for him by the man of the family. Animals and birds were taught him in a graded series beginning with those most easily taken, and as he brought in his first of each species his family duly made a feast of it, accepting his contribution as gravely as the buffalo his father brought. When he finally killed a buffalo, it was only the final step of his childhood conditioning, not a new adult role with which his childhood experience had been at variance.

DOMINANCE-SUBMISSION

Dominance-submission is the most striking of those categories of behavior where like does not respond to like, but where one type of behavior stimulates the opposite response. It is one of the most prominent ways in which behavior is patterned in our culture. When it obtains between classes, it may be nourished by continuous experience; the difficulty in its use between children and adults lies in the fact that an individual conditioned to one set of behavior in childhood must adopt the opposite as an adult. Its opposite is a pattern of approximately identical reciprocal behavior; the societies which rely upon continuous conditioning characteristically invoke this pattern. In some primitive cultures, the very terminology of address between father and son, and, more commonly, between grandchild and grandson or uncle and nephew, reflects this attitude. In such kinship terminologies, one reciprocal expresses each of these relationships so that son and father, for instance, exchange the same term with one another, just as we exchange the same term with a cousin. The child later will

exchange it with his son. "Father-son," therefore, is a continuous relationship he enjoys throughout life. The same continuity, backed up by verbal reciprocity, occurs far oftener in the grandchild-grandson relationship or that of mother's brother-sister's son. When these are "joking" relationships, as they often are, travellers report wonderingly upon the liberties and pretensions of tiny toddlers in their dealing with these family elders. In place of our dogma of respect to elders, such societies employ in these cases a reciprocity as nearly identical as may be. The teasing and practical joking the grandfather visits upon his grandchild, the grandchild return in like coin; he would be led to believe that he failed in propriety if he did not give like for like. If the sister's son has right of access without leave to his mother's brother's possessions, the mother's brother has such rights also to the child's possessions. They share reciprocal privileges and obligations which in our society can develop only between age mates.

From the point of view of our present discussion, such kinship conventions allow the child to put in practice from infancy the same forms of behavior which it will rely upon as an adult, behavior is not polarized into a general requirement of submission for the child and dominance for the adult.

It is clear from the techniques described above, by which the child is conditioned to a responsible status role, that these depend chiefly upon arousing in the child the desire to share responsibility in adult life. To achieve this, little stress is laid upon obedience but much stress upon approval and praise. Punishment is very commonly regarded as quite outside the realm of possibility, and natives in many parts of the world have drawn the conclusion from our usual disciplinary methods that white parents do not love their children. If the child is not required to be submissive, however, many occasions for punishment melt away; a variety of situations which call for it do not occur.

CONTRASTED SEXUAL ROLE

Continuity of conditioning in training the child to assume responsibility and to behave no more submissively than adults is quite possible in terms of the child's physiological endowment if his participation is suited to his strength. Because of the late development of the child's reproductive organs, continuity of conditioning in sex experience presents a difficult problem. So far as their belief that the child is anything but a sexless being is concerned, they are probably more nearly right than we are with an opposite dogma. But the great break is presented by the universally sterile unions before puberty and the presumably fertile ones after maturation. This physiological fact no amount of cultural manipulation can minimize or alter, and societies, therefore, which stress continuous conditioning most strongly sometimes do not expect children to be interested in sex experience until they have matured physically. This is striking among American Indian tribes like the Dakota; adults observe great privacy in sex acts and in no way stimulate children's sexual activity. There need be no discontinuity, in the sense in which I have used the term, in such a program if the child is taught nothing it does not have to unlearn later. In such cultures, adults view children's experimentation as in no way wicked or dangerous, but merely as innocuous play which can have no serious consequences. In some societies such play is minimal and the children manifest little interest in it. But the same attitude may be taken by adults in societies where such play is encouraged and forms a major activity among small children. This is true among most of the Melanesian cultures of Southeast New Guinea; adults go as far as to laugh off sexual affairs within the prohibited class, if the children are not mature, saying that since they cannot marry there can be no harm done.

DISCONTINUITY IN CONDITIONING

Even from this very summary statement of continuous conditioning, the economy of such mores is evident. In spite of the obvious advantages, however, there are difficulties in its way. Many primitive societies expect as different behavior from an individual as child and as adult as we do, and such discontinuity involves a presumption of strain.

Many societies of this type, however, minimize strain by the techniques they employ; and some techniques are more successful than

others in ensuring the individual's functioning without conflict. It is from this point of view that age-grade societies reveal their fundamental significance. Age-graded cultures characteristically demand different behavior of the individual at different times of his life and persons of a like age-grade are grouped into a society whose activities are all oriented toward the behavior desired at that age. Individuals "graduate" publicly and with honor from one of these groups to another. Where age society members are enjoined to loyalty and mutual support, and are drawn not only from the local group but from the whole tribe, as among the Arapaho, or even from other tribes as among the Wagawaga of Southeast New Guinea, such an institution has many advantages in eliminating conflicts among local groups and fostering intratribal peace. This seems to be also a factor in the tribal military solidarity of the similarly organized Masai of East Africa. The point that is of chief interest for our present discussion, however, is that by this means an individual who at any time takes on a new set of duties and virtues is supported not only by a solid phalanx of age mates but by the traditional prestige of the organized "secret" society into which he has now graduated. Fortified in this way, individuals in such cultures often swing between remarkable extremes of opposite behavior without apparent psychic threat. For example, the great majority exhibit prideful and non-conflicted behavior at each stage in the life cycle, even when a prime of life devoted to passionate and aggressive head hunting must be followed by a later life dedicated to ritual and to mild and peaceable civic virtues.

Our chief interest here, however, is in discontinuity which primarily affects the child. In many primitive societies, such discontinuity has been fostered not because of economic or political necessity or because such discontinuity provides for a socially valuable division of labor, but because of some conceptual dogma. The most striking of these are the Australian and Papuan cultures where the ceremony of the "Making of Man" flourishes. In such societies it is believed that men and women have opposite and conflicting powers, and male children, who are of undefined status, must be initiated into the male role. In Central Australia the boy child is of the woman's side, and women are taboo in the final adult stages of tribal ritual. The elaborate and protracted initiation ceremonies of the Arunta, therefore, snatch the boy from the mother, dramatize his gradual repudiation of her. In a final ceremony he is reborn as a man out of the men's ceremonial "baby pouch." The men's ceremonies are ritual statements of a masculine solidarity, caried out by fondling one another's *Churingas*, the material symbol of each man's life, and by letting out over one another blood drawn from their veins. After this warm bond among men has been established through the ceremonies, the boy joins the men in the men's house and participates in tribal rites. The enjoined discontinuity has been tribally bridged.

I have chosen illustrations of discontinuous conditioning where it is not too much to say that the cultural institutions furnish adequate support to the individual as he progresses from role to role or interdicts the previous behavior in a summary fashion. The contrast with arrangements in our culture is very striking, and against this background of social arrangements in other cultures the adolescent period of *Sturm und Drang* with which we are so familiar becomes intelligible in terms of our discontinuous cultural institutions and dogmas rather than in terms of physiological necessity.

It is even more pertinent to consider these comparative facts in relation to maladjusted persons in our culture who are said to be fixated at one or another pre-adult level. It is clear that if we were to look at our social arrangements as an outsider, we should infer directly from our family institutions and habits of child training that many individuals would not "put off childish things"; we should have to say that our adult activity demands traits that are interdicted in children, and that, far from redoubling efforts to help children bridge this gap, adults in our culture put all the blame on the child when he fails to manifest spontaneously the new behavior or, overstepping the mark, manifests it with untoward belligerence. It is not surprising that in such a society many individuals fear to use behavior which has up to that time been under a ban and trust instead, though at great psychic cost, to attitudes that have been exercised with approval during their formative years. Insofar as we invoke a physiological scheme to account for these neurotic adjustments, we are led to overlook the possibility of developing social institutions which would lessen the social cost we now pay; instead, we elaborate a set of dogmas which prove inapplicable under other social conditions.

THE
MOTIVATION
OF
BEHAVIOR

3

In searching to understand our own behavior and the behavior of others, we often ask the question, "Why did I do that?" In posing this question we are raising the problem of what motivates or moves us to certain actions. The term "motivation" itself reflects the nature of our problem in that it derives from the Latin verb *moveo*, meaning "to move." In the development of all animals the earliest motives which arouse and sustain activity are physiologically based. The infant is activated primarily by such drives as hunger, thirst, and pain, and he continues to make his needs known until they are relieved by those around him. As adults we tend to take for granted that we feel hungry when our body needs food, but if we stop to examine the question, "How do I know when I need food?" we find that the solution is by no means obvious. A not uncommon response to this question might take this form: "I know I'm hungry when I feel hunger pangs [stomach contractions]."

BIOLOGICAL FACTORS

Such a reply represents a somewhat oversimplified statement of the view proposed some thirty years ago by the eminent physiologist Walter B. Cannon. In attempting to determine the critical mechanisms which instigate physiological drives, Cannon focused on peripheral factors such as stomach contractions. Although this peripheral theory of hunger motivation appeals to common-sense experience, a wide variety of evidence indicates that it is faulty; for example, patients who have had their stomachs removed and thus cannot have stomach contractions seem to have normal hunger cycles. As a result, physiologists and psychologists began to look for mechanisms of motivation in portions of the central nervous system. In a paper entitled "Central Stimulation and Other New Approaches to Motivation and Reward," Selection 14, Dr. Neal Miller describes a variety of fascinating experiments which indicate that the critical mechanisms by which the organism "knows" that it is hungry, thirsty, etc. are to be found in subcortical regions of the brain. He points out that the new science of psychopharmacology has great potential for furthering our understanding of the biologically determined motivations "of mice and men." We are just beginning to open an exciting new chapter in the understanding of behavior![1]

PSYCHOLOGICAL FACTORS

There is no doubt that research such as Miller's greatly extends our understanding of the nature of physiological drives. However, despite the importance of this type of research, such an approach is incomplete since most human behavior is aroused and sustained by social motives or other learned motives. In Selection 15, Dr. Robert White reviews several trends within psychology which indicate a general dissatisfaction with the orthodox view of human motivation which would model all motives after the pattern of primary drives such as hunger and thirst. Within animal

[1] In 1965, Dr. Miller was one of a select group of ten distinguished scientists who received the National Medal of Science. This medal was established by the Eighty-sixth Congress to be awarded for "outstanding contributions to knowledge in the physical, biological, mathematical, or engineering sciences." Dr. Miller was cited "for sustained and imaginative research on principles of learning and motivation and illuminating behavioral analysis of the effects of direct electrical stimulation of the brain."

psychology it has become increasingly apparent that the primary-drive model is not adequate to account for such behavior as exploration, activity, and manipulation. A similar trend is discernible in psychoanalytic theory. Although Freud had recognized certain motive powers associated with the ego, he did not place great emphasis on these ego instincts. On the other hand, later psychoanalytic writers have tended to attach increasing importance to the motivation provided by the individuals need to master his environment. Several complementary trends are apparent in general psychology (e.g., in Hebb's discussion of arousal and novelty, and in Young or McClelland's hedonic arousal theories of motivation). White maintains that the common property in these superficially diverse behaviors is the motivation to interact competently with the environment. Although such *effectance* motivation has clear biological advantages in terms of adaptation, it is most poignantly represented in the "playful and investigatory activities of young animals and children."

Like White, Dr. Abraham Maslow takes execption to the traditional behavioristic view that complex human motives are derived from primary drives. He also criticizes the tendency of many psychologists to base their interpretations of normal motivations primarily upon clinical data from neurotic and psychotic patients. The essentials of Maslow's theory of motivation are presented in Selection 16 in which he proposes that human motivations can be meaningfully arranged into a hierarchy of prepotency or urgency. The most basic, or immediately urgent, motives are associated with physiological needs and safety needs. However, if our society arranges a benevolent environment, we are then freed to develop and satisfy the higher-order needs of self-esteem and love. Maslow's highest-level motive, which he calls self-actualization, is in some respects similar to White's concept of competence. However, self-actualization would appear to be a more general concept. Throughout his discussion Maslow notes interpersonal factors which can facilitate or inhibit satisfaction of these basic needs. His approach may thus provide the basis for a synthesis of biological, psychological, and social determinants of motivation.

SOCIOCULTURAL FACTORS

The experimental analysis of the learned motivation to achieve has been advanced by a large number of researchers since the publication of *The Achievement Motive* by McClelland and his associates in 1953. The basic technique by which need achievement (*n* Ach) is measured is to have the subject tell stories in response to a set of pictures. The stories are then scored for themes which indicate achievement strivings. It may be seen that *n* Ach may vary with the instructions given the subject, with whether or not the subject tends to be high or low in achievement striving, with the sex of the subject, and perhaps even the sex of the figures in the cards. Lesser, Krawitz, and Packard (Selection 17) studied the effect of achievement-oriented instructions in a group of females who were academic achievers or underachievers. Their results did not support the original hypothesis that achievement-oriented instructions would uniformly increase achievement motivation. However, as often happens, an unexpected finding made considerable sense. They found that achieving girls displayed the expected increase in *n* Ach scores under achievement-oriented instructions when they were telling stories in which the central character was a female; underachieving girls showed a similar increase in response to pictures portraying males. The authors show how a social-role model can explain the findings. They suggest that ". . . the achieving girls perceive intellectual-achievement goals as relevant to their own female role; in contrast, the underachieving girls perceive intellectual-achievement roles as more relevant to the male role than to their own female role." These results emphasize that such complex behavior as academic achievement has multiple determinants.

Selection **14** | CENTRAL STIMULATION AND OTHER NEW APPROACHES TO MOTIVATION AND REWARD*

NEAL E. MILLER
Yale University

The focus of my paper will be that of determining how motivations and rewards produce their effects. While the immediate practical implications will not be so obvious, it is a well-known fact that the deeper understanding of basic phenomena almost always leads to significant practical applications, frequently being the necessary foundation for radical innovations.

You are well aware that problems of motivation and reward, which incidentally shade off into mood and temperament, have wide clinical, social, and educational implications. I believe we are at last developing new techniques for getting inside of the organism, manipulating and measuring some of the simpler, more basic things that are going on there, and thus are laying the foundations for fundamental advances in our understanding of the mechanisms of motivation and reward.

The recent spurt of fruitful research on the mechanisms of motivations has emerged as a result of the convergence of two lines of development. Physiologists, pharmacologists, and biochemists have been developing new and subtler tools for radically affecting and measuring organic processes. At the same time, experimental psychologists have been developing a variety of more effective techniques for measuring drives. The combination of techniques from these two sources is beginning to yield results which have exciting potentialities.

In this brief presentation I can only sample a few of these results. I shall include some pictures to give you a firsthand impression of the work.

* Abridged from Neal E. Miller, "Central Stimulation and Other New Approaches to Motivation and Reward," *American Psychologist,* **13**: 100–108, 1958. Copyright 1958 by the American Psychological Association and reproduced by permission. The paper has been slightly rewritten.

An early study of hunger

Using the improved electrolytic technique for making lesions deep in the more primitive structures of the brain, Hetherington and Ranson found that lesions in the region of the ventromedial nuclei of the hypothalamus would cause albino rats to overeat enormously so that, as Fig. 1 shows, they became very fat. But Bailey, Stevenson, and I used behavioral tests to show that these lesions do not necessarily always potentiate hunger. Although our rats would eat more, they would not work as hard for food. Furthermore, they were stopped by smaller doses of quinine. Thus the additional behavioral tests did not support the original inference of increased hunger drawn from the measure of amount of food consumed. It seemed more reasonable to assume that the lesion interfered with complete satiation.

In the foregoing study, the single test of amount of food consumed disagreed with the rate of bar pressing and a number of other behavioral measures. Other studies, summar-

Figure 1 Effects of overeating, produced by lesions in the region of the ventromedial nuclei of the hypothalamus.

ized elsewhere, show that certain circumstances can affect the rate of bar pressing, so the results of this test will disagree with those of a number of different tests. Discrepancies among tests purporting to measure the same thing raise important problems which the aptitude testers have long since explored: namely, problems of general versus specific factors, and of the purity of various measures of such factors. But our main point for the moment is that it is prudent and extremely fruitful to use a variety of behavioral tests in studying a drive such as hunger. We are just beginning to cash in on the potentialities of these tests; to date, most studies of the physiological mechanisms of hunger are still limited to the single measure of the amount of food consumed.

Sample of other brain-lesion studies

Lesions in the same general region as those producing overeating can markedly change the temperament of the rat. Anand and Brobeck found that such lesions in the hypothalamus could make rats far more aggressive (a finding which Bailey, Stevenson, and I confirmed on our fingers) and that lesions in the region of the amygdala could abolish this hyperaggressiveness. Similarly, Brady and Nauta have shown that lesions in the septal region can produce heightened startle responses and, with the interesting exception of conditioned suppression (CER), a variety of other indications of increased emotionality. An abstract by King indicates that his paper shows that such emotionality can also be counteracted by lesions in the amygdaloid complex.

In addition to making the animals much tamer, lesions in the region of the amygdala can also produce marked hypersexuality. This is part of the classical Klüver-Bucy syndrome which has been one of the points of departure for many excellent studies of the effects of brain lesions on motivation.

In the past, the combination of the ablation technique with behavioral tests has been found to be a powerful method for studying sensory, perceptual, and motor functions of the brain. The same combination is becoming a powerful technique for studying also the motivational and emotional functions of the brain. I have cited only a small sample out of the increasingly impressive population of sophisticated studies by able men in this field.

Drive elicited by electrical stimulation

Electrical stimulation of specific points has been another classical technique for studying brain function. Originally, this technique was used to study motor effects on anaesthetized animals. In his classic work, Hess refined this technique by permanently implanting electrodes in the brains of cats so that they could be stimulated in the normal unanaesthetized state. In addition to eliciting complex motor and postural responses, which were less like reflexes and more like acts, Hess discovered that stimulation in the hypothalamus produced a variety of apparently motivational effects such as rage, flight, and eating. His trailblazing results, which were limited to naturalistic observation, have provided an excellent point of departure for recent studies using a variety of more rigorous behavioral tests.

Turning now to some work in collaboration with E. E. Coons, we see in Fig. 2 a rat with electrodes placed in a region where stimulation elicits eating. This rat has been thoroughly satiated on food. Soon after stimulation is turned on, the rat starts to eat; soon after it is turned off, he stops. Again, the demonstration is very effective.

These rats, like Hess's cats, will sometimes also gnaw at inedible objects such as pieces of wood. Therefore, we wonder whether the centrally elicited eating has the properties of normal hunger or is mere reflex gnawing. As a test, we thoroughly trained rats, when thirsty, to get water from a spout above; and, when hungry, to get food by pushing aside a little hinged door below. Then, after thorough satiation, we tested the effects of electrical stimulation. The stimulation can cause a moderately thirsty rat to leave the water spout where he has been drinking and go to a different place to perform the instrumental response of pushing back the hinged door which he has learned as a means of getting food. The fact that the rat stops drinking shows that the effects of stimulation are not mere indiscriminate activation. The fact that the stimulation elicits the learned response of pushing aside the hinged door shows that it has at least some of the

Figure 2 Electrical stimulation of the brain causes a thoroughly satiated rat to eat.

more general motivating properties of normal hunger.

In order to make the results completely official, we also trained the rats, when hungry, to secure food by pressing a Skinner bar which delivered small pellets on a variable-interval schedule. Fig. 3 shows the effects of brain stimulation on a thoroughly satiated rat. (Each time the rat presses the bar, the recording lever moves upwards slightly. Each time a bar press actually delivers food, the pen draws a downward spike.) Horizontal sections of the cumulative record show that the satiated rat did relatively little work at the bar during two-minute periods of nonstimulation. The upward steps show that, during the two minutes when the stimulation was on, the rat worked at the bar which occasionally delivered food. Thus we have further evidence that electrical stimulation in the areas that induce eating will also motivate the performance of learned instrumental responses that have been reinforced by food. The results are convincing pictorially; they also are statistically reliable.

Continuing our program of testing point-by-point whether the motivation elicited by the electrical stimulation of the brain has all of the properties of normal hunger, Coons and I found that its effects were not limited to the gnawing of solid foods; it caused a satiated rat to drink milk. In control tests the stimulation did not elicit similar sustained drinking of water. Furthermore, the stimulation could be used to motivate the rat to run a T maze with the termination of the stimulation serving as a reward to produce highly reliable choice of the endbox in which the stimulation was turned off. In short, the termination of centrally stimulated "hunger" by turning off the switch seems to have the same rewarding effects as the eating of food which ordinarily terminates normally elicited hunger.

Let us turn now to a different type of motivation: a pain—fear-like emotional disturbance which can be elicited by electrical stimulation

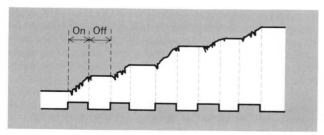

Figure 3 Stimulation in the hypothalamus elicits the learned response of bar pressing in a satiated rat. Each bar press moves the pen up a little. The rat has been trained on a variable-interval schedule; each spike below the record indicates when a bar press actually delivers food.

in a number of regions deep in the brain. Does this emotional reaction have all of the functional properties of normally aroused pain and fear? Some of these properties are: (a) Pain and fear can motivate, and their termination reinforce, trial-and-error learning. (b) They can be used to establish a conditioned response. (c) They can serve as a punishment to establish an approach-avoidance conflict so that a hungry animal will avoid food.

The purpose of the experiments is to demonstrate point-by-point that central stimulation of the critical places in the brain has all of the foregoing properties.

Figure 4 illustrates the first of these experiments. It shows a cat with chronic Delgado-type electrodes ending in subminiature tube sockets into which are plugged the wires bearing the stimulation. This cat first learned to rotate a paddle wheel to turn off electric shock. Then he was tested with brain stimulation. As soon as the stimulation was delivered, the cat became active and, after a few irrelevant responses, rotated the wheel which turned off the stimulation and thus rewarded the response of rotating the wheel. After a few trials, facilitated by transfer from the previous training, the cat learned to rotate the wheel as soon as the stimulation was turned on. Fig. 4 shows him performing this habit motivated by electrical stimulation of the brain.

In the next experiment, preliminary tests showed that a tone was a neutral stimulus which produced no obvious response. Then for a number of trials the tone was immediately followed by the brain stimulation which elicited wheel turning. After a few such trials, the wheel turning was conditioned: the tone alone,

without brain stimulation, caused the cat to turn the wheel.

In the final experiment, we find that stimulation in the sensorimotor area of a hungry control cat, which was eating, produced a violent withdrawal from food; but even after repeated stimulation, the control animals promptly returned to eat. By contrast, experimental cats, stimulated once or twice with a lower voltage in the critical area of the brain, learned to avoid the food.

These experiments have shown that brain stimulation at critical points can have a number of the significant properties of normally elicited pain and fear. In addition to illustrating a general approach to the problem of investigating motivational factors elicited by electrical stimulation of the brain, experiments of the foregoing type may yield information which will help us in knowing where to place lesions in order to relieve certain hitherto hopeless patients from the acute misery of intractable pain.

Similar experiments on centrally aroused aggression have elicited a spectacular and relatively well-integrated cluster of symptoms of rage—hissing, spitting, clawing, etc.—which suggest that rage contains some integrated motor components different from fear. So far, however, Warren Roberts and I have confirmed Masserman's results in that we have not been able to condition such responses. This raises an interesting question. Is anger a distinctive drive whose mechanisms we have simply failed to date to locate, or are the motor components involved in rage organized without any separate, distinctive drive so that they must be motivated by other drives such as fear, hunger, or sex?

Figure 4 Electrical stimulation of a pain-fear area in a cat's brain elicits a learned response: rotating a wheel which turns off the stimulation. Stimulation is turned on between the first and second pictures. (From a motion picture by Miller, Delgado, and Robert, shown by the author at the 1953 meeting of the APA.)

The results of these experiments are enough to illustrate that the combination of the physiological technique of electrical stimulation with various behavioral techniques for measuring the effects of such stimulation is turning out to be a powerful new tool for investigating the motivational functions of the brain.

Reward effects of electrical stimulation

The combination of the techniques for stimulating the brains of unanesthetized animals with those of exact behavioral testing led Olds and Milner to a completely unexpected discovery. They found that electrical stimulation of certain areas of the brain would act as a powerful reward. This reward could be used to cause animals to choose the correct side of a T maze or to press a bar in a Skinner box. Often in the history of science, the unexpected discovery of a novel phenomenon, such as X-rays or radioactivity, has forced drastic revisions in current theory and ultimately led to important practical developments. While it is too early to be certain exactly how important will be the effects of this unexpected discovery by Olds and Milner, I suspect they will be considerable.

On the theoretical front, the rewarding effect of central stimulation tends to revive hedonistic theories of reinforcement. As I have pointed out elsewhere, however, the results known to date can be fitted in fairly well with any of the current theories of reinforcement, and the drive-reduction hypothesis suggests a number of interesting lines of investigation in the area of centrally rewarding effects. The important thing is that we have here a genuinely novel phenomenon and a completely new technique for investigating the mechanism of reward and its relationship to various drives.

This new discovery has touched off a flurry of research which is still mounting with positive acceleration. Olds has shown that there are certain regions of the hypothalamus where the rate of bar pressing increases with hunger much as it would if the animals were receiving a food reward. In a slightly different area, the rate of bar pressing varies positively with sex— being reduced by castration and increased by androgen therapy. Furthermore, different drugs, such as tranquilizers, seem to have differential effects on the reward phenomenon elicited by stimulation in different parts of the brain. Thus, we probably have here a technique for learning more about how drugs affect different parts of the brain and also for screening drugs in order to discover ones that have more specific psychological effects.

Motivational effects of drugs

One of my students, Robert Kirschner, used an apparatus having two bars diagonally across a corner from each other in order to equalize the skill and effort required to turn the stimulation on or off. Studying the effects of methamphetamine and chlorpromazine, he found that 2 mg/k of the former and 4 mg/k of the latter produced roughly equivalent reductions in the total number of bar presses.

But, when the rewarding and aversive effects were analyzed separately, these two drugs had strikingly different effects. The methamphetamine increased the time to turn the stimulation off while decreasing the time to turn it on. By contrast, the chlorpromazine produced a great increase in the time to turn the stimulation on and also some increase in the time to turn it off. One interpretation of these results is that methamphetamine was accentuating the positive rewarding effects and minimizing the negative punishing ones—a result congruent with its clinical euphoric effects. Chlorpromazine seemed to be reducing reward more than the aversion—a result congruent with the fact that it sometimes causes patients to feel depressed.

The organic chemists are turning out thousands of new compounds and are able to produce at will slight modifications in known drugs. Similarly, the biochemists are learning more about vital hormones, enzymes, enzyme inhibitors, and other powerful agents of metabolism. But one of the chief bottlenecks to the discovery of superior psychotropic drugs is the difficulty in efficiently and safely testing for the psychological effects of all these new compounds. Perhaps this test, along with many other ingenious ones recently devised by experimental psychologists, will help us in finding drugs which have more potent therapeutic effects with fewer harmful side effects. Although the current enthusiasm for the tranquilizing drugs may have the same rocketing rise and frustrating fall as other "wonder cures" for schizophrenia, I believe that the recent signs of vigorous growth of a new infant science of psychopharmacology afford a reasonable ground for eventual hope.

For the rapid growth of psychopharmacology to be healthy, however, I believe that it should soon advance beyond the stage where a single test is widely used for screening merely on the basis of its face validity. The standards and methods of modern aptitude testing should be adapted to this new area. Batteries of tests should be tried out and validated, first by the criterion of internal consistency and eventually by the criterion of predicting clinically useful effects. Both screening tests and drugs might eventually be factor analyzed. At the same time that we are refining our sceening instruments, we should also be conducting pure-science studies to analyze how well-known drugs achieve their psychological effects. We need to discover fundamental laws to develop a basic science of psychopharmacology. Such a science should provide a rational basis for practical applications to mental hygiene in the same way that organic chemistry provides a basis for the analysis and synthesis of new compounds.

In connection with the problem of drugs, let me emphasize that there is no necessary incompatibility between organic and functional approaches to the problem of mental disease. As you know, I find it useful to describe neurosis and psychotherapy in terms of learning theory. But the book which Dollard and I wrote on this topic contains a chapter on drugs and brain lesions. It is entirely possible that people differ, for example, in the strength of the innate mechanisms for fear, guilt, and anxiety just as they vary in physical size and strength. A person with unusually strong emotional mechanisms of this kind would be especially susceptible to learning strong fears and guilts by traumatic incidents. These unusually strong fears and guilts might directly elicit certain psychosomatic symptoms, produce strong conflicts, or motivate the learning of functional symptoms. It is quite conceivable that chronic medication by suitable drugs could reduce this special susceptibility to irrationally strong fears and guilts much as insulin enables the diabetic to tolerate a diet containing more carbohydrates.

Furthermore, drug effects have the great advantage over certain other forms of organic intervention in that they are reversible. Some interesting results have already been secured by combining the use of barbiturates with psychotherapy. It is conceivable that a superior drug will be produced which will be a much more effective aid to emotional re-education. Indeed, it is conceivable that radically improved results with certain forms of mental disease may be achieved by an unconventional combination of drug therapy, individual therapy, group therapy, training in social skills, and temporary manipulation of the environment.

Biochemical stimulation

In addition to electrical techniques of stimulation, new biochemical techniques (which obviously have implications also for psychopharmacology) have recently been exploited. For example, Andersson has shown that minute injections of salt solution into the region of the third ventricle can cause excessive drinking in goats. Conversely, our group has shown that minute injections of water into the brain can cause a thirsty cat to stop drinking. Furthermore, we have shown that the minute salt injections increase, while the water ones decrease, the rate of performing a learned response to get water. Therefore, these minute injections into the brain have some of the more general effects of normal increases or reductions of thirst.

Similarly, Alan Fisher has shown that a minute injection of male hormone into a specific site in the brain can induce complex sexual, and in some instances maternal, behavior as though it had a motivating effect. Since similar effects were not produced by electrical stimulation of the same sites, there is reason to believe that, in some instances at least, the chemical stimulation may be more effective and selective than the electrical technique. Here again, we have a powerful new tool, the potentialities of which are just beginning to be explored.

Electrical recording of brain activity

The converse of the stimulation technique is that of recording electrical activity of the brain and other parts of the nervous system. This technique has been used with great success in tracing sensory systems and has recently produced some quite exciting results which may help to explain the mechanism for the relationship between motivation and attention. For example, it has been found that stimulation of the reticular system in the brain can actually reduce the transmission of sensory impulses from the end organs and through lower relay centers, thus partially shielding the brain from certain sources of stimulation. As Livingston has pointed out, this finding produces a radical change in our previous notions of sensory neurophysiology.

Can these new techniques be applied to other motivational phenomena? For example, Pavlov reports that, when a somewhat painful stimulus is made the conditioned stimulus for food, all of the obvious emotional responses to pain seem to drop out. By using suitable recording techniques, could we demonstrate that the pain impulses themselves are reduced before they reach the highest centers? Would we have an experimental method for producing and studying a phenomenon analogous to hysterical anaesthesia?

Although techniques for recording the electrical activity of the nervous system have been used very successfully in the study of sensory mechanisms, they have not been used much in the study of drive and reward. Here seems a promising new area of application, although there are technical difficulties to overcome. For example, if an animal's motor responses (which disturb electrical recording) were eliminated by one of the improved curare derivatives, such as flaxidil, would we find that the electrical activity in different tracts and centers of the brain is altered when the animal is hungry, thirsty, or suffering painful stimulation? What would be the effects of rewards such as water injected directly into the blood stream of a thirsty animal, if indeed it can be demonstrated that such injections function as a reward? Would there be any effects specific to stimulation of the brain at points where such stimulation is rewarding and different from those at points where it is neutral or aversive? Any such differences are likely to give us significant clues to the basic mechanisms of motivation and reward.

OTHER PROMISING APPROACHES

Now fasten your seat belts for a final spurt through a number of different approaches for which the brevity of listing does not mean any inferiority in merit.

Recently Roger Russell's group has been studying the effects of what might be called biochemical lesions of the brain, while David Krech and Mark Rosenzweig have been pursuing the relationships among brain chemistry, heredity, and behavior. While these new lines of work have been aimed chiefly at cognitive functions, they could easily turn up facts which would lead directly into problems of motivation and reward.

Most of the studies I have sampled thus far have involved relatively direct approaches to the brain. The combination of exact behavioral tests with various "intermediate" techniques has also proved fruitful. Some of the techniques used in this way have been a fistula into the stomach, a cannula into a vein, a subcutaneous saline injection, enzyme inhibitors, and unusual substances which are similar to a metabolite in one respect but different in others. Programs involving such work are well under way in Mayer's laboratory at Harvard, Stellar's at Pennsylvania, and our own laboratory at Yale. Similarly, Beach and his students are introducing a greater variety of behavioral techniques into the study of sex.

Thus far, various approaches usually have been used in relative isolation. Additional advances may be expected when more use is made of systematic combinations of these approaches. For example, appropriately placed lesions might be used in the analysis of the systems involved in the drive or reward effect of brain stimulation or of the different effects of distending the stomach with either food or a balloon.

Finally, a completely different and highly promising development has been the use of behavioral techniques to bring new drives into the laboratory: first fear, than curiosity, and most recently social deprivation. We can and should extend the range of drives experimentally studied. But that is another story.

Selection **15**

MOTIVATION RECONSIDERED: THE CONCEPT OF COMPETENCE*

ROBERT W. WHITE
Harvard University

When parallel trends can be observed in realms as far apart as animal behavior and psychoanalytic ego psychology, there is reason to suppose that we are witnessing a significant evolution of ideas. In these two realms, as in psychology as a whole, there is evidence of deepening discontent with theories of motivation based upon drives. Despite great differences in the language and concepts used to express this discontent, the theme is everywhere the same: Something important is left out when we make drives the operating forces in animal and human behavior.

The chief theories against which the discontent is directed are those of Hull and of Freud. In their respective realms, drive-reduction theory and psychoanalytic instinct theory, which are basically very much alike, have acquired a considerable air of orthodoxy. Both views have an appealing simplicity, and both have been argued long enough so that their main outlines are generally known. In decided contrast is the position of those who are not satisfied with drives and instincts. They are numerous, and they have developed many pointed criticisms, but what they have to say has not thus far lent itself to a clear and inclusive conceptualization. Apparently there is an enduring difficulty in making these contributions fall into shape.

In this paper I shall attempt a conceptualization which gathers up some of the important things left out by drive theory. To give the concept a name I have chosen the word

* Abridged from R. W. White, "Motivation Reconsidered: The Concept of Competence," *Psychological Review*, **66**: 297–333, 1959. Copyright 1959 by the American Psychological Association and reproduced by permission.

competence, which is intended in a broad biological sense rather than in its narrow everyday meaning. As used here, competence will refer to an organism's capacity to interact effectively with its environment. In organisms capable of but little learning, this capacity might be considered an innate attribute, but in the mammals and especially man, with their highly plastic nervous systems, fitness to interact with the environment is slowly attained through prolonged feats of learning. In view of the directedness and persistence of the behavior that leads to these feats of learning, I consider it necessary to treat competence as having a motivational aspect, and my central argument will be that the motivation needed to attain competence cannot be wholly derived from sources of energy currently conceptualized as drives or instincts. We need a different kind of motivational idea to account fully for the fact that man and the higher mammals develop a competence in dealing with the environment which they certainly do not have at birth and certainly do not arrive at simply through maturation. Such an idea, I believe, is essential for any biologically sound view of human nature.

As a first step, I shall briefly examine the relevant trends of thought in several areas of psychology. From this it will become clear that the ideas advanced in this paper have already been stated, in one way or another, by workers in animal behavior, child development, cognitive psychology, psychoanalytic ego psychology, and the psychology of personality. If there is novelty in this essay, it lies in putting together pieces which are not in themselves new. They already lie before us on the table, and perhaps by looking once more we can see how to fit them into a larger conceptual picture.

THE TREND IN ANIMAL PSYCHOLOGY

One of the most obvious features of animal behavior is the tendency to explore the environment. Cats are reputedly killed by curiosity, dogs characteristically make a thorough search of their surroundings, and monkeys and chimpanzees have always impressed observers as being ceaseless investigators.

Some theorists reasoned that activity of this kind was always in the service of hunger, thirst, sex, or some other organic need, but this view was at least shaken by the latent learning experiments, which showed that animals learned about their surroundings even when their major needs had been purposely sated. Shortly before 1950 there was a wave of renewed interest not only in exploratory behavior but also in the possibility that activity and manipulation might have to be assigned the status of independent motives.

Exploratory behavior

In 1953 Butler reported an experiment in which monkeys learned a discrimination problem when the only reward was the opening of a window which permitted them to look out upon the normal comings and goings of the entrance room to the laboratory. The discriminations thus formed proved to be resistant to extinction. In a later study, Butler and Harlow (1957) showed that monkeys could build up a series of four different discriminations solely for the sake of inspecting the entrance room. Butler concluded that "monkeys—and presumably all primates—have a strong motive toward visual exploration of their environment and that learning may be established on the basis of this motive just as it may be established on the basis of any motive that regularly and reliably elicits responses." Montgomery, in 1954, reported a study with rats in which the animals, their major organic needs satiated, learned to avoid the short arm of a Y maze and to take the path which led them into additional maze territory suitable for exploration. Similar findings have been described by Myers and Miller (1954), whose rats learned to press a bar for the sake of poking their heads into a new compartment and sniffing around.

These experiments make a strong case for an independent exploratory motive. The nature of this motive can be more fully discerned in situations in which the animals are allowed a varied repertory of behavior. In 1950 Berlyne published a searching paper on curiosity, a theme which he further developed in subsequent years (1955, 1957, 1958). The rats in his experiments were confronted with an unfamiliar space and later with various novel objects placed in it. Approaching sniffing, and examining were readily elicited by each novelty,

were fairly rapidly extinguished, but were restored nearly to original strength when a fresh novelty was added. Exploration on the part of chimpanzees has been studied by Welker (1956), who put various pairs of objects before the animals and observed the course of their interest. The objects were often first approached in a gingerly manner, with signs of uneasiness, then examined and handled quite fully, then discarded. Introducing a new pair of objects promptly reproduced the whole sequence, just as it did with the rats in Berlyne's experiments. Welker used pairs of objects to find out whether or not the chimpanzees would have common preferences. Bigness and brightness evoked more interest, and greater time was spent upon objects which could be moved, changed, or made to emit sounds and light.

Recent reviews by Butler (1958) and Cofer (1959) show that a great deal of similar work is going on in animal laboratories, generally with similar results.

Exploration as a drive

The designers of these experiments have favored the idea that exploration should be listed as an independent primary drive. In all cases the experimental plan calls for the elimination of other primary drives by satiation. It is recognized, however, that a confirmed advocate of orthodoxy might bring up two objections to the proposed enlargement of the list of primary drives. He might claim that exploratory behavior could be explained as a consequence of secondary reinforcement, or he might contend that it is reinforced by reduction of anxiety.

Both hypotheses thus far examined—secondary reinforcement and anxiety reduction—require us to make improbable assumptions. There remains the possibility that exploration should simply be added to the list of primary drives and otherwise treated in orthodox fashion. Myers and Miller (1954) suggest that this is the appropriate course, provided the new drive shows the same functional properties as those already known. "If an exploratory tendency can produce learning like other drives such as hunger, and also show a similar pattern of satiation and recovery, these functional parallels to already known drives would help to justify its classification in the same category." Logically the problem can be dealt with in this way, but we must consider very carefully what happens to the category of drive if we admit this new applicant to membership.

Using hunger as the chief model, the orthodox conception of drive involves the following characteristics: (a) there is a tissue need or deficit external to the nervous system which acts upon that system as a strong persisting stimulus; (b) this promotes activity which is terminated by a consummatory response with consequent reduction of need; (c) the reduction of need brings about the learning which gradually shapes behavior into an economical pursuit of suitable goal objects. In this scheme the tension of an aroused drive is interpreted as unpleasant, at least in the sense that the animal acts in such a way as to lower the drive and becomes quiescent when it is lowered. There are probably no living champions of so simple an orthodoxy, yet the scheme remains pervasive, and it is therefore worth while to observe that the proposed exploratory drive hardly fits it at all.

In the first place, the exploratory drive appears to bear no relation whatever to a tissue need or deficit external to the nervous system. It is, of course, clearly related to certain characteristics of stimulation from the external environment, a source of motivation which Harlow (1953) would like to see restored to a serious place in contemporary psychology; but it certainly cannot be correlated with a visceral need comparable to hunger, thirst, or sex. Considering the pattern of satiation and recovery shown by Welker's chimpanzees, Woodworth (1958) remarks that "what becomes satiated is not the exploratory tendency in general, but the exploring of a particular place or object." It is possible, as Hebb (1955) has pointed out, that the so-called "reticular activation system" in the brain stem creates a kind of general drive state, and this mechanism might indeed be flexibly responsive to changes in sensory stimulation. This interesting suggestion, however, is still a far cry from viscerogenic drives; it commits us instead to the novel idea of a neurogenic motive, one in which the state of the nervous system and the patterns of external stimulation conspire to produce motivated behavior. There is even a good deal of trouble in

supposing that the adequate stimuli for exploration are either strong or persistent. Novelty certainly cannot be equated with strength or persistence, and animals seem readily able to disregard the stimuli to exploration when they are weary.

In the second place, exploratory behavior cannot be regarded as leading to any kind of consummatory response. It is usual for the animal's investigation to subside gradually. If the animal at some point turns away and leaves the once novel object we may say that its curiosity is "satisfied," but we do not mean by this that the equivalent of a consummatory response has just taken place. The sequence suggests rather that curiosity wears out and slowly falls to a level where it no longer guides behavior, at least until a fresh novelty comes into view.

Finally, in the case of exploratory behavior there is real difficulty in identifying reinforcement with need reduction. Montgomery (1954), describing the learning of the Y maze, points out that the short arm essentially a dead end, would tend to reduce the exploratory drive, whereas the long arm, itself a complex maze, would increase it—but the long arm is chosen. If the long arm functions as a reinforcing agent, "the mechanism underlying this reinforcement is an *increase*, rather than a decrease, in the strength of the exploratory drive." In this experiment, as in their natural habitat, animals do not wait to have novelty thrust upon them, nor do they avoid situations in which novelty may be found. Such behavior can be most readily conceptualized by admitting that under certain circumstances reinforcement can be correlated with an increase in arousal or excitement rather than a decrease. A drive which has no consummatory climax seems almost to require this formulation. It is distinctly implausible to connect reinforcement with the waning of an agreeable interest in the environment or with a general progress from zestful alertness to boredom.

If we admit exploration to the category of drive we are thus committing ourselves to believe that drives need have no extraneural sources in tissue deficits or visceral tensions, that they are not necessarily activated by strong or persistent stimuli, that they do not require consummatory responses, and that drive increase can sometimes be a mechanism of reinforcement.

Activity and manipulation

Exploration is not the only motive proposed by critics of drive orthodoxy, and novelty is not the only characteristic of the environment which appears to incite motivated behavior. Some workers have suggested a need for activity, which can be strengthened by depriving animals of their normal opportunities for movement.

Harlow and his associates (Harlow, 1953; Harlow, Harlow, & Meyer, 1950) maintain that there is also a manipulative drive. It is aroused by certain patterns of external stimulation and reduced by actively changing the external pattern. The experiments were done with rhesus monkeys, and they involve the solving of a mechanical problem which, however, leads to no further consequences or rewards.

The addition of activity and manipulation to the list of primary drives can only make more serious the difficulties for the orthodox model that resulted from admitting exploration. But recent research with animals has put the orthodox model on the defensive even on its home grounds. It has become increasingly clear that hunger, thirst, and sex cannot be made to fit the simple pattern that seemed so helpful 40 years ago.

Changing conceptions of drive

In a brief historical statement, Morgan (1957) has pointed out that the conception of drive as a noxious stimulus began to lose its popularity among research workers shortly after 1940. "On the whole," he says, "the stimulus concept of drive owed more to wishful thinking than to experimental fact." When technical advances in biochemistry and brain physiology made it possible to bring in an array of new facts, there was a rapid shift toward the view that "drives arise largely through the internal environment acting on the central nervous system." One of the most influential discoveries was that animals have as many as a dozen specific hungers for particular kinds of food,

instead of the single hunger demanded by Cannon's model of the hunger drive. If an animal's diet becomes deficient in some important element such as salt, sugar, or the vitamin-B complex, foods containing the missing element will be eagerly sought while other foods are passed by, a selectivity that obviously cannot be laid to contractions of the stomach. Similarly, a negative food preference can be produced by loading either the stomach or the blood stream with some single element of the normal diet.

New methods of destroying and of stimulating brain centers in animals have had an equally disastrous effect on the orthodox drive model. The nervous system, and especially the hypothalamus, appears to be deeply implicated in the motivational process. Experimental findings on hypothalamic lesions in animals encourage Stellar (1954) to believe that there are different centers "responsible for the control of different kinds of basic motivation," and that in each case "there is one main excitatory center and one inhibitory center which operates to depress the activity of the excitatory center." As research findings accumulate, this picture may seem to be too cleanly drawn. Concerning sexual behavior, for example, Rosvold (1959) concludes a recent review by rejecting the idea of a single center in the cerebrum; rather, the sex drive "probably has a wide neural representation with a complex interaction between old and new brain structures and between neural and humoral agents." Nevertheless, Miller's (1958) careful work seems to leave little doubt that motivated behavior in every way similar to normal hunger and normal pain-fear can be elicited by electrical stimulation of quite restricted areas of the hypothalamus. It is clear that we cannot regress to a model of drives that represents the energy as coming from outside the nervous system. Whatever the effects of peripheral stimulation may be, drives also involve neural centers and neural patterns as well as internal biochemical conditions.

What sort of model becomes necessary to entertain these newly discovered facts?

Morgan, in 1943, undertook to capture the facts in a systematic theory which seems to have been well sustained by subsequent research (Morgan, 1957). He distinguished two types of process which he called *humoral motive factors* and *central motive states*. The humoral factors consist of chemical or hormonal constituents of the blood and lymph, and they are conceived to influence behavior chiefly by a direct sensitizing action on neural centers. The central motive states have several properties: They are partly self-maintaining through neural circuits, they tend to increase the organism's general activity, they evoke specific forms of behavior not strongly controlled by the environment, and they prime or prepare consummatory responses which will occur when adequate stimulation is found. This is a far cry from the orthodox model, but we must nowadays admit that the orthodox model is a far cry from the facts.

Twenty years of research have thus pretty much destroyed the orthodox drive model. It is no longer appropriate to consider that drives originate solely in tissue deficits external to the nervous system, that consummatory acts are a universal feature and goal of motivated behavior, or that the alleviation of tissue deficits is the necessary condition for instrumental learning. Instead we have a complex picture in which humoral factors and neural centers occupy a prominent position; in which, moreover, the concept of neurogenic motives without consummatory ends appears to be entirely legitimate. Do these changes remove the obstacles to placing exploration, activity, and manipulation in the category of drives?

Perhaps this is no more than a question of words, but I should prefer at this point to call it a problem in conceptual strategy. I shall propose that these three new "drives" have much in common and that it is useful to bring them under the single heading of competence. Even with the loosening and broadening of the concept of drive, they are still in important respects different from hunger, thirst, and sex. In hunger and thirst, tissue deficits, humoral factors, and consummatory responses retain an important position. The mature sex drive depends heavily on hormonal levels and is sharply oriented toward consummation. Tendencies like exploration do not share these characteristics, whatever else they have in common with the better known drives. It is in order to emphasize their intrinsic peculiarities, to get them considered in their own right without a cloud of surplus meanings, that I prefer in this essay to speak of the urge that makes for competence simply as motivation rather than as drive.

THE TREND IN PSYCHOANALYTIC EGO PSYCHOLOGY

Rather an abrupt change of climate may be experienced as we turn from the animal laboratory to the psychoanalytic treatment room, but the trends of thought in the two realms turn out to be remarkably alike. Here the orthodox view of motivation is to be found in Freud's theory of the instincts—they might be known to us as drives if an early translator had been more literal with the German *Trieb*.

Up to 1914 Freud used a two-fold classification of sexual instincts and ego instincts. The ego instincts made their appearance in his case histories in a somewhat moral character, being held responsible for the disastrous repression of sexual needs, but in systematic usage they were conceived as serving the goal of self-preservation, and hunger was generally taken as an appropriate model. In 1914, when he evolved the concept of narcissism and saw that it threatened to blur the line between sexual and ego tendencies, Freud (1925b) still expressed himself as unwilling to abandon an idea which followed the popular distinction of love and hunger and which reflected man's dual existence "as reproducer and as one who serves his own ends." Various facts, particularly those of sadism and masochism, served to overcome his reluctance, so that he finally united self-preservation and preservation of the species under the heading of Eros or life instincts, establishing destructiveness or the death instinct as the great antagonist in a profound biological sense (Freud, 1948). This highly speculative step proved to be too much for some of his otherwise loyal followers, and the earlier orthodoxy did not become entirely extinct.

It is easier to follow Freud's reasoning when we bear in mind the simultaneous development of his ideas about the mental apparatus. Bibring (1941) points out that even in his early thinking a sharp contrast was always drawn between instinct and mental apparatus.

Instinct supplied the energy in the form of powerful, persisting internal stimuli; the apparatus guided it into channels which produced organized behavior and eventually put a stop to the persisting stimulation. In 1915 Freud wrote:

The nervous system is an apparatus having the function of abolishing stimuli which reach it or of reducing excitation to the lowest possible level; an apparatus which would even, if this were feasible, maintain itself in an altogether unstimulated condition. . . . The task of the nervous system is—broadly speaking—to *master stimuli* (Freud, 1925c, p. 63).

During the next decade there was a considerable growth in his ideas about the mental apparatus, culminating in the well known division into id, ego, and superego. The activities of the ego now received much fuller recognition. Freud (1927) assigned to it "the task of self-preservation," which it accomplished through its several capacities of perception, memory, flight, defense, and adaptive action. One can see Freud's thought moving from a mechanical analogy—an engine and its fuel—toward a much more adaptational conception of the mental apparatus. Ego instincts did not wholly disappear, but the decline in their systematic importance was compensated by the insight that self-preservative tendencies were to some extent built into the whole living system. It is significant that as he took this course he came to question the earlier tension-reduction theory. In the last year of his life he declared it to be probable "that what is felt as pleasure or unpleasure is not the *absolute* degree of the tensions but something in the rhythm of their changes" (Freud, 1949).

Freud's tendency to revise his thinking makes it difficult to pin down an orthodox doctrine, but most workers will probably agree that his main emphasis was upon somatically based drives, a mental apparatus which received its power from the drives, and, of course, the multitude of ways in which the apparatus controlled, disguised, and transformed these energies. His treatment of the ego was far from complete, and it was not long before voices were raised against the conception that so vital and versatile a part of the personality could be developed solely by libidinal and aggressive energies.

An instinct to master

In 1942 Hendrick proposed that this difficulty be met by assuming the existence of an additional major instinct. "The development of ability to master a segment of the environment," he wrote, and the need to exercise such functions, can be conceptualized as an "instinct to master," further characterized as "an inborn drive to do and to learn how to do." The aim of this instinct is "pleasure in exercising a function successfully, regardless of its sensual value." The simpler manifestations are learning to suck, to manipulate, to walk, to speak, to comprehend and to reason; these functions and others eventually become integrated as the ego. "The central nervous system is more than a utility," Hendrick declared. The infant shows an immediate desire to use and perfect each function as it ripens, and the adult secures gratification from an executive function efficiently performed regardless of its service to other instincts.

Hendricks' procedure in this and two supporting papers (1943a, 1943b) is quite similar to that of the animal psychologists who propose listing exploration as an additional primary drive. The instinct to master has an aim—to exercise and develop the ego functions—and it follows hedonic principles by yielding "primary pleasure" when efficient action "enables the individual to control and alter his environment." It is to this extent analogous to the instincts assumed by Freud. But just as an exploratory drive seemed radically to alter the whole conception of drive, so the instinct to master implied a drastic change in the psychoanalytic idea of instinct.

It is of interest that Fenichel (1945), who definitely rejected Hendrick's proposal, gives us another close parallel to the animal work by attributing mastering behavior to anxiety-reduction. He argued that mastery is "a general aim of every organism but not of a specific instinct." He agreed that there is "a pleasure of enjoying one's abilities," but he related this pleasure to cessation of the anxiety connected with not being able to do things. "Functional pleasure," he wrote, "is pleasure in the fact that the exercise of a function is now possible without anxiety," and he contended that when anxiety is no longer present, when there is full confidence that a given situation can be met, then action is no longer accompanied by functional pleasure. We must certainly agree with Fenichel that anxiety *can* play the part he assigns it, but the proposal that all pleasure in ego functions comes from this source raises the same difficulties we have already considered in connection with exploratory behavior. That we exercise our capacities and explore our surroundings only to reduce our fear of the environment is not, as I have already argued, an assumption that enjoys high probability on biological grounds.

Hartmann on the ego

A less radical change in the orthodox model is proposed by Hartmann, who, in a series of papers since 1939, often in conjunction with Kris and Loewenstein, has been refining and expanding Freud's views on the ego and the instincts. While the ego is conceived as a "substructure" of the personality, this term is somewhat metaphorical because in practice the ego has to be defined by its functions. The list of functions, which includes grasping, crawling, walking, perceiving, remembering, language, thinking, and intention, covers much the same ground that was indicated by Hendrick, but Hartmann does not attribute their growth to an instinct. On the other hand, Hartmann (1950) early came to the conclusion that development could not be explained, as Freud had seemed to conceive it, simply as a consequence of conflict between instinctual needs and frustrating realities. The instincts alone would never guarantee survival; they require mediation by the innate ego apparatus if they are to meet "the average expectable environmental conditions." He therefore proposed that we conceive of an autonomous factor in ego development, an independent maturation of functions taking place in a "conflict-free ego sphere." Functions such as locomotion ripen through maturation and through learning even when they are not caught up in struggles to obtain erotic and aggressive gratification or to avoid anxiety. As Anna Freud (1952) has

pointed out, walking becomes independent of instinctual upheavals a few weeks after its beginning; thereafter, it serves the child impartially in situations of conflict and those that are free from conflict.

Hartmann's idea of autonomous ego development has of course been assumed all along by workers in child psychology, but it is an important step to relate it to Freud's disclosures concerning unconscious motivation. In what now looks like an excess of enthusiasm for his own concepts, Freud (1925a) undertook to explain the outgrowing of the pleasure principle and the substituting of the reality principle as a simple and direct consequence of the frustration of instinctual needs. However, the reality principle contained the idea of postponing an immediate gratification in favor of a future one, and Hartmann (1956) properly notes that the capacities for postponement and anticipation cannot be conjured into existence simply by the collision of frustrating reality and ungratified need. Important as frustrations may be, these capacities must already be available, "some preparedness for dealing with reality" must already exist, before the frustration can produce its momentous educative effect. It can be seen from this example that Hartmann's analysis opens the way for profitable commerce between developmental psychologies inside and outside of psychoanalysis.

Hartmann's emphasis on adaptation permits him to perceive much more that is autonomous about the ego than was ever seriously included in Freud's systematic thought. He allows, for instance, that aims and interests which develop in the beginning as defenses against instincts may later become part of conflict-free spheres of activity—become interests in their own right—and thus achieve "secondary autonomy," a concept very close to Allport's (1937) functional autonomy of motives (Hartmann, 1950).

Motility and a sense of industry

The trend away from instinct orthodoxy is illustrated by the work of Kardiner (1947) on what he calls "the development of the effective ego." Kardiner's reflections arose from his work on the tramatic neuroses of war. In these disorders the main threat is to self-preservation, and some of the most important symptoms, such as defensive rituals and paralyses, are lodged in the action systems that normally bring about successful adaptive behavior. It thus becomes pertinent to study the growth of action systems, to discover how they become integrated so as to maintain "controlled contact" with the environment and "controlled exploitation of objects in the outer world," and to work out the conditions which either favor or disrupt this acquired integration. Thinking along these lines, Kardiner is led to conclusions just about the opposite of Freud's: It is the successful and gratifying experiences, not the frustrations, that lead to increasingly integrated action and to the discrimination of self from outer world. Frustration produces chiefly disruptions and inhibitions which are unfavorable to the early growth of the ego. Children are gratified when they discover the connection between a movement executed and the accompanying and subsequent sensations. They are still more gratified when they carry out actions successfully; this "gives rise to the triumphant feeling of making an organ obedient to the will of the ego." Such experiences build up "a definite self- or body-consciousness which becomes the center and the point of reference of all purposeful and coördinated activity." Growth of the ego, in short, depends heavily upon action systems and the consequences of action. The course and vicissitudes of this development have to be studied in their own right, and they cannot be understood as side effects of the stages of libidinal development.

A similar theme is pursued to even more radical conclusions by Mittelmann (1954) in his paper on motility. Mittelmann regards motility, which manifests itself most typically in skilled motor actions such as posture, locomotion, and manipulation, as an "urge in its own right" in the same sense that one speaks of oral, excretory, or genital urges. From about 10 months of age it has a distinctly "driven" character, and there is restlessness and anger if it is blocked. During the second and third years the motor urge "dominates all other urges," so that it is proper to "consider this period the motor level of ego and libido development." The child makes tremendous efforts to learn to walk, and to walk well, and he exhibits joyous laughter as he attains these ends. Restrictions of motility may occur be-

cause the parents are anxious or because the child's assertiveness troubles them, and a lasting injury to the parent-child relationship may result. Clumsiness in motor or manipulative accomplishments may lead to self-hatred and dependence, for "the evolution of self-assertiveness and self-esteem is intimately connected with motor development." Motility is of central importance in many of the most characteristic functions of the ego. Partly by its means the infant differentiates himself from other objects, and the child's knowledge of objects depends on an extensive activity of manipulation and examination. "Thus motility becomes one of the most important aspects of reality testing." Because it is an element in all cognitive behavior, it can also be considered "the dominant integrative function." Mittelmann bases motor development, in short, on an independent urge, and he sees this urge as the really crucial motive behind the development of the ego.

Even more influential in this respect is the work of Erikson (1953), who has given a highly detailed timetable of ego development. Erikson stays with the libido theory as far as it will go, but he passes beyond its reach in his account of the latency period and some of the later crises of growth. It is clear that something more than the orthodox instincts is involved in the "enormous value" with which the child in the second year "begins to endow his autonomous will." Something more would seem to be implied in the expanding imagination and initiative of the "phallic" child. Certainly more is involved during the school years, when children address themselves to motor, manual, and intellectual achievements and need "a sense of being able to make things and make them well and even perfectly: this is what I call the *sense of industry.*" Erikson's (1952) theory of play is also influenced by the idea that learning to deal with the animate and inanimate worlds is an important preoccupation of childhood: "the playing child advances forward to new stages of real mastery." Action systems, motility, and a sense of industry all direct our attention to behavior which can scarcely be contained in the old bottle of instinct theory.

Glancing back over these trends in psychoanalytic ego psychology, we cannot fail to be impressed by striking similarities to the trend in animal work. Using Reik's familiar metaphor, we might say that those who listen with their two ears and those who listen with the third ear have apparently been hearing much the same sounds. In both realms there is discontent with drive orthodoxy. In both there is persistent pointing to kinds of behavior neglected or explained away by drive orthodoxy: exploration, activity, manipulation, and mastery. Similar theories have been proposed to account for the energies in such behavior: (a) they are derived or transformed in some way from the primary drives or instincts (secondary reinforcement, neutralization of drive energies); (b) they are powered by the need to reduce anxiety; (c) they can be accounted for only by postulating a new primary drive (exploratory drive, instinct to master). When these explanations are considered to have failed, the one remaining course is to work out a different idea of motivation.

I believe that the difficulties in this undertaking can be greatly reduced by the concept of competence, to which we shall shortly turn.

RELATED DEVELOPMENTS IN GENERAL PSYCHOLOGY

If a systematic survey were in order, it would be easy to show a parallel drift of opinion in other parts of the psychological realm. Discontent with drive orthodoxy has long been expressed by Allport (1937, 1946), who not only argues for a functional autonomy of motives from their infantile roots in primary drives but also seriously questions the law of effect, the very cornerstone of reinforcement theory. Little comfort for the orthodox can be found in Murray's (1938) detailed taxonomy of needs, especially when it comes to needs such as achievement and construction, which can be tied to primary drives only by conceptual acrobatics. Murray and Kluckhohn (1953), moreover, have made a case for pleasure in activity for its own sake, reviving the *Funktionslust* proposed many years ago by Karl Bühler (1924) and recently developed in some detail by French (1952). They also argue for intrinsic mental needs: "the infant's mind is not acting most of the time as the instrument of some urgent animal drive, but is preoccupied with *gratifying itself*." Murphy (1947) takes the view

that all tissues can become seats of tension and thus participants in drive; in addition to visceral drives, he postulates two independent forms, activity drives and sensory drives. Then there are workers such as Goldstein (1939) who approach the whole problem with a holistic philosophy which precludes the dictatorship of any isolated or partial drives. Goldstein (1940) assumes one master tendency, that toward self-actualization, of which the so-called visceral drives are but partial and not really isolated expressions, and which can find expression also in an urge toward perfection—toward completing what is incomplete, whether it be an outside task or the mastery of some function such as walking. It has been shown by the Ansbachers (1956) that Adler, never a friend of instinct orthodoxy, in his later years reached an idea very similar to the urge toward perfection. Maslow (1954, 1955), too, belongs with the heterodox. He insists that we should take account of growth motivation as well as the deficiency motivation implied in the visceral drives, and he offers the valuable idea of a hierarchy of motives, according to which the satisfaction of "lower" needs makes it possible for "higher" needs to emerge and become regnant in behavior.

Mention of these names must suffice here to show that the trends observed in animal psychology and psychoanalytic ego psychology are pervasive in contemporary psychological thought. Doubtless the same controversies and problems could be pointed out in child development, in cognitive psychology, and in other fields. But in order to advance to my main theme, I shall select only certain developments which bear directly on the concept of competence.

Needs for excitement and novelty

Human experience provides plentiful evidence of the importance of reducing excessive levels of tension. Men under wartime stress, men under pressure of pain and extreme deprivation, men with excessive work loads or too much exposure to confusing social interactions, all act as if their nervous systems craved that utterly unstimulated condition which Freud once sketched as the epitome of neural bliss. But if these same men be granted their Nirvana they soon become miserable and begin to look around for a little excitement. Human experience testifies that boredom is a bad state of affairs about which something must be done. Hebb (1949) has been particularly insistent in reminding us that many of our activities, such as reading detective stories, skin-diving, or driving cars at high speeds, give clear evidence of a need to raise the level of stimulation and excitement. Men and animals alike seem at times bent on increasing the impact of the environment and even on creating mild degrees of frustration and fear.

In recent papers Young (1949, 1955) has argued for an hedonic theory of motivation, one in which affective processes "constitute a form of primary motivation." According to Young's theory, "an organism behaves so as to maximize positive affective arousal (delight, enjoyment) and to minimize negative arousal (distress)." McClelland (1953) has offered a version of hedonic theory which is of particular value in understanding the significance of novelty. Affective arousal occurs when a stimulus pattern produces a discrepancy from the existing adaptation level. Small discrepancies produce pleasant affect and a tendency to approach; large ones produce unpleasantness and a tendency toward avoidance. The child at play, like the young chimpanzee and the exploring rat, needs frequent novelty in the stimulus field in order to keep up his interest—in order to maintain pleasant discrepancies from whatever adaptation level he has reached. Hebb's (1949) theory of the neurological correlates of learning also deals with novelty, though in a somewhat different way. He equates sustained interest with a state of neural affairs in which "phase sequences" are relatively complex and are growing, in the sense of establishing new internal relations. Such a state follows most readily from a stimulus field characterized by difference-in-sameness; that is, containing much that is familiar along with certain features that are novel. If the field is entirely familiar, phase sequences run off quickly, are short-circuited, and thus fail to produce sustained interest. Hebb's theory, which has the engaging quality of being able to explain why we enjoy reading a detective story once but not right over again, expresses in a neurological hypothesis the familiar fact that well-learned, habituated processes do not in themselves greatly interest us. Interest seems to require elements of unfamiliarity: of something still to be found out and of learning still to be done.

It seems to me that these contributions, though differing as to details, speak with unanimity on their central theme and would force us, if nothing else did, to reconsider seriously the whole problem of motivation. Boredom, the unpleasantness of monotony, the attraction of novelty, the tendency to vary behavior rather than repeating it rigidly, and the seeking of stimulation and mild excitement stand as inescapable facts of human experience and clearly have their parallels in animal behavior. We may seek rest and minimal stimulation at the end of the day, but that is not what we are looking for the next morning. Even when its primary needs are satisfied and its homeostatic chores are done, an organism is alive, active, and up to something.

Dealing with the environment

If we consider things only from the viewpoint of affect, excitement, and novelty, we are apt to overlook another important aspect of behavior, its effect upon the environment. Moving in this direction, Diamond (1939) invites us to consider the motivational properties of the sensorineural system, the apparatus whereby higher animals "maintain their relations to the environment." He conceives of this system as demanding stimulation and as acting in such a manner as to "force the environment to stimulate it." Even if one thinks only of the infant's exploring eyes and hands, it is clear that the main direction of behavior is by no means always that of reducing the impact of stimulation. When the eyes follow a moving object, or when the hand grasps an object which it has touched, the result is to preserve the stimulus and to increase its effect. In more elaborate explorations the consequence of a series of actions may be to vary the manner in which a stimulus acts upon the sense organs. It is apparent that the exploring, manipulating child produces by his actions precisely what Hebb's theory demands as a basis for continuing interest: he produces differences-in-sameness in the stimulus field.

Being interested in the environment implies

having some kind of satisfactory interaction with it. Several workers call attention to the possibility that satisfaction might lie in having an effect upon the environment, in dealing with it, and changing it in various ways. Groos (1901), in his classical analysis of play, attached great importance to the child's "joy in being a cause," as shown in making a clatter, "hustling things about," and playing in puddles where large and dramatic effects can be produced. "We demand a knowledge of effects," he wrote, "and to be ourselves the producers of effects." Piaget (1952) remarks upon the child's special interest in objects that are affected by his own movements. This aspect of behavior occupies a central place in the work of Skinner (1953), who describes it as "operant" and who thus "emphasizes the fact that the behavior *operates* upon the environment to generate consequences." Skinner finds it "difficult, if not impossible, to trace these reinforcing effects to a history of conditioning." "We may plausibly argue," he continues, "that a capacity to be reinforced by any feedback from the environment would be biologically advantageous, since it would prepare the organism to manipulate the environment successfully before a given state of deprivation developed."

Woodworth's behavior-primacy theory

The most far-reaching attempt to give these aspects of behavior a systematic place in the theory of motivation is contained in Woodworth's recent book, *Dynamics of Behavior* (1958). Woodworth takes his start from the idea that a great deal of human behavior appears to be directed toward producing effects upon the environment without immediate service to any aroused organic need. "Its incentives and rewards are in the field of behavior and not in the field of homeostasis." This is illustrated by exploratory behavior, which is directed outward toward the environment.

Its long-range value as the means of making the child acquainted with the world he has to deal with later, and so equipping him through play for the serious business of life, can scarcely lie within the little child's horizon. His goals are more limited and direct: to see this or that object more closely, to

find what is behind an obstacle, to hear the noise an object makes when it strikes the floor, to be told the name of a thing or person (Woodworth, 1958, p. 78).

More complex play, such as building with blocks, illustrates the same outgoing tendency and reveals more plainly the element of finding out what one can and cannot do with objects. Even social play falls into the pattern. Playmates do not chiefly supply affection or satisfy organic needs; rather, they "afford the opportunity to do something interesting in the environment."

COMPETENCE AND THE PLAY OF CONTENTED CHILDREN

A backward glance at our survey shows considerable agreement about the kinds of behavior that are left out or handled poorly by theories of motivation based wholly on organic drives. Repeatedly we find reference to the familiar series of learned skills which starts with sucking, grasping, and visual exploration and continues with crawling and walking, acts of focal attention and perception, memory, language and thinking, anticipation, the exploring of novel places and objects, effecting stimulus changes in the environment, manipulating and exploiting the surroundings, and achieving higher levels of motor and mental coordination. These aspects of behavior have long been the province of child psychology, which has attempted to measure the slow course of their development and has shown how heavily their growth depends upon learning. Collectively they are sometimes referred to as adaptive mechanisms or as ego processes, but on the whole we are not accustomed to cast a single name over the diverse feats whereby we learn to deal with the environment.

I now propose that we gather the various kinds of behavior just mentioned, all of which have to do with effective interaction with the environment, under the general heading of competence. According to Webster, competence means fitness or ability, and the suggested synonyms include capability, capacity, efficiency, proficiency, and skill. It is therefore a suitable word to describe such things as grasping and exploring, crawling and walking, attention and perception, language and thinking, manipulating and changing the surroundings, all of which promote an effective—a competent —interaction with the environment. It is true, of course, that maturation plays a part in all these developments, but this part is heavily overshadowed by learning in all the more complex accomplishments like speech or skilled manipulation. I shall argue that it is necessary to make competence a motivational concept; there is a *competence motivation* as well as competence in its more familiar sense of achieved capacity. The behavior that leads to the building up of effective grasping, handling, and letting go of objects, to take one example, is not random behavior produced by a general overflow of energy. It is directed, selective, and persistent, and it is continued not because it serves primary drives, which indeed it cannot serve until it is almost perfected, but because it satisfies an intrinsic need to deal with the environment.

No doubt it will at first seem arbitrary to propose a single motivational conception in connection with so many and such diverse kinds of behavior. What do we gain by attributing motivational unity to such a large array of activities? We could, of course, say that each developmental sequence, such as learning to grasp or to walk, has its own built-in bit of motivation—its "aliment," as Piaget (1952) has expressed it. We could go further and say that each item of behavior has its intrinsic motive—but this makes the concept of motivation redundant. On the other hand, we might follow the lead of the animal psychologists and postulate a limited number of broader motives under such names as curiosity, manipulation, and mastery. I believe that the idea of a competence motivation is more adequate than any of these alternatives and that it points to very vital common properties which have been lost from view amidst the strongly analytical tendencies that go with detailed research.

In order to make this claim more plausible, I shall now introduce some specimens of playful exploration in early childhood. I hope that these images will serve to fix and dramatize the concept of competence in the same way that other images—the hungry animal solving problems, the child putting his finger in the candle flame, the infant at the breast, the child on the toilet, and the youthful Oedipus caught

in a hopeless love triangle—have become memorable focal points for other concepts. For this purpose I turn to Piaget's (1952) studies of the growth of intelligence from its earliest manifestations in his own three children. The examples come from the first year of life, before language and verbal concepts begin to be important. They therefore represent a practical kind of intelligence which may be quite similar to what is developed by the higher animals.

As early as the fourth month, the play of the gifted Piaget children began to be "centered on a result produced in the external environment," and their behavior could be described as rediscovering the movement which by chance exercised an advantageous action upon things" (1952, p. 151). Laurent, lying in his bassinet, learns to shake a suspended rattle by pulling a string that hangs from it. He discovers this result fortuitously before vision and prehension are fully coordinated. Let us now observe him a little later when he has reached the age of three months and ten days.

I place the string, which is attached to the rattle, in his right hand, merely unrolling it a little so that he may grasp it better. For a moment nothing happens. But at the first shake due to chance movement of his hand, the reaction is immediate: Laurent starts when looking at the rattle and then violently strikes his right hand alone, as if he felt the resistance and the effect. The operation lasts fully a quarter of an hour, during which Laurent emits peals of laughter (Piaget, 1952, p. 162).

Three days later the following behavior is observed.

Laurent, by chance, strikes the chain while sucking his fingers. He grasps it and slowly displaces it while looking at the rattles. He then begins to swing it very gently, which produces a slight movement of the hanging rattles and an as yet faint sound inside them. Laurent then definitely increases by degrees his own movements. He shakes the chain more and more vigorously and laughs uproariously at the result obtained. (Piaget, 1952, p. 185).

Very soon it can be observed that procedures are used "to make interesting spectacles last." For instance, Laurent is shown a rubber monkey which he has not seen before. After a moment of surprise, and perhaps even fright, he calms down and makes movements of pulling the string, a procedure which has no effect in this case, but which previously has caused interesting things to happen. It is to be noticed that "interesting spectacles" consist of such things as new toys, a tin box upon which a drumming noise can be made, an unfolded newspaper, or sounds made by the observer such as snapping the fingers. Commonplace as they are to the adult mind, these spectacles enter the infant's experience as novel and apparently challenging events.

Moving ahead to the second half of the first year, we can observe behavior in which the child explores the properties of objects and tries out his repertory of actions upon them. This soon leads to active experimentation in which the child attempts to provoke new results. Again we look in upon Laurent, who has now reached the age of nine months. On different occasions he is shown a variety of new objects—for instance a notebook, a beaded purse, and a wooden parrot. His carefully observing father detects four stages of response: (a) visual exploration, passing the object from hand to hand, folding the purse, etc.; (b) tactile exploration, passing the hand all over the object, scratching, etc.; (c) slow moving of the object in space; (d) use of the repertory of action: shaking the object, striking it, swinging it, rubbing it against the side of the bassinet, sucking it, etc., "each in turn with a sort of prudence as though studying the effect produced" (1952, p. 255).

Here the child can be described as applying familiar tactics to new situations, but in a short while he will advance to clear patterns of active experimentation. At 10 months and 10 days Laurent, who is unfamiliar with bread as a nutritive substance, is given a piece for examination. He manipulates it, drops it many times, breaks off fragments and lets them fall. He has often done this kind of thing before, but previously his attention has seemed to be centered on the act of letting go. Now "he watches with great interest the body in motion; in particular, he looks at it for a long time when it has fallen, and picks it up when he can." On the following day he resumes his research.

He grasps in succession a celluloid swan, a box, and several other small objects, in each case stretching out his arm and letting them fall. Sometimes he stretches out his arm vertically, sometimes he holds it obliquely in front of or behind his eyes. When the object falls in a new position (for example on his pillow) he lets it fall two or three times more on the same place, as though to study the spatial relation; then he modifies the situation. At a certain moment the swan falls near his mouth; now he does not suck it (even though this object habitually serves this purpose), but drops it three times more while merely making the gesture of opening his mouth (Piaget, 1952, p. 269).

These specimens have a meaningful unity when seen as transactions between the child and his environment, the child having some influence upon the environment and the environment some influence upon the child. Laurent appears to be concerned about what he can do with the chain and rattles, what he can accomplish by his own effort to reproduce and to vary the entertaining sounds. If his father observed correctly, we must add that Laurent seems to have varied his actions systematically, as if testing the effect of different degrees of effort upon the bit of environment represented by the chain and rattles. Kittens make a similar study of parameters when delicately using their paws to push pencils and other objects ever nearer to the edge of one's desk. In all such examples it is clear that the child or animal is by no means at the mercy of transient stimulus fields. He selects for continuous treatment those aspects of his environment which he finds it possible to affect in some way. His behavior is selective, directed, persistent—in short, motivated.

Motivated toward what goal? In these terms, too, the behavior exhibits a little of everything. Laurent can be seen as appeasing a stimulus hunger, providing his sensorium with an agreeable level of stimulation by eliciting from the environment a series of interesting sounds, feels, and sights. On the other hand we might emphasize a need for activity and see him as trying to reach a pleasurable level of neuromuscular exercise. We can also see another possible goal in the behavior: the child is achieving knowledge, attaining a more differentiated cognitive map of his environment and thus satisfying an exploratory tendency or motive of curiosity. But it is equally possible to discern a theme of mastery, power, or control, perhaps even a bit of primitive self-assertion, in the child's concentration upon those aspects of the environment which respond in some way to his own activity. It looks as if we had found too many goals, and perhaps our first impulse is to search for some key to tell us which one is really important. But this, I think, is a mistake that would be fatal to understanding.

We cannot assign priority to any of these goals without pausing arbitrarily in the cycle of transaction between child and environment and saying, "This is the real point." I propose instead that the real point is the transactions as a whole. If the behavior gives satisfaction, this satisfaction is not associated with a particular moment in the cycle. It does not lie solely in sensory stimulation, in a bettering of the cognitive map, in coordinated action, in motor exercise, in a feeling of effort and of effects produced, or in the appreciation of change brought about in the sensory field. These are all simply aspects of a process which at this stage has to be conceived as a whole. The child appears to be occupied with the agreeable task of developing an effective familiarity with his environment. This involves discovering the effects he can have on the environment and the effects the environment will have on him. To the extent that these results are preserved by learning, they build up an increased competence in dealing with the environment. The child's play can thus be viewed as serious business, though to him it is merely something that is interesting and fun to do.

Bearing in mind these examples, as well as the dealings with environment pointed out by other workers, we must now attempt to describe more fully the possible nature of the motivational aspect of competence. It needs its own name, and in view of the foregoing analysis I propose that this name be *effectance*.

EFFECTANCE

The new freedom produced by two decades of research on animal drives is of great help in this undertaking. We are no longer obliged to look for a source of energy external to the nervous system, for a consummatory climax, or for a fixed connection between reinforce-

ment and tension-reduction. Effectance motivation cannot, of course, be conceived as having a source in tissues external to the nervous system. It is in no sense a deficit motive. We must assume it to be neurogenic, its "energies" being simply those of the living cells that make up the nervous system. External stimuli play an important part, but in terms of "energy" this part is secondary, as one can see most clearly when environmental stimulation is actively sought. Putting it picturesquely, we might say that the effectance urge represents what the neuromuscular system wants to do when it is otherwise unoccupied or is gently stimulated by the environment. Obviously there are no consummatory acts; satisfaction would appear to lie in the arousal and maintaining of activity rather than in its slow decline toward bored passivity. The motive need not be conceived as intense and powerful in the sense that hunger, pain, or fear can be powerful when aroused to high pitch. There are plenty of instances in which children refuse to leave their absorbed play in order to eat or to visit the toilet. Strongly aroused drives, pain, and anxiety, however, can be conceived as overriding the effectance urge and capturing the energies of the neuromuscular system. But effectance motivation is persistent in the sense that it regularly occupies the spare waking time between episodes of homeostatic crisis.

In speculating upon this subject we must bear in mind the continuous nature of behavior. This is easier said than done; habitually we break things down in order to understand them, and such units as the reflex arc, the stimulus-response sequence, and the single transaction with the environment seem like inevitable steps toward clarity. Yet when we apply such an analysis to playful exploration we lose the most essential aspect of the behavior. It is constantly circling from stimulus to perception to action to effect to stimulus to perception, and so on around; or, more properly, these processes are all in continuous action and continuous change. Dealing with the environment means carrying on a continuing transaction which gradually changes one's relation to the environment. Because there is no consummatory climax, satisfaction has to be seen as lying in a considerable series of transactions, in a trend of behavior rather than a goal that is achieved. It is difficult to make the word "satisfaction" have this connotation, and we shall do well to replace it by "feeling of efficacy" when attempting to indicate the subjective and affective side of effectance.

It is useful to recall the findings about novelty: the singular effectiveness of novelty in engaging interest and for a time supporting persistent behavior. We also need to consider the selective continuance of transactions in which the animal or child has a more or less pronounced effect upon the environment—in which something happens as a consequence of his activity. Interest is not aroused and sustained when the stimulus field is so familiar that it gives rise at most to reflex acts or automatized habits. It is not sustained when actions produce no effects or changes in the stimulus field. Our conception must therefore be that effectance motivation is aroused by stimulus conditions which offer, as Hebb (1949) puts it, difference-in-sameness. This leads to variability and novelty of response, and interest is best sustained when the resulting action affects the stimulus so as to produce further difference-in-sameness. Interest wanes when action begins to have less effect; effectance motivation subsides when a situation has been explored to the point that it no longer presents new possibilities.

We have to conceive further that the arousal of playful and exploratory interest means the appearance of organization involving both the cognitive and active aspects of behavior. Change in the stimulus field is not an end in itself, so to speak; it happens when one is passively moved about, and it may happen as a consequence of random movements without becoming focalized and instigating exploration. Similarly, action which has effects is not an end in itself, for if one unintentionally kicks away a branch while walking, or knocks something off a table, these effects by no means necessarily become involved in playful investigation. Schachtel's (1954) emphasis on focal attention becomes helpful at this point. The playful and exploratory behavior shown by Laurent is not random or casual. It involves focal *attention* to some object—the fixing of some aspect of the stimulus field so that it stays relatively constant—and it also involves the focalizing of *action* upon this object. As Diamond (1939) has expressed it, response under these conditions is "relevant to the stimulus," and it is change in the *focalized* stimulus that so strongly affects the level of interest. Dealing with the environment means directing focal attention to some part of it and organizing actions to have some effect on this part.

THE BIOLOGICAL SIGNIFICANCE OF COMPETENCE

The conviction was expressed at the beginning of this paper that some such concept as competence, interpreted motivationally, was essential for any biologically sound view of human nature. This necessity emerges when we consider the nature of living systems, particularly when we take a longitudinal view. What an organism does at a given moment does not always give the right clue as to what it does over a period of time. Discussing this problem, Angyal (1941) has proposed that we should look for the general pattern followed by the total organismic process over the course of time. Obviously this makes it necessary to take account of growth. Angyal defines life as "a process of self-expansion"; the living system "expands at the expense of its surroundings," assimilating parts of the environment and transforming them into functioning parts of itself. Organisms differ from other things in nature in that they are "self-governing entities" which are to some extent "autonomous." Internal processes govern them as well as external "heteronomous" forces. In the course of life there is a relative increase in the preponderance of internal over external forces. The living system expands, assimilates more of the environment, transforms its surroundings so as to bring them under greater control. "We may say," Angyal writes, "that the general dynamic trend of the organism is toward an increase of autonomy. . . . The human being has a characteristic tendency toward self-determination, that is, a tendency to resist external influences and to subordinate the heteronomous forces of the physical and social environment to its own sphere of influence." The trend toward increased autonomy is characteristic so long as growth of any kind is going on, though in the end the living system is bound to succumb to the pressure of heteronomous forces.

Of all living creatures, it is man who takes the longest strides toward autonomy. This is not because of any unusual tendency toward bodily expansion at the expense of the environment. It is rather that man, with his mobile hands and abundantly developed brain, attains an extremely high level of competence in his transactions with his surroundings. The building of houses, roads and bridges, the making of tools and instruments, the domestication of plants and animals, all qualify as planful changes made in the environment so that it comes more or less under control and serves our purposes rather than intruding upon them. We meet the fluctuations of outdoor temperature, for example, not only with our bodily homeostatic mechanisms, which alone would be painfully unequal to the task, but also with clothing, buildings, controlled fires, and such complicated devices as self-regulating central heating and air conditioning. Man as a species has developed a tremendous power of bringing the environment into his service, and each individual member of the species must attain what is really quite an impressive level of competence if he is to take part in the life around him.

Under primitive conditions survival must depend quite heavily upon achieved competence. We should expect to find things so arranged as to favor and maximize this achievement. Particularly in the case of man, where so little is provided innately and so much has to be learned through experience, we should expect to find highly advantageous arrangements for securing a steady cumulative learning about the properties of the environment and the extent of possible transactions. Under these circumstances we might expect to find a very powerful drive operating to insure progress toward competence, just as the vital goals of nutrition and reproduction are secured by powerful drives, and it might therefore seem paradoxical that the interests of competence should be so much entrusted to times of play and leisurely exploration. There is good reason to suppose, however, that a strong drive would be precisely the wrong arrangement to secure a flexible, knowledgeable power of transaction with the environment. Strong drives cause us to learn certain lessons well, but they do not create maximum familiarity with our surroundings.

This point was demonstrated half a century ago in some experiments by Yerkes and Dodson (1908). They showed that maximum motivation did not lead to the most rapid solving of problems, especially if the problems were complex. For each problem there was an optimum level of motivation, neither the highest nor the lowest and the optimum was lower for more complex tasks. The same problem has been discussed more recently by Tolman (1948) in his paper on cognitive maps. A cognitive map can be narrow or broad, depending upon the range of cues picked up in the course of learning. Tolman suggests that one of the conditions which tend to narrow the range of cues is a high level of motivation. In everyday terms, a man hurrying to an important business conference is likely to perceive only the cues that help him to get there faster, whereas a man taking a stroll after lunch is likely to pick up a substantial amount of casual information about his environment. The latent learning experiments with animals, and experiments such as those of Johnson (1953) in which drive level has been systematically varied in a situation permitting incidental learning, give strong support to this general idea. In a recent contribution, Bruner, Matter, and Papanek (1955) make a strong case for the concept of breadth of learning and provide additional evidence that it is favored by moderate and hampered by strong motivation. The latter "has the effect of speeding up learning at the cost of narrowing it." Attention is concentrated upon the task at hand and little that is extraneous to this task is learned for future use.

These facts enable us to see the biological appropriateness of an arrangement which uses periods of less intense motivation for the development of competence. This is not to say that the narrower but efficient learnings that go with the reduction of strong drives make no contribution to general effectiveness. They are certainly an important element in capacity to deal with the environment, but a much greater effectiveness results from having this capacity fed also from learnings that take place in quieter times. It is then that the infant can attend to matters of lesser urgency, exploring the properties of things he does not fear and does not need to eat, learning to gauge the force of his string-pulling when the only penalty for failure is silence on the part of the attached rattles, and generally accumulating for himself a broad knowledge and a broad skill in dealing with his surroundings.

The concept of competence can be most easily discussed by choosing, as we have done, examples of interaction with the inanimate environment. It applies equally well, however, to transactions with animals and with other human beings, where the child has the same problem of finding out what effects he can have upon the environment and what effects it can have upon him. The earliest interactions with members of the family may involve needs so strong that they obscure the part played by effectance motivation, but perhaps the example of the well fed baby diligently exploring the several features of his mother's face will serve as a reminder that here, too, there are less urgent moments when learning for its own sake can be given free rein.

In this closing section I have brought together several ideas which bear on the evolutionary significance of competence and of its motivation. I have sought in this way to deepen the biological roots of the concept and thus help it to attain the stature in the theory of behavior which has not been reached by similar concepts in the past. To me it seems that the most important proving ground for this concept is the effect it may have on our understanding of the development of personality. I believe it can be shown that existing explanations of development are not satisfactory and that the addition of the concept of competence cuts certain knots in personality theory. But this is not the subject of the present communication, where the concept is offered much more on the strength of its logical and biological probability.

SUMMARY

The main theme of this paper is introduced by showing that there is widespread discontent with theories of motivation built upon primary drives. Signs of this discontent are found in realms as far apart as animal psychology and psychoanalytic ego psychology. In the former, the commonly recognized primary drives have proved to be inadequate in explaining exploratory behavior, manipulation, and general activity. In the latter, the theory of basic instincts has shown serious shortcomings when it is stretched to account for the development of the effective ego. Workers with animals have attempted to meet their problem by invoking secondary reinforcement and anxiety reduction, or by adding exploration and manipulation to the roster of primary drives. In parallel fashion, psychoanalytic workers have relied upon the concept of neutralization of instinctual energies, have seen anxiety reduction as the central motive in ego development, or have hypothesized new instincts such as mastery. It is argued here that these several explanations are not satisfactory and that a better conceptualization is possible, indeed that it has already been all but made.

In trying to form this conceptualization, it is first pointed out that many of the earlier tenets of primary drive theory have been discredited by recent experimental work. There is no longer any compelling reason to identify either pleasure or reinforcement with drive-reduction, or to think of motivation as requiring a source of energy external to the nervous system. This opens the way for considering in their own right those aspects of animal and human behavior in which stimulation and contact with the environment seem to be sought and welcomed, in which raised tension and even mild excitement seem to be cherished, and in which novelty and variety seem to be enjoyed for their own sake. Several reports are cited which bear upon interest in the environment and the rewarding effects of environmental feedback. The latest contribution is that of Woodworth (1958), who makes dealing with the environment the most fundamental element in motivation.

The survey indicates a certain unanimity as to the kinds of behavior that cannot be successfully conceptualized in terms of primary drives. This behavior includes visual exploration, grasping, crawling and walking, attention and perception, language and thinking, exploring novel objects and places, manipulating the surroundings, and producing effective changes in the environment. The thesis is then proposed that all of these behaviors have a common biological significance: they all form part of the process whereby the animal or child learns to interact effectively with his environment. The word *competence* is chosen as suitable to indicate this common property. Further, it is maintained that competence cannot be fully acquired simply through behavior instigated by drives. It receives substantial contributions from activities which, though playful and exploratory in character, at the same time show direction, selectivity, and persistence in interacting with the environment. Such activities in the ultimate service of competence must therefore be conceived to be motivated in their own right. It is proposed to designate this motivation by the term effectance, and to characterize the experience produced as a *feeling of efficacy*.

In spite of its sober biological purpose, effectance motivation shows itself most unambiguously in the playful and investigatory behavior of young animals and children. Specimens of such behavior, drawn from Piaget (1952), are analyzed in order to demonstrate their constantly transactional nature. Typically they involve continuous chains of events which include stimulation, cognition, action, effect on the environment, new stimulation, etc. They are carried on with considerable persistence and with selective emphasis on parts of the environment which provide changing and interesting feedback in connection with effort expended. Their significance is destroyed if we try to break into the circle arbitrarily and declare that one part of it such as cognition alone or active effort alone, is the real point, the goal, or the special seat of satisfaction. Effectance motivation must be conceived to involve satisfaction—a feeling of efficacy—in transactions in which behavior has an exploratory, varying, experimental character and produces changes in the stimulus field. Having this character, the behavior leads the organism to find out how the environment can be changed and what consequences flow from these changes.

In higher animals and especially in man, where so little is innately provided and so much has to be learned about dealing with the environment, effectance motivation independent of primary drives can be seen as an arrangement having high adaptive value. Considering the slow rate of learning in infancy and the vast amount that has to be learned before there can be an effective level of interaction with surroundings, young animals and children would simply not learn enough unless they

worked pretty steadily at the task between episodes of homeostatic crisis. The association of interest with this "work," making it play and fun, is thus somewhat comparable to the association of sexual pleasure with the biological goal of reproduction. Effectance motivation need not be conceived as strong in the sense that sex, hunger, and fear are strong when violently aroused. It is moderate but persistent, and in this, too, we can discern a feature that is favorable for adaptation. Strong motivation reinforces learning in a narrow sphere, whereas moderate motivation is more conducive to an exploratory and experimental attitude which leads to competent interactions in general, without reference to an immediate pressing need. Man's huge cortical association areas might have been a suicidal piece of specialization if they had come without a steady persistent inclination toward interacting with the environment.

REFERENCES

Allport, G. W. *Personality: A psychological interpretation.* New York: Holt, 1937.

Allport, G. W. Effect: A secondary principle of learning. *Psychol. Rev.,* 1946, **53,** 335–347.

Angyal, A. *Foundations for a science of personality.* New York: Commonwealth Fund, 1941.

Ansbacher, H. L., & Ansbacher, R. R. (Eds.) *The individual psychology of Alfred Adler.* New York: Basic Books, 1956.

Beach, F. A. Analysis of factors involved in the arousal, maintenance and manifestation of sexual excitement in male animals. *Psychosom. Med.,* 1942, **4,** 173–198.

Beach, F. A. Instinctive behavior: Reproductive activities. In S. S. Stevens (Ed.), *Handbook of experimental psychology.* New York: Wiley, 1951. Pp. 387–434.

Berlyne, D. E. Novelty and curiosity as determinants of exploratory behavior. *Brit. J. Psychol.,* 1950, **41,** 68–80.

Berlyne, D. E. The arousal and satiation of perceptual curiosity in the rat. *J. comp. physiol. Psychol.,* 1955, **48,** 238–246.

Berlyne, D. E. Attention to change, conditioned inhibition (sIR) and stimulus satiation. *Brit. J. Psychol.,* 1957, **48,** 138–140.

Berlyne, D. S. The present status of research on exploratory and related behavior. *J. indiv. Psychol.,* 1958, **14,** 121–126.

Bibring, E. The development and problems of the theories of the instincts. *Int. J. Psychoanal.,* 1941, **22,** 102–131.

Bruner, J. S., Matter, J., & Papanek, M. L. Breadth of learning as a function of drive level and mechanization. *Psychol. Rev.*, 1955, **62**, 1–10.

Buhler, C. The reality principle. *Amer. J. Psychotherap.*, 1954, **8**, 626–647.

Bühler, K. *Die geistige Entwicklung des Kindes.* (4th ed.) Jena: Gustav Fischer, 1924.

Butler, R. A. Discrimination learning by rhesus monkeys to visual-exploration motivation. *J. Comp. physiol. Psychol.*, 1953, **46**, 95–98.

Butler, R. A. Exploratory and related behavior: A new trend in animal research. *J. indiv. Psychol.*, 1958, **14**, 111–120.

Butler, R. A. & Harlow, H. F. Discrimination learning and learning sets to visual exploration incentives. *J. gen. Psychol.*, 1957, **57**, 257–264.

Cofer, C. N. Motivation. *Ann. Rev. Psychol.*, 1959, **10**, 173–202.

Colby, K. M. *Energy and structure in psychoanalysis.* New York: Ronald, 1955.

Dashiell, J. F. A quantitative demonstration of animal drive. *J. comp. Psychol.*, 1925, **5**, 205–208.

Diamond, S. A neglected aspect of motivation. *Sociometry*, 1939, **2**, 77–85.

Dollard, J., & Miller, N. E. *Personality and psychotherapy.* New York: McGraw-Hill, 1950.

Erikson, E. H. *Childhood and society.* New York: Norton, 1952.

Erikson, E. H. Growth and crises of the healthy personality. In C. Kluckhohn, H. A. Murray, & D. Schneider (Eds.), *Personality in nature, society, and culture.* (2nd ed.) New York: Knopf, 1953. Pp. 185–225.

Fenichel, O. *The psychoanalytic theory of neurosis.* New York: Norton, 1945.

French, T. M. *The integration of behavior.* Vol. I. *Basic postulates.* Chicago: Univer. Chicago Press, 1952.

Freud, A. The mutual influences in the development of ego and id: Introduction to the discussion. *Psychoanal. Stud. Child*, 1952, **7**, 42–50.

Freud, S. *Wit and its relation to the unconscious.* New York: Moffat, Yard, 1916.

Freud, S. Formulations regarding the two principles in mental functioning. *Collected papers.* Vol. 4. London: Hogarth Press and Institute of Psychoanalysis, 1925. Pp. 13–21. (a)

Freud, S. On narcissism: An introduction. *Collected papers.* Vol. 4. London. Hogarth Press and Institute of Psychoanalysis, 1925. Pp. 30–59 (b)

Freud, S. Instincts and their vicissitudes. *Collected papers.* Vol. 4 London: Hogarth Press and Institute of Psychoanalysis, 1925. Pp. 60–83. (c)

Freud, S. *The ego and the id.* (Trans. by J. Riviere) London: Hogarth Press, 1927.

Freud, S. *Beyond the pleasure principle.* London: Hogarth Press, 1948.

Freud, S. *An outline of psycho-analysis.* (Trans. by J. Strachey) New York: Norton, 1949.

Goldstein, K. *The organism.* New York: American Book, 1939.

Goldstein, K. *Human nature in the light of psychopathology.* Cambridge, Mass.: Harvard Univer. Press, 1940.

Gross, K. *The play of man.* (Trans. by E. L. Baldwin) New York: D. Appleton, 1901.

Harlow, H. F. Mice, monkeys, men and motives. *Psychol. Rev.*, 1953, **60**, 23–32.

Harlow, H. F., Harlow, M. K., & Meyer, D. R. Learning motivated by a manipulation drive. *J. exp. Psychol.*, 1950, **40**, 228–234.

Hartmann, H. Comments on the psychoanalytic theory of the ego. *Psychoanal. Stud. Child*, 1950, **5**, 74–95.

Hartmann, H. Notes on the theory of sublimation. *Psychoanal. Stud. Child*, 1955, **10**, 9–29.

Hartmann, H. Notes on the reality principle. *Psychoanal. Stud. Child*, 1956, **11**, 31–53.

Hartmann, H. *Ego psychology and the problem of adaptation.* (Trans. by D. Rapaport) New York: International Univer. Press, 1958.

Hartmann, H., Kris, E., & Loewenstein, R. Notes on the theory of aggression. *Psychoanal. Stud. Child*, 1949, **3/4**, 9–36.

Hebb, D. O. *The organization of behavior.* New York: Wiley, 1949.

Hebb, D. O. Drives and the c.n.s. (conceptual nervous system). *Psychol. Rev.*, 1955, **62**, 243–254.

Hebb, D. O. The motivating effects of exteroceptive stimulation. *Amer. Psychologist*, 1958, **13**, 109–113.

Hebb, D. O., & Thompson, W. R. The social significance of animal studies. In G. Lindzey (Ed.), *Handbook of social psychology.* Vol. 1. Cambridge, Mass., Addison-Wesley, 1954. Pp. 532–561.

Hendrick, I. Instinct and the ego during infancy. *Psychoanal. Quart.*, 1942, **11**, 33–58.

Hendrick, I. Work and pleasure principal. *Psychoanal. Quart.*, 1943, **12**, 311–329. (a)

Hendrick, I. The dicussion of the 'instinct to master.' *Psychoanal. Quart.*, 1943, 12, 561–565. (b)

Hill, W. F. Activity as an autonomous drive. *J. comp. physiol. Psychol.*, 1956, **49**, 15–19.

Johnson, E. E. The role of motivational strength in latent learning. *J. comp. physiol. Psychol.*, 1953, **45**, 526–530.

Kagan, J. Differential reward value of incomplete and complete sexual behavior. *J. comp physiol. Psychol.*, 1955, **48**, 59–64.

Kagan, J. & Berkun, M. The reward value of running activity. *J. comp. physiol. Psychol.*, 1954, **47**, 108.

Kardiner, A. & Spiegel, H. War stress and neurotic illness. New York: Hoeber, 1947.

Lashley, K. S. Experimental analysis of instinctive behavior. *Psychol. Rev.*, 1938, **45**, 445–471.

Lashley, K. S. The problem of cerebral organization in vision. In H. Klüver, *Visual mechanisms.* Lancaster, Pa.: Jaques Cattell, 1942. Pp. 301–322.

Leuba, C. Toward some integration of learning theories: The concept of optimal stimulation. *Psychol. Rev.*, 1955, **1**, 27–33.

Lilly, J. C. Mental effects of reduction of ordinary levels of physical stimuli on intact, healthy persons. *Psychiat. res. Rep.*, 1956, No. 5.

Maslow, A. H. *Motivation and personality.* New York: Harper, 1954.

Maslow, A. H. Deficiency motivation and growth motivation. In M. R. Jones (Ed.), *Nebraska symposium on motivation 1955.* Lincoln, Neb.: Univer. Nebraska Press, 1955. Pp. 1–30.

McClelland, D. C. Atkinson, J. W. Clark, R. A. & Lowell, E. I. *The achievement motive.* New York: Appleton-Century, 1953.

McDougall, W. *Introduction to social psychology.* (16th ed.) Boston: John Luce, 1923.

McReynolds, P. A restricted conceptualization of human anxiety and motivation. *Psychol. Rep.*, 1956, **2**, 293–312. Monogr. Suppl. 6.

Miller, N. E. Learnable drives and rewards. In S. S. Stevens (Ed.), *Handbook of experimental psychology.* New York: Wiley, 1951. Pp. 435–472.

Miller, N. E. Central stimulation and other new approaches to motivation and reward. *Amer. Psychologist*, 1958, **13**, 100–108.

Mittelmann, B. Motility in infants, children, and adults. *Psychoanal. Stud. Child,* 1954, **9**, 142–177.

Montgomery, K. C. The role of the exploratory drive in learning. *J. comp. physiol. Psychol.*, 1954, **47**, 60–64.

Montgomery, K. C., & Monkman, J. A. The relation between fear and exploratory behavior. *J. comp. physiol. Psychol.*, 1955, **48**, 132–136.

Morgan, C. T. *Physiological psychology.* New York: McGraw-Hill, 1943.

Morgan, C. T. Physiological mechanisms of motivation. In M. R. Jones (Ed.), *Nebraska symposium on motivation 1957.* Lincoln, Neb.: Univer. Nebraska Press, 1957. Pp. 1–35.

Mowrer, O. H. *Learning theory and personality dynamics.* New York: Ronald, 1950.

Munroe, R. *Schools of psychoanalytical thought.* New York: Dryden, 1955.

Murphy, G. *Personality: A biosocial approach to origins and structure.* New York: Harper, 1947.

Murray, H. A. *Explorations in personality.* New York & London: Oxford Univer. Press, 1938.

Murray, H. A. & Kluckhohn, C. Outline of a conception of personality. In C. Kluckhohn, H. A. Murray, & D. M. Schneider (Eds.), *Personality in nature, society, and culture.* (2nd ed.) New York: Knopf, 1953.

Myers, A. K. & Miller, N. E. Failure to find a learned drive based on hunger; evidence for learning motivated by "exploration." *J. comp. physiol. Psychol.*, 1954, **47**, 428–436.

Nissen, H. W. A study of exploratory behavior in the white rat by means of the obstruction method. *J. genet. Psychol.*, 1930, **37**, 361–376.

Olds, J., & Milner, P. Positive reinforcement produced by electrical stimulation of septal area and other regions of rat brain. *J. comp. physiol. Psychol.*, 1954, **47**, 419–427.

Piaget, J. *The origins of intelligence in children.* (Trans. by M. Cook) New York: International Univer. Press, 1952.

Rapaport, D. *Organization and pathology of thought.* New York: Columbia Univer. Press, 1951.

Rapaport, D. On the psychoanalytic theory of thinking. In R. P. Knight & C. R. Friedman (Eds.), *Psychoanalytic psychiatry and psychology.* New York: International Univer. Press, 1954. Pp. 259–273.

Rapaport, D. The theory of ego autonomy: A generalization. *Bull. Menninger Clin.*, 1958, **22**, 13–35.

Rosvold, H. E. Physiological psychology. *Ann. Rev. Psychol.*, 1959, **10**, 415–454.

Schachtel, E. G. The development of focal attention and the emergence of reality. *Psychiatry*, 1954, **17**, 309–324.

Sheffield, F. D., & Roby, T. B. Reward value of a nonnutritive sweet taste. *J. comp. physiol. Psychol.*, 1950, **43**, 471–481.

Sheffield, F. D., Roby, T. B., & Campbell, B. A. Drive reduction vs. consummatory behavior as determinants of reinforcement. *J. comp. physiol. Psychol.*, 1954, **47**, 349–354.

Sheffield, F. D., Wulff, J. J., & Backer, R. Reward value of copulation without sex drive reduction. *J. comp. physiol. Psychol.*, 1951, **44**, 3–8.

Skinner, B. F. *Science and human behavior.* New York: Macmillan, 1953.

Steller, E. The physiology of motivation. *Psychol. Rev.*, 1954, **61**, 5–22.

Tolman, E. C. Cognitive maps in rats and men. *Psychol. Rev.*, 1948, **55**, 189–208.

Welker, W. L. Some determinants of play and exploration in chimpanzees. *J. comp. physiol. Psychol.*, 1956, **49**, 84–89.

Whiting, J. W. M. & Mowrer, O. H. Habit progression and regression—a laboratory study of some factors relevant to human socialization. *J. comp. Psychol.*, 1943, **36**, 229–253.

Wolfe, J. B., & Kaplon, M. D. Effect of amount of reward and consummative activity on learning in chickens. *J. comp. Psychol.*, 1941, **31**, 353–361.

Woodworth, R. S. *Dynamics of behavior.* New York: Holt, 1958.

Yerkes, R. M. & Dodson, J. D. The relation of strength of stimulus to rapidity of habit-formation. *J. comp. Neurol. Psychol.,* 1908, **18,** 459–482.

Young, P. T. Food-seeking drive, affective process and learning. *Psychol. Rev.* 1949, **56,** 98–121.

Young, P. T. The role of hedonic processes in motivation. In M. R. Jones (Ed.), *Nebraska symposium on motivation 1955.* Lincoln, Neb.: Univer. Nebraska Press, 1955. Pp. 193–238.

Zimbardo, P. G., & Miller, N. E. Facilitation of exploration by hunger in rats. *J. comp. physiol. Psychol.,* 1958, **51,** 43–46.

Selection **16** | A THEORY OF HUMAN MOTIVATION*

A. H. MASLOW
Brandeis University

THE BASIC NEEDS

The "physiological" needs The needs that are usually taken as the starting point for motivation theory are the so-called physiological drives. Two recent lines of research make it necessary to revise our customary notions about these needs, first, the development of the concept of homeostasis, and second, the finding that appetites (preferential choices among foods) are a fairly efficient indication of actual needs or lacks in the body.

Homeostasis refers to the body's automatic efforts to maintain a constant, normal state of the blood stream. Cannon has described this process for (1) the water content of the blood, (2) salt content, (3) sugar content, (4) protein content, (5) fat content, (6) calcium content, (7) oxygen content, (8) content hydrogen-ion level (acid-base balance) and (9) constant temperature of the blood. Obviously this list can be extended to include other minerals, the hormones, vitamins, etc.

*Abridged from A. H. Maslow, "A Theory of Human Motivation," *Psychological Review*, 50: 370–396, 1943. Copyright 1943 by the American Psychological Association and reproduced by permission.

Young in a recent article has summarized the work on appetite in its relation to body needs. If the body lacks some chemical, the individual will tend to develop a specific appetite or partial hunger for that food element.

Thus it seems impossible as well as useless to make any list of fundamental physiological needs for they can come to almost any number one might wish, depending on the degree of specificity of description. We can not identify all physiological needs as homeostatic. That sexual desire, sleepiness, sheer activity and material behavior in animals, are homeostatic, has not yet been demonstrated. Furthermore, this list would not include the various sensory pleasures (tastes, smells, tickling, stroking) which are probably physiological and which may become the goals of motivated behavior.

In a previous paper it has been pointed out that these physiological drives or needs are to be considered unusual rather than typical because they are isolable, and because they are localizable somatically. That is to say they are relatively independent of each other, of other motivations and of the organism as a whole, and secondly, in many cases, it is possible to demonstrate a localized, underlying, somatic base for the drive. This is true less generally than has been thought (exceptions are fatigue, sleepiness, material responses) but it is still true in the classic instances of hunger, sex, and thirst.

Undoubtedly these physiological needs are the most prepotent of all needs. What this means specifically is, that in the human being who is missing everything in life in an extreme fashion, it is most likely that the major motivation would be the physiological needs rather than any others. A person who is lacking food, safety, love, and esteem would most probably hunger for food more strongly than for anything else.

If all the needs are unsatisfied, and the organism is then dominated by the physiological needs, all other needs may become simply nonexistent or be pushed into the background. But what happens to man's desires when there is plenty of bread and when his belly is chronically filled?

At once other (and "higher") needs emerge and these, rather than physiological hungers, dominate the organism. And when these in turn are satisfied, again new (and still "higher") needs emerge and so on. This is what we mean by saying that the basic human needs are organized into a hierarchy of relative prepotency.

One main implication of this phrasing is that gratification becomes as important a concept as deprivation in motivation theory, for it releases the organism from the domination of a relatively more physiological need, permitting thereby the emergence of other more social goals. The physiological needs, along with their partial goals, when chronically gratified cease to exist as active determinants or organizers of behavior. They now exist only in a potential fashion in the sense that they may emerge again to dominate the organism if they are thwarted. But a want that is satisfied is no longer a want. The organism is dominated and its behavior organized only by unsatisfied needs. If hunger is satisfied, it becomes unimportant in the current dynamics of the individual.

The safety needs If the physiological needs are relatively well gratified, there then emerges a new set of needs, which we may categorize roughly as the safety needs. All that has been said of the physological needs is equally true, although in lesser degree, of these desires. The organism may equally well be wholly dominated by them. They may serve as the almost exclusive organizers of behavior, recruiting all the capacities of the organism in their service, and we may then fairly describe the whole organism as a safety-seeking mechanism. Again we may say of the receptors, the effectors, of the intellect and the other capacities that they are primarily safety-seeking tools. Again, as in the hungry man, we find that the dominating goal is a strong determinant not only of his current world-outlook and philosophy but also of his philosophy of the future. Practically everything looks less important than safety, (even sometimes the physiological needs which being satisfied, are now underestimated). A man, in this state, if it is extreme enough and chronic enough, may be characterized as living almost for safety alone.

Although in this paper we are interested primarily in the needs of the adult, we can approach an understanding of his safety needs perhaps more efficiently by observation of infants and children, in whom these needs are much more simple and obvious. One reason for the clearer appearance of the threat or danger reaction in infants, is that they do not inhibit this reaction at all, whereas adults in our society have been taught to inhibit it at all costs. Thus even when adults do feel their safety to be threatened we may not be able to see this on the surface. Infants will react in a total fashion and as if they were endangered, if they are disturbed or dropped suddenly, startled by loud noises, flashing light, or other unusual sensory stimulation, by rough handling, by general loss of support in the mother's arms, or by inadequate support.

The central role of the parents and the normal family setup are indisputable. Quarreling, physical assault, separation, divorce or death within the family may be particularly terrifying. Also parental outbursts of rage or threats of punishment directed to the child, calling him names, speaking to him harshly, shaking him, handling him roughly, or actual physical punishment sometimes elicit such total panic and terror in the child that we must assume more is involved than the physical pain alone. While it is true that in some children this terror may represent also a fear of loss of parental love, it can also occur in completely rejected children, who seem to cling to the hating parents more for sheer safety and protection than because of hope of love.

The healthy, normal, fortunate adult in our culture is largely satisfied in his safety needs. The peaceful, smoothly running, "good" society ordinarily makes its members feel safe enough from wild animals, extremes of temperature, criminals, assault and murder, tyranny, etc. Therefore, in a very real sense he no longer has any safety needs as active motivators. Just as a sated man no longer feels hungry, a safe man no longer feels endangered. If we wish to see these needs directly and clearly we must turn to neurotic or nearneurotic individuals, and to the economic and social underdogs. In between these extremes, we can perceive the expressions of safety needs only in such phenomena as, for instance, the common preference for a job with tenure and protection, the desire for a savings account, and for insurance of various kinds (medical, dental, unemployment, disability, old age).

Some neurotic adults in our society are, in many ways, like the unsafe child in their desire for safety, although in the former it takes on a somewhat special appearance. Their reaction is often to unknown, psychological dangers in a world that is perceived to be hostile, overwhelming and threatening. Such a person behaves as if a great catastrophe were almost always impending, *i.e.*, he is usually responding as if to an emergency. His safety needs often find specific expression in a search for a protector, or a stronger person on which he may depend, or perhaps, a Fuehrer.

The love needs   If both the physiological and the safety needs are fairly well gratified, then there will emerge the love and affection and belongingness needs, and the whole cycle already described will repeat itself with this new center. Now the pesron will feel keenly, as never before, the absence of friends, or a sweetheart, or a wife, or children. He will hunger for affectionate relations with people in general, namely, for a place in his group, and he will strive with great intensity to achieve this goal. He will want to attain such a place more than anything else in the world and may even forget that once, when he was hungry, he sneered at love.

In our society the thwarting of these needs is the most commonly found core in cases of maladjustment and more severe psychopathology. Love and affection, as well as their possible expression in sexuality, are generally looked upon with ambivalence and are customarily hedged about with many restrictions and inhibitions. Practically all theorists of psychopathology have stressed thwarting of the love needs as basic in the picture of maladjustment. Many clinical studies have therefore been made of this need and we know more about it perhaps than any of the other needs except the physiological ones.

One thing that must be stressed at this point is that love is not synonymous with sex. Sex may be studied as a purely physiological need. Ordinarily sexual behavior is multi-

determined, that is to say, determined not only by sexual but also by other needs, chief among which are the love and affection needs. Also not to be overlooked is the fact that the love needs involve both giving *and* receiving love.

The esteem needs   All people in our society (with a few pathological exceptions) have a need or desire for a stable, firmly based, (usually) high evaluation of themselves, for self-respect, or self-esteem, and for the esteem of others. By firmly based self-esteem, we mean that which is soundly based upon real capacity, achievement and respect from others. These needs may be classified into two subsidiary sets. These are, first, the desire for strength, for achievement, for adequacy, for confidence in the face of the world, and for independence and freedom. Secondly, we have what we may call the desire for reputation or prestige (defining it as respect or esteem from other people), recognition, attention, importance or appreciation. These needs have been relatively stressed by Alfred Adler and his followers, and have been relatively neglected by Freud and the psychoanalysts. More and more today however there is appearing widespread appreciation of their central importance.

Satisfaction of the self-esteem need leads to feelings of self-confidence, worth, strength, capability and adequacy of being useful and necessary in the world. But thwarting of these needs produces feelings of inferiority, of weakness and of helplessness. These feelings in turn give rise to either basic discouragement or else compensatory or neurotic trends. An appreciation of the necessity of basic self-confidence and an understanding of how helpless people are without it, can be easily gained from a study of severe traumatic neurosis.

The need for self-actualization   Even if all these needs are satisfied, we may still often (if not always) expect that a new discontent and restlessness will soon develop, unless the individual is doing what he is fitted for. A musician must make music, an artist must paint, a poet must write, if he is to be ultimately happy. What a man *can* be, he *must* be. This need we may call self-actualization.

This term, first coined by Kurt Goldstein, is being used in this paper in a much more specific and limited fashion. It refers to the desire for self-fulfillment, namely, to the tendency for him to become actualized in what he is potentially. This tendency might be phrased as the desire to become more and more what one is, to become everything that one is capable of becoming.

The specific form that these needs will take will of course vary greatly from person to person. In one individual it may take the form of the desire to be an ideal mother, in another it may be expressed athletically, and in still another it may be expressed in painting pictures or in inventions. It is not necessarily a creative urge although in people who have any capacities for creation it will take this form.

The clear emergence of these needs rests upon prior satisfaction of the physiological, safety, love and esteem needs. We shall call people who are satisfied in these needs, basically satisfied people, and it is from these that we may expect the fullest (and healthiest) creativeness. Since, in our society, basically satisfied people are the exception, we do not know much about self-actualization, either experimentally or clinically. It remains a challenging problem for research.

The preconditions for the basic need satisfactions There are certain conditions which are immediate prerequisites for the basic need satisfactions. Danger to these is reacted to almost as if it were a direct danger to the basic needs themselves. Such conditions as freedom to speak, freedom to do what one wishes so long as no harm is done to others, freedom to express one's self, freedom to investigate and seek for information, freedom to defend one's self, justice, fairness, honesty, orderliness in the group are examples of such preconditions for basic need satisfactions. Thwarting in these freedoms will be reacted to with a threat or emergency response. These conditions are not ends in themselves but the are *almost* so since they are so closely related to the basic needs, which are apparently the only ends in themselves. These conditions are defended because without them the basic satisfactions are quite impossible, or at least very severely endangered.

Selection **17** | EXPERIMENTAL AROUSAL OF ACHIEVEMENT MOTIVATION IN ADOLESCENT GIRLS* [1]

GERALD S. LESSER
Hunter College

RHODA N. KRAWITZ
Mount Sinai Hospital, New York City

RITA PACKARD
Hunter College

2 groups of female high school students (40 achievers and 40 underachievers, matched for IQ) were exposed to 2 experimental conditions (Neutral and Achievement Oriented) and 2 types of pictures (those depicting males and those depicting females). The overall effect of the experimental achievement arousal conditions for all girls was nonsignificant. However, a highly significant 2nd-order interaction effect was obtained: the achievement motivation scores of achievers increased significantly in response to Achievement Oriented conditions when they produced stories to pictures of females but did not increase in response to pictures of males; by contrast, the achievement motivation scores of underachievers increased significantly in response to Achievement Oriented conditions when they produced stories to pictures of males but did not increase in response to pictures of females.

An impressive body of theoretically consistent information has accumulated which describes the operation of achievement motivation in male subjects. Studies of achievement motivation in men have demonstrated increases

* Reprinted from Gerald S. Lesser, Rhoda N. Krawitz, and Rita Packard, "Experimental Arousal of Achievement Motivation in Adolescent Girls," *Journal of Abnormal and Social Psychology,* 66: 59–66, 1963. Copyright 1963 by the American Psychological Association and reproduced by permission.
[1] This study was supported in part by the National Institute of Mental Health, United States Public Health Service, under Research Grant M–3607 to Elizabeth G. French and Gerald S. Lesser.

in achievement motivation scores in response to experimental achievement arousal conditions which stress intelligence and leadership ability and have described significant relationships between achievement motivation and risk taking behavior, conformity, work partner selection, problem solving effectiveness, academic performance, learning, speech behavior, etc. However, the few comparable studies of achievement motivation in female subjects have shown neither consistency with the findings for men nor internal consistency with each other. The general theory of achievement motivation which has evolved to date (Atkinson, 1957, 1958; McClelland, Atkinson, Clark, & Lowell, 1953) confines its empirical supports to research with men and is forced to ignore the dynamics of achievement motivation in women because of the scarcity, ambiguity, and inconclusiveness of the empirical findings. This, of course, has been a formidable restriction on comprehensive theory construction.

One area of confusion in the results on samples of women (e.g., Veroff et al., 1953) is the apparent failure of female subjects to show the expected increase in n Achievement scores when exposed to experimental achievement arousal conditions which stress "intelligence and leadership ability." Almost a decade ago, McClelland et al. (1953) stated:

Women do not show an increase in n Achievement scores as a result of achievement-involving instruction. . . . Why then don't women's scores increase under experimental arousal? This is the puzzler. Two possible explanations—invalidity of the scoring for women, scores too high to go higher—have been eliminated. Apparently the usual arousal instructions simply do not increase achievement striving in women . . ." (p. 178).

Substantially the same unresolved state of affairs remains today. In general, we know very little about the operation of achievement motivation in female subjects, and, specifically, the lack or response to experimental achievement arousal conditions has not been explained. Field (1951) supplied some clarification of the experimental arousal issue by demonstrating that, although manipulating achievement orientation by reference to intelligence and leadership does not increase achievement motivation scores in women, experimental conditions which arouse a concern about social acceptance produce increases in their n Achievement scores.

One research result has been reported in the literature on achievement motivation which suggests that, for certain female samples, the experimental instructions which appeal to intelligence and leadership ability can produce an increase in achievement motivation scores. Angelini (1955), employing a sample of Brazilian college women, found significant increases in n Achievement following experimental instructions which appeal to intelligence and leadership ability, and also found that this increase exceeded the increase produced by experimental conditions which arouse concern about social acceptance. Angelini explains the discrepancy between the results on Brazilian and American college women by indicating that in Brazil, where opportunities for higher education are greatly limited, only highly competitive girls who have placed great stress on intellectual accomplishment will succeed in enrolling in a university. It is reasonable to conclude that the achievement goals of Angelini's sample of Brazilian college women are more career or intellectually oriented than the more socially oriented objectives of the average American female subject.

Thus, it appears possible that the failure to demonstrate increases in achievement motivation in American women in response to experimental conditions stressing intelligence and leadership ability is related to the fact that the female subjects employed were insufficiently concerned with standards of intellectual excellence and with achieving through the development of intellectual skills. There are, of course, certain settings in which great emphasis is placed upon the intellectual accomplishments of girls. One such institution is the Hunter High School for intellectually gifted girls; this is a seventh through twelfth grade demonstration school associated with Hunter College of the City University of New York. Hunter High School sets extremely high expectations and demands for intellectual achievement, provides intense scholastic stimulation, and emphasizes competitive achievement goals which require long-range planning and persistence, including the pursuit of college training.

The presence of a strong intellectual achievement orientation at Hunter High School is reflected in the following facts: (a) admission is highly competitive—only outstanding elementary school students are advised to apply and from this highly selected group of about 4000 candidates, approximately 150 are admitted; (b) more than 99% of Hunter High School girls proceed to college (and, of the remaining few, most choose other forms of advanced training, such as nursing); (c) no high school in New York State receives a higher percentage of State Regents Scholarships; ordinarily, about 75% of Hunter High School's graduating seniors receive this competitive award; (d) although no precise tabulations exist, a very large percentage of graduates win scholastic recognition in college and proceed to professional careers.

Girls attending Hunter High School might, thus, be expected to display a concern for competitive standards of excellence and achievement comparable to the concern of the Brazilian college women in Angelini's (1955) sample, and it was hypothesized that Hunter High School students would display the same increases in achievement motivation scores in response to experimental conditions emphasizing intelligence and leadership ability which were shown by previous samples of men and by Brazilian college women. While no specific direction of results was predicted, it was further expected that academic "achievers" and "underachievers" might respond differently to the experimental achievement arousal conditions and to pictures depicting male or female characters.

METHOD

Subjects

The subjects were 80 juniors and seniors (ranging in age from 15–8 to 18–3 years) at Hunter High School.[2] These girls are primarily from middle-class families.

Because it appeared likely that there would be

[2] The cooperation of the Hunter High School administration is gratefully acknowledged. Cyril W. Woolcock, Mildred A. Busch, Della B. Meehan, Harriet Schueler, and many others contributed much valuable advice and assistance.

differences in response to experimental instructions stressing intelligence and leadership ability between girls who were successfully meeting the academic demands of the school and girls who were not, the 80 students were divided into two equal matched groups of 40 achievers and 40 underachievers. Achievers in the junior class had cumulative scholastic grade averages in the first quartile for the four preceding semesters and in the senior class had first quartile grades for five of six preceding semesters; underachievers in the junior class had cumulative scholastic grade averages in the fourth quartile for the four preceding semesters and in the senior class had fourth quartile grades for five of the six preceding semesters.

Achievers were individually matched with underachievers for IQ score—Terman-McNemar (1941) Test of Mental Ability. The mean IQ score for the 40 achievers was 132.36 ($SD = 6.40$) and for the 40 underachievers was 131.86 ($SD = 7.42$); thus, the groups did not differ significantly in IQ ($t = 0.71$, $p > .05$).

In order to accumulate a sufficient number of matched subjects, the experiment was spread over a 2-year period. In 1958, 20 achievers and 20 underachievers were drawn from the junior and senior classes, and, again in 1960, 40 matched subjects were drawn from the junior and senior grades. All experimental sessions were conducted by the same female experimenter (assisted by another female experimenter) in 1958 and in 1960 under identical classroom conditions.

Experimental Conditions

Each student was exposed to two group experimental sessions separated by one week, the first under Neutral conditions and the second under Achievement Oriented conditions. The Neutral and Achievement Oriented conditions employed in this experiment were identical to those described originally by McClelland et al. (1953, pp. 101–104) and used widely thereafter (e.g., Atkinson & Reitman, 1956; Martire, 1956). In general, the neutral condition is one in which no experimental attempt is made either to arouse achievement motivation or to create an especially relaxed condition; the objective is to elicit the normal motivation level of the subject in an everyday school setting. The achievement oriented condition introduces strong achievement cues in the form of special instructions in order to arouse achievement related motives.

Measure of n Achievement

Content analysis of thematic stories provided the measure of achievement motivation. The group testing procedure which was followed for collecting the stories is described in detail elsewhere (Atkinson, 1958, p. 837; McClelland et al., 1953, pp. 97–99).

Each of the 80 subjects wrote 12 thematic stories, 6 under neutral experimental conditions (3 to pictures in which a male was the central figure and 3 in which a female was the central figure), and 6 different stories under achievement arousal conditions (3 to pictures of males and 3 to pictures of females).

The 12 pictures were selected from those used in previous research on achievement motivation. The 6 pictures depicting females as central figures were derived from the research of Veroff, Atkinson, Feld, and Gurin (1960, pp. 3–4), and the 6 pictures of males are described by McClelland et al. (1953, p. 375). These 12 pictures were divided into the following four sets of 3 pictures each:

Female Set A

Woman (mother) seated by a young girl reclining in chair.

Group of four women, one standing, the others seated facing each other.

Woman kneeling and applying a cover to a chair.

Female Set B

Two women preparing food in a kitchen.

Two women standing by a table in a laboratory; one woman is working with test tubes.

A woman in the foreground with a man standing behind and to the side.

Male Set C

Two men ("inventors") in a shop working at a machine.

Boy in foreground with vague operation scene in background.

Father and son.

Male Set D

Two men, in colonial dress, printing in a shop.

"Lawyer's" office: two men talking in a well-furnished office.

"Cub reporter" scene—older man handing papers to a younger man.

The thematic stories were scored according to the method of content analysis (Scoring System C) also described in detail elsewhere (Atkinson, 1958, pp. 179–204, 685–735; McClelland et al., 1953, pp. 107–138, 335–374). Interjudge scoring reliability (Spearman rank-order correlation coefficient) was .93 for the six-story protocols of 30 subjects.[3]

Design

Both groups of female subjects (achievers and underachievers) were exposed to both experimental conditions. (Neutral and Achievement Oriented) and both types of pictures (those depicting males and those depicting females). For the variable of groups each achieving subject was matched for IQ with an underachieving control. For the variables of experimental conditions and pictures each subject was

[3] We wish to acknowledge the assistance of Arlene Benson (Survey Research Center, University of Michigan) and Shirley Feltman (Hunter College) in scoring test protocols.

Table 1 | MEAN *n* ACHIEVEMENT SCORES OF ACHIEVING AND UNDERACHIEVING GIRLS UNDER NEUTRAL AND ACHIEVEMENT ORIENTED EXPERIMENTAL CONDITIONS TO PICTURES CONTAINING FEMALE AND MALE CHARACTERS

Group	N	Experimental Conditions								Total for all experimental conditions and pictures	
		Neutral				Achievement oriented					
		Three female pictures		Three male pictures		Three female pictures		Three male pictures			
		M	SD	M	SD	M	SD	M	SD	M	SD
Achievers	40	4.80	2.39	5.43	2.61	6.03	2.82	4.78	2.17	5.26	2.56
Underachievers	40	2.93	2.40	4.18	2.82	2.25	2.22	6.20	2.47	3.89	2.91
Total for all subjects	80	3.86	2.58	4.80	2.56	4.14	2.91	5.49	2.44		

used as his own control, being exposed to both experimental sessions and to both male and female pictures. Thus, since there were one between subjects variable (groups) and two within-subjects variables (experimental conditions and pictures), a $2 \times 2 \times 2$ Type VI analysis of variance design described by Lindquist (1956) was employed.

A succession of studies has shown the crucial influence upon the motivational content of stories of the cue strength of the thematic apperception pictures. No fully adequate technique for comparing and equating the relative cue strengths of thematic pictures has as yet been developed. In order to be able to unequivocally attribute any observed increases in achievement motivation scores to the experimental conditions rather than to the differential cue strength of the pictures used under Neutral and Achievement Oriented conditions, the sets of pictures were counterbalanced. Since the total experimental procedure was conducted first in 1958 and then repeated in 1960 with samples of equal

size, the counterbalancing of sets of pictures was used; the data from the two administrations were then pooled in the Type VI analysis of variance design described. The effect of order of presentation for different combination of sets of pictures could not be computed because all possible combinations of order of presentation were not represented; that is, the combinations A-B, C-D and B-A, D-C were used in counterbalancing, but A-B, D-C and B-A, C-D did not appear.

RESULTS

Table 1 presents the mean achievement motivation scores for the eight subgroups. Bartlett's test for homogeneity of variance indicated that analysis of variance was not inappropriate for these data.

Table 2 presents the analysis of variance. This table indicates that the overall effect of the experimental conditions was nonsignificant; thus, the major expectation of this study, that experimental conditions stressing intelligence and leadership ability would produce an increase in achievement motivation scores for this sample of girls, was not confirmed. Also, the experimental conditions were apparently no more effective in producing an increase in the achievement motivation scores of the achievers than of the underachievers (i.e., the interaction between experimental conditions and groups was also nonsignificant). However, the second order interaction effect of Pictures $\times$ Experimental Conditions $\times$ Groups was highly significant ($F = 44.73$, $p < .001$). Thus, the achievement motivation scores of achievers increase significantly in response to Achievement Oriented conditions when they produce stories to pictures of females but do not increase in response to pictures of males; by contrast, the achievement motivation scores of underachievers increase significantly in response to Achievement Oriented conditions when they produce stories to pictures of males but do not increase in response to pictures of females. The other significant results presented in Table 2 indicate that the achievers have higher n Achievement scores than underachievers for all experimental conditions and types of pictures combined ($F = 16.60$, $p < .001$), the pictures depicting males produce higher n

Table 2 | ANALYSIS OF VARIANCE OF n ACHIEVEMENT SCORES OF ACHIEVING AND UNDERACHIEVING GIRLS UNDER NEUTRAL AND ACHIEVEMENT ORIENTED EXPERIMENTAL CONDITIONS TO PICTURES CONTAINING FEMALE AND MALE CHARACTERS

Source	SS	df	MS	F
Between subjects				
Groups (G)	149.88	1	149.88	16.60*
Error (b)	704.72	78	9.03	
Total between	854.60	79		
Within subjects				
Pictures (P)	104.66	1	104.66	15.06*
Experimental conditions (E)	18.53	1	18.53	2.53
P $\times$ E	3.40	1	3.40	1.45
P $\times$ G	169.65	1	169.65	24.41*
E $\times$ G	3.00	1	3.00	0.41
P $\times$ E $\times$ G	104.66	1	104.66	44.73*
Error$_1$ (w)	542.44	78	6.95	
Error$_2$ (w)	571.22	78	7.32	
Error$_3$ (w)	182.19	78	2.34	
Error$_T$ (w)	1295.85	234	5.54	
Total within	1699.75	240		
Total	2554.35	319		

* $p. < .001$.

Achievement scores than pictures depicting females for all groups and experimental conditions combined ($F = 15.06$, $p < .001$); however, this difference is attributable to the scores of underachievers and not of achievers, since for both experimental conditions combined, achievers produce higher n Achievement scores to female pictures than to male pictures while underachievers produce higher n Achievement scores to male pictures than to female pictures ($F = 24.41$, $p < .001$).

Numerous studies (e.g., Veroff et al., 1960) have demonstrated the importance of controlling for individual differences in verbal fluency in computing scores derived from thematic content. However, the correlation coefficient obtained in the present study between n Achievement scores and number of words in the story protocols ranged from $-.01$ to $-.10$. These negligible coefficients may have resulted from the fact that word fluency showed little variability; all of the subjects in this experiment showed great verbal fluency and very few brief protocols were obtained. This finding is consistent with earlier reports in which negligible correlation coefficients were found between n Achievement scores and length of protocol when the sample was homogeneous and structuring questions were used in the test administration. Since the correlation coefficients in the present study were so small (accounting for no more than 1% of the shared variance between n Achievement scores and length of protocol), no attempt was made to correct for individual differences in verbal fluency.

DISCUSSION

Contrary to expectation, the experimental introduction of Achievement Orientation conditions did not produce an overall increase in achievement motivation scores for this sample of girls. However, a highly significant second order interaction effect emerged: achieving girls did display the expected increase in achievement motivation scores under achievement orienting conditions, but only when responding to stimuli depicting females; underachieving girls also displayed the expected increase in achievement motivation scores under achievement orienting conditions, but only when responding to stimuli depicting males.

A suggested interpretation is that the achieving girls perceive intellectual achievement goals as a relevant part of their own female role; in contrast, the underachieving girls perceive intellectual achievement goals as more relevant to the male role than to their own female role. Since the achievers and underachievers have equivalent intellectual capabilities, the discrepancy between them in their perception of the strivings and behaviors relevant to female and male roles may also represent a reasonable explanation for their differential academic performance. These interpretations are consistent with growing evidence that the production of thematic material is strongly influenced by the subject's conception of what behaviors are appropriate to the hero's social roles.

The application of such a social role model to the finding that achieving girls respond to experimental arousal conditions with increased achievement imagery when reacting to female figures but not when reacting to male figures is relatively direct. The achievement strivings of these girls are aroused by the experimental instructions stressing intelligence and leadership, and this increase in achievement motivation is expressed imaginally in response to the female figures since these female characters and their activities are most directly related to the girls' own strivings.

The concept of achievement motivation as a generalized pattern of strivings must be added to the social role interpretation when it is applied to the finding that the underachieving girls respond to experimental arousal conditions with increased achievement imagery only to male figures. If achievement motivation in this sample of underachieving girls is composed of generalized strivings to excel, then these generalized achievement strivings, when aroused, will be expressed imaginally by assigning increased achievement directed activity to the male figures for whom achievement behaviors are considered more appropriate. Thus, this social role interpretation suggests that when the achievement imagery of underachieving subjects is engaged by experimental instructions stressing intelligence and leadership, the increased generalized achievement imagery is attached to the figures whom the underachievers perceive to be the usual and proper agents for action directed toward achievement.

Margaret Mead (1949) has observed that

the adolescent girl in our society begins to realize that her attempts to achieve place her in competition with men and elicit negative reactions from them; our society, thus, defines out of the female role ideas and strivings for intellectual achievement. The results of the present research suggest that these social conditions have different impacts upon different girls. It appears that the girl who retains a perception of the female role as including intellectual achievement goals succeeds intellectually under conditions of strong academic competition with other girls; by comparison, the girl who accepts the social prescription that intellectual achievement striving are relevant to the male role and not the female role does not succeed as well in intellectual competition with other girls.

Other results of the present study are consistent with a social role interpretation and may help to explain previously reported findings on samples of women. Veroff et al. (1953) report that female high school students produce greater n Achievement scores to pictures of men than to pictures of women, while Angelini (1955) reports higher scores for Brazilian college women responding to pictures of females than for Brazilian college men responding to pictures of men. In the present study, the pictures of men elicited more achievement imagery than pictures of women only for the underachievers and not for the achievers. Table 1 shows that for the underachievers, the mean n Achievement score to pictures of men significantly exceeds the mean score to pictures of women under both Neutral and Achievement Orientation conditions. However, for the achievers, the mean *n* Achievement score to pictures of men was significantly lower than the mean score to pictures of women under Achievement Orientation conditions, and under Neutral conditions the mean scores to pictures of men and women were not significantly different.[4]

However, no matter what theoretical *model*

is applied, it is apparent that attempts to clarify the impact of experimental achievement arousal conditions upon female subjects must consider the interaction among the nature of the experimental conditions, the characteristics of the stimuli used to elicit thematic material, and the relative accomplishment of the subjects in achievement performance.

One further comparison should be noted between the present results and the findings of earlier research. While a recent study by Pierce and Bowman (1960) on a sample of gifted high school girls reports the absence of a significant relationship between achievement motivation scores and academic performance (when only pictures of men were used in assessing achievement motivation of the female subjects), studies relating academic performance to achievement motivation in samples of men have reported either strong relationships (e.g., McClelland et al., 1953; Pierce & Bowman, 1960); or at least moderate relationships.

The present study obtained a highly significant difference between achieving and underachieving girls in their achievement motivation scores, even with IQ controlled through the matching of subjects. The significant interaction of Pictures × Groups reported in Table 2 indicates that the difference in achievement motivation scores between achievers and underachievers occurred in response to pictures of females but did not occur in response to pictures of males. Thus, the discrepancy between the positive findings of this study and the negative results of Pierce and Bowman in relating achievement motivation to academic performance in girls may be explained by the absence in the latter study of stimuli which allow the relationship to be displayed. Despite the present evidence, Atkinson's (1958, p. 605) caution is still appropriate: that no simple explanation of the complex behaviors referred to by the variable of academic achievement can be expected through the consideration of the strength of any single motive alone.

---

[4] In the absence of additional empirical evidence on the operation and achievement motivation in women, the social role explanation is not more fully developed here. However, this theoretical approach is being expanded in a study of the characteristic of achievement motivation in college women conducted currently by Elizabeth G. French and the senior author of this paper.

REFERENCES

Angelini, A. L. Um nove metodo para avaliar a motivacal human! (A new method of evaluating human motivation) *Bol. Fac. Filos. Cienc. S. Paulo.*, 1955, No. 207.

Atkinson, J. W. Motivational determinants of risk-taking behavior. *Psychol Rev.*, 1957, **64**, 359–372.

Atkinson, J. W. (Ed.) *Motives in fantasy, action, and society.* Princeton: Van Nostrand, 1958.

Atkinson, J. W., & Reitman, W. R. Performance as a function of motive strength and expectancy of goal attainment. *J. abnorm. soc. Psychol.*, 1956, **53**, 361–366.

Field, W. F. The affects of thematic apperception upon certain experimentally aroused needs. Unpublished doctoral dissertation, University of Maryland, 1951.

Lindquist, E. F. *Design and analysis of experiments in psychology and education.* Boston: Houghton Mifflin, 1956.

Martire, J. G. Relationships between self-concept and differences in the strength and generality of achievement motivation. *J. Pers.*, 1956, **24**, 364–375.

McClelland, D. C., Atkinson, J. W., Clark, R. A. & Lowell, E. L. *The achievement motive.* New York: Appleton-Century-Crofts, 1953.

Mead, Margaret. *Male and female.* New York: Morrow, 1949.

Pierce, J. V., & Bowman, P. H. Motivation patterns of superior high school students. *Coop. res. Mongr.*, 1962, No. 2, 33–66. (USDHEW Publ. No. OE–35016)

Veroff, J., Wilcox, Sue, & Atkinson, J. W. The achievement motive in high school and college age women. *J. abnorm. soc. Psychol.*, 1953, **48**, 108–119.

Veroff, J., Atkinson, J. W., Feld, S. C., & Gurin, G. The use of thematic apperception to assess motivation in a nationwide interview study. *Psychol. Monogr.*, 1960, **74** (12, Whole No. 499).

4

Surprisingly enough, the study of emotion has traditionally been relegated to a position secondary to that of motivation. However, it is at times quite difficult to differentiate emotion and motivation. As a result, we have recently begun to view emotions as special types of motives. The previous dearth of information and interest in the scientific study of emotions has stemmed in part from the difficulty inherent in investigating such a highly subjective phenomenon under controlled laboratory conditions. In addition, emotions have often been thought of as having a disorganizing effect on behavior. As a result, emotions have been primarily the concern of clinical psychologists who are typically more interested in the modification of a specific person's disorganized behavior, rather than in a scientific study of emotion per se.

BIOLOGICAL FACTORS

Fortunately, in the last few years there has been an increased interest in understanding the physiological mechanisms underlying specific emotional states. The work of Dr. Daniel H. Funkenstein, and his associates (Selection 18), has not only served to further our basic knowledge but promises to provide a new approach to the study of mental illness. On the basis of an extensive and diverse experimental program, Dr. Funkenstein presents evidence to indicate that under stress lower animals, normal human beings, and psychotics behave in one of three ways. They direct their anger outward, or they direct it inward and become depressed, or they become anxious. His measures of the relative amounts of adrenalin and noradrenalin in the three cases support the generalization that *the outward expression of anger is related to secretion of noradrenaline while anger-in and anxiety are associated with the secretion of adrenalin.*

PSYCHOLOGICAL FACTORS

Although noradrenalin and adrenalin seem to be associated with different emotions, it would appear that both the emotional experience and the behavior associated with injections of epinepherine (adrenalin) also depend upon the cognitive interpretations of the situation which are made by the subject. Schachter and Singer[1] suggest

. . . that emotional states may be considered a function of a state of physiological arousal and of a cognition appropriate to this state of arousal. From this follows these propositions:
1. Given a state of physiological arousal for which an individual has no immediate explanation, he will label this state and describe his feeling in terms of the cognitions available to him. To the extent that cognitive factors are potent determiners of emotional states, it should be anticipated that precisely the same state of physiological arousal could be labeled "joy" or "fury" or "jealousy" or any of a great diversity of emotional labels depending on the cognitive aspects of the situation.
2. Given a state of physiological arousal for which an individual has a completely appropriate explanation, no evaluative needs will arise and the individual is unlikely to label his feelings in terms of the alternative cognitions available.
3. Given the same cognitive circumstances, the individual will react emotionally or describe

---
[1] S. Schachter and J. F. Singer, "Cognitive, Social, and Physiological Determinants of Emotional State," *Psychological Review,* **69:** 379–399, 1962.

his feelings as emotions only to the extent that he experiences a state of physiological arousal.

Schachter and Singer report an experiment in which, just prior to the injection of epinepherine, subjects were either informed, misinformed, or uninformed about the bodily experiences which they would have following the injection. They were then placed into a room with a trained stooge who reacted either euphorically or angrily. Under these conditions the misinformed and the ignorant subjects tended to feel the suggested emotional state and to behave in accordance with that state to a greater extent than the informed subjects. For example, the misinformed subjects behave and feel somewhat more euphoric than the ignorant subjects, who in turn behave and feel somewhat more euphoric than the informed subjects. These results support propositions 1 and 2.

In Selection 19 Schachter and Wheeler provide a direct test of proposition 3, and the results tend to support its validity. Appended to the end of the Schachter and Wheeler article is the final portion of the discussion section from Schachter and Singer in which the overall implications of the several experiments are considered.

It has been a common assumption of behavioristic psychology that complex social motives and emotions are conditioned to previously neutral stimuli by being associated with a reduction in an appetitional drive such as hunger or with increases in a noxious drive such as pain. In a similar vein, Freud's phsychoanalytic interpretation of the development of love assumed that a child's love for its mother was dependent on its receiving food in her presence and satisfying an innate need for sucking. In his article on "The Nature of Love" (Selection 20), Dr. Harry Harlow has made two major contributions. The first is in terms of method; he has perfected laboratory techniques for investigating the development of the affectional bonds between a child and its mother. The second is a substantive contribution; he has shown that love is much more dependent on the satisfaction of the need for physical body contact than it is on the satisfaction of the hunger drive or the need for oral gratification.

SOCIOCULTURAL FACTORS

In the process of socializing or training, our culture not only teaches the individual new ways to behave but also teaches him to delay or to inhibit his emotions. It is, of course, necessary for the welfare of the group that the individual learn to avoid the unbridled expression of such emotions as anger or the indiscriminate gratification of the sex drive. However, the inhibition of expression and gratification is often overlearned. As a result, the individual often is left with a feeling of emptiness. He becomes aware of a lack of meaningfulness in his life. He often reacts to this condition of "emotional poverty" by seeking excessive gratification from external sources. In Selection 21 Leeper and Madison note that among other things excessive dependence on material comforts, on sexual gratification, and on other people are symptoms of this emotional deprivation. This tendency to throw oneself into excessive living when there is strong emotional insecurity is reminiscent of the sensuous orgies held by the Romans during the decadent period of the Empire. Leeper and Madison examine some of the facets of our own culture which tend to create an inability to satisfy emotional needs. Two cultural factors which operate all too often among college students are conformity pressures and the desire to obtain symbols of knowledge, such as grades, rather than knowledge itself. Leeper and Madison refer to this later tendency as "blue-ribbon motivation."[2]

2 The student should also refer to Dr. Karen Horney's article on cultural factors in neurosis, Selection 66, to see how the tendency toward emotional poverty associated with blue-ribbon motivation may be related to the cultural emphasis on competition.

Selection **18** | THE PHYSIOLOGY
OF FEAR AND
ANGER*

DANIEL H. FUNKENSTEIN
*Boston Psychopathic
Hospital*

When the late Walter B. Cannon, by his historic experiments nearly half a century ago, showed a connection between emotions and certain physiological changes in the body, he opened a new frontier for psychology and medicine. His work, coupled with that of Sigmund Freud, led to psychosomatic medicine. It also made the emotions accessible to laboratory measurement and analysis. Within the last few years there has been a keen revival of interest in this research, because of some important new discoveries which have sharpened our understanding of specific emotions and their bodily expressions. It has been learned, for instance, that anger and fear produce different physiological reactions and can be distinguished from each other. The findings have given us a fresh outlook from which to study mental illnesses.

The best way to begin the account of this recent work is to start with Cannon's own summary of what he learned. Cannon found that when an animal was confronted with a situation which evoked pain, rage or fear, it responded with a set of physiological reactions which prepared it to meet the threat with "fight" or "flight." These reactions, said Cannon, were mobilized by the secretion of adrenalin: when the cortex of the brain perceived the threat, it sent a stimulus down the sympathetic branch of the autonomic nervous system to the adrenal glands and they secreted the hormone. Cannon graphically described the results as follows:

"Respiration deepens; the heart beats more rapidly; the arterial pressure rises; the blood is shifted away from the stomach and intestines to the heart and central nervous system and the muscles; the processes in the alimentary canal ease; sugar is freed from the reserves in the liver; the spleen contracts and discharges its content of concentrated corpuscles, and adrenin is secreted from the adrenal medulla. The key to these marvelous transformations in the body is found in relating them to the natural accompaniments of fear and rage—running away in order to escape from danger, and attacking in order to be dominant. Whichever the action, a life-or-death struggle may ensue.

"The emotional responses just listed may reasonably be regarded as preparatory for struggle. They are adjustments which, so far as possible, put the organism in readiness for meeting the demands which will be made upon it. The secreted adrenin cooperates with sympathetic nerve impulses in calling forth stored glycogen from the liver, thus flooding the blood with sugar for the use of laboring muscles; it helps in distributing the blood in abundance to the heart, the brain, and the limbs (*i.e.*, to the parts essential for intense physical effort) while taking it away from the inhibited organs in the abdomen; it quickly abolishes the effects of muscular fatigue so that the organism which can muster adrenin in the blood can restore to its tired muscles the same readiness to act which they had when fresh; and it renders the blood more rapidly coagulable. The increased respiration, the redistributed blood running at high pressure, and the more numerous red corpuscles set free from the spleen provide for essential oxygen and for riddance of acid waste, and make a setting for instantaneous and supreme action. In short, all these changes are directly serviceable in rendering the organism more effective in the violent display of energy which fear or rage may involve."

Cannon recognized that among all these physiological changes there were a few which could not be ascribed directly to the action of adrenalin. He therefore postulated that the hormone was supplemented by two additional substances from the sympathetic nerves. An active agent, distinguishable from adrenalin, was eventually identified in 1948, when B. F. Tullar and M. L. Tainter at length succeeded in preparing the optically active form of the substance. It proved to be a second hormone secreted by the adrenal medulla. Called nor-adrenalin, it differs markedly from adrenalin in its physiological effects. Whereas adrenalin elicits profound physiological changes in almost every system in the body, nor-adrenalin

* Daniel H. Funkenstein, "The Physiology of Fear and Anger," *Scientific American*, **192**:74–80, 1955. Reprinted with permission.

apparently has only one important primary effect: namely, it stimulates the contraction of small blood vessels and increases the resistance to the flow of blood.

An animal exhibits only two major emotions in response to a threatening situation: namely, rage and fear. A man, however, may experience three: anger directed outward (the counterpart of rage), anger directed toward himself (depression) and anxiety, or fear. In studies of physiological changes accompanying various emotional states among patients at the New York Hospital, H. G. Wolff and his co-workers noticed that anger produced effects quite different from those of depression or fear. For example, when a subject was angry, the stomach lining became red and there was an increase in its rhythmic contractions and in the secretion of hydrochloric acid. When the same subject was depressed or frightened, the stomach lining was pale in color and there was a decrease in peristalic movements and in the hydrochloric acid secretion.

The experiments of Wolff, the evidence that the adrenal medulla secreted two substances rather than one and certain clinical observations led our group at the Harvard Medical School to investigate whether adrenaline and nor-adrenaline might be specific indicators which distinguished one emotion from another. The clinical observations had to do with the effects of a drug, mecholyl, on psychotic patients. We had been studying their blood-pressure responses to injections of adrenalin, which acts on the sympathetic nervous system, and mecholyl, which stimulates the parasympathetic system. On the basis of their blood-pressure reactions, psychotic patients could be classified into seven groups. This test had proved of value in predicting patients' responses to psychiatric treatments, such as electric shock and insulin: certain groups responded better to the treatments than others. But more interesting was the fact that psychotic patients with high blood pressure reacted to the injection of mecholyl in two distinctly different ways. In one group there was only a small drop in the blood pressure after the injection, and the pressure returned to the usually high level within three to eight minutes. In the other group the blood pressure dropped markedly after the injection and remained below the preinjection level even after

25 minutes. Not only were the physiological reactions quite different, but the two groups of patients also differed in personality and in response to treatment. Thirty-nine of 42 patients whose blood pressure was sharply lowered by mecholyl improved with electric shock treatment, whereas only three of the 21 in the other group improved with the same treatment. Further, the two groups showed distinctly different results in projective psychological tests such as the Rorschach.

All this suggested that the two groups of patients might be differentiated on the basis of emotions. Most psychotic patients in emotional turmoil express the same emotion constantly over a period of days, weeks or months. Psychiatrists determined the predominant emotion expressed by each of 63 patients who had been tested with mecholyl, without knowing in which physiological group they had been classified. When the subjects' emotional and physiological ratings were compared, it turned out that almost all of the patients who were generally angry at other people fell in Group N (a small, temporary reduction of blood pressure by mecholyl), while almost all those who were usually depressed or frightened were in Group E (sharp response to mecholyl). In other words, the physiological reactions were significantly related to the emotional content of the patients' psychoses.

The next step was to find out whether the same test could distinguish emotions in normal, healthy people, using medical students as subjects. They were studied at a time when they were under stress—while they were awaiting the decisions of hospitals on their applications for internships. As the competition among the students for the hospitals of their choice is keen, the period just prior to such announcements is a time of emotional turmoil for the men. A group of students who responded to this situation with elevated blood pressure was given the standard dose of mecholyl. The results were the same as for the psychotic patients: students who were angry at others for the situation in which they found themselves had a Type N physiological reaction; those who felt depressed (angry at themselves) or anxious showed a Type E physiological reaction. The reaction was related only to their temporary emotional state; after the internships were settled and their blood pressures had returned to pre-stress levels, all the students reacted the same way to the injection of mecholyl.

It was at this point that we undertook to investigate the comparative effects of adrenalin and nor-adrenalin. A group of workers at the Presbyterian Hospital in New York had shown that injections of nor-adrenalin and adrenalin produced two different types of rise in blood pressure, one due to contraction of blood vessels and the other to faster pumping by the heart. Upon learning of this work, we designed experiments to test the hypothesis that the two types of elevated blood pressure differentiated by us on the basis of mecholyl tests, indicated in one instance excessive secretion of nor-adrenalin and in the other excessive secretion of adrenalin. Healthy college students were first given a series of intravenous injections of salt water to accustom them to the procedure so that it would not disturb them. Then each subject was tested in the following way. He was given an injection of nor-adrenalin sufficient to raise his blood pressure by 25 per cent. Then, while his blood pressure was elevated, he received the standard dose of mecholyl, and its effects on the blood pressure were noted. The next day the subject was put through the same procedure except that adrenalin was given instead of nor-adrenalin to raise the blood pressure.

Ten students were studied in this way, and in every instance the effect of nor-adrenalin was different from that of adrenalin. When the blood pressure was elevated by nor-adrenalin, mecholyl produced only a small drop in pressure, with a return to the previous level in seven to 10 minutes. This reaction was similar to the Type N response in psychotic patients and healthy students under stress. In contrast, when the blood pressure was elevated by adrenalin, mecholyl produced the Type E response: the pressure dropped markedly and did not return to the previous level during the 25-minute observation period.

These results suggested, in the light of the earlier experiments, that anger directed outward was associated with secretion of nor-

adrenalin, while depression and anxiety were associated with secretion of adrenalin. To check this hypothesis, another series of experiments was carried out.

A group of 125 college students were subjected to stress-inducing situations in the laboratory. The situations, involving frustration, were contrived to bring out each student's habitual reaction to stresses in real life; that the reactions actually were characteristic of the subjects' usual responses was confirmed by interviews with their college roommates. While the subjects were under stress, observers recorded their emotional reactions and certain physiological changes—in the blood pressure, the pulse and the so-called IJ waves stemming from the action of the heart. This test showed that students who responded to the stress of anger directed outward had physiological reactions similar to those produced by injection of nor-adrenalin, while students who responded with depression or anxiety had physiological reactions like those to adrenalin.

There remained the question: Does the same individual secrete unusual amounts of nor-adrenalin when angry and of adrenalin when frightened? Albert F. Ax, working in another laboratory in our hospital, designed experiments to study this question. He contrived laboratory stressful situations which were successful in producing on one occasion anger and on another occasion fear in the same subjects. His results showed that when a subject was angry at others, the physiological reactions were like those induced by the injection of nor-adrenalin; when the same subject was frightened, the reactions were like those to adrenalin. This indicated that the physiology was specific for the emotion rather than for the person.

In all these experiments the evidence for excessive secretion of nor-adrenalin and adrenalin was based on the physiological changes being similar to those which can be produced by the intravenous injection of nor-adrenalin and adrenalin. Since the substances involved have not been identified chemically, and the evidence is entirely physiological, at the present time we prefer to limit ourselves to the statement that the reactions are *like* those to the two hormones. However, nothing in our experiments would contradict the hypothesis that these substances are actually adrenalin and nor-adrenalin.

What is the neurophysiological mechanism whereby different emotions evoke different adrenal secretions? Although no conclusive work in this area is yet available, some recent investigations suggest a possible answer. U. S. von Euler in Sweden found that stimulation of certain areas of the hypothalamus caused the adrenal gland to secrete nor-adrenalin, whereas stimulation of other areas caused it to secrete adrenalin. These areas may correspond to those which the Nobel prize winner W. R. Hess of Zurich stimulated to produce aggressive behavior and flight, respectively, in animals. The experiments suggest that anger and fear may activate different areas in the hypothalamus, leading to production of nor-adrenalin in the first case and adrenalin in the second. Until more experiments are made, these possibilities must remain suppositions.

Some of the most intriguing work in this field was recently reported by von Euler. He compared adrenal secretions found in a number of different animals. The research material was supplied by a friend who flew to Africa to obtain the adrenal medullae of wild animals. Interpreting his findings, J. Ruesch pointed out that aggressive animals such as the lion had a relatively high amount of nor-adrenalin, while in animals such as the rabbit, which depend for survival primarily on flight, adrenalin predominated. Domestic animals, and wild animals that live very social lives (e.g., the baboon), also have a high ratio of adrenalin to nor-adrenalin.

These provocative findings suggest the theory that man is born with the capacity to react with a variety of emotions (has within him the lion and the rabbit), and that his early childhood experiences largely determine in which of these ways he will react under stress. Stated in another way, the evolutional process of man's emotional development is completed in the bosom of the family. We have found in other studies that individuals' habitual emotional reactions have a high correlation with their perceptions of psychological factors in their families.

This entire series of experiments yielded data which can be understood in the frame of reference of psychoanalytical observations. According to theory, anger directed outward is more characteristic of an earlier stage of childhood than is anger directed toward the self or anxiety (conflicts over hostility). The latter two emotions are the result of the acculturation of the child. If the physiological development of the child parallels its psychological development, then we should expect to find that the ratio of nor-adrenalin to adrenalin is higher in infants than in older children. Bernt Hokfelt and G. B. West established that this is indeed the case: at an early age the adrenal medulla has more nor-adrenalin, but later adrenalin becomes dominant.

Paranoid patients show a greater degree of regression to infantile behavior than do patients with depression or anxiety neurosis. And it will be recalled that in our test paranoid patients showed signs of excessive secretion of nor-adrenalin, while depressed and anxious patients exhibited symptoms of adrenalin secretion.

These parallels between psychological and physiological development suggest further studies and some theories for testing. Standing on the shoulders of Cannon and Freud, we have extended our view of human behavior and discovered fertile new fields for exploration.

Selection **19** | EPINEPHRINE, CHLORPROMAZINE, AND AMUSEMENT*

STANLEY SCHACHTER
Columbia University

LADD WHEELER
University of Minnesota

In their study of cognitive and physiological determinants of emotional states, Schachter and Singer (1962) have demonstrated that cognitive processes play a major role in the development of emotional states. Given a common state of physiological arousal, subjects can be readily induced into states of euphoria or of anger by means of cognitive manipula-

* Abridged from Stanley Schachter and Ladd Wheeler, "Epinephrine, Chlorpromazine and Amusement," *Journal of Abnormal and Social Psychology*, **65**: 121—128, 1962. Copyright 1962 by the American Psychological Association and reproduced by permission.

tions. To what extent the state of physiological arousal is a necessary component of an emotional experience is not, however, completely clear in that study.

The technique employed by Schachter and Singer (1962) to produce a state of physiological arousal was simply the injection of the sympathomimetic amine, epinephrine. With slight exceptions, this agent provokes a pattern of physiological activation which is a virtual replica of the state produced by active discharge of the sympathetic nervous system. In experimental situations designed to make subjects euphoric, those subjects who received injections of epinephrine were, on a variety of indices, somewhat more euphoric than subjects who received placebo injection. Similarly, in situations designed to make subjects angry, and irritated, those who received ephinephrine were somewhat angrier than subjects who received placebo. In both sets of conditions, however, these differences between epinephrine and placebo subjects were significant, at best, at borderline levels of statistical significance.

Assuming, for the moment, that physiological arousal is a necessary component of emotional states, one of the factors that might account for this failure to find larger differences between epinephrine and placebo subjects seems reasonably apparent. The experimental situations employed were fairly effective. The injection of placebo does not, of course, prevent the subject from self-arousal of the sympathetic system, and indeed there is considerable evidence (Woodworth & Schlosberg, 1958) that the arousal of an emotional state is accompanied by general excitation of the sympathetic nervous system.

A test of the proposition at stake, then, would require comparison of subjects who have received injections of epinephrine with subjects who, to some extent, are rendered incapable of self-activation of the sympathetic nervous system. Thanks to a class of drugs known generally as autonomic blocking agents, such blockade is, to some degree, possible. If the proposition that a state of sympathetic discharge is a necessary component of an emotional experience is correct, it should be anticipated that whatever emotional state is experimentally manipulated, it should be most intensely experienced by subjects who have received epinephrine, next by placebo subjects, and least of all by subjects who have received injections of an autonomic blocking agent.

Procedure

In order to conceal the purposes of the study and the nature of the injection, the experiment was cast in the framework of a study of the effects of vitamins on vision. As soon as the subject arrived, he was taken to a private room and told by the experimenter:

> I've asked you to come today to take part in an experiment concerning the effects of vitamins on the visual processes. We know a great deal about vision, but only night vision has been studied in relation to nutrition. Our experiment is concerned with the effects of suproxin on vision. Suproxin is a high concentrate vitamin C derivative. If you agree to take part in the experiment, we will give you an injection of suproxin and then subject your retina to about 15 minutes of continuous black and white stimulation. This is simpler than it sounds; we'll just have you watch a black and white movie. After the movie, we'll give you a series of visual tests.
>
> The injection itself is harmless and will be administered by our staff doctor. It may sting a little at first, as most injections do, but after this you will feel nothing and will have no side effects. We know that some people dislike getting injections, and if you take part in the experiment, we want it to be your own decision. Would you like to? [All subjects agreed to take part.]

This much said, the experimenter gave the subject a test of visual acuity and color vision, took the subject's pulse and left the room. Shortly thereafter, the doctor arrived, gave the subject a quick ophthalmoscopic examination, then gave him an injection and informed him that the experimenter would be back for him shortly "in order to take you and some other subjects who have also received shots of suproxin into the projection room."

Injections

There were three forms of suproxin administered —epinephrine, placebo, and chlorpromazine.

1. Epinephrine: Subjects in this condition received a subcutaneous injection of ½ cubic centi-

meter of a 1:1000 solution of Winthrop Laboratory's Suprarenin.

2. Placebo: Subjects in this condition received a subcutaneous injection of ½ cubic centimeter of saline solution.

3. Chlorpromazine: Subjects in this condition received an intramuscular injection of a solution consisting of 1 cubic centimeter (25 milligrams) of Smith, Kline, and French Thorazine and 1 cubic centimeter of saline solution.

The choice of chlorpromazine as a blocking agent was dictated by considerations of safety, ease of administration, and known duration of effect. Ideally, one would have wished for a blocking agent whose mechanism and effect was precisely and solely the reverse of that of epinephrine—a peripherally acting agent which would prevent the excitation of sympathetically innervated structures. Though it is certainly possible to approach this ideal more closely with agents other than chlorpromazine, such drugs tend to be dangerous, or difficult to administer, or of short duration.

Chlorpromazine is known to act as a sympathetic depressant. It has a moderate hypotensive effect, with a slight compensatory increase in heart rate. It has mild adrenergic blocking activity for it reverses the pressor effects of small doses of epinephrine and depresses responses of the nictitating membrane to preganglionic stimulation. Killam (1959) summarizes what is known and supposed about the mechanism of action of chlorpromazine as follows:

> Autonomic effects in general may be attributed to a mild peripheral adrenergic blocking activity and probably to central depression of sympathetic centers, possibly in the hypothalamus (p. 27).

Popularly, of course, the compound is known as a "tranquilizer."

It is known that chlorpromazine has effects other than the sympatholytic effect of interest to us. For purposes of experimental purity this is unfortunate but inevitable in this sort of research. It is clear, however, that the three conditions do differ in the degree of manipulated sympathetic activation.

Subjects

Subjects were male college students taking classes in introductory psychology at the University of Minnesota. Some 90% of the students in these classes

volunteer for a subject pool, for they receive two extra points on their final exam for every hour that they serve as experimental subjects. The records of all potential subjects were cleared with the Student Health Service in order to insure that no harmful effects would result from injections of either epinephrine or chlorpromazine.

Each experimental group was made up of three subjects—one from each of the injection conditions. Their appointments were staggered slightly so as to insure sufficient time for the particular drug to be absorbed. Thus, the chlorpromazine subject received his injection about 15 minutes before the movie began. Pretests had revealed that, with this dosage and mode of administration, about this time interval was required for the onset of sympathetic effects. Placebo subjects were injected 5–10 minutes before onset of the movie. Epinephrine subjects were injected immediately before the movie so that at most 3–4 minutes went by between the time they were injected and the beginning of the film. Pretests had shown that the effects of epinephrine began within 3–5 minutes of injection. It was, of course, basic to the experimental design that these effects begin only after the movie had started.

Film

Rather than the more complicated devices employed in the Schachter and Singer (1962) experiment, an emotion inducing film was used as a means of manipulating the cognitive component of emotional states. In deciding on the type of film, two extremes seemed possible—a horror, fright, or anxiety provoking film or a comic, amusement provoking film. Since it is a common stereotype that adrenalin makes one nervous and that the tranquilizer, chlorpromazine, makes one tranquil and mildly euphoric, the predicted pattern of results with a horror film would be subject to alternative interpretation. It was deliberately decided, then, to use a comedy. If our hypothesis is correct, it should be anticipated that epinephrine subjects would find the film somewhat funnier than placebo subjects who, in turn, would be more amused than chlorpromazine subjects.

The film chosen was a 14-minute 40-second excerpt from a Jack Carson movie called *The Good Humor Man.* This excerpt is a self-contained, comprehensible episode involving a slapstick chase scene.

The projection room was deliberately arranged

so that the subjects could neither see nor hear one another. Facing the screen were three theatre-type seats separated from one another by large, heavy partitions. In a further attempt to maintain the independence of the subjects, the sound volume of the projector was turned up so as to mask any sounds made by the subjects.

Measurement

Observation During the showing of the movie an observer, who had been introduced as an assistant who would help administer the visual tests, systematically scanned the subjects and recorded their reactions to the film. He observed each subject once every 10 seconds, so that over the course of the film 88 units of each subject's behavior were categorized. The observer simply recorded each subject's reaction to the film according to the following scheme.

1. Neutral: Straight-faced watching the film with no indication of amusement.
2. Smile.
3. Grin. A smile with teeth showing.
4. Laugh: A smile or grin accompanied by bodily movements usually associated with laughter, e.g., shaking shoulders, moving head, etc.
5. Big laugh: Belly laugh—a laugh accompanied by violent body movement such as doubling up, throwing up hands, etc.

In a minute by minute comparison, two independent observers agreed in their categorization of 90% of the 528 units recorded in six different reliability trials. Lumping Categories 2 through 5 together, the two observers agreed on 93% of the units jointly recorded.

The observer, of course, never knew which subject had received which injection.

Evaluation of the film The moment the movie ended the lights were turned on and the experimenter proceeded:

> Before beginning the visual tests, we want your eyes to recover somewhat from the constant stimulation they've just received. The rate of neuro-limnal recovery under conditions of perfectly normal lighting and coloring is of major interest to us. The recovery will have begun in about 12 minutes, and after that time, Dr. Mena will give you the more precise visual examination.
>
> In the meantime, I'd like to ask your help. As I told you, we need about 15 minutes of retinal stimulation, for which purpose we use a movie. Obviously, it doesn't matter at all to us which movie we use, so long as it is black and white. We can use one movie just as easily as another, but we do want to use a film that you like. I'm sure that you can see the necessity of using a film which our subjects will like. Of course, the only way to find out if you like it is to ask you. We're just beginning this experiment and will have many more subjects like you. Since you are one of the first groups, it will be a big help if you will give us your personal reactions to the film. If you like it, we'll keep it and if you don't like it, we can just as easily get another. If you'll use these mimeographed questionnaires, it will make it easier for us.

The experimenter then handed out a questionnaire whose chief items, for present purposes, were as shown below:

The figures in brackets represent the values used in computing the means presented in later tables.

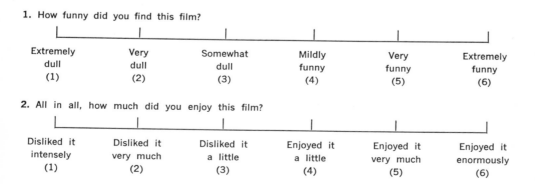

1. How funny did you find this film?

| Extremely dull (1) | Very dull (2) | Somewhat dull (3) | Mildly funny (4) | Very funny (5) | Extremely funny (6) |

2. All in all, how much did you enjoy this film?

| Disliked it intensely (1) | Disliked it very much (2) | Disliked it a little (3) | Enjoyed it a little (4) | Enjoyed it very much (5) | Enjoyed it enormously (6) |

3. Would you recommend that we should show this particular film to our future subjects?

(3) ——— Strongly recommend keeping this film.
(2) ——— moderately recommend keeping this film.
(1) ——— recommend you get another film.

Physical condition In order to check on whether or not the drugs were having the desired effect on the subject's internal state, after the subjects had evaluated the film, the experimenter continued with the following spiel:

> Before we begin the eye tests, we need a bit more information about you. Earlier studies on the visual processes have shown that a person's physical and emotional states influence the visual process. Because of this it is necessary to know how you feel physically and emotionally at this time. We know, for example, that certain states such as hunger, or fatigue, or boredom, do have a noticeable effect on these processes. Naturally, we have to know these things about you in order to interpret the results we will obtain from each of you, and the only way we can find out such things is to ask you.

A bit more on this line and the experimenter then handed round a questionnaire whose chief items were the following:

A. For evaluation of the effects of epinephrine:
  1. Have you experienced any palpitation (consciousness of your own heartbeat) during the last half hour or so?

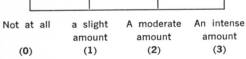

Not at all   a slight   A moderate   An intense
              amount   amount   amount
(0)   (1)   (2)   (3)

  2. Have you felt any tremor (involuntary shaking of the hands, arms, or legs) during the last half hour or so?

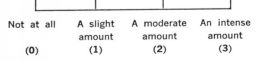

Not at all   A slight   A moderate   An intense
              amount   amount   amount
(0)   (1)   (2)   (3)

B. For evaluation of the effects of chlorpromazine:

Any direct measure (such as blood pressure) of the effects of the chlorpromazine injection on each subject was pretty much out of the question owing to limitations of time and personnel. It is known, however, that chlorpromazine does have somewhat of a dehydrating effect. As some indication that within the experimental time interval the chlorpromazine had been absorbed, the following questions were asked:

1. Does your mouth feel dry?

Not at   A little   Somewhat   Very   Extremely
all dry   dry   dry   dry   dry
(0)   (1)   (2)   (3)   (4)

2. Does your nose feel stuffy?

Not at all   A little   Somewhat   Very   Extremely
stuffy   stuffy   stuffy   stuffy   stuffy
(0)   (1)   (2)   (3)   (4)

Film detail questionnaire

Since it is known that chlorpromazine produces drowsiness, it seemed possible that experimental differences might be due to the fact that subjects had simply not watched the film. In order to check on this, a 10-item multiple-choice test concerned with small details of the film was administered. This test was rationalized to the subjects as a means of measuring the amount of time they had watched the movie, therefore, the amount of retinal stimulation received. Presumably the more they had watched the screen the more details they would remember.

Following this test the purpose of the experiment was disclosed, the deception was explained in detail, and the subjects were sworn to secrecy. Finally, the subjects filled out a brief questionnaire concerned with their past experiences with adrenalin and tranquilizers and with their suspicion, if any, of the experiment.

RESULTS

Physical effects of the injections

Evaluating, first, the effects of the injections, it can be seen in Table 1 that there are good indications that epinephrine has produced the required pattern of sympathetic activation. On self-reports of palpitation and tremor, subjects in the epinephrine condition report considerably more disturbance than subjects in either the placebo or chlorpromazine condition. On pulse measures, epinephrine subjects increase significantly when compared with placebo subjects. A subject's pulse was measured immediately before the injection and shortly after the movie. Pulse increased for some 63% of the epinephrine subjects and for 28% of the placebo subjects.

As to the effects of chlorpromazine, it can be seen in Table 1 that subjects in this condition report considerably more nose stuffiness and mouth dryness than subjects in the placebo or epinephrine conditions. This may be taken as indirect evidence that within the time limits of the experiment, chlorpromazine was taking effect. The increase in pulse rate (61% of chlorpromazine subjects increase) is a standard reaction to chlorpromazine and appears to be compensatory for the decreased blood pressure caused by this agent. It should be noted, however, that unlike epinephrine subjects the chlorpromazine subjects were unaware of this increased heart rate, for on the palpitation scale they are quite similar to subjects in the placebo condition.

Six subjects (included in Table 1) in the epinephrine condition were unaffected by the injection. They reported virtually no palpitation or tremor and their pulses were not markedly affected. Since for these subjects the necessary experimental state was not produced, they are not included in any further presentation of data.

Effects of drowsiness

It is known that chlorpromazine produces drowsiness, a state which in this experimental context might mean that the subjects paid less attention to the movie. Differences between chlorpromazine subjects and those in the other two conditions in reaction to the film could then be due to differential attention rather than to the factors presumably being tested. In order to check for this, the film details questionnaire, described earlier, was administered shortly after the movie. The results of this questionnaire are presented in Table 2 where the figures represent the mean number of correct answers in each of the conditions. It can be immediately seen that the three conditions are virtually identical. None of these figures is significantly different from one another and any differences in reaction to the film cannot, then, be attributed to differences in attention.

Overt reactions to the film

The observation record provides a continuous record of each subject's reaction to the film. As an overall index of amusement, the number of units in which a subject's behavior was recorded in the categories Smile, Grin, Laugh, and Big Laugh are summed together. The means of this amusement index are presented in Table 3. The larger the figure, the more amusement was manifest. Differences are in

Table **1** | PHYSICAL EFFECTS OF THE INJECTIONS

Condition	N	Pulse		Palpita-tion	Tremor	Mouth dry	Nose stuffy
		Pre-injection	Post-injection				
Epinephrine	44	81.4	87.3	2.00	1.86	0.72	0.39
Placebo	42	78.7	75.5	0.30	0.12	0.30	0.68
Chlorpromazine	46	81.4	86.0	0.52	0.26	1.12	2.16
p value							
Epinephrine versus Placebo				<.001	<.001	<.01	ns
Epinephrine versus Chlorpromazine				<.001	<.001	.07	<.001
Placebo versus Chlorpromazine				ns	ns	<.001	<.001

the anticipated direction. Epinephrine subjects gave indications of greater amusement than did placebo subjects who, in turn, were more amused than chlorpromazine subjects. The *U* test was used to test for significance of differences since the variance in the epinephrine condition was significantly greater than that in either the placebo or chlorpromazine condition. The means of both the epinephrine and the placebo conditions are significantly greater than the mean of the chlorpromazine condition.

Though the trend is clearly in the predicted direction, epinephrine and placebo subjects do not differ significantly in this overall index. The difference between these two groups, however, becomes apparent when we examine strong reactions to the film. Considering just the categories Laugh and Big Laugh, as indicating strong reactions to the film, we find an average of 4.84 such units among the epinephrine subjects and of only 1.83 such units among placebo subjects. This difference is significant at better than the .05 level of significance. Epinephrine subjects tend to be openly amused at the film, placebo subjects to be quietly amused. Some 16% of epinephrine subjects reacted at some point with belly laughs while not a single placebo subject did so. It should be noted that this is much the state of affairs one would expect from the disguised injection of epinephrine—a manipulation which, as Schachter and Singer (1962) have suggested, creates a bodily state "in search of" an appropriate cognition. Certainly laughter can be considered a more appropriate accompaniment to the state of sympathetic arousal than can quietly smiling.

It would appear, then, that degree of overt amusement is directly related to the degree of manipulated sympathetic activation.

Table **2** | MEAN NUMBER OF CORRECT ANSWERS ON THE FILM DETAILS QUESTIONNAIRE

Condition	N[a]	Mean number correct
Epinephrine	38	9.29
Placebo	41	9.15
Chlorpromazine	45	9.38

[a] One subject in the placebo and one in the chlorpromazine condition did not answer this questionnaire.

Table **3** | THE EFFECTS OF EPINEPHRINE, PLACEBO, AND CHLORPROMAZINE ON AMUSEMENT

Condition	N	Mean amusement index
Epinephrine	38	17.79
Placebo	42	14.31
Chlorpromazine	46	10.41
p value		ns
Epinephrine versus Placebo		ns
Epinephrine versus Chlorpromazine		.01
Placebo versus Chlorpromazine		.05

Evaluation of the film

Responses to the postmovie questionnaire in which the subjects evaluated the film are presented in Table 4. The column heading Funny includes answers to the questions "How funny did you find this film?"; the heading Enjoy includes answers to the question "All in all, how much did you enjoy the film?"; and the heading Recommend presents answers to the question, "Would you recommend that we show this particular film to our future subjects?"

For all three questions, the trend is in precisely the same direction, epinephrine subjects like the film slightly more than do placebo subjects who like it more than do chlorpromazine subjects. On all questions, however, the differences between conditions are small and, at best, significant at only borderline probability levels.

The fact that between-condition differences are large on the behavioral measure and quite small on the attitude scales administered after the film is an intriguing one. The most reasonable explanation comes from the subjects themselves. For example, after the experiment an epinephrine subject said,

I just couldn't understand why I was laughing during the movie. Usually, I hate Jack Carson and this kind of nonsense and that's the way I checked the scales.

For this subject, then, his long time preferences determined his answers to the questions whereas his immediate bodily state seems to have determined his reaction while watching the movie. If this is widespread, it should be

Table **4** | EVALUATION OF THE FILM

Condition	N	Funny	Enjoy	Recommend
Epinephrine	38	4.09	3.99	2.04
Placebo	42	4.01	3.95	1.93
Chlorpromazine	46	3.85	3.85	1.85

anticipated that there will be relatively little relationship between past preferences and overt behavior in the epinephrine condition and a considerably stronger relationship in the placebo condition. For chlorpromazine, too, one should anticipate slight relationship between past preferences and behavior. No matter what the long time feeling about such films the immediate reaction to the movie should be restrained owing to lack of sympathetic activity. However, as pointed out earlier, chlorpromazine is a weak blocker and, most reasonably, one should expect a somewhat weaker relationship with this drug than with the placebo.

As a measure of general attitude toward the sort of film shown, at the time that they were evaluating the film the subjects also answered the question, "In general, how well do you like this kind of slapstick film?" by checking one of five points along a scale ranging from "Slapstick is the kind of film I like least" to "Slapstick is my favorite kind of film." The relationship of attitude to this sort of film to reactions to this particular film in each of the drug conditions is presented in Table 5. These subjects are divided into two groups—those who dislike slapstick and those who like it as much or more than they do other kinds of films. The entries in the table are the mean laugh indices for each of the breakdowns.

It is evident that there is a very strong relationship between general attitude toward such films and laughter in the placebo condition, a considerably weaker relationship in the chlorpromazine condition, and the weakest relationship of all in the epinephrine condition.

DISCUSSION

The overall pattern of experimental results of this study and the Schachter and Singer (1962) experiment gives consistent support to general formulation of emotion as a function of a state of physiological arousal and of an appropriate cognition. The fact that the epinephrine-placebo difference in this study, though in the proper direction, was not larger must be considered within the context of other relevant studies. As noted earlier, Schachter and Singer obtained similar results in their tests of the effects of epinephrine on euphoria and anger. In their attempt to account for their results, they identify two factors which could attenuate the differences between subjects injected with epinephrine and those receiving a placebo. One of these factors—the self-arousal of placebo subjects—has been tested in the present study. The second factor they identify is what they call the "self-informing" tendency of epinephrine subjects. To understand this notion will require a brief review of the formulation proposed by Schachter (1959) who has suggested that an emotion be considered a joint function of a state of physiological arousal and of a cognition appropriate to this state. Given a state of physiological arousal for which an individual has no immediate explanation, he will "label" this state and describe his feeling in terms of the cognitions available to him. Given a state of arousal for which an individual has a completely appropriate explanation (e.g., "I feel this way because I have just received an injection of adrenalin.") no evaluative needs will arise and he is unlikely to label his feelings in terms of the alternative cognitions available. These propositions are strongly supported in the Schachter-Singer study where subjects, injected with epinephrine and told precisely what they would feel and why, were

Table **5** | RELATIONSHIP BETWEEN LAUGHTER AND PREVIOUS ATTITUDE TOWARD SLAPSTICK FILMS

Attitude to slapstick	Epinephrine		Placebo		Chlorpromazine	
	N^a	Laugh index	N^a	Laugh index	N^a	Laugh index
Dislike	25	15.12	29	10.52	29	7.34
Like	12	21.75	12	23.25	16	14.69
t		1.18		3.40		2.04
p		ns		.001		.05

[a] One subject in each condition did not answer the question concerned with general attitude to such films.

considerably less emotional (either angry or euphoric) than were subjects injected with epinephrine and told simply that they would experience no side effects. Inevitably, however, some of the subjects in this latter condition were self-informed; that is, on their own, they attributed their states of arousal to the injection. Consistent with expectations, such "self-informed" subjects proved to be considerably less emotional than subjects in the same condition who were not self-informed. To the extent, however, that this self-informing tendency operates, the differences between placebo and epinephrine conditions will, then, be attenuated. There is little question that such a tendency also operated in the present study and we suggest, of course, that this is one of the chief factors limiting the magnitude of differences between the epinephrine and the placebo conditions. Such a self-informing tendency will probably operate in any experiment on humans which employs an injection technique.

In order to make the epinephrine-placebo comparison under conditions which would rule out the operation of any "self-informing" tendency, two experiments were conducted on rats. In one of these, Singer (1961) demonstrated that under fear inducing conditions, rats injected with epinephrine were considerably more frightened than rats injected with a placebo. In another study, Latané and Schachter (1962) demonstrated that rats injected with epinephrine were notably more capable of avoidance learning than were rats injected with a placebo. Viewed together this series of experiments on rats and humans give clear support to the hypothesis that "emotionality" is, in part, a function of degree of sympathetic excitation.

Let us examine the implications of these findings and of this line of thought for problems in the general area of the physiology of the emotions.[1] We have noted in the introduction that the numerous studies on physiological differentiators of emotional states have, viewed en masse, yielded quite inconclusive results. Most, though not all, of these studies have

indicated no differences among the various emotional states. Since as human beings, rather than as scientists, we have no difficulty identifying, labeling, and distinguishing among our feelings, the results of these studies have long seemed rather puzzling and paradoxical. Perhaps because of this, there has been a persistent tendency to discount such results as due to ignorance or methodological inadequacy and to pay far more attention to the very few studies which demonstrate *some* sort of physiological differences among emotional states than to the very many studies which indicate no differences at all. It is conceivable, however, that these results should be taken at face value and that emotional states may, indeed, be generally characterized by a high level of sympathetic activation with few if any physiological distinguishers among the many emotional states. If this is correct, the findings of the present study may help to resolve the problem. Obviously this study does *not* rule out the possibility of physiological differences among the emotional states. It is the case, however, that given precisely the same state of epinephrine-induced sympathetic activation, we have, by means of cognitive manipulations, been able to produce in our subjects the very disparate states of euphoria and anger. It may indeed be the case that cognitive factors are major determiners of the emotional labels we apply to a common state of sympathetic arousal.

Let us ask next whether our results are specific to the state of sympathetic activation or if they are generalizable to other states of physiological arousal. It is clear that from our experiments proper, it is impossible to answer the question for our studies have been concerned largely with the effects of an epinephrine created state of sympathetic arousal. We would suggest, however, that our conclusions are generalizable to almost any pronounced internal state for which no appropriate explanation is available. This suggestion receives some support from the experiences of Nowlis and Nowlis (1956) in their program of research on the effects of drugs on mood. In their work the Nowlises typically administer a drug to groups of four subjects who are physically in one another's presence and free to interact. The Nowlises describe some of their results with these groups as follows:

---

[1] The remaining portion of this selection is abridged from Stanley Schachter and Jerome E. Singer. "Cognitive, social and physiological determinants of emotional state." *Psychological Review*, 1962, **69**, 379–399. Reprinted by permission of the author and the American Psychological Association.

At first we used the same drug for all 4 men. In those sessions seconal, when compared with placebo, increased the checking of such words as expansive, forceful, courageous, daring, elated, and impulsive. In our first statistical analysis we were confronted with the stubborn fact that when the same drug is given to all 4 men in a group the N that has to be entered into the analysis is 1, not 4. This increases the cost of an already expensive experiment by a considerable factor, but it cannot be denied that the effects of these drugs may be and often are quite contagious. Our first attempted solution was to run tests on groups in which each man had a different drug during the same session, such as 1 on seconal, 1 on benzedrine, 1 one dramamine, and 1 on placebo. What does seconal do? Cooped up with, say, the egotistical benzedrine partner, the withdrawn, indifferent dramimine partner, and the slightly bored lactose man, the seconal subject reports that he is distractible, dizzy, drifting, glum, defiant, languid, sluggish, discouraged, dull, gloomy, lazy, and slow! This is not the report of mood that we got when all 4 men were on seconal. It thus appears that the moods of the partners do definitely influence the effect of seconal (p. 350).

It is not completely clear from this description whether this "contagion" of mood is more marked in drug than in placebo groups, but should this be the case, these results would certainly support the suggestion that our findings are generalizable to internal states other than that produced by an injection of epinephrine.

SUMMARY

An experiment is described which was designed to test the proposition that "emotionality" is, in part, a function of the degree of excitation of the sympathetic nervous system. The degree of sympathetic activation was manipulated by injections of (a) the sympathomimetic agent—epinephrine, (b) a placebo, and (c) the sympatholytic drug—chlorpromazine. The effects of these drugs on amusement were tested by exposing subjects to a slapstick film. Epinephrine subjects were more amused than were placebo subjects who, in turn, were more amused than chlorpromazine subjects.

It is suggested that emotional states may be considered a function of a state of physiological arousal and of a cognition appropriate to this state of arousal. From this follows these propositions:

1. Given a state of physiological arousal for which an individual has no immediate explanation, he will label this state and describe his feelings in terms of the cognitions available to him. To the extent that cognitive factors are potent determiners of emotional states, it should be anticipated that precisely the same state of physiological arousal could be labeled "joy" or "fury" or "jealousy" or any of a great diversity of emotional labels depending on the cognitive aspects of the situation.
2. Given a state of physiological arousal for which an individual has a completely appropriate explanation, no evaluative needs will arise and the individual is unlikely to label his feelings in terms of the alternative cognitions available.
3. Given the same cognitive circumstances, the individual will react emotionally or describe his feelings as emotions only to the extent that he experiences a state of physiological arousal.

An experiment is described which, together with the results of other studies, supports these propositions.

REFERENCES

1. Hunt, J. McV., Cole, M. W., & Reis, E. E. Situational cues distinguishing anger, fear, and sorrow. *Amer. J. Psychol.*, 1958, **71**, 136–151.
2. Latane, B., & Schachter, S. Adrenalin and avoidance learning. *J. comp. physiol. Psychol.*, 1962, **55**, 369–372.
3. Lindsley, D. B. Emotion. In S. S. Stevens (Ed.), *Handbook of experimental psychology.* New York: Wiley, 1951. Pp. 473–516.
4. Nowlis, V., & Nowlis, H. H. The description and analysis of mood. *Ann. N. Y. Acad. Sci.*, 1956, **65**, 345–355.
5. Schachter, S. *The psychology of affiliation.* Stanford, Calif.: Stanford Univer. Press, 1959.
6. Schachter, S., & Singer, J. E. Cognitive, social, and physiological determinants of emotional state. *Psychol. Rev.*, 1962, **69**, 379–399.

Selection **20** | THE NATURE
OF LOVE*

HARRY F. HARLOW
University of Wisconsin

Love is a wondrous state, deep, tender, and rewarding. Because of its intimate and personal nature it is regarded by some as an improper topic for experimental research. But, whatever our personal feelings may be, our assigned mission as psychologists is to analyze all facets of human and animal behavior into their component variables. So far as love or affection is concerned, psychologists have failed in this mission. The little we know about love does not transcend simple observation, and the little we write about it has been written better by poets and novelists. But of greater concern is the fact that psychologists tend to give progressively less attention to a motive which pervades our entire lives. Psychologists, at least psychologists who write textbooks, not only show no interest in the origin and development of love or affection, but they seem to be unaware of its very existence.

The apparent repression of love by *modern* psychologists stands in sharp contrast with the attitude taken by many famous and normal people. The word "love" has the highest reference frequency of any word cited in Bartlett's book of *Familiar Quotations*. It would appear that this emotion has long had a vast interest and fascination for human beings, regardless of the attitude taken by psychologists; but the quotations cited, even by famous and normal people, have a mundane redundancy. These authors and authorities have stolen love from the child and infant and made it the exclusive property of the adolescent and adult.

Thoughtful men, and probably all women, have speculated on the nature of love. From the developmental point of view, the general plan is quite clear: the initial love responses of the human being are those made by the infant

* Abridged from H. F. Harlow, "The Nature of Love," *American Psychologist*, 13: 673–685, 1958. This paper was presented as the address of the President of the sixty-sixth annual convention of the American Psychological Association, Washington, D.C., August 31, 1958. Copyright 1958 by the American Psychological Association and reproduced by permission.

to the mother or some mother surrogate. From this intimate attachment of the child to the mother, multiple learned and generalized affectional responses are formed.

Unfortunately, beyond these simple facts we know little about the fundamental variables underlying the formation of affectional responses and little about the mechanisms through which the love of the infant for the mother develops into the multifaceted response patterns characterizing love or affection in the adult. Because of the dearth of experimentation, theories about the fundamental nature of affection have evolved at the level of observation, intuition, and discerning guesswork, whether these have been proposed by psychologists, sociologists, anthropologists, physicians or psychoanalysts.

The position commonly held by psychologists and sociologists is quite clear: the basic motives are for the most part, the primary drives —particularly hunger, thirst, elimination, pain, and sex—and all other motives, including love or affection, are derived or secondary drives. The mother is associated with the reduction of the primary drives—particularly hunger, thirst, and pain—and through learning, affection or love is derived.

It is entirely reasonable to believe that the mother through association with food may become a secondary-reinforcing agent, but this is an inadequate mechanism to account for the persistence of the infant-maternal ties. There is a spate of researches on the formation of secondary reinforcers to hunger and thirst reduction. There can be no question that almost any external stimulus can become a secondary reinforcer if properly associated with tissue-need reduction, but the fact remains that this redundant literature demonstrates unequivocally that such derived drives suffer relatively rapid experimental extinction. Contrariwise, human affection does not extinguish when the mother ceases to have intimate association with the drives in question. Instead, the affectional ties to the mother show a lifelong, unrelenting persistence and, even more surprising, widely expanding generality.

Oddly enough, one of the few psychologists who took a position counter to modern psychological dogma was John B. Watson, who believed that love was an innate emotion elicited by cutaneous stimulation of the erogenous zones. But experimental psychologists, with their peculiar propensity to discover facts that are not true, brushed this theory aside by demonstrating that the human neonate had no differentiable emotions, and they established a fundamental psychological law that prophets are without honor in their own profession.

The psychoanalysts have concerned themselves with the problem of the nature of the development of love in the neonate and infant, using ill and aging human beings as subjects. They have discovered the overwhelming importance of the breast and related this to the oral erotic tendencies developed at an age preceding their subjects' memories. Their theories range from a belief that the infant has an innate need to achieve and suckle at the breast to beliefs not unlike commonly accepted psychological theories. There are exceptions, as seen in the recent writings of John Bowlby, who attributes importance not only to food and thirst satisfaction, but also to "primary object-clinging," a need for intimate physical contact, which is initially associated with the mother.

As far as I know, there exists no direct experimental analysis of the relative importance of the stimulus variables determining the affectional or love responses in the neonatal and infant primate. Unfortunately, the human neonate is a limited experimental subject for such researches because of his inadequate motor capabilities. By the time the human infant's motor responses can be precisely measured, the antecedent determining conditions cannot be defined, having been lost in a jumble and jungle of confounded variables.

Many of these difficulties can be resolved by the use of the neonatal and infant macaque monkey as the subject for the analysis of basic affectional variables. It is possible to make precise measurements in this primate beginning at two to ten days of age, depending upon the maturational status of the individual animal at birth. The macaque infant differs from the human infant in that the monkey is more mature at birth and grows more rapidly; but the basic responses relating to affection, including nursing, contact, clinging, and even visual and auditory exploration, exhibit no fundamental differences in the two species. Even the development of perception, fear, frustration, and learning capability follows very similar sequences in rhesus monkeys and human children.

Three years' experimentation before we started our studies on affection gave us experience with the neonatal monkey. We had separated more than 60 of these animals from their mothers 6 to 12 hours after birth and suckled them on tiny bottles. The infant mortality was only a small fraction of what would have obtained had we let the monkey mothers raise their infants. Our bottle-fed babies were healthier and heavier than monkey-mother-reared infants. We know that we are better monkey mothers than are real monkey mothers thanks to synthetic diets, vitamins, iron extracts, penicillin, chloromycetin, 5% glucose, and constant, tender, loving care.

During the course of these studies we noticed that the laboratory-raised babies showed strong attachment to the cloth pads (folded gauze diapers) which were used to cover the hardware-cloth floors of their cages. The infants clung to these pads and engaged in violent temper tantrums when the pads were removed and replaced for sanitary reasons. Such contact-need or responsiveness had been reported previously by Gertrude van Wagenen for the monkey and by Thomas McCulloch and George Haslerud for the chimpanzee and is reminiscent of the devotion often exhibited by human infants to their pillows, blankets, and soft, cuddly stuffed toys.

We had also discovered during some allied observational studies that a baby monkey raised on a bare wire-mesh cage floor survives with difficulty, if at all, during the first five days of life. If a wire-mesh cone is introduced, the baby does better; and, if the cone is covered with terry cloth, husky, healthy, happy babies evolve. It takes more than a baby and a box to make a normal monkey. We were impressed by the possibility that, above and beyond the bubbling fountain of breast or bottle, contact comfort might be a very important variable in the development of the infant's affection for the mother.

At this point we decided to study the development of affectional responses of neonatal and infant monkeys to an artificial, inanimate mother, and so we built a surrogate mother which we hoped and believed would be a good surrogate mother. In devising this surrogate mother we were dependent neither upon the capriciousness of evolutionary processes nor upon mutations produced by chance radioactive fallout. Instead, we designed the mother surrogate in terms of modern human-engineering principles. We produced a perfectly proportioned, streamlined body stripped of unnecessary bulges and appendices. Redundancy in the surrogate mother's system was avoided by reducing the number of breasts from two to one and placing this unibreast in an upper-thoracic, sagittal position, thus maximizing the natural and known perceptual-motor capabilities of the infant operator. The surrogate was made from a block of wood, covered with sponge rubber, and sheathed in tan cotton terry cloth. A light bulb behind her radiated heat. The result was a mother, soft, warm, and tender, a mother with infinite patience, a mother available twenty-four hours a day, a mother that never scolded her infant and never struck or bit her baby in anger. Furthermore, we designed a mother-machine with maximal maintenance efficiency since failure of any system or function could be resolved by the simple substitution of black boxes and new component parts. It is our opinion that we engineered a very superior monkey mother, although this position is not held universally by the monkey fathers.

Before beginning our initial experiment we also designed and constructed a second mother surrogate, a surrogate in which we deliberately

Figure 1 Wire and cloth mother surrogates.

built less than the maximal capability for contact comfort. This surrogate mother is illustrated in Figure 1. She is made of wire-mesh, a substance entirely adequate to provide postural support and nursing capability, and she is warmed by radiant heat. Her body differs in no essential way from that of the cloth mother surrogate other than in the quality of the contact comfort which she can supply.

In our initial experiment, the dual mother-surrogate condition, a cloth mother and a wire mother were placed in different cubicles attached to the infant's living cage as shown in Figure 1. For four newborn monkeys the cloth mother lactated and the wire mother did not; and, for the other four, this condition was reversed. In either condition the infant received all its milk through the mother surrogate as soon as it was able to maintain itself in this way, a capability achieved within two or three days except in the case of very immature infants. Supplementary feedings were given until the milk intake from the mother surrogate was adequate. Thus, the experiment was designed as a test of the relative importance of the variables of contact comfort and nursing comfort. During the first 14 days of life the monkey's cage floor was covered with a heating pad wrapped in a folded gauze diaper, and thereafter the cage floor was bare. The infants were always free to leave the heating pad or cage floor to contact either mother, and the time spent on the surrogate mothers was automatically recorded. Figure 2 shows the total time spent on the cloth and wire mothers under the two conditions of feeding. These data make it obvious that contact comfort is a variable of overwhelming importance in the development of affectional responses, whereas lactation is a variable of negligible importance. With age and opportunity to learn, subjects with the lactating wire mother showed decreasing responsiveness to her and increasing responsiveness to the nonlactating cloth mother, a finding completely contrary to any interpretation of derived drive in which the mother-form becomes conditioned to hunger-thirst reduction. The persistence of these differential responses throughout 165 consecutive days of testing is evident in Figure 3.

One control group of neonatal monkeys was

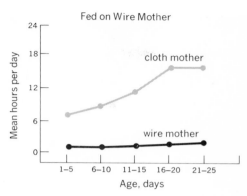

Figure 2 Time spent on cloth and wire mother surrogates.

raised on a single wire mother, and a second control group was raised on a single cloth mother. There were no differences between these two groups in amount of milk ingested or in weight gain. The only difference between the groups lay in the composition of the feces, the softer stools of the wire-mother infants suggesting psychosomatic involvement. The wire mother is biologically adequate but psychologically inept.

We were not surprised to discover that con-

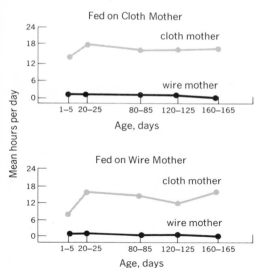

Figure 3 Long-term contact time on cloth and wire mother surrogates.

tact comfort was an important basic affectional or love variable, but we did not expect it to overshadow so completely the variable of nursing; indeed, the disparity is so great as to suggest that the primary function of nursing as an affectional variable is that of insuring frequent and intimate body contact of the infant with the mother. Certainly, man cannot live by milk alone. Love is an emotion that does not need to be bottle- or spoon-fed, and we may be sure that there is nothing to be gained by giving lip service to love.

A charming lady once heard me describe these experiments; and, when I subsequently talked to her, her face brightened with sudden insight: "Now I know what's wrong with me," she said, "I'm just a wire mother." Perhaps she was lucky. She might have been a wire wife.

We believe that contact comfort has long served the animal kingdom as a motivating agent for affectional responses. Since at the present time we have no experimental data to substantiate this position, we supply information which must be accepted, if at all, on the basis of face validity.

One function of the real mother, human or subhuman, and presumably of a mother surrogate, is to provide a haven of safety for the infant in times of fear and danger. The frightened or ailing child clings to its mother, not its father; and this selective responsiveness in times of distress, disturbance, or danger may be used as a measure of the strength of

Figure 4 Typical response to cloth mother surrogate fear test.

affectional bonds. We have tested this kind of differential responsiveness by presenting to the infants in their cages, in the presence of the two mothers, various fear-producing stimuli. A typical response to a fear stimulus is shown in Figure 4, and the data on differential responsiveness are presented in Figure 5. It is apparent that the cloth mother is highly preferred over the wire one, and this differential selectivity is enhanced by age and experience. In

this situation, the variable of nursing appears to be of absolutely no importance: the infant consistently seeks the soft mother surrogate regardless of nursing condition.

Similarly, the mother or mother surrogate provides its young with a source of security, and this role or function is seen with special clarity when mother and child are in a strange situation. At the present time we have completed tests for this relationship on four of our eight baby monkeys assigned to the dual mother-surrogate condition by introducing them for three minutes into the strange environment of a room measuring six feet by six feet by six feet (also called the "open-field test") and containing multiple stimuli known to elicit curiosity-manipulatory responses in baby monkeys. The subjects were placed in this situation twice a week for eight weeks with no mother surrogate present during alternate sessions and the cloth mother present during the others. A cloth diaper was always available as one of the stimuli throughout all sessions. After one or two adaptation sessions, the infants always rushed to the mother surrogate when she was present and clutched her, rubbed their bodies against her, and frequently manipulated her body and face. After a few additional sessions, the infants began to use the mother surrogate as a source of security, a base of operations.

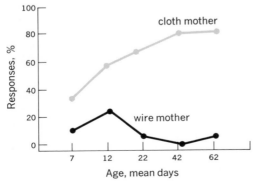

Figure 5 Differential responsiveness in fear tests.

Figure 6 Response in the open-field test in the absence of the mother surrogate.

They would explore and manipulate a stimulus and then return to the mother before adventuring again into the strange new world. The behavior of these infants was quite different when the mother was absent from the room. Frequently they would freeze in a crouched position, as illustrated in Figure 6. Emotionality indices such as vocalization, crouching, rocking, and sucking increased sharply. Total emotionality score was cut in half when the mother was present. In the absence of the mother some of the experimental monkeys would rush to the center of the room where the mother was customarily placed and then run rapidly from object to object, screaming and crying all the while. Continuous, frantic clutching of their bodies was very common, even when not in the crouching position. These monkeys frequently contacted and clutched the cloth diaper, but this action never pacified them. The same behavior occurred in the presence of the wire mother. No difference between the cloth-mother-fed and wire-mother-fed infants was demonstrated under either condition.

We have already described the group of four control infants that had never lived in the presence of any mother surrogate and had demonstrated no sign of affection or security in the presence of the cloth mothers introduced in test sessions. When these infants reached the age of 250 days, cubicles containing both a cloth mother and a wire mother were attached to their cages. There was no lactation in these mothers, for the monkeys were on a solid-food diet. The initial reaction of the monkeys to the alterations was one of extreme disturbance. All the infants screamed violently and made repeated attempts to escape the cage whenever the door was opened. They kept a maximum distance from the mother surrogates and exhibited a considerable amount of rocking and crouching behavior, indicative of emotionality. Our first thought was that the critical period for the development of maternally directed affection had passed and that these macaque children were doomed to live as affectional orphans. Fortunately, these behaviors continued for only 12 to 48 hours and then gradually ebbed, changing from indifference to active contact on, and exploration of, the surrogates. The home-cage behavior of these control monkeys slowly became similar

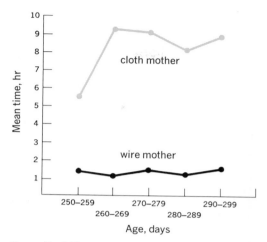

Figure 7 Differential time spent on cloth and wire mother surrogates by monkeys started at 250 days of age.

to that of the animals raised with the mother surrogates from birth. Their manipulation and play on the cloth mother became progressively more vigorous to the point of actual mutilation, particularly during the morning after the cloth mother had been given her daily change of terry covering. The control subjects were now actively running to the cloth mother when frightened and had to be coaxed from her to be taken from the cage for formal testing.

Objective evidence of these changing behaviors is given in Figure 7, which plots the amount of time these infants spent on the mother surrogates. Within 10 days mean contact time is approximately nine hours, and this measure remains relatively constant throughout the next 30 days, Consistent with the results on the subjects reared from birth with dual mothers, these late-adopted infants spent less than one and one-half hours per day in contact with the wire mothers, and this activity level was relatively constant throughout the test sessions. Although the maximum time that the control monkeys spent on the cloth mother was only about half that spent by the original dual mother-surrogate group, we cannot be sure that this discrepancy is a function of differential early experience. The control monkeys were about three months older when the mothers were attached to their cages than the experimental animals had been when their mothers were removed and the retention tests begun. Thus, we do not know what the amount of contact would be for a 250-day-old animal raised from birth with surrogate mothers. Nevertheless, the magnitude of the differences and the fact that the contact-time curves for the mothered-from-birth infants had remained constant for almost 150 days suggest that early experience with the mother is a variable of measurable importance.

That the control monkeys develop affection or love for the cloth mother when she is introduced into the cage at 250 days of age cannot be questioned. There is every reason to believe, however, that this interval of delay depresses the intensity of the affectional response below that of the infant monkeys that were surrogate-mothered from birth onward. In interpreting these data it is well to remember that the control monkeys had had continuous opportunity to observe and hear other monkeys housed in adjacent cages and that they had had limited opportunity to view and contact surrogate mothers in the test situations, even though they did not exploit the opportunities.

During the last two years we have observed the behavior of two infants raised by their own mothers. Love for the real mother and love for the surrogate mother appear to be very similar. The baby macaque spends many hours a day clinging to its real mother. If away from the mother when frightened, it rushes to her and in her presence shows comfort and composure. As far as we can observe, the infant monkey's affection for the real mother is strong, but no stronger than that of the experimental monkey for the surrogate cloth mother, and the security that the infant gains from the presence of the real mother is no greater than the security it gains from a cloth surrogate. Next year we hope to put this problem to final, definitive, experimental test. But, whether the mother is real or a cloth surrogate, there does develop a deep and abiding bond between mother and child. In one case it may be the call of the wild and in the other the McCall of civilization, but in both cases there is "togetherness."

In spite of the importance of contact comfort, there is reason to believe that other variables of measurable importance will be discovered. Postural support may be such a variable, and it has been suggested that, when we build arms into the mother surrogate, 10 is the minimal number required to provide adequate child care. Rocking motion may be such a variable, and we are comparing rocking and stationary mother surrogates and inclined planes. The differential responsiveness to cloth mother and cloth-covered inclined plane suggests that clinging as well as contact is an affectional variable of importance. Sounds, particularly natural, maternal sounds, may operate as either unlearned or learned affectional variables. Visual responsiveness may be such a variable, and it is possible that some semblance of visual imprinting may develop in the neonatal monkey. There are indications that this becomes a variable of importance during the course of infancy through some maturational process.

Since we can measure neonatal and infant affectional responses to mother surrogates, and since we know they are strong and persisting, we are in a position to assess the effects of feeding and contactual schedules; consistency and inconsistency in the mother surrogates; and early, intermediate, and late maternal deprivation. Again, we have here a family of problems of fundamental interest and theoretical importance.

If the researches completed and proposed make a contribution, I shall be grateful: but I have also given full thought to possible practical applications. The socioeconomic demands of the present and the threatened socioeconomic demands of the future have led the American woman to displace, or threaten to displace, the American man in science and industry. If this process continues, the problem of proper child-rearing practices faces us with startling clarity. It is cheering in view of this trend to realize that the American male is physically endowed with all the really essential equipment to compete with the American female on equal terms in one essential activity: the rearing of infants. We now know that women in the working classes are not needed in the home because of their primary mammalian capabilities; and it is possible that in the foreseeable future neonatal nursing will not be regarded as a necessity, but as a luxury—to use Veblen's term—a form of conspicuous consumption limited perhaps to the upper classes.

But whatever course history may take, it is comforting to know that we are now in contact with the nature of love.

Selection **21** | EMOTIONAL RICHNESS AND EMOTIONAL POVERTY*

ROBERT WARD LEEPER
Universtiy of Oregon

PETER MADISON
Swarthmore College

We are likely to react with surprised disbelief to the idea that modern living may often leave us emotionally starved. We so habitually evaluate the adequacy of a culture in terms of its industrial development or of material wealth that we are sure anyone who disputes this self-evident goodness must have some peculiar and cranky streak in his nature making him want to belittle what we have achieved.

One does not need to belittle the material accomplishments of our society (incidentally, these are *not* our personal accomplishments, yours and mine) to see that there can be intense motivational satisfactions in ways of living that look extremely meager to sophisticated eyes. Nor do we need naively to urge man to return to the life of Rousseau's noble savage. In fact, in primitive life, the very lack of material resources must often have resulted in an existence dominated by fears and bitter frustrations. Our material achievements are not to be depreciated. They conceivably can yet give us the means of a life richer, even in most emotional respects, than any primitive could ever have known.

To say that such a thing is possible is not the same as conceding, however, that we have achieved this result so far. Great numbers of people brought up in modern civilized surroundings are showing, either directly or indirectly, that something is wrong.

* Abridged from Robert Ward Leeper and Peter Madison, *Toward Understanding Human Personalities*, Appleton-Century-Crofts, Inc., New York, 1959, pp. 249–267. Reprinted by permission of Appleton-Century-Crofts, Division of Meredith Publishing Company.

SOME INDIRECT EXPRESSIONS OF THIS FEELING OF EMOTIONAL POVERTY

Right now a lot more effort might be directed toward meeting this need for emotionally rich experience if more people saw clearly, and admitted, that there is something lacking in modern life. But, most often, the feeling of lack does not express itself in clearly conscious form. The discontent shows up more in indirect ways. It may be worthwhile looking into some of the indirect forms that emotional poverty may take. Let us examine six of these, even though this list is surely far from complete.

Pseudo-hungers for food as an expression of emotional poverty One of the simplest indirect expressions of emotional poverty is a craving for food that the individual does not really need and would not eat were it not for his emotional hungers. Thus, one college teacher observed this about himself:

It's not very long after Jane is gone that I often get intensely hungry. I wander around the house for a while, maybe, and get my desk organized for an evening's work. Sometimes, then, I feel suddenly tired. Other times I get hungry for cornflakes and milk. It's absurd. I've had a good dinner; but that insistent craving starts, and I can't get to work until I pour myself a huge bowl of the stuff and eat it while arranging my work. Once I get started, the work carries itself along, and time passes quickly. But, particularly if the work is a bit of a chore, or something I can't too well see my way through, I'm likely to get hungry, no matter how recently I've eaten.

Here you have only one case, but what it reports is typical of a good many persons—in short, it is a good instance of an expression of emotional deprivation.

An exorbitantly increased demand for closer human relationships as one effect of emotional poverty Emotional hungers may find an outlet through our dependence upon and demand for more satisfaction from our close human relationships than we can reasonably expect. In marriage and in other close relationships, some people tend to want others almost to revere them and to share with them all their ideals, ideas, and interests. Such a demand is exceedingly egotistical, not wholly unlike that of a small child who feels that his mother should think only of him. In all soberness we have no right even to imagine that any other person would respect us on some matters, love us for some reasons, or share some of our activities, because each of us is complex and each of us inevitably will differ somewhat from every other person. One wonders if it is not some unfulfilled emotional hunger on our part that makes us expect more from a marriage or from any other relationship than it can be expected to yield except under the rarest circumstances—except when both persons involved are of the most unusual fineness and when their natures are complementary in some fullest sense.

Overdependence on sexual satisfactions as a consequence of emotional poverty   No one would think of denying that the sex motive is a strong one simply in its own right. The satisfactions of sex are vital in themselves, just as the satisfaction of hunger is vital in itself. Given its proper development and place in relation to all the other components of a full life, the sex motive becomes part of an enduring and profound love-relationship. As such it is part of a complex of motives that is anything but simple.

Because the sex motive has a strong physiological basis, it is a rare person who, as an adolescent and adult, has not depended to some considerable extent either on sexual relations with others or, if his upbringing and social ideals or his situation have made that sort of expression inappropriate, on autoerotic satisfactions. One fact tending to work in this direction is that, unlike many other motives such as the enjoyment of music that requires long training to develop adequately, the sex motive provides intensely pleasurable effects even when the richer forms of satisfaction of this motive—its fusion with the rich emotional elements of shared lives—have not been achieved.

However, even when all this is recognized, it must be definitely recorded that the sex motive is not as imperiously strong as it sometimes seems to be when its expression occurs under those conditions we have termed conditions of emotional poverty, or when it is accom-

panied by fear, sense of guilt, or some other intense and negative motive.

Many psychotherapists have come to the conclusion that most of what appears as excessively strong sexual motivation in human beings must be similarly explained. Karen Horney was expressing the views of many of such workers when she wrote as follows:[1]

. . . just as "all is not gold that glitters," so also "all is not sexuality that looks like it." A great part of what appears as sexuality has in reality very little to do with it, but is an expression of the desire for reassurance. If this is not taken into consideration one is bound to overestimate the role of sexuality.

The individual whose sexual needs are enhanced under the unrecognized stress of anxiety is inclined naively to ascribe the intensity of his sexual needs to his innate temperament, or to the fact that he is free from conventional taboos . . . an individual who needs sexuality as an outlet for the sake of allaying anxiety will be particularly incapable of enduring any abstinence, even of short duration.

. . . a great deal of sexual activity today is more an outlet for psychic tensions than a genuine sexual drive, and is therefore to be regarded more as a sedative than as genuine sexual enjoyment or happiness. . . .

It is one of the great achievements of Freud that he contributed so much to giving sexuality its due importance. In detail, however, [within psychoanalytic views] many phenomena are accepted as sexual which are really the expression of complex neurotic conditions, mainly expressions of the neurotic need for affection.

It is not surprising, then, that the research of Kinsey on sex behavior in human beings should show, in a somewhat similar vein, that the socially and economically underprivileged classes in our society are more sexually active than is, for example, the professional class. The difference may not lie in the greater virility of lower class groups, or in some supposed repression of sex in professional groups, but in the over-all differences with respect to emotional satisfactions that their everyday lives provide.

[1] Karen Horney, *The Neurotic Personality of Our Time,* W. W. Norton & Company, Inc., New York, 1937, pp. 157–159. Reprinted by permission of the publisher.

The powerful and insistent demands for material comforts and material products that characterize our society may be an expression of emotional deprivation in other respects Many persons who study our society come to feel that our interest in the material products of our technology far exceeds their value as the means of a fuller life. Material goods, they feel, come to be wanted with an irrational intensity bewildering to the detached onlooker.

There is, for instance, our tremendous itch to own the newest, biggest, most powerful, and showiest car, an urge that goes far beyond any simple need for going places. One automobile executive remarked that if sales appeal were the sole basis for deciding what next year's car was to be like, it would have 500 horsepower and be made of solid chrome.

No one denies that a car is what most people need for getting quickly to work; it may allow a family to live in beautiful country though the breadwinner works a long distance away. It is wonderful for a trip to the coast or mountains on weekends, for vacation exploring. Going up 12,000 feet over Trail-Ridge Road in Rocky Mountain National Park, or over Tioga Pass in Yosemite, can be a never-to-be-forgotten thrill—an experience alive with adventure and beauty. But why must one have a car loaded with expensive chrome? Why must one have 285 horsepower rather than a mere 250 or 150? Why a new car every second year?

Often it seems that people are misled in judging how much emotional value they can get from the ownership of material goods— cars and other things—acquired at great sacrifice. Some questions need looking into. Is it true, for example, that we especially enjoy and like people who own luxury homes and big cars? Do we feel any unusual sense of warm human interest in them when we are with them? Can it make a difference in the quality of friendship they extend to us if we arrive in the latest and biggest model of a car?

Or do we remember and like those people who are most human, friendly, and interested in us, and who are unpretentious, and warmly and simply welcoming and hospitable? Isn't it likely that if we go in for exaggerated material ostentation, it will arouse envy and competitive counterreactions rather than the kind of humanness we really want from others—despite

the reactions that advertisers lead us to feel we will surely get if we arrive in a Cadillac?

Here, it would seem, is a fine instance of how basic, unfilled human hungers for companionship and appreciation, for being wanted, liked, valued, for feeling close to others, get sidetracked and replaced by a need for material things that we want so desperately as supposed means of gratifying these basic desires. But somehow the supposed means turn out to separate us even further from the kind of fundamental human responsiveness we want from others.

Much interest in violence (directly or through phantasy) may be an expression of emotional poverty It is sobering to look at the activities of many teen-age gangs in cities such as New York and Philadelphia. One news item told about a teen-age youth, the leader of a street gang, who had shot and killed an innocent boy. He had mistaken the boy for the leader of a rival teen-age gang that his group were fighting over the question of whether the other group could wear jackets colored like their own. As he was led away by police, a group of teen-agers followed him, cheering him loudly. The girls in the group shouted, "We love you, Tarzan!" Several days later they assembled at the funeral of the innocent victim and booed and threatened the police there, loudly defending the act of their leader. That he had killed someone added to his stature in their eyes. Another report told of an unbelievable incident in which some boys drenched a child with gasoline and set fire to their screaming victim. One youth, arrested for knifing a perfectly innocent person, was asked why he had done such a horrible thing. He replied that he wanted to feel the thrill of his knife going through bone! Unbelievable? One need only read the newspaper reports to find similar incidents every week among teen-age gangs in our cities.

It may even be that war appeals to us because we are emotionally starved in peacetime Many writers have pointed out that it is not the whole truth to say we fear and hate war; in many ways we like it. Some of them have concluded, as Freud did, that man is equipped with a fundamentally aggressive need that is almost bound at times to find an outlet in war if it cannot be successfully drained off by less horrible substitutes. Another possibility may be, though, that wars come partly from other indirect emotional sources. In war some men attain their deepest emotional experiences—in heroism, generosity, companionship, courage, and self-sacrifice. One need only read Winston Churchill's account of the "finest hour" of the British people subjected to Hitler's all-out bombardment of London in World War II to realize what wars can bring in the way of emotional values that continue to be celebrated in movies and fiction for long afterwards. When people so docilely support the aggressive military programs of their countries, it may not be entirely from a feeling of helplessness in the face of such a waste of treasure, but rather because the idea of a struggle for national survival has its positive emotional appeal, particularly in view of the dearth of meaning in much of peacetime existence. If so, the transforming of modern life to make it emotionally more rich is not something of merely individual concern, but is one of the major social needs of our modern world!

It would be possible to mention a number of other indications of emotional poverty in modern life. The high frequency of alchoholism may be one such indicator. The increasing reliance on cocktail parties as a means of making social life "sufficiently interesting" may be another. Sensationalistic newspapers may be still another.

The problem is extensive and serious enough, at any rate, that it is well worth our asking about the factors that produce emotional poverty in modern life and about the resources that we might use to foster emotionally rich experiences, instead.

FACTORS PRODUCTIVE OF EMOTIONAL POVERTY

Conformity pressures In a country founded in part on a belief in rugged individualism, it is a curious fact that, with every passing year, it seems to become more difficult to be one's own individual self. It is commonly pointed out that we have been moving rapidly toward an "organizational" society where the individual tends to become lost in the large-scale unit such as a corporation, union, bureaucratic government, university, or church. The structure of

such organizations is designed to meet the goals of the group, and before he knows it the individual finds himself falling in line with group pressures regardless of whether it is in his own fundamental interest to do so or not.

The young executive may want to live in New England where he grew up and where he deeply enjoys living, but he knows he has to take the offered transfer to Kansas if his career is not to be blocked. He wants to spend his evenings and week ends with his wife and children, but instead brings home a brief case full of work in order to meet the pressures that come down on him from above. He enjoys good literature and the theater, but the circle of associates who hold the reins to his future favor evenings of canasta, bridge, and social drinking. He dislikes parties, but knows that not to be seen at the organizational gatherings would be fatal.

The scientist is subject to the same forces. We may have always thought that research flourishes in proportion as the individual genius is free and that the fundamental premise of the laboratory is that the inquirer must be his own judge of what he considers the most promising line of work. But it is the relatively rare scientist who can do just what he wants. He too must conform to views of the large foundation or government bureau as to what deserves research funds. Too often our scientists find themselves offered large grants to work on something considered valuable by someone else but are unable to get a few thousand dollars for research on their own ideas.

These influences tend to dry up the wells of rich emotional living. It is the essence of such full living that the particular nature of each person and his interests serve as the basis for decision in choosing what he should do or not do. This does not mean that we are each to develop without contact or influence from others. But it does mean that we must have freedom to be attracted to this or that work or person in accord with the character of our own selves, rather than according to the dictates of conformity to an external value-standard set up by authority.

Blue-ribbon motivation and emotional poverty The following conversation was reported by a father of a girl who was near the end of her first grade in school:

"Daddy," she said, "you have to get me some books that I can read myself."

The father, pleased at such an early interest in reading, smiled benignly, "Well, if you like reading that well, we'll certainly have to get you some books."

"Yes," little Marguerite went on, "Dorothy's already got five stars on her reading chart, and I haven't got any yet."

"Reading chart? Stars? What's that got to do with wanting books to read?"

"Well, you see Daddy, I'm in the fast reading group, along with Dorothy Harlan, Sally Evans, and Jeanie Scott—those three are the best readers—and they're in our 'sharp eye' group, which is the best in the first grade. This week the teacher put up a big chart on the wall. She said that now that we could read, we would all have to read books on our own, outside of class. Everytime we read a book, we tell her, and she marks another star by our name. Dorothy gets two or three stars every day, and I haven't got a one yet."

While this is a schoolroom example, the practice of giving recognition to those who are to be considered first in any activity is not limited to child education. In our culture the question too often is: "Are you *first*? Are you the *top* in your field? Are you the *best* there is?"

This is "blue-ribbon motivation." The character of the work itself, its interest for you, its importance to society, are all secondary, or not even asked about. The only question is whether, by some external, tangible criterion, you have, in some sense, won first, or at least ranked high, in competition against the rest of the field. To some extent, it doesn't even matter too much what the competition is about. It may be for making the best pie at the fair or the best model of a nineteenth-century sailing ship, for being president of the largest manufacturing plant in the whole country; or it may be that you came in first in a hamburger-eating contest.

Throughout our whole society it is remarkable to what extent such extrinsic, tacked-on, blue-ribbon evaluation is the main basis for undertaking what people do. Listen, sometime, to parents talking about their children who are away at the university. You will find them telling of their son's or daughter's being elected to class presidency, or some club presidency,

or being on the honor roll, or getting a prize for being the best freshman engineering student, or what not. How rare it is, instead, to hear a parent rejoice because Mary or Ronnie has a brand new area of interest that fills her or his letters home—just that, and no blue ribbon!

It is very hard, in our society, to continue to like doing something for itself, for its intrinsic merits. Such an interest is regarded as an indulgence. Even hobbies too often become competitive. Sometimes we allow art to become an intrinsic interest, providing it is understood to be distinctly amateurish. But, most of us are a little mystified by the person who says he is doing something merely because it is interesting. He doesn't make money at it, he isn't very good at it, but he likes it—something surely a little odd about such a fellow!

Oversatiation of major interests Pressures to conform and to succeed have another insidious effect. Even when they do not keep us from pursuing our major interests, they tend to produce an excessive concentration on one single activity and tend to have corrosive effects on the emotional satisfactions inherent in this activity.

Professional activities tend to be self-chosen, and when a person has gone into science, teaching, business, or the ministry as something he preferred to do above everything else in life, it is hard to imagine that doing it could have harmful side effects. In fact, if such activities were limited to a 40-hour week, they wouldn't. But whereas the 40-hour week is standard in working-class lives, the professional and business-managerial groups in our society are fortunate if they have less than a 60-hour or 65-hour week.

Any mother of three or four little children can tell you about satiation effects, though she may not call it by that name. For, in our contemporary kind of servantless middle-class society, where families live long distances from any relatives who could help, and where the husband typically is gone from breakfast time until the children's bedtime, the mother may find that she has spent well over 80 hours per week in caring for her children and running her home.

She loves her children. But still it is true that any activity, when engaged in too persistently, tends to lose its interest, except when a person has unusual emotional resources.

The neglect and belittling of concrete perceptual experiences is another source of emotional poverty in our culture Modern Western society is highly advanced in technology and scientific understanding. Our culture has laid stress upon abstract knowledge and standardization. These things have some real emotional value for us, and they are not solely the servants of material ends. But they fall far short of serving our emotional needs in a full way. Some of our emotional experience must spring from things around us that impinge directly, immediately, concretely upon us, that are perceived as having color, warmth, and vitality and are likely to be down-to-earth—as the play of color and form in the fireplace, the feel of the winds, and skies, the alternation of lights and shade in a forest, being surrounded with friends.

There is even a lot of tacit disapproval of living in the present in our middle-class culture. It is as if we had some leftovers from past religious prohibitions against investing too heavily in present earthly pleasures. Of course, we need abstractions, we need to have a future orientation, and so on, else we would be a nation of sensualists bent only on immediate pleasures. But we also ought to be able to shuck off regularly all these necessaries and immerse ourselves in fuller realities and concrete joys of life.

Emotional poverty may spring from the failure to develop the neural mechanisms for some satisfactions It is amazing how we seem to assume that our children will grow, without any special help on the part of the older generation, into adults who will have the motivational mechanisms for a resourceful and satisfying adult life. Here is the family of another vacationer whom one of the writers had a chance to observe:

They were a family of three staying in a cottage among the mountains for several weeks. The father was a college professor. He and his wife were never seen outside their cottage except as they emerged in order to get into their car periodically, drive into town, and back again.

On the first day, their 11-year-old boy appeared outside carrying three toy rifles, a cartridge belt, and two cap pistols. Each day he appeared, armed to the teeth, and proceeded to play, as best he could, with his guns.

Across the road there was an inviting-looking livery where even small children could learn to ride horses. There were plenty of fishing streams nearby, a lake, beautiful trails. Never once did the father take his boy out to sample any of these interesting activities. The boy happened to be playing among rocks that would have been fascinating to collect and study, with trees and flowers around that fairly begged to be observed in their beauty. The general scenery was awe-inspiring, or so it seemed until perhaps we chanced to remember that it isn't the eyes that see, but the habits of the beholder. As far as we, his neighbors, could see, those five guns were the sole interest that the boy had.

What will such a boy be able to find deeply satisfying at age 30 or 40? What is he prepared for except to sit and watch some of those 588 killings and other crimes that the National Association for Better Radio and Television workers tallied in one week of watching seven TV stations?

How are people to be made less blind to their responsibilities for helping their children to develop, to grow, psychologically? Rich positive motives do not simply unfold by themselves without somebody's making the effort to care about them, to implant and foster them. The development of strong and diversified motives is one of society's main tasks and it requires stupendous efforts in comparison with what we as a people have done in the past.

As a result of continued interactions with his environment, the individual learns to value and to want to obtain a wide variety of objects, activities, and symbols. When the possibility of attaining these goals is temporarily or permanently blocked, we speak of frustration. Common barriers to goal attainment are restrictions imposed by authorities, restricted socioeconomic opportunities, and inadequate personal ability. Since our wants are so diverse and heterogeneous, it is understandable that these wants often compete and are in conflict with each other. Such motivational conflict constitutes an especially important source of frustration. Whatever the source, frustration always involves an increase in emotionality, typically an arousal of anger, and fear or anxiety.

BIOLOGICAL FACTORS

Extensive investigations of experimentally induced conflicts in lower animals have been performed by Dr. Neal E. Miller and his colleagues at Yale University. His most recent experiments have focused on the effects of certain drugs in modifying the fear-motivated behavior resulting from approach-avoidance conflicts (Selection 22). Dr. Miller first demonstrated that sodium amytal appeared to have fear-reducing effects on rats similar to its effects on human beings. After establishing this basis for generalizing his results, he attempted to determine more precisely the mechanisms of the apparent fear-reducing property of the drug. In addition to his specific findings, the experimental program as a whole illustrates "a type of work which is needed on a variety of selected drugs each of which has well established, but different, psychological effects on the human subject."

It will be noted that the experiments reported by Miller typically generate a conflict between avoidance tendencies (fear motivation) and approach tendencies (incentive motivation). Dr. Allan Wagner, a colleague of Miller, has extended the analysis to the emotions involved in frustration (Selection 23). It is regularly observed that animals which receive reward only 50 percent of the time respond faster than those which are rewarded on every trial. One interpretation of this partial reinforcement effect is that the 50 percent group runs faster because frustration is added to the drive level already present due to the hunger drive and the animals are thus generally more motivated than those in the 100 percent group. Wagner hypothesized that if this interpretation were correct, rats which were trained under 50 percent reinforcement after being injected with sodium amytal should *not* show superior performance to the 100 percent group since the sodium amytal would reduce the frustration. As may be seen in Fig. 1, the drug not only eliminated the superiority of the 50 percent group but in fact reversed the relationship so that the 100 percent group was significantly faster than the 50 percent group. Wagner explains this reversal as being due to stronger anticipation of reward (incentive motivation) under 100 percent reinforcement than under 50 percent reinforcement.

PSYCHOLOGICAL FACTORS

So far we have indicated only one component of reactions to frustration—the emotional component. In Selection 24, Dr. S. Stansfeld Sargent outlines a hypothesis about the behavior resulting from frustration which attempts to take into account several additional determinants of the overt response. He states that the internal emotional response is the first stage in the reaction sequence; in fact, without the emotional reaction it does not seem meaningful to infer that frustration has occurred. The specific kind of emotion which occurs depends on how the person perceived the situation, especially his perception of the source of the frustration. An understanding of the overt response to frustration must also take into account the habits which the individual has built up in reacting to previous frustration. It is at this stage of the sequence that learned mechanisms of defense come into play. The last stage, overt behavior, is determined by interaction of the intervening organismic factors of perception, emotion, and habit.

SOCIOCULTURAL FACTORS

If it is necessary to take into account the processes of frustration and conflict in order to understand normal human behavior, it is even more necessary for the understanding of that portion of each person's behavior which could be described as neurotic. Although neurosis itself will be considered in more detail in Chapter 13, we can at this point make use of Dr. Karen Horney''s insight into neurotic conflicts to help us understand conflicts in general (Selection 25). Horney emphasizes that the really important conflicts are generated by our interactions with other people, especially our parents or parent substitutes. From them we learn our basic attitudes about the world. If, as children, our interactions with parents are characterized by rejection, lack of warmth, inconsistency, etc., then a feeling of basic anxiety is generated. The child becomes hostile, but because the expression of hostility will cause further rejection, he tends to project this hostility out onto the external world and comes to perceive other people as basically untrustworthy. He thus feels isolated and estranged from others. The child may attempt to cope with this threatening environment in three ways: he "may move toward people, against them, or away from them. . . . In each of these attitudes one of the elements involved in basic anxiety is overemphasized: helplessness in the first, hostility in the second, and isolation in the third." In the normal person these three tendencies complement each other for effective behavior. In the neurotic these are irreconcilable, and he is caught in a severe conflict. Horney contends that this type of conflict constitutes the core of neurosis. She calls it the *basic conflict*.

Selection **22**

SOME RECENT
STUDIES OF
CONFLICT
BEHAVIOR AND
DRUGS*

NEAL E. MILLER
Yale University

Clinical studies of mental disease indicate the extreme importance of fear and conflict, two factors which usually are closely interrelated. Studies of men in combat show clearly that practically all of the common symptoms of neuroses, and even psychoses, can be produced by intense fear and conflict. Similarly, experimental studies on animals show that fear and conflict can produce behavioral disturbances, and even psychosomatic symptoms such as stomach acidity, ulcers, cardiac symptoms, and increased susceptibility to infection. Even in normal life, fear and conflict contribute significantly to human physical and mental fatigue.

My earlier work on conflict behavior was closely integrated by theory. I started with principles which had been abstracted from results of experiments in the simplified conditioning situation, and made a few additional assumptions. First, very simple deductions from these principles were tested in very simple experimental situations. Then, step by step, attempts were made to apply the joint action of a number of principles to more complex situations with additional experimental checks at each successive stage of development. The studies I am talking about here are related to the same theory; but they also attempt to investigate new variables which ultimately should be incorporated into the theory, after we have enough data to formulate reasonably probable principles. Since I am investigating a variety of such variables, the studies are somewhat heterogeneous.

In both the former work and these studies, I have benefited greatly by interaction with my

* Abridged from Neal E. Miller, "Some Recent Studies of Conflict Behavior and Drugs," *American Psychologist*, **16**: 12–24, 1961. Copyright 1961 by the American Psychological Association and reproduced by permission.

students. The work I report here is that of the entire group in my laboratory. It continues to be a great pleasure to work with such wonderful groups of students and collaborators.

EFFECTS OF SODIUM AMYTAL ON CONFLICT

First, I shall describe some studies of effects of drugs on fear and conflict done in collaboration with Herbert Barry, III. One of our purposes is to study how performance in a number of experimental situations which presumably measure fear is changed by various drugs which presumably affect fear. We want to see whether fear behaves as a single unitary variable, or whether certain drugs have more effect on the crouching-freezing pattern, while others have more effect on startle and avoidance responses, or whether the results are still more complex.

In the course of this work, we have devised a number of techniques for getting repeated measures of conflict behavior, so that each animal can be used as his own control, and so that a variety of drugs can be tested with the same group of animals.

Another of our purposes (which is the basis of the work to be exemplified here) is to make analytical studies of the behavioral effects of certain drugs which are definitely known to have interesting effects on human behavior. I shall illustrate our work by presenting some results of an analytical series of experimental studies still in progress on one of the drugs with interesting clinical effects, amobarbital sodium, commonly called sodium amytal. I believe that in a modest and incomplete way the studies of this drug illustrate a type of work which is needed on a variety of selected drugs, each of which has well-established, but different, psychological effects on the human subject.

A decade ago, John Dollard and I advanced the hypothesis that the therapeutic effects of this drug, which are especially notable in combat neuroses, are produced by reducing the avoidance component of an approach-avoidance conflict more than the approach one. In fairly extensive exploratory work on rats, Bailey and I were unable to demonstrate such an effect, but we did readily get the fear-reducing effect in an experiment on cats. In the current experiments on rats under the supervision of Barry, this drug has produced unusually consistent effects in ameliorating approach-avoidance conflict. The unexplained discrepancy with the early exploratory results on rats is puzzling and indicates the danger of generalizing too widely from observations of drug effects in a single experimental situation.

Figure 1 shows the effects of an intraperitoneal injection of 20 mg/kg of amobarbital sodium, commonly called sodium amytal, on a variety of experimental tests of fear and conflict in the albino rat. Let me briefly describe the tests.

In the *telescope alley* test, on the first trial, the rats run 1 foot to the reward, where they never receive electric shock. (Therefore this trial is labeled "0" on the ordinate which indicates threat of shock.) On each successive trial, the rats are required to run an additional foot and occasionally receive the shocks at the goal which, when they occur, are stronger the longer the distance to the goal. Incidentally, the shocks in all of our experiments are given

through a series resistance of approximately 200,000 ohms, which accounts for the high voltages. The current is 60 cycle ac.

In this test the cues for danger are primarily proprioceptive and visual. The response, which is running, involves considerable movement and is rewarded every trial.

In the *automated conflict* test, the rats press a bar for a reward on a variable interval schedule. The first 2 minutes are safe, but after that, an increasingly loud tone signals unpredictable shocks on the bar which, when they occur, are increasingly strong the louder the tone. For the last 2 minutes, the tone and shock are turned off. The cues for danger are primarily auditory, the test chamber severely limits movement, and the response of standing on the hind legs and pressing a bar is rewarded on a variable interval schedule.

The *conditioned suppression* test is similar except that the shock is delivered via the grid floor and is inescapable, so that we are measuring conflict with "freezing," rather than with active withdrawal from the bar. Except for the

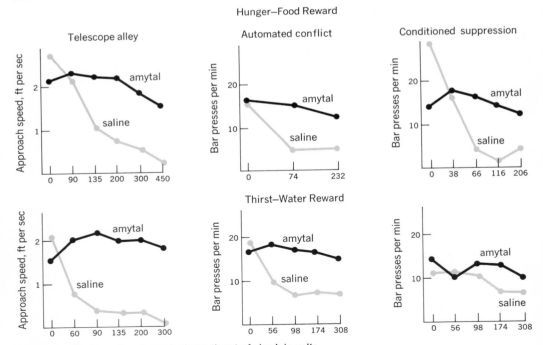

Figure 1 Abscissa of each graph shows threat of shock in volts.

minor innovation of the gradually increasing tone correlated with increasingly strong shocks, this last test is identical, of course, with the conditioned emotional response (CER) which has been developed out of Estes and Skinner's classic paper and has been extensively used by Hunt, Brady, and others.

On the test trials shown in Figure 1, no electric shocks were given, so we are dealing with the effects of fear, rather than of pain plus fear. In order to control for any effects specific to the approach drive, animals in the experiments represented in the top row were motivated by hunger and rewarded by food, while those in the bottom row were motivated by thirst and rewarded by water.

It can be seen that the results under all of these various conditions were highly similar. Looking at the beginning of each curve, which represents performance with little or no fear, it can be seen that, in general, the amytal reduced performance below the placebo level. This part of the test acts as a control to show that the effects of the amytal were not simply to produce an increase in the approach drive, or to act as a general stimulant. As the rats encountered cues to which increasingly strong fear had been conditioned, the performance following placebo was markedly reduced. But the performance under sodium amytal was not affected nearly as much by the fear-inducing cues. Thus, amytal improved the performance under fear.

The fact that so similar results appear in tests involving different cues, different responses, and different drives, makes it unlikely that the effects are specific to the peculiarities of a certain testing situation. The remarkable agreement in the results of the six different experiments makes it clear that sodium amytal definitely reduced the relative strength of fear in our different conflict situations.

Having experimentally demonstrated a striking effect on rats consonant with clinical observations on people, the next step is to determine how this effect is produced. More precise knowledge of the detailed behavioral effects of this drug is needed in order to know under what circumstances a fear-reducing effect can be expected to occur. It is also needed as a basis for relating behavioral effects to results secured with powerful new neurophysiological

and biochemical techniques for studying the action of drugs on different parts of the brain.

Primacy of habit versus direct action on fear

In all the preceding experiments, the amytal improved performance by reducing the relative strength of the fear-motivated habit. How was this effect achieved: directly by a selective action on the brain mechanisms involved in fear, or indirectly by other means? For example, in all of these experiments, as well in all other experiments that I know of on the effects of drugs on conflict, the habit of approach was established first, and the habit of avoidance second. Perhaps the drug reduced the fear-motivated avoidance not because it has a selective effect on certain fear centers, but rather because it has a selective effect on the more recently established habit.

Perhaps there is something special about the first habit to be established in any situation that makes it more resistant to drug effects—and also to other interventions. In their trail blazing papers on primary inhibition, Szwejkowska and Konorski and Szwejkowska have shown that whether a cue is first presented in an excitatory or inhibitory role makes a great deal of difference in the ease of subsequent excitatory or inhibitory conditioning, even after several reversals of the role. Perhaps primacy is more important than we have realized. How can we test for its effects in our experiments on drugs?

In the simplest of a series of experiments on this problem, we trained an animal first to go right in a T maze and then to go to the left. After the second habit was fairly well established, we tested with injections of drug or saline. The sodium amytal produced an increase in errors which would be consistent with the primacy hypothesis. Since the errors did not reliably exceed the 50% that would be expected by chance, we were unable to discriminate a differential resistance of the first-established habit to the drug for a mere increase in random behavior.

In another experiment, we tried establishing the fear of the tone in a Skinner box first before we trained the animal to press a bar to secure food there. In the hope of attaching the fear specifically to the tone, and avoiding too much fear of the whole situation, we started out with weak shocks first and gradually increased them after the animal had a chance to learn the discrimination. This procedure apparently was reasonably successful, because it was not extraordinarily difficult subsequently to train the animals to eat and then to press the bar during silent periods in the Skinner box. Then we tested for the effects of sodium amytal. If this drug primarily affects fear, results should be similar to our previous ones, but if it primarily affects the most recent habit, our results should be completely reversed.

Figure 2 shows the results. You can see that the results were similar to our previous ones; the sodium amytal had the greater effect on fear, even though it was the first-established habit. In this experiment we may have had some residual fear of the general testing situation. Such fear would account for the low initial rate of bar pressing and for the fact that the amytal had some beneficial effect on performance even before the fear-evoking tone was sounded.

In another experiment on the same topic, we used a technique analogous to our telescope alley. We used a shuttle alley 8 feet long with a light bulb at either end. Five seconds after the light at one end started flashing, an electric shock was delivered through the sections of the grid floor. This shock was strongest at the lighted end and progressively weaker in farther

sections, with the one at the opposite end having no shock. In this way, we trained the rats to shuttle from one end of the alley to the other, always staying away from the flashing light. After they had learned this, we gave the hungry rats trials of being started at alternate ends of the darkened alley, and finding food pellets in tiny cups in the center of each 1-foot section. Then they were given trials with the light flickering at the far end from the start. On these trials shocks occurred on the grid at unpredictable times, being stronger, as before, nearer to the flashing light. The rat was taken out after he had been in the alley 2 minutes, or had taken the pellet in the section nearest the flashing light.

Following this training, the animals were given the drug and placebo tests. During these test trials, no shock was actually given. The results are presented in Figure 3. It can be seen that under amytal, the animals approached farther toward the flashing light into sections with a higher threat of shock than they did after a placebo. Since the habit of approaching was established after the fear of the sections near the flashing light, we would expect exactly the *opposite* results if the main effect of the amytal had been to weaken most the most recently established habit.

The results of these two different experiments indicate that the amytal did not produce its fear-reducing effects merely by weakening the more recently established habit.

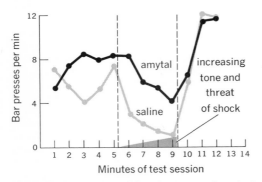

Figure 2 In the conditioned suppression test, sodium amytal affects the habit motivated by fear rather than the habit established most recently. (The rats had learned to fear the tone before they learned to press the bar.)

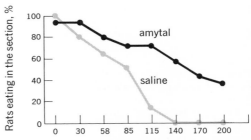

Figure 3 In the shuttle alley, sodium amytal reduces the strength of the originally learned habit of avoiding electric shock associated with a flashing light more than it does that of the subsequently learned habit of advancing to eat pellets of food found in cups spaced at 1-foot intervals.

Transfer of fear-reduction from drugged to sober state

If a drug produces a differential reduction in fear, by any one of a number of mechanisms, it may have some therapeutic usefulness as a chronic medication for people who need to have all of their fears reduced somewhat or may help to tide a person over a transient situation which is producing too much general anxiety.

In many cases, however, it is necessary to reduce a specific unrealistic fear which is far too strong without producing an equivalent reduction in realistic fears, such as those of reckless driving. Since we cannot expect any drug to have such a discriminative action tailored to the needs of the culture at a given moment in history, the patient can only be helped by retraining or, in other words, psychotherapy. Even here, a temporary use of the drug might theoretically be useful in order to help the person to become able to practice the responses he needs to learn. But as John Dollard and I pointed out, such new learning under the influence of the drug will not be useful unless it ultimately can be transferred to the normal nondrugged state. Perhaps drugs differ in this significant aspect of their effectiveness. How can we test for this?

In one of the few studies on this problem, Hunt recently found that experimental extinction of fear under chlorpromazine did not transfer effectively to the normal state. But human patients usually are not merely extinguished on their fears; they also are rewarded for performing the correct response in spite of fear. Thus the approach-avoidance conflict situation seemed to me more relevant than simple experimental extinction. It also seemed more likely to show a positive transfer effect because the reward would be expected to add counter-conditioning to the extinction of fear.

Hungry ablino rats were trained to press a bar with food as a reward on a 100% schedule. Then the bar was electrified for unpredictable brief periods approximately half of the time. The strength of these shocks was increased until such a strong conflict was established that the rats would not press the bar.

After this conflict had been set up, the rats were given a retraining session in the appara-

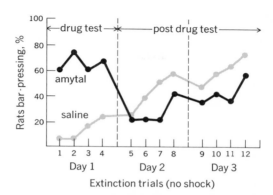

Figure 4 The therapeutic effects of sodium amytal fail to transfer from the drugged to the nondrugged condition.

tus with the shock turned off. During this session half of them had received a dose of amytal, and the other half a placebo injection. Figure 4 shows the results. You can see that during the extinction session, labeled "Drug Test," more of the amytal than the control animals resumed pressing the bar. On another day, the rats were given post-drug tests to see whether the superiority during retraining with drug transferred to the normal nondrugged state. You can see that it did not. But the apparent inferiority of the drug group is not statistically reliable.

Figure 5 shows the results of a simlar experiment with 2 mg/kg of chlorpromazine. Al-

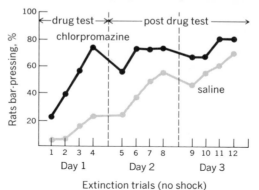

Figure 5 While chlorpromazine (2 mg/kg administered intraperitoneally 45 minutes before the test) produces less initial improvement than does sodium amytal, more of the gain seems to persist during subsequent tests without drugs.

though the initial fear-reducing effects with this drug do not seem to be as striking as those with sodium amytal, there is less loss with transfer to the normal state. The superiority of the chlorpromazine group on the post-drug test approaches statistical reliability. We are performing dose-response studies essential to establish more definitely the apparent difference in transfer of the effects of these two drugs. If indeed there is less decrement in the transfer of training from the drugged to the normal state with chlorpromazine, this difference may be related to the fact that this drug has less extensive effects on the reticular formation than does sodium amytal.

Meanwhile, these experiments clearly show that it is unsafe to assume that therapeutic transfer will occur from the drugged to the nondrugged state. It is also unsafe to assume that the drug which produces the greatest effect on immediate performance will have the greatest ultimate effect on learning transferred to the normal state. Perhaps some drugs will be discovered which are markedly superior in this crucial respect. Such a drug could make a major contribution to psychotherapy.

NEED FOR BASIC STUDIES TO ESTABLISH A SCIENCE OF PSYCHOPHARMACOLOGY

The work I have just described is a progress report rather than a completed program. By now it should be clear that an adequate study of even certain aspects of the behavioral effects of a single drug is a major project. Nevertheless, I believe it is necessary for us to take the time to be analytical and precise in determining the exact behavioral effects of a variety of drugs already known in a general way to have interesting clinical effects. Then we should advance to the further step of trying to find lawful relationships between these behavioral effects and the action of the drug on different parts of the brain as determined by techniques of neurophysiology, biochemistry, and biophysics. Out of such work may come a better understanding of how the brain functions to control behavior. Out of such work may emerge a basic science of psychopharmacology. As I have said before, the principles of such a basic science should eventually supply a rational basis for practical applications to mental health in the same way that organic chemistry provides a rational basis for the synthesis of new compounds.

DOES FEAR BECOME CONSOLIDATED WITH TIME?

In lay and clinical experience there are two schools of thought which make different assumptions concerning the setting or forgetting of fear after a traumatic event. One school of thought recommends that a person suffering a fear-inducing accident when practicing an activity, such as flying an airplane or riding a horse, should go back to it immediately before the fear has a chance to become set. The opposite school of thought recommends an immediate rest to allow the fear to subside. Of course, these human examples may be complicated by the effects of verbal rehearsal during the intervening intervals. Nevertheless, the notion has been advanced by a number of different people that a basic physiological process of consolidation occurs shortly after a new learning experience. Thus it seemed worthwhile to Edgar Coons, James Faust, and me to investigate this problem with animals.

In the first experiment, hungry rats received 30 trials at the rate of 5 a day running down an elevated strip to food. Then they were divided into two matched groups. On the first trial of the next day, upon touching the food, each rat received a traumatic electric shock at the goal and then was immediately removed to its home cage. Thirty seconds later the rats in the first group were returned to the runway for a test, while those in the second group were tested 24 hours later. The time required to touch food was recorded with a 5-minute maximum limit. It can be seen from the left-hand side of Figure 6 that the rats tested 24 hours later required twice as long to go back to touch the food than those tested 30 seconds afterwards. Since the difference is highly reliable, we may conclude that the relative strength of avoidance, and hence presumably of fear, increased during the 24-hour interval immediately following the strong electric shock.

We have considered a number of hypotheses to explain these results. One is that the fear is consolidated during the interval. Another is that the excitement produced by the electric shock has a dynamogenic effect that increases the rat's tendency to run up to the goal immediately afterwards. Another is that under the particular conditions of this experiment, the stimulus conditions for the 30-second group differed more than did those for the 24-hour group from the ones immediately preceding the strong shock. Then it follows that the greater stimulus change for the 30-second group should produce a greater decrement in avoidance than in approach, so that this group would reach the goal sooner.

To describe this stimulus-change hypothesis in more detail, let us note that, when the animals received their shock, it was the first trial of the day, and they had not received any immediately preceding shock. For these animals tested 24 hours later, it was again the first trial of the day, and as before, they had not received any immediately preceding shock. But for the 30-second group the conditions were different in that it was the second trial of the day and they had just received an electric shock. Assuming that some sort of after-effects from the immediately preceding trial and/or shock persist, these would be expected to change the stimulus situation. These changes should produce a greater decrement in the avoidance motivated by fear than in the approach motivated by hunger. Therefore, these animals should show relatively less avoidance.

How can we test this hypothesis? Suppose we change the conditions so that the two factors—an immediately preceding trial and an immediately preceding shock—make the training and test conditions more similar for the 30-second group instead of for the 24-hour one. Then, we will expect the direction of the difference of the two groups to be reversed. The other two hypotheses would not predict such a reversal.

To test this prediction, we ran additional animals in another experiment exactly similar to the foregoing one, except that, instead of giving them their shock in the runway on the first trial of the day, we gave it to them on the third trial. We also gave them a shock in a quite different apparatus 30 seconds before their shock trial in the alley. When these animals were being trained to avoid the goal by

being shocked there, they had the stimulus after-effects of an immediately preceding trial and shock. But when tested 24 hours later, they were in a somewhat different stimulus context of no immediately preceding trials and no immediately preceding shock. Therefore, we would expect their avoidance to be relatively weaker on this test 24 hours later, so that the results would be completely opposite to those of the preceding experiment.

The right-hand side of Figure 6 shows the results of the second experiment. It can be seen that the results are opposite to those in the first experiment. The difference is highly reliable ($p < .01$). Instead of being consolidated with time, the relative strength of fear was reduced in the second experiment. The stimulus-change hypothesis was confirmed. Under the conditions of these experiments, differences in the stimulus traces were shown to be more important than any setting or forgetting of fear with time.

The results of these two experiments impress us with the importance of trying to analyze the exact stimulus conditions under which the fear was originally established and those under which it is tested.

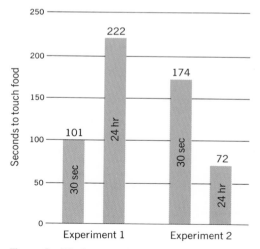

Figure 6 Whether or not a 24-hour interval produces consolidation or forgetting of fear depends upon details of the experimental situation, which were designed to affect the degree to which the interval of time restored or altered the pattern of cues present when the traumatic shock was received.

LEARNING RESISTANCE TO STRESS

The final experiments I shall describe have to do with learning resistance to pain and fear in an approach-avoidance conflict situation. Can resistance to stressful situations be learned? If such learning is possible, what are the laws determining its effectiveness and generality?

In one experiment on this topic, which is reported in more detail elsewhere, albino rats were trained to run down an alley for food. Their criterion task was to continue running in spite of 400-volt electric shocks administered through a 250,000-ohm series resistance for .1 second immediately after they reached the goal. Some of these animals were introduced to the shock suddenly, other were given special training to resist the shock by receiving first mild shocks at the goal, followed by trials with shocks of gradually increasing strength.

The results are presented in Figure 7. You can see that the animals that had been habituated to gradually increasing shocks in the alley continued to run much faster than those in the sudden groups which had not received the same type of training.

Was the superior performance of the gradually habituated group a general effect of mere exposure to the shocks, or, as our theoretical analysis demanded, was it an effect dependent upon specific rewarded training in the criterion situation? This was tested by giving another group the same gradual habituation to the same shocks administered at a different time of day in a distinctive box outside of the alley. You can see that this group was not appreciably helped. Apparently, mere exposure to tough treatments will not necessarily improve resistance to stress in a different criterion situation.

As a control for the effect of additional training trials in the alley, we ran one group which was suddenly exposed to 400-volt shocks at the goal on the same trial that the gradual group received its first mild shocks, and we ran another group which was suddenly exposed to the 400-volt shocks at the same time that the gradual group reached the level of 400 volts. As you have already seen, the

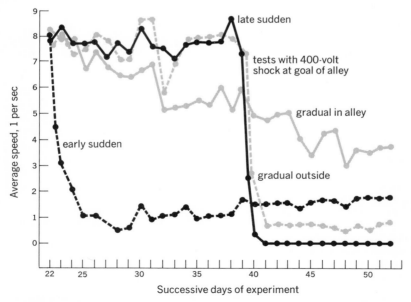

Figure 7 Hungry rats may be trained to resist stress by continuing to run down an alley to a goal where they receive both food and electric shock. Under these conditions, previous overlearning of the habit of running to food decreases, rather than increases, resistance to stress.

performance of both of these groups was poorer than that of the rats receiving the gradually increasing shocks at the goal of the alley. But looking at the curves for these two groups immediately after the sudden shocks were introduced, we can see a surprising fact. The speed of the group shocked late in training falls off much more rapidly than that of the one shocked early in training. This difference, which is reliable at the .02 level of confidence, confirms earlier suggestive results in our laboratory by Eileen Karsh. It is directly contrary to the widely-held notion that overtraining will increase resistance to stress.

The results of the foregoing experiment suggest that it should be feasible and profitable to analyze further at both the animal and human level, the laws governing the learning of resistance to stresses, such as pain, fear, fatigue, frustration, noise, nausea, and extremes of temperature.

Two of my colleagues, David Williams and Herbert Barry III, have already performed an interesting experiment providing behavioral evidence for the counterconditioning of fear. Rats were trained on a variable interval schedule of food reward. On exactly the same variable interval schedule, they were given a gradually increasing series of electric shocks for pressing the bar. For one group the food and shock schedules were in phase, so that every time they got a shock, a pellet of food was promptly delivered; for the other group, the schedules were out of phase, so that they received the same number and distribution of shocks, but at times when food was not delivered. You should note that for each bar press in both groups, the probability of food or shock was equally great and equally unpredictable. Nevertheless, the correlation of shock with food apparently rendered shock less disrupting to the rat, because the animals in the in-phase group continued pressing through considerably higher levels of shock than those in the out-of-phase group.

At present we are trying to secure objective measures of the counterconditioning of physiological responses to pain, a phenomenon suggested by Pavlov. If we succeed, we want to study this phenomenon in greater detail to determine how it is affected by factors such as strength of drive, amount and schedule of reward, and experimental extinction.

SUMMARY

In the first part of this paper I have described a series of experiments analyzing how a drug with well-established clinical effects on human behavior may act to achieve some of these effects. Amobarbital sodium, commonly called sodium amytal, was the drug selected for this first series of experiments. As the first step, we established that we could produce in experiments on rats, effects which appear to parallel the fear-reducing effects of this drug in human conflict situations. These effects were repeated in experiments in three different types of apparatus with the approach motivated by two different drives. We also found that it was not primarily due to a greater effect of the drug on the more recently established habit of avoidance; similar effects were secured when avoidance was learned first.

One series of experiments suggested that the fear-reducing effects of the drug in the Skinner box were not due merely to interference with the rat's ability to discriminate the tone used as a cue for danger in that situation. But another experiment in the alley situation showed that the drug either did interfere with discrimination, or produced recovery from experimental extinction. Thus, although a number of indirect modes of action have been ruled out, we have not yet decisively narrowed down the drug's fear-reducing effects to a direct action on the fear mechanism.

Finally, we found that the beneficial effects of the sodium amytal on relearning in a conflict situation did not generalize from the drugged to the normal state. Chlorpromazine yielded more promising results on this crucial test. Dose-response studies are in progress to determine the generality of the difference between the drugs in this respect.

We have also seen that some conditions can produce an apparent consolidation of fear with the passing of time, while other conditions produce an apparent forgetting of fear. In these experiments, the crucial factor seems to be the extent to which the elapsed time changes or restores the cues present immediately before the traumatic electric shock.

Finally, we have seen that it is possible to increase the resistance to the stress of pain and fear by appropriate training. But one of the most obvious methods, overlearning, can reduce, rather than improve, the resistance of the habit to disruption by fear.

Selection 23 | SODIUM AMYTAL AND PARTIALLY REINFORCED RUNWAY PERFORMANCE*

ALLAN R. WAGNER

Yale University

Acquisition performance of rats in a simple runway was investigated as a function of percentage reinforced trials (100% vs. 50%) and injection solution received prior to daily training (sodium amytal vs. isotonic saline) in a 2 × 2 factorial design. The results obtained from 4 groups of 12 Ss showed 50% reinforcement to lead to faster final speeds than 100% reinforcement with saline control injections; whereas this order was reversed under training with sodium amytal. The results were predicted from a frustration theory interpretation of random partial reinforcement and the assumption that anticipatory frustration is particularly susceptible to the depressant action of sodium amytal.

A relatively consistent finding in appetitional runway studies (e.g., Goodrich, 1959; Haggard, 1959; Wagner, 1961; Weinstock, 1958) is that rats will attain faster running speeds over all but the last segments of an alley, if rewards are received on only a random 50% of the trials than if they are received on every trial. Theoretical interpretations of this finding have frequently appealed to motivational differences associated with the anticipatory goal responses conditioned under the two reinforcement schedules. For example, Wagner (1961) has assumed that while *anticipatory reward*, or incentive motivation, is greater under continuous reinforcement, a motivational advantage remains under partial reinforcement, due to the added drive effects of *anticipatory frustration*.

* Reprinted from Allan R. Wagner, "Sodium Amytal and Partially Reinforced Runway Performance," *Journal of Experimental Psychology*, 65: 474–477, 1963. Copyright 1963 by the American Psychological Association and reproduced by permission.

This position, in conjunction with the familiar assumption (e.g., Wilson, Weiss, & Amsel, 1955) that partially reinforced Ss learn to approach in the presence of anticipatory frustration as well as anticipatory reward, allows the deduction that partially reinforced Ss will approach faster than continuously reinforced Ss. The position also suggests, however, that if the drive effects of anticipatory frustration were removed, partially reinforced Ss would respond slower than continuously reinforced Ss.

In a recent report Barry, Wagner, and Miller (1962) advanced the argument that anticipatory frustration, like fear, may be particularly susceptible to the depressant action of alcohol and sodium amytal. If this argument is sound, a manipulation is available for reducing anticipatory frustration, and consequently for testing the above prediction. That is, while partially reinforced Ss should run faster, asymptotically, than continuously reinforced Ss following saline control injections, they should run slower following similar injections of either alcohol or sodium amytal. The following experiment was designed to evaluate this prediction in the case of the latter drug.

METHOD

Subjects The Ss were 48 experimentally naive, male albino rats of Sprague-Dawley strain, purchased from the Charles River Breeding Laboratories. Their ages ranged from 100 to 110 days at the beginning of experimental training.

Apparatus The apparatus was an enclosed, straight alley with gray, pine, side and end walls and hardware cloth ceiling and floor. The alley was 3½ in. wide and 4 in. high throughout, and divided by guillotine doors into three sections, a 15-in. start box, a 39-in. runway, and an 18-in. goal box. Two measures of locomotor performance were provided. Starting time was recorded from the raising of the start door until the interruption of a light beam 6 in. distant. Running time was recorded from the breaking of the first beam until the interruption of a second beam located 12 in. from the end wall of the goal box. A metal food cup, 1¼ in. in diameter, was permanently affixed to the end wall.

The apparatus was located in a quiet, dimly illuminated room maintained at approximately 72° F.

The Ss were also housed, in individual cages, in this same room throughout the experiment.

Procedure Eight days prior to acquisition training Ss were placed on a 24-hr. deprivation schedule. Each S received 12 gm. Purina lab chow checkers each day, 1 hr. after its daily training. Water was freely available. During the course of these 8 days Ss were habituated to the experimental situation by systematic handling, exposure to the reward pellets (.045 gm. each, purchased from the P. J. Noyes Company) scattered on a raised platform, exposure to the runway in groups of 3, and finally, a direct placement in the goal box with seven reward pellets in the food cup.

This preliminary training was followed by a total of 64 acquisition trials in the alley, 2 trials on Days 1 and 2, and 4 trials on subsequent days. On each day of acquisition S was given an intraperitoneal injection of drug or saline and replaced in its home cage. Ten minutes later S was introduced into the start box. After approximately 5 sec. the start-box door was raised, allowing S to traverse the runway. When S entered the goal box, the goal-box door was lowered to prevent retracing. The S was removed from the goal box immediately after eating, or in the case of nonreward trials, after 20 sec., and returned to its home cage. The Ss were run in squads of 6, each trial in rotation. This produced an average intertrial interval of 4–5 min., and allowed all daily trials to be run within the 10–30 min. period following injection.

Twelve Ss were assigned to each of four experimental groups, distinguished by the combination of reinforcement schedule and injection solution received. Two groups received injections of 20 mg/kg sodium amytal (2 ml/kg of a 10 mg/ml solution of isotonic saline) while the other two received equal volumes of isotonic saline. These dosages were the same as those used by Barry, Wagner, and Miller (1962). Within each injection condition one group received 100% reinforcement in the alley and the other 50%. The schedule of rewards for the 50% groups over the 64 trials was obtained by repeating the following sequence: + − + − − + + − − − + + + − − +. All Ss received seven pellets on rewarded trials.

The experiment was conducted in two replications, 3 mo. apart, by different Es each running 6 of the Ss in each of the experimental groups.[1]

[1] The first replication was run by Merle F. Goldstein, the second by Mary W. Miller.

RESULTS AND DISCUSSIONS

For purposes of analysis each S's individual starting and running times were converted to speeds in ft/sec. Since the two response measures yielded essentially identical results, only one measure will be reported here. Running speed was chosen for presentation since it was less likely to be influenced by inter- or intra-E variability in placement of Ss in the start box or in operation of the start door.

Figure 1 presents, for the two replications combined, the mean running speeds of the four experimental groups over successive blocks of eight acquisition trials. As may be observed, the two sodium amytal groups were not only slower than the two saline control groups, but the final order of the 50% and 100% groups was reversed in the two injection conditions. Whereas the 50% saline group ran faster than its corresponding 100% group, the 50% sodium amytal group ran slower than its corresponding 100% group.

Analysis of variance appropriate for a factorial design was performed on the mean speeds over the last 16 trials. The results of this analysis support the reliability of both the overall depressing effect of sodium amytal, $F (1, 40) = 67.81$, $p < .001$, and the interaction of this effect with the reinforcement schedule, $F (1, 40) = 7.64$, $p < .01$. Subsequent t tests relevant to this interaction, employing the within-cells MS as the estimate of error variance, revealed 50% reinforcement to produce significantly faster speeds than 100% reinforcement under saline, $t (40) = 2.26$, $p < .025$, one-tailed, but significantly slower speeds than 100% reinforcement under sodium amytal, $t (40) = 1.70$, $p < .05$, one-tailed.

A comparison of the results from the two replications further attests to the stability of these findings. The general picture presented in Fig. 1 was obtained in each replication, with no statistically significant difference between the two in overall drug effect, $F (1, 40) = 2.75$, $p < .10$, or in the Solution × Reinforcement Schedule interaction ($F < 1$), although the absolute speeds obtained by one E were consistently higher than those obtained by the other E, $F (1, 40) = 27.75$, $p < .001$.

The results are clearly in accord with the pre-

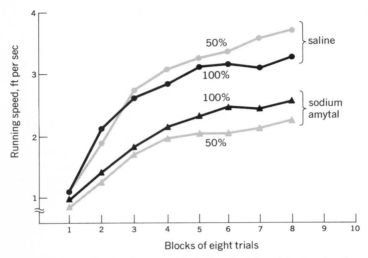

Figure 1 Mean running speeds in blocks of eight trials for the four experimental groups.

diction made. The general reduction in running speeds produced by sodium amytal is consistent with the drug's classification (e.g., Goodman & Gilman, 1955, Ch. 9) as a central nervous system depressant. The exaggeration of this effect under partial, as compared to continuous, reinforcement training, however, requires a more detailed theoretical interpretation. The dual assertion, that partially reinforced approaching is in part mediated and energized by anticipatory frustration, and that sodium amytal selectively reduces this emotional response, provides such an interpretation. The observation that partially reinforced Ss ran slower than continuously reinforced Ss, when the effects of anticipatory frustration had presumably been reduced via sodium amytal, is also in agreement with the assumption that anticipatory reward is lower under partial than under continuous reinforcement.

It should not be overlooked that random partial reinforcement has been specifically treated (e.g., Wagner, 1961) as a special case in which Ss are reinforced for continuing to approach in the presence of anticipatory frustration. Without such special training, anticipatory frustration has been assumed (e.g., Wagner, 1961) to elicit avoidance responses. Consequently, a reduction in anticipatory frustration should, by reducing avoidance behavior, more

typically produce an increase in previously frustrated responses. Barry, Wagner, and Miller (1962), for example, observed that administration of sodum amytal was followed by an increase in performance previously reduced by experimental extinction.

Considering both the present results and those obtained by Barry, Wagner, and Miller within the context of existing frustration theory, the single assumption, that sodium amytal reduces anticipatory frustration, is able to account for empirically quite diverse effects of the drug. This fact is, at least, encouraging to the sodium amytal assumption as well as to the several tenets of frustration theory involved.

REFERENCES

Barry, H., III, Wagner, A. R., & Miller, N. E. Effects of alcohol and amobarbital on performance inhibited by experimental extinction. *J. comp. physiol. Psychol.*, 1962, **55**, 464–468.

Goodman, L. S., & Gilman, A. *The pharmacological basis of therapeutics.* (2nd ed.) New York: Macmillan, 1955.

Goodrich, K. P. Performance in different segments of an instrumental response chain as a function of reinforcement schedule. *J. exp. Psychol.*, 1959, **57**, 57–63.

Haggard, D. F. Acquisition of a simple running response as a function of partial and continuous schedules of reinforcement. *Psychol. Rec.,* 1959, **9,** 11–18.

Wagner, A. R. Effects of amount and percentage of reinforcement and number of acquisition trials on conditioning and extinction. *J. exp. Psychol.,* 1961, **62,** 234–242.

Weinstock, S. Acquisition and extinction of a partially reinforced running response at a 24-hr. inter- trial interval. *J. exp. Psychol.,* 1958, **56,** 151– 159.

Wilson, W., Weiss, I. J., & Amsel, A. Two tests of the Sheffield hypothesis concerning resistance to extinction, partial reinforcement, and distri- bution of practice. *J. exp. Psychol.,* 1955, **50,** 51–60.

Selection **24** | REACTION TO FRUSTRATION— A CRITIQUE AND HYPOTHESIS*

S. STANSFELD SARGENT
Columbia University

The problem of frustration has commanded considerable attention during the last decade. Not only psychiatrists and specialists in clinical and abnormal psychology, but also students of personality and social psychology have become interested in frustration. The *Frustration and Aggression* volume by the Yale collaborators, Dollard, Doob, Miller, Mowrer and Sears, has helped focus attention on the subject, as have papers by Maslow, Rosenzweig and others.

While dealing with the concept of frustra- tion in a course in Social Psychology, I became convinced that current treatments of frustra- tion still lack a systematic framework and a clear definition of terms. The major concepts which are used lack integration; for example, frustration, conflict, motives, emotions, de- fense mechanisms, habit patterns, personality factors of many kinds, and situational influ- ences. Several instances might be cited to il- lustrate confusion in usage of terms. 'Frustra-

* Reprinted from S. Stansfeld Sargent, "Reaction to Frustration—A Critique and Hypothesis," *Psycho- logical Review*, 55: 108–114, 1948. Copyright 1948 by the American Psychological Association and repro- duced by permission.

tion' usually refers to environmental blocking of motives, but sometimes to an unpleasant emotional state resulting from the blocking. At times 'hostility' seems to mean actual be- havior; again it signifies a strong feeling under- lying behavior. 'Inferiority,' 'insecurity,' 'anxi- ety,' 'guilt' and many other concepts are frequently employed in ways which are unclear psychologically. Probably the worst of all is 'aggression,' which sometimes seems to mean a motive, sometimes an emotional state akin to anger, sometimes a habit of mechanism, and sometimes a type of overt behavior!

I wish to propose a rather simple conceptual scheme for describing behavior resulting from frustration. It is presented as a hypothesis which seems reasonably consistent with clini- cal and experimental data and also with many of the theoretical formulations which have been advanced.

Briefly the hypothesis is this: frustration evokes a patterned sequence of behavior whose chief stages or aspects are indicated by the terms *frustration, emotion, habit or mecha- nism,* and *overt behavior.* The nature of each stage of the total process is determined by the interaction of two major factors: the indi- vidual's past experience, and the present situa- tion as perceived or defined by the individual. Let us consider each of these in more detail.

It is well agreed that frustration involves the thwarting or blocking of a person's dominant motives, needs, drives, desires or purposes. However, some psychologists place greater stress upon the thwarting than upon the indi- vidual's reaction to it. For example, the Yale group defines frustration as "that condition which exists when a goal-response suffers in- terference." In his recent book Symonds defines it as "the blocking or interference of the satisfaction of an aroused need through some barrier or obstruction." Others empha- size not so much the thwarting, *per se,* as the significance of the thwarting to the individual. Maslow insists that frustration involves two concepts—deprivation, and threat to the per- sonality. Sexual deprivation, for example, does not necessarily constitute frustration, but when such deprivation is felt by the individual to represent rejection by the opposite sex, inferi- ority, or lack or respect, it becomes seriously frustrating. Similarly, Rosenzweig distinguishes between 'need-persistive' and 'ego-defensive' reactions, the latter representing greater frustration. Zander maintains that frustration occurs only when there is interference with "a goal believed important and attainable by a given person." In all probability future studies of frustration will take into account such subjective individual differences as are mentioned by Maslow, Rosenzweig and Zander.

In any event, we turn next to the question, What is the immediate psychological consequence of frustration? It is definitely not aggression, as most readers of *Frustration and Aggression* might assume. Nor is it the adoption of some handy defense mechanism, as others might conclude. First in time, and foremost in significance, frustration arouses a *pronounced emotional reaction.*

Most students of frustration refer to concomitant emotional tensions, but they seldom make emotion a central aspect of the whole reaction pattern. According to the present hypothesis, emotion is the core of reaction to frustration. If no emotion is aroused, there is no frustration—at least not in any psychologically meaningful sense.

Furthermore, the emotion aroused may be broad and diffuse, like a generalized anger or fear, or it may be fairly specific, like hostility, jealousy, inferiority or shame. Whether the emotion is general or specific depends largely upon the nature of the whole precipitating situation as interpreted by the individual.

It is clearly established that strong emotional reactions upset the organism and tend to pass over into overt behavior. However, the form of the resultant behavior is not, *ipso facto*, determined by the kind and intensity of the emotion. Behavior is, of course, partly dependent upon the emotion which agitates the organism; anger is more likely to work itself out in aggressive behavior than is anxiety or shame. But the form of the overt reaction is importantly affected by the individual's adjustive habits or mechanisms, and by the way he interprets the situation.

The above analysis agrees rather well with Rosenzweig's interpretation. In studying reactions to frustration, according to Rosenzweig, we must be concerned not with what is objectively present, but instead with what the individual emphasizes or reads into the situation according to his personality needs and traits. He finds three main types of reaction

to frustration. The 'extrapunitive' is an aggressive reaction toward others. It arises from anger and indignation and from the individual's judgment which blames others; "I'll get you!" is its thesis. Thus, if snubbed by a friend, the extrapunitive reaction is to regard him as ill-bred and ungrateful. The 'intropunitive' is an aggressive reaction directed toward the self. It comes from feelings of humiliation and guilt, and from judgments of self-blame. The intropunitive reaction to a snub is to regard oneself as inferior and unworthy. The 'impunitive' reaction is unaggressive. It arises from feelings of embarrassment and shame and from the judgment "It can't be helped." A friend's snub would be condoned or glossed over as an oversight.

More than any other interpreter of frustration, Rosenzweig stresses the importance of both emotional and 'apperceptive' or judgmental factors. I feel, however, that he has made the latter too conscious. According to my hypothesis there is a continuously operating, relatively unconscious perceptual process which may be called 'defining the situation.'

This term is taken from the sociologist, W. I. Thomas. It was used by him and by others to designate the process of perceiving and interpreting, and also of exploring the behavior possibilities of a social situation. It has elements in common with Lewin's 'psychological environment' and with Sherif's 'frames of reference.' But 'defining the situation' is more than perceiving; it is a kind of active perceiving, interpreting and sizing up a situation with reference to one's potential behavior in it. We cannot know how a given situation influences an individual unless we know how he defines it for himself.

Strong emotions, then, tend toward overt behavior, but always directed and limited by the individual's adjustive habits and by the way he defines the situation. He may customarily express his emotions freely, or he may repress them. Or he may be adept at utilizing substitute forms—*i.e.*, mechanisms—for expressing his strong emotions which are the essence of frustration. Generally speaking, the more stress or threat he reads into the immediate social situation, the more inhibited and disguised his expressive behavior will be.

Our analysis will be made clearer by the use of an example and a diagram [see Fig. 1]. An

Frustrated Motive   Emotion, "Feeling"   Habit or Mechanism   Overt Behavior

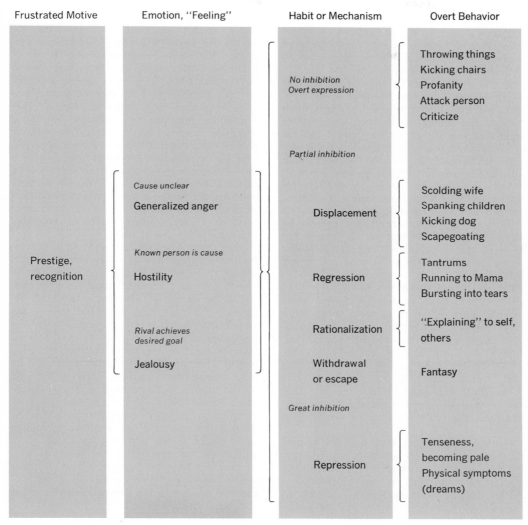

Figure 1   Reaction to frustration.

individual intent upon an important promotion in his business or profession learns the promotion has been won by another person, which produces real frustration. He becomes emotional—but how? If the event is unexpected and the cause unclear, the emotion is a generalized sort of anger. If he knows, or thinks he knows, whose efforts defeated him, his emotional reaction takes the more specific form of hostility or hatred, quite possibly with components of jealously. Psychologically this is a different phenomenon from generalized anger (though it may be similar physiologically) since it is directed toward a particular individual.

Let us assume, however, that our individual has no detailed information about the events leading up to the loss of his expected promotion and that, therefore, he is in a state of generalized anger. Then what? If he characteristically expresses emotion in an uninhibited way, he may throw things, kick chairs around and curse vehemently. But he is less likely to do this if persons whose opinions he values are present. If they are, he might rather engage in some substitute type of expression, such as rationalizing or seeking sympathy.

On the other hand, he may be the kind of person who seldom gives free vent to his emotions. He may then displace his anger upon his wife and children if they are present. He might kick the dog or cat, or 'take it out' on a clumsy delivery boy, all depending upon who is present at the time and what his relationship to them happens to be. Or if he were a person of violent prejudices, he might displace his anger upon 'the Jews,' 'the Reds,' 'the Catholics' or some other handy scapegoat. Again, he might regress; if his mother were present he might burst into tears and put his face in her lap as he always did when a child. Or he might engage in one or another kind of comforting fantasy.

Actually he would probably utilize more than one kind of defense mechanism. Seldom does a single outlet relieve all of one's strong emotional tensions. An immediate emotional outburst might well be followed by rationalizing, fantasy, or some kind of compensatory behavior. Clinical data suggest that as children most of us acquire quite a repertory of forms of substitute expression. Hence the particular one or ones we employ depend in large measure upon the social situation as we interpret it.

Another possibility is that, because of past training and/or a very stringent social situation, an individual may inhibit or repress nearly all overt behavior. If so, we would expect some sort of delayed overt expression, possibly in disguised form, as in dreams or physical symptoms of illness.

Does frustration eventuate in aggression? At the beginning of their book the Yale psychologists proposed "that the existence of frustration always leads to some form of aggression." This thesis is hard to defend, as two of the authors, Miller and Sears, point out in subsequent articles.[1]

Much behavior resulting from frustration is, of course, aggressive. Probably the Yale group arrived at their sweeping conclusion partly because the cases they considered were dramatic, short-time, anger-producing kinds of frustration—the young man who was bawled out by the traffic cop while driving with his girl, the boarders and the delayed dinner, and so on. Clinical data, however, suggest that frustration may produce different emotional reactions, such as fear, anxiety, inferiority or shame, sometimes without any trace of anger, hostility or jealously. Symonds considers anxiety a very common reaction to frustration. In fact, he defines anxiety as a "mental distress with respect to some anticipated frustration." Rosenzweig, as already mentioned, notes that frustration may produce emotional reactions like humiliation and shame.

What kind of overt behavior occurs when frustration gives rise to other emotions than anger? Consider an example, diagrammed in Fig. 2. Here is a 'rejected' child—a child frustrated by denial of affection and social response. If the situation is unclear to him, his emotional reaction is one of general anxiety or insecurity. What does he do? He may, indeed, compensate and engage in bullying, boasting and other kinds of aggressive behavior. But he may instead compensate by making a friend of the teacher or by forming a strong attachment for an older boy or girl. He may seek satisfaction through identification—either by playing the role of a 'big shot' or by joining some social group with prestige value. If he withdraws and daydreams, his fantasies may or may not be of an aggressive sort. In other words, we suggest that aggression is not necessarily present in the compensatory or other substitute behavior.

Here again, past experience and the prevailing social situation are both important. The child's behavior is partly a function of the kind of emotion aroused, partly of his training—whether or not he has learned to express himself aggressively, for example—and partly of

---

[1] The first part of the same proposition is "that the occurrence of aggressive behavior always presupposes the existence of frustration." We shall not discuss the subject here, except to suggest that it is also difficult to defend as a general statement. Certain kinds of behavior which are definitely aggressive seem to be the socially sanctioned ways of behaving in some communities (e.g., a tough city slum area or a primitive culture). Such behavior may well be learned and practiced without having its origin, necessarily in frustration.

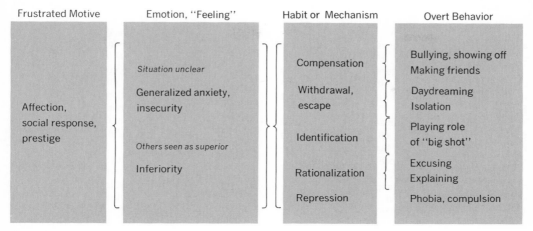

Figure 2 Reaction to frustration.

his interpretation of the situation, such as whether or not he defines it as containing a potentially sympathetic person.

What about the relation between 'frustration' and 'conflict'? Frustration is usually considered an objective or environmental kind of thwarting; conflict is a subjective clash of incompatible motives. The current tendency seems to be to consider conflict a special case of frustration. Many psychologists, however, treat frustration and conflict separately and do not attempt to relate them. In terms of the present hypothesis the important point is that both frustration and conflict involve dynamic and highly upsetting emotional states which impel the organism toward some sort of overt behavior. Reaction to conflict, as to frustration, follows the same sequence: emotion, habit or mechanism, and overt behavior. For instance, conflict arising from performance of an act considered immoral may arouse a feeling of generalized anxiety, or a more specific feeling of guilt, embarrassment or shame. Habits and mechanisms come into play. Through sublimation the emotional reaction may impel one toward religious or altruistic activity; through projection, toward gossip or scandal-mongering; through repression, toward phobia or compulsion; through a kind of displacement toward masochism or other self-directed aggression. The nature of the frustration largely determines the basic emotional reaction, and the resultant

behavior depends upon existing habit-patterns operating in the individually defined social situation.

The above discussion has omitted many important aspects of the problem of frustration. It has not dealt with the efficacy of resultant behavior in reducing emotional tensions evoked by frustration. It has neglected the important matters, so ably treated by the Yale group, of the effects of differing degrees and strengths of instigation, or the effects of anticipated punishment. Nor has it dealt with the concept of 'frustration tolerance' which is taken up by Rosenzweig and others.

The critique and hypothesis presented above is a systematic contribution designed to fill in certain gaps and to fit loose ends together. Some psychologists may object to such an analysis, *per se*, as violating the essential unity or Gestalt-character of behavior. The only answer, I suppose, is that some kinds of behavior are too complex to be treated as a whole; they have to be analyzed, though efforts must be made to put the pieces together again. Other psychologists will undoubtedly object to certain of the statements and interpretations. The whole hypothesis needs, of course, to be verified by clinical or experimental methods.

In addition to setting up the four stage scheme of frustration-mechanism-overt behavior, the hypothesis proposes the following things:

It makes emotion the central dynamic factor in reaction to frustration, and distinguishes between generalized emotional states (e.g., anger, anxiety) and more specific and directed states or 'feelings' (e.g., hostility, jealousy, inferiority).

It stresses the interoperation of both past experience and present situations as determining the form and content of resulting overt behavior.

Furthermore, it emphasizes that the crucial present factor is not the situation as it exists in some objective sense, but rather as the individual defines and interprets it.

Most of all, perhaps, this paper represents a protest against what Leeper calls 'peripheralism' in psychology; that is to say, the description of behavior chiefly in terms of stimuli and overt responses, to the neglect of intervening organismic factors. Hence it is, in brief, an attempt to describe all the significant psychological variables which interoperate when a person is frustrated.

Selection 25 | OUR INNER CONFLICTS*

| KAREN HORNEY
| *New York City*

Let me say to begin with: It is not neurotic to have conflicts. At one time or another our wishes, our interests, our convictions are bound to collide with those of others around us. And just as such clashes between ourselves and our environment are a commonplace, so, too, conflicts within ourselves are an integral part of human life.

An animal's actions are largely determined by instinct. Its mating, its care for its young, its search for food, its defenses against danger are more or less prescribed and beyond individual decision. In contrast, it is the prerogative as well as the burden of human beings to be able to exert choice, to have to make decisions. We may have to decide between desires that lead in opposite directions. We may, for instance, want to be alone but also want to

be with a friend; we may want to study medicine but also to study music. Or there may be a conflict between wishes and obligations: we may wish to be with a lover when someone in trouble needs our care. We may be divided between a desire to be in accord with others and a conviction that would entail expressing an opinion antagonistic to them. We may be in conflict, finally, between two sets of values, as occurs when we believe in taking on a hazardous job in wartime but believe also in our duty to our family.

The kind, scope, and intensity of such conflicts are largely determined by the civilization in which we live. If the civilization is stable and tradition bound, the variety of choices presenting themselves are limited and the range of possible individual conflicts narrow. Even then they are not lacking. One loyalty may interfere with another; personal desires may stand against obligations to the group. But if the civilization is in a stage of rapid transition, where highly contradictory values and divergent ways of living exist side by side, the choices the individual has to make are manifold and difficult. He can conform to the expectations of the community or be a dissenting individualist, be gregarious or live as a recluse, worship success or despise it, have faith in strict discipline for children or allow them to grow up without much interference; he can believe in a different moral standard for men and women or hold that the same should apply for both, regard sexual relations as an expression of human intimacy or divorce them from ties of affection; he can foster racial discrimination or take the stand that human values are independent of the color of skin or the shape of noses—and so on and so forth.

When conflicts center about the primary issues of life, it is all the more difficult to face them and resolve them. But provided we are sufficiently alive, there is no reason why in principle we should not be able to do so. Education could do much to help us to live with greater awareness of ourselves and to develop our own convictions. A realization of the significance of the factors involved in choice would give us ideals to strive for, and in that a direction for our lives.[1]

---

* From Karen Horney, *Our Inner Conflicts*, W. W. Norton & Company, Inc., New York, 1945. Reprinted by permission of the publisher.

[1] To normal persons merely dulled by environmental pressures, a book like Harry Emerson Fosdick's *On Being a Real Person* would be of considerable profit.

The difficulties always inherent in recognizing and resolving a conflict are immeasurably increased when a person is neurotic. Neurosis, it must be said, is always a matter of degree—and when I speak of "a neurotic" I invariably mean "a person to the extent that he is neurotic." For him awareness of feelings and desires is at a low ebb. Often the only feelings experienced consciously and clearly are reactions of fear and anger to blows dealt to vulnerable spots. And even these may be repressed. Such authentic ideals as do exist are so pervaded by compulsive standards that they are deprived of their power to give direction. Under the sway of these compulsive tendencies the faculty to renounce is rendered impotent, and the capacity to assume responsibility for oneself all but lost.

Neurotic conflicts may be concerned with the same general problems as perplex the normal person. But they are so different in kind that the question has been raised whether it is permissible to use the same term for both. I believe it is, but we must be aware of the differences. What, then, are the characteristics of neurotic conflicts?

Conflicts play an infinitely greater role in neurosis than is commonly assumed. To detect them, however, is no easy matter—partly because they are essentially unconscious, but even more because the neurotic goes to any length to deny their existence. What, then, are the signals that would warrant us to suspect underlying conflicts? In the examples cited [in an earlier chapter] their presence was indicated by two factors, both fairly obvious. One was the resulting symptoms—fatigue in the first case, stealing in the second. The fact is that every neurotic symptom points to an underlying conflict; that is, every symptom is a more or less direct outgrowth of a conflict. We shall see gradually what unresolved conflicts do to people, how they produce states of anxiety, depression, indecision, inertia, detachment, and so on. An understanding of the causative relation here helps direct our attention from the manifest disturbances to their source—though the exact nature of the source will not be disclosed.

The other signal indicating that conflicts were in operation was inconsistency. In the first example we saw a man convinced of a procedure being wrong and of injustice done him, making no move to protest. In the second a person who highly valued friendship turned to stealing money from a friend. Sometimes the person himself will be aware of such inconsistencies; more often he is blind to them even when they are blatantly obvious to an untrained observer.

Inconsistencies are as definite an indication of the presence of conflicts as a rise in body temperature is of physical disturbance. To cite some common ones: A girl wants above all else to marry, yet shrinks from the advances of any man. A mother oversolicitous of her children frequently forgets their birthdays. A person always generous to others is niggardly about small expenditures for himself. Another who longs for solitude never manages to be alone. One forgiving and tolerant toward most people is oversevere and demanding with himself.

I see the basic conflict of the neurotic in the fundamentally contradictory attitudes he has acquired toward other persons. Before going into detail, let me call attention to the dramatization of such a contradiction in the story of Dr. Jekyll and Mr. Hyde. We see him on the one hand delicate, sensitive, sympathetic, helpful, and on the other brutal, callous, and egotistical. I do not, of course, mean to imply that neurotic division always adheres to the precise line of this story, but merely to point to a vivid expression of basic incompatibility of attitudes in relation to others.

To approach the problem genetically we must go back to what I have called basic anxiety,[2] meaning by this the feeling a child has of being isolated and helpless in a potentially hostile world. A wide range of adverse factors in the environment can produce this insecurity in a child: direct or indirect domination, indifference, erratic behavior, lack of respect for the child's individual needs, lack of real guidance, disparaging attitudes, too much admiration or the absence of it, lack of reliable warmth, having to take sides in parental disagreements, too much or too little responsibility, over-protection, isolation from other children, injustice, discrimination, unkept promises, hostile atmosphere, and so on and so on.

[2] Karen Horney, *The Neurotic Personality of Our Time,* W. W. Norton, 1937.

The only factor to which I should like to draw special attention in this context is the child's sense of lurking hypocrisy in the environment: his feeling that the parents' love, their Christian charity, honesty, generosity, and so on may be only pretense. Part of what the child feels on this score is really hypocrisy; but some of it may be just his reaction to all the contradictions he senses in the parents' behavior. Usually, however, there is a combination of cramping factors. They may be out in the open or quite hidden, so that in analysis one can only gradually recognize these influences on the child's development.

Harassed by these disturbing conditions, the child gropes for ways to keep going, ways to cope with this menacing world. Despite his own weakness and fears he unconsciously shapes his tactics to meet the particular forces operating in his environment. In doing so, he develops not only *ad hoc* strategies but lasting character trends which become part of his personality. I have called these "neurotic trends."

If we want to see how conflicts develop, we must not focus too sharply on the individual trends but rather take a panoramic view of the main directions in which a child can and does move under these circumstances. Though we lose sight for a while of details we shall gain a clearer perspective of the essential moves made to cope with the environment. At first a rather chaotic picture may present itself, but out of it in time three main lines crystallize: a child can move *toward* people, *against* them, or *away from* them.

When moving *toward* people he accepts his own helplessness, and in spite of his estrangement and fears tries to win the affection of others and to lean on them. Only in this way can he feel safe with them. If there are dissenting parties in the family, he will attach himself to the most powerful person or group. By complying with them, he gains a feeling of belonging and support which makes him feel less weak and less isolated.

When he moves *against* people he accepts and takes for granted the hostility around him, and determines, consciously or unconsciously, to fight. He implicitly distrusts the feelings and intentions of others toward himself. He rebels in whatever ways are open to him. He wants to be the stronger and defeat them, partly for his own protection, partly for revenge.

When he moves *away from* people he wants neither to belong nor to fight, but keeps apart. He feels he has not much in common with them, they do not understand him anyhow. He builds up a world of his own—with nature, with his dolls, his books, his dreams.

In each of these three attitudes, one of the elements involved in basic anxiety is overemphasized: helplessness in the first, hostility in the second, and isolation in the third. But the fact is that the child cannot make any one of these moves wholeheartedly, because under the conditions in which the attitudes develop, all are bound to be present. What we have seen from our panoramic view is only the predominant move.

From the point of view of the normal person there is no reason why the three attitudes should be mutually exclusive. One should be capable of giving in to others, of fighting, and of keeping to oneself. The three can complement each other and make for a harmonious whole. If one predominates, it merely indicates an over-development along one line.

But in neurosis there are several reasons why these attitudes are irreconcilable. The neurotic is not flexible; he is driven to comply, to fight, to be aloof, regardless of whether the move is appropriate in the particular circumstance, and he is thrown into a panic if he behaves otherwise. Hence when all three attitudes are present in any strong degree, he is bound to be caught in a severe conflict.

Another factor, and one that considerably widens the scope of the conflict, is that the attitudes do not remain restricted to the area of human relationships but gradually pervade the entire personality, as a malignant tumor pervades the whole organic tissue. They end by encompassing not only the person's relation to others but also his relation to himself and to life in general. If we are not fully aware of this all-embracing character, the temptation is to think of the resulting conflict in categorical terms, like love *versus* hate, compliance *versus* defiance, submissiveness *versus* domination, and so on. That, however, would be as misleading as to distinguish fascism from democracy by focusing on any single opposing feature, such as their difference in approach to religion or power. These are differences certainly, but exclusive emphasis upon them would serve to obscure the point that democracy and fascism are worlds apart and represent two philosophies of life entirely incompatible with each other.

It is not accidental that a conflict that starts with our relation to others in time affects the whole personality. Human relationships are so crucial that they are bound to mold the qualities we develop, the goals we set for ourselves, the values we believe in. All these in turn react upon our relations with others and so are inextricably interwoven.[3]

My contention is that the conflict born of incompatible attitudes constitutes the core of neurosis and therefore deserves to be called *basic*. And let me add that I use the term *core* not merely in the figurative sense of its being significant but to emphasize the fact that it is the dynamic center from which neuroses emanate. This contention is the nucleus of a new theory of neurosis whose implications will become apparent in what follows. Broadly considered, the theory may be viewed as an elaboration of my earlier concept that neuroses are an expression of a disturbance in human relationships.[4]

---

[3] Since the relation to others and the attitude toward the self cannot be separated from one another, the contention occasionally to be found in psychiatric publications, that one or the other of these is the most important factor in theory and practice is not tenable.

[4] This concept was first presented in *The Neurotic Personality of Our Time* and elaborated in *New Ways in Psychoanalysis and Self-Analysis*.

PERCEPTION AND BEHAVIOR | 6

The term "perception" refers to the complex processes which begin with the stimulation of a sense organ and end with an interpretation of the resulting neural activity by the organism, that is, with the "meaning of the stimulus." However, since this inner meaning is entirely personal and subjective, it cannot be observed directly by another person; therefore, the psychologist must infer the characteristics of these intervening processes from the behavior of the individual.

BIOLOGICAL FACTORS

Even casual analysis of the perceptual process reveals that the meaning of a stimulus pattern depends on such biological characteristics as the capacities of the receptor organs through which we are sensitive to stimulation. Some 300 years ago a British philosopher, John Locke, made explicit the position that there is nothing in the mind which was not first in the senses. Thus, in attempting to understand man's behavior we must know something about the characteristics of his receiving mechanisms, that is, his sense organs. Certainly our world would be a quite different one if we were not able to be sensitive to light waves via our visual receptors; similarly our behavior would undoubtedly be different if we were able to be directly sensitive to radio waves! However, the ability of our receptors to be excited by external stimuli is not the whole story. Sensory stimulation is modified greatly by the characteristics of our nervous system. The nerve fibers do not conduct a miniature image of an external object to the brain; rather, this information is coded into a series of neural impulses. In Selection 26 Dr. Clifford T. Morgan, a physiological psychologist, helps us to understand some of the structural factors which influence our perception.[1] Morgan points out that our ability to differentiate sensory qualities such as red from blue, and pain from touch, is not dependent simply on which receptor organ is stimulated. Rather, the receptor organs such as the eye contain millions of specific receptor elements which respond differentially to certain types of stimuli, that is, they serve as analysers. He goes on to show that several receptor elements often attach to the same individual nerve fiber, and thus, perception depends on "very complex patterns of signals coming from receptors."

Morgan briefly alludes to inhibitory mechanisms which operate in the nervous system to prevent some nerve fibers from firing. It is this inhibitory capacity which seems to serve as the basic physiological correlate of the psychological process of attention. Clearly, the organism does not perceive all of the potential stimuli which surround it from moment to moment. The term "attention" refers to the selection process whereby some stimuli are "let through" and others "cut out." Hernández-Peón and his associates have demonstrated (Selection 27) that when an animal is attending to stimuli in one sense modality, such as vision, there is considerable inhibition of transmission in the auditory pathways. (Thus perhaps the daydreaming student who is unable to answer his instructor's question is being truthful when he says, "I didn't hear you.")

[1] Since Morgan's discussion assumes some familiarity with the "basic physics of stimuli, the anatomy of our sense organs and neurology of sensory systems . . . ," the student would be well-advised to read this selection after he has mastered the discussion of the senses and neural transmission in his text. He will then be in a better position to understand some of the complexities of the problem of how we experience different sensory qualities.

PSYCHOLOGICAL FACTORS

Perception not only depends on functioning sense organs and the neural mechanisms of attention, but is extensively determined by the previous experiences that the individual has had with similar stimuli. In other words, our ability to extract "meaning" from raw stimulation depends on the previous transaction that we have had with the stimulus. In Selection 28 Drs. Ittelson and Kilpatrick show that seemingly simple perceptions such as object size are based on a variety of cues. The organism seems to implicitly weigh these cues in coming up with a prediction about (perception of) object size.

Several important generalizations about perception are suggested by Ittelson and Kilpatrick's paper: (1) *Perception is predictive (probabilistic); (2) perception is functional; (3) the results of the perceptual processes vary with previous experience; (4) perception is organismic; and (5) perception defines for the individual the nature of external reality.*

SOCIOCULTURAL FACTORS

The generalization that perception is organismic is implied by Ittleson and Kilpatrick's statement that "The thing perceived is an inseparable part of the function of perceiving, which in turn includes all aspects of the total process of living." Consistent with this organismic view, recent experiments in the "New Look" in perception have emphasized the role which motives, attitudes, and personality characteristics play in determining what we perceive. Some of the major experiments in this research area are discussed by Dr. Jerome S. Bruner in Selection 30. One of the major subissues in the "New Look" movement concerned the concept of perceptual defense. Bruner and his colleagues found that words which seemed to arouse negative emotions or connotations required significantly longer tachistoscopic exposures in order to be recognized than did neutral words. These results, Bruner inferred, imply some kind of process whereby the subjects tended to avoid or delay perceiving stimuli which aroused feelings of anxiety or guilt (i.e., perceptual defense). However, it soon became apparent that there were at least two possible alternative explanations of Bruner's results which would not require that the person have the capacity for perceptual defense. These alternative explanations were based on the fact that two other variables were confounded with the independent variable in Bruner's experiments. One possibility was that the effect was due to the fact that the frequency of usage of the tabu words in written discourse was considerably less than that of the neutral words; and it has been shown that more frequently appearing words are recognized faster. A second confounding variable was related to the possibility that the subjects were more reluctant to verbalize the tabu words even though they perceived them just as rapidly as they did the neutral words, i.e., the effect is due to response inhibition rather than to perceptual defense. Several experiments have attempted to untangle these factors. One such experiment by Dr. Fred H. Nothman is reported in Selection 29. Nothman hypothesizes that if the apparent phenomenon of perceptual defense is real (i.e., a valid concept), then the difference in recognition threshold between neutral and tabu words should not be influenced by the kind of response which the subject uses to communicate to the experimenter what he perceives. Nothman's results do not support the hypothesis since he found that the differences in threshold between tabu and neutral words are greater for oral responding than for written responding. This finding also explains apparently contradictory results obtained by previous experimenters. Nothman thus concludes that the difference in recognition thresholds is really due to reluctance to verabalize the tabu words rather than to perceptual defense.

The other side of the coin in the "New Look" view of perception is represented by the concept of perceptual readiness. In Selection 30 Bruner shows that the human tends to structure his perception in part on the basis of his needs and interests and in part on the basis of the desire to accurately predict the nature of "external reality." In both of these sets of determiners the sociocultural factors play an important role. The effect of sociocultural factors is, of course, most pronounced in our perception of other people. Also, as Bruner points out, our perceptions are influenced by our conceptions, that is, by the categories into which we place certain objects or persons. Now any concept must, by its very nature, leave out certain characteristics in order to include other characteristics. Stereotypes, as special kinds of concepts, not only leave out information about *individuals* in that category but also add certain bits of misinformation. This misinformation, like accurate information, is often based on sociocultural factors which serve to satisfy the perceiver's needs and to keep his perception of other people consistent with his conceptions of them.

Selection **26** | SOME STRUCTURAL FACTORS IN PERCEPTION*

CLIFFORD T. MORGAN
University of Wisconsin

Perception has its substrate in structure. We can only see and feel what our sense organs and nervous system let us sense. It is natural, therefore, that this chapter should deal with anatomical and structural factors in perception. It will provide a background of the facts and present conception of how physiological structures function in perception.

In setting out on this task there is obviously no point in repeating the many details of anatomy, physiology, and psychology that can be found in the various textbooks. In fact, acquaintance with the basic physics of stimuli, the anatomy of our sense organs, and the neurology of sensory systems must be assumed. Having these fundamentals in mind, however, it is possible to work toward two goals in this chapter.

One is to bring the discussion up to date on the results of recent research. Many of these results really upset our old ideas and make us take new views of the anatomy of perception.

The second goal will be to look at perceptual mechanisms as a whole. When we study some one part of a sensory system, say the retina, we often "cannot see the woods for the trees." If we stand off a bit, however, and look at all the senses together, we begin to be able to make some general rules and principles about the mechanisms of perception.

That will be attempted in this chapter—at the risk sometimes of suggesting ideas that not everyone will agree with.

THE QUALITIES OF EXPERIENCE

We see with our eyes, hear with our ears, and feel with our skins, and it is obvious in each

* Abridged from Clifford T. Morgan, "Some Structural Factors in Perception," *Perception: An Approach to Personality*, Robert R. Blake and Glenn V. Ramsey, eds., The Ronald Press Company, New York, 1951, pp. 23–37. Copyright 1951 by The Ronald Press Company.

case that the structure of the sense organ has a lot to do with what we perceive through it. More than a hundred years ago, however, Müller carried the anatomical approach far beyond the obvious and gave us his now famous doctrine of specific nerve energies. We see red or blue, hear high tones or low tones, feel pain or heat, he said, only because each of these perceptions involves different sensory paths. Thus he gave us an anatomical explanation for qualities of experience.

Hardly any suggestion could have been taken so seriously by so many persons for so many years. Even today some physiologists take it as an axiom, rather than a hypothesis, and try to prove other notions by it. Many specific theories of sensory functions have been based upon it, and a good many of them have been wrong. Müller's general idea, however, still looks like a good one. We have simply had to revise again and again our specific notions of how the idea works in practice.

The shape of receptors

Take the question of structure of receptors. It would have been very handy not only for Müller's doctrine to prove right but for every receptor to have some unusual shape or color that would let us tell it from other receptors for other experiences. Our wishful thinking on this score has made us waste a lot of research time and peddle some bad notions. They tell us in the elementary textbooks, for example, that we have two kinds of receptors in our eyes, one for twilight vision and the other for color vision. We have been taught, too, that there are different kinds of receptors for skin perception—Meissner corpuscles for touch, Krause end-bulbs for cold, Ruffini cylinders for warmth, and free nerve endings for pain. It would indeed be nice if anatomy were that good to us—if each receptor had its trademark of experience on it—but we are gradually learning to be wary of such notions.

Visual receptors Take as an example the matter of visual receptors. In Figure 1 you see drawings of the photoreceptors of four different vertebrate animals. In A are those of the frog,

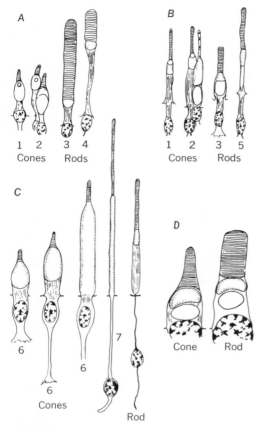

Figure 1 Rods and cones found in the eyes of different vertebrates: A, the leopard frog; B, the house sparrow; C, man; and D, the mud puppy; 1, typical cones; 2, so-called twin cone; 3, typical red rod; 4, green rod; 5, rod from the central area; 6, cones from different regions of the periphery of the retina; and 7, cone from the fovea. (Based on the work of L. B. Arey and G. L. Walls. From E. N. Willmer, *Retinal Structure and Colour Vision*, New York, Cambridge University Press, 1946, p.2. By permission of the publisher.)

and they divide themselves fairly well into cones and rods, just as the classical doctrine says they should. In B are the rods and cones of the house sparrow. Again they look somewhat as they are supposed to, but the rods look something like cones and the cones look like rods. In C we meet a disturbing situation, for these are the receptors of man. Many of the

cones from the peripheral retina look like cones and the rods look like rods, but notice what is supposed to be a cone from the fovea centralis —the all-cone area of our fovea. It outdoes the rods in being long, cylindrical, and rodlike. The best excuse for calling it a cone is that our theory of duplicity says that it should be a cone. Anatomy certainly does not justify the label.

These are just a few examples of the problem. There are other animals in which it is hard to make out rods and cones. In some cases, like that of the lizard *Gecko*, the animal seems to have all rods in its eye, yet reacts to visual objects as though it had only cones. In other cases, histologists have a hard time deciding whether there are any cones in an animal's eye, when electrical records of the eye's behavior make it quite certain that "cones" are there. Finally, some vision scientists have reason to believe that our perception of the color blue may rest not upon the cones, as we have so long thought, but rather upon some kind of rod.

So the duplicity theory seems to be passing on toward its death. It gave us a kind of anatomical explanation for one aspect of perception which would have been very nice if true. Indeed, we may even go on teaching students this theory for years to come as a sort of teaching device that may be partly true. It is not true enough, however, to depend on to make correct guesses about perception. We cannot tell about the color perception of an animal by the looks of the receptors in its eyes.

Skin receptors We are being even more rudely disappointed by the skin senses. The physiologists and psychologists used to assign these receptors to different experiences. Some in fact still do. The common scheme is to assign the Meissner corpuscle to the experience of touch or pressure, the Krause end-bulb to cold, the Ruffini cylinder to warmth, and the free nerve ending to pain. The reason for this kind of scheme is that one kind of receptor seems to be in greater numbers in regions of the skin where one experience may be more prominent. Other arguments can and have been made with great vigor.

The only trouble—and the big trouble—is that these receptors are not always present where they ought to be. It is, of course, a simple matter to make a map of the skin, marking just where we feel various experiences. When a spot seems to give one experience much more than another, we can do a biopsy on the spot, that is, cut out a piece of skin and see what receptors we have been able to trap. Such experiments have often been done in the last seventy years, and the result all too often is that the receptors our anatomical scheme calls for are missing. We do not always find Meissner corpuscles under pressure spots, Krause end-bulbs under cold spots, and so on. We can swear in fact that they very often are not there.

What scientists always do find when they make biopsies is a network of nerve fibers and blood vessels. This is not strange, of course, because our skin needs blood and so do the nerve fibers. Nerve fibers are also needed to control the dilation and contraction of blood vessels. More than that, however, these networks obviously supply the skin with a good many free nerve endings. These endings, in fact, are about the only possible receptors in many areas of the skin. We can be very sure that they serve as pain receptors and as pressure receptors. The experiments leave little doubt about that. They strongly suggest, too, even if they do not prove, that we can experience cold and warmth with free nerve endings. Perhaps some of the fancier corpuscles also get involved in our experiences of touch and temperature, but they are certainly not the sole receptors.

We should not get into too many details here. The upshot of the matter is that one cannot tell much about perception from the anatomy of receptors in the skin. A free nerve ending is just as likely to give one kind of experience as another. The beautifully designed corpuscles such as the Meissner or Krause bodies do not stand for a particular experience. It would have been very nice—in fact, it would often be very helpful—if each receptor in the skin had a different function. Alas, it is not so.

The receptors as analyzers

Even though the receptors do not wear uniforms that tell us their duties, Müller could still be right. Which receptor gets stimulated could still decide what we perceive. The differences in receptors might be chemical or electrical rather than anatomical. There may very well be a receptor in the eye for red, another for blue, and so on without our being able to tell it by looking at them. So, too, with the skin receptors. All the receptors have to do is respond differently to different stimuli, and then make the proper connections in the sensory pathways so that the brain can keep their identities straight. If they do that, then Müller's theory is right.

Specificity vs. pattern As we know, research workers have divided into two camps on this issue. Natanson, Helmholtz, Von Frey, Hecht, Stevens, and Dallenbach—to mention but a few—have stood by Müller. Lotze, Hering, Goldscheider, Wever, and Nafe are some who departed a little or a lot from the anatomical point of view. They have held that receptors can send in to the nervous system different kinds of messages and that these messages, and not just the receptors that sent them, affect our experiences. Wever used to say, for example, that the frequency of impulses in the auditory nerve had something to do with whether we hear a high tone or a low tone. Hering believed that the same receptor could make us see red acting in one way and, sending in another kind of message, could make us see green. Nafe has been saying that what receptors *do*, not just which ones they are, determines our perception.

When people argue long and loud about something, there is a fair chance that both sides are partly right, partly wrong. So it seems to be in this case. Research has been telling us enough lately to let us make some decisions about these issues, and it looks more and more as though both camps are partly right. With very small electrodes and the right electrical systems, physiologists have been finding out just what receptors do when they are stimulated. Many facts of great interest have come out of their work. Let us spend just a little time hitting their high points.

Kinds of receptors It looks as though we have two kinds of receptors in all the senses. One kind responds in about the same way as does the sense organ as a whole. The eye, for example, can see wave lengths of light as long as 760 mμ and as short as 380 mμ. Some of the individual receptors in the eye do exactly the same thing. When plotted on a graph, their response looks about the same as the over-all response of the eye. In hearing, too, some of the receptors of the ear are aroused by about the same range of stimuli as is the whole ear, namely, 20 cps to 20 kcps. In taste, too, there are receptors that give impulses to almost any kind of chemical stimulus, whether it be sour, salt, or bitter. Receptors such as these may be very good for telling us about the intensity of a stimulus and are thus of help in perception. They cannot tell us much, however, about the nature of a stimulus. A receptor that reacts just as does the eye as a whole, or the ear, or the tongue, is not good for quality of perception. It does not let us perceive different colors or pitches or tastes.

Besides these broad-band receptors, however, we have some narrow-band receptors—cells that pick out only some of the spectrum of stimuli that hit the receptors. Granit, for example, has put his electrodes in the retinas of various animals and gotten the records

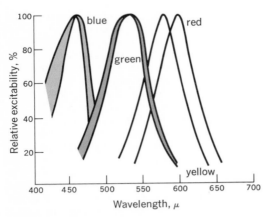

Figure 2 Relative excitability of four types of receptors found by Granit in different mammalian eyes. The cross-hatched and stippled portions of the "blue" and "green" receptors indicate variability in the exact forms of these curves. (From C. T. Morgan and E. Stellar, *Physiological Psychology*, 2d ed., New York, McGraw-Hill Book Company, 1950. By permission of the publisher.)

shown in Figure 2. Some of the nerve cells he records from have peak responses at 600 mμ, and he calls them red elements. Some have peaks at 530 mμ in the green, 580 mμ in the yellow, and 450 mμ in the blue. Galambos, making the same kind of experiments in a cat, finds nerve cells that react to a small part of the acoustic spectrum. And from the cat's tongue, Pfaffmann has picked up cells that respond more to bitter than to salt or more to salt than to bitter. Those are the only experiments we have now, but we shall probably hear before long of similar results in smell or the skin senses.

Physiology is now giving us an answer to the long debated question whether receptors are at the root of the different qualities of experience we have. Müller was at least partly right. Receptors are analyzers. One receptor picks out some stimuli to respond to more than others, and they somehow or other keep themselves identified upstream in the nervous system. We can perceive different colors, tones, tastes, and probably odors because different anatomical receptors send in messages. There is little doubt about that.

Patterns for messages The story, however, is not as simple as it might seem at first glance. We do not have receptor A sending in its private message over line A, and receptor B talking to the nervous system over line B. The notion of private lines from receptors to the brain is simple and attractive. Unfortunately, however, it is not true. Instead, receptors get hooked up with each other, so different receptors are talking to the nervous system at the same time. Their talk makes a complex pattern that must be uncoded by the nervous system before we can perceive their meaning.

To make this point clear, let us turn to some examples. Take first Pfaffmann's study of the taste receptors of the cat. All the fibers that he got under his microelectrodes would respond to acids. They were, one might say, sour receptors. Some of the fibers would respond only to acid. Another type of fiber, however, responded to both acid and bitter stimuli. Still a third class reacted to acid and salt. So there are at least three classes of taste receptors in the cat. They let the cat perceive different tastes, but not in the simple way we might expect. Instead, the cat tastes "salt" when fiber *A* is sending in messages, "bitter" when fiber *B* is signaling, but "sour" when all three fibers—*A*, *B*, and *C*, are firing. Thus it is a pattern of impulses that comes into the nervous system and that makes the basis for perceiving different tastes.

Coupling of receptors   Pfaffmann's records of taste receptors come from fibers heading into the nervous system which have not yet made synapses. At the first synapse, there are a lot of possibilities for matters to get more mixed up. Perhaps the different classes of taste fibers— *A*, *B*, and *C*—make connections at these synapses that make the pattern much more complicated. Certainly that happens in the eye and the ear. For example, the records of Galambos and of Granit, referred to above, probably come from nerve cells that have had synapse since the messages left the eye and ear. Granit's records probably come from the third order ganglion cells of the eye, and Galambos' from second order neurons of the cochlear nucleus. Both scientists report complex patterns of response in the nerve cells that gave them their records.

In the eye we see receptors getting coupled together in various ways. Receptors, each responding to a narrow band of the spectrum, hook into the same neurons after one or two synapses are passed. Sometimes a green and a blue receptor are coupled together, sometimes a blue and a yellow, and sometimes there are other combinations. There are certainly cases in which many are ganged together in different ways. That can be proved by bleaching out some receptors with one wave length of light and then seeing what records the remaining receptors give. Some day, with the right facts in hand, we may be able to say exactly how the coupling of receptors makes us see different colors. So far we know only that the receptors are coupled in many ways.

Inhibition by receptors   Life would be simple if receptors were coupled together in only one way, so that their responses added up. Thus it would be nice if a red and a green receptor were so hooked onto the same bipolar or ganglion cell that their responses simply added together. Sadly enough, though, receptors not only add together, they also subtract from each other's effects. That is to say, when receptors are coupled together, one receptor sometimes inhibits or stops the effects of the other.

We find this sort of coupling turning up in other kinds of experiments with the eye. From electrodes in the optic nerve or in the ganglion cells of the retina, we can see several kinds of reactions to light. As is shown in Figure 3, some nerve cells "go on," that is, give impulses, when a light comes on. Some are in spontaneous activity while the eye is in the dark and stop firing when a light comes on. Still others go on when the light goes on, then stop while the light is on, and finally start firing again when the light goes off. The main point is that turning on a light can inhibit or stop impulses that have been started by other lights or in some other way. Thus we are led to believe that receptors are coupled not only by adding but also by subtracting, that is, by inhibiting arrangements of various sorts.

We do not understand just how the receptors add and subtract in perception. We are starting to get the general idea though, and we are making progress year by year. As matters now stand, we know this much: One cannot tell what a receptor does by the way it is built or how it looks. Receptors have different features that do not meet the eye. Some act like the sense organ as a whole, but others pick out only part of the sensory gamut of stimuli to react to. We can perceive different tones, colors, and tastes by what receptors signal that they are responding to. The signals, however, are not simple. In the synapses between the receptors and the brain, receptors get coupled to the same nerve cells. Sometimes this coupling adds up to signals from different receptors. Sometimes it causes a nerve cell to be inhibited by a receptor. Our perception thus

Maintained,   On-off, Y type   Off, Z type
  X type

Figure 3   Activity of three types of ganglion cells distinguished in the vertebrate eye by Hartline. (From S. H. Bartley, "Some Factors in Brightness Discrimination," *Psychological Review.* **46**: 340, 1939. By permission of the author and the publisher.)

rests on very complex patterns of signals coming from receptors.

Selection 27 | MODIFICATION OF ELECTRIC ACTIVITY IN COCHLEAR NUCLEUS DURING "ATTENTION" IN UNANESTHETIZED CATS*

RAÚL HERNÁNDEZ-PEÓN
HAROLD SCHERRER
MICHEL JOUVET
*School of Medicine,
University of California,
Los Angeles*

Attention involves the selective awareness of certain sensory messages with the simultaneous suppression of others. Our sense organs are activated by a great variety of sensory stimuli, but relatively few evoke conscious sensation at any given moment. It is common experience that there is a pronounced reduction of extraneous sensory awareness when our attention is concentrated on some particular matter. During the attentive state, it seems as though the brain integrates for consciousness only a limited amount of sensory information, specifically, those impulses concerned with the object of attention.

An interference with impulses initiated by sensory stimuli other than those pertaining to the subject of attention seems to be an obvious possibility. It is clear that this afferent blockade might occur at any point along the classical sensory pathways from receptors to the cortical receiving areas, or else perhaps in the recently disclosed extra-classical sensory paths that traverse the brain-stem reticular system.

Recent evidence indicates the existence of

* Reprinted from Raúl Hernández-Peón, Harold Scherrer, and Michel Jouvet, "Modification of Electric Activity in Cochlear Nucleus during 'Attention' in Unanesthetized Cats," *Science,* 123: 331–332, 1956. Reprinted by permission of the authors and the publisher.

central mechanisms that regulate sensory transmission. It has been shown that appropriate stimulation of the brain-stem reticular system will inhibit afferent conduction between the first- and second-order neurons in all three principal somatic paths. During central anesthesia, the afferent-evoked potentials in the first sensory relays are enhanced. This appears to be due to the release of a tonic descending inhibitory influence that operates during wakefulness and requires the functional integrity of the brain-stem reticular formation.

The possibility that a selective central inhibitory mechanism might operate during attention for filtering sensory impulses was tested by studying afferent transmission in the second- or third-order neurons of the auditory pathway (cochlear nucleus) in unanesthetized, unrestrained cats during experimentally elicited attentive behavior. Bipolar stainless steel electrodes with a total diameter of 0.5 mm were implanted stereotaxically in the dorsal cochlear nucleus through a small hole bored in the skull. The electrodes were fixed to the skull with dental cement. A minimum of 1 week elapsed between the operation and the first electroencephalographic recordings. Electric impulses in the form of short bursts of rectangular waves (0.01 to 0.02 sec) at a frequency of 1000 to 5000 cy/sec were delivered to a loudspeaker near the cats at an intensity comfortable to human observers in the same environment.

Three types of sensory modalities were used to attract the animal's attention: visual, olfactory, and somatic. As is illustrated in Fig. 1, during presentation of visual stimuli (two mice in a closed bottle), the auditory responses in the cochlear nucleus were greatly reduced in comparison with the control responses; they were practically abolished as long as the visual stimuli elicited behavioral evidence of attention. When the mice were removed, the auditory responses returned to the same order of magnitude as the initial controls. An olfactory stimulus that attracted the animal's attention produced a similar blocking effect. While the cat was attentively sniffing tubing through which fish odors were being delivered, the auditory potential in the cochlear nucleus was practically absent. After the stimulus had been removed and when the cat appeared to be relaxed once more, the auditorily evoked re-

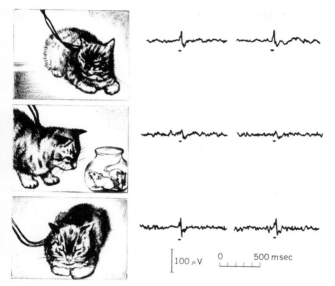

Figure 1 Direct recording of click responses in the cochlear nucleus during three periods; the photographs were taken simultaneously. Top and bottom, cat is relaxed; the click responses are large. Middle: while the cat is visually attentive to the mice in the jar, the click responses are diminished in amplitude.

sponses in the cochlear nucleus were of the same magnitude as they had been prior to the olfactory stimulation. Similarly, a nociceptive shock delivered to the forepaw of the cat—a shock that apparently distracted the animal's attention—resulted in marked reduction of auditorily evoked responses in the cochlear nucleus.

If this sensory inhibition during attentive behavior, as demonstrated in the auditory pathway, occurs in all other sensory paths except the ones concerned with the object of attention, such an inhibitory mechanism might lead to favoring of the attended object by the selective exclusion of incoming signals. It is conceivable not only that such a selective sensory inhibition might operate simultaneously for various sensory modalities, leaving one or more unaffected but that the selectivity could extend to some discriminable aspects of any single modality—for example, to one tone and not to others. This suggestion finds support in the recent demonstration that sensory "habituation" may occur to a particular tone—that is, a slowly developing inhibitory effect on audi-

torily evoked potentials observed in the cochlear nucleus on prolonged repetition of a given tone, an influence that does not affect other frequencies that are novel to the animal. The pathway by which this inhibitory influence acts on incoming auditory impulses remains to be determined, but experiments now in progress have shown that during electric stimulation of the midbrain reticular formation, the auditory potential in the cochlear nucleus is depressed.

The present observations suggest that the blocking of afferent impulses in the lower portions of a sensory path may be a mechanism whereby sensory stimuli out of the scope of attention can be markedly reduced while they are still in their trajectory toward higher levels of the central nervous system. This central inhibitory mechanism may, therefore, play an important role in selective exclusions of sensory messages along their passage toward mechanisms of perception and consciousness. In a recent symposium on brain mechanisms and consciousness, Adrian pointed out that "the signals from the sense organs must be treated differently when we attend to them and when we do not, and if we could decide where and how the divergence arises we should be nearer to understanding how the level of consciousness is reached."

Selection **28** | EXPERIMENTS IN PERCEPTION*

W. H. ITTELSON
Brooklyn College

F. P. KILPATRICK
Princeton University

What is perception? Why do we see what we see, feel what we feel, hear what we hear? We act in terms of what we perceive; our acts lead to new perceptions; these lead to new acts, and so on in the incredibly complex process that constitutes life. Clearly, then, an understanding of the process by which man becomes aware of himself and his world is basic to any adequate understanding of human behavior. But the problem of explaining how and why we perceive in the way we do is one of the most controversial fields in psychology. We shall describe here some recent experimental work which sheds new light on the problem and points the way to a new theory of perception.

The fact that we see a chair and are then able to go to the place at which we localize it and rest our bodies on a substantial object does not seem particularly amazing or difficult to explain—until we try to explain it. If we accept the prevailing current view that we can never be aware of the world as such, but only of the nervous impulses arising from the impingement of physical forces on sensory receptors we immediately face the necessity of explaining the correspondence between what we perceive and whatever it is that is there.

An extremely logical, unbeatable—and scientifically useless—answer is simply to say there is no real world, that everything exists in the mind alone. Another approach is to postulate

the existence of an external world, to grant that there is some general correspondence between that world and what we perceive and to seek some understandable and useful explanation of why that should be. Most of the prominent theories about perception have grown out of the latter approach. These theories generally agree that even though much of the correspondence may be due to learning, at some basic level there exists an absolute correspondence between what is "out there" and what is in the "mind." But there is a great deal of disagreement concerning the level at which such innately determined correspondence occurs. At one extreme are theorists who believe that the correspondence occurs at the level of simple sensations, such as color, brightness, weight, hardness, and so on, and that out of these sensations are compounded more complex awarenesses, such as the recognition of a pencil or a book. At the other extreme are Gestalt psychologists who feel that complex perceptions such as the form of an object are the result of an inherent relationship between the properties of the thing perceived and the properties of the brain. All these schools seem to agree, however, that there is some perceptual level at which exists absolute objectivity; that is, a one-to-one correspondence between experience and reality.

This belief is basic to current thinking in many fields. It underlies most theorizing concerning the nature of science, including Percy W. Bridgman's attempt to reach final scientific objectivity in the "observable operation." In psychology one is hard put to find an approach to human behavior which departs from this basic premise. But it leads to dichotomies such as organism v. environment, subjective v. objective. Stimuli or stimulus patterns are treated as though they exist apart from the perceiving organism. Psychologists seek to find mechanical relationships or interactions between the organism and an "objectively defined" environment. They often rule out purposes and values as not belonging in a strictly scientific psychology.

The experiments to be described here arose from a widespread and growing feeling that such dichotomies are false, and that in practice it is impossible to leave values and purposes out of consideration in scientific observation. The experiments were designed to re-examine some of the basic ideas from which these problems stem.

During the past few years Adelbert Ames, Jr., of the Institute for Associated Research in Hanover, N. H., has designed some new ways of studying visual perception. They have resulted in a new conception of the nature of knowing and of observation. This theory neither denies the existence of objects nor proposes that they exist in a given form independently, that is, apart from the perceiving organism. Instead, it suggests that the world each of us knows is a world created in large measure from our experience in dealing with the environment.

Let us illustrate this in specific terms through some of the demonstrations. In one of them the subject sits in a dark room in which he can see only two star points of light. Both are equidistant from the observer, but one is brighter than the other. If the observer closes one eye and keeps his head still, the brighter point of light looks nearer than the dimmer one. Such apparent differences are related not only to brightness but also to direction from the observer. If two points of light of equal brightness are situated near the floor, one about a foot above the other, the upper one will generally be perceived as farther away than the lower one; if they are near the ceiling, the lower one will appear farther away.

A somewhat more complex experiment uses two partly inflated balloons illuminated from a concealed source. The balloons are in fixed positions about one foot apart. Their relative sizes can be varied by means of a lever control connected to a bellows, and another lever controls their relative brightness. When the size and brightness of both balloons are the same, an observer looking at them with one eye from 10 feet or more sees them as two glowing spheres at equal distances from him. If the brightnesses are left the same and the relative sizes are changed, the larger balloon appears to nearly all observers somewhat nearer. If the size lever is moved continuously, causing continuous variation in the relative size of the balloons, they appear to move dramatically back and forth through space, even when the observer watches with both eyes open. The result is similar when the sizes are kept equal and the relative brightness is varied.

With the same apparatus the effects of size and brightness may be combined so that they supplement or conflict with each other. When they supplement each other, the variation in apparent distance is much greater than when either size or brightness alone is varied. When conflict is introduced by varying size and brightness in opposition to each other, the relative change in distance is considerably less than when they act in combination or alone. Most people, however, give more weight to relative size than they give to brightness in judging distance.

These phenomena cannot be explained by referring to "reality," because "reality" and perception do not correspond. They cannot be explained by reference to the pattern in the retina of the eye, because for any given retinal pattern there are an infinite number of brightness-size-distance combinations to which that pattern might be related. When faced with such a situation, in which an unlimited number of possibilities can be related to a given retinal pattern, the organism apparently calls upon its previous experiences and assumes that what has been most probable in the past is most probable in the immediate occasion. When presented with two star-points of different brightness, a person unconsciously "bets" or "assumes" that the two points, being similar, are probably identical (*i. e.*, of equal brightness), and therefore that the one which seems brighter must be nearer. Similarly the observed facts in the case of two star-points placed vertically one above the other suggest that when we look down we assume, on the basis of past experience, that objects in the lower part of the visual field are nearer than objects in the upper part; when we look up, we assume the opposite to be true. An analogous explanation can be made of the role of relative size as an indication of relative distance.

Why do the differences in distance seem so much greater when the relative size of two objects is varied continuously than when the size difference is fixed? This phenomenon, too, apparently is based on experience. It is a fairly common experience, though not usual, to find that two similar objects of different sizes are actually the same distance away from us. But it is rare indeed to see two stationary objects at the same distance, one growing larger and the other smaller; almost always in everyday life when we see two identical or nearly identical objects change relative size they are in motion in relation to each other. Hence under the experimental conditions we are much more likely to assume distance differences in the objects of changing size than in those of fixed size. In other words, apparently we make use of a weighted average of our past experience in interpreting what we see. It seems that the subject relates to the stimulus pattern a complex, probability-like integration of his past experience with such patterns. Were it not for such integrations, which have been labeled assumptions, the particular perceptual phenomenon would not occur. It follows from this that the resulting perceptions are not absolute revelations of "what is out there" but are in the nature of probabilities or predictions based on past experience. These predictions are not always reliable, as the demonstrations make clear.

Visual perception involves an impression not only of *where* an object is but of *what* it is. From the demonstrations already described we may guess that there is a very strong relationship between localization in space ("thereness") and the assignment of objective properties ("thatness"). This relationship can be demonstrated by a cube experiment.

Two solid white cubes are suspended on wires that are painted black so as to be invisible against a black background. One cube is about 3 feet from the observer and the other about 12 feet. The observer's head is in a headrest so positioned that the cubes are almost in line with each other but he can see both, the nearer cube being slightly to the right. A tiny metal shield is then placed a few inches in front of the left eye. It is just big enough to cut off the view of the far cube from the left eye. The result is that the near cube is seen with both eyes and the far cube with just the right eye. Under these conditions the observer can fix the position of the near cube very well,

because he has available all the cues that come from the use of the two eyes. But in the case of the far cube seen with only one eye, localization is much more difficult and uncertain.

Now since the two cubes are almost in line visually, a slight movement of the head to the right will cause the inside vertical edges of the cubes to coincide. Such coincidence of edge is strongly related to an assumption of "togetherness." Hence when the subject moves his head in this way, the uncertainly located distant cube appears to have moved forward to a position even with the nearer cube. Under these conditions not only does the mislocated cube appear smaller, but it appears different in shape, that is, no longer cubical, even though the pattern cast by the cube on the retina of the eye has not changed at all.

The same point can be illustrated most dramatically by experiments in which the subject wears a pair of glasses fitted with so-called aniseikonic lenses, which are ground in such a way that they give images of different size and shape to the two retinas. This produces very marked distortions of any objects which the subject visualizes mainly through the use of two-eyed stereoscopic vision. In an ordinary environment there are generally enough one-eye cues, such as shadow, overlay, familiar objects of known size, and so on, to suppress the binocular cues and hold the visual world "in shape." But in an environment poor in one-eye cues the observer is forced to rely on binocular cues, and under these circumstances the distortion is enhanced for anyone wearing such glasses. It has been found that if an ordinary square room is lined with tree leaves, which reduce monocular cues to a minimum by covering the flat wall spaces, most observers looking through aniseikonic lenses perceive a great deal of distortion of the room and the leaves. To an observer looking at the room as a whole through certain glasses of this type the walls appear to slant inward from floor to ceiling, the ceiling seems much lower than it is and its leaves look very small. The floor, which is the object of interest in this particular analysis, appears to be much farther away than its true position, and the leaves covering it look huge. Now, if the observer wearing the same glasses looks at just the floor instead of the room in general, the floor changes markedly in appearance. It appears to be much nearer than before, and instead of being level it seems to rise from front to back at a pitch of about 45 degrees. The leaves, however, now look more nearly normal in size.

These perceptions can be explained in terms of the geometry of stereoscopic vision. The stimulus patterns on the retinas of the eyes are the geometric projections of an external surface. But identical projections may be produced by surfaces of different kinds. In this case a distant surface that is nearly horizontal, a closer surface that is slightly tipped and a very near surface that is sharply tipped all produce the same stereoscopic stimulus patterns. When the observer looks at the whole room, he "chooses" the nearly horizontal faraway floor surface as the focus of perception, probably because he cannot make a room out of the pattern if the floor is sharply tipped up. When he limits his gaze to the floor, he no longer needs to make a room of what he is looking at, and he sees the floor sharply tipped, perhaps because the leaves now appear more nearly the size he assumes them to be.

In the everyday environment outside the laboratory the wearing of these glasses produces similarly interesting illusions. For example, a large body of water such as a lake appears horizontal and farther away than its real position, but a large expanse of level lawn looks tipped and nearer than its real position. Presumably this happens because the observer brings to these occasions the assumptions, based on past experience, that the probability of a lake surface being other than horizontal is almost zero, while the probability of a grass surface being a slope is fairly high.

The most reasonable explanation of these visual phenomena seems to be that an observer unconsciously relates to the stimulus pattern some sort of weighted average of the past consequences of acting with respect to that pattern. The particular perception "chosen" is the one that has the best predictive value, on the basis of previous experience, for action in carrying out the purposes of the organism. From this one may make two rather crucial deductions: (1) an unfamiliar external configuration which yields the same retinal pattern

as one the observer is accustomed to deal with will be perceived as the familiar configuration; (2) when the observer acts on his interpretation of the unfamiliar configuration and finds that he is wrong, his perception will change even though the retinal pattern is unchanged.

Let us illustrate with some actual demonstrations. If an observer in a dark room looks with one eye at two lines of light which are at the same distance and elevation but of different lengths, the longer line will look nearer than the shorter line. Apparently he assumes that the lines are identical and translates the difference in length into a difference in position. If the observer takes a wand with a luminous tip and tries to touch first one line and then the other, he will be unable to do so at first. After repeated practice, however, he can learn to touch the two lines quickly and accurately. At this point he no longer sees the lines as at different distances; they now look, as they are, the same distance from him. He originally assumed that the two lines were the same length because that seemed the best bet under the circumstances. After he had tested this assumption by purposive action, he shifted to the assumption, less probable in terms of past experience but still possible, that the lines were at the same distance but of different lengths. As his assumption changed, perception did also.

There is another experiment that demonstrates these points even more convincingly. It uses a distorted room in which the floor slopes up to the right of the observer, the rear wall recedes from right to left and the windows are of different sizes and trapezoidal in shape. When an observer looks at this room with one eye from a certain point, the room appears completely normal, as if the floor were level, the rear wall at right angles to the line of sight and the windows rectangular and of the same size. Presumably the observer chooses this particular appearance instead of some other because of the assumptions he brings to the occasion. If he now takes a long stick and tries to touch the various parts of the room, he will be unsuccessful, even though he has gone into the situation knowing the true shape of the room. With practice, however, he becomes more and more successful in touching what he wants to touch with the stick. More important, he sees the room more and more in its true shape, even though the stimulus pattern on his retina has remained unchanged.

By means of a piece of apparatus called the "rotating trapezoidal window" it has been possible to extend the investigation to complex perceptual situations involving movement. This device consists of a trapezoidal surface with panes cut in it and shadows painted on it to give the appearance of a window. It is mounted on a rod connected to a motor so that it rotates at a slow constant speed in an upright position about its own axis. When an observer views the rotating surface with one eye from about 10 feet or more or with both eyes from about 25 feet or more, he sees not a rotating trapezoid but an oscillating rectangle. Its speed of movement and its shape appear to vary markedly as it turns. If a small cube is attached by a short rod to the upper part of the short side of the trapezoid, it seems to become detached, sail freely around the front of the trapezoid and attach itself again as the apparatus rotates.

All these experiments, and many more that have been made, suggest strongly that perception is never a sure thing, never an absolute revelation of "what is." Rather, what we see is a prediction—our own personal construction designed to give us the best possible bet for carrying out our purposes in action. We make these bets on the basis of our past experience. When we have a great deal of relevant and consistent experience to relate to stimulus patterns, the probability of success of our prediction (perception) as a guide to action is extremely high, and we tend to have a feeling of surety. When our experience is limited or inconsistent, the reverse holds true. According to the new theory of perception developed from the demonstrations we have described, perception is a functional affair based on action, experience and probability. The thing perceived is an inseparable part of the function of perceiving, which in turn includes all aspects of the total process of living. This view differs from the old rival theories: the thing perceived is neither just a figment of the mind nor an innately determined absolute revelation of a reality postulated to exist apart from the perceiving organism. Object and percept are part and parcel of the same thing.

This conclusion of course has far-reaching implications for many areas of study, for some assumption as to what perception is must underly any philosophy or comprehensive theory of psychology, of science or of knowledge in general. Although the particular investigations involved here are restricted to visual perception, this is only a vehicle which carries us into a basic inquiry of much wider significance.

Selection **29** | THE INFLUENCE OF RESPONSE CONDITIONS ON RECOGNITION THRESHOLDS FOR TABU WORDS*

FRED H. NOTHMAN
American University

A perceptual defense hypothesis was first formulated by Bruner and Postman (1947), and Postman, Bruner, and McGinnies (1948), to explain the higher recognition thresholds that were found in the case of emotionally charged or negatively valued words. They suggested that a person "unconsciously" attempts to delay recognition of "anxiety laden" stimuli as long as possible. But they also recognized that this formulation raised the question: "How does the subject 'know' that a word should be avoided? In order to 'repress' he must first recognize it for what it is" (p. 153). McGinnies tried to resolve this dilemma.

In a study in which he compared recognition thresholds for socially tabu and socially neutral words, McGinnies (1949) found that tabu words were more difficult to recognize than neutral words, and that GSRs prior to

* Reprinted from Fred H. Nothman, "The Influence of Response Conditions on Recognition Thresholds for Tabu Words," *Journal of Abnormal and Social Psychology*, **65**: 154–161, 1962. Copyright 1962 by the American Psychological Association and reproduced by permission.

the recognition of tabu words were greater than prior to the recognition of neutral words. McGinnies postulated the operation of some special perceptual mechanisms of an organismic nature to account for the process of perceptual defense.

Howes and Solomon (1950; Solomon & Howes, 1951) suggested a more plausible and more parsimonious way of accounting for McGinnies' (1949) results, by pointing out that the tabu words used by McGinnies were, on the basis of the Thorndike-Lorge (1944) semantic count, much less familiar words, and that McGinnies' experimental situation of "scientific respectability" would tend to "set" subjects to inhibit overt verbal reports of tabu words, until they were ". . . more certain before reporting it" (Howes & Solomon, 1950, p. 233). Thus perceptual defense, or whatever is left of it after equating for word familiarity, would be explainable in terms of selective reporting or response inhibition.

Postman (Postman, Bronson, & Gropper, 1953) experimentally tested some of the Solomon-Howes' assertions. He equated McGinnies' tabu words with neutral words of equal familiarity on the basis of the Thorndike-Lorge (1944) semantic count. Postman's data show absence of the perceptual defense phenomenon. However, he had introduced some additional changes from the McGinnies' procedure. He gave advance information as to the kinds of stimuli to be shown tachistoscopically. Several other investigators (Cowen & Beier, 1950; Cowen & Obrist, 1958; Freeman, 1954; Lacy, Lewinger, & Adamson, 1953) have discovered that advance information regarding tabu word stimuli will significantly reduce or eliminate the perceptual defense phenomenon. Postman also changed the oral mode of responding used in McGinnies' study by obtaining written responses from groups of subjects. Thus his work does not constitute a test of the McGinnies' position.

The present experiment is similar in most respects to the earlier work by McGinnies (1949) and Postman et al. 1953), but in this study other modes of responding are used in addition to the oral one employed by McGinnies and the written one employed by Postman. Under these treatment conditions and on the basis of the previous considerations the following predictions are made: If, as McGinnies believes, the process of perceptual defense is mediated by modification of visual perception in response to inimical or tabu stimuli, then the institution of different overt behavioral response conditions should not be expected to bring about any changes in the perceptual defense phenomenon, since distortion occurs at the perceptual level, and not at the level of overt responding. If, on the other hand, the process of "perceptual defense" is mediated through response inhibition, then variations in response conditions may be expected to affect this response inhibition.

In this experiment, the method by which the subject identifies the word consists of (a) oral responding, that is, pronouncing the word in full; (b) writing the whole word; (c) spelling parts of the word orally; and (d) spelling parts of the word in writing.

It appears that not only response conditions but also the sex of subjects may be related to differences between neutral and tabu word recognition thresholds. Some investigators report that women show significantly greater differences between neutral and tabu word recognition thresholds than men (Cowen & Obrist, 1958; Freeman, 1955; Postman et al., 1953). On the other hand, McGinnies (1949) and Cowen and Beier (1954) find no such differences. In view of these conflicting reports, it seemed important to allow for an evaluation of the sex variable in the present design.

METHOD

Subjects

The subjects were 60 male and 24 female students from the introductory psychology courses at Indiana University.

Apparatus

The apparatus consisted of a modified Dodge tachistoscope similar to the electronic tachistoscope designed by Kupperian and Golin (1951), except that optical glass having 33% transmission, 33% reflection, and 34% absorption was substituted for the half-silvered mirrors used in their design. Another innovation was the use of two polaroid disks which were inserted in the eyepiece in such a way that when one of them was rotated, while the other remained stationary, the amount of illumination was reduced for the subject. The position of the rotating disk was set before the beginning of the experiment and was left unchanged for all subjects. Four thousand 500-degree phosphorescent coated mercury vapor tubes were employed to illuminate the exposure and pre-exposure fields. Illumination of the pre-exposure field brought into view a stimulus card on which the fixation point was drawn. In the course of the switching process the pre-exposure field was darkened, and the exposure field was illuminated, presenting the stimulus material for a set period of time. The electronic timer was designed for exposure durations to be varied in 1 millisecond steps from 1 to 1,099 milliseconds.

Two aluminium chutes, one attached to the front and the other to the left side of the tachistoscope, were used to convey 3 inch × 5 inch cards between the experimenter and the subject. The front chute was placed almost vertically, 12 inches to the right of the eyepiece of the tachistoscope, with the chute bottom within easy reach of the subject. This chute served for the transfer of cards from the experimenter to the subject. The side chute was placed on the left side of the tachistoscope so that the entrance of the chute at the front left of the tachistoscope, in relation to the table on which is was located, was 18.5 inches high and flush at the rear. This arrangement allowed the cards to slide easily down the chute from the subject to the experimenter.

Room conditions

The experimental room was not sound insulated or air conditioned, but little or no interference occurred from the outside. The room was dimly illuminated by a 7.5-watt bulb painted red.

Materials

The materials consisted of 17 stimulus cards for use in the tachistoscope, each stimulus card having 1 of the 17 stimulus words printed on it in plain black type ³⁄₁₆ inch high. The five-letter stimulus words consisted of 5 neutral training words and 12 test words, 6 tabu and 6 neutral. The tabu and neutral words were matched for frequency value on the basis of the Thorndike-Lorge (1944) semantic count. The tabu words, listed in Table 1, with one exception, are identical to the words used by both McGinnies (1949) and Postman et al. (1953).

For the experimental response conditions of pronouncing, writing, and spelling, subjects were given salmon colored 3 inch × 5 inch cards to use. Salmon colored rather than white cards were used to reduce the brightness of the cards.

Table **1** | LIST OF STIMULUS WORDS AND THEIR FREQUENCY VALUES[a]

Tabu word	Frequency value	Neutral word	Frequency value	Training word	Frequency value
Penis	1[b]	Mixer	1	Tacit	13
Bitch	4	Album	4	Tonic	11
Belly	47	Noted	45	Folio	12
Raped	13	Photo	11	Chute	11
Filth	4	Fried	4	Prune	12
Whore	4	Tally	4		

[a] Frequency of occurrence in 4.5 million words according to the Thorndike-Lorge (1944) semantic count.
[b] Estimated frequency (Postman, Bronson & Gropper, 1953, p. 217).

Procedure

The subjects were divided into four different response groups: Group I, pronouncing the whole word; Group II, writing the whole word; Group III, spelling the word components orally; Group IV, spelling the word components in writing.

Each group consisted of 21 subjects, 15 males and 6 females. The subjects were randomly assigned to the four response groups with the restriction that each group gain one subject per multiple of four subjects of each sex assigned.

Thresholds were obtained first on four of the five training words. The training words were followed by eight test words, four tabu and four neutral. Finally every subject was presented with one more neutral word.

The method of selection of sequences of training words was as follows: 15 different training words sequences were randomly chosen. Each sequences was used once in each response group of 15 males. Six of the 15 word sequences were each used once in each response group of females.

The method of selection of neutral and tabu words for presentation to a subject was as follows: of the 12 test words used in this experiment, each subject was given a randomly selected sample of 8, 4 neutral and 4 tabu words, with the restrictions that (a) no subject receive the same neutral or tabu word twice; (b) for each subject, the neutral words in his particular sample be those matched in frequency value to the tabu words selected; and (c) for the first three male subjects and every subsequent three male subjects assigned to a treatment group, each test word be used twice. The same restriction is applied to the females in each treatment group.

Thus in a group of 21 subjects (15 males, 6 females), each test word was used 14 times (10 times for males, 4 times for females).

Following the selection of test words, the order of presentation was randomly determined. This order was different for each one of the 15 male subjects in a group. The same 15 sequences were used for all groups, with the restriction that not more than two neutral or two tabu words follow each other. Six of the 15 sequences selected for males were used for females. The same 6 sequences were repeated in each treatment group of females.

After presentation of the training words, the test words were first shown 60 milliseconds below the lowest threshold obtained on the training words.

Intertrial intervals were approximately 10–15 seconds.

For the determination of recognition thresholds, a modified method of limits was used by employing an ascending order of presentation only. Step intervals were 10 milliseconds. Every stimulus word was presented until the recognition threshold was reached. For each additional presentation of a stimulus word, the exposure time was increased by 10 milliseconds.

The criterion of threshold was one correct spoken, written, or spelled identification of the word.

The use of cards was necessitated by the response requirements of this experiment; that is, writing and spelling. In the course of establishing recognition thresholds for the training and test words, these cards were used in all groups under the following conditions:

Group I—Pronouncing the Whole Word (Oral-Whole) Following each presentation of the stimulus word, the subject received a 3 inch × 5 inch card (described under Materials) and was instructed to look at the card while pronouncing the word he saw or thought he saw previously exhibited in the tachistoscope. Subjects in Group I were given cards for the methodological purpose of equalizing the conditions for the four treatment groups with respect to the handling of cards and the different eye adjustments necessary for looking through the tachistoscope and looking at the cards.

Group II—Writing the Whole Word (Written-Whole) Following each presentation of the stimulus word, the subject received a card and was instructed to look down at the card and to write on the card the word he saw or thought he saw previously exhibited in the tachistoscope.

Group III—Spelling the Word Components Orally (Oral-Components) Following each presentation of the stimulus word, the subject received a card and was instructed to look down at the card while pronouncing the letters of the word he saw or thought he saw previously exhibited in the tachistoscope. The cards the subject received had the numbers 1 through 5 written on them; these numbers corresponded to the five letters of the word presented. Any one card had, on the basis of random determination, either two or three letters on it. The cards were made up in pairs, so that if a subject were first presented with a two-number unit, this was followed by a card bearing the three remaining numbers. Thus all the letters of the word were called for over every pair of odd-even trials.

Group IV—Spelling the Word Components in Writing (Written-Components) Following each presentation of the stimulus word, the subject received a card and was instructed to look down at the card and to write on the card the letters of the word he saw or thought he saw previously exhibited in the tachistoscope. The cards the subject received had the numbers 1 through 5 written on them; these numbers corresponded to the five letters of the word presented. Any one card had, on the basis of random determination, two or three letters on it. The cards were made up in pairs, so that if a subject were first presented with a two-number unit, this was followed by a card bearing the three remaining numbers. Thus all the letters of the word were called for over every pair of odd-even trials.

The cards were delivered through the chute in front of the tachistoscope following presentation of a stimulus word. After responding the subjects returned the cards to the experimenter via the chute at the side of the tachistoscope.

RESULTS

The primary data of the present experiment consist of the four thresholds for tabu words and four thresholds for neutral words for each subject. The group means, in milliseconds, of the thresholds for both types of words for both sexes separately and pooled are presented in Table 2.

The first question asked of these data was whether or not there was a significant difference between the groups with respect to neu-

Table **2** | MEAN RECOGNITION THRESHOLDS IN MILLISECONDS FOR NEUTRAL AND TABU WORDS BY RESPONSE GROUPS AND SEXES

Sex	N	Group I		Group II		Group III		Group IV	
		Neutral	Tabu	Neutral	Tabu	Neutral	Tabu	Neutral	Tabu
Male	15	102.8	136.3	108.3	104.0	152.8	162.2	131.5	138.2
Female	6	85.4	133.3	120.0	148.8	113.3	125.0	98.3	109.6
Combined	21	97.9	135.5	111.7	116.7	141.6	151.6	122.0	130.0

tral word thresholds. This question is of some theoretical importance, because if there were a significant difference between the groups for both tabu *and* neutral word thresholds, any resultant differences in the perceptual defense measure could not be ascribed exclusively to either response inhibition or perceptual alteration.

Accordingly an analysis of variance was made of the neutral words thresholds for the four groups with sexes pooled. A Bartlett's test indicated a significant lack of homogeneity of variance, the chi square of 10.744 for 3 df being significant beyond the 5% level. A Kruskal-Wallis nonparametric one-way analysis of variance (Siegel, 1956) was made and resulted in an H of 3.843. This value of H is not significant at the 5% level (7.82 for 3 df).

The data used in the statistical evaluation to follow are mean differences in milliseconds between tabu and neutral word thresholds. These differences were obtained by averaging the four thresholds for tabu words and the four thresholds for neutral words for each subject, and taking the differences between the two averages. When the average tabu word threshold was smaller than the average neutral word threshold, a minus sign was assigned to the difference.

The mean differences between neutral and tabu word recognition thresholds and the standard deviations of the differences for the various groups are presented in Table 3. The means are smaller for Groups II, III, and IV than for Group I in the case of both sexes; this indicates that the perceptual defense phenomenon measured by neutral-tabu word threshold differences decreased when procedures other than the customary oral response were employed. It is to be noted also in Table 3 that the average threshold differences of females are higher in all treatment groups than those of the males.

Prior to testing for statistical signficance, the data were examined to determine whether average differences between neutral and tabu word recognition thresholds were independent of the height of average thresholds, and also whether homogeneity of variance was within acceptable limits.

Accordingly, product-moment correlation coefficients were computed for each treatment group by correlating average threshold difference between tabu and neutral words with average tabu and neutral word thresholds. These correlation coefficients are presented in Table 4. None of these correlation coefficients were significant at the 5% level, indicating

Table **3** | MEAN AND STANDARD DEVIATIONS OF AVERAGE THRESHOLD DIFFERENCES IN MILLISECONDS BETWEEN NEUTRAL AND TABU WORDS

Sex	N	Group I (Oral-Whole)		Group II (Written-Whole)		Group III (Oral-Components)		Group IV (Written-Components)		Total	
		M	SD	M	SD	M	SD	M	SD	M	SD
Male	15	33.5	17.2	−4.3[a]	26.7	9.3	18.0	6.7	27.4	11.3	26.0
Female	6	47.9	32.1	28.3	21.4	11.7	14.1	11.3	13.4	24.8	24.8
Combined	21	37.6	22.6	5.0	29.0	10.0	16.7	8.0	24.0	15.2	26.4

[a] Minus signs indicate that neutral word thresholds were on the average higher than tabu word thresholds; otherwise, tabu word thresholds were on the average higher than neutral word thresholds.

Table **4** | CORRELATION BETWEEN AVERAGE DIF-
FERENCES AND AVERAGE THRESHOLDS

Treatment groups	Correlation between average differences and average thresholds	t
Group I (Oral-Whole)	0.247	1.108
Group II (Written-Whole)	−0.149	0.656
Group III (Oral-Components)	−0.157	0.695
Group IV (Written-Components)	0.195	0.866

that the mean difference score is independent of the magnitude of the average threshold.

Next, homogeneity of variance was tested by Bartlett's test. For the four treatment groups with sexes pooled, a chi square of 5.956 was obtained, which is not significant at the 5% level (7.815 for 3 *df*). Another homogeneity of variance test was made after dividing each treatment group by sex of subject. The resulting chi square based on eight groups was 10.343, which again is not significant at the 5% level (14.067 for 7 *df*).

Next, a factorial analysis of variance was made by using a triple $2 \times 2 \times 2$ classification (Edwards, 1950). The summary of this analysis is exhibited in Table 5. Each of the three variables had a significant effect on recognition thresholds. Specifically, significant differences

are obtained at better than the .001 level between the oral (Groups I and III) and written (Groups II and IV) modes of response; and significant differences at better than the .025 level were obtained between the whole (Groups I and II) and components (Groups III and IV) modes of response. Males and females differ significantly at better than the .025 level in respect to mean threshold differences.

Testing for interaction effects between the experimental variables indicates that a significant interaction exists at better than the .005 level between oral-written and whole-components conditions (A $\times$ B). The interactions between sexes and modes of response (A $\times$ C, B $\times$ C) are not significant, indicating that the differential responding of the sexes to tabu and neutral words was not dependent on the different modes of response.

The triple interaction between sexes, written-oral, and whole-components conditions is likewise not significant. This indicates that changes in any one of these variables are independent of changes in the other two.

In order to determine whether the perceptual defense phenomenon, as measured by the mean difference between tabu and neutral word thresholds, was present or absent in the various treatment groups, the mean difference for each group was tested by a t test against a theoretical mean of zero. Three *t*'s were computed in each treatment group, one for each sex and one for the sexes combined. The results of these t tests are presented in Table 6.

Table **5** | ANALYSIS OF VARIANCE OF AVERAGE DIFFERENCES BETWEEN TABU AND NEUTRAL WORD
RECOGNITION THRESHOLDS

Source	SS	df	MS	F
Oral versus Written (A)	6300.670	1	6300.670	12.422***
Whole versus Components (B)	3188.170	1	3188.170	6.286*
Males versus Female subjects (C)	3124.286	1	3124.286	6.160*
A $\times$ B	4914.360	1	4914.360	9.689**
A $\times$ C	450.267	1	450.267	0.888
B $\times$ C	1728.601	1	1728.601	3.408
A $\times$ B $\times$ C	274.306	1	274.306	0.541
Within groups	38,548.730	76	507.220	
Total	58,529.390	83		

* Significant at better than the .025 level.
** Significant at better than the .005 level.
*** Significant at better than the .001 level.

Table **6** | SIGNIFICANCE TESTS OF THE DIFFERENCES BETWEEN THE AVERAGE TABU AND NEUTRAL WORD THRESHOLDS

Response conditions	Male		Female		Combined	
	N	t	N	t	N	t
Group I (Oral-Whole)	15	7.538***	6	3.651**	21	7.631***
Group II (Written-Whole)	15	0.629	6	3.239*	21	0.790
Group III (Oral-Components)	15	2.009	6	2.025	21	2.751**
Group IV (Written-Components)	15	0.941	6	2.057	21	1.523

* Significant at better than the .05 level.
** Significant at better than the .02 level.
*** Significant at better than the .001 level.

Males show significant mean differences between tabu and neutral word thresholds at better than the .001 level only in Group I (oral-whole). Males in the other three groups did not attain a significant t. But one should note that Group III (oral-components) just fails to reach significance at the .05 level.

Females show significant mean differences between tabu and neutral word thresholds at better than the .02 level in Group I (oral-whole), and at better than the .05 level in Group II (written-whole).

The combined t's for males and females of the different treatment groups indicate that Group I shows significant mean threshold differences between tabu and neutral word thresholds at better than the .001 level, and Group III at better than the .02 level. Significant differences were not obtained between tabu and neutral word thresholds for Groups II and IV.

DISCUSSION

The results support the response inhibition hypothesis rather than a perceptual defense hypothesis, since they show that the use of different response conditions had the effect of significantly lowering mean threshold differences between tabu and neutral words without producing significant differences in neutral word thresholds. The important and determining role that response conditions play in the evocation of the perceptual defense phenomenon is pointed up by these findings. A concept of perceptual defense becomes a misnomer in that the differential height of tabu to neutral word thresholds is specific to the response conditions employed, and that these mean differences can be satisfactorily interpreted in terms of response inhibition.

A major finding of this study is that Postman's and McGinnies' results are not irreconcilable. When the response condition consisted of words reported orally and in full, as in Group I, the results follow closely McGinnies' (1949) findings. But when the response conditions were made more like those that prevailed in Postman's (Postman et al., 1953) experiment, by instituting written response conditions, as in Groups II and IV, the results follow more closely those reported by Postman; namely, the perceptual defense phenomenon disappeared. The data at hand show, therefore, that substitution of different response conditions resolve the seemingly contradictory results of McGinnies and Postman. Furthermore, the principle of response inhibition can cover both situations parsimoniously.

With respect to the sex variable, no differential effect was found when different response conditions were used; the analysis of variance indicated that the interaction between sexes and modes of response is not significant. However, the sex variable, with response conditions pooled, does have a significant effect on recognition thresholds in that females show significantly higher mean differences between neutral and tabu words than males.

These results in respect to the sex variable are in agreement with the findings of other investigators (Cowen & Obrist, 1958; Freeman, 1955; Postman et al., 1953). It is uncertain what may cause these sex differences. It has been suggested that the sex of the experimenter (male) in an experiment where female subjects are used may be a variable, but

Postman, who investigated the experimenter variable by using both male and female experimenters, did not find any significant interaction between sex of experimenter and sex of subject. Postman has suggested that females may be less familiar with tabu words, and less ready to report them; that is, they require a higher degree of certainty. Even so, the underlying causes for the behavior noted still remain to be specified.

In the light of the results of this experiment, response inhibition may be viewed as a complex function of oral versus written and whole versus components conditions, and the interaction between them. It would seem that the optimal conditions for the evocation of response inhibition, in a perceptual defense situation, are oral responding and whole word responding; and the minimal conditions for the evocation of response inhibition are written responding and spelling components of words.

An explanation for these findings may be sought in the cultural conditioning of the subjects. It is conceivable that in the course of his reactional biography, the individual in our culture learns that the consequences of *speaking* tabu words are much more severe than the consequences of *writing* or *spelling* or expressing tabu words in some other indirect fashion.

SUMMARY

It was hypothesized that the perceptual defense phenomenon can be accounted for on the basis of response inhibition. Therefore, it was predicted that under response conditions other than the customary pronouncing of neutral and tabu words in full, the differences between neutral and tabu word thresholds would significantly diminish.

The effects of four modes of response on recognition thresholds were investigated by using four groups consisting of 21 subjects each (15 males, 6 females). The modes of response were (a) the customary oral responding, that is, pronouncing in full the tachistoscopically presented word; (b) writing the whole word; (c) spelling the word components orally; and (d) spelling the word components in writing.

The test stimuli consisted of six tabu words and six neutral words (equated in familiarity), and were exhibited tachistoscopically. Recognition thresholds for the words presented were determined by a modified method of limits.

The findings are:

1. Oral responding resulted in significantly greater mean differences between neutral and tabu word thresholds than written responding.
2. Whole word responding resulted in significantly greater mean differences between neutral and tabu word thresholds than responding by spelling components of words.
3. Females showed significantly greater mean differences between neutral and tabu word thresholds than males.
4. The interaction effects between oral versus written and between whole versus components were significant.
5. The interaction between the sexes and modes of response was not significant.

The results are interpreted as lending support to the response inhibition hypothesis.

REFERENCES

Bruner, J. A., & Postman, L. Emotional selectivity in perception and reaction. *J. Pers.*, 1947, **16**, 69–77.

Cowen, E. L., & Beier, E. G. The influence of "threat expectancy" on perception. *J. Pers.*, 1950, **19**, 85–94.

Cowen, E. L., & Beier, E. G. Threat-expectancy, word frequencies, and perceptual prerecognition hypotheses. *J. abnorm. soc. Psychol.*, 1954, **49**, 178–182.

Cowen, E. L., & Obrist, P. A. Perceptual reactivity to threat and neutral words under varying experimental conditions. *J. abnorm. soc. Psychol.*, 1958, **56**, 305–310.

Edwards, A. L. *Experimental design in psychological research.* New York: Rinehart, 1950.

Freeman, J. T. Set of perceptual defense. *J. exp. Psychol.*, 1954, **48**, 283–288.

Freeman, J. T. Set versus perceptual defense: A confirmation. *J. abnorm. soc. Psychol.*, 1955, **51**, 710–712.

Howes, D. H., & Solomon, R. L. A note on McGinnies' "Emotionality and perceptual defense." *Psychol. Rev.*, 1950, **57**, 229–234.

Kantor, J. R. *A survey of the science of psychology.* Bloomington, Ind.: Principia, 1933.

Kupperian, J. E., Jr., & Golin, E. An electronic tachistoscope. *Amer. J. Psychol.,* 1951, **64,** 274–276.

Lacy, O. W., Lewinger, N., & Adamson, J. F. Foreknowledge as a factor affecting perceptual defense and alertness. *J. exp. Psychol.,* 1953, **45,** 169–174.

McGinnies, E. M. Emotionality and perceptual defense. *Psychol. Rev.,* 1949, **56,** 244–251.

Postman, L., Bronson, Wanda C., & Gropper, G. L. Is there a mechanism of perceptual defense? *J. abnorm. soc. Psychol.,* 1953, **48,** 215–224.

Postman, L., Bruner, J. S., & McGinnies, E. Personal values as selective factors in perception. *J. abnorm. soc. Psychol.,* 1948, **43,** 142–154.

Siegel, S. *Nonparametric statistics for the behavioral sciences.* New York: McGraw-Hill, 1956.

Solomon, R. L., & Howes, D. H. Word frequency, personal values, and visual duration thresholds. *Psychol. Rev.,* 1951, **58,** 256–270.

Thorndike, E. L., & Lorge, I. *The teachers' word book of 30,000 words.* New York: Teachers Coll., Columbia Univer., Bureau of Publications, 1944.

Selection **30** | SOCIAL PSYCHOLOGY AND PERCEPTION*

JEROME S. BRUNER
Harvard University

Contemporary social psychology, one finds in looking through the contents of its professional journals, is much concerned, indeed even preoccupied, with problems of perception. There is constant reference to the manner in which subjects in experiments "perceive the situation." The term "social perception" has come widely into use to describe the manner in which one person perceives or infers the traits and intentions of another, and there is a steady flow of experimental studies on the manner in which social factors induce types of selectivity in what a person perceives and how he interprets it. Social attitudes are defined as a readiness to experience events in certain

* Reprinted from Jerome S. Bruner, "Social Psychology and Perception," in Eleanor E. Maccoby, Theodore M. Newcomb, Eugene L. Hartley, etc., *Readings in Social Psychology,* 3d ed., Holt, Rinehart and Winston, Inc., New York, 1958, pp. 85–94. Reprinted by permission of the author and publisher.

consistent and selective ways, and the most recent writings on the psychology of language, inspired by Benjamin Lee Whorf, urge that the structure of a language and its lexical units determine or at least influence what one habitually notices in the world about one. Without appropriate attitudes and an appropriate linguistic structure, one does not readily register upon certain events in the environment that another person, appropriately armed with attitudes and a language, would notice as salient.

While this point of view about the central importance of perception has always to some measure been a feature of social psychology —McDougall in his classic textbook of 1912, for example, was sharply aware of the role of social sentiments in biasing the selectivity of attention, and Thomas and Znaniecki made "the definition of the situation" a key concept in their pioneering acculturation study of *The Polish Peasant*—it is only within the last ten or 15 years that the role of perception and "selective registration" has come to be dominant in social psychological theory. In the pages that follow, we shall examine the backgrounds of this emphasis, some of the reasons why perceptual concepts are indispensable to the social psychologist, and the nature of these concepts as they have emerged in the last decade or so.

To the uninitiated, one with a background neither in psychology nor in classical philosophy, perceiving may pose no problems. The simple view, sometimes called naïve realism, would hold that there are objects and events in the external world and that somehow representations of these, called *Eidola* by the pre-Socratic philosophers, emanate from the things in the world and find their way into the nervous system and eventually into consciousness. Such, however, is not the case save in the most metaphoric sense; rather, the problem is how we integrate into a unitary percept the myriad of sensory stimuli that come from our specialized sense organs. In most instances, there are more things to be noticed than one can possibly register upon simultaneously—as when one walks into a room full of people with several conversations going on at once—and even when the stimulus input is fairly simple, there are various ways in which it can be "looked at" or organized. A tree can be perceived from the point of view of the soundness of its wood, the seasonal status of its foliage, its species, its shade-giving quality, and so on. Perhaps we can notice four or five or six of these features at once, but rarely do we register on more of them. For the abiding fact about the process of knowing, of which perceiving is one aspect, is that organisms have a highly limited span of attention and a highly limited span of immediate memory. Selectivity is forced upon us by the nature of these limitations, and indeed, even if we should operate at maximum capacity (estimated to be an ability to notice and keep in mind about seven independent things simultaneously), the cost in cognitive strain would be considerable.

In the interests of economizing effort we do three things. On the one hand, we narrow the selectivity of attention more or less to those things that are somehow essential to the enterprises in which we are engaged. In social situations, we register on the color of people's skins, but not on the texture. Moreover, we simplify even here and may register solely on whether they are white or colored. Secondly, we "recode" into simpler form the diversity of events that we encounter so that our limited attention and memory span can be protected. Instead of trying to remember how far falling bodies fall, we simply commit to memory the formula $S = \frac{gt^2}{2}$, which preserves the necessary information and allows us to recreate any specific information about distance we want. Sometimes these recodings of information serve their economical function but lead to a serious loss of information, as when we recode information in terms of what Walter Lippmann long ago called a "stereotype." We see a Negro sitting on a park bench, a Jew or Texan changing a check at a bank window, a German dressing down a taxicab driver, and allocate each experience to an established and well-memorized stereotype: lazy Negro, mercenary Jew, rich Texan, bullying German. The behavior is perceived according to the formula, the person saved from having to do much perceptual work aside from picking up a few cues. Not only is information lost but misinformation is added: the person "sees" the stereotyped individuals he has created—"Why, I saw a big healthy Negro sitting there idle in the park doing nothing the other day," and the behavior is perceived as lazy rather than, perhaps, that the Negro worked the swing shift and was enjoying his hours off in the park. Finally, we deal with the overload of information provided by the environment, the overload relative to our limited capacities for noticing and registering and remembering, by the use of technological aids, aids that are designed to lengthen the noticing process. A simple example of such an aid is pencil and paper: trying to list all that is before us from every point of view. Or we use a camera in the hope of being able to go back over the picture and extract the last ounce of meaning from an event. All of these methods help. None of them can succeed fully, for as Robert Oppenheimer has noted about the cognitive processes, in order to know anything we must somehow give up the aspiration of knowing everything about a particular situation.

All of the ways in which we deal with environmental complexity at the perceptual level are deeply tinged with the hues of the society in which we live. That we notice skin color and not skin texture results from the nature of social customs. Yet, it is curious that closely below the level of habitual awareness there is also a kind of "noticing" of socially less relevant things. Morphologists tell us, for example, that human skin texture can be divided roughly and metaphorically into three types: apple skins, onion skins, and orange skins, the first associated with round pyknic physiques, the second with thin or "scrawny" types, the last with athletic builds. The moment this is mentioned, you have what Herman Melville once called a "shock of recognition"—you somehow knew these types but did not quite recognize them explicitly. So it is, too, with recording information: new methods of organizing experience, once one can break through the old methods, are "obvious." A mother has been seeing her obstreperous child as "naughty" or "rebellious." A psychologist explains to her that it is five o'clock and that the child is principally tired. If this new way of organizing the welter of movements and expressions that constitute a child's behavior can be accepted by the mother, likely as not she will say, "Of course, but I should have thought of that." The alternative ways of organizing a percept seem somehow to be there in nascent form. So, too, with technological aids like languages and cameras and lists. A photographic plate is immensely limited: the noises that make a Roman street so memorable do not register, no matter how fine-grained the film. But, as in the other two modes of dealing with stimulation overload, technological aids also produce a surplus beyond what is immediately "used" consciously.

I have mentioned the "nascent surplus" of information one obtains in encounters with the environment even though one has been highly selective in noticing things, because it is important from the point of view of creativity and social change and innovation. If it is true that people are selective, must be selective to match their limited cognitive capacities to the complexities of the social and physical environment, it is also true that they are not completely trapped in this selectivity, that the conditions for producing a change in perceiving and thinking about events are there.

The reader will properly ask at this point, "But *is* selectivity forced on a person by the nature of his cognitive apparatus? Can he not take his time and perceive more carefully and comprehensively and get a better sense of what things really mean around him?" The question is a good one, indeed a deep one, and can be answered in several ways. First, there are great individual differences between people in the degree to which they "gamble" in their selectivity, some seemingly content with noticing only a few relevant-to-them things about events they encounter, others being much more deliberate and aware about alternatives and sutleties. Elsewhere in this volume, for example, the reader will find discussions of the authoritarian personality, one of whose notable characteristics is a proneness to seeing things very selectively, in black and white unrelieved by gray. It is also worth remembering that a constant regimen of close inspection of events, a devotion to the alternative ways in which events can be perceived, may conflict with requirements for action. We are forced to decide whether a man is honest or not, whether a group is friendly toward us. If we are to adjust to problems of segregation and desegregation, we must notice whether skins are white or colored. We cannot, like Hamlet, remain long in the state of being "sicklied o'er with the pale cast of thought"—not if we are to act. Finally, there are times when the world is too much like one of Rorschach's ink blots, with

ambiguity prevailing. The cues we are forced to use are highly random and probabilistic. We must often decide whether a man is friendly or not on the basis of a cue no more trustworthy than whether or not he is smiling, and are thus forced to fall back on what may be a groundless stereotype. In such situations, perceptual inference may reflect little more than the social conventions or the particular strategy a person uses for coping with his difficulties. It is characteristic, for example, that people are inaccurate, indeed only a bit better than chance, in being able to recognize those members of a group who dislike them—far less good at it than in telling whether others like them. The masking of cues by politesse— we are subtle about showing dislike—plus the protective need of avoiding the sense of being disliked lead perception into all sorts of traps. We end up by seeing those people as disliking us whom we ourselves dislike.

THE "NEW LOOK" IN PERCEPTION

Perhaps the immediate impetus to contemporary concern with the role of perceptual processes in social behavior came from a series of experiments on determinants of perceptual organization—determinants that could be called "behavioral" which relate to such influences as need, social values, attitudes, stress, cultural background, etc., in contrast to "autochthonous" which refers to stimulus factors. These experiments, taken as a sequence, came rather waggishly, to be called the "New Look" in perception. A sampling of some of the principal studies carried out will serve to highlight some of the critical problems that have faced the theorist concerned with formulating a model of the perceptual process that has some relevance to the understanding of social behavior. In the final section we shall return to the nature of such a theoretical model.[1]

The early studies were principally concerned

[1] Since there have appeared several hundred experimental investigations of motivational and social determinants of perception, it is indeed difficult and certainly arbitrary to select a few for special mention. The choice of the experiments is based partly on their importance, partly upon the degree to which they illustrate basic theoretical issues, and partly on expository convenience—in about that order.

with showing the nature of "distortion" in perception and the sources of perceptual inaccuracy and were, in the main, influenced by thinking imported from clinical psychiatry where such doctrines as "autistic thinking," "defense," "primary process" (hypothesized infantile wishful hallucination) had become dominant as a result of Freud's pioneering work. The studies of Gardner Murphy and his colleagues are a case in point. Levine, Chein, and Murphy[2] showed their subjects a set of food pictures behind a ground-glass screen that obscured them to the point of ambiguity. The subjects were then asked to give the first association that the obscured pictures brought to mind. They found that associations connected with food and eating increased as the hours of food deprivation of the subjects increased, reaching a maximum around ten to 12 hours of starvation. After this, the number of food associations declined. The authors attempted to explain the finding in terms of the pleasure principle operating under conditions of mild drive, being supplanted by the reality principle when hunger became severe. Like many pioneering experiments, there was much wrong with the design of this study—the kind of associational response employed, the fact that the subjects knew they would be fed after the requisite number of hours being without food, etc. But it stimulated many follow-up studies. We now know that the results of Levine, Chein, and Murphy are a special case of a more general one whose nature is not yet clear.

McClelland and Atkinson,[3] for example, worked with subjects who were unaware of the relation between their hunger and the perceptual test they were being given. The subjects, sailors at a submarine base, were asked to "recognize" "barely perceptible" objects on a screen. Actually the screen was blank. The men showed an increase in instrumental food response—seeing eating utensils and the like—but no increase with hours of deprivation in the number of consummatory food objects seen.

Yet, in another study, under conditions of prolonged and chronic semistarvation, conscientious objectors show no increase at all in the number or quality of food associations or readiness to perceive food objects (see the wartime work of Brosek and his colleagues[4]). Here the question may well have been one of pride: these dedicated young men were doing their service by serving as subjects in an experiment. Giving in to hunger may have been something to avoid as almost a matter of honor. With respect to chronically food-deprived prisoners of war and concentration camp victims that I have interviewed shortly after release, one finds that there is repeated mention of two extreme types: those preoccupied with food and those who avoid the topic as much as possible. One can cite other studies that add further subtleties to the complex pattern that seems to emerge, but there is now enough evidence before us to suggest that not the *amount* of need but the *way* in which a person learns to *handle* his needs determines the manner in which motivation and cognitive selectively will interact. Autism or wishful thinking are scarcely universal modes of coping with one's needs. It is conceivable that in a culture or in a family setting where emphasis is placed upon asceticism and denial of needs, autism would be the exception. On the whole, then, selectivity reflects the nature of the person's mode of striving for goals rather than the amount of need which he seems to be undergoing.

Closely related to this line of investigation are studies on the role of interest, value, and attitude, and this work brings up several additional subtleties. The experimental work of Postman, Bruner, and McGinnies[5] indicated that the speed and ease with which words were recognized when briefly presented in a fast-exposure apparatus (tachistoscope) was a function of the value areas these words represented and of the interest the subjects in

[2] R. Levine, I. Chein, and G. Murphy, "The Relation of the Intensity of a Need to the Amount of Perceptual Distortion, a Preliminary Report," *J. Psychol.*, 1942, **XIII**, 283–293.

[3] D. C. McClelland and J. W. Atkinson, "The Projective Expression of Needs: I. The effect of different Intensities of the Hunger Drive on Perception," *J. Psychol.*, 1948, **XXV**, 205–222.

[4] J. Brozek, H. Guetzkow, and M. G. Baldwin, "A Quantitative Study of Perception and Association in Experimental Semi-starvation." *J. Pers.*, 1951, **XIX**, 245–264.

[5] L. Postman, J. S. Bruner, and E. McGinnies, "Personal Values as Selective Factors in Perception," *J. Abnorm. Soc. Psychol.*, 1948, **XXCIII**, 148–153.

the experiment evinced in these various value areas as measured by the Allport-Vernon Study of Values which tests for the relative dominance of religious, esthetic, political, social, theoretical, and economic interests. The general finding was that the greater the dominance of a value in the person, the more rapidly he would recognize words representing that area. The authors found that the hypotheses offered by subjects prior to correct recognition were particularly revealing, suggesting that in the presence of low-value words there was some form of defensive avoidance—the perceiving of blanks, scrambled letters, or even derogatory words which the authors called "contravaluant hypotheses." With high-value words, on the contrary, subjects tended in excess of chance to propose guesses that were in the value area of the stimulus word prior to correct recognition, in keeping with a subsequent finding of Bricker and Chapanis[6] that subjects can obtain partial information from words when they are presented below threshold. Later studies by Bruner and Postman[7] on blocks in perceiving personally threatening words and by McGinnies[8] on the raising of identification thresholds for taboo words led to the development of the concept of "perceptual defense," a kind of blocking of recognition for classes of materials that were personally and/or culturally unacceptable to the perceiver, a "proscribed list" at the entry port so to speak.

It was argued by Solomon and Howes[9] that the findings on the effect of values could be accounted for by a factor of frequency—that the person interested in religion was more likely to have selective exposure to religious words and symbols. Howes[10] then went on to show that the amount of time required to recognize a word in the English language could be expressed rather precisely as a function of the logarithm of the frequency with which the word appeared in printed English as recorded in the useful Thorndike-Lorge frequency count.[11] But since economic words are likely to be more frequently encountered in printed English than theoretical words, the general frequency of words in English would not be sufficient grounds to explain why some individuals, high in theoretical interests, recognize theoretical words more quickly than economic words such as "money" or "price." We must invoke a notion of "idiosyncratic frequency," an individual's frequency of encounter without regard to frequency in English. Indeed, Postman and Schneider[12] showed that for very common words drawn from the six value-areas of the Allport-Vernon test, the relative position of the values for the subject made little difference. With rarer words it did, with the more valued ones being recognized more easily.

The upshot of this debate, it would appear, is twofold and of considerable significance. Perceptual readiness, the ease with which items are recognized under less than optimal viewing conditions, seems to reflect not only the needs and modes of striving of an organism but also to reflect the requirement that surprise be minimized—that perceptual readiness be predictive in the sense of being tuned to what is likely to be present in the environment as well as what is needed for the pursuit of our enterprises. The predictive nature of perceptual readiness, however, reflects more than the frequency with which things occur. Rather, it is best thought of as the matching of perceptual readiness to the probable *sequences* of events in the environment. We come to learn what goes with what. We *hear* the approaching whistle of a train and are readied to *see* the train. We learn, if you will, the probabilistic texture of the world, conserve this learning, use it as a guide to tuning our perceptual readiness to what is most likely next. It is this that permits us to "go beyond the information given." That there is danger is using such a guide is illustrated in a study by Bruner and

[6] P. D. Bricker and A. Chapanis, "Do Incorrectly Perceived Tachistoscopic Stimuli Convey Some Information?," *Psychol. Rev.*, 1953, **LX**, 181–188.

[7] J. S. Bruner and L. Postman, "Emotional Selectivity in Perception and Reaction," *J. Pers.*, 1947, **XVI**, 69–77.

[8] E. McGinnies, "Emotionality and Perceptual Defense," *Psychol. Rev.*, 1949, **LVI**, 244–251.

[9] R. L. Solomon and D. W. Howes, "Word Frequency, Personal Values, and Visual Deviation Thresholds," *Psychol. Rev.*, 1951, **LVIII**, 256–270.

[10] D. Howes, "On the Interpretation of Word Frequency as a Variable Affecting Speed of Recognition," *J. Exp. Psychol.*, 1954, **XLVIII**, 106–122.

[11] E. L. Thorndike and I. Lorge, *The Teacher's Word Book of 30,000 Words* (New York: Teachers College, Columbia University, 1944).

[12] L. Postman and B. Schneider, "Personal Values, Visual Recognition, and Recall," *Psychol. Rev.*, 1951, **LVIII**, 271–284.

Postman on the perception of incongruity.[13] If playing cards with suit and color reversed —a red four of clubs say—are presented to subjects for brief intervals of a few milliseconds, what occurs is perceptual completion according to high probability linkages we have already learned; the subject "sees" a red four of hearts or a black four of clubs. Thresholds of identification increase grossly: when subjects are presented with these incongruous stimuli, it takes them an inordinately long exposure time to "see" what is actually there. But human organisms unlearn and learn quickly: having seen the incongruity finally, later instances are much more rapidly identified correctly.

It is characteristic of perceptual identification of things that the larger the number of alternatives the person is expecting, the more difficult it is to recognize any single one of the alternatives that does occur. In an experiment by Bruner, Miller, and Zimmerman[14] it was found that it is much easier to recognize a word when it is one of four that may occur than when it is one of eight or 16 or 32 that may occur. This suggests that where speed is required in perception—as under stress conditions or under conditions of exigent motivation —that the likelihood of erroneous perception increases. That is to say, to gain speed, we limit the alternative hypotheses that we are willing to entertain. In the event of ambiguous stimulation, as in social perception generally, such speed-producing monopolistic hypotheses are likely to be confirmed. We expect, for example, a hostile action from a disliked person; he does something equivocal; we "see" it as a hostile act and thus confirm our expectation. It is the case, moreover, that under conditions where alternative expectancies must be limited, we will be more likely to adopt socially conventional expectancies or ones that reflect our more basic needs. It is in this sense that stress and social pressure serve to reduce the subtlety of the registration process.

One final matter must be mentioned before turning briefly to theory. It has to do with the perception of magnitude, a subject which does not at first seem closely related to social psychology. An early study by Bruner and Goodman[15] opened the issue. The study was simply conceived—in both a good and a bad sense. Children, ages 10 to 11, divided into those from fairly prosperous homes and those from a slum settlement house, were given the task of adjusting a variable patch of light to the sizes of pennies, nickels, dimes, quarters, and half dollars. Half the subjects worked with coins in hand, half from memory. Control groups adjusted the light patch to cardboard discs of the same sizes. The findings, in general, were that the sizes of the more valuable coins were overestimated, of less valuable coins underestimated. The effects were greater for the memory condition than for the condition with coin present. No significant effect was found for paper discs. In general, the economically well-to-do children showed less of the value-distortion effect than the poor children.

The study has been repeated several times, and as McCurdy[16] and Tajfel[17] point out, the same effect found more often than not under a variety of conditions. One experiment by Carter and Schooler[18] found somewhat contrary results. The same trends were observed, but they fell short of statistical significance save for the condition where size was estimated from memory, where significant results were observed. A later study by Bruner and Rodrigues[19] pointed up one faulty assumption of the earlier studies mentioned. Overestimation and underestimation of size is always stated with respect to the measured sizes of the coins, the "physically accurate" size. This is a psychologically naïve way of describing

[13] J. S. Bruner and L. Postman, "On the Perception of Incongruity: A Paradigm," *J. Pers.,* 1949, **XVIII,** 206–223.

[14] J. S. Bruner, G. A. Miller, and C. Zimmerman. "Discriminative Skill and Discriminative Matching in Perceptual Recogniton," *J. Exp. Psychol.,* 1955, **XLIX,** 187–192.

[15] J. S. Bruner and C. C. Goodman, "Value and Need as Organizing Factors in Perception," *J. Abnorm. & Soc. Psychol.,* 1947, **XLII,** 33–44.

[16] H. G. McCurdy, "Coin Perception Studies and the Concept of Schemata," *Psychol. Rev.,* 1956, **LXIII,** 160–168.

[17] H. Tajfel, "Value and the Perceptual Judgment of Magnitude," *Psychol. Rev.,* 1957, **LXIV,** 192–204.

[18] L. F. Carter and K. Schooler, "Value, Need and Other Factors in Perception," *Psychol. Rev.,* 1949, **LVI,** 200–207.

[19] J. S. Bruner and J. S. Rodrigues, "Some Determinants of Apparent Size," *J. Abnorm. & Soc. Psychol.,* 1953, **XLVIII,** 17–24.

what goes on in judgement of magnitude. Rather, one should ask about the *relative* subjective sizes of coins of different value. The study by Bruner and Rodrigues had as its principal object to show that there was a *greater separation* in subjective size between a nickel and a quarter than there was for comparable-sized while metal discs. Tajfel[20] has developed this point in an interesting theoretical paper, pointing out that it is one of the functions of perceptual judgement to accentuate the apparent difference in magnitudes between objects that differ in value, provided that the difference in magnitude is associated with the difference in value—as if, so to speak, the two attributes, value and magnitude, are confounded in a way to point up and accentuate value difference. In short, even in the estimation of magnitude, judgmental processes reflect the social conventions that establish values for various elements of the environment.[21]

ON THEORETICAL MODELS OF PERCEPTION

Given the operation of behavioral factors in perceiving and cognizing generally, including the operation of social factors, what can be said about a theoretical model of perception that would be of relevance to the social psychologist? It is quite clear at the outset that the psychologist principally concerned with perception cannot work with one kind of theory and the social psychologist, interested in the effects of perceptual selectivity on social behavior and in the cultural patterning of perception as well, work with yet another theory of perception. Let me briefly outline, in conclusion, some of the features that I believe a theory of perception must have in order to do justice to the concerns of both kinds of psychologists. For a fuller account of the points to be made, the reader is referred to Bruner.[22]

The first, and perhaps most self-evident point upon reflection, is that perceiving or registering on an object or an event in the environment involves an act of categorization. We "place" things in categories. That is a "man" and he is "honest" and he is now "walking" in a manner that is "leisurely" with the "intention" of "getting some relaxation." Each of the words in quotation marks involves a sorting or placement of stimulus input on the basis of certain cues that we learn how to use. Now it is of great importance to bear in mind that most of the categories into which we sort for identification are learned on the basis of experience, by virtue of our membership in a culture and a linguistic community, and by the nature of the needs we must fulfill in order to exist beyond some degraded level. Not only are the categories learned, but we learn to estimate the likelihood that placement of an event into a category on the basis of a few cues will be "accurate"—by which we mean, *predictive* in the sense that a closer look will bear it out or that it will be consensually validated when other perceivers come on the scene or it will be confirmed by technological inspection.

We may take it as self-evident that some categories we employ are more amenable to check by prediction. The cues we use for judging an object "distant" or a surface "impenetrable" are checked a thousand times a day in getting about: walking, driving, reaching. Others are less readily checked. Whether, on the basis of a few signs, we can judge whether a man is "honorable," given the difficulty of establishing a quick and adequate criterion, is questionable. The category, established by a culture in response to its social needs, resists validation. It is perhaps the case that modes of categorizing that are amenable to firm and immediate validation with respect to predictiveness are the ones that are more universal to the human race, more easily diffused and learned. The less readily a form of categorizing is able to be predictively validated, the more will it reflect the idiosyncrasies of a culture. It is not surprising that the famous Cambridge expedition to the Torres Straits[23] at the opening of the century found so few differences in the

20 Tajfel, *op. cit.*
21 So brief a summary of a field of research as complicated as magnitude estimation and the role of value factors in it is bound to be oversimplified. For a fuller account, the reader is referred to the excellent papers of Tajfel, *op. cit.*, and McCurdy, *op. cit.*
22 J. S. Bruner, "On Perceptual Readiness," *Psychol. Rev.*, 1957, **LXIV**, 123–152.

23 W. H. R. Rivers, "Vision," *Reports of the Cambridge Anthropological Expedition to Torres Straits*, 1901, **II**, 1–132.

perception of distance, size, etc. in comparing primitive Pacific Islanders and English undergraduates.

It is also apparent that the categories of events with which we become accustomed to dealing are organized into systems or structures, bound together in various ways: by virtue of the fact that one class of events is likely to follow another or because classes of events are closely bound by some other principle than mere association as, for example, that several are required in order for certain objectives to be reached. Thus, displacement of a dot from one position to another is categorized as "a dot moving" and not as "first a dot in position A, then another dot at position B." As we have noted before, recoding into systems serves to keep mental life from becoming burdened with a diversity of unrelated particulars. Highly practiced perception is a case in point. A practiced baseball spectator joins and meshes a highly complex set of categorized events into a structure called a "double play."

In addition to the problem of categories and category systems and how they are formed, there is also a question of the accessibility of such categories for use by a perceiver. It is often the case that we fail to identify an event properly although we are knowledgeable about the class of events which it exemplifies; fail to do so even though the cues are clear. And as the work cited earlier in this paper has shown, certain categories manifest their accessibility by permitting rapid identification of relevant objects under conditions of very brief or very "fuzzy" exposure. What makes certain kinds of categorizing responses sometimes available and sometimes not? What can be said in general is that category accessibility reflects two sets of factors. Need and interest states, as we have implied, increase accessibility of those categories of objects that relate to their fulfillment or furthering—not necessarily in a wish-fulfilling or autistic way, as noted before, but in a manner consonant with achieving realistically a desired goal. The second set of factors governing category accessibility has to do with the predictive requirements of perception and the need to avoid disruptive mistakes. These requirements tune the readiness of the perceiver to match the likelihood of events in the environment. When we are hungry, we tend to be alerted to signs of restaurants, if we usually assuage hunger in restaurants. We notice ones we have never noticed before. Our "restaurant" category has become highly "available." But we look for and expect restaurants at the street level and not in the sky or atop trees. It is this balancing of need-induced alertness and event-matching expectancy that makes it possible for perception to act in the service of needs and interests and, at the same time, with due regard for reality.

In conclusion, perceptual readiness reflects the dual requirements of coping with an environment—directedness with respect to goals and efficiency with respect to the means by which the goals can be attained. It is no matter of idle interest that a religious man picks up perceptually things that are relevant to his interest more easily and more quickly than other things, and at the same time, this efficiency continues to reflect what is likely to occur in his surroundings. What it suggests is that once a society has patterned a man's interests and trained him to expect what is likely in that society, it has gained a great measure of control not only on his thought processes, but also on the very material on which thought works—the experienced data of perception. It is not surprising, then, that the social psychologist has shown a renewed interest in the process of perceiving. To understand the manner in which man responds to and copes with his social environment we must know what that environment is *to him*. The physicist provides a description of the nature of stimulation in such terms as wave lengths, radiant energy, chemical compounds. Nobody confuses these descriptions with what we experience—colors, brightnesses, tastes. The student of society like the physicist, provides descriptions of the "external environment" in terms of stratification, totemic clans, moities. The question is how people perceive or register upon these features of the social environment. That is what is crucial in determining how we respond.

BIOLOGICAL FACTORS

In our previous selections we have seen that development of complex motivations and of even rudimentary perceptions is dependent on the ability of the organism to be modified by interactions with its environment, that is, to learn from experience. In this chapter we are concerned with the nature of the modification process per se. When we observe a change in behavior over a period of time, which we call learning, we make the assumption that the behavioral change reflects some more or less permanent modification of the central nervous system. Even though this assumption seems eminently reasonable, we are in the unfortunate position of having relatively little empirical knowledge concerning the nature of this neurological change. However, in the past few years much excitement has been created in scientific circles by experiments which have shown that brain chemistry and brain structure may be modified by certain kinds of learning experiences. One approach to this problem is represented by cooperative research programs between biochemists and psychologists (see Selection 39 for one of a series of experiments by University of California researchers). A molecular approach has been taken by Dr. Holger Hyden, a neurophysiologist who has shown changes in molecular structure of ribonucleic acid following learning. A more behavioral approach has been followed by a group of psychologists at the University of Michigan. Dr. James V. McConnell and his colleagues have shown that a small flatworm known as a planarian can be classically conditioned. In addition to this rudimentary learning ability, the planarian has the capacity of regeneration if cut into two parts. McConnell and his colleagues have shown that both halves retain the original learning. They have further shown that if untrained planaria are fed conditioned worms which had been ground, these planaria will learn a conditioned response faster than worms that have been fed untrained worms. In Selection 31, Dr. Allan L. Jacobson reviews this research and then indicates how he and his colleagues have transferred responses from trained organisms to untrained organisms by injecting RNA-rich substances extracted from trained animals. Although several other experimenters have obtained similar transfer effects, as of this writing (June 1966) about an equal number have failed to obtain the effect.[1] However, it seems likely that in this fast-moving research area the answer regarding the reliability of this transfer-via-injection effect will be emerging within a year or two. If it is a reliable phenomenon, it will then be the psychologist's task to demonstrate its generality or specificity to a variety of psychological effects, such as generalization, extinction, and partial reinforcement. It will be the biochemists' task to determine the specific molecular process which is the transmitting agent. Hopes are high for a major breakthrough on the biochemical basis for learning and memory.

PSYCHOLOGICAL FACTORS

At the psychological level there is no lack of experiments exploring those variables which influence learning. In fact, probably more papers are published every year on the topic of learning than on any other basic psychological process. Despite the

[1] Two reports which have presented negative results are (a) M. Luttges, T. Johnson, C. Buck, J. Holland, and J. McGough, "An Examination of 'Transfer of Learning' by Nucleic Acid," *Science*, **151**: 834–837, 1966; and (b) J. A. Corson, and H. E. Enesce, "Some Effects of Injections of Ribonucleic Acid," *Psychonomic Science*, **5**: 217–218, 1966.

vast amount of data, there is still no basic agreement on such fundamental questions as, "What is it that is learned when learning takes place?" In general, there are two major theoretical positions: the *stimulus-response* theories (as represented by Clark Hull) hold that what is learned is an association between a stimulus and the response which the subject makes; the *cognitive* theories (represented by Edward C. Tolman) hold that the making of an overt response is not necessary for learning, but rather the organism is said to learn the relationship between two sets of stimuli, that is, "what leads to what." In an experiment reported as Selection 32, McNamara, Long, and Wike attempt to determine if lower animals can learn the locus of food without actually making the instrumental response required to come in contact with the food. The results indicate that rats *can* learn without overt performance, but only if they have the stimulus-support of extra maze cues.

All too often the student taking an introductory psychology course completes his assigned reading on the learning process with the feeling that the material has little relevance to everyday practical learning problems. Each of the remaining selections in this chapter has been selected to dispel this notion. Each of them has rather clear implications for learning in the "real life" situation. In Selection 33, Honig and Slivka present an experimental analysis of the generalization effects of punishment. The procedures used are those of operant conditioning, which involves precise stimulus-response-reinforcement contingencies. The experimental report is highly descriptive and noninterpretive, in contrast to the theoretically based research and discussion represented in Selection 32. These characteristics are typical of research conducted within the framework of the experimental analysis of behavior advocated by B. F. Skinner. The substantive results of the experiment indicate that the performance depression which is conditioned to punishment of a response tends to generalize to stimuli which are similar to those which are present during the original conditioning. This experimental finding is consistent with the clinical finding of generalization of phobic reactions to objects which are similar in some way to the object which was focally present during an early traumatic experience. It is also consistent with the common observation that children who are reared in families in which the father is a frequent and severe punisher tend to generalize their emotional reactions from the father to authority figures in general. Thus, one of the difficulties with punishment as a technique for eliminating responses and modifying behavior is that the punished response may generalize much too broadly, or that the child may fail to understand the contingency between his response and the punishment and may thus interpret the punishment to imply that he is a bad person or that other people are generally to be feared. An alternative technique for behavioral modification is to extinguish the response by eliminating its reinforcers. In Selection 34, Dr. Carl D. Williams demonstrates the application of this principle to the practical problem of eliminating tantrum behavior in children.

A person's response repertoire is modified not only by positive or negative reinforcement and by extinction but also by the process of forgetting. In Selection 35, Dr. Benton J. Underwood reviews the previous research which had been conducted on forgetting of verbal material. The previously dominant explanation of the large amount of forgetting which occurred within twenty-four hours after learning was based on the notion of retroactive interference. That is, something which the subject learned in his daily activities between the time of learning and the time of recall interfered with the retention of the original learning. Underwood proposes that, on the contrary, the explanation should be based upon the notion of *proactive interference;* that is, learning which took place prior to participating in the experiment is primarily responsible for the forgetting. Underwood also reviews several variables which influence the amount of proactive interference. The two most important variables are similarity of material and situation and associative strength (level of original learning). In another paper,[2] Underwood elaborates the effect of associative strength by noting that the rate of forgetting is determined by the final level of learning rather than the rate of learning. This principle is contrary to two common-sense notions about forgetting: (a) that material which is easy to learn is easy to remember, and (b) that slow (or fast) learners forget what they learn faster than those who learn at a normal rate.

In Selection 36 Professor B. F. Skinner points out that the usual classroom learning situation falls short of the ideal conditions in several respects, especially in terms of the lack of control over the relationship between the responses and the reinforcement. He argues that in order to obtain the necessary response-reinforcement contingencies we must use mechanical devices which have come to be known as "teaching machines." In addition to indicating the basic principles which must be implemented by such a machine, he also replies to some questions which have been raised about their use.

SOCIOCULTURAL FACTORS

From Skinner's discussion it should be clear that any event which will change the probability of a response is a reinforcer. Thus, it is not only the behavior of a rat in a maze or of a student operating a teaching machine which can be shaped by reinforcement. On the contrary, much of our everyday behavior is shaped and modified by other people. In fact such social reinforcers are probably the primary source of behavior modification for human adults. In Selection 37, Dr. Norman S. Endler hypothesized that "Reinforcement is an important force in shaping (i.e., in forming and altering) social behavior, including conformity." His results showed that verbal reinforcement by a status figure is quite effective in modifying the behavior of an individual so that he will either agree or disagree with a contrived group consensus, depending on what the experimenter reinforces.

Further analysis of the effectiveness of verbal reinforcers in a social situation has been obtained by Drs. Norma McCoy and Edward Zigler (Selection 38). They show that an adult's effectiveness as a social reinforcer depends on whether he is valued positively or negatively by the child.

[2] B. J. Underwood, "Forgetting," *Scientific American*, **210**: 91–99, 1964.

Selection **31** | CHEMICAL TRANSFER OF LEARNING*

ALLAN L. JACOBSON
*University of California,
Los Angeles*

Scientists may be on the verge of a major break-through in the problem of memory. For at least a hundred years, physiologists and psychologists have pondered over and investigated the manner in which an organism's experience is stored and later used. Certain general features of the process have been worked out, but the nature of the hypothetical "memory trace" or "engram" has remained frustratingly elusive. In the 1930s and 1940s, Karl Lashley, an eminent neuropsychologist, conducted an extensive series of investigations aimed at discovering just where memory is stored in the brain. One of Lashley's basic techniques involved ablating or removing cortical tissues from various parts of rats' brains and finding out whether these lesions interfered with the animals' memory for previously-learned tasks. But Lashley's search for the engram failed: although he found deficits in performance, they appeared to be more related to the *amount* of cortical tissue removed than to the particular location of the tissue. This work suggested that the engram, whatever its nature, must be rather widely represented in the brain. Later investigations have shown that the amount of memory impairment produced by such lesions depends on several variables, including the nature of the task employed.

This question of localization of memories has also been investigated by electrophysiological techniques. Dr Wilder Penfield of McGill University in Montreal, in the course of his neurosurgical operations on conscious humans, has discovered that direct electrical stimulation of certain portions of the brain can evoke particular experiences or memories in great detail. Penfield reports, "The sights and sounds, and the thoughts, of a former day pass through the man's mind again." In contrast to

*From A. L. Jacobson, "Chemical Transfer of Learning," *Discovery*, 27: 11–16, 1966. Reprinted with permission of the author and the publisher.

Lashley's results, this finding suggests particular locations in the brain for at least certain memories.

Two brains in one

Quite recently, the above ablation technique has been employed in a somewhat different way. Cutting the corpus callosum, the major bundle of nerve fibres connecting the two cerebral hemispheres, produces a *split-brain* preparation. An animal treated in this way behaves essentially normally in most situations, since the input to the two hemispheres is the same. However, if a particular input is given to only *one* hemisphere, the habit taught is apparently restricted to that particular half of the brain; if the stimulus is given to the other hemisphere, the animal reveals no indication of prior training. In fact, the two hemispheres can be taught diametrically opposed solutions to the same problem; the animal's response is then determined by which side of the brain receives the triggering stimulus.

Much of the split-brain research has been conducted by Dr Roger Sperry of the California Institute of Technology. The usual subjects have been cats and monkeys, but Dr Sperry has also studied the behaviour of two humans, who had had a split-brain operation to reduce the intensity of epileptic seizures. These patients, though normal in their everyday behavior, show 'dissociation' effects in the laboratory similar to those of split-brain animals— so much so that Dr Sperry claims these subjects appear to have two separate "spheres of consciousness." One example will suffice. In humans, the speech function is typically confined to one hemisphere. When Sperry blindfolded one of his subjects and placed an object in the hand connected to the "mute" hemisphere, the subject could use the object appropriately, but was totally unable to identify it verbally. The information reaching the mute hemisphere was quite unavailable to the hemisphere controlling speech.

The ablation technique, then, has revealed many aspects of brain functioning and has suggested how different parts of the brain interact in the process of memory storage. But it tells us little about the actual nature of this process or about the nature of the engram itself. One approach, the *consolidation hy-*

pothesis has thrown some light on the former problem. Proposed in 1900, this hypothesis asserts that, following a learning experience, a period of time is required for the effects of the experience to become established in the brain via continuing neural activity. Such an explanation has been used to account for the limited amnesias of human accident victims—a traumatic experience during the consolidation period might disrupt the laying down of the memory trace. The consolidation hypothesis has been tested by administering electroconvulsive shocks (ECS) to the brains of rats shortly after a learning experience. In one recent experiment, for example, this treatment interfered with learning if the ECS was given as much as 30 seconds after a training trial, but not if the delay was 60 seconds or more.

Another intriguing implication of the consolidation hypothesis is that appropriate action after the learning experience may help, rather than hinder, the process of learning. And, in fact, post-trial injection of the neural stimulant strychnine sulphate does produce more rapid learning in some cases, presumably by virtue of its effect on the neural activity involved in consolidation.

Does RNA "encode" memory?

Such experiments provide us with valuable information about the laying down of the memory trace. But what, exactly, is being laid down or consolidated? Here we must resort primarily to theory, for experimental facts are scarce. The most dominant view for many years has been that the behavioural changes we call learning are correlated with some physiological change within our brains, most probably at the synapse—the junction between two neurons. Since behaviour is dictated by neural activity, changes in behaviour must involve changes in neural activity. And the synapse, as the key decision point in a neural network, is a logical site for such neural changes. These changes would make the passage of impulses across particular synapses more efficient, and thus selectively aid the activation of hypothetical neural chains mediating certain behaviours.

The very vagueness of the above explanation reflects our ignorance in this critical area. Observation of synaptic changes accompanying learning is extremely difficult—where, for instance, should one look? The mammalian brain is discouragingly complex. One way to get around this problem is to study simpler organisms which are still capable of learning. Thus, Dr J. V. Luco has studied the manner in which a cockroach, deprived of its forelegs, learns to use its middle legs efficiently in cleaning the antennae. Dr Luco has observed that accompanying this behavioural change is a change in the electrical reaction of the cockroach's nervous system, which he interprets as an effect occurring at a single synapse. Such correlations of behavioural change and synaptic change are rarely found, however, and suggestive at best. Lowered synaptic resistance is generally conceded to be a likely basis for memory, but we must not lose sight of the fact that data in support of this contention are practically non-existent.

Around 1950, a new way of thinking arose which may one day be considered the turning point in man's understanding of his own brain. Molecular biologists had identified DNA as the carrier of genetic instructions, and certain of them had noted a basic conceptual similarity between heredity and memory: namely, that both involve information storage. The information in one case is passed on from generation to generation, while in the other it concerns the experience of the individual organism. This similarity suggested that the information storage or coding process in the two cases might be at least analogous.

Of all the possible chemical substances which might encode memory, ribonucleic acid, or RNA, appears in many respects the most attractive candidate. RNA is a large molecule present in all living cells and similar in structure to DNA. Furthermore, in theory RNA has a large enough storage capacity for information to account for the facts of memory, and it does not directly serve as a repository of genetic information in the same manner as DNA. For these reasons, the hypothesis that RNA encodes memory was proposed. Of course this hypothesis does not contradict the notion of synaptic change as a basis of learning; even if experience is encoded in RNA, one must still explain the manner in which such stored information exerts an influence on subsequent behaviour—an explanation which might well include changes in neural action. The RNA hypothesis, as typically stated, asserts that learning produces changes in RNA which then mediate or monitor (via protein synthesis) the synaptic alterations which presumably underlie modifications of behaviour.

In the last ten years a number of experiments have been performed which seem to implicate RNA in learning and memory functions. Noteworthy among these is the work of Dr Holger Hydén of Sweden, who has found changes in the RNA in the brains of rats occurring at the same time as behavioural changes. Another line of research has shown that chemical agents which interfere with RNA activity also have adverse effects on learning. The approach which will be the concern of the remainder of this article, however, is quite different. Recent experiments have demonstrated that material transferred from trained animals can produce specific behavioural changes in untrained animals, such that the recipient animals appear to have acquired some of the training of the donors. The evidence gathered so far suggests that in many of these cases RNA is involved in the transfer process.

Pavlovian worms

The planarian is a common, water-dwelling flatworm, about half an inch long, which has a rudimentary nervous system (including a brain) and also has remarkable powers of regeneration—if a planarian is cut into several pieces, each piece will regenerate into a complete planarian. Some ten years ago, Dr James McConnell and Dr Robert Thompson at the University of Texas reported that they had successfully established a Pavlovian-type conditioned response in planarians. Initially, if they presented a light flash, the animals made little obvious response. An electric current passed through the water, however, would evoke a contraction of the planarian's body. If the light flash was now repeatedly presented immediately before the shock, the planarians came to make more and more observable responses to the light, *before* the shock was given. It appeared, in other words, as though they were "anticipating" the shock, much as Pavlov's dogs "anticipated" food when a tone was sounded.

Several years later McConnell, Daniel Kimble

and I conditioned planarians in the fashion described above, and then cut each conditioned planarian in half across the body. After each half had regenerated, we trained the "new" planarians in the same manner as the original worms. These regenerated worms, whether derived from the head half or tail half of the original worms, acquired the conditioned response much faster than had the originals. Thus, to some extent, the tendency to react to the light had apparently been passed on to both "offspring."

McConnell proposed that the conditioning process had produced some *chemical* change in the animal, and he posed a further question: could the response to light produced by training be transferred to an entirely different planarian, rather than to an asexual offspring? McConnell, R. Jacobson and B. Humphries tested this notion by taking advantage of the fact that hungry planarians will eat other planarians—particularly if the latter are damaged. They conditioned one group of worms, then cut them up and fed them to untrained cannibal worms (identified as group 1). A second group of victim worms which received no training was fed to a second group of untrained cannibal worms (group 2). When the cannibal worms were subsequently tested, the group 1 animals were significantly more responsive to the light than were group 2 worms. Clearly, the cannibals' ingestion of the trained worms had affected their response to light. Incidentally, I should add that this study was conducted in "blind" fashion—that is, the experimenter did not know during testing whether a given cannibal had ingested trained or untrained victims. Such a procedure lessens the chance of the results being inadvertently biased.

This cannibalism study raised a question of interpretation: was the observed behavioural effect actually an instance of true learning being transferred from one animal to another, or might the same effect have been observed if control victims, instead of being untreated, had been stimulated with shock and light but not specifically trained? In other words, did the transfer effect depend on training or only on sheer stimulation of the victim worms? In addition, could the transfer effect be ascribed to a particular chemical substance, possibly RNA in the victim worms' bodies?

Inducing a response by injection

Drs E. R. John and W. Corning, at the University of Rochester, reasoned that if the RNA hypothesis is correct, then it might be possible to "erase" memories by applying a chemical substance which breaks down RNA. Their experiment showed, in fact, that such a substance, the enzyme ribonuclease, apparently does "wipe out" a classically-conditioned response in regenerating planarians.

These findings led C. Fried, S. Horowitz and me to perform an experiment designed to analyze the role of RNA in the planarian transfer effect more thoroughly. We trained one group of planarians (classically-conditioned, or CC) to respond to light by pairing the light with electric shock. A second group (pseudo-conditioned, or PC), we gave randomly interspersed lights and shocks, and a third group (non-conditioned, or NC) received no training at all. Thus, at the end of this stage of the experiment only the first group was responding to the light (see *Fig. 1*). We then extracted RNA from each of the three groups, and injected it into three groups of 25 untrained planarians.

Each of these 75 injected planarians was then given 25 exposures to the light and was scored on whether or not it responded to each exposure. Naturally, we ran this part of the experiment 'blind'. The result (see *Fig. 2*) was that planarians which received RNA from the CC group consistently made more responses to the light than did recipients of RNA from the two control groups, PC and NC. We have repeated this experiment successfully and have done other tests which suggest more strongly that RNA is the effective agent. We have, it seems, induced a response to a stimulus by injection!

Acquisition of a conditioned response, however, is only one aspect of behavioural change. Horowitz, Fried, and I wondered how the loss (or extinction) of the conditioned response might depend on RNA changes. We trained two groups of planarians as before, one with paired (CC) and the other with randomly interspersed light and shock (PC). Immediately before RNA extraction, we gave one half of the CC group an extended series of light bursts which were *not* followed by an electric shock. This process extinguished the conditioned response; that is,

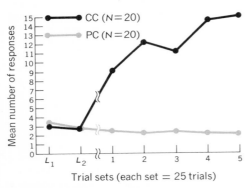

Mean Number of Responses per Set of 25 Trials for Groups CC and PC

Figure 1 Classical conditioning in planarians. Group CC (classically-conditioned) worms were trained to respond to light by pairing the light with an electric shock, while group PC (pseudo-conditioned) received randomly interspersed light and shock. Only the classically-conditioned worms learned the response, "anticipating" the electric shock. L_1 and L_2 are trial sets during which no shock was given.

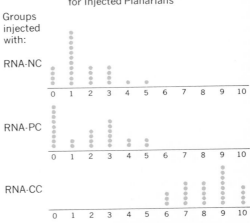

Distribution of Scores (Responses per 25 Trials) for Injected Planarians

Figure 2 Responses to light of untrained planarians which have been injected with RNA from donor worms. Three groups of donor worms were used; classically-conditioned (CC), pseudo-conditioned (PC) and non-conditioned (NC). The injected worms receiving RNA from the classically-conditioned group were markedly more responsive to the light than were the others.

the planarians ceased to respond to the light. We then extracted RNA, injected, and tested as before. Once again, the recipients from CC worms were more responsive to the light than were recipients from PC worms. But the recipients from CCE worms (conditioned, then extinguished) were just as responsive as the CC recipients (see *Fig. 3*)! The extinction process, although it had wiped out the donors' response to light, had not reduced the RNA transfer effect. The interpretation of this finding will require considerable further analysis, but it certainly appears that in this case extinction is not simply an 'undoing' of the presumed chemical changes produced during acquisition.

Rats in place of worms

The planarian makes an ideal simple system for the study of learning. Recently, however, experiments on mammals analogous to those on planarians have been reported from several laboratories. Dr. D. Albert performed one of the first of these studies. His basic experiment is quite ingenious. A treatment known as "spreading depression" can put one hemisphere of a rat's brain temporarily out of action. If one hemisphere (say hemisphere A) is made nonfunctional in this way, and the rat then learns an avoidance task, only hemisphere B receives the training. Thus, when the rat is later tested with hemisphere B out of action it behaves like an untrained animal, taking just as long to learn the task the second time as it did the first. Albert removed tissue from the trained hemisphere B and injected it back into the donor rat, with the result that the second learning, with hemisphere A, was markedly faster. He also found that only tissue from a certain region of the trained hemisphere would produce this facilitation effect—an interesting contrast to Lashley's work. Albert then investigated the effects of different treatments on the brain tissue before it was injected. He found that ribonuclease eliminated the transfer effect, whereas the enzyme trypsin, which breaks down proteins, did not—a strong indication that RNA rather than a protein was producing the transfer effect.

In our laboratories at the University of California, we have conducted several experiments on the transfer of behaviour in rats. My wife Ann and I collaborated on this work with F. Babich and S. Bubash, who started the project and discovered the basic phenomenon. In our first experiment, we trained rats to run to the food cup of an experimental chamber (Skinner box) when a distinct click was sounded. With each click, a small pellet of food dropped

Groups injected with:

RNA-PC

| 1 | 2 | 3 | 4 | 5 | 6 | 7 | 8 | 9 | 10 | 11 | 12 | 13 |

RNA-CC

| 1 | 2 | 3 | 4 | 5 | 6 | 7 | 8 | 9 | 10 | 11 | 12 | 13 |

RNA-CCE

| 1 | 2 | 3 | 4 | 5 | 6 | 7 | 8 | 9 | 10 | 11 | 12 | 13 |

Figure 3 Extinguishing the conditioned response of the donor worms (by giving repeated presentations of light without shock) before RNA extraction, appears not to reduce the RNA transfer effect in recipient worms (CCE). Recipients of RNA from both CC and CCE groups of donor worms made a greater number of responses than recipients of RNA from control worms.

Distribution of Scores (Responses per 25 Trials) for Injected Rats

Rat donor   • = Experimental S_S
           ○ = Control S_S

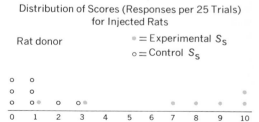

| 0 | 1 | 2 | 3 | 4 | 5 | 6 | 7 | 8 | 9 | 10 |

Figure 4 Distribution of scores for recipient rats approaching the food cup in a Skinner box. Each animal was given 25 clicks and was scored each time on whether or not it approached the cup. The experimental rats, injected with RNA from the brains of trained rats, scored much higher than the control animals which received RNA from untrained rats.

into the food cup, rewarding the rat for its approach. When training was completed, these animals were killed, and RNA extracted from their brains was injected into the body cavities of other, untrained rats. A control group of rats received RNA from the brains of rats which had not been trained in the Skinner box. We then tested the experimental and control recipients in blind fashion in the Skinner box to see whether the click had any effect. Each animal was given 25 clicks (but no pellets) and was scored each time on whether or not it approached the cup area. Overall, the experimental rats approached the cup far more often than did control rats (*see Fig. 4*). We concluded tentatively that the original training had changed the brain RNA, which in turn had exerted effects on the behaviour of the injected animals. We did not rule out the possibility, however, that traces of other material in the extract had produced the effects.

Transfer of specific effects

But what sort of effects? Were these effects specific or general? Was it in fact *learning* that we were transferring? We attempted in two further experiments to answer these questions —at least in part. In the first we trained two groups of rats to approach the food cup, one in response to the click and the other in response to a blinking light. As before, RNA from these rats was injected into untrained rats. We then tested each untrained rat with both the click and the blinking light, and on the average the animals responded predominantly to the stimulus with which their particular donor rats had been trained (*see Fig. 5*). That is, when the donors had been trained with the click, the recipients responded more to the click than to the light, and conversely for training with the light. Thus, to some extent the transfer effect was specific—a conclusion which strengthens the hypothesis that the effect being transferred is related to learning.

In a second experiment a discrimination apparatus rather than a Skinner box was used. Together with C. Goren, we trained one group of rats with food reward to select alternative A, and another group to select alternative B, in a type of simple maze. Alternatives A and B

Total Number of Responses per Animal
on the 25 Test Trials with Click (C)
and on the 25 Test Trials with Light (L)

Group receiving RNA-C		Group receiving RNA-L	
R's to C	R's to L	R's to C	R's to L
2	3	0	7
3	4	0	7
5	2	0	3
5	2	1	3
6	1	0	2
7	1	0	2
7	0	0	1
11	2	7	5
46	15	8	30

Figure 5 Transfer of specific learning is shown by training the donor rats to respond specifically to either a light or a click. Rats injected with RNA taken from donors trained with a click (left side of chart) show a greater response to a click than a light. The opposite occurs when the donor rats are trained with a light (right).

were differentiated by several cues, including floor colour, position, and so on. When the task was well learned, we extracted RNA from the brains of the trained rats and injected it into untrained rats. Each untrained rat was then placed in the maze 25 times and allowed to select one alternative each time. We gave no food reward during testing—as in both the planarian studies and the rat Skinner box studies, we did not allow new learning to occur. Each injected rat was said to have a 'preference' for the alternative it chose 13 or more times (out of the 25 choices) during testing. On the whole, recipient rats tended to 'prefer' the alternative which their respective donors had been trained to select. Thus we have additional evidence that the RNA transfer effect is specific in nature, and also that it can occur in different behavioural situations.

Since RNA injections affect behaviour in animals as disparate as rats and planarians, it would seem theoretically possible to use recipients and donors of different species. We attempted to do this. The experiment was similar to our first rat experiment in the Skinner box, except that in this case the donor animals were hamsters. And, as was predicted, rats receiving RNA from trained hamsters approached the food cup much more than rats receiving RNA from untrained hamsters (see *Fig. 6*). We had succeeded in transferring "learning" from one species to another!

Crucial questions for the future

Not uncommonly in science a discovery is made simultaneously in independent laboratories. This is not entirely accidental—the activities of the various investigators have in such cases often been inspired by the same previous experimental findings or theory. Thus in the present situation, the findings of Dr G. Ungar and C. Oceguera-Navarro of Baylor University and of Drs H. H. Roigaard-Petersen, E. J. Fjerdingstad, and Th. Nissen of the University of Copenhagen should be mentioned. Drs Ungar and Oceguera-Navarro adapted rats to a repeated mechanical stimulus, then injected tissue from their brains into mice. These mice were found to adapt more quickly to the stimulus than were control mice. The Danish group trained rats to select either the lighted or dark path in a discrimination apparatus. RNA from the brains of these rats helped recipient rats to learn this same discrimination. These different research groups were all apparently unaware of each other's activities; the major catalysts of this particular coincidence were the RNA hypothesis and the cannibalistic transfer results in planarians.

Hamster donor

Figure 6 Scores for recipient rats approaching the food cup as in Figure 4 above. This time however the donor animals were hamsters. Rats receiving RNA from trained hamsters approached the food cup much more than rats receiving injections of RNA from untrained hamsters. Thus it would appear that "learning" has been transferred from one species to another.

A further aspect of the "chemical transfer of learning" must be considered. Since the experiments mentioned above, other laboratories have undertaken similar investigations. Not all of them have been successful, and some with negative results regard their results as casting doubt upon the successful efforts. However, the growing number of positive results is encouraging, and we believe that the inconsistency of findings simply reflects our incomplete knowledge of the critical variables rather than a fundamental misconception. When we know enough to reconcile the successes with the failures, we will be well on our way to understanding the transfer effects.

Certain crucial questions still remain. What is the precise nature of the behavioural effects transferred and can we attribute them to learning? What produces the effects—are we sure it is RNA and only RNA? Although I have spoken glibly of "RNA" being extracted and injected, typically such RNA preparations contain traces of other substances as well. At the moment we do not have definite evidence that these substances can be safely disregarded. For example, Ungar and Oceguera-Navarro believe that in their experiment the effective transfer agent was some small protein. Finally, even if we were quite convinced that the effect transferred is a specific learned response, and even if we could identify the effective agent in each experiment beyond doubt, we are still faced with bewildering theoretical questions. How does the injected material act upon the recipient animal? How does training affect RNA or protein so as to make the transfer effect possible? How might alterations in RNA or protein affect synaptic resistance? How can we account for the specificity of neural circuits that would seem necessary in learning?

In 1950, considering his 30 years · of brilliant work, Karl Lashley mused, "I sometimes feel, in reviewing the evidence on the localization of the memory trace, that the necessary conclusion is that learning just is not possible." The problem of learning and memory is no less complex today than it ever was; indeed, it may appear that the new biochemical approaches raise more questions than they answer. But a more important consideration is that the new questions show promise of being the right ones to ask.

Selection **32** | LEARNING WITHOUT RESPONSE UNDER TWO CONDITIONS OF EXTERNAL CUES*

HAROLD J. MCNAMARA
JOHN B. LONG
EDWARD L. WIKE
University of Kansas

In 1946 Thorndike critically examined Tolman's concept of expectancy and proposed a number of experiments to evaluate this viewpoint. Bugelski and his co-workers mention some unpublished research, using Thorndike's situations, which failed to provide support for the expectancy interpretation. More recently, Gleitman has demonstrated place learning without performance in an elevated T maze with rats that had been drawn along a path in a "cable car" and shocked during transit. Learning was observed only when the locus of the T maze coincided with the path which the Ss had traversed.

The first situation suggested by Thorndike was:

. . . put the rat in a little wire car, in the entrance chamber of a maze, run it through the correct path of a simple maze and into the food compartment. Release it there and let it eat the morsel provided. Repeat 10 to 100 times according to the difficulty of the maze under ordinary conditions. The rat had an opportunity to form expectancies that presence in the food compartment is followed by food, that the correct turn is followed by the food chamber, and so on. Then put it in the entrance chamber free to go wherever it is inclined and observe what it does. Compare the behavior of such rats with that of rats run in the customary manner.

The present experiments follow rather closely Thorndike's suggested procedure except that the performance on a number of extinction trials is utilized as an indicant of learning. In

* From Harold J. McNamara, John B. Long, and Edward L. Wike, "Learning without Response under Two Conditions of External Cues," *Journal of Comparative and Physiological Psychology*, 49:477–480, 1956. Copyright 1956 by the American Psychological Association and reproduced by permission.

addition, each S in the experimental ("basket") group is matched with a control S in terms of the number and pattern of rewarded and nonrewarded responses; and, instead of a complex maze, the learning task is a single-unit elevated T maze.

Thus, the experimental question becomes: Is execution of running and turning responses necessary in order for rats to learn the locus of food in an elevated T maze? If learning involves the establishment of S-R connections by means of drive-reduction, then we should expect that the Ss that are conveyed about the maze in a wire basket would show little or no learning, since the running and turning responses are not made contiguously with the eliciting cues and reinforcement. On the other hand, if the learning consists of the development of field expectancies, then there is no obvious reason why the conveyed animals should not acquire a *representation* of the situation if there are sufficient differential cues to serve as environmental supports and the Ss frequently have access to these discriminanda. Accordingly, in experiment I, it is anticipated that Ss which have been transported about an elevated T maze in a basket will go to the correct side as often on the extinction trials as control Ss which have previously learned the maze under normal running conditions.

The purpose of Experiment II is to determine the influence of an extensive reduction in the extra-maze cues upon the learning of a basket-transported group and a normally run group of Ss. With the extramaze cues at a minimum, it is expected that the control Ss will select the formerly rewarded side more frequently in extinction than the transported Ss. With decreased external cues the learning is probably dependent to a greater degree on internal, response-produced cues, and since these cues are not available to the conveyed Ss, their extinction performance should be inferior.

EXPERIMENT I: METHOD

Subjects Twenty-four experimentally naive Long-Evans strain hooded male rats were used. They were bred in the University of Kansas laboratory and were four or five months of age at the start of the experiment.

Apparatus The elevated T maze, which was constructed of 3.75-in. black wooden strips, had a 51-in.

stem, 31-in. side arms, and stood 30-in. from the floor. A flat black metal tray, 3.75 in. by 3.75 in. by .25 in. served as a food dish. It was clipped to either side arm and was not visible from the choice point.

The basket, which was used to transport the Ss of the experimental group along the maze had a floor consisting of a 9-in. by 4-in. sheet of transparent plastic. A piece of .5-in.-sq. hardware cloth bent in the shape of a half-cylinder was fastened to the basket floor so as to make a cage with 6-in. walls. The ends of the basket were also constructed of .5-in.-sq. hardware cloth, and one end was hinged to permit the entrance and exit of S.

The maze was placed in the center of a room measuring 10 ft. by 10 ft. by 8.5 ft. Although the walls and ceiling were uniformly white, differential cues were provided by a radiator and window opposite the left arm and a large, black multicelled cage opposite the right arm. The floor of the room provided the possibilities for other gross visual cues since the left half was unpainted while the right half was black. The room was illuminated by the sunlight from the window on the left and by a fluorescent lamp with two 90-w. bulbs which was attached to the ceiling directly over the center of the maze and aligned with the stem.

Procedure The Ss were place on a 22-hr. hunger cycle five days before the beginning of maze adaptation by limiting them to a daily 1-hr. feeding session in the living cages. Water was always available in these cages, and Purina Layena pellets were employed as the maintenance food and as an incentive in the maze. During this period, each S was handled for several minutes per day.

In the adaptation phase the Ss were accustomed to the elevated apparatus. The starting half of the stem was detached from the T and aligned in the direction of the stem proper. The purpose of this arrangement was to provide rewarded adaptation without the concurrent induction of directional habits. The reward tray was attached to the end of the stem section, and S was permitted to explore the stem and eat freely for 5 min. daily. After seven days the adaptation was terminated because the Ss ate and moved along the stem without timidity. Four Ss were discarded in this phase when they displayed continued emotionality, leaving a total of 10 Ss in each treatment.

The maze training extended over four days until a group criterion of 95 per cent correct was attained by the control Ss. The control Ss learned a position response by running the maze in the traditional,

noncorrection fashion. Four trials were given each day with a 30-sec. intertrial interval. Half the Ss in each group found food on the right side and half on the left. When an S placed all four paws on either side arm, it was prevented from retracing by E's blocking the choice with a wooden paddle. A correct choice resulted in 30-sec. feeding at the food tray, and an incorrect turn led to 60-sec. confinement on that arm of the maze.

The Ss in the experimental group were placed in the basket at the start of the stem, the basket was gently slid along the top of the maze, and they were released from the basket at the end of the side arm. Each experimental S was given the same experiences of right and wrong choices, reward, and confinement, and was rewarded on the same side of the maze as its matched control S. Both groups were subjected to a 30-min. waiting period following the completion of the last trial before being fed their daily ration.

On the following day, extinction trials were administered to both groups in the same manner. The S was placed at the start of the stem, and the direction of choice was recorded. Retracing was again prevented by blocking off the choice point, the same response criterion was utilized, and the Ss were confined on the selected side arm for a 60-sec. period. Whenever S failed to make a choice within 300 sec., it was placed on a side arm by E for the regular confinement period, and the trial was scored as an error. The S was arbitrarily placed on the right arm after the first no-choice trial, on the left arm after the second, and so on. The Ss received eight extinction trials on the first day and eight more trials on the second. The intertrial interval of 30 sec. was maintained throughout extinction.

EXPERIMENT II: METHOD

Subjects There were three replications with 10 Wistar albino rats, six males and four females, in the first, 12 male hooded rats in the second, and 14 male hooded rats in the third. The albino rats were purchased from a local vender, and the Long-Evans strain Ss were from the University of Kansas laboratory. The Ss had not been used in an experiment previously and were three to five months of age.

Apparatus The T maze described above was employed. To decrease the extra-maze cues, the total room was painted flat black. The window on the left side of the room was covered completely by a plywood sheet and sealed to prevent the passage of light. The maze was enclosed in a rectangular wooden framework, 8 ft. by 6 ft. by 8.5 ft., and black cheesecloth was fastened to the frame. To reduce the illumination, the overhead fluorescent light was covered by a black cheesecloth panel. The light intensities, as measured by a photoelectric photometer, were 14.4 ft.-c. at the start of the stem, 13.5 ft.-c. at the choice point, 8.8 ft.-c. at the end of the left arm, and 8.5 ft.-c. at the end of the right arm. The greatest intensity difference between corresponding points on the side arms was 0.8 ft.-c. which was present at the mid-point of the side arm.

Procedure The procedure was almost identical to that of Experiment I except that the Ss in the third replication received three additional days of training after attaining the criterion of 95 per cent correct, and Ss in all replications had only eight extinction trials. One pair of Ss was discarded from the third replication when a control S failed to learn the maze.

RESULTS

The percentages of correct responses for the successive quarters of extinction in experiment I are shown in Table I. The average percentage correct was 66.25 for the experimental group and 64.38 for the control group. The difference between these two values was evaluated by the sign test and was not significant ($p > .30$). In addition, none of the tests at the separate quarters of extinction was significant at less than the .30 level. We may conclude that, with the number of correct responses in extinction serving as a measure of previous learning, there were no reliable differences between the Ss that ran the maze and those that traversed the maze in a basket.

A further question which can be raised is: Did the performance of the groups in extinc-

| Table 1 | PERCENTAGES OF CORRECT RESPONSES DURING EXTINCTION IN EXPERIMENT I |

Group	N	Trials			
		1–4	5–8	9–12	13–16
C (run)	10	65	60	67.5	65
E (carry)	10	60	65	65	75

| Table 2 | PERCENTAGES OF CORRECT RESPONSES DURING EXTINCTION IN EXPERIMENT II |

Group	N	Trials			
		1–2	3–4	5–6	7–8
C (run)	17	85	62	50	59
E (carry)	17	44	59	56	32

tion differ from chance? To answer this question, the number of Ss in the combined groups which ran to the correct side more than eight times and the number of Ss that ran to the correct side equal to, or less than, eight times were found. On an a priori basis, if no learning occurred, we should expect 10 Ss in each category. Actually there were 17 Ss in the "above" category and 3 Ss in the "below." The resulting χ^2 of 8.45 is significant at less than .01 level of confidence—the Ss manifested a significant preference for the formerly rewarded side in extinction.

The three replications of Experiment II were tested for homogeneity of their means and variances. Since the differences among the replications were within the limits of sampling, they were pooled. The combined extinction data in the form of the percentages of correct turns for the four quarters of extinction are presented in Table 2. When the external cues were reduced, the transported Ss scored 47.75 per cent correct choices in extinction, and the regularly run Ss made 64 per cent correct turns. Eleven of the Ss in the latter condition went to the correct side more often than their matched mates, one regularly run S was inferior to its mate, and in five instances there were no differences between Ss in the two treatments. Disregarding the ties, the probability of such an outcome is .01.

It is clear from Table 2 that the experimental Ss did not deviate from chance on the extinction trials. If assignment is made at random of the 5 control Ss that ran to the correct side on half the trials, there were 14 Ss in the above-chance category and 3 Ss in the below-chance category. The significance of this outcome is less than the .02 level of confidence. In summary, then, in Experiment II the regularly run animals gave evidence, in extinction, of learning, whereas the transported Ss did not.

DISCUSSION

The results of Experiment I confirm Gleitman's finding that place learning in an elevated T maze can occur without performance. However, when the extramaze cues are reduced (Experiment II), performance appears to be necessary for place learning. The finding that place learning without performance is demonstrable is congruent with *our* interpretation of Tolman's system as given in the introduction.

This same finding is not readily reconcilable with those aspects of Hull's system which conceive of learning as habit formation via drive reduction. For, in the case of the basket Ss, the response component of the cue pattern-response-reinforcement paradigm is not present. To encompass these findings, the Hullian theorist must, as in some latent learning studies, call upon fractional antedating goal reactions and/or secondary reinforcement to account for the results. To us, at present, the linkages of these constructs with independent and dependent variables seem to be as programmatic as the coordinating definitions of cognitive map, expectancy, etc. The hopeful feature of this situation is, as Hilgard points out, that with an increased emphasis in *S-R* theory on secondary reinforcement the differences between field and association theory become more blurred and the possibilities for a fruitful *rapprochement* may be seen.

SUMMARY

Two experiments were performed to determine whether or not place learning is possible without performance. In Experiment I ten Ss were regularly run in an elevated T maze, and ten Ss were transported about the maze in a basket. In the extinction trials there were no reliable differences between the two groups in the frequency of correct choices. In Experiment II carried out under the conditions of reduced external cues, the run Ss displayed significantly more learning than the transported Ss. It was concluded that: (a) Gleitman's finding that place learning can occur without performance was confirmed; and (b) when the extramaze cues are minimized, performance is necessary for learning.

Selection **33** │ STIMULUS GENERALIZATION OF THE EFFECTS OF PUNISHMENT*

WERNER K. HONIG
ROBERT M. SLIVKA
Denison University

Three pigeons were trained to respond to seven spectral stimulus values ranging from 490 to 610 mμ and displayed in random order on a response key. After response rates had equalized to these values, a brief electric shock was administered when the subject (S) responded to the central value (550 mμ) while positive reinforcement for all values was maintained. Initially, there was broad generalization of the resulting depression in response rate, but the gradients grew steeper in the course of testing. When punishment was discontinued, the rates to all values recovered, and equal responding to all stimuli was reattained by two of the Ss. Stimulus control over the effects of punishment was clearly demonstrated in the form of a generalization gradient; this probably resulted from the combined effects of generalization of the depression associated with punishment and discrimination between the punished value and neutral stimuli.

This study sought to explore stimulus control over the effects of punishment by obtaining generalization gradients for the decrement in response rate induced by response-contingent shocks. The general procedure was similar in many ways to the methods which have yielded reliable generalization gradients following acquisition with positive reinforcement (e.g., Guttman and Kalish, 1956). Gradients of response decrement are inverted with respect to the usual gradients of response strength. The effect of punishment on responding to any given stimulus value must be assessed against a baseline of response rates obtained prior to punishment from a number of stimuli lying on the continuum. Gradients of response decrement have been obtained by a similar method

* Reprinted from Werner K. Honig and Robert M. Slivka, "Stimulus Generalization of the Effects of Punishment," *Journal of the Experimental Analysis of Behavior,* 7: 21–25, 1964. Reprinted by permission of the author and publisher.

around a stimulus associated with extinction (Honig, 1961). With different techniques, other gradients of decrement have been studied for the negative stimulus used in discrimination training (Honig, Boneau, Burstein, and Penny-packer, 1963; Jenkins and Harrison, 1962) and for a stimulus used in association with an unavoidable shock to develop a conditioned suppression (Hoffman and Fleshler, 1961).

Discriminative stimulus control over punishment effects has been shown in operant situations by Azrin (1956) and Dinsmoor (1952). In Azrin's study, pigeons were used, and responding in the presence of an orange stimulus light was markedly depressed when this light signalled periods in which a response-contingent shock was scheduled; this was readily discriminated from a blue light projected on the response key during safe periods. Dinsmoor used rats which learned to discriminate safe periods correlated with onset of a light which illuminated the animal's chamber, from punishment periods in the dark. Neither of these experimenters attempted to obtain generalization gradients from stimulus values lying between those used in discrimination training. But their demonstrations of discriminative control, together with the variety of generalization gradients which have been generated in operant situations after various kinds of training, led us to expect that orderly punishment gradients could be obtained.

METHOD

Subjects

Three fully-grown White King pigeons were used throughout the study at 75% of their free-feeding weight. They had been rejected from another study in which they were reinforced for standing still, a task for which they demonstrated little aptitude.

Apparatus

A two-key operant behavior box was used; it is described elsewhere (Honig, 1962). Spectral values were produced by passing white light through Bausch and Lomb monochromatic interference filters and projecting it on the key. A yellow (Wratten K-2) filter was inserted in the beam with values greater than 570 mμ to eliminate the visible second-order spectrum. Only the right key of the apparatus was used for the present research.

The method of administering shock was adapted

from Hoffman (1960). Chrome-plated bead chain of 0.156 in. diameter was wrapped twice around the base of each wing. The down under the wing was plucked to insure good contact between the bead chain and the skin. A flexible connector could be attached to each chain by a pair of Muller test clips. The shock was provided by a variable transformer ("Variac") at a setting of 50 v, and with a 50,000 ohm resistance in series with the bird, about 0.75 ma were delivered. The shock duration was 0.6 sec.

Procedure

Preliminary training was carried out in successive sessions as follows. First, S was allowed to eat from the open food magazine for 3 min. Second, S was trained to eat during the 4-sec magazine cycle. Third, S was taught by successive approximations to peck at the key illuminated by 550 mμ and was given 50 continuous reinforcements immediately following conditioning. Fourth, S received 10 continuous reinforcements with each of the seven stimulus values displayed on the key in randomized order. On the fifth day, S was reinforced five times on a FR 5 schedule for pecking at each of the stimulus values displayed in a random order, and this procedure was repeated with a FR 10 schedule.

During the VI training, punishment, and recovery phases of the study, seven stimulus values ranging in 20 mμ steps from 490 to 610 mμ were employed. Each training session consisted of 28 periods of 1 min each of stimulus presentation followed by 10 sec of blackout. The seven stimulus values were each presented four times, once in each of four randomized blocks.

A VI 30-sec schedule programmed reinforcement for training sessions 1-6; this was changed to VI 75 sec for sessions 7-19; from session 20 to the end of the study, the mean inter-reinforcement interval was reduced to 37.5 sec, since rates did not stabilize well under the VI 75-sec program. As extinction of positive reinforcement was not used during this study, a relatively short VI interval did not detract from efforts to obtain generalization gradients.

Wing bands were attached after 16 training sessions, and from session 25 on, the clips were fastened to the bands at the start of each session. The birds could move freely about the box, and the attachment had no noticeable effect on response rate.

Beginning with session 31, punishment was automatically administered for nine sessions whenever S responded to the 550 mμ stimulus (but not for responses to other stimuli). Reinforcements were scheduled as before for all stimulus values. Beginning with session 40, punishment was discontinued for nine sessions in order to observe the recovery of response rate. All other conditions remained the same.

RESULTS

The combined results are presented for the three Ss in Fig. 1 and 2 in terms of mean response rates per minute. In each figure, the VI baseline is based on the mean rates for the last six days of training preceding the introduction of punishment. Under this condition the rates are quite similar for the seven stimulus values. In Fig. 1, both the effects of punishment at 550 mμ and the generalization of response decrement to other values is shown for three blocks of three sessions each. Responding to 550 mμ dropped to zero as soon as punishment was introduced. While the other values were also affected, a progressive increase in rate can be seen both as a function of the difference between 550 mμ and the other

stimuli, and as a function of time, since the response rates increased during the three successive blocks. Recovery data are similarly presented in Fig. 2. Rates to 550 mμ and adjacent values recover fastest, flattening the gradient. For the last three sessions, recovery is almost complete; the terminal gradient is close to the VI baseline save for a small depression remaining at 550 mμ.

Results for the three Ss are individually presented in Fig. 3. The VI baseline is presented for each bird, together with mean rates obtained for the nine sessions of punishment and the nine sessions of recovery. Each S shows a different individual pattern of stimulus control. For S1, the punishment gradient is very steep and attains the level of the VI baseline at both ends. The recovery gradient is almost parallel to the punishment gradient, except that it is displaced upward so that some of it is below and some of it is above the VI baseline. For S2, the punishment gradient is much flatter and the recovery gradient is almost identical to the VI baseline. For S3, a third pattern

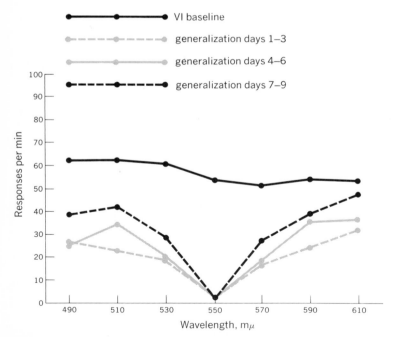

Figure 1 Mean response rates obtained for different values during nine sessions while punishment was in effect at 550 mμ.

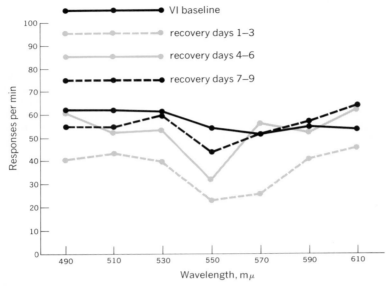

Figure 2 Mean response rates obtained for different stimulus values during nine sessions after punishment at 550 mμ was discontinued.

appears; the punishment gradient is intermediate in slope to those of the other two, and, while the recovery gradient is quite flat, it remains well below the overall level of responding indicated by the VI baseline. The general form of all punishment gradients is concave downward for all birds, although the slopes differ. But the recovery gradients are very different both in form and overall response level, and the similarity of the mean recovery gradient to the VI baseline (see Fig. 2) may be a coincidence due to averaging across Ss.

A temporal analysis of the effect of punishment is presented in Fig. 4. Here, the mean response rates are presented for the three 1-min periods immediately preceding and immediately following each punishment period as averaged across the various spectral values presented in these periods.[1] These data are presented for three blocks of three punishment sessions each. In the 3 min preceding

[1] Due to the random order of stimuli, two punishment periods could be close together, so that the periods immediately following one would overlap those immediately preceding the next. For this reason, only those punishment periods were used in this analysis which were separated from the preceding and succeeding punishment periods by at least 4 min.

each period of punishment, response rates are about equal. Following each period of punishment, the rates are depressed. This is most marked for sessions 1-3 where the depression extends to the 3 min following punishment, but recovery is increasingly rapid for days 4-6 and 7-9. For the latter two blocks, the rates during the second and third minutes following punishment are equal to the rates preceding punishment. It is likely that if the punishment procedure had continued, the rate for the first period following punishment would have recovered to an equal extent.

DISCUSSION

From these analyses, it appears that during any given stage of the generalization-punishment procedure, two major variables affected the rate of responding: (1) the difference between a given stimulus value and 550 mμ (stimulus effect), and (2) the interval between the presentation of that value and the preceding punishment period (temporal effect). These two effects were randomly combined in that neither stimulus value nor punishment-stimulus interval was held constant while the other was

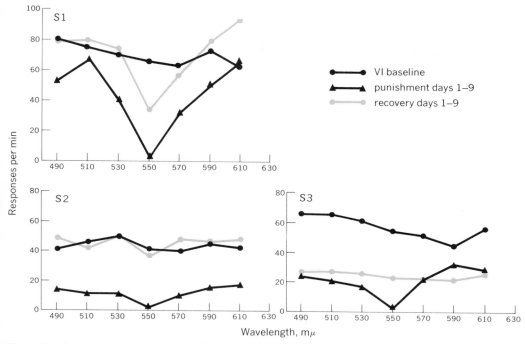

Figure 3 Mean response rates obtained from the three individual Ss during the last six sessions of VI training, nine sessions of punishment, and nine sessions of recovery.

varied; since the stimulus values were randomized, the rates obtained for each temporal interval reflect the temporal effect in combination with the mean of the set of stimulus effects produced by the different values.

Initially, neither of these effects was great enough to eliminate the depression of rate due to punishment, since the generalization and temporal gradients do not approach the VI baseline. But both effects change systematically in the course of punishment. The stimulus effect becomes more pronounced, in that response rates to values other than 550 mµ increase; in other words, the Ss appeared to be developing a stimulus discrimination. The temporal effect becomes less important as stimulus control increases; by the end of the punishment sequence, this effect extended only to the period directly following punishment. It is unlikely that the temporal effect decreased in importance because Ss were receiving fewer actual shocks during punishment periods in the course of the punishment sequence; each response was punished, and the

response rate to 550 mµ was close to zero during the whole time that punishment was in effect. The shift in control over response rate from a temporal to a stimulus basis is therefore genuine and reflects a process of stimulus discrimination. A similar steepening can be obtained for positive generalization gradients if the reinforced value is embedded between two or more stimuli in the presence of which reinforcement is not available (Hanson, 1961).

It is of particular interest to compare the present results with those of Hoffman and Fleshler (1961), since these experimenters also used a noxious stimulus to induce a response decrement. They presented a 1,000-cycle tone in advance of an unavoidable shock of 8-sec duration. After complete suppression of responding in the presence of this stimulus, shocks were discontinued while test tones ranging from 300 to 3,400 cycles were presented. At first, generalization of suppression was almost complete for all the test tones, but the rate of recovery was directly related to the differences between each test tone and

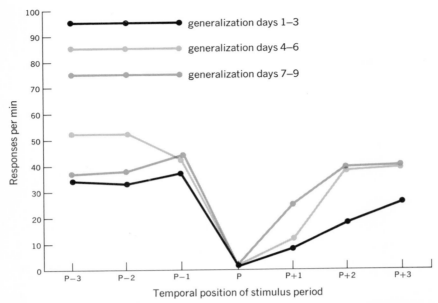

Figure 4 Mean response rates obtained for the stimulus periods immediately preceding and following each punishment period (P).

the 1,000-cycle training tone, yielding orderly gradients of response decrement. Their gradients, therefore, reflect different rates of extinction of the suppression in the presence of different test values. Our gradients also grew steeper in the course of testing, but this may have been due to the opportunity for explicit discrimination learning provided by the fact that in the presence of one stimulus, punishment was maintained during the testing procedure. When punishment was discontinued, the gradients grew flatter, at least for two Ss, as the decrement extinguished at 550 mμ and adjacent stimuli. A similar result was obtained by Hoffman, Fleshler, and Jensen (1962) in a continuation of the earlier study, where the birds were retested after two and one half years away from the experimental situation.

Clearly, the design of the conditioned suppression and the punishment studies should be made more similar to determine whether the obtained similarities in results are genuine or fortuitous. It remains to be seen whether the steepening of the punishment gradient would be obtained where explicit discrimination training is not provided. Once a baseline is established, this can be done by punishing

responding to 550 mμ without the presentation of the other values used to establish the VI baseline. Then the complete set of stimuli would be reintroduced after punishment is discontinued. Attention is now being given to this problem.

REFERENCES

Azrin, N. H. Some effects of two intermittent schedules of immediate and non-immediate punishment. *J. Psychol.*, 1956, **42**, 3–21.

Dinsmoor, J. A. A discrimination based on punishment. *Quart. J. exp. Psychol.*, 1952, **4**, 27–45.

Guttman, N. and Kalish, H. I. Discriminability and stimulus generalization. *J. exp. Psychol.*, 1956, **51**, 79–88.

Hanson, H. M. Stimulus generalization following three-stimulus discrimination training. *J. comp. Physiol. Psychol.*, 1961, **54**, 181–185.

Hoffman, H. S. A flexible connector for delivering shock to pigeons. *J. exp. Anal. Behav.*, 1960, **3**, 330.

Hoffman, H. S. and Fleshler, M. Stimulus factors in aversive controls: The generalization of conditioned suppression. *J. exp. Anal. Behav.*, 1961, **4**, 371–378.

Hoffman, H. S., Fleshler, M., and Jensen, P. K. Aversive training: Long-term effects. *Science,* 1962, **138**, 1269–1270.

Honig, W. K. Generalization of extinction on the spectral continuum. *Psychol. Rec.,* 1961, **11**, 269–278.

Honig, W. K. Prediction of preference, transposition, and transposition-reversal from the generalization gradient. *J. exp. Psychol.,* 1962, **64**, 239–248.

Honig, W. K., Boneau, C. A., Burstein, K. R., and Pennypacker, H. S. Positive and negative generalization gradients obtained after equivalent training conditions. *J. comp. physiol. Psychol.,* 1963, **56**, 111–116.

Jenkins, H. M. and Harrison, R. H. Generalization gradients of inhibition following auditory discrimination learning. *J. exp. Anal. Behav.,* 1962, **5**, 435–441.

Selection **34** | THE ELIMINATION OF TANTRUM BEHAVIOR BY EXTINCTION PROCEDURES*

CARL D. WILLIAMS
University of Miami

This paper reports the successful treatment of tyrant-like tantrum behavior in a male child by the removal of reinforcement. The subject (S) was approximately 21 months old. He had been seriously ill much of the first 18 months of his life. His health then improved considerably, and he gained weight and vigor.

S now demanded the special care and attention that had been given him over the many critical months. He enforced some of his wishes, especially at bedtime, by unleashing tantrum behavior to control the actions of his parents.

The parents and an aunt took turns in putting him to bed both at night and for S's afternoon nap. If the parent left the bedroom after putting S in his bed, S would scream and

fuss until the parent returned to the room. As a result, the parent was unable to leave the the bedroom until after S went to sleep. If the parent began to read while in the bedroom, S would cry until the reading material was put down. The parents felt that S enjoyed the control over them and that he fought off going to sleep as long as he could. In any event, a parent was spending from one-half to two hours each bedtime just waiting in the bedroom until S went to sleep.

Following medical reassurance regarding S's physical condition, it was decided to remove the reinforcement of this tyrant-like tantrum behavior. Consistent with the learning principle that, in general, behavior that is not reinforced will be extinguished, a parent or the aunt put S to bed in a leisurely and relaxed fashion. After bedtime pleasantries, the parent left the bedroom and closed the door. S screamed and raged, but the parent did not re-enter the room. The duration of screaming and crying was obtained from the time the door was closed.

The results are shown in Fig. 1. It can be seen that S continued screaming for 45 min. the first time he was put to bed in the first extinction series. S did not cry at all the second time he was put to bed. This is perhaps attributable to his fatigue from the crying of Occasion 1. By the tenth occasion, S no

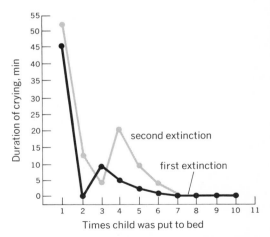

Figure 1 Length of crying in two extinction series as a function of successive occasions of being put to bed.

longer whimpered, fussed, or cried when the parent left the room. Rather, he smiled as they left. The parents felt that he made happy sounds until he dropped off to sleep.

About a week later, S screamed and fussed after the aunt put him to bed, probably reflecting spontaneous recovery of the tantrum behavior. The aunt then reinforced the tantrum behavior by returning to S's bedroom and remaining there until he went to sleep. It was then necessary to extinguish this behavior a second time.

Figure 1 shows that the second extinction curve is similar to the first. Both curves are generally similar to extinction curves obtained with subhuman subjects. The second extinction series reached zero by the ninth occasion. No further tantrums at bedtime were reported during the next two years.

It should be emphasized that the treatment in this case did not involve aversive punishment. All that was done was to remove the reinforcement. Extinction of the tyrant-like tantrum behavior then occurred.

No unfortunate side- or aftereffects of this treatment were observed. At three and three-quarters years of age, S appeared to be a friendly, expressive, outgoing child.

Selection **35** | INTERFERENCE AND FORGETTING*

BENTON J. UNDERWOOD[1,2]
Northwestern University

I know of no one who seriously maintains that interference among tasks is of no consequence in the production of forgetting. Whether forgetting is conceptualized at a strict psychological level or at a neural level (e.g., neural memory trace), some provision is made for

* From Benton J. Underwood, "Interference and Forgetting," *Psychological Review*, **64**: 50–60, 1957. Copyright 1957 by the American Psychological Association and reproduced by permission.
[1] Address of the president, Midwestern Psychological Association, St. Louis, Missouri, May, 1956.
[2] Most of the data from my own research referred to in this paper were obtained from work done under Contract N7 onr-45008, Project NR 154-057, between Northwestern University and The Office of Naval Research.

interference to account for at least some of the measured forgetting. The many studies on retroactive inhibition are probably responsible for this general agreement that interference among tasks must produce a sizable proportion of forgetting. By introducing an interpolated interfering task very marked decrements in recall can be produced in a few minutes in the laboratory. But there is a second generalization which has resulted from these studies, namely, that most forgetting must be a function of the learning of tasks which interfere with that which has already been learned (19). Thus, if a single task is learned in the laboratory and retention measured after a week, the loss has been attributed to the interference from activities learned outside the laboratory during the week. It is this generalization with which I am concerned in the initial portions of this paper.

Now, I cannot deny the data which show large amounts of forgetting produced by an interpolated list in a few minutes in the laboratory. Nor do I deny that this loss may be attributed to interference. But I will try to show that use of retroactive inhibition as a paradigm of forgetting (via interference) may be seriously questioned. To be more specific: if a subject learns a single task, such as a list of words, and retention of this task is measured after a day, a week, or a month, I will try to show that very little of the forgetting can be attributed to an interfering task learned outside the laboratory during the retention interval. Before pursuing this further, I must make some general comments by way of preparation.

Whether we like it or not, the experimental study of forgetting has been largely dominated by the Ebbinghaus tradition, both in terms of methods and materials used. I do not think this is due to sheer perversity on the part of several generations of scientists interested in forgetting. It may be noted that much of our elementary knowledge can be obtained only by rote learning. To work with rote learning does not mean that we are thereby not concerning ourselves with phenomena that have no counterparts outside the laboratory. Furthermore, the investigation of these phenomena can be handled by methods which are acceptable to a science. As is well known, there are periodic verbal revolts against the Ebbinghaus tradition (e.g., 2, 15, 22). But for some reason nothing much ever happens in the laboratory as a consequence of these revolts. I mention these matters neither by way of apology nor of justification for having done some research in rote learning, but for two other reasons. First, it may very well be true, as some have suggested (e.g., 22), that studies of memory in the Ebbinhaus tradition are not getting at all of the important phenomena of memory. I think the same statement—that research has not got at all of the important processes—could be made about all areas in psychology; so that the criticism (even if just) should not be indigenous to the study of memory. Science does not deal at will with all natural events. Science deals with natural events only when ingenuity in developing methods and techniques of measurement allow these events to be brought within the scope of science. If, therefore, the studies of memory which meet scientific acceptability do not tap all-important memorial processes, all I can say is that this is the state of the science in the area at the moment. Secondly, because the bulk of systematic data on forgetting has been obtained on rote-learned tasks, I must of necessity use such data in discussing interference and forgetting.

Returning to the experimental situation, let me again put in concrete form the problem with which I first wish to deal. A subject learns a single task, such as a list of syllables, nouns, or adjectives. After an interval of time, say, 24 hours, his retention of this list is measured. The explanatory problem is what is responsible for the forgetting which commonly occurs over the 24 hours. As indicated earlier, the studies of retroactive inhibition led to the theoretical generalization that this forgetting was due largely to interference from other tasks learned during the 24-hour retention interval. McGeoch (20) came to this conclusion, his last such statement being made in 1942. I would, therefore, like to look at the data which were available to McGeoch and others interested in this matter. I must repeat that the kind of data with which I am concerned is the retention of a list without formal interpolated learning introduced. The interval of retention with which I am going to deal in this, and several subsequent analyses, is 24 hours.

First, of course, Ebbinghaus' data were available and in a sense served as the reference point for many subsequent investigations. In terms of percentage saved in relearning, Ebbinghaus showed about 65 per cent loss over 24 hours (7). In terms of recall after 24 hours, the following studies are representative of the amount forgotten: Youtz, 88 per cent loss (37); Luh, 82 per cent (18); Krueger, 74 per cent (16); Hovland, 78 per cent (11); Cheng, 65 per cent and 84 per cent (6); Lester, 65 per cent (17). Let us assume as a rough average of these studies that 75 per cent forgetting was measured over 24 hours. In all of these studies the list was learned to one perfect trial. The percentage values were derived by dividing the total number of items in the list into the number lost and changing to a percentage. Thus, on the average in these studies, if the subject learned a 12-item list and recalled three of these items after 24 hours, nine items (75 per cent) were forgotten.

The theory of interference as advanced by McGeoch, and so far as I know never seriously challenged, was that during the 24-hour interval subjects learned something outside the laboratory which interfered with the list learned in the laboratory. Most of the materials involved in the investigations cited above were nonsense syllables, and the subjects were college students. While realizing that I am viewing these results in the light of data which McGeoch and others did not have available, it seems to me to be an incredible stretch of an interference hypothesis to hold that this 75 per cent forgetting was caused by something which the subjects learned outside the laboratory during the 24-hour interval. Even if we agree with some educators that much of what we teach our students in college is nonsense, it does not seem to be the kind of learning that would interfere with nonsense syllables.

If, however, this forgetting was not due to interference from tasks learned outside the laboratory during the retention interval, to what was it due? I shall try to show that most of this forgetting was indeed produced by interference—not from tasks learned outside the laboratory, but from tasks learned previously in the laboratory. Following this I will show that when interference from laboratory tasks is removed, the amount of forgetting which occurs is relatively quite small. It then becomes more plausible that this amount could be produced by interference from tasks learned outside the laboratory, although as I shall also point out, the interference very likely comes from prior, not interpolated, learning.

In 1950 a study was published by Mrs. Greenberg and myself (10) on retention as a function of stage of practice. The orientation for this study was crassly empirical; we simply wanted to know if subjects learn how to recall in the same sense that they learn how to learn. In the conditions with which I am concerned, naive subjects learned a list of ten paired adjectives to a criterion of eight out of ten correct on a single trial. Forty-eight hours later this list was recalled. On the following day, these same subjects learned a new list to the same criterion and recalled it after 48 hours. This continued for two additional lists, so that the subjects had learned and recalled four lists, but the learning and recall of each list was complete before another list was learned. There was low similarity among these lists as far as conventional symptoms of similarity are concerned. No words were repeated and no obvious similarities existed, except for the fact that they were all adjectives and a certain amount of similarity among prefixes, suffixes, and so on must inevitably occur. The recall of these four successive lists is shown in Fig. 1.

As can be seen, the more lists that are learned, the poorer the recall, from 69 per cent recall of the first list to 25 per cent recall of the fourth list. In examining errors at recall, we found a sufficient number of intrusion re-

sponses from previous lists to lead us to suggest that the increasing decrements in recall were a function of proactive interference from previous lists. And, while we pointed out that these results had implications for the design of experiments on retention, the relevance to an interference theory of forgetting was not mentioned.

Dr. E. J. Archer has made available to me certain data from an experiment which still is in progress and which deals with this issue. Subjects learned lists of 12 serial adjectives to one perfect trial and recalled them after 24 hours. The recall of a list always took place prior to learning the next list. The results for nine successive lists are shown in Fig. 2. Let me say again that there is no laboratory activity during the 24-hour interval; the subject learns a list, is dismissed from the laboratory, and returns after 24 hours to recall the list. The percentage of recall falls from 71 per cent for the first list to 27 per cent for the ninth.

In summarizing the more classical data on retention above, I indicated that a rough estimate showed that after 24 hours 75 per cent forgetting took place, or recall was about 25 per cent correct. In viewing these values in the light of Greenberg's and Archer's findings, the conclusion seemed inescapable that the classical studies must have been dealing with subjects who had learned many lists. That is to say, the subjects must have served in many

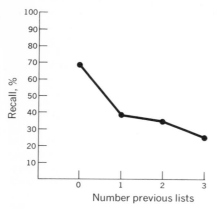

Figure 1   Recall of paired adjectives as a function of number of previous lists learned.

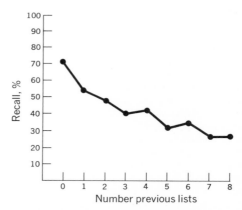

Figure 2   Recall of serial adjective lists as a function of number of previous lists learned. Unpublished data, courtesy of Dr. E. J. Archer.

conditions by use of counterbalancing and repeated cycles. To check on this I have made a search of the literature on the studies of retention to see if systematic data could be compiled on this matter. Preliminary work led me to establish certain criteria for inclusion in the summary to be presented. First, because degree of learning is such an important variable, I have included only those studies in which degree of learning was one perfect recitation of the list. Second, I have included only studies in which retention was measured after 24 hours. Third, I have included only studies in which recall measures were given. (Relearning measures add complexities with which I do not wish to deal in this paper.) Fourth, the summary includes only material learned by relatively massed practice. Finally, if an investigator had two or more conditions which met these criteria, I averaged the values for presentation in this paper. Except for these restrictions, I have used all studies I found (with an exception to be noted later), although I do not pretend to have made an exhaustive search. From each of these studies I got two facts: first, the percentage recalled after 24 hours, and second, the average number of previous lists the subjects had learned before learning the list on which recall after 24 hours was taken. Thus, if a subject had served in five experimental conditions via counterbalancing, and had been given two practice lists, the average number of lists learned before learning the list for which I tabulated the recall was four. This does not take into account any previous experiments in rote learning in which the subject might have served.

For each of these studies the two facts, average number of previous lists learned and percentage of recall, are related as in Fig. 3. For example, consider the study by Youtz. This study was concerned with Jost's law, and had several degrees of learning, several lengths of retention interval, and the subjects served in two cycles. Actually, there were 15 experimental conditions and each subject was given each condition twice. Also, each subject learned six practice lists before starting the experimental conditions. Among the 15 conditions was one in which the learning of the syllables was carried to one perfect recitation and recall was taken after 24 hours. It is this particular condition in which I am interested. On the average, this condition would have been given at the time when the subject had learned six practice lists and 15 experimental lists for a total of 21 previous lists.

The studies included in Fig. 3 have several different kinds of materials, from geometric forms to nonsense syllables to nouns; they include both paired-associate and serial presentation, with different speeds of presentation and different lengths of lists. But I think the general relationship is clear. The greater the number of previous lists learned the greater the forgetting. I interpret this to mean that the greater the number of previous lists the greater the *proactive* interference. We know this to be true (26) for a formal proactive-inhibition paradigm; it seems a reasonable interpretation for the data of Fig. 3. That there are minor sources of variance still involved I do not deny. Some of the variation can be rationalized, but that is not the purpose of this report. The point I wish to make is the obvious one of the relationship between number of previous lists learned—lists which presumably had no intentionally built-in similarity—and amount of forgetting. If you like to think in correlational terms, the rank-order correlation between the two variables is − .91 for the 14 points of Fig. 3.

It may be of interest to the historian that, of the studies published before 1942 which met the criteria I imposed, I did not find a single one in which subjects had not been given at least one practice task before starting experimental conditions, and in most cases the subjects had several practice lists and several experimental conditions. Gibson's study (1942) was the first I found in which subjects served in only one condition and were not given practice tasks. I think it is apparent that the design proclivities of the 1920s and 1930s have been largely responsible for the exaggerated picture we have had of the rate of forgetting of rote-learned materials. On the basis of studies performed during the 1920s and 1930s, I have given a rough estimate of forgetting as being 75 per cent over 24 hours, recall being 25 per cent. On the basis of modern studies in which the subject has learned no previous lists—where there is no proactive inhibition from previous laboratory

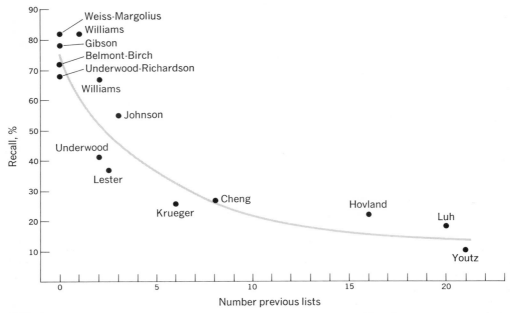

Figure 3 Recall as a function of number of previous lists learned as determined from a number of studies. From left to right: Weiss and Margolius (35), Gibson (9), Belmont and Birch (3), Underwood and Richardson (33), Williams (36), Underwood (27, 28, 29, 30), Lester (17), Johnson (14), Krueger (16), Cheng (6), Hovland (11), Luh (18), Youtz (37).

tasks—a rough estimate would be that forgetting is 25 per cent; recall is 75 per cent. The values are reversed. (If in the above and subsequent discussion my use of percentage values as if I were dealing with a cardinal or extensive scale is disturbing, I will say only that it makes the picture easier to grasp, and in my opinion no critical distortion results.)

Before taking the next major step, I would like to point out a few other observations which serve to support my general point that proactive inhibition from laboratory tasks has been the major cause of forgetting in the more classical studies. The first illustration I shall give exemplifies the point that when subjects have served in several conditions, forgetting after relatively short periods of time is greater than after 24 hours if the subject has served in only one condition. In the Youtz study to which I have already referred, other conditions were employed in which recall was taken after short intervals. After 20 minutes recall was **74** percent, about what it is after 24 hours if the

subject has not served in a series of conditions. After two hours recall was 32 per cent. In Ward's (34) well-known reminiscence experiment, subjects who on the average had learned ten previous lists showed a recall of only 64 per cent after 20 minutes.

In the famous Jenkins-Dallenbach (13) study on retention following sleep and following waking, two subjects were used. One subject learned a total of 61 lists and the other 62 in addition to several practice lists. Roughly, then, if the order of the conditions was randomized, approximately 30 lists had been learned prior to the learning of a list for a given experimental condition. Recall after eight waking hours for one subject was 4 per cent and for the other 14 per cent. Even after sleeping for eight hours the recall was only 55 per cent and 58 per cent.

I have said that an interpolated list can produce severe forgetting. However, in one study (1), using the A-B, A-C paradigm for original and interpolated learning, but using subjects who had never served in any previous conditions, recall of the original list was 46 per cent after 48 hours, and in another comparable study (24), 42 per cent. Thus, the loss is not nearly as great as in the classical studies I have cited where there was no interpolated learning in the laboratory.

My conclusion at this point is that, in terms of the gross analysis I have made, the amount of forgetting which might be attributed to interference from tasks learned outside the laboratory has been "reduced" from 75 per cent to about 25 per cent. I shall proceed in the next section to see if we have grounds for reducing this estimate still more. In passing on to this section, however, let me say that the study of factors which influence proactive inhibition in these counterbalanced studies is a perfectly legitimate and important area of study. I mention this because in the subsequent discussion I am going to deal only with the case where a subject has learned a single list in the laboratory, and I do not want to leave the impression that we should now and forevermore drop the study of interference produced by previous laboratory tasks. Indeed, as will be seen shortly, it is my opinion that we should increase these studies for the simple reason that the proactive paradigm provides a more realistic one than does the retroactive paradigm.

When the subject learns and recalls a single list in the laboratory, I have given an estimate of 25 per cent as being the amount forgotten over 24 hours. When, as shown above, we calculate percentage forgotten of lists learned to one perfect trial, the assumption is that had the subjects been given an immediate recall trial, the list would have been perfectly recalled. This, of course, is simply not true. The major factor determining how much error is introduced by this criterion-percentage method is probably the difficulty of the task. In general, the overestimation of forgetting by the percentage method will be directly related to the difficulty of the task. Thus, the more slowly the learning approaches a given criterion, the greater the drop on the trial immediately after the criterion trial. Data from a study by Runquist (24), using eight paired adjectives (a comparatively easy task), shows that amount of forgetting is overestimated by about 10 per

cent. In a study (32) using very difficult consonant syllables, the overestimation was approximately 20 per cent. To be conservative, assume that on the average the percentage method of reporting recall overestimates the amount forgotten by 10 per cent. If we subtract this from the 25 per cent assumed above, the forgetting is now re-estimated as being 15 per cent over 24 hours. That is to say, an interference theory, or any other form of theory, has to account for a very small amount of forgetting as compared with the amount traditionally cited.

What are the implications of so greatly "reducing" the amount of forgetting? There are at least three implications which I feel are worth pointing out. First, if one wishes to hold to an interference theory of forgetting (as I do), it seems plausible to assert that this amount of forgetting could be produced from learning which has taken place outside of the laboratory. Furthermore, it seems likely that such interference must result primarily from proactive interference. This seems likely on a simple probability basis. A 20-year-old college student will more likely have learned something during his 20 years prior to coming to the laboratory that will interfere with his retention than he will during the 24 hours between the learning and retention test. However, the longer the retention interval the more important will retroactive interference become relative to proactive interferences.

The second implication is that these data may suggest greater homogeneity or continuity in memorial processes than hitherto supposed. Although no one has adequately solved the measurement problem of how to make comparisons of retention among conditioned responses, prose material, motor tasks, concept learning, and rote-learned tasks, the gross comparisons have indicated that rote-learned tasks were forgotten much more rapidly than these other tasks. But the rote-learning data used for comparison have been those derived with the classical design in which the forgetting over 24 hours is approximately 75 per cent. If we take the revised estimate of 15 per cent, the discrepancies among tasks becomes considerably less.

The third implication of the revised estimate of rate of forgetting is that the number of variables which appreciably influence rate of forgetting must be sharply limited. While this statement does not inevitably follow from the analyses I have made, the current evidence strongly supports the statement. I want to turn to the final section of this paper which will consist of a review of the influence of some of the variables which are or have been thought to be related to rate of forgetting. In considering these variables, it is well to keep in mind that a variable which produces only a small difference in forgetting is important if one is interested in accounting for the 15 per cent assumed now as the loss over 24 hours. If appropriate for a given variable, I will indicate where it fits into an interference theory, although in no case will I endeavor to handle the details of such a theory.

Time Passage of time between learning and recalls is the critical defining variable for forgetting. Manipulation of this variable provides the basic data for which a theory must account. Previously, our conception of rate of forgetting as a function of time has been tied to the Ebbinghaus curve. If the analysis made earlier is correct, this curve does not give us the basic data we need. In short, we must start all over and derive a retention curve over time when the subjects have learned no previous materials in the laboratory. It is apparent that I expect the fall in this curve over time to be relatively small.

In conjunction with time as an independent variable, we must, in explanation of forgetting, consider why sleep retards the processes responsible for forgetting. My conception, which does not really explain anything, is that since forgetting is largely produced by proactive interference, the amount of time which a subject spends in sleep is simply to be subtracted from the total retention interval when predicting the amount to be forgotten. It is known that proactive interference increases with passage of time (5); sleep, I believe, brings to a standstill whatever these processes are which produce this increase.

Degree of learning We usually say that the better or stronger the learning the more or better the retention. Yet we do not know whether or not the *rate* of forgetting differs for items of different strength. The experimental problem is a difficult one. What we need is to have a subject learn a single association and measure its decline in strength over time. But this is difficult to carry out with verbal material, since almost of necessity we must have the subject learn a series of associations, to make it a reasonable task. And, when a series of associations are learned, complications arise from interaction effects among associations of different strength. Nevertheless, we may expect, on the basis of evidence from a wide variety of studies, that given a constant degree of similarity, the effective interference varies as some function of the strength of associations.

Distribution of practice It is a fact that distribution of practice during acquisition influences retention of verbal materials. The facts of the case seem to be as follows. If the subject has not learned previous lists in the laboratory, massed practice gives equal or better retention than does distributed practice. If, on the other hand, the subject has learned a number of previous lists, distributed practice will facilitate retention (32). We do not have the theoretical solution to these facts. The point I wish to make here is that whether or not distribution of learning inhibits or facilitates retention depends upon the amount of interference from previous learning. It is reasonable to expect, therefore, that the solution to the problem will come via principles handling interference in general. I might also say that a theoretical solution to this problem will also provide a solution for Jost's laws.

Similarity Amount of interference from other tasks is closely tied to similarity. This similarity must be conceived of as similarity among materials as such and also situational similarity (4). When we turn to similarity within a task, the situation is not quite so clear. Empirically and theoretically (8) one would expect that intratask similarity would be a very relevant variable in forgetting. As discussed elsewhere (31), however, variation in intratask similarity almost inevitably leads to variations in intertask similarity. We do know from a recent study (33) that with material of low meaningfulness forgetting is significantly greater with high intralist similarity than with low. While the difference in magnitude is only about 8 per cent, when we are trying to account for a total loss of 15 per cent, this amount becomes a major matter.

Meaningfulness   The belief has long been held that the more meaningful the material the better the retention—the less the forgetting. Osgood (21) has pointed out that if this is true it is difficult for an interference theory to handle. So far as I know, the only direct test of the influence of this variable is a recent study in which retention of syllables of 100 per cent association value was compared with that of zero association value (33). There was no difference in the recall of these syllables. Other less precise evidence would support this finding when comparisons are made among syllables, adjectives, and nouns, as plotted in Fig. 3. However, there is some evidence that materials of very low meaningfulness are forgotten more rapidly than nonsense syllables of zero association value. Consonant syllables, both serial (32) and paired associates (unpublished) show about 50 per cent loss over 24 hours. The study using serial lists was the one mentioned earlier as knowingly omitted from Fig. 3. These syllables, being extremely difficult to learn, allow a correction of about 20 per cent due to criterion overestimation but even with this much correction the forgetting (30 per cent) is still appreciably more than the estimate we have made for other materials. To invoke the interference theory to account for this discrepancy means that we must demonstrate how interference from other activities could be greater for these consonant syllables than for nonsense syllables, nouns, adjectives, and other materials. Our best guess at the present time is that the sequences of letters in consonant syllables are contrary to other well-established language habits. That is to say, letter sequences which commonly occur in our language are largely different from those in consonant syllables. As a consequence, not only are these consonant syllables very dfficult to learn, but forgetting is accelerated by proactive interference from previously well-learned letter sequences. If subsequent research cannot demonstrate such a source of interference, or if some other source is not specified, an

interference theory for this case will be in some trouble.

Affectivity   Another task dimension which has received extensive attention is the affective tone of the material. I would also include here the studies attaching unpleasant experiences to some items experimentally and not to others, and measuring retention of these two sets of items. Freud is to a large extent responsible for these studies, but he cannot be held responsible for the malformed methodology which characterizes so many of them. What can one say by way of summarizing these studies? The only conclusion that I can reach is a statistical one, namely, that the occasional positive result found among the scores of studies is about as frequent as one would expect by sampling error, using the 5 per cent level of confidence. Until a reliable body of facts is established for this variable and associated variables, no theoretical evaluation is possible.

Other variables   As I indicated earlier, I will not make an exhaustive survey of the variables which may influence rate of forgetting. I have limited myself to variables which have been rather extensively investigated, which have immediate relevance to the interference theory, or for which reliable relationships are available. Nevertheless, I would like to mention briefly some of these other variables. There is the matter of *warm-up* before recall; some investigators find that this reduces forgetting (12); others, under as nearly replicated conditions as is possible to obtain, do not (23). Some resolution must be found for these flat contradictions. It seems perfectly reasonable, however, that inadequate set or context differences could reduce recall. Indeed, an interference theory would predict this forgetting if the set or context stimuli are appreciably different from those prevailing at the time of learning. In our laboratory we try to reinstate the learning set by careful instructions, and we simply do not find decrements that might be attributed to inadequate set. For example, in a recent study (33) subjects were given a 24-hour recall of a serial list after learning to one perfect trial. I think we would expect that the first item in the list would suffer the greatest decrement due to inadequate set, yet this item showed only .7 per cent loss. But let it be clear that when we are attempting to account for the 15 per cent loss over 24 hours, we should not overlook any possible source for this loss.

Thus far I have not said anything about forgetting as a function of characteristics of the subject, that is, the personality or intellectual characteristics. As far as I have been able to determine, there is not a single valid study which shows that such variables have an appreciable influence on forgetting. Many studies have shown differences in learning as a function of these variables, but not differences in rate of forgetting. Surely there must be some such variables. We do know that if subjects are severely insulted, made to feel stupid, or generally led to believe that they have no justification for continued existence on the earth just before they are asked to recall, they will show losses (e.g., 25, 38), but even the influence of this kind of psychological beating is short lived. Somehow I have never felt that such findings need explanation by a theory used to explain the other facts of forgetting.

Concerning the causes of forgetting, let me sum up in a somewhat more dogmatic fashion than is probably justified. One of the assumptions of science is finite causality. Everything cannot influence everything else. To me, the most important implication of the work on forgetting during the last ten years is that this work has markedly *reduced* the number of variables related to forgetting. Correspondingly, I think the theoretical problem has become simpler. It is my belief that we can narrow down the cause of forgetting to interference from previously learned habits, from habits being currently learned, and from habits we have yet to learn. The amount of this interference is primarily a function of similarity and associative strength, the latter being important because it interacts with similarity.

SUMMARY

This paper deals with issues in the forgetting of rote-learned materials. An analysis of the current evidence suggests that the classical Ebbinghaus curve of forgetting is primarily a function of interference from materials learned previously in the laboratory. When this source of interference is removed, forgetting decreases from about 75 per cent over 24 hours to about 25 per cent. This latter figure can be reduced by at least 10 per cent by other methodological considerations, leaving 15 per cent as an estimate of the forgetting over 24 hours. This estimate will vary somewhat as a function of intratask similarity, distributed practice, and with very low meaningful material. But the over-all evidence suggests that similarity with other material and situational similarity are by far the most critical factors in forgetting. Such evidence is consonant with a general interference theory, although the details of such a theory were not presented here.

REFERENCES

1. Archer, E. J., & Underwood, B. J. Retroactive inhibition of verbal associations as a multiple function of temporal point of interpolation and degree of interpolated learning. *J. exp. Psychol.*, 1951, **42**, 283–290.
2. Bartlett, F. C. *Remembering: a study in experimental and social psychology.* London: Cambridge Univer. Press, 1932.
3. Belmont, L., & Birch, H. G. Re-individualizing the repression hypothesis. *J. abnorm. soc. Psychol.*, 1951, **46**, 226–235.
4. Bilodeau, I. McD., & Schlosberg, H. Similarity in stimulating conditions as a variable in retroactive inhibition. *J. exp. Psychol.*, 1951, **41**, 199–204.
5. Briggs, G. E. Acquisition extinction, and recovery functions in retroactive inhibition. *J. exp. Psychol.*, 1954, **47**, 285–293.
6. Cheng, N. Y. Retroactive effect and degree of similarity. *J. exp. Psychol.*, 1929, **12**, 444–458.
7. Ebbinghaus, H. *Memory: a contribution to experimental psychology.* (Trans. by H. A. Ruger, and C. E. Bussenius) New York: Bureau of Publications, Teachers College, Columbia Univer., 1913.
8. Gibson, Eleanor J. A systematic application of the concepts of generalization and differentiation to verbal learning. *Psychol. Rev.*, 1940, **47**, 196–229.
9. Gibson, Eleanor J. Intra-list generalization as a factor in verbal learning. *J. exp. Psychol.*, 1942, **30**, 185–200.
10. Greenberg, R., & Underwood, B. J. Retention as a function of stage of practice. *J. exp. Psychol.*, 1950, **40**, 452–457.
11. Hovland, C. I. Experimental studies in rote-

learning theory. VI. Comparison of retention following learning to same criterion by massed and distributed practice. *J. exp. Psychol.*, 1940, **26**, 568–587.

12. Irion, A. L. The relation of "set" to retention. *Psychol. Rev.*, 1948, **55**, 336–341.

13. Jenkins, J. G., & Dallenbach, K. M. Oblivescence during sleep and waking. *Amer. J. Psychol.*, 1924, **35**, 605–612.

14. Johnson, L. M. The relative effect of a time interval upon learning and retention. *J. exp. Psychol.*, 1939, **24**, 169–179.

15. Katona, G. *Organizing and memorizing: studies in the psychology of learning and teaching.* New York: Columbia Univer. Press, 1940.

16. Krueger, W. C. F. The effect of over-learning on retention. *J. exp. Psychol.*, 1929, **12**, 71–78.

17. Lester, O. P. Mental set in relation to retroactive inhibition. *J. exp. Psychol.*, 1932, **15**, 681–699.

18. Luh, C. W. The conditions of retention. *Psychol. Monogr.*, 1922, **31**, No. 3 (Whole No. 142).

19. McGeoch, J. A. Forgetting and the law of disuse. *Psychol. Rev.*, 1932, **39**, 352–370.

20. McGeoch, J. A. *The psychology of human learning.* New York: Longmans, Green, 1942.

21. Osgood, C. E. *Method and theory in experimental psychology.* New York: Oxford Univer. Press, 1953.

22. Rapaport, D. Emotions and memory. *Psychol. Rev.*, 1943, **50**, 234–243.

23. Rockway, M. R., & Duncan, C. P. Pre-recall warming-up in verbal retention. *J. exp. Psychol.*, 1952, **43**, 305–312.

24. Runquist, W. Retention of verbal associations as a function of interference and strength. Unpublished doctor's dissertation. Northwestern Univer., 1956.

25. Russell, W. A. Retention of verbal material as a function of motivating instructions and experimentally-induced failure. *J. exp. Psychol.*, 1952, **43**, 207–216.

26. Underwood, B. J. The effect of successive interpolations on retroactive and proactive inhibition. *Psychol. Monogr.*, 1945, **59**, No. 3 (Whole No. 273).

27. Underwood, B. J. Studies of distributed practice: VII. Learning and retention of serial nonsense lists as a function of intralist similarity. *J. exp. Psychol.*, 1952, **44**, 80–87.

28. Underwood, B. J. Studies of distributed practice: VIII. Learning and retention of paired nonsense syllables as function of intralist similarity. *J. exp. Psychol.*, 1953, **45**, 133–142.

29. Underwood, B. J. Studies of distributed practice: IX. Learning and retention of paired adjectives as a function of intralist similarity. *J. exp. Psychol.*, 1953, **45**, 143–149.

30. Underwood, B. J. Studies of distributed practice: X. The influence of interalist similarity on learning and retention of serial adjective lists. *J. exp. Psychol.*, 1953, **45**, 253–259.

31. Underwood, B. J. Intralist similarity in verbal learning and retention. *Psychol. Rev.*, 1954, **3**, 160–166.

32. Underwood, B. J., & Richardson, J. Studies of distributed practice: XIII. Interlist interference and the retention of serial nonsense lists. *J. exp. Psychol.*, 1955, **50**, 39–46.

33. Underwood, B. J., & Richardson, J. The influence of meaningfulness, intralist similarity, and serial position on retention. *J. exp. Psychol.* 1956, **52**, 119–126.

34. Ward, L. B. Reminiscence and rote learning. *Psychol. Monogr.*, 1937, **49**, No. 4 (Whole No. 220).

35. Weiss, W., & Margolius, G. The effect of context stimuli on learning and retention. *J. exp. Psychol.*, 1954, **48**, 318–322.

36. Williams, M. The effects of experimentally induced needs upon retention. *J. exp. Psychol.*, 1950, **40**, 139–151.

37. Youtz, Adella C. An experimental evaluation of Jost's laws. *Psychol. Monogr.*, 1941, **53**, No. 1 (Whole No. 238).

38. Zeller, A. F. An experimental analogue of repression: III. The effect of induced failure and success on memory measured by recall. *J. exp. Psychol.*, 1951, **42**, 32–38.

Selection **36** | THE SCIENCE OF LEARNING AND THE ART OF TEACHING*

B. F. SKINNER
Harvard University

Some promising advances have recently been made in the field of learning. Special techniques have been designed to arrange what are called "contingencies of reinforcement"—the relations which prevail between behavior on the one hand and the consequences of that behavior on the other—with the result that a much more effective control of behavior has been achieved. It has long been argued that

* Abridged from B. F. Skinner, "The Science of Learning and the Art of Teaching," *Harvard Educational Review*, **24**:86–97, 1954. Reprinted by permission of the author and the publisher.

an organism learns mainly by producing changes in its environment, but it is only recently that these changes have been carefully manipulated. In traditional devices for the study of learning—in the serial maze, for example, or in the T-maze, the problem box, or the familiar discrimination apparatus—the effects produced by the organism's behavior are left to many fluctuating circumstances. There is many a slip between the turn-to-the-right and the food-cup at the end of the alley. It is not surprising that techniques of this sort have yielded only very rough data from which the uniformities demanded by an experimental science can be extracted only by averaging many cases. In none of this work has the behavior of the individual organism been predicted in more than a statistical sense. The learning processes which are the presumed object of such research are reached only through a series of inferences. Current preoccupation with deductive systems reflects this state of the science.

Recent improvements in the conditions which control behavior in the field of learning are of two principal sorts. The Law of Effect has been taken seriously; we have made sure that effects *do* occur and that they occur under conditions which are optimal for producing the changes called learning. Once we have arranged the particular type of consequence called a reinforcement, our techniques permit us to shape up the behavior of an organism almost at will. It has become a routine exercise to demonstrate this in classes in elementary psychology by conditioning such an organism as a pigeon. Simply by presenting food to a hungry pigeon at the right time, it is possible to shape up three or four well-defined responses in a single demonstration period—such responses as turning around, pacing the floor in the pattern of a figure-8, standing still in a corner of the demonstration apparatus, stretching the neck or stamping the foot. Extremely complex performances may be reached through successive stages in the shaping process, the contingencies of reinforcement being changed progressively in the direction of the required behavior. The results are often quite dramatic. In such a demonstration one can see learning take place. A significant change in behavior is often obvious as the result of a single reinforcement.

A second important advance in technique permits us to maintain behavior in given states of strength for long periods of time. Reinforcements continue to be important, of course, long after an organism has learned *how* to do something, long after it has acquired behavior. They are necessary to maintain the behavior in strength. Of special interest is the effect of various schedules of intermittent reinforcement. Charles B. Ferster and the author are currently preparing an extensive report of a five-year research program, sponsored by the Office of Naval Research, in which most of the important types of schedules have been investigated and in which the effects of schedules in general have been reduced to a few principles. On the theoretical side we now have a fairly good idea of why a given schedule produces its appropriate performance. On the practical side we have learned how to maintain any given level of activity for daily periods limited only by the physical exhaustion of the organism and from day to day without substantial change throughout its life. Many of these effects would be traditionally assigned to the field of motivation, although the principal operation is simply the arrangement of contingencies of reinforcement.

These new methods of shaping behavior and of maintaining it in strength are a great improvement over the traditional practices of professional animal trainers, and it is not surprising that our laboratory results are already being applied to the production of performing animals for commercial purposes. In a more academic environment they have been used for demonstration purposes which extend far beyond an interest in learning as such. We have trained two pigeons to coordinate their behavior in a cooperative endeavor with a precision which equals that of the most skillful human dancers. In a more serious vein these techniques have permitted us to explore the complexities of the individual organism and to analyze some of the serial or coordinate behaviors involved in attention, problem solving, various types of self-control, and the subsidiary systems of responses within a single organism called "personalities." Some of these are exemplified in what we call multiple schedules of reinforcement. In general a given schedule has an effect upon the rate at which a response is emitted. Changes in the rate from moment to moment show a pattern typical of the schedule. The pattern may be as simple as a constant rate of responding at a given value, it may be a gradually accelerating rate between certain extremes, it may be an abrupt change from not responding at all to a given stable high rate, and so on. It has been shown that the performance characteristic of a given schedule can be brought under the control of a particular stimulus and that different performances can be brought under the control of different stimuli in the same organism. At a recent meeting of the American Psychological Association, Dr. Ferster and the author demonstrated a pigeon whose behavior showed the pattern typical of "fixed-interval" reinforcement in the presence of one stimulus and, alternately, the pattern typical of the very different schedule called "fixed ratio" in the presence of a second stimulus. In the laboratory we have been able to obtain performances appropriate to *nine* different schedules in the presence of appropriate stimuli in random alternation. When Stimulus 1 is present, the pigeon executes the performance appropriate to Schedule 1. When Stimulus 2 is present, the pigeon executes the performance appropriate to Schedule 2. And so on. This result is important because it makes the extrapolation of our laboratory results to daily life much more plausible. We are all constantly shifting from schedule to schedule as our immediate environment changes, but the dynamics of the control exercised by reinforcement remain essentially unchanged.

One of the most dramatic applications of these techniques has recently been made in the Harvard Psychological Laboratories by Floyd Ratliff and Donald S. Blough, who have skillfully used multiple and serial schedules of reinforcement to study complex perceptual processes in the infrahuman organism. They have achieved a sort of psychophysics without verbal instruction. In a recent experiment by Blough, for example, a pigeon draws a detailed dark-adaptation curve showing the characteristic breaks of rod and cone vision. The curve is recorded continuously in a single experimental period and is quite comparable with the curves of human subjects. The pigeon behaves in a way which, in the human case, we would not hesitate to describe by saying that it adjusts a very faint patch of light until it can just be seen.

In all this work, the species of the organism has made surprisingly little difference. It is true that the organisms studied have all been vertebrates, but they still cover a wide range. Comparable results have been obtained with pigeons, rats, dogs, monkeys, human children, and most recently, by the author in collaboration with Ogden R. Lindsley, human psychotic subjects. In spite of great phylogenetic differences, all these organisms show amazingly similar properties of the learning process. It should be emphasized that this has been achieved by analyzing the effects of reinforcement and by designing techniques which manipulate reinforcement with considerable precision. Only in this way can the behavior of the individual organism be brought under such precise control. It is also important to note that through a gradual advance to complex interrelations among responses, the same degree of rigor is being extended to behavior which would usually be assigned to such fields as perception, thinking, and personality dynamics.

From this exciting prospect of an advancing science of learning, it is a great shock to turn to that branch of technology which is most directly concerned with the learning process—education. Let us consider, for example, the teaching of arithmetic in the lower grades. The school is concerned with imparting to the child a large number of responses of a special sort. The responses are all verbal. They consist of speaking and writing certain words, figures, and signs which, to put it roughly, refer to numbers and to arithmetic operations. The first task is to shape up these responses—to get the child to pronounce and to write responses correctly, but the principal task is to bring this behavior under many sorts of stimulus control. This is what happens when the child learns to count, to recite tables, to count while ticking off the items in an assemblage of objects, to respond to spoken or written numbers by saying "odd," "even," "prime," and so on. Over and above this elaborate repertoire of numerical behavior, most of which is often dismissed as the product of rote learning, the teaching of arithmetic looks forward to those complex serial arrangements of responses involved in original mathematical thinking. The child must acquire responses of transposing, clearing fractions, and so on, which modify the order or pattern of the original material so that the response called a solution is eventually made possible.

Now, how is this extremely complicated verbal repertoire set up? In the first place, what reinforcements are used? Fifty years ago the answer would have been clear. At that time educational control was still frankly aversive. The child read numbers, copied numbers, memorized tables, and performed operations upon numbers to escape the threat of the birch rod or cane. Some positive reinforcements were perhaps eventually derived from the increased efficiency of the child in the field of arithmetic and in rare cases some automatic reinforcement may have resulted from the sheer manipulation of the medium—from the solution of problems or the discovery of the intricacies of the number system. But for the immediate purposes of education the child acted to avoid or escape punishment. It was part of the reform movement known as progressive education to make the positive consequences more immediately effective, but any one who visits the lower grades of the average school today will observe that a change has been made, not from aversive to positive control, but from one form of aversive stimulation to another. The child at his desk, filling in his workbook, is behaving primarily to escape from the threat of a series of minor aversive events —the teacher's displeasure, the criticism or ridicule of his classmates, an ignominious showing in a competition, low marks, a trip to the office "to be talked to" by the principal, or a word to the parent who may still resort to the birch rod. In this welter of aversive consequences, getting the right answer is in itself an insignificant event, any effect of which is lost amid the anxieties, the boredom, and the aggressions which are the inevitable by-products of aversive control.

Secondly, we have to ask how the contingencies of reinforcement are arranged. When is a numerical operation reinforced as "right"? Eventually, of course, the pupil may be able to check his own answers and achieve some sort of automatic reinforcement, but in the early stages the reinforcement of being right is usually accorded by the teacher. The contingencies she provides are far from optimal. It can easily be demonstrated that, unless explicit

mediating behavior has been set up, the lapse of only a few seconds between response and reinforcement destroys most of the effect. In a typical classroom, nevertheless, long periods of time customarily elapse. The teacher may walk up and down the aisle, for example, while the class is working on a sheet of problems, pausing here and there to say right or wrong. Many seconds or minutes intervene between the child's response and the teacher's reinforcement. In many cases—for example, when papers are taken home to be corrected—as much as 24 hours may intervene. It is surprising that this system has any effect whatsoever.

A third notable shortcoming is the lack of a skillful program which moves forward through a series of progressive approximations to the final complex behavior desired. A long series of contingencies is necessary to bring the organism into the possession of mathematical behavior most efficiently. But the teacher is seldom able to reinforce at each step in such a series because she cannot deal with the pupil's responses one at a time. It is usually necessary to reinforce the behavior in blocks of responses—as in correcting a work sheet or page from a workbook. The responses within such a block must not be interrelated. The answer to one problem must not depend upon the answer to another. The number of stages through which one may progressively approach a complex pattern of behavior is therefore small, and the task so much the more difficult. Even the most modern workbook in beginning arithmetic is far from exemplifying an efficient program for shaping up mathematical behavior.

Perhaps the most serious criticism of the current classroom is the relative infrequency of reinforcement. Since the pupil is usually dependent upon the teacher for being right, and since many pupils are usually dependent upon the same teacher, the total number of contingencies which may be arranged during, say, the first four years, is of the order of only a few thousand. But a very rough estimate suggests that efficient mathematical behavior at this level requires something of the order of 25,000 contingencies. We may suppose that even in the brighter student a given contingency must be arranged several times to place the behavior well in hand. The responses to be set up are not simply the various items in tables of addition, subtraction, multiplication, and division; we have also to consider the alternative forms in which each item may be stated. To the learning of such material we should add hundreds of responses concerned with factoring, identifying primes, memorizing series, using short-cut techniques of calculation, constructing and using geometric representations or number forms, and so on. Over and above all this, the whole mathematical repertoire must be brought under the control of concrete problems of considerable variety. Perhaps 50,000 contingencies is a more conservative estimate. In this frame of reference the daily assignment in arithmetic seems pitifully meagre.

The result of all this is, of course, well known. Even our best schools are under criticism for their inefficiency in the teaching of drill subjects such as arithmetic. The condition in the average school is a matter of widespread national concern. Modern children simply do not learn arithmetic quickly or well. Nor is the result simply incompetence. The very subjects in which modern techniques are weakest are those in which failure is most conspicuous, and in the wake of an ever-growing incompetence come the anxieties, uncertainties, and aggressions which in their turn present other problems to the school. Most pupils soon claim the asylum of not being "ready" for arithmetic at a given level or, eventually, of not having a mathematical mind. Such explanations are readily seized upon by defensive teachers and parents. Few pupils ever reach the stage at which automatic reinforcements follow as the natural consequences of mathematical behavior. On the contrary, the figures and symbols of mathematics have become standard emotional stimuli. The glimpse of a column of figures, not to say an algebraic symbol or an integral sign, is likely to set off —not mathematical behavior—but a reaction of anxiety, guilt, or fear.

There would be no point in urging these objections if improvement were impossible. But the advances which have recently been made in our control of the learning process suggest a thorough revision of classroom practices and, fortunately, they tell us how the revision can be brought about. This is not, of course, the first time that the results of an experimental science have been brought to bear upon the practical problems of education. The modern classroom does not, however, offer much evidence that research in the field of learning has been respected or used. This condition is no doubt partly due to the limitations of earlier research. But it has been encouraged by a too hasty conclusion that the laboratory study of learning is inherently limited because it cannot take into account the realities of the classroom. In the light of our increasing knowledge of the learning process we should, instead, insist upon dealing with those realities and forcing a substantial change in them. Education is perhaps the most important branch of scientific technology. It deeply affects the lives of all of us. We can no longer allow the exigencies of a practical situation to suppress the tremendous improvements which are within reach. The practical situation must be changed.

There are certain questions which have to be answered in turning to the study of any new organism. In the first place, what reinforcements are available? What does the school have in its possession which will reinforce a child? We may look first to the material to be learned, for it is possible that this will provide considerable automatic reinforcement. Children play for hours with mechanical toys, paints, scissors and paper, noise-makers, puzzles—in short, with almost anything which feeds back significant changes in the environment and is reasonably free of aversive properties. The sheer control of nature is itself reinforcing. This effect is not evident in the modern school because it is masked by the emotional responses generated by aversive control. It is true that automatic reinforcement from the manipulation of the environment is probably only a mild reinforcer and may need to be carefully husbanded, but one of the most striking principles to emerge from recent research is that the *net* amount of reinforcement is of little significance. A very slight reinforcement may be tremendously effective in controlling behavior if it is wisely used.

If the natural reinforcement inherent in the subject matter is not enough, other reinforcers must be employed. Even in school the child is occasionally permitted to do "what he wants to do," and access to reinforcements of many sorts may be made contingent upon the more immediate consequences of the behavior to be established. Those who advocate competition as a useful social motive may wish to use the reinforcements which follow from excelling others, although there is the difficulty that in this case the reinforcement of one child is necessarily aversive to another. Next in order we might place the good will and affection of the teacher, and only when that has failed need we turn to the use of aversive stimulation.

In the second place, how are these reinforcements to be made contingent upon the desired behavior? There are two considerations here—the gradual elaboration of extremely complex patterns of behavior and the maintenance of the behavior in strength at each stage. The whole process of becoming competent in any field must be divided into a very large number of very small steps, and reinforcement must be contingent upon the accomplishment of each step. This solution to the problem of creating a complex repertoire of behavior also solves the problem of maintaining the behavior in strength. We could, of course, resort to the techniques of scheduling already developed in the study of other organisms but in the present state of our knowledge of educational practices, scheduling appears to be most effectively arranged through the design of the material to be learned. By making each successive step as small as possible, the frequency of reinforcement can be raised to a maximum, while the possible aversive consequences of being wrong are reduced to a minimum. Other ways of designing material would yield other programs of reinforcement. Any supplementary reinforcement would probably have to be scheduled in the more traditional way.

These requirements are not excessive, but they are probably incompatible with the current realities of the classroom. In the experimental study of learning it has been found that the contingencies of reinforcement which are most efficient in controlling the organism cannot be arranged through the personal mediation of the experimenter. An organism is affected by subtle details of contingencies which are beyond the capacity of the human organism to arrange.

If our current knowledge of the acquisition and maintenance of verbal behavior is to be applied to education, some sort of teaching machine is needed.[1] Contingencies of reinforcement which change the behavior of lower organisms often cannot be arranged by hand; rather elaborate apparatus is needed. The human organism requires even more subtle instrumentation. An appropriate teaching machine will have several important features. The student must *compose* his response rather than select it from a set of alternatives, as in a multiple-choice self-rater. One reason for this is that we want him to recall rather than recognize—to make a response as well as see that it is right. Another reason is that effective multiple-choice material must contain plausible wrong responses, which are out of place in the delicate process of "shaping" behavior because they strengthen unwanted forms. Although it is much easier to build a machine to score multiple-choice answers than to evaluate a composed response, the technical advantage is outweighed by these and other considerations.

A second requirement of a minimal teaching machine also distinguishes it from earlier versions. In acquiring complex behavior the student must pass through a carefully designed sequence of steps, often of considerable length. Each step must be so small that it can always be taken, yet in taking it the student moves somewhat closer to fully competent behavior. The machine must make sure that these steps are taken in a carefully prescribed order.

Several machines with the required characteristics have been built and tested. Sets of separate presentations or "frames" of visual material are stored on disks, cards, or tapes. One frame is presented at a time, adjacent frames being out of sight. In one type of machine the student composes a response by moving printed figures or letters. His setting is compared by the machine with a coded response. If the two correspond, the machine automatically presents the next frame. If they do not, the response is cleared, and another must be composed. The student cannot proceed to a second step until the first has been taken. A machine of this kind is being tested

[1] The remaining portion of this selection is abridged from B. F. Skinner, "Teaching Machines," *Science*, 128:969–977, 1958. Reprinted by permission of the author and the publisher.

in teaching spelling, arithmetic, and other subjects in the lower grades.

For more advanced students—from junior high school, say, through college—a machine which senses an arrangement of letters or figures is unnecessarily rigid in specifying form of response. Fortunately, such students may be asked to compare their responses with printed material revealed by the machine. In the machine, material is printed in 30 radial frames on a 12-inch disk. The student inserts the disk and closes the machine. He cannot proceed until the machine has been locked, and, once he has begun, the machine cannot be unlocked. All but a corner of one frame is visible through a window. The student writes his response on a paper strip exposed through a second opening. By lifting a lever on the front of the machine, he moves what he has written under a transparent cover and uncovers the correct response in the remaining corner of the frame. If the two responses correspond, he moves the lever horizontally. This movement punches a hole in the paper opposite his response, recording the fact that he called it correct, and alters the machine so that the frame will not appear again when the student works around the disk a second time. Whether the response was correct or not, a second frame appears when the lever is returned to its starting position. The student proceeds in this way until he has responded to all frames. He then works around the disk a second time, but only those frames appear to which he has not correctly responded. When the disk revolves without stopping, the assignment is finished. (The student is asked to repeat each frame until a correct response is made to allow for the fact that, in telling him that a response is wrong, such a machine tells him what is right.)

The machine itself, of course, does not teach. It simply brings the student into contact with the person who composed the material it presents. It is a labor-saving device because it can bring one programmer into contact with an indefinite number of students. This may suggest mass production, but the effect upon each student is surprisingly like that of a private tutor. The comparison holds in several respects. (i) There is a constant interchange between program and student. Unlike lectures, textbooks, and the usual audio-visual aids, the machine induces sustained activity. The student is always alert and busy. (ii) Like a good tutor, the machine insists that a given point be thoroughly understood, either frame by frame or set by set, before the student moves on. Lectures, textbooks, and their mechanized equivalents, on the other hand, proceed without making sure that the student understands and easily leave him behind. (iii) Like a good tutor the machine presents just that material for which the student is ready. It asks him to take only that step which he is at the moment best equipped and most likely to take. (iv) Like a skillful tutor the machine helps the student to come up with the right answer. It does this in part through the orderly construction of the program and in part with techniques of hinting, prompting, suggesting, and so on, derived from an analysis of verbal behavior. (v) Lastly, of course, the machine, like the private tutor, reinforces the student for every correct response, using this immediate feedback not only to shape his behavior most efficiently but to maintain it in strength in a manner which the layman would describe as "holding the student's interest."

CAN MATERIAL BE TOO EASY?

The traditional teacher may view these programs with concern. He may be particularly alarmed by the effort to maximize success and minimize failure. He has found that students do not pay attention unless they are worried about the consequences of their work. The customary procedure has been to maintain the necessary anxiety by inducing errors. In recitation, the student who obviously knows the answer is not too often asked; a test item which is correctly answered by everyone is discarded as nondiscriminating; problems at the end of a section in a textbook in mathematics generally include one or two very difficult items; and so on. (The teacher-turned-programmer may be surprised to find this attitude affecting the construction of items. For example, he may find it difficult to allow an item to stand which "gives the point away." Yet if we can solve the motivational problem with other means, what is more effective than giving a point away?) Making sure that the student knows he doesn't know is a technique concerned with motivation, not with the learning process. Machines solve the problem of motivation in other ways. There is no evidence that what is easily learned is more readily forgotten. If this should prove to be the case, retention may be guaranteed by subsequent material constructed for an equally painless review.

The standard defense of "hard" material is that we want to teach more than subject matter. The student is to be challenged and taught to "think." The argument is sometimes little more than a rationalization for a confusing presentation, but it is doubtless true that lectures and texts are often inadequate and misleading by design. But to what end? What sort of "thinking" does the student learn in struggling through difficult material? It is true that those who learn under difficult conditions are better students, but are they better because they have surmounted difficulties or do they surmount them because they are better? In the guise of teaching thinking we set difficult and confusing situations and claim credit for the students who deal with them successfully.

The trouble with deliberately making education difficult in order to teach thinking is (i) that we must remain content with the students thus selected, even though we know that they are only a small part of the potential supply of thinkers, and (ii) that we must continue to sacrifice the teaching of subject matter by renouncing effective but "easier" methods. A more sensible program is to analyze the behavior called "thinking" and produce it according to specifications. A program specifically concerned with such behavior could be composed of material already available in logic, mathematics, scientific method, and psychology. Much would doubtless be added in completing an effective program. The machine has already yielded important relevant by-products. Immediate feedback encourages a more careful reading of programmed material than is the case in studying a text, where the consequences of attention or inattention are so long deferred that they have little effect on reading skills. The behavior involved in observing or attending to detail—as in inspecting charts and models or listening closely to recorded speech—is efficiently shaped by the contingencies arranged by the machine. And when an immediate result is in the balance, a student will be more likely to learn how to marshal relevant material, to concentrate on specific features of a presentation, to reject irrelevant materials, to refuse the easy but wrong solution, and to tolerate indecision, all of which are involved in effective thinking.

Part of the objection to easy material is that the student will come to depend on the machine and will be less able than ever to cope with the inefficient presentations of lectures, textbooks, films, and "real life." This is indeed a problem. All good teachers must "wean" their students, and the machine is no exception. The better the teacher, the more explicit must the weaning process be. The final stages of a program must be so designed that the student no longer requires the helpful conditions arranged by the machine. This can be done in many ways—among others by using the machine to discuss material which has been studied in other forms. These are questions which can be adequately answered only by further research.

No large-scale "evaluation" of machine teaching has yet been attempted. We have so so far been concerned mainly with practical problems in the design and use of machines, and with testing and revising sample programs. Material has been prepared and tested with the collaboration of Lloyd E. Homme, Susan R. Meyer, and James G. Holland. Nearly 200 students completed 48 disks (about 1400 frames) prepared with the collaboration of Holland. The factual core of the course was covered, corresponding to about 200 pages of the text. The median time required to finish 48 disks was $14\frac{1}{2}$ hours. The students were not examined on the material but were responsible for the text which overlapped it. Their reactions to the material and to self-instruction in general have been studied through interviews and questionnaires. Both the machines and the material are now being modified in the light of this experience, and a more explicit evaluation will then be made.

Meanwhile, it can be said that the expected advantages of machine instruction were generously confirmed. Unsuspected possibilities were revealed which are now undergoing further exploration. Although it is less convenient to report to a self-instruction room than to pick up a textbook in one's room or elsewhere, most students felt that they had much to gain in studying by machine. Most of them worked for an hour or more with little effort, although they often felt tired afterwards, and they reported that they learned much more in less time and with less effort than in conventional ways. No attempt was made to point out the relevance of the material to crucial issues, personal or otherwise, but the students remained interested. (Indeed, one change in the reinforcing contingencies suggested by the experiment is intended to *reduce* the motivational level.) An important advantage proved to be that the student always knew where he stood, without waiting for an hour test or final examination.

SOME QUESTIONS

Several questions are commonly asked when teaching machines are discussed. Cannot the results of laboratory research on learning be used in education without machines? Of course they can. They should lead to improvements in textbooks, films, and other teaching materials. Moreover, the teacher who really understands the conditions under which learning takes place will be more effective, not only in teaching subject matter but in managing the class. Nevertheless, some sort of device is necessary to arrange the subtle contingencies of reinforcement required for optimal learning if each student is to have individual attention. In nonverbal skills this is usually obvious; texts and instructor can guide the learner but they cannot arrange the final contingencies which set up skilled behavior. It is true that the verbal skills at issue here are especially dependent upon social reinforcement, but it must not be forgotten that the machine simply mediates an *essentially verbal* relation. In shaping and maintaining verbal knowledge we are not committed to the contingencies arranged through immediate personal contact.

Machines may still seem unnecessarily complex compared with other mediators such as workbooks or self-scoring test forms. Unfortunately, these alternatives are not acceptable. When material is adequately programmed, adjacent steps are often so similar that one frame reveals the response to another. Only some sort of mechanical presentation will make successive frames independent of each other. Moreover, in self-instruction an automatic record of

the student's behavior is especially desirable, and for many purposes it should be fool-proof. Simplified versions of the present machines have been found useful—for example, in the work of Ferster and Sapon, of Porter, and of Gilbert—but the mechanical and economic problems are so easily solved that a machine with greater capabilities is fully warranted.

Will machines replace teachers? On the contrary, they are capital equipment to be used by teachers to save time and labor. In assigning certain mechanizable functions to machines, the teacher emerges in his proper role as an indispensable human being. He may teach more students than heretofore—this is probably inevitable if the world-wide demand for education is to be satisfied—but he will do so in fewer hours and with fewer burdensome chores. In return for his greater productivity he can ask society to improve his economic condition.

The role of the teacher may well be changed, for machine instruction will affect several traditional practices. Students may continue to be grouped in "grades" or "classes," but it will be possible for each to proceed at his own level, advancing as rapidly as he can. The other kind of "grade" will also change its meaning. In traditional practice a C means that a student has a smattering of a whole course. But if machine instruction assures mastery at every stage, a grade will be useful only in showing *how far* a student has gone. C might mean that he is halfway through a course. Given enough time he will be able to get an A; and since A is no longer a motivating device, this is fair enough. The quick student will meanwhile have picked up A's in other subjects.

Differences in ability raise other questions. A program designed for the slowest student in the school system will probably not seriously delay the fast student, who will be free to progress at his own speed. (He may profit from the full coverage by filling in unsuspected gaps in his repertoire.) If this does not prove to be the case, programs can be constructed at two or more levels, and students can be shifted from one to the other as performances dictate. If there are also differences in "types of thinking," the extra time available for machine instruction may be used to present a subject in ways appropriate to many types.

Each student will presumably retain and use those ways which he finds most useful. The kind of individual difference which arises simply because a student has missed part of an essential sequence (compare the child who has no "mathematical ability" because he was out with the measles when fractions were first taken up) will simply be eliminated.

CONCLUSION

An analysis of education within the framework of a science of behavior has broad implications. Our schools, in particular our "progressive" schools, are often held responsible for many current problems—including juvenile delinquency and the threat of a more powerful foreign technology. One remedy frequently suggested is a return to older techniques, especially to a greater "discipline" in schools. Presumably this is to be obtained with some form of punishment, to be administered either with certain classical instruments of physical injury—the dried bullock's tail of the Greek teacher or the cane of the English schoolmaster—or as disapproval or failure, the frequency of which is to be increased by "raising standards." This is probably not a feasible solution. Not only education but Western culture as a whole is moving away from aversive practices. We cannot prepare young people for one kind of life in institutions organized on quite different principles. The discipline of the birch rod may facilitate learning, but we must remember that it also breeds followers of dictators and revolutionists.

In the light of our present knowledge a school system must be called a failure if it cannot induce students to learn except by threatening them for not learning. That this has always been the standard pattern simply emphasizes the importance of modern techniques. John Dewey was speaking for his culture and his time when he attacked aversive educational practices and appealed to teachers to turn to positive and humane methods. What he threw out should have been thrown out. Unfortunately he had too little to put in its place. Progressive education has been a temporizing measure which can now be effectively supplemented. Aversive practices can not only be replaced, they can

be replaced with far more powerful techniques. The possibilities should be thoroughly explored if we are to build an educational system which will meet the present demand without sacrificing democratic principles.

Selection **37** | THE EFFECTS OF VERBAL REINFORCEMENT ON CONFORMITY AND DEVIANT BEHAVIOR*

NORMAN S. ENDLER
York University

INTRODUCTION

There are a number of factors that influence conforming behavior. These include (a) the stimulus variables used to elicit the conforming behavior; (b) group properties: i.e., group structure and function; and (c) individual differences or personality factors. A fourth phenomenon related to both (a) and (b), yet operating as a factor in its own right, is (d) the situational factor or the conditions under which conforming behavior occurs.

Conformity is not a general factor that occurs indiscriminately, but is partially determined by the situational context in which it occurs. If, in a group situation, the individual is reinforced for conforming; his conforming behavior will increase. If he is reinforced for being deviant, his conforming behavior will decrease. As Oliver and Alexander state, ". . . conforming responses are seen as voluntary behavior whose occurrence is under the control of reinforcing stimuli that follow them, and discriminative stimuli or cues that precede them" (17, p. 3). They go on to say that "In social interaction, the behaviors of individuals or groups may serve as reinforcing stimuli, or they may serve as discriminative stimuli" (17, p. 3).

Conforming behavior can be manipulated

* Norman S. Endler, "The Effects of Verbal Reinforcement on Conformity and Deviant Behavior," which appeared in *The Journal of Social Psychology*, **66**: 147–154, 1965.

like any other class of behavior (21). It is an instrumental act that leads to need satisfaction and goal attainment, with reinforcement playing a crucial role in the need → instrumental act → goal, behavioral sequence (21). If conforming behavior is followed by positive reinforcement the probability of its reoccurrence is increased; if deviation from a group norm is followed by positive reinforcements the probability of nonconformity is increased. Reinforcement is an important force in shaping (i.e., in forming and altering) social behavior, including conformity.

In a conformity situation there are a number of sources of social reinforcement, including the individuals comprising the group and the experimenter (E). Crutchfield (9), for example, had E inform the Ss of the correct answers (i.e., the false group consensus) to various items immediately after the responses to each slide. The reinforcement by E (an authority figure) in conjunction with the group consensus increased the degree of conformity. Schein (18) found that reward facilitated learned imitation, but that this did not generalize to all types of problems. Jones, Wells, and Torrey (14) found that feedback by E in terms of group consensus had little or no effect on conformity, but that feedback in terms of objective reality reduced conforming behavior. However, when E stressed the importance of group accuracy and social conformity, feedback by E in terms of group consensus increased conforming behavior; and reinforcement by E of independence still reduced conformity but to a lesser extent.

The present study was designed to study the effects on conforming behavior of feedback by E. The proposition tested was that verbal reinforcement for agreeing with a contrived group consensus increases conformity, while reinforcement for disagreeing increases deviant behavior (i.e., decreases conformity).

Furthermore, because a number of investigators (1, 3, 5, 9, 19) have found that females conform more frequently than males, sex differences in conforming behavior were also examined. Bass (4) attempts to explain these differences in terms of motivational orientation, stating that men are more task-oriented while women are more social-interaction oriented. Because women are more concerned than men with receiving social approval from other individuals, women tend to conform more.

As a side issue, the present study also investigated the effects of the type of stimulus on conforming behavior. There are at least two dimensions to the stimulus factor: (a) ambiguity and (b) personal commitment. Luchins (16), Asch (2), Blake, Helson, and Mouton (7), and Endler (10) have shown that the more ambiguous the stimulus the greater proportion of Ss conforming to the objectively incorrect judgment of the confederates. Crutchfield (9) found that conformity is least common for items involving personal commitment, such as personal preferences and attitudes.

In the present study, three types of stimulus items were used: verbal (obscure facts), perceptual (geometrical forms), and attitudes. Because the obscure facts (verbal items) would be most ambiguous for S, and because the attitude items involve personal or emotional commitment, we would expect most conformity to the verbal items, least conformity to the attitude items, and an intermediate degree of conformity to the perceptual items.

This study deals primarily with the effects of the situational factor on conformity (reinforcement) and secondarily with the effects of individual differences (sex) and stimulus factors.

METHOD

Subjects

Forty male and 35 female college freshmen were randomly assigned to one of three experimental conditions: conformity reinforcement (CR), 14 males and 12 females; neutral (N), 12 males and 10 females; and deviancy reinforcement (DR), 14 males and 13 females. There were three approximately equal groups of males; and three, of females.

Three male college sophomores served as confederates, and E (Ss' psychology instructor) served as the source of verbal reinforcement. The three confederates had prestige value in that one was the president of the students' council and was majoring in psychology, a second was editor of the student periodical, and the third was majoring in psychology.

Procedure

Each S was tested separately by E, but in the presence of the three male confederates. A series of 36 slides, consisting of 20 critical (conformity) items and 16 buffer items was used to measure conforming behavior. The 20 critical items, which were of the multiple-choice type, included eight information (verbal), nine perceptual, and three attitude items. The series of slides was programmed so that after the first three buffer items there were never more than two consecutive buffer items or two consecutive critical items. Slide Numbers 4, 5, 7, 8, 10, 12, 13, 15, 17, 18, 20, 22, 23, 25, 27, 28, 30, 32, 33, and 35 served as the critical items. Base rates in responding to these items were determined by administering them to a control group.

The 36 two-inch by two-inch slides were projected (one at a time) on a screen six feet in front of the respondents. The confederates and S were seated behind tables, and each individual had a pencil and a data recording sheet on which to record his answers. E projected the slide on to the screen and then told each individual when to respond. Each individual was required to announce his response. For the buffer or neutral items, E randomized the order in which the individuals responded. For each critical item, S was required to respond after hearing the responses of the three confederates. Previously, the confederates had been instructed how to respond to the critical items. The conformity score for each S was the number of times he agreed with the contrived consensus of the confederates on the critical items.

Ss were randomly assigned to one of three experimental conditions: conformity reinforcement (CR), neutral (N), and deviancy reinforcement (DR). Ss in the CR group were verbally reinforced by E saying, "*Good, that is right*," every time they *agreed* with the contrived consensus of the confederates on the critical items. Ss in the DR group were similarly reinforced by E every time they *disagreed* with the confederates on the critical items. Ss in the N group were not explicitly reinforced by E. Nothing was said after the buffer items, nor did the confederates at any time comment on an S's responses. The independent variable was the experimental treatment; the dependent variable was the S's conformity score.

RESULTS

To test the hypotheses of differences in conforming behavior due to experimental conditions and sex, the data were analyzed by means of a two-way (conditions-by-sex) analysis of variance with unequal Ns (12 pp. 234–245). Table 1 shows that the observed differences among the several subclasses are significant ($p < .01$) indicating that at least one of the components (experimental conditions, sex, or interaction) is significant. Therefore, specific tests of the hypotheses concerning conditions, sex, and interaction were made, and the analysis of variance for this also appears in Table 1. The only significant factor is that among conditions CR, N, and DR ($F = 15.56$, $p < .01$). There are no significant sex or interaction differences. Since there were no significant sex differences, the male and female samples were combined, and Tukey's gap tests (20) for comparing means in the analysis of variance reveal that Ss in the CR group conformed significantly more ($p < .01$) than those in the N group, who conformed significantly more ($p < .01$) than those in the DR group. Table 2 contains the means and standard deviations for the various subgroups.

To test the hypothesis that the verbal items elicit the greatest degree of conformity, that attitude items elicit the least degree of conformity and that the perceptual (geometrical) items elicit an intermediate degree of conformity, the Jonckheere distribution (13)—free k-sample test against ordered alternatives—was performed for the CR, N, and DR conditions separately, yielding Z values of 3.64, 6.94, and 12.08 respectively ($p < .01$).

DISCUSSION

The results indicate that verbal reinforcement for *agreeing* with a contrived group consensus increases the degree of conforming behavior.

Table 1 | **TWO-WAY (EXPERIMENTAL CONDITIONS*-BY-SEX) ANALYSIS OF VARIANCE OF CONFORMITY SCORES (FOR UNEQUAL Ns)**

Source	Sum of squares	df	Mean square	F	p
Experimental conditions	375.69	2	187.85	15.56	< .01
Sex	14.88	1	14.88	1.23	
Interaction	16.53	2	8.26	.68	
Among subclasses	407.10	5	81.42	6.75	< .01
Within-subclasses	833.03	69	12.07		
Total	1240.13	74			

* The experimental conditions are conformity reinforcement (CR), neutral (N), and deviancy reinforcement (DR).

Table **2** | MEANS AND STANDARD DEVIATIONS OF CONFORMITY SCORES FOR MALE, FEMALE, AND COMBINED SAMPLES UNDER THREE EXPERIMENTAL CONDITIONS

Sample	Experimental Conditions						Deviancy reinforcement		
	Conformity reinforcement			Neutral					
	N	*M*	*S.D.*	*N*	*M*	*S.D.*	*N*	*M*	*S.D.*
Male	14	10.43	3.79	12	6.17	3.08	14	4.14	1.96
Female	12	8.25	3.27	10	6.20	4.85	13	3.62	2.17
Combined	26	9.42	3.72	22	6.18	3.99	27	3.89	2.08

Similarly, reinforcement for *disagreeing* with a contrived group consensus decreases the degree of conformity (i.e., increases deviant behavior).

Verbal reinforcement is a potent force in shaping social behavior, often more potent than the objective state of affairs. From an early age, when a child is undergoing the socialization process, he is rewarded for imitating others and is often punished for attempting to be different: e.g., for not listening to his parents. Much of the individual's behavior (as he goes through grade school, high school, and college) is similarly shaped by reward and punishment. Likewise, the individual's behavior outside of classes is shaped by reward and punishment. Campbell (8) has pointed out that the more an individual is rewarded for nonconformity, the less often he will conform; and the more he is punished for nonconformity, the more he will conform.

In the experimental conformity situation the individual is faced with a discrepancy between the confederates' responses and what he knows or believes to be true. This discrepancy induces a conflict or a state of cognitive dissonance for S (11). (Another potential source of dissonance is between what a person privately believes to be true and what he publicly expresses.) The individual can reduce his dissonance via rationalizing: i.e., by redefining the situation and conforming.

In the neutral (N) situation, there are only two sets of opposing forces: the responses required by the stimulus materials and the responses required by the group pressure. For the Conformity-reinforcement (CR) and Deviancy-reinforcement (DR) groups, a third force is present: the reinforcing responses of the experimenter.

In the CR Group, the group pressures summate or interact with the pressures created by E's verbal reinforcement for conforming; and this tends to maximize conformity pressure and produce the greatest amount of conforming behavior. In the DR Group, the group conformity pressures oppose those created by E's verbal reinforcement for disagreeing with the group. Furthermore, in this case, E's reinforcements are congruent with what S believes to be the objective state of affairs. This tends to minimize conformity pressure and produce the least amount of conforming behavior. In the N Group, there is no reinforcement from E. The only pressures to conform come from the confederates, and the only pressures to deviate come from S himself. There is still conforming behavior because S, in his previous life history, has been reinforced for conforming and punished for nonconformity. However, the conforming behavior is less than that for the CR Group, but greater than that for the DR Group.

Sex differences in conforming behavior did not occur. Most other investigators (3, 9) have found that females conform more than males do. However, in most of these cases the sex of the S has been the same as that of the confederates. In this present study, all the confederates were males while there were both male and female Ss. It is possible that females conform less to male confederates than they do to female confederates. This may be because they identify more with other females and are more concerned with receiving social approval from females as a group than from males as a group. The presence of male confederates, therefore, may have reduced the conforming behavior of the females to the conformity level of the males.

In terms of the amount of conforming behavior, the type of stimulus material was also a factor. For all three experimental groups

(CR, N, and DR), there was the greatest amount of conformity to the verbal items; the least amount, to the attitude items; and an intermediate amount, to the perceptual (geometrical) items. The verbal items were composed primarily of obscure facts, and S was not expected to know or be able immediately to verify the correct answers. Therefore S, presumably, would be willing to conform to the answers of the confederates who had both prestige value and more educational experience than Ss. Since individuals have a strong emotional or personal commitment to their attitudes, these would be most resistant to change and, for these items, pressure would produce the least amount of conforming behavior. Since Ss, presumably, could verify the perceptual items via visual inspection these items would also be resistant to change. However, S would have no strong personal or emotional commitment to these items and, therefore, would be more likely to conform to these than to the attitude items. The results of the relative effects of the different kinds of stimuli on conforming behavior can be considered only as exploratory since there were only eight verbal, nine perceptual, and three attitude items.

In general, conformity is found to be greatest when Ss are verbally reinforced (by E) for agreeing with a contrived group consensus and is least when Ss are reinforced for disagreeing with the group. It is intermediate when Ss are not reinforced by E. There were no sex differences in conformity, but the type of stimulus material affects the amount of conforming behavior.

REFERENCES

1. Applezweig, M. H., & Moeller, G. Conforming behavior and personality variables. Tech. Rep. No. 8, Contract No. NR 996 (02), Connecticut College, New London, Conn., 1958.
2. Asch, S. E. Effects of group pressure upon the modification and distortion of judgments. In H. Guetzkow (Ed.), *Groups, Leadership and Men*. Pittsburgh: Carnegie Press, 1951.
3. ————. Studies of independence and conformity: I. A minority of one against a unanimous majority. *Psychol. Monog.*, 1956, **70**, Whole No. 416.

4. Bass, B. M. Conformity, deviation and a general theory of interpersonal behavior. In I. A. Berg & B. M. Bass (Eds.), *Conformity and Deviation*. New York: Harper, 1961. Pp. 38–100.
5. Beloff, H. Two forms of social conformity: Acquiescence and conventionality. *J. Abn. & Soc. Psychol.*, 1958, **56**, 99–104.
6. Berg, I. A. & Bass, B. M. Conformity and Deviation. New York: Harper, 1961.
7. Blake, R. R., Nelson, H., & Mouton, J. The generality of conformity behavior as a function of factual anchorage, difficulty of task and amount of social pressure. In R. R. Blake & H. Helson (Eds.), *Adaptability Screening of Flying Personnel: Situational and Personal Factors in Conforming Behavior*. Randolph Field, San Antonio, Texas: School of Aviation Medicine, USAF, 1956. Pp. 27–34.
8. Campbell, D. T. Conformity in psychology's theories of acquired behavioral dispositions. In I. A. Berg & B. M. Bass (Eds.), *Conformity and Deviation*. New York: Harper, 1961. Pp. 101–142.
9. Crutchfield, R. S. Conformity and character. *Amer. Psychologist,* 1956, **10**, 191–198.
10. Endler, N. S. Social conformity in perception of the autokinetic effect. *J. Abn. & Soc. Psychol.*, 1960, **60**, 489–490.
11. Festinger, L. A. Theory of Cognitive Dissonance. Stanford, Calif.: Stanford Univer. Press, 1957.
12. Johnson, P. O., & Jackson, R. W. B. Modern Statistical Methods: Descriptive and Inductive. Chicago: Rand McNally, 1959.
13. Jonckheere, A. R. A distribution-free k-sample test against ordered alternatives. *Biometrika,* 1954, **41**, 133–145.
14. Jones, E. E., Wells, H. H., & Torrey, R. Some effects of feedback from the experimenter on conformity behavior. *J. Abn. & Soc. Psychol.*, 1958, **57**, 207–213.
15. Krech, D., Crutchfield, R. S., & Ballachey, E. L. Individual in Society. New York: McGraw-Hill, 1962.
16. Luchins, A. S. On agreement with another's judgment. *J. Abn. & Soc. Psychol.*, 1944, **39**, 97–111.
17. Oliver, B., & Alexander, S. Reinforcing effects of congruent group judgments on conforming behavior. Paper read at the annual meeting of the Midwestern Psychological Association, Chicago, May 4, 1963.
18. Schein, E. H. The effect of reward on adult imitative behavior. *J. Abn. & Soc. Psychol.*, 1954, **49**, 389–395.
19. Tuddenham, R. D. Some correlates of yielding to a distorted group norm. Tech. Rep. No.

8, Contract NR 170–159, University of California, Berkeley, 1958.

20. Tukey, J. W. Comparing individual means in a analysis of variance. *Biometrics*, 1949, **5,** 99–114.

21. Walker, E. L., & Heyns, R. W. An Anatomy for Conformity. Englewood Cliffs, N.J.: Prentice-Hall, 1962.

Selection **38**

SOCIAL
REINFORCER
EFFECTIVENESS AS
A FUNCTION OF
THE RELATIONSHIP
BETWEEN CHILD
AND ADULT*

NORMA McCOY
EDWARD ZIGLER
Yale University

The hypothesis tested was that the child's positive- and negative-reaction tendencies interact to determine an adult's effectiveness as a reinforcer. Before administering a simple 2-part satiation task under conditions of positive reinforcement, 36 grade-school boys were divided randomly into 3 conditions. In the stranger (St) condition Ss had no prior contact with E. In the familiar-neutral (FN) imprint condition Ss participated in 3 sessions at weekly intervals during which E provided attractive art materials but interacted minimally. The familiar-positive (FP) was identical to the FN condition except that E interacted freely and positively with Ss. Results showed that the FP group elected to play the experimental game significantly longer than the FN group (p < .05) which played significantly longer than the St group (p < .001). The pattern of results in time spent in Part I vs. Part II suggested that the experimental conditions influenced both the child's positive- and negative-reaction tendencies.

Considerable evidence has now been presented indicating that a number of verbal responses, for example, "good," "right,"

* Reprinted from Norma McCoy and Edward Zigler, "Social Reinforcer Effectiveness as a Function of the Relationship between Child and Adult," *Journal of Personality and Social Psychology*, 1: 604–612, 1965. Copyright 1965 by the American Psychological Association and reproduced by permission.

emitted by adults are effective in influencing children's behavior. Attention has been given recently to the degree to which a variety of situational, subject, and experimenter variables influence the effectiveness of these social reinforcers (Gewirtz, 1954; Gewirtz & Baer, 1958a, 1958b; Gewirtz, Baer, & Roth, 1958; Patterson, 1959; Patterson, Littman, & Hinsey, in press; Patterson & Ludwig 1961; Stevenson, 1961; Stevenson, Hickman, & Knights, 1963; Walters & Ray, 1960; Zigler, 1961, 1963b, in press; Zigler & Kanzer, 1962; Zigler & Williams, 1963). Although the effects of a number of variables have been demonstrated, the process or processes by which these verbal responses of an adult acquire their reinforcing properties are far from clear. The simplest and most commonly advanced view is that parents or caretakers frequently pair positive verbal responses with primary reinforcers, and these responses thus acquire their reinforcing property. This view further holds that through generalization, these responses are also reinforcing when employed by other adults.

The difficulty in testing this position can be seen in recent studies which compare the effectiveness of social reinforcers dispensed by the mother or father of the child being reinforced or by a strange adult (Patterson, 1959; Patterson et al., in press; Patterson & Ludwig, 1961; Stevenson et al., 1963). The most logical prediction generated by the number-of-pairings position is that social reinforcers dispensed by parents would be more effective than social reinforcers dispensed by strange adults. However, Patterson (1959) found that although both fathers and strangers were positively reinforcing, fathers were not generally more reinforcing than were strange adults. Taking a somewhat different tack, Stevenson et al. (1963) predicted that parents would be less effective social reinforcers than would strange adults. Although subscribing to the number-of-pairings position, these investigators felt that the continuous supportive role played by parents results in the child being relatively satiated on his parents' supportive comments. Although Stevenson et al. did find that strangers were more effective reinforcing agents than were parents, their results remain surprising. These investigators, employing a measure involving the change in the rate of responding with the onset of reinforcement, found that the fathers' supportive comments were negative reinforcers for both boys and girls and that the mothers' supportive comments were negative reinforcers for boys and positive reinforcers for girls. These findings are hardly in keeping with the number-of-pairings hypothesis even when augmented by the satiation notion. In order to explain their findings, Stevenson et al. suggested that fathers in particular and men in general induced anxiety in children which inflated the rate of responding during the base period. The view that greater identification exists between girls and their mothers than between boys and either their mothers or fathers was employed to explain the finding that mothers and female adults were effective positive reinforcers with girls.

These explanations certainly suggest that it is inappropriate to view social reinforcers as operating in an automatic or mechanical manner or that the key variable is simply the number of pairings that these reinforcers have had with primary reinforcement. It would appear, rather, that the reinforcing agent and the responses he makes are complex stimuli which activate a variety of emotional, motivational, and cognitive responses. Depending upon the particular measure of reinforcer effectiveness employed, the responses of the child thus activated can result in either a facilitation or an attenuation in the effectiveness of the adults' supportive comments. Although reporting certain findings not in keeping with those of Stevenson et al. (1963), Patterson et al. (in press) have also taken the view that the reinforcing adult is best conceptualized as being both a general reinforcer and a complex cue eliciting a wide array of responses.

The problem in conceptualizing the reinforcing adult as the elicitor of responses is the difficulty in predicting just what responses he elicits and how such responses influence his effectiveness as a generalized reinforcer. The complexity of this problem has been noted by Patterson et al. (in press), and their effort to unravel it by investigating the relationship between parental practices in the home and the effectiveness of parents as reinforcers has been truly pioneering work.

Zigler and his colleagues (cf. Zigler, 1963b, in press) have also asserted that the typical experimental situation in which an adult verbally reinforces a child must be viewed as a complex interaction between adult and child. While also treating the adult as an elicitor, they have not been concerned with the entire spectrum of responses which are elicited in the child as a function of his total social conditioning history. Instead they have focused on those general tendencies elicited by the reinforcing adult which influence the adult's effectiveness as a reinforcer independent of the particular task being employed to assess this effectiveness. The view here is that while the adult is both an elicitor and a reinforcer, it should be possible to deduce certain general principles which determine the adult's reinforcer effectiveness. These investigators have argued that the history of every child is such that any adult elicits both a positive (approach) and negative (avoidance) reaction tendency. Thus, every interaction between an adult and child is viewed as a conflict situation for the child.

Stating that the reinforcing adult elicits a positive-reaction tendency in the child is simply another way of asserting that the history of all children is such that adults have been paired with primary or secondary reinforcers frequently enough to make adults general-positive reinforcers. What has received minimal attention in the literature is that parents and adults are not only general-positive reinforcers but through their history of pairings with punishing events, are general-negative reinforcers as well. Thus, how reinforcing the adult is for the child will depend on the interaction between both these positive and negative tendencies. Clearly, then, the relative magnitude of the tendencies will depend on the relative amount of positive and negative experiences the child has had with adults. Within such a framework the child minimally affected by social reinforcers would not necessarily be viewed as having low motivation for social reinforcers; he could be one whose negative-reaction tendency inhibits him from freely responding in order to secure positive reinforcement.

In the present study, the hypothesis was tested that the child's positive- and negative-reaction tendencies interact in determining an adult's effectiveness as a reinforcer. The assumption was made that the magnitude of these tendencies is affected by the general quality of the relationship existing between the reinforcing adult and the child. Three experimental conditions were employed. In the first, the reinforcing adult was a stranger; in the second, she was a familiar but neutral person; and in the third, she was a familiar and positive person. The general prediction tested was that the adult would be least reinforcing in the first condition, more reinforcing in the second condition, and most reinforcing in the third condition. This prediction was derived from the position that the strange adult would elicit the child's negative-reaction tendency which in turn would reduce the adult's effectiveness as a social reinforcer. In the familiar-neutral condition, the child would have learned that this particular adult was not a punishing agent; and this knowledge would reduce the child's negative-reaction tendency towards the adult prior to the reinforcing situation. The familiar-positive condition was viewed as one in which not only the negative-reaction tendency would be reduced but one in which the positive tendency would be enhanced as well.

A test of this position demands independent measures of both the child's positive and negative tendencies. As in previous studies (Zigler, 1961; Zigler, Hodgden, & Stevenson, 1958), the total time the child elected to play a two-part satiation task was employed as the measure of his positive-reaction tendency. A cosatiation index, that is, a score reflecting the relative amount of time spent playing each part of the game, was employed to assess the child's negative-reaction tendency. That this score is a valid measure of a child's negative-reaction tendency is suggested by a number of earlier studies in which relatively low cosatiation scores were found for subjects whose life histories were characterized by a high incidence of negative social encounters (Kounin, 1941; Zigler, 1961; Zigler et al., 1958). The rationale of this measure as advanced by Zigler (1961) is as follows: If the child has no negative-reaction tendency, he should play the first part of the game until he is satiated on the social reinforcers being dispensed. Such a child should play the second part for a shorter period of time than the first. The greater the negative-reaction tendency of the child, the shorter should be the time he spends on the first part. However, during the first part he is socially reinforced;

he learns that the adult is not punishing and furthermore, he discovers upon the termination of the first part that he can indeed end the interaction whenever he likes. This should reduce the negative-reaction tendency with which he begins the second part. How long such a child plays the second part depends upon how large a negative-reaction tendency was present to be reduced during the first part. The greater the child's initial negative-reaction tendency, the greater the likelihood that he will play the second part longer than the first.

Further evidence that the cosatiation index is a valid measure of the child's negative-reaction tendency was provided by Shallenberger and Zigler (1961). These investigators found that both normal and retarded children who received the negative pretraining condition prior to the two-part game had lower cosatiation scores than children in a positive pretraining condition. For normal children, evidence to date suggests that the reduction in the negative-reaction tendency during Part I of the game is balanced by the satiation effects. Such children play Part II for about the same length of time as Part I. Thus, employing the two-part cosatiation procedure, the specific prediction made was that children in the stranger condition should play Part II about as long as Part I, while both familiar groups should show a marked decrease in playing time from Part I to Part II.

METHOD

Subjects

The sample consisted of 36 first- and second-grade boys attending the Edgewood Elementary School in New Haven, Connecticut. The school was located in a middle-class neighborhood having a predominantly Jewish population. Subjects were picked at random from all first- and second-grade boys with the restriction that no boy was included who was judged a behavior problem by the teacher or principal. The mean age of the group was 7.2 years. The sample was restricted to boys in order to avoid the complications of sex effects.

Experimenter

The experimenter was a 28-year-old female PhD in child psychology who had had considerable experience testing subjects in studies investigating social reinforcement effects on children. The experimenter was aware of the hypothesis under test, and any bias that this may have produced must be considered an uncontrolled variable in this experiment. In order to diminish the effect of any such bias, a highly structured procedure was employed during the administration of the experimental game. Considering the care exercised by the experimenter, it is the authors' belief that any examiner bias had minimal effect on the findings.

Experimental manipulations

The sample was divided randomly into three groups of 12 boys each with the restriction that the mean CA of the groups be approximately equal. The three experimental conditions were:

Stranger (St). The experimenter had no contact with any of the subjects in this condition prior to the administration of the experimental task.

Familiar-Neutral (FN). On three occasions the 12 subjects of this condition were taken from the classroom in two groups of 6 subjects each. The three sessions were separated by intervals of 1 week. Each group of 6 subjects was taken to an empty classroom and given drawing paper and attractive art materials consisting of pastels in 12 colors in Session 1, felt-top markers in 6 colors in Session 2, and presto paints in 6 colors in Session 3.

The instructions were as follows:

> Hello. As you remember [Sessions 2 and 3 only] my name is Miss —— and I've brought some things for you to have some fun with. I will give each of you some of these pastels [markers, paints] and some paper and you can make a picture of anything you like. You can begin as soon as you get some materials.

Following the instructions the experimenter distributed the art materials and told the subjects that she was going to be busy at her desk (located in the front of the room) and requested that they work quietly until it was time to return to their classroom. Any further comments by a child were reacted to minimally or not at all. Questions were answered briefly and the child was reminded to work quietly because the experimenter was very busy. If the children attempted to interact among themselves, the experimenter again requested that they work quietly. Very few children made more than one attempt to interact with the experimenter, and very little effort was required to keep the children quiet.

Familiar-Positive (FP). The initial procedure for this group was the same as for the FN group. Following the instructions, however, the experimenter responded at some length to all questions and comments as she passed out the materials. As the children began to work, the experimenter approached each boy individually and talked with him about what he was drawing. The experimenter then continued to interact with each subject attempting to establish a warm, positive relationship by being complimentary, helpful, and responsive. By the end of the three sessions the experimenter was employing the subjects' first names in her interactions with them. One boy in this group was absent from Session 3 but was retained in the study. Another boy was withdrawn from school during the course of the study; and this group, therefore, had 11 rather than 12 subjects.

Experimental game (marble-in-the-hole)

The experimental game was a two-part satiation task consisting of a simple monotonous repetitive game called Marble-in-the-Hole which has been described previously (Zigler, 1961, 1963a). The game was made up of a wooden box having two holes on top. Inside the box was a chute connecting the holes with a single opening at the bottom of the box. The opening was filled with green and yellow marbles, thus insuring the subject a steady supply of marbles. The apparatus was automated so that it recorded the length of time the child played and the number of marbles he inserted. The subject's task was to insert a marble of one color into one hole and a marble of another color into the other hole.

Part I The game was placed in front of the subject with the experimenter directly behind it and facing the child. The experimenter said:

> Hello. As you remember [with FN and FP subjects only] my name is Miss ——, and we are going to play some games today. This is a game we call Marble-in-the-Hole. I'll tell you how to play it. You see these marbles. Some of them are green and some of them are yellow. They go in these holes. The green ones go in this hole [the experimenter's left] and the yellow ones go in this hole [the experimenter's right] [the experimenter pointed to the appropriate holes]. Now show me a green marble. Put it in the hole it goes in. Now show me a yellow marble. Put it in the hole it goes in. You can put as many marbles in the holes as

you want to. You tell me when you want to stop. Remember, when you want to stop, just tell me. OK, ready? Begin.

The subject then played the game until he indicated that he wished to stop, either by telling the experimenter he wanted to stop or by not inserting a marble for 30 seconds. A 15-minute time limit was used.

Part II   After the subject indicated that he wished to stop, the experimenter said:

> Now I'll tell you how to play *this* game. This time we put the yellow marbles in this hole [the experimenter's left] and the green marbles in this hole [the experimenter's right]. Put a yellow marble where it goes. You can put as many marbles in the holes as you want to. You tell me when you want to stop. Remember, when you want to stop just tell me. OK, ready? Begin.

The subject again played the game until he indicated that he wished to stop, either by telling the experimenter he wanted to stop or by not inserting a marble for 30 seconds. A 15-minute time limit again was employed.

Procedure

The St subjects were administered the Marble-in-the-Hole game prior to any contact between the experimenter and FN and FP subjects. This was done so that none of the St subjects would become familiar with the experimenter by seeing her in the school or by hearing about her from subjects in the other groups. The FN and FP subjects were administered the Marble-in-the-Hole game 1 week following their third experimental session.

The subjects were tested individually in a small conference room. The subject was verbally reinforced twice a minute for as long as he played either part of the game. (The decision to verbally reinforce the child rather than to employ attention alone as a reinforcer was made in light of studies which have indicated that an attention-only condition has differential effects depending upon the reinforcement condition that has preceded it—Crandall, 1963; Stevenson & Snyder, 1960. While it might appear that an attention-only condition would provide the purest measure of the child's reaction tendencies, the particular contrast effects introduced by such a procedure mitigated against its use.) Reinforcements were administered approximately at the 15-second and 45-second points within each minute. Five statements were used: "You're doing very well," "That's very good," "You know how to play this game very well," "That's fine," and "You're really good at this game." These statements were made in a predetermined random order established separately for each subject. The experimenter was warm and friendly, smiling and nodding when administering the praise; but she did not respond to any attempts by the subject to engage her in conversation. If the subject dropped a marble on the floor, he was told not to pursue it but simply to continue playing the game.

RESULTS

The three groups' time scores are presented in Table 1 and Figure 1. Since the means and variances of these scores were correlated, a logarithmic transformation of the time scores (log $X + 1$) was made. The log times spent by each group on each part of the game were subjected to a Lindquist Type I analysis of variance (Lindquist, 1956). The method of unweighted means was used to handle the unequal number of subjects in three groups. The results of this analysis are presented in Table 2.

A Pearson r of .977 was found between the subject's total time scores and the total num-

Table **1 |** PERFORMANCE OF THE THREE GROUPS ON THE EXPERIMENTAL GAME

| Group | N | Mean Time | | | | | | Part I — Part II | Part I — Part II |
| | | Part I | | Part II | | Total | | Part II | Part I + Part II |
		Minutes	Log minutes	Minutes	Log minutes	Minutes	Log minutes		
Stranger	12	1.22	.3095	1.31	.3193	2.53	.6288	−.10	.0071
Familiar-neutral	12	6.72	.7327	2.85	.4702	9.57	1.2029	3.87	.3203
Familiar-positive	11	7.96	.8725	5.39	.6815	13.35	1.5540	2.56	.2455

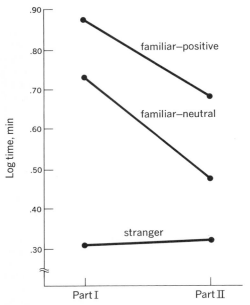

Figure 1   Mean log time spent by the three groups in Part I and Part II of Marble-in-the-Hole game.

ber of marbles inserted. An analysis of the number-of-marbles-inserted data resulted in findings highly similar to those found with the time scores.

As can be seen in Figure 1, the significant groups effect supported the prediction concerning how the groups would differ in the total time spent on the game. Further analyses of the total log-time scores using the between-subjects mean square as the estimate of error variance revealed that each group differed significantly from the other two. The FP group played significantly longer than both the FN ($t = 2.23$, $p < .05$) and St ($t = 5.88$, $p < .001$) groups. The St group also differed significantly from the FN group ($t = 3.73$, $p < .001$). The significant Parts effect reflected the overall tendency of the three groups to play Part I (M log $= .6315$) longer than Part II (M log $= .4849$). However, the St group did not contribute to this effect; and it was the failure of this group to decrease from Part I to Part II that resulted in the significant Conditions × Parts interaction. The performance pattern of the three groups on the two parts of the game

supported the prediction that the two familiar groups would evidence a greater decrease from Part I to Part II than would the St group.

The prediction concerning the decrease from Part I to Part II was tested further through a direct examination of difference scores for each subject. A variation of Kounin's (1941) cosatiation index was employed to compute relative difference scores (Part I − Part II/Part I + Part II). Mean relative difference scores for each of the three groups are presented in Table 1. A simple one-way analysis of variance of these scores was significant ($F_{2/32} = 3.64$, $p < .05$). Further analyses revealed that the FN group had a significantly ($t = 2.59$, $p < .02$) greater decrease from Part I to Part II than did the St group. The difference between the FP and FN groups was not significant ($t < 1$), while the difference between the FP and St groups reached a borderline level of significance ($t = 1.93$, $p < .10$).

An examination was made of the number of subjects in each group who played Part II longer than Part I. As noted earlier, this pattern has been found in socially deprived children and in normal children who had negative experiences with an adult prior to being reinforced on the Marble-in-the-Hole game. The number of children playing Part II longer than Part I in the St, FN, and FP groups was seven, one, and two, respectively. The familiar groups were combined and a 2 × 2 contingency table was set up. Employing the Fisher exact test, this difference was found to be significant ($p < .01$). However, one subject in each of the familiar groups played both parts of the game for the total time allowed (15 minutes). Since it was possible that these two subjects might have played Part II longer than Part I had longer playing times been permitted, the analysis reported immediately above was recomputed with these two subjects excluded. The resulting differences remained significant ($p < .02$).

DISCUSSION

The findings of the present study clearly indicate that the nature of the relationship between a child and an adult influences how effective the adult will be in reinforcing the child's behavior. The experimenter was found to be significantly more reinforcing in the FP than in the FN condition. In turn, the experimenter was significantly more reinforcing in the FN than in the St condition. The significant differences between the groups in the decrease in playing time from Part I to Part II lent support to the view that one factor resulting in an increase in an adult's effectiveness as a social reinforcer is a decrease in the child's negative-reaction tendency, that is, wariness of and/or reluctance to interact with an adult. However, the total pattern of performance of the three groups on the two parts of the game indicated that the enhanced effectiveness of the adult cannot be attributed solely to the reduction of the negative tendency.

If a reduction in the negative tendency were the only pertinent factor, then the FP group would show a greater decrease from Part I to Part II than would the FN group. However, the FP group not only played the total game longer than the FN group but also did not evidence any greater decrease from Part I to Part II. The overall findings thus suggest that the increased effectiveness of the adult in the FP condition was due to both a reduction in the negative-reaction tendency and to an increase in the positive-reaction tendency. It would appear that the reinforcers dispensed by the experimenter take on increased reinforcement value if the adult has been associated with warm, positive experiences in the child's recent past. This seems to be such a straightforward explanation that one is tempted to explain all the findings in terms of differential increase in the positive tendency.

Thus, one could argue that the differences in total time found between the three groups reflect differences in the positive-reaction tendency and that the large decrease between Part I and Part II found for the familiar groups reflects nothing but fatigue and other satiation effects caused by playing Part I of the game so long. However, the finding that over half of the subjects in the St group play Part II longer than Part I constitutes strong evidence against this more simple view. The very nature of the game is such that one would expect every child to play the second part of the game for a shorter period than the first due to satiation and fatigue effects. No argument employing the positive tendency alone is capable of encompassing the finding that the majority of the children in the St group played Part II longer than Part I. As demonstrated by Shallenberger and Zigler (1961), playing the second part longer than the first is the clearest indication that a negative-reaction tendency is present. It would thus appear that the most appropriate conclusion derivable from the findings is that the treatment conditions differentially affected both the positive- and negative-reaction tendencies of the groups.

The results of the present study appear capable of shedding light on the effectiveness of parents versus strangers as social reinforcers. If it is assumed that parents have been more frequently associated with punishing events than have strange adults, then one would expect the negative-reaction tendency elicited by parents to be higher than that elicited by strange adults. It would be quite possible for this negative tendency to interfere with the parent's effectiveness as a reinforcer and given our usual experimental procedures, make him appear less effective as a social reinforcer than he really is. Given differences in the age of their children, their procedures, and the actual parents employed, it is not surprising that investigators have found that parents can be either negative or positive reinforcers (Patterson et al., in press; Stevenson et al., 1963). Certainly the context in which the parent serves as a reinforcer for his child and the particular child-rearing practices that have been employed by that parent would be factors influencing the magnitude of the child's negative-reaction tendency during the experimental task.

The findings of the present study also appear to be related to those of Sacks (1952) who investigated the effect of treatment con-

Table **2** | ANALYSIS OF VARIANCE OF LOG-TIME SCORES

Source	df	MS	F
Conditions (A)	2	1.2622	8.87**
Between subjects	32	.1422	
Parts (B)	1	.3761	13.51**
A × B	2	.1190	4.28*
Within subjects	32	.0278	

* $p < .025$.

** $p < .001$.

ditions very similar to those employed in the present study on intelligence test performance. Three groups of children were tested. Following this, one group had positive interactions with the examiner, a second group had interactions similar to those employed in our neutral condition, and a third group had no interactions with the examiner. Upon retest, Sacks found that subjects in the first group showed the greatest increment; subjects in the second group the next largest increment; and those in the control group, the smallest increment in mean IQ. These findings suggest that negative-reaction tendencies evoked by a strange examiner interfere with children's test performance. Very high negative-reaction tendencies could explain the large discrepancies that have been reported (Sarason & Gladwin, 1958) between the test performance of institutionalized retardates, typically obtained while the child is interacting with a stranger, and the retardate's day-to-day capabilities, typically assessed through the child's interactions with familiar adults. Further investigations of the relative magnitudes of the positive- and negative-reaction tendencies referred to in this paper should also aid us in our understanding of the autistic child as well as illuminating the current controversy over whether extreme social deprivation leads to an increase in the interaction of the socially deprived individual or whether such deprivation leads to apathy and/or withdrawal (Cox, 1953; Goldfarb, 1953; Irvine, 1952; Wittenborn & Myers, 1957).

One final note is in order. Throughout this study longer playing time of the child has been interpreted as being due to the greater reinforcer effectiveness of the adult. The argument can be made that while longer playing time may reflect a heightened positive tendency towards the adult, it does not necessarily indicate that the adult has taken on greater social reinforcer effectiveness. The central issue here is whether the adult is effective only in maintaining the child's interaction with him or whether the adult has acquired a generally enhanced reinforcer effectiveness in respect to specific responses of the child. The investigation of the relationship between the child's positive or negative feelings towards an adult and that adult's effectiveness in shaping various behaviors of the child would appear to be an inviting area of future research.

REFERENCES

Cox, F. The origins of the dependency drive. *Australian Journal of Psychology*, 1953, **5**, 64–73.

Crandall, Virginia C. Reinforcement effects of adult reactions and nonreactions on children's achievement expectations. *Child Development*, 1963, **34**, 335–354.

Gewirtz, J. L. Three determinants of attention-seeking in young children. *Monographs of the Society for Research in Child Development*, 1954, **19** (2).

Gewirtz, J. L., & Baer, D. M. Deprivation and satiation of social reinforcers as drive conditions. *Journal of Abnormal and Social Psychology*, 1958, **57**, 165–172. (a)

Gewirtz, J. L., & Baer, D. M. The effect of brief social deprivation on behaviors for a social reinforcer. *Journal of Abnormal and Social Psychology*, 1958, **56**, 49–56. (b)

Gewirtz, J. L., Baer, D. M., & Roth, C. H. A note on the similar effects of low social availability of an adult and brief social deprivation on young children's behavior. *Child Development*, 1958, **29**, 149–152.

Goldfarb, W. The effects of early institutional care on adolescent personality. *Journal of Experimental Education*, 1953, **12**, 106–129.

Irvine, E. Observations on the aims and methods of child rearing in communal settlements in Israel. *Human Relations*, 1952, **5**, 247–275.

Kounin, J. Experimental studies of rigidity: I. The measurement of rigidity in normal and feeble-minded persons. *Character and Personality*, 1941, **9**, 251–273.

Lindquist, E. F. *Design and analysis of experiments in psychology and education.* Boston: Houghton Mifflin, 1956.

Patterson, G. R. A preliminary report: Fathers as reinforcing agents. Paper read at Western Psychological Association, San Diego, April 1959.

Patterson, G. R., Littman, R. A., & Hinsey C. Parents as social stimuli. *Child Development*, in press.

Patterson, G. R., & Ludwig, M. Parents as reinforcing agents. Paper read at Oregon Psychological Association, Eugene, April 1961.

Sacks, Elinor L. Intelligence scores as a function of experimentally established social relationships between child and examiner. *Journal of Abnormal and Social Psychology*, 1952, **47**, 354–358.

Sarason, S. B., & Gladwin, T. Psychological and cultural problems in mental subnormality: A review of research. *Genetic Psychology Monographs*, 1958, **57**, 7–269.

Shallenberger, Patricia, & Zigler, E. Rigidity, negative reaction tendencies, and cosatiation effects in normal and feebleminded children. *Journal* of *Abnormal and Social Psychology*, 1961, **63**, 20–26.

Stevenson, H. W. Social reinforcement with children as a function of CA, sex of *E*, and sex of *S*. *Journal of Abnormal and Social Psychology*, 1961, **63**, 147–154.

Stevenson, H. W., Hickman, R. K., & Knights, R. M. Parents and strangers as reinforcing agents for children's performance. *Journal of Abnormal and Social Psychology*, 1963, **67**, 183–189.

Stevenson, H. W., & Synder, Lelia C. Performance as a function of the interaction of incentive conditions. *Journal of Personality*, 1960, **28**, 1–11.

Walters, R., & Ray, E. Anxiety, isolation, and reinforcer effectiveness. *Journal of Personality*, 1960, **28**, 258–367.

Wittenborn, J., & Myers, B. *The placement of adoptive children*. Springfield, Ill.: Charles C. Thomas, 1957.

Zigler, E. Social deprivation and rigidity in the performance of feebleminded children. *Journal of Abnormal and Social Psychology*, 1961, **62**, 413–421.

Zigler, E. Rigidity and social reinforcement effects in the performance of institutionalized and non-institutionalized normal and retarded children. *Journal of Personality*, 1963, **31**, 258–269. (a)

Zigler, E. Social reinforcement, environmental conditions, and the child. *American Journal of Orthopsychiatry*, 1963, **33**, 614–623. (b)

Zigler, E. The effect of social reinforcement on normal and socially deprived children. *Journal of Genetic Psychology*, in press.

Zigler, E., Hodgden, L., & Stevenson, H. W. The effect of support on the performance of normal and feebleminded children. *Journal of Personality*, 1958, **26**, 106–122.

Zigler, E., & Kanzer, P. The effectiveness of two classes of verbal reinforcers on the performance of middle- and lower-class children. *Journal of Personality*, 1962, **30**, 157–163.

Zigler, E., & Williams, Joanna. Institutionalization and the effectiveness of social reinforcement: A three-year follow-up study. *Journal of Abnormal and Social Psychology*, 1963, **66**, 197–205.

THINKING, REASONING, AND PROBLEM SOLVING

8

Although the experimental evidence indicates that lower animals are capable of rudimentary representational processes, man is superior to his mammalian relatives in his ability to manipulate symbols of objects and relationships in his environment, that is, to think. Defining thinking as the covert manipulation of symbols makes the term include a wide variety of mental activity ranging from the visual imagery characteristic of dreams and fantasy to the manipulation of verbal symbols involved in problem solving. In this chapter we are concerned primarily with the latter type of thinking. Such thinking makes use of the results of previous learning so that certain neural correlates of symbols are activated in sequences. In the case of concept formation and other creative thinking, the symbols are put together in new and unique ways.

BIOLOGICAL FACTORS

Earlier research by Dr. Edward L. Bennett, a biochemist, and psychologists David Krech and Mark R. Rosenzweig had indicated that being raised in an enriched environment resulted in an increase in the total amount of brain cholinesterase, a substance which is important in synaptic transmission. In the experiment reported as Selection 39, Krech, Rosenzweig, and Bennett attempted to replicate this finding and to determine if these biochemical changes are related to enhanced problem-solving ability. They varied the early experience of two groups by raising one group in an enriched environment and the other in an impoverished environment. The rats were then tested on a problem-solving task involving discrimination reversal. Their results clearly indicate that the animals which were raised in the complex environment solved the discrimination reversal better than the isolated control animals. Furthermore, they obtained a high correlation between both morphological (brain size) and biochemical (cholinesterase ratios) indices and problem-solving ability. When added to the experiments discussed by Jacobson (Selection 31), by Miller (Selections 14 and 22), and by Heath (Selection 62), these results support the expectation that even more significant discoveries regarding the biochemical basis of behavior will be emerging within the next decade.

PSYCHOLOGICAL FACTORS

An equally exciting area of research which promises great breakthroughs in the near future and which has already greatly boosted our knowledge store is the computer simulation of psychological processes. The importance of such simulation is indicated by Dr. Carl I. Hovland (Selection 40). He points out that if a computer can be programmed in such a way as to reproduce the behavioral outcome of human beings in problem-solving tasks, then indeed we know a good deal about the process of problem solving. This is to say that computer simulation can serve as a test of the accuracy of our theoretical models of behavior. It should be noted in this context that it would be just as troublesome to the computer-simulation scientist if the computer did better than human subjects as if it did worse. Both events would indicate that something was wrong with the simulation program. A second important advantage of computer simulation is its predictive capacity. New behaviors may be tested by modifications of the program. And third, many complex variables may be manipulated at once. In concluding, Hovland puts down the specter that "thinking" machines will eventually displace man. On the contrary, they will free him to be truly human by relieving him from machinelike functions.

In Selection 41, Dr. Ian M. L. Hunter presents evidence that specific sets facilitate the solution of anagram problems. It is likely that this facilitation is dependent upon the activation of verbal mediators.[1] Thus if you tell a person that the anagram spells the name of an animal, he no longer has to try out and discard possible solutions regarding plants, trees, etc.

SOCIOCULTURAL FACTORS

In many actual problem-solving situations, the solution is not attained or is greatly retarded because the correct general category of ideas or associations is not emitted. Sometimes the person tends to block, to run dry of possible solutions, or to become fixated on a wrong approach. His "guessing" or hypothesizing becomes prematurely narrowed to a small set of ideas which excludes the category of ideas which, if explored, might lead to successful solution. In such problem situations a reasonable approach would seem to be to rely on a group of persons rather than a single individual. We would thus expect that there would be a better chance of "getting in the right ball park." A particular approach to group problem solving which has received considerable attention in business and industry has been called "brainstorming." Consistent with the above analysis, Taylor, Berry, and Block (Selection 42) note that the basic assumption of brainstorming is that the larger the number of ideas produced, the greater the probability of achieving an effective solution.

Taylor et al. point out that common sense and informal experience with this technique seem to indicate that groups do produce more ideas and are thus more effective than individuals. However, a scientific evaluation of brainstorming requires more adequately controlled experimentation and statistical evaluation. They also note that it is not adequate simply to compare average group performance to average individual performances, since by virtue of being composed of several individuals the group should most certainly produce more ideas than the average individual. Thus, they make use of a "nominal-group" control procedure in which persons who have actually worked on the problems alone are combined at random to form a "group" equal in size to the real groups which performed together. Their results indicate that, as expected, the real groups produced more ideas than did the individuals. However, when the real groups were compared with the "nominal groups," the results were contrary to expectation, that is, the nominal groups produced significantly more ideas than did the real groups. Further, analysis of the results indicated that the real groups were also inferior to the nominal groups in terms of uniqueness and quality of ideas. The authors conclude that to the extent that the results may be generalized, brainstorming inhibits rather than facilitates creative thinking. They further suggest that the inhibition may be due to a reduction of the variety of ideas produced. The curious student may wonder if this factor of reduction of the variety of ideas was not, in fact, especially important in this experiment since the subjects were a relatively homogeneous group. It may well be that in a setting where individuals with a wide variety of backgrounds (for example, electrical engineers, aeronautical engineers, physicists, and psychologists) are composed into groups to solve an applied problem, the brainstorming technique may facilitate problem solution. The answer to this question awaits further research.

[1] The student may obtain more information regarding the role of verbal responses as mediators of problem solving by reading: Charles N. Cofer, "Reasoning as an Associative Process: III. The Role of Verbal Responses in Problem Solving," *The Journal of General Psychology*, 57: 55–68, 1957. (Selection 36 in the first edition of the present text.)

Selection **39**

RELATIONS BETWEEN BRAIN CHEMISTRY AND PROBLEM-SOLVING AMONG RATS RAISED IN ENRICHED AND IMPOVERISHED ENVIRONMENTS*

DAVID KRECH
MARK R. ROSENZWEIG
EDWARD L. BENNETT
*University of California,
Berkeley*

We have recently reported on a series of experiments which investigated the effects of varying the rat's environment upon changes in the biochemistry and morphology of the brain. In the first report of this series (Krech, Rosenzweig, & Bennett, 1960) it was shown for six strains of rats that, with an increase in the animal's environmental complexity and training (ECT), there was a *drop* in specific cholinesterase (ChE) activity of the sensory cortex and an *increase* in the specific ChE activity of the subcortex. (Specific ChE activity was measured in terms of moles of acetylcholine, ACh, hydrolyzed per minute per milligram of tissue.) The clearest effect of ECT, therefore, was to decrease the cortical-subcortical (CS) ratio of specific ChE activity.

A later finding, reported in the second article in this series (Rosenzweig, Krech, Bennett, & Diamond, 1962), helped to explain, in part, the puzzle of the drop in the specific ChE of the cortex. We found that *total* ChE of the cortex (total ChE activity taken without regard to the weight of the tissue) actually increased somewhat in the ECT animals as compared with their littermates, but that the *weight* of the cortex increased to a greater degree. Thus *specific* ChE (ChE per unit weight)

* Reprinted from David Krech, Mark R. Rosenzweig, and Edward L. Bennett, "Relations between Brain Chemistry and Problem-solving among Rats Raised in Enriched and Impoverished Environments," *Journal of Comparative and Physiological Psychology,* 55: 801–807, 1962. Copyright 1962 by the American Psychological Association and reproduced by permission.

had decreased even though *total* ChE had increased.

The present experiment was designed to measure the learning ability of young animals immediately after 1 mo. of exposure to our complex environmental situation—an exposure period which Zolman and Morimoto (1962) had shown was sufficient to lower the CS ratio of ChE. The ECT conditions were originally adopted in our program because many studies from other laboratories (e.g., Bingham & Griffiths, 1952; Forgays & Forgays, 1952; Hymovitch, 1952) had shown that training and opportunities for experience can produce changes in learning capacity. But, as we stated at the 1958 Pittsburgh Symposium, ". . . the mechanism of these effects has not been explained. In this connection we will want to consider whether effects of training can be detected in changes in brain chemistry" (Rosenzweig, Krech, & Bennett, 1961, p. 90). Having now established that our enriched environmental conditions can induce cerebral changes, it is still necessary to demonstrate that these environmental conditions can enhance learning capacity. The necessity for this is underscored by the fact that the interpretation of the evidence from other laboratories on the enhancing effects of enriched environment is now being challenged. Thus Woods, Fiske, and Ruckelshaus concluded that the characteristically poor maze-solving performance of the animals brought up in a restricted environment ". . . is not due to a deficiency in intelligence or maze-solving ability, but more likely due to a heightened exploratory drive" (1961, p. 169). Furthermore, a number of experiments claiming to have demonstrated the beneficial effects of early experience have neglected certain important precautions, thus rendering the results equivocal.

Our experimental design, detailed in Method, was intended to overcome three major difficulties which have made the interpretation of other experiments ambiguous: (*a*) The prejudicing of the results by the unwitting bias of *E* who, when testing the learning capacity of the animal, is fully aware which animal comes from the enriched environment, which from the impoverished; (*b*) the possibility of confusing increased learning ability with effects of specific positive transfer to handling, due to the experimental animal's being handled by the same *E* during the "enriched environment" phase and the learning-testing phase; and (c) the confounding of exploratory behavior with error scores. Because we wanted a problem-solving test which would make a "heavy" demand on the animal's capacity for adaptive behavior, we chose a visual reversal discrimination test.

METHOD

Subjects

Male rats of the S₁ strain were weaned at 21 to 28 days of age and placed in the experimental conditions. This strain had shown marked effects of enriched environment on brain chemistry and morphology in our previous work. Fifteen pairs of littermates were used, each pair taken from a different litter. Three subgroups were run in succession, 6 pairs in the first group, 4 in the second, and 5 in the third. One animal of each pair, chosen at random, was assigned to the Environmental Complexity (EC) conditions, and its littermate was assigned to the Isolated Control (IC) conditions.

EC and IC conditions

In the EC condition, the animals lived 10 to a large cage (Extra rats of the same strain, age, and sex were added to each subgroup to bring the number up to 10.) The cage contained a small maze, and each day two wooden "toys" from a set of seven were placed in the cage. For 30 min. daily, the rats explored the Hebb-Williams apparatus with the pattern of barriers changed daily. Unlike our previous experiments, no formal training was given, so this condition is called EC rather than ECT as in our previous experiments.

The IC animals lived in individual cages where they could not see or touch another rat. Both the IC and EC animals had food and water ad lib. Both conditions lasted for 30 days. During this period the IC animals were handled only six times, for weighing.

At the end of the 30-day period, the *E* in charge of this first phase recaged the rats, three to a usual colony cage, so that some cages contained one EC and two IC rats, while the others contained two EC and one IC rat. The extra rats living in the EC condition were caged separately and retained as weight controls for the EC and IC animals. The rats, identified only by code numbers that did not reveal their group, were then turned over to a second *E* for the second phase of the experiment.

Reversal discrimination

In the second phase the animals were run for food reward on a reversal discrimination schedule in the Krech Hypothesis Apparatus—which consists, essentially, of four successive units of two-choice discrimination boxes (see Fig. 1, Krech, Rosenzweig, & Bennett, 1956). A 10-day pretraining period accustomed the animals to the 24-hr. deprivation schedule, trained them in a pretraining apparatus to leave the start box, run through doorways, and enter the goal box, and give the previously restricted animals a period of social and environmental exploration before the start of testing. A daily session during the testing period of 18 days consisted of 10 trials, comprising 40 choices.

The reversal discrimination schedule followed that used by Krechevsky (1932). The animals were first trained on a light-correct problem. Criterion was not more than 1 error in 5 successive trials, i.e., 19 correct choices out of 20. As soon as an animal reached criterion, it was started on the first *reversal* problem, dark-correct. Training on dark-correct was continued until the same criterion was reached, whereupon the problem was switched to light-correct, etc. At the end of the 18-day testing period, animals were run for 2 control days, with the doors open in the same daily sequence as before but with both alleys lighted at each choice point.

It was hoped that exploratory behavior was restricted both by the design of the apparatus and by the motivating conditions. Over the 18 days of testing, the animal divides its 720 choices among the same 8 alleys. Furthermore, the 24-hr. deprivation schedule produces strong motivation in young animals, and this should compete successfully with the exploratory drive.

Control of weight

While the EC and IC rats were receiving training and testing, the weight-control rats continued to receive food and water ad lib. and gained about 40% during this 30-day period. The weights of the EC and IC rats were stabilized during testing at about 88% of that of the weight-control group. The EC and IC rats ended the 30-day period about 16% heavier than they had begun. They always ran well and never appeared to be seriously undernourished.

Careful control of food deprivation was essential both to treat EC and IC animals similarly and to preclude retardation of growth of the brain in young animals. As we have shown elsewhere (Rosenzweig et al., 1961), underfeeding may produce significant loss of brain weight and may result in striking changes in labile constituents of the brain.

Chemical analysis

Within 3 days after the end of the testing period, the animals, now aged from 84 to 90 days, were sacrificed for chemical analysis of their brains. The brain of each animal was dissected into five parts: (*a*) a sample from the visual cortex of both hemispheres (V) weighing on the average 52 g.; (*b*) a sample from the somesthetic cortex of both hemispheres, weighing about 45 g. (S); (*c*) the remaining dorsal cortex; (*d*) the ventral cortex and contiguous tissue, and (*e*) the rest of the brain, including the cerebellum. This last sample will be referred to as "subcortex II." The V and S samples, taken together, will be referred to as "sensory cortex." These tissue samples have been defined more fully and their location shown by diagrams in a previous report (Rosenzweig et al., 1962).

Littermates were sacrified and analyzed consecutively, with the sequence randomized as between the EC and IC member of each pair. The analysts did not know to which group any animal belonged. For each tissue sample, three measures were obtained: (*a*) wet weight, determined to 0.1 g., (*b*) total ChE activity. This is expressed in terms of moles acetylcholine (ACh) $\times 10^8$ hydrolyzed per minute. (*c*) Specific ChE activity, which is total ChE activity divided by the weight of the tissue sample. Specific ChE activity is expressed in terms of moles ACh $\times 10^{10}$ hydrolyzed per minute per milligram of tissue. The analytical procedures, using an automatic titrator, have been reported previously (Rosenzweig, Krech, & Bennett, 1958).

RESULTS

Comparison of performance of EC and IC groups

The main results of the behavioral testing are shown in Figure 1. The initial light-correct problem was relatively simple, and there was practically no difference in the mean numbers of errors made by the EC and IC groups. The first *reversal* problem, dark-correct, was slightly more difficult for the EC animals but was considerably more difficult for the IC animals; the 51% difference between groups was not, however, statistically significant. The second reversal problem was still more difficult

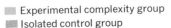

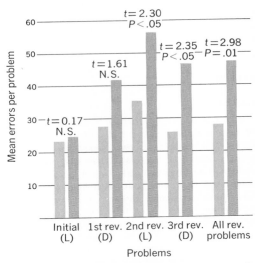

Figure 1 Mean errors per problem made by rats of the EC and IC groups.

than the preceding problem, and one IC animal failed to master it by the end of the 18-day experimental period; the computations are therefore based on 14 littermate pairs, eliminating the unsuccessful IC rat and its littermate. The difference between the EC and IC groups (54%) is significant for this second reversal problem at the .05 level. For the third reversal problem, the difference between groups (now 79%) is significant at the .05 level. Two IC rats failed on this problem, so they and their littermates had to be dropped from these calculations. The elimination of the unsuccessful IC animals from the second and third reversal problems minimized the differences between groups, since these animals were slow learners and made many errors. The EC littermates of these two IC animals showed scores very close to the mean of the other EC animals.

The mean number of reversal problems solved by the EC animals was 6.1 and by the IC group, 4.5, a difference short of significance ($p < .10$). The last set of bars in Figure 1 shows the mean number of errors per problem for *all* reversal problems attempted by each animal. For this measure, the difference between groups (68%) reaches the .01 level of significance.

It is clear that the animals exposed to a complex environment for 30 days performed better on the reversal discrimination problems than did their littermates kept in isolation for 30 days.

During the 18 days the animals had confronted the same sequence of 40 right and left opened alleys—no matter whether they were working on a light-correct or a dark-correct problem. The possibility remains therefore that the animals had been gradually learning this spatial sequence rather than solving visual reversal discrimination problems. One check of this possibility comes from the data from Days 19 and 20. During these control days, the animals were run in the apparatus with the doors open in the same daily sequence as before, but with both alleys lighted at each choice point. If the animals had by this time learned the spatial sequence, then under these control conditions they should have been able to do better than chance in choosing the open alley. Since each animal was given a total of 80 choices in this control situation, the score to be expected by chance alone was 40. The results of this control test are unequivocal. The mean number of choices of the open alley was 39.7 for the EC group, and 40.5 for the IC group. It would appear, then, that at the end of the 18-day period the animals were still attacking the problem in terms of the visual discriminanda.

Brain weight and ChE

The brains of the EC and IC groups were compared for all the biochemical and morphological indices which, on the basis of previous work (Krech et al., 1960; Rosenzweig et al., 1962), have significantly differentiated animals reared for 80 days under our ECT and IC conditions. The results of this comparison are presented in Table 1.

The total ChE activity of the EC group exceeds that of the IC group by 3% in the sensory cortex and by 4% in the total cortex. There is practically no difference between the groups in subcortex II. In weight, the EC group exceeds the IC group by 2% in the sensory cortex and by 3% in total cortex, with almost no difference in the subcortex. While these differences in ChE activity and cortical weight are consistent with our previous findings between ECT and IC animals, none of them is statistically significant.

The other comparisons yield results which differ from that of our other work. Thus, the increase of weight of the cortex (EC over that of IC) is no greater than the increase of total ChE activity of the cortex, where in our previous work cortical weight consistently showed the greater increase. In consequence, specific ChE (total ChE divided by tissue weight) does not differentiate between EC and IC groups for the cortex, nor does it for the subcortex. This again differs from our findings with our ECT and IC groups where the specific ChE was lower for the ECT group in the sensory cortex and higher in the subcortex. As a final consequence of this, the CS ratio of specific ChE— the index which best differentiates between ECT and IC groups in all of our previous experiments—here does not discriminate at all between the EC and IC groups: The EC group shows a ratio of .381 and the IC, of .380.

The cortical-subcortical weight ratio does, however, show much the same differentiation between our present EC and IC groups as it has between our former ECT and IC groups (Rosenzweig et al., 1962). Weight of the total

Table 1 | MEAN VALUES OF CEREBRAL CHOLIN-ESTERASE AND WEIGHT FOR EC AND IC ANIMALS

Measure	Group	Sensory cortex[a]	Total cortex[b]	Subcortex II[c]
Total ChE	EC	67.5	613.6	1827.1
	IC	65.7	588.3	1820.1
Weight (in mg.)	EC	97.8	647.4	919.4
	IC	95.6	630.6	916.9
Specific ChE	EC	69.7	94.8	198.8
	IC	69.2	93.3	198.5

[a] Sensory cortex is composed of the samples from the visual and somesthetic areas of cerebral cortex.
[b] Total cortex comprises sensory cortex, remaining dorsal cortex, and ventral cortex.
[c] Subcortex II is what remains of the brain after total cortex has been removed.

cortex divided by weight of subcortex II shows the EC group greater by 2.5% than the IC group, but this difference is short of significance ($p = .10$, two-tailed t test).

Correlations of performance and cerebral measures

It remains to be determined whether the individual differences in problem solving are related to individual differences in brain measures.

The behavioral index employed was the mean number of errors per reversal problem attempted by the animal. This ratio reflects the two basic performance measures: the total errors made on reversal problems and the total number of successive reversal problems the animal tackled during the training period. It will be recalled that by this ratio, the EC group was significantly superior to the IC group (see Fig. 1).

On the physiological side we also used ratios—the CS ratios of specific ChE and of weight discussed previously. These ratios were used because, as has been indicated, each of these had been shown in our previous work to differentiate between animals brought up under enriched environments and animals brought up under impoverished environments.

The 15 littermate pairs, it will be remembered, were run in three subgroups of 6, 4, and 5 pairs, separated widely in time. Since small variations in the processes of enzymic assay render somewhat questionable the comparison of absolute biochemical values obtained weeks or even months apart, we therefore determined the correlations between performance and cerebral measures separately for the three successive subgroups. The three correlations were then combined, using Fisher's r to z transformation, after statistical tests indicated that such combinations were legitimate.

The correlation of the CS weight ratio against the performance measure was $-.77$ for the EC group (significant at better than the .01 level of confidence), and for the IC group it was $-.15$ (nonsignificant). The sign of the correlations is what should have been expected from theory: Since the performance measure is an error measure, and the effect of enriched experience is to *increase* the cortical weight in relation to the subcortical weight, the error

score should decrease as the CS weight ratio increases.

For the CS ratio of specific ChE activity, the correlations with performance records were surprisingly high. For the EC group the correlation was .81 (significant at better than the .01 level of confidence), and for the IC group it was .53 (significant at better than the .05 level). Here, the correlations are positive since the CS ratio of specific ChE has always been found to *decrease* with enriched experience, and therefore the lower the ratio, the fewer the errors. Figure 2, the scatterplot for the EC data, illustrates the stable and reproducible nature of these correlations. It can be seen from Figure 2 that each subgroup had a high positive correlation. The same was true of the EC correlations involving the weight ratio.

It is clear from this correlational analysis that for animals raised in an enriched environment during infancy there is a substantial and stable relation between performance measures on the reversal discrimination problem and those morphological and biochemical measures of the rat's brain which are most affected by the enriched environment. For the rats raised in an impoverished environment during infancy, correlations of the same sign are also present, but of a lower magnitude.

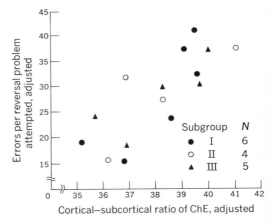

Figure 2 Scatterplot of cortical-subcortical ratio of specific ChE versus mean errors per reversal problem. (For both variables, the values were adjusted so that the means of each subgroup equalled the overall mean.)

DISCUSSION

Our data seem to support three major conclusions and pose one major paradox:

We have shown that exposure of 1 mo. to enriched or impoverished environment for weanling rats is sufficient to bring about significant differences in their ability to cope with a series of reversals of discrimination. The use of two different E for the two phases of the experiment precluded the possibility of E's biasing the results and of benefiting the frequently handled EC rats through specific positive transfer to the E's handling from one experimental phase to the other. It would also seem difficult to attribute the inferior performance of our IC group to "a heightened exploratory drive," as Woods, Fiske, and Ruckelshaus (1961) have done in the case of their restricted-environment group. The two groups did equally well on the initial discrimination problem and began to grow apart in performance only during the succeeding days as the difficulty of the problem increased—by which time the same eight alleys of the apparatus had already been traversed hundreds of times.

We have found substantial and significant correlations between two indices of brain morphology and biochemistry and the animal's problem-solving ability. The two physiological indices (CS ratios of ChE activity and of weight) are the ones which have most consistently differentiated between rats reared in an enriched environment and rats reared in an impoverished environment. The problem-solving measure against which these indices have been correlated (errors per reversal problem) is also the measure which most clearly and most significantly differentiates our EC rats from our IC rats. And in each case, the records of the EC rats yielded higher correlations than did those of the IC.

The biochemical and morphological differences between the EC and the IC rats were highly attenuated in comparison with all of our previous findings on the effect of environment on brain physiology. For one of these measures—the CS ratio of brain weight—the difference was slight and significant at only the .10 level of confidence. For the other

measure—CS ratio of specific ChE—there was almost no difference at all.

The paradox derives from a consideration of the three findings taken together: The EC rats are clearly superior problem-solvers to the IC rats, and the problem-solving performance of all the animals is correlated with those morphological and biochemical indices which normally differentiate "enriched" and "impoverished" animals, *but these very indices* do not clearly differentiate the EC from the IC rats!

In order to resolve this paradox, let us first consider some of our results in relation to some of those of Zolman and Morimoto (1962). They assigned one littermate of each of 15 pairs of S_1 weanlings to the ECT condition and the other to the IC condition. At the end of 30 days the ECT littermate was found in 14 of 15 pairs to have the lower CS ratio of specific ChE activity (as in our previous experiments). The mean values of the CS ratios for these ECT and IC groups are shown by the two points to the left in Figure 3 (55 days). Their ECT condition differed from our EC condition only in including one trial a day in the Lashley III maze during the last 8 days. At the age of 55 days, our rats in the present experiment presumably had CS ratios very close to those

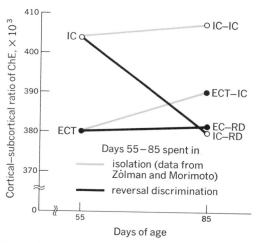

Figure 3 Mean cortical-subcortical ratios of specific ChE ($\times 10^3$) for groups of S_1 rats exposed to different experimental conditions.

of the corresponding groups of Zolman and Morimoto, since the animals were alike in strain, age, and sex, and since the IC conditions of the two experiments were identical while the EC and ECT conditions were very similar.

In another part of their experiment, Zolman and Morimoto ran 15 littermate pairs in ECT or IC conditions for 30 days and then kept both groups in isolation for another 30 days before sacrificing them at 85 days of age. It will be seen that an additional 30 days of isolation had little effect on the group that had been isolated since weaning—the line across the top of the figure from IC to IC-IC is almost flat. The isolation had more effect on the CS ratio of the group originally exposed to the ECT condition, as is shown by the upward slope of the line from ECT to ECT-IC.

Now consider the results of the present experiment in the light of the others: At the lower right of Figure 3 are shown the mean CS ratios of the group given EC and then tested on reversal discrimination (EC-RD) and of the group first isolated and then tested on reversal discrimination (IC-RD). The mean value of the EC group is almost identical to that of the corresponding IC group. For the group exposed from weaning to a complex environment, the effect of presenting the animals with a complex task was only to keep the CS ratio at about the level that it had at the end of the first phase—the line across the bottom of the graph from ECT to EC-RD is almost horizontal. For the group started in the IC condition, however, the switch to the reversal discrimination situation caused a relatively large drop in the CS ratio (IC to IC-RD).

Both analyses suggest that CS ratios of specific ChE and weight are not immutably fixed after a 30-day enriched or impoverished environment. To some degree, the changes induced by an enriched environment can be lost if the animal is placed in an impoverished environment, and to a much greater extent, the originally impoverished animal's brain can be brought to the status of the enriched animal through intensive training on complex problems.

Now we are in a position to understand how the CS ratio could correlate with behavior of the animals within a group (and especially strongly within the EC group) and yet not differentiate between the EC and IC groups. The CS ratio of the EC group, as we have seen in Figure 3, presumably remained rather stable throughout the learning phase; therefore, the value obtained at the end was representative of the level existing throughout the behavioral testing, and a high correlation with the behavioral scores was possible. The CS ratio values for the IC animals, on the other hand, must have been changing during the learning phase, and the values determined at the end of the experiment could not so adequately represent this varying course, hence no very high correlation with the behavioral measure could be anticipated.

SUMMARY AND CONCLUSIONS

Fifteen littermate pairs of male rats of the S_1 strain were used, one member of each pair being assigned at weaning to the environmental complexity (EC) situation and the littermate to the isolated control (IC) situation. The EC or IC experience lasted for 30 days, and then during a second period of 30 days the animals of both groups were pretrained and tested on reversal discrimination problems under condition of food deprivation. The EC group was significantly superior to the IC group on this test. Within the EC group, high and significant correlations were found between the behavioral scores and the cortical-subcortical ratios of cholinesterase and between the behavioral scores and the cortical-subcortical ratios of brain weight. Within the IC group the corresponding correlations were lower, and only the first of them was significant. Differences between the EC and IC groups on brain measures were small and insignificant. Presumably the EC and IC groups differed in brain measures at the end of the phase of differential environmental treatment, as found in related experiments. Partially as a consequence of these cerebral differences, the EC animals had an initial advantage in problem-solving ability over the IC animals. As training progressed, the brain values of the IC group approached those of the EC group. Since analyses of the brains could be done only at the end of the experiment, these end-point values showed little or no differences between the two groups. Furthermore, such end-point determinations presumably reflected rather accurately the relatively stable cerebral values of the EC group during the problem-solving phase and less accurately the changing values of the IC group, thus permitting higher correlations of brain measures with behavior for the EC than for the IC group.

REFERENCES

Bingham, W. E., & Griffiths, W. J. The effect of differential environments during infancy on adult behavior in the rat. *J. comp. physiol. Psychol.*, 1952, **45**, 307–312.

Forgays, D. G., & Forgays, J. W. The nature of the effects of free-environmental experience on the rat. *J. comp. physiol. Psychol.*, 1952, **45**, 322–328.

Hymovitch, B. The effects of experimental variations on problem-solving in the rat. *J. comp. physiol. Psychol.*, 1952, **45**, 313–321.

Krech, D., Rosenzweig, M. R., & Bennett, E. L. Dimensions of discrimination and level of cholinesterase activity in the cerebral cortex of the rat. *J. comp. physiol. Psychol.*, 1956, **49**, 261–266.

Krech, D., Rosenzweig, M. R., & Bennett, E. L. Effects of environmental complexity and training on brain chemistry. *J. comp. physiol. Psychol.*, 1960, **53**, 509–519.

Krechevsky, I. Antagonistic visual discrimination habits in the white rat. *J. comp. Psychol.*, 1932, **14**, 263–277.

Rosenzweig, M. R., Krech, D., & Bennett, E. L. Brain enzymes and adaptive behaviour. In, *Ciba Foundation: Symposum on neurological basis of behaviour.* London, England: Churchill, 1958. Pp. 337–355.

Rosenzweig, M. R., Krech, D., & Bennett, E. L. Heredity, environment, brain biochemistry, and learning. In, *Current trends in psychological theory.* Pittsburgh: Univer. Pittsburgh Press, 1961. Pp. 37–110.

Rosenzweig, M. R., Krech, D., Bennett, E. L., & Diamond, M. C. Effects of environmental complexity and training on brain chemistry and anatomy: A replication and extension. *J. comp. physiol. Psychol.*, 1962, **55**, 429–437.

Woods, P. J., Fiske, A. S., & Ruckelshaus, S. I. The effects of drives conflicting with exploration on the problem-solving behavior of rats reared in free and restricted environments. *J. comp. physiol. Psychol.*, 1961, **54**, 167–169.

Zolman, J. F., & Morimoto, H. Effects of age of training on cholinesterase activity in the brains of maze-bright rats. *J. comp. physiol. Psychol.*, 1962, **55**, 794–800.

Selection 40 | COMPUTER SIMULATION OF THINKING* [1]

CARL I. HOVLAND
Yale University

It is commonplace in the history of science for developments in one field of knowledge to have profound effects on other related areas. The dramatic influence of advances in atomic physics on biology, genetics, and medicine is a good case in point. We are currently witnessing a similar phenomenon in the repercussions of high speed computer technology on research in the behavioral sciences. The initial impact came from the computational efficiency of these devices which permitted calculations formerly prohibitive in terms of time and effort. A more recent and less direct effect has been in simulating machine-like methods of analysis of human thought and behavior through simulation on high speed computers. It is these newer techniques and their applicability to psychological problems that is the topic of the present paper.

The analogy between the high speed computer and human thinking has long been noted. We frequently see the Univacs, Johniacs, Illiacs referred to in the popular press as "giant brains" or "thinking machines." In most uses of high speed computers, however, there is an attempt to attain objectives beyond the scope of human capabilities, either because of their speed or their extensive storage capacity (called, interestingly enough, their "memory"). But in the investigations I shall be describing, the utilization is quite different. Here we are primarily concerned with the use of computing machines to simulate in exact fashion the way a human solves a problem. Both human weaknesses, such as limited and fallible memory, and strengths, such as the ability to

* From Carl I. Hovland, "Computer Simulation of Thinking," *The American Psychologist*, 1960, 11: 687–693. Copyright 1960 by the American Psychological Association and reproduced by permission.
[1] Adapted from a talk given over the *Voice of America* in September 1959. Unrestricted use of this material is available to the United States Government without cost.

choose an efficient solution out of innumerable alternatives, must be represented. We say that we can simulate human problem solving when we are able to specify both the prior information a human possesses and the sequence of steps by which he utilizes this information in the solution of the problem. We are then able to set up a computing machine to carry out this same sequence of operations.

Those familiar with the operation of high speed computers will readily understand the way in which simulation proceeds. Just as in ordinary operations of a computer, one gives the machine a set of "instructions" to execute. These constitute a "program." In arithmetical operations these are sentences like the following: "square the product of the first and second number," "store the product in memory," "compare the first and second number," "select the larger of the two numbers compared." Or such instructions as: "find the number of dollars paid to the individual last month," "add to this amount the number of dollars earned this month," and so forth. The machine then executes each of these instructions through an intricate electronic system, printing out its answers on an electric typewriter. Sequences of instructions can then solve the most complicated numerical problems, such as making out a payroll with each individual working different numbers of hours, at different wage rates, with advance payments to some workers, with different deductions for subscriptions to health and accident insurance, different income tax credits, and so forth. The nub of the simulation problem involves the use of similar types of "programs" of "instructions" to the machine in order to reproduce the steps an individual goes through in thinking out the solution to a difficult problem. One specifies the steps the individual uses by stating them in an unambiguous way so that a computing machine is able to carry them out. These may be instructions like: "store the answer to the last problem," "determine whether you have stored in memory any similar problems," "if so, what are the differences between the past problem and the present problem," "see if applying Rule A will convert the old problem into the new one," and "apply Rule B" to convert the answer to the former problem into the solution to the present one. Thus the computer can be given information

which is exactly equivalent to that of the human problem solver; as well as a specification of the way the human goes about processing that information to reach a solution.

The obvious point is that if we can be precise enough about a process to describe it in terms which can be programed and executed by a machine, we indeed know quite a bit about that process. And if we can specify singly each of the subprocesses involved, we can determine the effects of combinations of them and of variations in order of execution of the steps. The outcomes are almost impossible to foresee without actually carrying out the combinations and variations.

Let me begin by giving a concrete example of the new techniques, namely, simulation of the solving of geometry problems. We certainly think of the solving of theorems in Euclidian geometry by a high school sophomore as constituting a clearcut example of intelligent human behavior. But Gelernter and Rochester (1958) of the International Business Machines Company have now successfully developed a program whereby a high speed computer is able to solve many of the theorems in Euclid's geometry, for example, that the diagonals of a parallelogram bisect one another. A human learner who tries to solve such a problem has usually been taught a series of fundamental principles, or axioms, together with a set of rules for inferring relationships by which the basic symbols in the system may be manipulated. He is then asked to prove a new theorem. He tries to find a way of transforming and combining previous axioms through the set of rules until he achieves the proof of the new theorem. Typically he starts out in rather routine fashion, then has a flash of insight as to a possible means of solution, and then methodically tests the adequacy of the solution. The geometry computing machine is set up to operate in an analogous fashion. It is given a set of basic formulas and axioms, together with rules as to possible ways of manipulating them in order to form new theorems. The new theorem is then presented to the machine to prove. The machine is equipped with a number of rules of thumb for possible ways of solving problems. For example, it is instructed that if the proposition to be proved involves parallel lines and equality of angles, there is a good chance that it may be useful to try the theorem: "If two parallel lines are intersected by a third line, the opposite interior angles are equal." This instruction constitutes a short-cut which often works well but is by no means sure to be of value. Successful solution typically involves setting up a series of subgoals which are then worked on in succession. For example, in the problem cited earlier the machine ascertains that it can solve the theorem if it can establish the fact that the distance from one corner of the base of the parallelogram to the point of intersection must equal the distance from the intersection to the opposite corner of the parallelogram. This is then a subgoal, which in turn can be proved if the triangle formed by the bisecting lines and one of the sides of the parallelogram is equal to the triangle formed by the opposite side and the corresponding bisects. A device is incorporated into the computer which makes constructions and measures lines and angles. This operates by means of coordinate geometry. Once the sequence of subgoals leads from the initial axioms to the theorem to be proved, the machine routinely tests the accuracy of the proof. This it can do in an exhaustive manner, since once one has a possible proof, checking it is largely clerical. The chief problem is to find a possible method of proceeding, out of the almost infinite number of alternatives. It is here that the short-cut methods operate. They permit the use of likely and plausible methods of solution, just the way a clever high school student would proceed. Once the proof has been verified, the machine prints QED. Throughout the entire operation the machine prints out on paper a complete tracing of the steps it tries—this is analogous to an individual's account of the way he solves a problem in geometry. Some of the machine's failures in finding proofs closely resemble those made by beginning geometry students.

It will be noted that the methods of solution built into the computer closely resemble those used by humans solving similar problems. Let me again call attention to the fact that in this way they differ from the usual uses of high speed computers which methodically go through every possible solution in a deliberate way. The complete methods guarantee that if there is a solution it will be found, although an extraordinary number of trials may be required. Solutions of this type are referred to as "algorithms." These are used here to check proofs. In contrast, finding a possible solution is facilitated by short-cuts and rules of thumb programed into the machine. In this way it simulates a human subject in making leaps in the solution and trying out schemes which have been successful in the past, rather than exhaustively trying out each possible alternative. Mathematicians call these short-cut solutions "heuristics."

One may wonder whether we have gained anything by the simulation since we initially derive processes from study of how students work and then program into the computer their ways of proceeding. In fact, at the outset, we may operate in a somewhat circular fashion—that is, we may only get out of the machine what we put into it. But as one proceeds, new combinations are tested which could not have been predicted from the individual steps. Some results, although strictly determined by the processes programed, are impossible to foresee because so many complex operations interact in the final solution. One can find out the effect of increased complexity of problems, and then determine with human subjects whether the order of difficulty is the same that would be predicted from the computer's information processing routines. In this way one is constantly working back and forth from experiments with human subjects to simulation on the computing machine. Furthermore one frequently finds that one must make assumptions about certain steps in the process to get the computer to execute its program correctly. Here the simulation comes first and suggests later experiments with human subjects.

The geometry machine just described involves solving problems rather than learning how to solve them, in the sense that the computer would solve the same problem in the same way on a second trial. Humans, of course, do learn and improve through practice. So the interesting task is to build into the computer this capability as well. Simulation of learning is one of the most interesting potential applications of computer simulation techniques, since the ability to learn is one of the clear-cut differences between human and machine performance. A number of different types of learning are currently being simulated. The first involves stimulus-response learning. It is rather simple to simulate this type of learning with rewards ("reinforcements") given when certain types of behavior occur and not given when other types of responses are made. The probability that the response followed by reward will occur on later trials can then be made to increase. Failure of reward, or punishment, can be made to lead to a decreased probability of response ("extinction"). The studies of Herman, a computing machine, carried out by Friedberg (1958), and of the Perceptron, investigated by Rosenblatt (1958), are interesting examples of artificial learning machines. Other related possibilities are discussed in Miller, Galanter, and Pribram (1960).

At a somewhat more complex level is the type of learning involved in recognizing patterns imbedded in complex stimuli. It seems a simple thing for a human to respond to a triangle as a triangle whether it is large or small, short or tall, tilted or upright, and to distinguish it clearly from a square. But to specify rigorously the criteria in such a way that a machine can learn to recognize it invariably is quite a job. And the difficulty clearly hints that there is a lot we do not understand about the phenomenon even at the human level where we take the process for granted. Selfridge (1955) and Dinneen (1955) have worked most extensively on this problem and have been able to develop methods for getting the salient features of patterns to stand out so that some uniform response is given to a particular pattern. With two techniques, one of "averaging," to get rid of random elements, and a second, of "edging," to maximize the most distinctive features, they are able to insure that a variety of different ways of writing the letter A, for example, are registered as the same letter in the computer as a basis for further processing.

The third type of learning is made possible by keeping records of success and failure attained when different methods are pursued and using these records to improve performance. Thus, in the case of the geometry computer it is possible to store theorems which have already been proved. Similar mechanisms have been incorporated into the General Prob-

lem Solver developed by Newell, Shaw, and Simon (1958). It is also possible for these machines to be selective in their choice of theorems for permanent storage, rejecting those which do not seem sufficiently general to be useful later on. The most highly developed simulation of this type of learning is that incorporated in a checker-playing machine developed by Samuel (1959). His machine utilizes a type of rote learning which stores all of the checkerboard positions it encounters in play, together with the outcomes following each move. In addition this machine has some capacity to generalize on the basis of past experience and to store the generalizations themselves. With these learning mechanisms it appears possible for the computer to learn in a short period of time to play a better game of checkers than can be played by the person who wrote the program.

Many of the formulations of learning are made without any special assumptions that learning processes are consistent with known neurophysiological mechanisms. A number of students are attempting to close this gap by simulation studies of the way in which nerve networks become organized into systems and are then modified through use. There is quite extensive investigation along these lines, some of it instigated by the speculations of Hebb about the nature of nervous organization. Suffice it to say that a number of researchers have been able to program computers to simulate the changing of neural organization patterns as a result of repeated simulation of nerve fibers and further work of a similar type is in progress (cf. Clark & Farley, 1955, and Rochester, Holland, Haibt, & Duda, 1956).

In the work in our laboratory the emphasis is on understanding and simulating the processes involved in acquiring complex concepts through experience (Hovland & Hunt, 1960). The learner acquires a particular concept when he is told which of a series of specific instances presented to him belong in the concept class and which do not. This is similar to the way in which a child learns the concept of "animate" through some experiences in which parents and teachers label a given stimulus as "animate" and others in which they label it as "inanimate" (Hovland, 1952).

Our type of problem is illustrated by a situation in which there are a large number of slides of cancer cells, some of which are known to be malignant and others nonmalignant. The task of the individual (or the machine) is one of inducing the base of difference between the two types and subsequently labeling correctly new slides previously unidentified. Medical pathologists have just such a task and have achieved considerable success, although not 100% accuracy, in making such distinctions. It is of interest in passing that there is a machine available which can make such a distinction on the basis of slides presented to it, but here the combination of characteristics (the "concept") was formulated by the scientist who developed the instrument (Tolles & Bostrom, 1956). The machine's task is to see whether the new specimen conforms to certain specifications, that is, whether on the basis of density and structure the cell belongs in the "malignant" or "normal" category. Thus it has the "concept" built into it, obviating the need to start from the beginning in order to induce it.

The input to the type of concept learning in which we are interested is a series of pictures, say flower designs (Hovland, 1953), some of which are labeled "positive" instances (examples of the concept) and some "negative" instances (examples of what the concept *is not*). The characteristics of the instances are represented as symbols for processing by the machine. It is hoped later to have this transformation automatic through the use of techniques developed at the Bell Telephone Laboratories which employ a television camera to convert the visual representation into electrical impulses as input to the computer. Thus the picture would become converted into one set of symbols representing the characteristics which constitute the instances of the concept (like A1B2C1D1E2F1G1H2), while another string of symbols will represent instances of what the concept *is not* (like A2B1C1D2E1F1G1H2).

Potentially, a machine can then consider combinations of all of these characteristics as possible ways of categorizing and distinguishing between the class of "A" and of "not A." Typically, human learners only attend to part of the potential set of characteristics because of perceptual limitations. We have devoted considerable research effort toward determining just how attention and perception vary during the course of learning. We have incorporated in the machine simulation a selective scanning of possible aspects of the complex stimuli with provision for the fact that some individuals see only some of the characteristics while other individuals pay attention to different aspects.

Human subjects, at least at the adult level, operate on material of this type by developing strategies involving some generalization as to what concepts are like. Some details of these strategies have been investigated by Bruner, Goodnow, and Austin (1956). The strategies may be different for different types of concepts. Logicians describe some concepts as being of the *conjunctive* type, where all the members of the class share certain common characteristics. For example, rubies share the characteristics of hardness, translucence, and redness. A second type of concept is called *disjunctive*, in which possession of either one characteristic or possession of a different characteristic makes the instance subsumable under the general class. This is illustrated by the concept of "strike" in American baseball which is either a pitched ball across the plate and between the batter's knees and shoulders *or*, alternatively, any pitch at which the batter strikes but fails to send into the field. A third type of concept is *relational*, where the instances of the concept share no common fixed characteristics but do have certain relationships in common. A sample would be the concept of "isosceles triangles." All instances of this concept involve triangles with two equal sides. But any fixed characteristics, such as lengths of the equal sides, lengths of the third side, or sizes of angles, are not an adequate basis for inclusion or exclusion in the concept class.

In preparation for later simulation, we have carried out extensive experimentation to determine the order in which these various types of concepts are considered by human learners. We find that for our type of stimulus materials, conjunctive and relational concepts are considered much more commonly than disjunctive ones (Hunt & Hovland, 1960). So our present machine will have built into it a hierarchy of responses in which the first attempts to organize the material will be in terms of shared characteristics—conjunctive type concepts. Alternatively the machine will consider concepts which are based on relationships between the stimuli. Only when these have been extensively and unsuccessfully explored will the machine try disjunctive concept patterns.

At present, then, we have the program for a machine which is able to receive drawings having a number of different dimensions. It is then able to try a number of possible ways of organizing into a concept the prior information it has received regarding confirming and non-confirming instances. First it considers possibilities of concepts which have various combinations of features. When none of these suffice, it considers relational concepts. When these are not successful, it considers various disjunctive concepts where one set of features or another alternative set define the concept. When a solution is reached the description of what constitutes a concept is printed out on tape and subsequent unlabeled instances are classified A's or non-A's. A scanning device is built into the machine to take into account only certain of the characteristics available for consideration. The present machine remembers all that has been presented to it. We are currently considering various devices to simulate the gradual loss of information, or forgetting, which is all too human a characteristic. Our experimental studies have indicated the overall mathematical form which the loss should take, but there are alternative means of producing such a loss (Cahill & Hovland, 1960). Each alternative represents a different theory of the way in which forgetting occurs and investigation of the different theories is of fundamental importance. Simulation again provides a powerful tool for specifying the operation of the process of forgetting.

A high proportion of our research effort goes into new experimentation with human learners to determine their methods of handling various aspects of the problem, as compared to other efforts which stress programing the actual simulation. It is expected that this type of imbalance in effort will continue, but we are perennially hopeful that as more and more information becomes available an increasing amount of our effort will go into the simulation itself.

Work has now progressed to the point where I think we can see more clearly both the opportunities provided by these methods and some of the difficulties involved. I hope that the foregoing discussion has suggested some of the advantages of these new techniques. Let me briefly summarize the potentialities. First, simulation methods have a tremendous role in sharpening our formulations concerning mental processes and phenomena. It is one thing to say, as earlier students have said, that problem solving involves a number of different stages, for example, those of preparation, incubation, illumination, and verification, and quite another thing for one to specify exactly what is involved in each stage. The pioneering studies by Newell, Shaw, and Simon (1958) on the General Problem Solver indicate the great forward strides which result from specifying the nature of these processes in such complete detail that a computer is able to solve problems by following the sequence of steps programed into the machine.

Closely related is the second advantage of the computer, the emphasis which it places on developing theories that have both descriptive and predictive power. Many of the theories which exist in psychology and sociology are so general and vague that they have little real predictive power. The program written for the computer to describe a particular process constitutes a theory which, if successful in carrying out the process in the same way as the human, is highly efficient in predicting the effects of changes in conditions and in specifying what other individuals will do under particular conditions.

Lastly, the simulation of human responses has the same overwhelming advantages for our understanding of behavioral phenomena as similar methods in other sciences. For example, the use of the wind tunnel represents a complex set of interacting conditions in actuality which could not be duplicated and whose effects could not be predicted from theory alone. Analogously in the present case, for single factors one can analyze effects without simulation, but when one seeks to understand the combined action of a number of factors interacting in complex ways, no satisfactory way of predicting the exact outcome may be possible. Those working on the geometry simulator, the General Problem Solver, and the chess and checker-playing machines, all testify to the fact that many of the moves made by the computer greatly surprised their inventors.

I hope that my remarks on the importance of simulation methods do not give rise to the feeling that these methods automatically lead to quick success in areas which have been investigated for decades using other techniques. Two examples of the difficulties confronting us may be mentioned. The first is the complexity of the process to be simulated. At present we consider ourselves fortunate if we can simulate on a machine the typical performance of a single individual in solving a particular problem. This is indeed a great step forward. But for simulation to be maximally effective we would like to be able to predict machine solutions which simulate not only a single individual under some specified condition, but also the effects for different individuals under different environmental conditions, and after various amounts of experience. To date, most simulation has been of the performance of one individual, either real or an imaginary average individual. It may prove to be extremely difficult to carry out the next step, that of specifying which characteristics must be known about each individual to be able to simulate the way he varies from the typical pattern. In addition, the effects of environmental variables, such as the effects of drugs on performance, or of pressure to complete a task, should then be simulated. Finally, the effects of experience should be specified, so that the way in which a problem is attacked is appropriately changed as a result of the machine's ability to learn. This leaves for the future such a complex problem as analysis of the interactions between type of individual and amount of learning under different environmental conditions. It is apparent that a long and difficult road lies ahead before we can accomplish successful simulation of a single type of task which has all of these variables programed. But when they can be successfully specified we will know a great deal about the problem. Most research generalizations in the social sciences are only true for a group of people, not for each individual. Computer methodology may make possible a broadening of our understanding of behavior by emphasizing the simulation of single individuals and then studying variations between them. The integration of these com-

plementary approaches in new computer work will help us to reduce the gap between group averages and individual processes.

A second example of the difficulties of machine simulation is attributable to the nature of the process with which we are concerned. Simulation methods have most successfully been employed where it is possible to define the final performance of a task as an outcome of a succession of single steps. Thus where the mental process involves steps in a sequence one can synthesize the process by having the computing machine work first on stage one, then stage two, etc. Much more difficult are those processes where a number of stages are going on simultaneously, in parallel fashion. It certainly appears that much of our perceptual and thought process operates in this way. Under these conditions it is much more difficult to untangle the processes at work prior to simulation. In addition, present machines are not as suitable for these purposes as they are for sequential operation. New and radically different machines may ultimately be required to cope with this problem. Most of our present work is being carried out with computers which were built for quite other purposes, namely, high speed arithmetical computation. It would be possible to design machines more closely simulating thought processes and more flexible in their operation, but they would be expensive to construct and would not have the large number of potential purchasers who ordinarily help defray the costs of development.

Despite the difficulties mentioned, work on simulation of complex psychological processes is yielding results of increasing importance. Processes which were thought to be understood turn out to require much more explicit statement. But along with the increased explicitness comes new understanding and precision. At present most computer programs grapple with only one phase of complex processes, but we are beginning to see common features in a number of different programs, permitting the construction of comprehensive programs from simpler subprograms. Work on simulation has also had a stimulating effect on research on the higher thought processes themselves. Attempts to program computers have repeatedly revealed that we lacked much information as to how humans carry out seemingly simple thought operations. This has led to the return of workers to the laboratory which in turn has further enriched our knowledge of the human thought process.

Let not this enthusiastic report on the scientific potentialities of simulation research arouse anxieties of the sort raised by Norbert Wiener (1960) and other writers that machines will take over our civilization and supplant man in the near future. Rather, I think, there is great hope that detailed knowledge of how humans learn, think, and organize will redound to human welfare in removing much of the mystery which surrounds these processes and in leading to better understanding of the limitations of current ways of solving problems. It may, of course, become possible for us to then build machines which will work out solutions to many problems which we now consider distinctively human and to do so in a manner surpassing present human performance. But that this will lead to the machine becoming master and the designer, slave, seems to me most unlikely. Rather it will free man for novel creative tasks which are progressively beyond the capability of machines designed by man.

REFERENCES

Bruner, J. S., Goodnow, Jacqueline, J., & Austin, G. A. *A study of thinking.* New Work: Wiley, 1956.

Cahill, H., & Hovland, C. I. The role of memory in the acquisition of concepts. *J. exper. Psychol.,* 1960, **59,** 137–144.

Clark, W. A., & Farley, B. G. Generalization of pattern recognition in a self-organizing system. In, *Proceedings of the Western Joint Computer Conference.* Institute of Radio Engineers, 1955. Pp. 86–91.

Dinneen, G. P. Programming pattern recognition. In, *Proceedings of the Joint Western Computer Conference.* Institute of Radio Engineers, 1955. Pp. 94–100.

Friedberg, R. M. A learning machine. Part I. *IBM J. Res. Develpm.,* 1958, **2,** 2–13. (Cf. also 1959, **3,** 282–287.)

Gelernter, H. L., & Rochester, N. Intelligent behavior in problem-solving machines. *IBM J. Res. Develpm.,* 1958, **2,** 336–345.

Hovland, C. I. A "communication analysis" of concept learning. *Psychol. Rev.,* 1952, **59,** 461–472.

Hovland, C. I. A set of flower designs for concept learning experiments. *Amer. J. Psychol.,* 1953, **66,** 140–142.

Hovland, C. I., & Hunt, E. B. Computer simulation of concept attainment. *Behav. Sci.,* 1960, **5,** 265–267.

Hunt, E. B., & Hovland, C. I. Order of consideration of different types of concepts. *J. exper. Psychol.,* 1960, **59,** 220–225.

Miller, G. A., Galanter, E., & Pribram, K. H. *Plans and the structure of behavior.* New York: Holt, 1960.

Newell, A., Shaw, J. C., & Simon, H. A. Elements of a theory of human problem solving. *Psychol. Rev.,* 1958, **65,** 151–166.

Rochester, N., Holland, J. H., Haibt, L. H., & Duda, W. L. Tests on a cell assembly theory of the action of the brain, using a large digital computer. *Trans. Info. Theory,* 1956, IT–2(3), 80–93.

Rosenblatt, F. The perceptron: A probabilistic model for information storage and organization in the brain. *Psychol. Rev.,* 1958, **65,** 386–408.

Samuel, A. L. Some studies in machine learning using the game of checkers. *IBM J. Res. Develpm.,* 1959, **3,** 211–229.

Selfridge, O. G. Pattern recognition and modern computers. In, *Proceedings of the Western Computer Conference.* Institute of Radio Engineers, 1955. Pp. 91–93.

Tolles, W. E., & Bostrom, R. C. Automatic screening of cytological smears for cancer: The instrumentation. *Annals NY Acad. Sci.,* 1956, **63,** 1211–1218.

Wiener, N. Some moral and technical consequences of automation. *Science,* 1960, **131,** 1355–1358.

Selection **41** | THE INFLUENCE OF MENTAL SET ON PROBLEM SOLVING*

IAN M. L. HUNTER
University of Edinburgh

In his laboratory manual, Foster includes an experiment which aims to demonstrate the influence of mental set on speed of problem-

* From Ian M. L. Hunter, "The Influence of Mental Set on Problem Solving," *British Journal of Psychology,* 47:63–64, 1956. Reprinted by permission of the author and publisher.

solving. He uses six different lists of five-letter anagrams. Two series, containing miscellaneous words, are presented with an indefinite set, the subject being told nothing about the general nature of the words involved. Two series comprise words which "have something to do with eating" and another two series contain words "representing things about the house." Before attempting these, the subject is informed of the classification. Foster reports only that 'typical results show that the median time with indefinite set is about 2.5 times as long as for definite set' and that 'a typical median time for transposing anagrams with indefinite set is 25 sec.; for transposing anagrams referring to eating, 10 sec.; for anagrams referring to house, 10 sec.'

It seems likely that these results demonstrate the facilitating effect of definite as opposed to indefinite set. Nevertheless, an unambiguous interpretation is difficult to make. There is no adequate control of practice and fatigue effects. Also the specified and unspecified series employ different anagrams and there is no guarantee that the difference between the times taken to solve these is not attributable to a mere difference in their intrinsic difficulty. This note reports a class experiment in which Foster's materials and design were modified. The result demonstrates, of course, only one of the ways in which set can be established, and only one of the ways in which its effects can be observed (other investigations of set have been reviewed recently by Johnson). However, the experiment confirms, under better-controlled conditions, Foster's original findings. Moreover, it provides an interesting and instructive experiment for use in the teaching of experimental psychology.

The experiment was carried out with four laboratory sections of a first-year class in experimental psychology. A total of seventy-two students (thirty-five men, thirty-seven women) took part. The students were divided into groups of three, each member of the group acting, in turn, as subject, experimenter, and recorder. The material consisted of fifty-four five-letter anagrams, each of which permitted of only one solution. The solutions were nouns which fell into nine different categories as follows:

1. Animals: sheep, horse, tiger, skunk, camel, zebra.
2. Trees: birch, rowan, aspen, beech, hazel, holly.
3. Musical instruments: piano, flute, cello, organ, banjo, viola.
4. Birds: stork, eagle, goose, robin, heron, raven.
5. Fruit: peach, grape, olive, lemon (melon), prune, apple.
6. Parts of the body: wrist, mouth, waist, ankle, thigh, chest.
7. Countries: India, Spain, Wales, Italy, Japan, Tibet.
8. Wearing apparel: glove, skirt, apron, scarf, dress, shirt.
9. Flowers: pansy, lilac, daisy, tulip, lupin, poppy.

Each subject attempted two lists of six anagrams, one specified and the other unspecified. The specified lists used, for example, by the first group were lists 1, 2, and 3 above, while each unspecified list contained six nouns, one selected from each of the remaining categories. Using twelve groups of three subjects, lists were prepared so that: over the thirty-six subjects, each noun occurred the same number of times, i.e. twice, as specified and as unspecified; practice and fatigue effects were counterbalanced, half of the subjects attempting a specified list followed by an unspecified, and half attempting first an unspecified and then a specified list; in no group did an experimenter or recorder experience a noun which he would encounter while acting as subject.

Each group was given a six-page booklet, on each page of which the appropriate list was typed in capital letters on heavy white paper. Each list was headed either "Unspecified" or given a specific title, e.g., "Animals." Over the first list, the experimenter placed a long strip of hard-board in the centre of which was an aperture just large enough to expose a single anagram. The experimenter then moved the aperture down to expose the heading and told the subject whether the list was unspecified or specified in a particular way. He then exposed the first anagram for 30 sec. If the solution was given in this time, the experimenter waited until the recorder had noted the time taken for solution and then exposed the second anagram. If the anagram was not successfully transposed in 30 sec., a failure was recorded and the next anagram exposed. This procedure was continued until the end of the list. The same subject then attempted the second list. Members of the group then exchanged functions and the next two lists were presented to a new subject. This done, the third subject attempted the last two lists. Throughout, the recorder was responsible for timing the experiment by stop-watch and for entering the results in a specially prepared table. An hour gave the students time to perform the experiment, calculate the results for their own group of three, and discuss both their findings and the design of the experiment.

The results from the seventy-two subjects were as follows:

Median time to solve ana- = 3 sec.
    grams in specified lists
Median time to solve ana- = 12.5 sec.
    grams in unspecified
    lists
Total number anagrams = 35 (8.10%)
    failed in specified lists
Total number anagrams = 129 (29.86%)
    failed in unspecified
    lists

These results show clearly that the more specific the set the easier is the problem to solve. It is to be noted that the set involved here may not derive entirely from the instructions given but may, in part, have been established in the course of transposing a series of homogeneous anagrams. Even without specific instructions, a subject might, after solving four or five "animal" anagrams, be set for an animal name in the sixth anagram. Such a task-induced set can easily be demonstrated in the classroom by means of the water-jar problems of Luchins. However, the design of the present experiment does not permit any conclusion regarding the extent to which set established in this way contributes, if at all, to the results obtained.

Selection **42** | DOES GROUP PARTICIPATION WHEN USING BRAINSTORMING FACILITATE OR INHIBIT CREATIVE THINKING?*

DONALD W. TAYLOR
PAUL C. BERRY
CLIFFORD H. BLOCK
Yale University

Brainstorming was originated and first used by Alex F. Osborn in 1939 in the advertising agency Batten, Barton, Durstine & Osborn, which he then headed. Within recent years its use has grown rapidly. A large number of major companies, units of the Army, Navy, and Air Force, and various federal, state, and local civilian agencies have employed the technique, and instruction has been given in a number of colleges and universities in its use. Although an occasional critical voice has been raised, brainstorming may be said to have achieved wide acceptance as a means of facilitating creative thinking.

The purpose of brainstorming is to free individuals from inhibition, self-criticism, and criticism by others in order that in response to a specific problem they may produce as many different ideas as possible. The assumption is that the larger the number of ideas produced, the greater the probability of achieving an effective solution. Brainstorming is characterized by four basic rules:

1. *Criticism is ruled out.* Adverse judgment of ideas must be withheld until later.
2. *"Free-wheeling" is welcomed.* The wilder the idea, the better; it is easier to tame down than to think up.
3. *Quantity is wanted.* The greater the num-

* Abridged from Donald W. Taylor, Paul C. Berry, and Clifford H. Block, "Does Group Participation When Using Brainstorming Facilitate or Inhibit Creative Thinking?" *Administrative Science Quarterly*, 3:23–47, 1958. Reprinted by permission of the author and the publisher.

ber of ideas, the more the likelihood of winners.

4. *Combination and improvement are sought.* In addition to contributing ideas of their own, participants should suggest how ideas of others can be turned into *better* ideas; or how two or more ideas can be joined into still another idea.

Brainstorming ordinarily involves not only following the four basic rules but also group collaboration in attacking the problem. Osborn emphasizes the value of group interaction in facilitating the flow of ideas. It was this characteristic of brainstorming which was of primary interest in the present study.

The present experiment employed a design previously developed by Taylor for use in studies of group problem solving where the problems involved have logically correct solutions. Earlier studies of such group problem solving were concerned with a comparison of the achievement of groups of various sizes with that of individuals. However, the performance of a group should be superior to that of an individual, simply because in the group more individuals are working on the problem. On the assumption of the appropriate null hypothesis, namely, that working in a group has no effect either positive or negative upon individual performance, Taylor and Lorge & Solomon independently have presented a simple mathematical model for predicting the performance of a group of a given size from a knowledge of individual performance. By comparing actual group achievement with that predicted from the model, one can determine whether group participation facilitates or inhibits problem solving.

Taylor has also developed an experimental design which provides an alternative method of testing the same null hypothesis as that represented by the model. Individuals are randomly assigned to work either alone or in groups of a given size on a series of problems. The number of individuals working alone should be about equal to that working in groups. After the experiment is completed, those who actually worked alone are divided at random into nominal groups of the same size as the real groups. The performance of the nominal groups

is then scored as though the members of the group had worked together. The achievement of the nominal groups thus provides a measure of the performance to be expected under the null hypothesis. If the performance of the real groups is superior to that of the nominal groups, group participation facilitates performance; if it is inferior, group participation inhibits it.

This design, with appropriate modification in the scoring of responses for nominal groups, was employed in the present experiment to provide an answer to the question: Does group participation when using brainstorming facilitate or inhibit creative thinking?

METHOD

Subjects   The ninety-six Yale juniors and seniors who served as subjects in this experiment were all at the time enrolled in a course in Psychology of Personnel Administration taught by the first author. Each week, in addition to two lectures to the entire class, the course included an analysis of a case carried out in small discussion groups; each group had its own student leader, this task being rotated among the members of the group. As a result of such case discussion and of the way in which subjects were assigned, each real group in the present experiment was not, as often must be the case in studies of group problem solving, an *ad hoc* group of individuals meeting for the first time; instead, each real group included men who not only knew each other but who also had worked together effectively in small-group discussion over a considerable period of time. At the same time, the procedure used in assigning subjects was such that those assigned to work in groups and those assigned to work alone could legitimately be regarded as random samples from the same population.

From each of the ten discussion groups in the class, four men were picked at random to form an experimental group, thus providing ten experimental groups; and from two of the ten discussion groups, an additional four men were picked at random to provide two more groups, for a total of twelve experimental groups. The remaining men in the ten discussion groups, forty-eight in all, served as individual subjects.

Problems   On the basis of pretesting, three problems were selected which seemed to be of interest to Yale students, productive of many and varied responses, and appropriate for use with brainstorming. The three problems were as follows:

1. Each year a great many American tourists go to visit Europe. But now suppose that our country wished to get many more European tourists to come to visit America during their vacations. What steps can you suggest that would get more European tourists to come to this country?

2. We don't think this is very likely to happen, but imagine for a moment what would happen if everyone born after 1960 had an extra thumb on each hand. This extra thumb will be built just as the present one is, but located on the other side of the hand. It faces inward, so that it can press against the fingers, just as the regular thumb does now. Here is a picture to help you see how it will be. (A line drawing of a hand with two thumbs was shown by the experimenter at this point in the reading of the problem and then left in full view on the table during the entire period of work on the problem.) Now the question is: What practical benefits or difficulties will arise when people start having this extra thumb?

3. Because of the rapidly increasing birth rate beginning in the 1940s, it is now clear that by 1970 public school enrollment will be very much greater than it is today. In fact, it has been estimated that if the student-teacher ratio were to be maintained at what it is today, 50 per cent of all individuals graduating from college would have to be induced to enter teaching. What different steps might be taken to insure that schools will continue to provide instruction at least equal in effectiveness to that now provided?

For brevity's sake, the three problems were referred to as "Tourist Problem," the "Thumbs Problem," and the "Teachers Problem."

Procedure In a single experimental session lasting about one hour, the three problems were presented in the order in which they are listed above to each of the twelve groups and to each of the forty-eight individuals. The second and third authors of the present report conducted the sessions, each one conducting six group and twenty-four individual sessions. The assignment of groups and individuals to experimenters was largely a matter of chance.

Group and individual sessions were alternated in such a way that on any given date about the same proportion of group and individual sessions had been completed.

Both experimenters were advanced graduate students in psychology. Both were familiar with Osborn's writing concerning brainstorming. Both had participated in the pretesting described above and thereby gained experience with the procedures of brainstorming. Both personally believed that group brainstorming was an effective procedure for facilitating the production of ideas.

Very shortly before the present experiment began, one lecture to the class as a whole was devoted to creative thinking, with particular attention to brainstorming. The origin, nature, and widespread use of brainstorming was described, the purpose being to create interest in the procedure and as favorable as possible an attitude toward it. The shortage of controlled experimental studies of this and similar procedures was described. Finally, the students were asked to participate as subjects in the experiment and were promised a report of the results when it was available.

During the pretesting, both with individuals and with small groups, attention was devoted to the question of what length of time should be allowed for work on each of the problems selected for use. What was wanted was a span of time long enough so that members of groups of four would have adequate opportunity to express all the ideas which occurred to them within the working period and at the same time short enough so that individuals would not become bored by being forced to continue work on a problem long after they had essentially exhausted their ideas. Pretesting showed that the rate at which ideas were produced on the problems decreased with time. A time limit of twelve minutes was finally selected as one which would permit group members to express all ideas occurring to them within the work period (though not to exhaust all possible ideas) and yet which would not result in excessive periods of silence for individual subjects. Actually, for both individuals and groups, appreciable periods of silence appeared between responses near the end of the twelve minutes.

RESULTS

The first step following the completion of the experimental sessions was the division of the forty-eight individual subjects into twelve nominal groups of four each. This was done in order to permit comparison of real group performance not only with that of individuals but also with that to be expected on the basis of the hypothesis that working in the group has no effect either positive or negative upon the performance of its members. A table of random numbers was employed to divide the twenty-four individual subjects who had worked with the first experimenter into six nominal groups of four; the same procedure was used to divide the twenty-four who had worked with the second experimenter into an additional six nominal groups. This particular procedure was necessary if a test were to be made of any possible difference between the two sets of six nominal groups resulting from differences between the experimenters. Inspection of the data later obtained, however, revealed no possible significant difference between experimenters in the results.

Table 1 presents the mean number of responses by individuals and real groups to each of the three problems. On each of the three problems, the mean number of ideas presented by real groups is much larger than that presented by individuals. The appropriate analysis of variance briefly summarized in Table 1 shows this difference between real groups and individuals with an F of 71.2 is significant at well beyond the .0001 level. The analysis also shows that the differences among the three problems in mean number of responses is significant at the .001 level and that the interaction between the two primary variables is also significant.

Table 2 shows that the mean number of responses produced by nominal groups was considerably larger than that produced by real groups on each of the three problems. The analysis of variance indicates that this superiority of nominal to real groups is significant at far beyond the .001 level. The difference among the three problems in number of responses is again significant, but in this case the interaction does not even approach significance.

It seemed important to compare the performance of real and nominal groups not only in terms of the number of ideas produced but also in terms of the originality and quality of these ideas. For this purpose, additional analyses were undertaken.

A large proportion of the responses to any one of the problems was, of course, produced by more than one of the nominal or real groups, a small number of the ideas on each of the problems being suggested by nearly all of the twenty-four groups. On each problem, however, an appreciable number of suggestions was made by only one of the twenty-four groups; these may be described as unique responses. The number of such unique ideas provides one satisfactory measure of the originality of the performance of a particular group.

In Table 3 are given the mean number of unique responses produced by real and nominal groups on each of the three problems. The superiority of the nominal to the real groups on this measure is significant at the .005 level. The difference among the three problems in mean number of unique responses is also significant, but the interaction is not.

Table 1 | **MEAN TOTAL NUMBER OF RESPONSES TO EACH PROBLEM BY INDIVIDUALS AND REAL GROUPS**

	Tourists	Thumbs	Teachers	Mean of means
Individuals	20.7	19.9	18.2	19.6
Real groups	38.4	41.3	32.6	37.5
Mean of means	29.6	30.6	25.4	

Analysis of variance	d. f.	F	p
Individuals *vs.* real groups	1, 58	71.2	.0001
Among problems	2, 116	8.5	.001
Interaction	2, 116	4.96	.01

Table 2 | MEAN TOTAL NUMBER OF RESPONSES TO EACH PROBLEM BY REAL GROUPS AND NOMINAL GROUPS

	Tourists	Thumbs	Teachers	Mean of means
Real groups	38.4	41.3	32.6	37.5
Nominal groups	68.3	72.6	63.5	68.1
Mean of means	53.4	57.0	48.0	
Analysis of variance	d. f.	F	p	
Real vs. nominal groups	1, 22	96.3	.0001	
Among problems	2, 44	7.8	.005	
Interaction	2, 44	.09	—	

Detailed examination of the 483 different suggestions for solution of the Tourists Problem and of the 513 different suggestions for solution of the Teachers Problem indicated that these suggestions differed in quality with respect to at least three dimensions: feasibility, effectiveness, and generality. Accordingly, five-step rating scales were constructed for use in measuring these three. The 791 different responses made to the Thumbs Problem differed from those made to the other two problems in that they represented anticipated consequences instead of suggested steps for solution. For this reason only one of the three rating scales constructed for rating responses to the other two problems, namely, generality, appeared equally applicable in the case of the Thumbs Problem. For this problem, however, analogous to feasibility and effectiveness on the other problems were the dimensions of probability and significance, respectively. Accordingly, two additional rating scales were constructed by

the same method to measure these latter variables.

The responses to each problem were rated on three different scales by three different raters, presumably increasing the independence of the ratings of the three characteristics. Each rater employed a different scale for each of the three problems, thus presumably minimizing the possibility that a single idiosyncratic interpretation of any of the scales would occur for all three problems.

One additional point concerning the procedure used in rating deserves emphasis. All ratings were made of the responses as they appeared on the master list for the given problem and without any knowledge of whether the response had been made by real or nominal groups. This was done, of course, to eliminate any possible tendency of any rater to bias his ratings to favor either real or nominal groups. The score for each group for a given problem and a given dimension was simply the sum of

Table 3 | MEAN NUMBERS OF UNIQUE RESPONSES TO EACH PROBLEM

	Tourists	Thumbs	Teachers	Mean of means
Real groups	7.5	17.7	7.3	10.8
Nominal groups	13.7	28.1	17.5	19.8
Mean of means	10.6	22.9	12.4	
Analysis of variance	d. f.	F	p	
Real vs. nominal groups	1, 22	11.4	.005	
Among problems	2, 44	42.1	.0001	
Interaction	2, 44	1.29	—	

the ratings on that dimension of the responses given by the group to that problem.

A comparison of the mean scores of real and nominal groups [shows that]: On each of the three dimensions for each of the three problems, the mean for the nominal groups is much larger than that for the real groups. The analyses of variance show that this superiority of the nominal to the real groups is significant well beyond the .0001 level for each of the three problems.

DISCUSSION

The first important finding was that on each of the three problems the mean total number of ideas produced by the twelve groups was considerably larger than the mean number produced by the forty-eight individuals, the difference being highly significant (Table I). It is true that the interaction is significant, indicating that the difference between real group and individual performance does vary among the three problems. But on all three problems group performance is clearly superior to individual performance. Such group superiority may very well account for the widespread impression that group participation does facilitate production of ideas. The individual who compares his own performance working alone with that of a group in which he participates at another time may understandably conclude that group interaction stimulates creative thinking, whether or not this is in fact the case. Many of those participating in the groups in the present experiment made comments indicating that they believed such participation had been stimulating.

The comparison of group performance with individual performance does not, however, provide an adequate answer to the question: Does group participation when using brainstorming facilitate or inhibit creative thinking? To answer this question, the performance of the twelve real groups was compared with that of the twelve nominal groups on each of the three problems with respect to (a) mean total number of ideas produced, (b) mean number of

unique ideas produced, and (c) the three measures which involved the weighting of the ideas with respect to quality. The results of these several analyses were both clear-cut and consistent.

The performance of the twelve real groups is markedly inferior to that of the twelve nominal groups both in terms of number of ideas produced (Table 2) and in terms of number of unique ideas produced (Table 3). Since in neither case was the interaction significant, these findings apply equally to all three problems. The mean scores of the real groups on the three weighted measures were also markedly inferior to those of the nominal groups for the Tourists, Thumbs, and Teachers Problem. In brief, the performance of the real groups is inferior to that of the nominal groups on all three problems with respect to each and all of the measures of performance employed.

To the extent that the results of the present experiment can be generalized, it must be concluded that group participation when using brainstorming *inhibits* creative thinking. What accounts for such inhibition? Although data are not available to provide an adequate answer, two suggestions may be made. In brainstorming strong emphasis is placed upon avoiding criticism both of one's own ideas and of the ideas of others. Nevertheless, it appears probable that the individual working in a group feels less free of possible criticism by others even when such criticism is not expressed at the time than does the individual working alone. To the extent that this is true, group participation is inhibiting. A second reason is that group participation may reduce the number of different ideas produced. A given number of individuals working in a group appear more likely to pursue the same train of thought—to have the same set or the same approach to the problem—than do the same number of individuals working alone. The greater the variety of set, train of thought, or approach, the greater would be the expected number of different ideas produced. To the extent that group participation reduces such variety, it inhibits production of ideas.

INTELLIGENCE | 9

After studying the chapter on intelligence in textbooks in introductory psychology, students often ask, "But what do you mean by the term 'intelligence?'" The professor may define the term in a way which is satisfactory to the student, but in all likelihood the definition is not entirely satisfactory to the professor himself. Definitions of "intelligence" have ranged from the ultra-operational definition that "intelligence is what is measured by intelligence tests," to rather vague statements to the effect that "intelligence refers to the ability of the individual to maintain a flexible adjustment to his environment." Like all other attempts to pin down the meaning of the term, these definitions are inadequate in that they refer to only part of what we mean by intelligence. In lieu of accepting any particular explicit definition of intelligence, perhaps it is more important to emphasize that "intelligence" is not some "thing" that a person *has*, but is rather something that he *does*. It is an abstraction from his characteristic ways of behaving. We thus see that intelligence tests are important in understanding intelligence in that, to the extent that they are valid, they help us to predict how satisfactorily the individual will interact with his environment in everyday life. That is, we are never concerned about a person's intelligence test score per se; we are concerned about the typical level with which he can bring previous learning to bear on solutions of problems in his everyday living. In our society the most culturally important forms of learning are those which involve manipulation of abstract symbols (thinking). It is thus reasonable that most intelligence tests place great emphasis on verbal abilities.

BIOLOGICAL FACTORS

In Selection 43, Dr. Theodosius Dobzhansky, an internationally known geneticist, points out that considerable heat has been generated in the controversy centering on the question of whether or not intelligence is inherited. Dobzhansky's view, based in part on the correlational analysis of the intelligences of twins, is that intelligence is determined jointly by genetic and environmental variables. The vast majority of psychologists would agree with his statement that "Any way you look at it, man is a creature of both his nature and his nurture. It is folly to disagree with either."

The question is often raised by layman and scientist alike, "What is the relationship of intellectual function to the structures and functioning of the brain?" In attempting to answer this question, the pseudoscience of phrenology assumed that (1) specific mental functions are localized in the brain; (2) the amount of brain tissue reflects the amount of mental ability; and (3) the shape of the skull indicates the amount of tissue and therefore the amount of ability. We now know that the latter two assumptions are most certainly wrong, and although there are specific areas of the brain which are related to specific functions, speech, for example, intelligence in general, or its subcomponents, does not seem to be so localized.

We have already seen that important work on this problem is being conducted by the interdisciplinary team at Berkeley (see Selection 39). In Selection 44 D. O. Hebb presents a hypothesis concerning the nature of adult intelligence which is based on examination of clinical and experimental data regarding the effects of brain injury on intelligence. He cites data to support the following empirical generalizations: (1) *The degree of intellectual loss resulting from brain injury depends on the age at which the injury occurs and the specific intellectual factor being tested.* (2) *Destruction of brain tissue early in life has a less selective and more general effect than similar injury as an adult.* (3) *In the adult, extensive portions of the brain may be removed or destroyed without great loss of verbal abilities.* On the basis of these empirical generalizations Hebb offers the hypothesis that intellectual functioning may depend on two factors: present intellectual power or ability to develop new patterns of response; and the functioning of those patterns of response which are already developed. Thus, the test performance of an adult who suffered brain injury as a child is lowered by inadequate previous development of response patterns as well as by reduction of present intellectual power. On the other hand, brain injury as an adult influences only present intellectual power, whereas previously learned response patterns may continue to function relatively unimpaired.

PSYCHOLOGICAL FACTORS

Dr. J. P. Guilford has devoted his research career to the determination of the structure of the intellect through the use of factor analysis. As a part of the more general structure of the intellect there exists a class of operations known as divergent thinking. It is within this class of operations that most of the creative abilities are to be found. Among the creativity factors which have thus far been isolated, Guilford includes sensitivity to problems, word fluency, ideational fluency, associational fluency, expressional fluency, spontaneous flexibility, adaptive flexibility, and originality. The question of the relationship between creativity and intelligence has been raised frequently in scholarly journals and in the public press. In Selection 45, Guilford points out that most intelligence tests do not sample the major aspects of creativity which are involved in divergent thinking. High IQ is neither a necessary nor a sufficient condition for creativity. Although hereditary factors may set the upper limits of the intellect, much can be done in the educational situation to increase the quality and quantity of creative behavior.

One of the inadequacies inherent in defining intelligence as the ability of the individual to adjust to his environment is indicated by the fact that even though two persons may have equivalent IQs, one may be highly neurotic and be making a poor adjustment, whereas the other may be making the most of his intellectual ability. It is thus clear that the level of intellectual functioning is greatly influenced by emotional factors. We make a grave error in our attempts to understand human behavior when we separate man's cognitive self from his emotional self. Behavior in the "microcosm" of the intelligence test situation is influenced by emotional factors, just as is behavior in "real life." Dr. Edith Weisskopf (Selection 46) presents a lucid discussion of the many facets of personality dynamics which may influence tested intelligence and intelligent behavior in general.

SOCIOCULTURAL FACTORS

A question which is often heatedly argued by the layman is whether or not there are innate intellectual differences between the races of men. On the basis of our previous discussion of the interaction of hereditary and environmental factors in the determination of behavior, the discerning student will recognize that this problem is likely to be quite difficult to investigate scientifically. Further, since motivations, emotions, attitudes, and other facets of personality dynamics greatly influence intellectual functioning, it is evident that any adequate investigation of the problem must attempt to hold constant or to evaluate sociocultural influences. McCord and Demerath (Selection 47) show how a widely publicized statement regarding Negro-white intellectual differences is an inadequate scientific report. In addition, they present a further empirical study which in no way supports innate racial differences when environmental differences are eliminated. A joint statement made by eighteen outstanding social scientists further supports this view (see Selection 48).

Selection **43** | GENETIC AND ENVIRONMENTAL DETERMINERS OF INTELLIGENCE*

THEODOSIUS DOBZHANSKY
Rockefeller University

Much discussion and polemics have centered on the problem of the inheritance of intelligence. Psychologists and educationists have worked out a technique of estimation of the so-called intelligence quotient, or I.Q. What is measured by the I.Q. is not necessarily the same as what is referred to in everyday language as intelligence, cleverness, aptitude, or wit. Still less does the I.Q. give an estimate of the value or worth of the person. The I.Q. as administered to school children is regarded as a measure of their ability to handle verbal symbols. This ability shows a fairly high correlation with scholastic success, and this is what makes the I.Q. measurements useful, but at the same time suggests the limitations of their usefulness. The I.Q. is certainly not independent of the environment, of the family background, schooling, and the circumstances under which the test is administered.

Identical twins perform appreciably more similarly in intelligence tests than do fraternal twins, and the latter only slightly more similarly than do siblings who are not twins. L. Erlenmeyer-Kimling and L. F. Jarvik have recently reviewed and summarized the data obtained in fifty-two different studies by different investigators. The mean correlation coefficient for the I.Q. scores of identical twins reared together is 0.87, and for those reared apart 0.75. A correlation coefficient of 1.00 would mean that the I.Q. measurement was absolutely precise and that the variations observed are entirely genotypic and not environmental. This is obviously not so, and particularly the fact that the twins reared apart show a lower correlation than those reared together is evidence that the I.Q. depends in part on environment. However,

the fraternal twins give a correlation of only 0.53, the value being almost the same for twins reared together and those reared apart. This value, 0.53, is only slightly greater than the 0.49 for siblings, brothers or sisters who are not twins, and significantly lower than the values for identical twins reared either together or apart. Important additional evidence comes from studies on the I.Q.'s of genetically unrelated persons reared together, such as children brought up in the same orphanage or foster home. Here the correlation falls to 0.23. The correlation between foster children and foster parents is only 0.20. The value of 0 would indicate, of course, no correlation at all.

The conclusion is inevitable that the performance on I.Q. tests is determined jointly by genotypic and environmental variables. The genetic component is, for this trait, appreciably greater than the environmental component in the materials covered by the studies. This last qualification is necessary and important. The point is this: Every one of the fifty-odd studies concerned itself with twins, or siblings, or foster children in the same country and usually within a rather limited section of the same country. The range of the environments to which the individuals studied were exposed was accordingly a limited one, much more limited than it could be if the persons reared apart where brought up in, for example, a Western country, China, or an Indian tribe, or at least in different social classes and different economic and educational groups. It is, indeed, evident that the more uniform the environment is the greater, relatively, is the role of genotype differences, and vice versa.

Intelligence, or whatever it is that the I.Q. scores measure, is an important but certainly not the only quality in which we are interested in our fellow men. Temperamental, emotional, and other personality traits may for some purposes and under some circumstances be equally or even more important. The handicap that has impeded scientific study of personality traits is the difficulty of reliably measuring them. Psychologists have, however, been making progress with such measurements, by means of a variety of questionnaires, personality inventories, projective tests, and so on. It is too early at present to reach firm conclusions in this difficult field.

* Abridged from T. Dobzhansky, *Heredity and the Nature of Man,* Harcourt, Brace and World, Inc., New York, 1964, pp. 62–64, 65, 67–68. Reprinted by permission of the author and publisher.

WHAT THE DATA ON TWINS DO NOT MEAN

Notwithstanding all their weaknesses and incompleteness, the studies of twins have laid a firm foundation on which to build an understanding of the roles of genotypic and environmental variables in human development. It is fair, I think, to say that, as a general rule, whenever a variable human trait, whether structural or physiological or psychological, was at all adequately studied, both genotypic and environmental causes proved to be involved to some extent. Any way you look at it, man is a creature of both his nature and his nurture. It is folly to disregard either.

Many social scientists, and also followers of some schools of psychoanalysis, feel nevertheless a compulsive distrust of any genetic determinism in man. When the evidence becomes overwhelming they try to patch things up by saying that the genetic differences between persons are, after all, very small. For example: "In a consideration of behavioral differences among people, therefore, we may regard the biological factor as a constant, and hence eliminate it from our calculations" (L. White). I can understand (and perhaps forgive) statements of this sort only as a reaction against the excesses of social Darwinists; scientists should, however, resist the temptation to oppose exaggerations by making exaggerations opposite in sign. It has, to be sure, been claimed that the studies on identical and fraternal twins prove that what man is or can become is settled and predestined by his heredity. Environment matters little; heredity is the "dice of destiny."

However, the data show that in some environments, and presumably in any environment, persons with similar genotypes are likely to be on the average more similar in their behavior than persons with different hereditary endowments. Heredity is not the destiny that foreordains that a person will behave in a certain way regardless of circumstances. Heredity does predispose him to behave this way, rather than that way, under a given set of circumstances. It is a conditioning that to a certain extent biases man's choices and efforts of will.

As stated previously, certain people like to exaggerate the deterministic role of heredity and to underestimate that of environment. Others are loath to believe that heredity can have any influence, at least on socially significant human qualities, such as intelligence and character. The antihereditarians fear that if the genes are shown to have anything to do with man's behavior, this will deprive us of our freedom, make us mere automata, and render futile all attempts to improve man by education and social betterment. These fears go hand in hand with a misunderstanding of what heredity really "determines." It has been said before, but it will bear repetition, that heredity, the genotype, the genes do not determine "characters," such as proneness to criminality or smoking habits; the genes determine the reactions of the organism to its environment.

Selection **44** | THE EFFECT OF EARLY AND LATE BRAIN INJURY UPON TEST SCORES AND THE NATURE OF NORMAL ADULT INTELLIGENCE*

D. O. HEBB
McGill University

THE EFFECT OF LATE INJURY OUTSIDE THE SPEECH AREAS

Since the characteristics of aphasia are so unlike those of nonaphasic deterioration, the **test scores** made by aphasic patients will be considered in a separate section. For the effect of brain injury without aphasia, there are several sources of information. One is the fairly large number of cases of brain operation in which the Stanford-Binet has been used, sometimes both before and after operation. Although there are serious drawbacks to its use for the purpose, the high validity of much of its con-

* Abridged from D. O. Hebb, "The Effect of Early and Late Brain Injury upon Test Scores, and the Nature of Normal Adult Intelligence," *Proceedings of the American Philosophical Society*, 85:275–292, 1942. Reprinted by permission of the author and publisher.

tent with normal subjects gives a special interest to the scores of brain-operated patients.

STANFORD-BINET SCORES IN CASES OF BRAIN OPERATION

I have been able to find reports of Stanford-Binet *IQ*'s after adult brain operation in 15 cases. The mean *IQ* for this group of 15 patients is 108, with scores ranging from 82 to 139 (not much weight can be given to the exact figures since in some cases the old Stanford-Binet was used, in others the new). In addition, I have records of 23 patients examined at the Montreal Neurological Institute with the new Stanford-Binet; the average here is 107, with scores ranging from 54 to 152. For the total group of 38 cases the mean score is 108. Since the true norm for adults is probably below 100, there is evidently some selection operating to give us an above-average group—how much above average, in original level, there is no way to tell.

Again, five of the writers cited above gave pre- and post-operative scores. In none was there post-operative loss. For 14 cases from the Montreal Neurological Institute with pre- and post-operative examination there was a mean loss of 1.3 points in *IQ* following operation. For the total group of 19 cases the mean drop in *IQ* is 1 point, the individual results ranging from a loss of 14 points to a gain of 11 points. Of the 19 cases, 7 show a loss, 6 a gain, and 6 no change following operation. Is this apparent lack of effect due to the compensating removal of dysfunction, with the effect of surgical destruction balanced by recovery from the pre-operative disturbance? To some extent, presumably; but in the cases from the Montreal Neurological Institute the pre-operative status was good (in each case the operation was for the purpose of removing scar tissue), and the case reports of other writers suggest the same thing. The data do not give an exact knowledge of the effect of cerebral destruction, *per se*, but they do suggest strongly that destruction outside the speech areas has no great effect on Binet score. We shall see later that this is not confined to cases of smaller excision.

INDIVIDUAL CASES OF LARGE LESION OR MARKED DETERIORATION

The evidence discussed so far has been from cases of diffuse pathological destruction or relatively small surgical removals, and cases in which deterioration is not outstanding but evaluated by taking averages for large groups. Another approach to the question of the effect of brain damage is found in cases of unusually large surgical destruction or cases in which there has been marked deterioration.

The outstanding case is that of Rowe. Dr. Rowe, in a personal communication, has furnished further details of the Stanford-Binet examination of his patient after removal of the entire right hemisphere above the basal ganglia. These details are very valuable. Dandy, Gardner and O'Brien have reported cases which are similar surgically, but without psychometric examination. In such cases the bare statement that the patient showed "no obvious mental defect" must be particularly unconvincing to a psychologist, and a common-sense appraisal of intellectual ability may be especially fallible after brain injury. Yet for certain aspects of intelligence it is impressive to find independent observers reporting that there was little or no mental change after operation. The repeated statements of relatives or acquaintances that they found no defects cannot be wholly dismissed: they indicate that some of the components of adult intellectual ability are at most slightly affected. The psychometric data given by Rowe support this strongly. His patient had unfortunately become sensitive about her intellectual powers (after loss of half the cerebral cortex!) and was also found to tire very easily; the examination was not completed, but the results, while they do not make it possible to calculate an *IQ*, are of great significance.

This was the third time the test had been given the patient (others before the complete hemi-decortication), but more than a year had elapsed since the second examination, and it seems impossible to explain such a performance by practice effect, in the presence of any serious, generalized intellectual loss. The repetition of digits, forward and backward, should alone be enough to show that for some things the patient's abilities were above the average for the general population. It is clear, of course, that these data do not mean that other abilities were unaffected. We have already seen that the retention of one ability does not mean that others are also equally retained, and the psychometrist's report, that the patient "fatigued fairly rapidly, both physically and mentally" is positive evidence that in certain other tests the patient would have made lower scores. The significant fact here is the objective evidence supporting the clinical opinion that the patient's abilities were in some respects well retained; and the fact that even if other test abilities were impaired the patient still had average or above-average ability in the kind of task which is the core of the Binet test. Such things as comprehension of words, differentiation of abstract terms, memory for complex verbal material and solution of reasoning problems, are the kind of task which is most successful in differentiating various levels of intellectual development in normal subjects.

SUMMARY OF TEST DATA IN NON-APHASIC CASES OF DETERIORATION

The evidence from the larger groups of cases, and from the individual cases cited here, agrees on one point. Ability to do certain tasks which form an important part of Binet-type tests may not be greatly affected even by large injuries to the mature brain: these tasks include word definition, comprehension of and memory for complex verbal material, and the solution of unspeeded verbal problems which are hard to classify apart from the fact that they appear to be of a familiar kind, dealing with matters of general significance (though even this may not be true in all instances). The evidence shows also that there is likely to be deterioration in other abilities, although the extent and kind of loss in any individual case is unpredictable. The particular tests which have been found to show the effect of late brain injury, in the various cases cited, include: maze tracing, sentence completion, differentiation of abstract words, giving of opposites, analogies, speeded block-manipulation tasks, and picture absurdities.

Vocabulary is most noteworthy as an ability which is at most slightly affected; in all probability there are other things which are as well retained, but which are not measured directly by existing tests. This is suggested by the repeated and emphatic clinical statement that "intelligence" has been unaffected by surgical removal of cerebral tissue. The statement cannot be taken at face value but it is presumptive evidence that important components of normal adult ability are well retained.

TEST SCORES AFTER INJURY TO THE INFANT BRAIN

The discussion here is confined to cases of "birth injury" in which test-score levels are not primary determined by sensory or motor defects. The patient with hemiparesis cannot carry out certain tasks properly because of his motor defect; his test score is not then representative of an intellectual level. As far as can be determined, the scores to be discussed were not directly affected by such handicaps.

This makes for a selected sample. Athetosis or hemiparesis is detectable, but a case of cortical destruction without gross symptoms may pass for normal. The known birth-injury population therefore may deviate systematically from the total birth-injury population, so that one cannot compare the average test score of the birth-injured with the average score in cases of adult injury. The unknown degree of selection in the clinical birth-injury population is the principal difficulty of this study, and I shall return to it again.

A less direct comparison may be made, however, through the pattern of test scores. We do not know that the birth-injury sample is representative; but we can ask whether the defects, *when they do occur*, are similar in cases of early and late injury. In adult injury there are two psychometric patterns: the non-aphasic syndrome, with vocabulary in particular high and other abilities low, and the aphasic syndrome, with non-verbal abilities markedly higher than verbal abilities. For all cases of adult deterioration there would be, therefore, a bi-modal distribution of vocabulary scores and of differences between verbal (Binet) and performance scores, one mode due to the inclusion of cases of aphasia, the other to cases of deterioration without aphasia. Are the defects due to early injury at all similar? The available data, in cases of birth injury, are for children or young adolescents, which is another difficulty in making a direct comparison; but it is possible to compare brain-injured children with normal children, and brain-injured adults with normal adults, to see if deviations from the normal in each case are of the same kind, and of the same extent.

By the kindness of Dr. Heinz Werner, I have obtained details of test data in a series of 32 cases of "exogenous" mental defect from the Wayne County Training School. These are not even representative of the known birth-injury cases without gross motor handicap, since those with Binet *IQ*'s below 50 were excluded. As it happens, however, the selection here is on the safe side since it operates against the conclusions of this paper—namely, that certain test levels are lower with early than with late injury.

Werner's data include Stanford-Binet scores (in some of the cases the old, in some the new form was used); year level of vocabulary score; Stanford-Binet scatter; and Arthur Performance Test score. With these data I have included four comparable records from the Montreal Neurological Institute. Strauss has described the Wayne County Training School group as including only higher grade defectives, without gross motor handicap. The lack of motor disability makes an important difference between this group and that of Doll, Phelps and Melcher, the object of whose study was of course different.

The chronological age range, in the combined groups, is from 10 to 19 years, and the range of Binet *IQ* from 43 to 99. Vocabulary scores are available for 32 of the 36 cases. Taking the maximal chronological age as 15, Table I gives the differences between chronological age and vocabulary age level. In one case only the vocabulary age is (6 months) higher than the chronological age; the median vocabulary retardation is between 5 and 6 years, the greatest 9 years. This is evidence that vocabulary is generally depressed by birth injury. Vocabulary, also, does not tend, as it does with mature injury, to be one of the high Stanford-Binet subtest scores. Two of 30 cases have vocabulary at the highest year-level of successes; 10, on the contrary, have vocabulary scores at the basal age, and the rest are nearer the basal age than the highest year-level of successes. Scatter seems to be somewhat greater than with normal children, but with vocabulary scores tending to be low it is not like the scatter that may be found in adult cases.

Obviously vocabulary is markedly depressed in these cases, and has not the relationship to other scores that is apt to be found in cases of adult deterioration. There is no evidence of a bi-modal vocabulary distribution, nor of a bi-modal distribution of the relationship between verbal and non-verbal ability. The low level of vocabulary score means that the "non-aphasic syndrome" of the adult is not to be found here.

Nor does the adult aphasic syndrome appear. "Speech-area" injury in the infant may affect later symbolic formulation and expression: indeed, it is possible that the more extreme defects of imbecility or idiocy (not repre-

Table 1 | DISTRIBUTION OF VOCABULARY RETARDATION IN MONTHS, OBTAINED BY SUBTRACTING VOCABULARY AGE LEVEL FROM CHRONOLOGICAL AGE[1] IN 32 CASES OF BIRTH INJURY (DATA IN 28 CASES PROVIDED BY WERNER)

CA–VA[2] (months)	No. of cases	CA–VA (months)	No. of cases
−12 to −1	1	60 to 71	9
0 to 11	1	72 to 83	3
12 to 23	1	84 to 95	5
24 to 35	1	96 to 107	1
36 to 47	4	106 to 119	3
48 to 59	3		

[1] Range of chronological age was actually 10 to 19, but 15 is taken as a maximum; vocabulary age ranged from less than 6 to 14.
[2] VA = vocabulary age.

sented in the group analyzed) may be the result of injury to what, in the adult, is the speech area. But it is characteristic of aphasics to have some non-verbal abilities well within the normal range, with the verbal abilities outside the normal range: in a large proportion, with a marked discrepancy between verbal and non-verbal abilities. No writer has discussed, as far as I am aware, the occurrence of aphasia as the result of birth injury (as distinct from lesions occurring or progressing after speech has developed), but it appears that when verbal defects are as serious as those of aphasia the level of other abilities is not far removed. In short, the only children whose verbal capacities are as poor as in the ordinary case of aphasia would be imbeciles at least. Doll refers to the effect of birth injury upon speech, pointing out that speech defects may be accompanied by normal ability elsewhere, but he appears to mean a kind of defect which is not at all like the aphasic disturbance of symbolic function. Such defects are to be thought of as disturbances of speech production, not of the cortical processes underlying speech organization (just as there are adult speech disturbances which have no relation to aphasia).

THE DEVELOPMENT AND RETENTION OF INTELLIGENCE

The weight of evidence points to a more widespread and less selective effect of the large infant injury than of the large adult injury. Unless known cases of exogenous mental defect involve lesions in the speech areas (the possibility already discussed), to account for the uniformly low vocabulary and verbal test scores, it must be that *low verbal test scores are produced by early lesions outside the speech areas*. With vocabulary at least it appears that a cerebral lesion may be deleterious at infancy and not at maturity, for such lesions at maturity do not affect vocabulary to a detectable degree. If this is so, the development and the retention of an ability may depend on the brain in different ways. An intact cerebrum is necessary for the normal development of certain test abilities, but not for their retention at a nearly normal level. In other words, *more cerebral efficiency or more intellectual power is needed for intellec-*

tual development than for later functioning at the same level.

Stating the problem in this way suggests a clue to a possible solution. The actual modifications of behavior which occur in intellectual development are mostly qualitative. Faced with a complex situation, the subject sees it in a new way and makes a new response—not more responses or harder responses. Now often in such modifications of behavior it is the first steps which demand intellectual capacity. Learning to solve a problem demands more intellectual effort than solving more problems of the same kind; this is obvious with formal problems, but it may also be true of the perception of relationships: in the figures used by the Gestalt psychologists, in puzzle pictures of the kind made to amuse children, in Street's Gestalt Completion test, there is ample evidence that the original perception of a relationship may make more intellectual demand than the same perception later. It is not far-fetched to suppose that this is also true of the perception of relationships in everyday events which the growing child does not set out consciously to master, as he must an arithmetic problem or a puzzle picture, but which make up the "problems" of everyday life. The intelligent child solves these problems without thinking of them as such, but nevertheless at a faster rate than the less intelligent: intellectual capacity must be important in the development and it is plausible to suppose that here, as in more formal intellectual undertakings, the first achievement is what requires the greater amount of intellect. The development of social appreciation, common sense and verbal comprehension, therefore, may demand an intact brain, while their retention does not.

Intellectual development then would involve stable, qualitative changes of behavior and perception, dependent for their first appearance upon more elaborate intellectual processes than for their later functioning. Physiologically, this implies that stable changes of neural organization may occur as the result of activity in other parts of the nervous system. Normal development of verbal comprehension demands an intact or almost intact cerebrum, but its persistence at a high level is possible after the removal of the right half of the cerebral cortex. This is accounted for on the supposition that the actual basis of the adult verbal response is in the middle regions of the left hemisphere (in right-handed individuals, of course), but that the physiological organization of this part of the brain is partly determined by earlier activities in the rest of the brain. The qualitatively good response is a modification due to an earlier and more elaborate kind of cerebral activity.

All this, however, emphasizes only one of the factors entering into test performance—the one accounting for high scores following mature brain injury. But verbal test indices, like non-verbal, vary in their susceptibility to the effect of injury outside the speech areas and no test is wholly unaffected. The stable qualitative changes of intellectual development are therefore not all that is rated by intelligence tests. To a varying degree, the tests must also measure something closer to the intellectual power that produced the qualitative changes in the first place.

An hypothesis can now be stated, to account for the high level of certain test scores following late brain injury, for the varying degree to which other test scores are affected, and for the differences of the effect of early and late injury:

In any test performance there are two factors involved, the relative importance of which varies with the test: one factor being present intellectual power, of the kind essential to normal intellectual development; the other being the lasting changes of perceptual organization and behavior induced by the first factor during the period of development. Roughly, the one concerns power of "reasoning," of synthesis and invention; the other skill (that is, a factor due to experience). The term "present intellectual power" is not altogether satisfactory; it is used in a special sense not equal to "present intellectual efficiency," since efficiency would be determined by both factors, not only one. The clinical data indicate that both are of essential importance in intelligence as it would be identified either by tests or by common sense. The contrast is not between intelligence and knowledge, but between capacity to develop new patterns of response and the functioning of those already developed.

Vocabulary, unspeeded verbal comprehension and so on may be regarded as primarily indices of a level of past development, while some other tests, more sensitive to the effect of injury to the mature brain, are better indices of "present intellectual power"; keeping in mind, however, the implication of the hypothesis presented—that adult intellectual efficiency in many matters is determined more by the highest past level of intellectual power than by the level of "present intellectual power." There are, in this view, two ways in which a test may function.

Weisenburg and McBride have made a somewhat similar distinction of test material, related to the familiarity or unfamiliarity of the task. Finding no evidence of loss, after right-sided cerebral destruction, in tests of sentence dictation, oral spelling, and vocabulary, they say:

It is noteworthy that these are language tests involving the reproduction of acquired knowledge in situations not unfamiliar to everyday experience. They [the patients] fall furthest below the normal on the Sentence Completion Test, which involves constructive synthetic mental activity in a situation which is not difficult for them to grasp, but still a less natural situation.

Emphasis here should be put on the kind and form of task rather than on "reproduction of acquired knowledge," if this phrase means the reproduction of material in the form in which it was learned. It must be insisted that in an oral vocabulary test the subject is not asked to repeat a form of words as he learned them, and a high score cannot be explained as due to rote memory. In spelling, this is often true; the child in school learns to repeat individual letters in the proper order; when he is tested as an adult he may make the same response from memory. Vocabulary tests are another matter. Common words are rarely learned by their definitions; still less are the definitions learned by heart. It is their use that is learned. The evidence in Rowe's case shows that comprehension and memory for complex verbal material heard *for the first time* are also insensitive to late injury. The kind of task is familiar; the specific content, and the actual response to be made, are not.

There is a still more cogent reason for not dismissing the vocabulary score of the adult brain-injured as a mere feat of memory. This is the correlation between vocabulary score and post-operative social competence, conversational ability (ability, that is, to understand and communicate ideas) and general level of functioning in ordinary life. I must revert here to the frequency with which relatives or friends, as well as the attending clinicians, report of the patient who has had successful removal of a large amount of cerebral tissue that his intelligence is unimpaired, and the inescapable conclusion that the patient has retained some essential and important part of his intellectual powers. Vocabulary score therefore would be a better index of level of functioning in such matters than test scores which are more sensitive to the effect of brain damage.

The implication of the hypothesis presented here is that the formation of the qualitative modifications of behavior may continue for some time after intellectual power has reached its peak, and that when tests of more genuinely adult interest are developed they may be found, unlike "power" tests but like vocabulary and some other tests, to continue to show a rise for some time after the onset of puberty. The functioning of intelligence in practice demands that these subjective products of earlier intellectual activity be available, that the understanding of common situations and the solution of routine problems occur without intellectual effort. The farther this process has gone, the more efficient intelligence will be. No amount of native mathematical aptitude, even to the extent of genius, will make original contributions to higher mathematics possible until the ideas of elementary algebra and geometry are second nature, so that real intellectual effort is saved for the advanced problem. Intellectual development, therefore, involves (a) the development of direct intellectual power, by neural maturation, and (b) the establishment of routine modes of response to common problems, or of perceptual and conceptual modifications leading to qualitative modifications of behavior.

The kind of test ability which is generally thought to reach its peak earliest, perhaps between the ages of 12 to 15 years, is the kind which is also more apt to be sensitive to the effect of brain injury after this period, and sensitive as well to the changes of senescence. Direct intellectual power, therefore, may be thought to be at a maximum before the age of 16 years. What we call intelligence, however, would involve both (a) and (b). It would therefore continue to rise to the point at which

declining intellectual power offset the increase of intellectual products. For some problems, this peak of efficiency would be reached early; for others late, depending on the extent to which subsidiary problems are involved in the solution of the more difficult problems. Pure puzzle-solving might reach its peak early, for each puzzle would be more or less isolated; but insight into social relationships or skill at dealing with other people might reach a peak very much later and then be maintained. It is granted at once that this high level of problem solving by older subjects is likely to be within a strictly limited range, but this does not justify the psychological conclusion that intelligence begins to decline with adolescence, nor the idea that the older subject gives only an appearance of intelligence. He may not function as well in a wide range of tasks, and may not maintain as high a level of efficiency over long periods; but in all that kind of comprehension which is commonly thought of as demanding maturity of judgment it is likely that the older man has as high a level of functioning as the younger man, if not in many matters a higher one. We have as yet no good measures of "the integrative mental processes interpretative of [adult] experience," but when these processes can be measured one may expect to see a more adequate picture of psychological maturity.

Selection **45** | CREATIVITY: ITS MEASUREMENT AND DEVELOPMENT*

J. P. GUILFORD
University of Southern California

Creativity is a most timely subject. Interest in creativity is evidently very widespread. Industries and governmental agencies are asking how they can promote a greater exhibition of creative performance in their personnel. They

* Adapted from an address presented to educators of Sacramento County, in Sacramento, Calif., Jan. 20, 1959. Reproduced by permission of the author.

are also asking why the graduates from our schools, although technically trained and generally informed, do not produce more in the way of original ideas.

With artificial satellites and even an artificial planet circling over our heads, the day of Buck Rogers is arriving with accelerated pace. The imagination of all of us is in for considerable stretching, just to keep up with developments of this kind. It is obvious that we are in a tight race with Russia with respect to these technological advances. It is almost as obvious that we are in competition with Russia also with respect to education, and in fact, with respect to other areas of social and economic progress. In many respects our adversary has shown more initiative and imagination than we have. It is not likely that our potential intellectual resources are inferior to those of Russia. We may well ask ourselves, therefore, what we are doing that is wrong and how we may promote better use of the intellectual resources that we have.

My own interest in creativity dates back many years. As a graduate student I had the very fruitful experience of serving in a psychological clinic, in connection with which I tested a great many children. I came away from this experience with the conviction that an IQ is a very inadequate item of information regarding a child and that IQ tests did not give adequate attention to such qualities as ingenuity, inventiveness, and originality of thinking. It was not until ten years ago, when funds became available, that I had an adequate opportunity to investigate the subject of creativity in a comprehensive manner. I should say that the study of creativity is only one aspect, but an important one, of a larger project that ranges over most of the area of intellectual abilities.[1]

It is my purpose today, to speak first of the various hypotheses we set up at the beginning of our investigations of abilities in the area of creativity and to report what has subsequently happened in testing those hypotheses. I shall then point out the relationships of creative abilities to other abilities and their place in the scheme of all intellectual abilities. The more obviously creative abilities take on added mean-

[1] Under Contract N6onr–23810 with the Office of Naval Research, entitled a Project on Aptitudes of High-Level Personnel.

ing and significance when seen as part of a larger organization of intellectual abilities. The restriction of my discussion to abilities involved in creativity does not mean that I believe other traits, of needs, interests, attitudes, and of temperament are unimportant. We have felt, however, that the study of creative abilities would be the most profitable place to begin.

THE MORE OBVIOUSLY CREATIVE ABILITIES

The best way known at present for determining what are the different kinds of abilities in an area is that of factor analysis. Each unique ability is found as a separate factor from the way in which test scores from a group of individuals intercorrelate. A good factor-analytic study begins with some guesses as to what unique abilities exist in an area and what kind of ability each one is. This means setting up some hypotheses. The factor analysis is then conducted in a way that should give the answer as to whether each hypothesis is probably correct or not correct.

Initial hypotheses

In our first study of creativity, we guessed that we should find at least seven distinct abilities. We thought that individuals differ with respect to their ability to sense problems that call for solution. Those individuals who are more alert to the existence of problems have occasion to go to work upon them, and if they do, they have increased probability of coming up with solutions.

We thought that individuals differ with respect to the rate with which they can produce ideas. Faced with a problem, and having defined it, we think of one possible solution after another. The person who can produce ten ideas per minute, as compared with the one who can produce only two per minute, should have the advantage, if the average level of quality of the ideas is the same for the two. In other words, we expected to find individual differences in *fluency* of thinking; the facility with which ideas can be generated.

We expected to find individual differences in *flexibility* of thinking. Some individuals are rigid or set in their ways of thinking and this shows up particularly where problems call for the rejection of habitual, conventional, or previously successful ways and the striking out in new directions. Popular conceptions include the idea that the creative person is an *original* thinker. He does not repeat the thinking of others around him. The ideas generated are new to him and perhaps to his culture.

We also thought that creative individuals are superior in their abilities to analyze information and particularly to synthesize information, for so many inventions involve simply putting the same old elements together in some new way. Borrowing a concept from Gestalt psychology, we thought that individuals may differ in their *ability to redefine* things; to transform the meaning or use or function of an object so as to give it a new role. Prior to our investigation, there had been some evidence to support the hypothesis that there are factors of fluency of thinking and of originality but not of the other kinds mentioned, at least in the category of thinking abilities.

Major results

Our results have well supported the existence of a separate ability to be aware of problems and it is called *sensitivity to problems*. It is measured best by means of two tests. One test calls for stating things that are wrong with common devices such as the telephone, the refrigerator, or the electric toaster. The other calls for things wrong with social institutions such as national elections, divorce laws, or tipping. Seeing defects or deficiencies seems to be the common feature of such tests.

The hypothesis of a trait of fluency of thinking was more than amply supported, in that we have found four abilities, all of which can be regarded as kinds of fluency. Prior factor-analytical results had partially prepared us for this outcome. *Word fluency* was discovered by L. L. Thurstone some 20 years ago (5). It is the ability to think of words rapidly, each word satisfying the same letter requirement or requirements, such as containing a stated letter or syllable or containing two given letters.

The factor of *ideational fluency* calls for tests involving the rapid listing of meaningful words in a specified category or the listing of ideas to meet meaningful requirements, for example, to list objects that are solid, white, and edible. In another test the examinee names as many uses as he can for a common brick. In still another he writes as many titles as he can think of for a given short story. In any test of ideational fluency, speed is important and quality does not matter, the score being the total number of acceptable responses. Winston Churchill must have had this ability to a high degree. Clement Attlee is reported to have said about him recently that no matter what problem came up, Churchill always seemed to have about ten ideas. The trouble was, Attlee continued, he did not know which was the good one.

Associational fluency is the ability to list words that bear some relation to a given word. The task is different from that in connection with ideational fluency, for in the latter the responses belong to a specified class. An example would be naming synonyms to the given word "dark." Other relations could be specified and would probably serve in a measure of associational fluency.

Expressional fluency is the ability to put words into organized phrases and sentences. In one test, the examinee is told to make four-word sentences and is given the same four initial letters of the words to be used in all his responses. Given the initial letters W_____ c_____ e_____ n_____, one might write: We can eat nuts, Whence came Eve Newton?, and so on. The test would work about as well without the four initial letters being given.

In the investigation of the hypothesis of flexibility of thinking we have found two different abilities. One of these we have designated as *spontaneous flexibility* and the other as *adaptive flexibility*. The reason for these particular qualifying adjectives, "spontaneous" and "adaptive," is that in the first case the thinker is flexible even when he has no need to be whereas in the second case he would fail to solve a problem if he were not flexible. I have mentioned the Brick Uses test as a measure of ideational fluency, in which the score is simply the number of uses listed. The examinee might write a set of responses that are all within one category: Build a house; build a barn; build a garage; build a school; build a church; build a walk; build a barbecue; build a chimney. On the other hand, in another paper every response might be in a different category:

Make a door stop; make a red powder; throw at a dog; make a paper weight; make a bookcase; drown a cat; drive a nail; use for baseball bases. Jumping from one category to another is an indication of spontaneous flexibility. It may indicate other qualities, also, but we are not concerned about this right now.

A good example of a test measuring adaptive flexibility is Match Problems. This is based upon the common game that uses squares the sides of which are formed by match sticks. The examinee is told to take away a given number of matches to leave a stated number of squares. Nothing is said about the sizes of the squares to be left. If the examinee imposes upon himself the restriction that the squares must be of the same size, he will fail in his attempts to do some of the items. Other odd kinds of solutions are introduced in other items, such as one square inside another or overlapping squares, and so on. In another variation of the Match Problems test, the examinee is told that there are two or more solutions to each item. After solving it one way, can he think of still different ways? Other tests of adaptive flexibility present what are called insight problems. There is some unusual trick required for the solution of each problem.

For the measurement of originality, quite a variety of tests will work. In every case some standard of quality has to be set up for acceptable responses or the task has very novel requirements for the examinee. The Plot Titles test presents a short story, the examinee being told to list as many titles as he can to head the story. One story is about a missionary who has been captured by cannibals in Africa. He is in the pot and about to be boiled when a Princess of the tribe obtains a promise for his release if he will become her mate. He refuses and is boiled to death.

In scoring the test, the responses are separated into two categories, clever and non-clever. Examples of non-clever titles are:

African Death
Defeat of a Princess
Eaten by Savages
The African Missionary
In Darkest Africa
Boiled by Savages

These titles are appropriate but commonplace.

The number of such responses serves as a score for ideational fluency. Examples of clever responses are:

Pot's plot
Potluck dinner
Stewed parson
Goil or boil
A mate worse than death
He left a dish for a pot
Chaste in haste
A hot price for freedom

Another test of originality presents a very novel task. It asks the examinee to invent simple line symbols to stand for meaningful ideas. For each verb and noun in the following items a symbol must be produced:

Ring the bell
Open the door
Look into the room
Close the window

Still another task calls for somewhat unusual responses each with at least a minimal degree of cleverness. In the Cartoons test the examinee is to write the "punch line" for each cartoon.

Thus far I have mentioned only positive findings. The hypotheses regarding sensitivity to problems, fluency of thinking, flexibility of thinking, and originality have been more than vindicated, in the sense that there were even more factors of these kinds than had been anticipated. Two hypotheses of expected factors were definitely not supported in spite of ample opportunity for such support. We found no unitary ability to analyze and none to synthesize. This may come as a surprise to you as it did to us.

Please note that this kind of result does not mean that we do not analyze in our thinking and that we do not synthesize, for we obviously perform operations that can be put in these categories. What the analytical results indicate is that each person is not at all uniformly able to analyze in all situations and with all kinds of material nor is he uniformly able to synthesize. His success in either respect is dependent upon the circumstances. Abilities to perform in tests involving analyzing are general aptitudes of various kinds, depending upon the task. The same may be said regarding tests involving synthesizing.

We have regarded the ordinary operations of planning as examples of creative thinking and have made one factorial study of this particular area. One of the hypothesized abilities involved that was supported by results is called "elaboration." It is measured by a test in which the examinee is given the bare outlines of a plan and is to supply the detailed steps that will make the plan work. It is also measured by a test in which the examinee is given a line or two and is told to construct on this foundation a complete object of some kind.

The question naturally arises, how do we know that the abilities measured by the tests are related to creative performances in everyday life. There is not time to present all the evidence, but there is increasing information to the effect that other, independent assessments of some of the same abilities and some performances in practice are correlated significantly and even substantially with scores from some of the tests. Some of the qualities assessed have been the creative performances of students of arts and of sciences, of military officers, and of engineers.

THE PLACE OF CREATIVE ABILITIES IN INTELLECT

I stated that the Aptitudes Project has as its major objective the exploration of all aspects of intelligence. In addition to creative abilities, we have investigated abilities in the areas of reasoning, evaluation, planning, and problem solving. In a broader sense, the developing picture of human intellect is more significant than that of creative abilities alone. Creative abilities also become more meaningful when we compare them with other kinds of abilities and find relations between them. Furthermore, it is becoming clear that creative performance in everyday life cannot be fully accounted for by such abilities as I have already indicated. Many other abilities may make their contributions, depending upon the situation and the task. Furthermore, some relationships among the factors strongly suggest that there are creative abilities yet to be discovered. It will be necessary to discuss briefly the entire struc-

ture of intellect to make these statements clear.

Classification of the intellectual factors

Attempts to classify the intellectual abilities as found by factor analysis have shown that there are three meaningful ways of grouping the factors of intellect. One way is in terms of the kind of operation required or performed. There are five fundamental kinds of operations—cognition, memory, divergent thinking, convergent thinking, and evaluation. Cognition means discovery or rediscovery or recognition. Memory means retention of what has been cognized. Two kinds of productive-thinking operations generate new information from known and remembered information. In divergent-thinking operations we think in different directions, sometimes searching, sometimes seeking variety. In convergent thinking the information can and does lead to one right answer or to a recognized best or conventional answer. In evaluation we reach decisions as to the goodness, correctness, suitability, or adequacy of what we know, what we remember, and what we produce in productive thinking.

A second way of classifying the intellectual factors is according to the kind of material or content involved. The factors known thus far involve three kinds of material or content— figural, symbolic, and semantic. Figural content is concrete material, with various properties of size, form, color, texture, and so on. Things we hear or feel would provide other examples of figural material. Symbolic content is composed of letters, digits, and other conventional signs. Semantic content is in the form of verbal meanings or ideas.

When a certain kind of operation is applied to a certain kind of content, as many as six general kinds of products may be involved. There is enough evidence available to suggest that regardless of which combination of operation and content is concerned (there are 15 combinations from the five operations and the three contents mentioned before), the same six kinds of products may be found associated. The kinds of products are: units, classes, relations, systems, transformations, and implications. So far as we have determined from factor analysis, these are the only fundamental kinds of products that we can know. Or, stated otherwise, we should be able to identify any item of information as belonging in one of these categories.

The structure of intellect

The three classifications of the intellectual abilities can be combined. As three cross classifications they provide a unified theory of intelligence that can be represented in a rectangular model as shown in Fig. 1. Each mode of classification becomes a parameter or dimension of the model. Every kind of content is shown combined with every kind of operation and each of these combinations is shown combined with every kind of product. The only aspect of the model not previously mentioned is the fourth kind of content—behavioral—which has been added on a purely theoretical basis. Behavioral content is information in the form of the actions, desires, intentions, thoughts, and feelings of people, which we can know, and we can use the information in dealing with people. The area is sometimes known as "social intelligence," which has not been investigated from the approach of factor analysis. The model predicts a number of abilities, parallel to those found applying to each of the other kinds of content.

Of the 90 different abilities represented in the three content areas that have been investigated, we now know more than half. Most of the creative abilities of fluency, flexibility, and originality that have already been mentioned, come in the category of divergent thinking. For tests of such abilities, there is no one right answer and a variety of answers gives a good score. In terms of the model, ideational fluency is interpreted as the ability to produce divergently a number of semantic (meaningful) units (ideas). Spontaneous flexibility is reinterpreted as the divergent production of classes. Recall that in scoring the Brick Uses test for flexibility it is the number of shifts from class to class that gives a score for this ability. Associational fluency is regarded as an ability to produce a variety of meaningful "correlates." Correlates are units of information that complete a relationship, when a relation and another unit are given. Thus, to the question "What words mean almost the opposite of 'soft'?" the responses might be: difficult, firm, solid, and so on.

The factor first called originality is now recognized as the ability to produce a variety of transformations. The clever plot titles men-

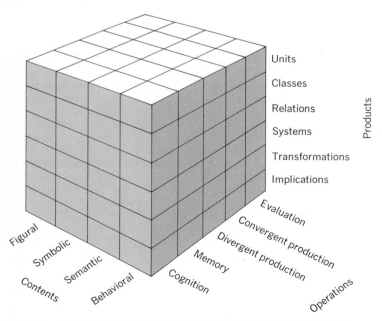

Figure 1 Theoretical model for the complete "Structure of Intellect."

tioned earlier usually involve some unusual interpretation of the story or of the characters, and make liberal use of puns, all of which are meaningful reinterpretations or transformations. The factor of elaboration is regarded as the divergent production of implications. Giving the details to complete a plan, or building complex, meaningful objects out of simple lines is a matter of producing many implications; one thing suggests another.

It is to be especially noted that the abilities just mentioned are all in the semantic or verbal category as to content. Their relations to creative writing and to meaningful planning and problem solving may be obvious. But the structure-of-intellect model suggests distinct abilities of similar nature for dealing with figural and symbolic material. We already know three such abilities. The factor of word fluency calls for a test of rapidly listing words (symbolic units) that have some specified spelling requirement. The factor of expressional fluency calls for a test of forming sentences. Considering that a sentence is a symbolic system, we can interpret this factor as the ability to produce divergent, symbolic systems. In the figural column would come the factor of adaptive flexibility that was shown in dealing with match problems, an ability to produce divergent transformations.

Thus, abilities to think divergently to produce results differ according to the kind of information with which the person deals. An all-round creative person is probably the exception rather than the rule. Leonardo da Vinci was one of those rare geniuses. In these days we have only to think of the synthetic nature of a motion picture or television production to realize that not all the creative talents come from the same person in arriving at highly successful results. The creative mathematician probably shines in the symbolic abilities and the creative visual artist in the figural abilities. For the composer we may suggest a completely different set of figural abilities having to do with sounds.

Other factors contributing to creative performances

I have indicated that the most obviously creative abilities are in the category of divergent thinking. It is necessary now to explain some exceptions. One of the creative-thinking abilities mentioned, *redefinition*, is classified with the convergent-thinking factors, a classification that may seem to be somewhat contradictory. But it is in the row for which the kind of product is that of transformations. Much creative effort is in the form of the transformation of something known into something else not previously known. The first redefinition factor that we found is in the semantic column and the characteristic test of it is called Gestalt Transformations. A sample item: "From which object could you most likely make a needle?," has the alternative answers: "cabbage, splice, steak, paper box; and fish." The most likely object is a fish, a bone of which might be adapted to make a needle. The essential step in solving this item is changing the meaning of an object or part of an object in order to adapt it to some new use.

There are two other redefinition factors that come in the same row with the factor of semantic redefinition. An example of a kind of test for measuring *symbolic redefinition* gives sentences in each of which the name of sport or a game is concealed. Some sample items are:

Cowardice is not a soldierly attribute. (dice)
To beat the Hun, tin goes a long way. (hunting)
One could tell he was a Mongol from his costume. (golf)
I am sorry, I did not know he was ailing. (sailing)

Familiar words must be broken down and the letters regrouped in order to answer the items.

A test of *figural redefinition* is called Hidden Figures. In this test, the same lines that function in certain ways in the complex figure must be given new functions as they become parts of new figures. In connection with all three redefinition factors, there is involved a freedom from what has been called "functional fixedness," a form of rigidity. We can give the redefinition factors a more positive interpretation, however, by saying that a kind of lability or flexibility is involved.

The factor of sensitivity to problems, one of the first creative-thinking abilities we hypothesized and found, is placed in the evaluation category. It is now regarded as the ability to evaluate semantic implications. Tests that ask what is wrong with devices or with institutions is asking what errors or flaws are suggested by those things under their present conditions. In general, evaluation means being sensitive to errors or shortcomings.

Granting creative properties to these transformation and evaluation factors thus enlarges the number of abilities that may contribute substantially to creative performances. As a matter of fact, most of the abilities in the structure of intellect may play appreciable roles in the complete operation of invention. The cognitive abilities are basic. Without having information there is no intellectual performance of any kind. Learned information is of no value later unless it is retained. Evaluative abilities are needed if there is any self-criticism, which there should be if the creative thinker is to complete his job.[2]

Creativity and the IQ

You have probably already wondered about the question of the relation of creativity to the IQ. I think that all teachers must have made the observation that not all children with high IQs are creative and on the other hand, not all the creative children have high IQs. It is said that Thomas A. Edison was by no means a genius from an academic point of view. Shakespeare and other creative geniuses had little schooling, although it is not known what their IQs were.

I think it can be safely said that IQ tests have been concentrated on a very few factors in the structure of intellect. The factors emphasized have differed somewhat in different IQ tests. The IQ for verbal intelligence, which correlates highest with academic grades, is usually dominated by one factor, that of *verbal comprehension*—the ability to cognize semantic units; in other words, the ability to know verbal concepts. Whatever the strong components of an IQ test, they are probably very much confined to the cognitive category. Certainly, there is usually almost nothing involved in the way of divergent thinking or of transformations. A high IQ may help a child to show excellence in the way of creative performances but it is not a sufficient condition. In singling out the gifted child, therefore, giftedness might be defined so as to emphasize either high IQ or high creative abilities, or both, depending upon where one wishes to place the emphasis.

[2] For a more complete description of the known factors of intellect, see (3).

DEVELOPMENT OF CREATIVITY

Can we, through any educational procedures, make our graduates any more creatively productive? Can we improve the status of our students in the various creative abilities? These two questions are not quite the same, but they are both pertinent. Would Shakespeare have done any better had he gone to college? Would engineering or scientific education have helped Edison? It is also pertinent to ask whether our nuclear scientists could have invented the atomic bomb and whether our rocketeers could have produced new satellites without having had college instruction. In connection with the last question, did the education merely furnish the inventors with the needed information and what did it do to their creative-thinking abilities?

Creativity and the nature-nurture problem

On the academic question as to whether individual positions on the primary intellectual abilities are determined by heredity or by environment there is opinion all the way between the two extremes, as you probably know. On the one hand there are those who will tell you that a creative genius is entirely due to a lucky accident of a certain unique combination of genes. I heard that statement from a professor of English who was discussing Shakespeare. At the other extreme there are those who say that the primary abilities are generalized, learned habits or skills, produced by certain kinds of practice. This view is proposed by the Canadian psychologist, G. A. Ferguson (1). My own position is somewhere between these two extremes. Heredity probably does determine limits, both upper and lower, within which development can occur. Experience or learning may have considerable room within which to operate and to produce results. The finding of a very large number of distinct intellectual abilities definitely means that the combined effects of heredity and learning do not produce uniform results in all areas of mental functioning.

The best working assumption to adopt is that education can do a great deal to promote the development of individuals in the way of preparing them to perform creatively, if not in the way of strengthening their creative abilities. What can we do to achieve these goals?

No one knows as yet how we can best educate for creativity. The better teachers have probably always made some contributions in these directions, often without being able to say explicitly just what they did or why. On the other hand, we suspect that poor teaching has actually many times put the brakes on development toward creativity, or, at best, has had no net effect one way or the other. It is likely that the normal conditions of mass education are on the whole inhibiting to the development of creative individuals, for creativity is highly individualistic. A few general suggestions can be ventured, without adequate empirical support for many of them.

Changed attitudes needed

My first suggestion is that the intellectual atmosphere of the country as a whole needs some serious changes. The forces of anti-intellectualism have subsided somewhat since the advent of the sputniks, but they are still with us. On the whole, as compared with other countries of the Western World, we have had a history of appreciation of brawn rather than of brain. Public acclaim has gone to the athlete rather than to the outstanding student of the arts, humanities, or sciences. No one knows better than teachers that we obtain development in those directions in which achievement is rewarded. What is even worse, the student who excels has often felt compelled to conceal his distinction, lest he be ridiculed.

There has also been an unfortunate and unusual drive toward mediocrity in all respects. I was very much depressed recently by an article in Look Magazine that described the students of a certain high school setting for themselves a general goal of mediocrity. I hope this school is not typical, but the report was that the students did not want to excel in *any* respect. In part, this attitude may stem from a mistaken idea about democracy as a social ideal; a belief that democracy means equality of ability as well as equality of rights. I am afraid that it also stems, in part, from the emphasis upon personal adjustment. If adjustment means the forcing of all individuals into a mold of mediocrity and if the emphasis upon adjustment has contributed to such a leveling process, it has done our country a grave disservice.

I do not wish to minimize the importance of dealing with maladjustment. But it seems to me that a more positive approach can be taken to the problem. What is often needed is the development of social and personal skills. Perhaps when we know much more about the components of social intelligence we shall be in a better position to decide in what respect such skills are deficient and knowing the properties of behavioral abilities we can take the appropriate steps. In the meantime, let us recognize that each individual has a unique personality and that in our democratic respect for the individual we should tolerate the right of each person to be different, within the limits of personal safety and welfare of those concerned.

Changes in the attitudes of many teachers toward creative signs in their pupils would be a great help toward the development of creativity. The sad fact is that teachers generally do not prefer the more creative students. Furthermore, they do not have much confidence in the future success of the more creative students. These conclusions are supported by some research of Getzels and Jackson (2). In a secondary school they selected a group of students who were in the highest fifth in terms of IQ, but not that high in a test of creative abilities. and another group of students who were in the highest fifth in the creative-ability test but not in IQ. While both groups made equally high achievement scores, the teachers stated that they liked the high-IQ students better and they expected higher future success from them. No doubt the more creative students are irritating at times and they are not as ready to conform to the usual standards. While both teachers and parents share the belief that creativity should be a recognized property of gifted children, along with high IQ and high grades, neither teachers nor parents expect as much success from creative children as they do from well-adjusted children.

Instruction for creativity

For the teacher who is concerned about promoting creativity in students, a knowledge of the various abilities contributing to creativity should be very helpful. If we wish to develop certain skills, it is very important to have a knowledge of the nature of those skills. Unless we know what a skill is like we do not have a very clear goal at which to aim. The same principle applies to the intellectual abilities less directly connected with creative performances. In other words, the promotion of intellectual development all along the line should be facilitated by knowing what intellectual abilities exist and what they are like.

One obvious practical approach that suggests itself would be to seek curriculum changes that might favor development of creativity. Are there certain areas of instruction now offered in which there are special opportunities to cultivate creative habits? If so, they could perhaps be given more emphasis. There is a suggestion that courses in art are the most obvious place for this, since students of art are thought to have more room for individual expression and originality may be expected of them and may be rewarded.

There is the broader educational question, however, whether creative habits learned in art courses will transfer to activities outside the art context. It is also possible for a teacher of art to be so insistent upon the conventional ways of doing things and upon rigid standards of evaluation that little encouragement is offered for students to develop creativity, even in art. The teacher would need to take full advantage of opportunities to foster creative attitudes and creative skills as well as to point out the parallels with other areas to which some transfer of those skills can be made.

Opportunities for teaching creative skills is by no means limited to courses in art. Such opportunities are perhaps most obviously encountered in courses in the sciences, in composition, and in mathematics. In most subjects, however, including those just mentioned, we have been prone to think that the child needs to spend his first 16 school years in learning what others have done and have found out, leaving the graduate-school level any serious encouragement for the student to produce something of his own. This policy will have to be materially changed, if we are to keep alive the natural creative inclinations with which the child starts at the bottom of the academic ladder. Some children, at least, could very well profit by having a part of their instruction in the form of seminars and some substitution of laboratory exercises of their own choosing for exercises that are ordinarily required.

Some high-school students having these kinds of opportunities in the Portland, Oregon, schools were reported to be distinctly better adapted than other students to college instruction at Reed College.[3]

The teacher who is alert to opportunities to stimulate creative thinking, whatever the course, can very likely find such occasions. This probably calls for new ways in which subject matter is presented. With the information that most of the creative-thinking abilities are in the divergent-thinking category, the teacher can seek opportunities to call for divergent thinking. In transmitting our culture to the younger generation, we naturally stress conventional answers to problems, hence we emphasize convergent thinking. In urging that we need more emphasis upon divergent thinking on the part of students, I am not advocating that we attempt to create a generation of young rebels. It should be possible to teach appreciation for those things from the past that are good as well as to encourage students to see how things might be done better.

To be more specific, and to give some attention to particular creative-thinking abilities, can we teach students to be more sensitive to problems? Can we teach them to see that a problem may have several different interpretations? Can we encourage practice in the generation of a multitude of ideas that might be pertinent in interpreting the problem or in reaching the solution? Even if there is only one right answer, as in mathematical problems, can the student solve the problem in a number of different ways? Can we train him to be less sensitive to ridicule of others when he has come up with what appears to be an outlandish idea? Can we teach him to be his own best critic so that he can depend upon his own judgment? In order to obtain the answers to these questions, we shall have to apply whatever procedures we believe will achieve the desired results and determine experimentally whether those procedures have been effective.

A general procedure that is becoming rather common is to give a special course on creative thinking. Such courses are given in colleges, in industries, and in governmental agencies, including the armed forces. The content and

[3] From a personal communication from Dr. Robert C. Wilson.

the methods of instruction differ in such courses. Some of the courses present information concerning the nature of thinking as we know it, pointing out the kinds of thinking operations and how they are applied. Most of them provide exercises in thinking of one kind or another.

Many of you have no doubt heard of the brainstorming session approach. This kind of exercise involves group thinking on a problem. A small group of similar individuals, perhaps ten or twelve, comes together to think up new ideas to solve a problem, for example, to find a name for a new product. All criticisms are strictly prohibited during the brainstorming session. Everyone is encouraged to feel free to suggest any idea, no matter how ridiculous it may sound. Evaluation of the ideas comes at a later session. It is claimed that exercise of this kind has a general effect upon an individual's ability to produce ideas in quantity. Some recent research at the University of Buffalo showed that individuals who had taken the course in which brainstorming was one of the popular methods could produce nearly twice as many "good" ideas in five minutes as a control group who had not taken the course. The goodness of ideas was judged in terms of uniqueness and usefulness (4).

After a short course on creative thinking by personnel in the Air Force, in which brainstorming and other exercises were utilized, a group of men showed a significant gain in a test of originality as compared with a control group. The trained group also showed a slight, but insignificant, loss in a test for ideational fluency. A similar result was obtained in a study with children who took a short course on creative writing. In both cases we may infer that the instruction emphasized quality of ideas at the expense of quantity, or at least it seemed to have that effect. In one of our own experiments we had two groups take the Plot Titles test, one with instruction to give clever responses and the other without this part of the instructions. The effect of the instructions was to improve the average score for originality and to reduce the score for ideational fluency.

The implication from all these experiments is that individuals are likely to show some gain in originality of responses if they are induced to give attention to being creative or clever. In the few cases in which actual measurements are obtained, there is evidence that special instruction and exercise in creative performances can lead to gains. The slight losses in speed of production is unimportant where there is ample time, at least when there is more time than the few minutes allowed in a test of fluency.

We need experiments that will also assess the possible benefits of teaching for creativity in connection with regular courses in sciences, mathematics, and the arts. It almost goes without saying that kinds of assessment of achievement should be different from that provided by most current marking practices. More than this, we shall need experiments upon transfer of the benefits of each kind of instruction for creativity. Whatever the outcomes, I suspect that many students will find these kinds of education exciting and rewarding.

A final thought would be that in an effort to improve the status of each student in a particular intellectual factor, we give him special exercises in tasks like the tests that have been found to measure that factor. Such a technique has been used on a trial basis at the earliest grade levels in Chicago, having been introduced by Thelma G. Thurstone (5). The technique could be tried at higher educational levels and with tasks that call for creative abilities, such as those of fluency, flexibility, and originality. I should not recommend this in the form of a regular diet, but a certain amount of exercise of this kind might yield important benefits, particularly to those students who may have a deficiency of experience involving certain abilities. The idea is somewhat revolutionary, but we should be ready to undertake experiments with novel methods. In these days of electronic marvels upon which we can draw if need be, we should expect to see some radical changes in educational procedures. If we are not ready to tolerate the idea of drastic changes, we are not ready for an age of creative education.

REFERENCES

1. Ferguson, G. A. On learning and human ability. *Canad. J. Psychol.*, 1954, **8**, 95–112.
2. Getzels, J. W. and Jackson, P. W. The highly creative and the highly intelligent adolescent. *Amer. Psychologist*, 1958, **13**, 336.

3. Guilford, J. P. *Personality*. New York: McGraw-Hill, 1959.
4. Parnes, S. J. *Compendium of research on creative imagination*. Buffalo, N.Y.: Creative Education Foundation, 1958.
5. Thurstone, Thelma G. *Learning to think series*. Chicago: Science Research Associates, 1947.
6. Thurstone, L. L. Primary mental ability. *Psychometric Mongr.*, No. 1, 1938.

Selection **46** | INTELLECTUAL MALFUNCTIONING AND PERSONALITY*

EDITH A. WEISSKOPF
Purdue University

It is one of the traditional tasks of the psychologist to evaluate the intellectual potentialities of individuals. The traditional tool for such evaluation is the intelligence test. At the same time, experience with the use of intelligence tests has shown that this instrument has serious limitations. If, for instance, of two individuals with the same IQ, one behaves considerably more "intelligently" outside the test situation than the other one, it becomes evident that intelligent behavior is affected by factors which may not be measured by traditional intelligence tests. More specifically, these factors are thought to be personality traits, such as persistence, emotional stability, curiosity, etc. However, it would be erroneous to say that these personality factors affect the degree to which an individual behaves intelligently outside the test situation without ever influencing the scores on intelligence tests. That psychometric performance also may be influenced by personality factors is a tacit assumption made by clinical psychologists and corroborated by various studies which submit the components of intelligence to factorial analysis.

Thus, a child with a comparatively high IQ,

* Abridged from Edith A. Weisskopf, "Intellectual Malfunctioning and Personality," *Journal of Abnormal and Social Psychology*, 46: 410–423, 1951. Copyright 1951 by the American Psychological Association and reproduced by permission.

who functions on a low academic level, may be handicapped by personality factors unfavorable for high academic achievement. In this case, these unfavorable personality factors depress the individual's academic achievement more than they depress his psychometric performance. Stoddard indicates that the nature of the psychometric situation prevents certain personality factors from having an effect on test scores, while the same factors may be of potent influence on intellectual achievement outside the test situation. The ability to concentrate one's effort and interest over a long period of time on a problem, for example, is a factor which may have little effect on psychometric performances, since each problem in such performances requires only a very short amount of time. On the other hand, the ability to make a persistent effort may be an important factor affecting intellectual achievement outside the test situation. In other cases, nonintellective factors may depress test scores as much as they depress performance outside the test situation. For example, this is the case with certain individuals who are described as being pseudofeebleminded. The test scores of such individuals fall within the feebleminded range. Their behavior outside the test situation is in agreement with the test scores, i.e., on a defective level. Yet, there may be indicators in these individuals' performance on tests and projective techniques as well as in their present and past behavior outside test situations which make the clinician suspect that nonintellective personality factors rather than low intellectual ability are responsible for the defective behavior. Such suspicion is, of course, of great practical importance to the clinician, since unfavorable personality traits may yield to therapeutic effort. Thus, in studying nonintellective factors inhibiting intellectual functioning, the psychologist should not limit himself to cases where he finds a discrepancy between psychometric score and performance outside the test situation.

It will be noted that no attempt has been made, thus far, to draw, by definition, a line of demarcation between intellective and nonintellective factors. Wechsler says, "personality traits *enter into* the effectiveness of intelligent behavior and, hence, into any global concept of intelligence itself." If this is the case, the question may arise how these personality traits can be distinguished from "intellective" factors. Probably the only way to distinguish the two kinds of factors is by enumeration, not by definition. We speak traditionally of the ability to do arithmetical computation or to grasp spatial relationships as intellective factors, while we do not include curiosity under the same heading. The recognition that intelligent behavior is influenced by every aspect of the personality may induce the psychologist to do away completely with any line of demarcation between intellective and nonintellective factors.

ETIOLOGICAL FACTORS

Lack of parental reward

It is well known that the emotional relationship of parents with their children may influence the children's intellectual efficiency. Thus, parental rejection may be a factor which blocks the child in the progress of his intellectual development. There are various possible connections between parental rejection and learning disabilities. The author has pointed out one connection in a previous treatment, the main points of which are as follows:

Learning processes of any kind and at any age are connected with frustration of more or less serious degree. The child feels frustrated when he has to learn to drink from a cup instead of a nipple. It is frustrating, too, for him to adjust the functioning of his bowels to the demands and taboos of the society in which he lives. Also, the acquisition of knowledge and skills at school is frustrating to a certain degree. What is it, then, that makes children put up with all the thwarting "do's and don'ts" which are impressed on them? It is obvious that children could never be induced to put on the tight corset of cultural demands unless they are given some reward which makes it worth while for them. Maybe the most powerful reward is love and approval, especially when given by the parents or parent substitutes. Thus, if the child develops intellectually, if he learns to master the three R's and to acquire the skill which enables him to perform the little tricks required by psychometric scales, he does it partly in exchange for ap-

proval, love, and security.[1] If he does not get this reward because he has no parents or parent substitutes, or because the responsible adults fail to give love and security, he may fail to learn what is expected from him by society and to develop intellectually in the desired direction. This is usually an unconscious psychological mechanism rather than conscious malingering. Such a child appears dull to the superficial observer. However, he may actually be like a good businessman who does not deliver the merchandise unless the price has been paid; sometimes it is smart to be dull.

Thus, if we encounter parents who seem to reject their children because they are dull and do not get along at school, we find frequently that the cart has been put before the horse. The children may not be rejected because they are dull, but they may be dull because they are rejected.

Desire to punish the parents

In our culture the most potent satisfiers of children's needs, namely the parents, are, at the same time, the most potent frustrators. Such a culture can be expected to create a frequent desire in children to punish their parents. This desire may be present even though the relationship between the parents and children is a "normal" one. It may become strongly enhanced by such maladaptive factors as domination, neglect, etc. Because of societal taboos and the child's dependence on his seemingly powerful, omnipotent parents, the hostile impulses of children against their parents remain frequently unconscious. For the same reason, punishing actions against the parents have often to be undertaken in an indirect, camouflaged manner whereby the connection between the action and its punishing significance may remain entirely unconscious. The refusal to eat, or to defecate regularly, is often an unconscious way of punishing parents, characteristic for the preschool child, but often carried on far beyond the first years

[1] This statement does not negate heredity as a factor in the determination of intellectual differences. However, this article is concerned with the effect of environmental rather than hereditary factors.

of life, and even into adulthood. The refusal to develop intellectually—for example, to progress at school—may have the same unconscious significance. The following example illustrates the above.

Shirley, an 18-year-old girl, was referred to the author for psychotherapy because of her inability to meet the academic requirements of a junior college. Her Wechsler-Bellevue IQ was 120. She showed considerable blocking in her social relationships. She was overcome with feelings of despair and anxiety whenever she was in social contact with contemporaries, but she felt perfectly at ease with her parents and their friends. Her academic difficulties at school, however, were probably not a mere outcome of her inability to associate with people of her own age, since she exhibited the same blocking towards academic achievement when taking individual instructions from a tutor. Shirley's mother underwent psychotherapy simultaneously with Shirley. She was a woman who had great difficulties in accepting a feminine role. Her marriage and pregnancy forced her to give up her aim of getting graduate academic training and becoming a lawyer. She unconsciously resented Shirley for this reason. When Shirley reached school age and proved to have good intellectual endowment, her mother transferred her professional ambitions from herself to her daughter, hoping that Shirley would get a higher education and reach the goal which she herself had to give up. Shirley's father was a pediatrician and very fond of children. He wanted to have another child, a desire which met with strong resistance on the part of the mother. Shirley remained the only child. The father's arguments in favor of having a second child centered especially around the idea that Shirley's development might suffer by her being the only child. The mother tried to pacify her feelings of guilt about the matter by making herself believe that Shirley would associate with many other children and never be lonely on account of her onliness. Thus, the mother had two main ambitions for her daughter. She wanted her to get a higher education, and she wanted her to be a sociable person who is surrounded by and enjoys the company of a large number of contemporaries.

It is remarkable that Shirley blocked in exactly the activities which were most important to her mother, namely, in her association with contemporaries and in her intellectual growth. In the course of Shirley's therapy it became apparent that behind a façade of extreme submission she harboured a tremendous amount of resentment against her mother. The material brought out in the course of her treatment suggested that the two main symptoms of her neurosis were partially determined by her unconscious desire to hit her mother's two most sensitive spots.

Desire for self-punishment

Like many other neurotic symptoms, intellectual blocking may be brought about by an unconscious desire for self-punishment and, thus, for atonement of guilt feelings. These guilt feelings may stem from some of the sources discussed in this paper, or from other sources. The fact that a very high prestige premium is put on intellectual achievement in certain strata of society facilitates the use of learning disabilities as a self-punishing device.

Individuals whose intellect serves in the function of self-punishment frequently torture themselves through many other devices besides failure; for example, by compulsive pedantry in their intellectual work, through exaggeratedly long studying hours, etc.

Desire to maintain an infantile level of gratification

Intellectual malfunctioning may be a manifestation of a conscious resistance against growing up. Every step which the child undertakes in his development toward maturity brings about the necessity to forego more infantile gratifications. Thus, developmental progress is often accompanied by considerable nostalgia. Growing up means losing the privilege of entertaining sweet, dependent, protected relationships which are based on self-centered receiving rather than on a give-and-take basis. For example, the satisfaction of passive, irresponsible sucking at the mother's breast has to be given up, first for the sake of more active, less convenient cup-and-spoon feeding, which lacks the intimate physical contact with the mother and burdens the child with heavy responsibility, and much later for the strenuous and inconvenient activity of making a living. Intellectual growth, too, means renouncement of the satisfaction of dependent needs. Learning to read may mean to a child not being read to; learning to think may mean not being thought for; learning to orient himself in his environment may mean not being guided and protected. The child who is excessively afraid of losing infantile gratifications may block in his intellectual development.

Mahler-Schoenberger reports on an 18-year-old boy suffering from pseudoimbecility. His behavior was seriously retarded. He walked with a shuffling gait like an automaton and sat with his arms listlessly hanging at his side. His mother and his siblings felt toward him as towards a small child and treated him accordingly. They exchanged kisses and caresses with him, a form of behavior in which they could not have indulged if the patient were a normal 18-year-old boy. Mahler-Schoenberger considers the desire of obtaining such infantile gratification one of the etiological factors of the boy's neurosis.

In this connection it may be interesting to note that clinical workers are frequently concerned as to whether the mentally retarded child will encounter rejection by his parents and whether the parents will show favoritism towards the normal siblings. The opposite danger is discussed less frequently, namely, that the parents, especially the mother, may develop an unduly strong attachment toward the defective child, so that the normal sibling may be at a disadvantage. In many ways mentally retarded children may offer certain libidinal satisfactions to parents which the normal child cannot supply, namely, complete, helpless dependence without the threat of a second childbirth, i.e., of a painful separation from the child at the time of adolescence. Such helplessness may satisfy the parents' need to protect, or to dominate. In a more indirect manner it may also satisfy the parents' dependency needs, since it offers them the possibility of identifying with a completely dependent individual. The parents may, thus, enjoy the care of a feebleminded child directly and vicariously. In this manner, *true* mental retardation may offer certain libidinal satisfactions to the child and to his parents.. *Pseudo*retardation, on the other hand, may be caused by the unconscious desire of the child to gain such satisfaction and unconsciously encouraged through the same desire in the parents.

A graduate student of the author who worked in an institution for the feebleminded remarked jokingly that if he would ever adopt a child, it would have to be a Mongolian imbecile. The remark was, of course, not serious, but humorous in a grim way. However, a genuine emotion may have given rise to his statement, namely, the sweet feeling of attachment which many adults experience towards creatures who are and will forever remain helpless. It is known that Mongolians with their characteristic clinging behavior often become the favorites of institutional staff members.

The previous discussion also throws some light on the problems of children who show intellectual regression, such as deterioration of speech, reading, or other mental skills, at the time of the birth of a younger sibling. At that time the advantages of the infant's way of life and the futility of trying to capture the parents' attention by "academic sophistication" seems especially apparent to the older child. If the child could express his feelings, he would say something like, "Why did I have to go through all the troubles of growing up, when this helpless and stupid baby receives so much affection?"

In this connection it may be enlightening to compare the attitude of adults toward children of very superior intelligence and toward less intelligent children. We often find that superior children are to a lesser degree recipients of adults' protective warmth. Many adults are inclined to handle superior children with objective detachment. Thus, the unconscious desire to avoid such curtailment in warmth and affection may result in intellectual blocking with children of superior ability. Gumpert says about the American woman that "she would rather be loved than respected." The same may be true for some children of superior intellect.

DISPLACEMENT[2] OF INHIBITIONS FROM SPECIFIC, THREATENING ASPECTS OF COGNITION TO INTELLECTUAL ACTIVITY IN GENERAL

Inhibitions caused by guilt feelings: (a) sexual curiosity In certain strata of society the attitude of adults toward children's sexual knowl-

---

[2] In many instances where the term "displacement" is used in this paper, it would be more correct to use the term "displacement or stimulus generalization" since the exact nature of the mechanism cannot be determined.

edge is, in many ways, diametrically the opposite of their attitude toward other kinds of knowledge. This rather obvious fact becomes especially apparent if we examine the literature on sex education written for parents and teachers of young children. Many authors, for example, make statements to this effect: A frank way of discussing the facts of life will, they say, stop the child's curiosity and interest in these matters and will put an end to his preoccupation and his questions. Now let us compare this alleged aim of sex education with the aim of any other branch of education. Is there any other field in which the teacher aims at squelching the children's intellectual thirst, at suffocating interest and curiosity, and at stopping further questions? On the contrary, educators measure the success of their teaching not so much according to the amount of knowledge or information they transmit, but according to the interest they create. Questions, stimulated curiosity, attempts to make further investigations are considered criteria of success in teaching. Thus, the aims of sex education appear to be the exact opposite of the aims of education in any other field.

It is no wonder that many children develop guilt feelings about their knowledge and curiosity concerning sexual matters. According to psychoanalytic theory, such guilt feelings do not always remain limited to knowledge about sex. Again, displacement upon similar stimuli may take place, i.e., the guilt feelings may spread to intellectual activity in general. Since the guilt is irrational, it usually remains unconscious, but may result in serious blocking of intellectual functioning.

The author treated an 11-year-old boy who was making poor progress at school. His school achievement improved considerably after treatment for several months. The main topic of conversation during the counseling sessions was "the facts of life." The boy had very drastic misconceptions about reproduction. His foster parents had never given him any sex information. He had acquired most of his knowledge from an older boy, whom he met secretly against the wish of his foster parents. He considered the conversations about sex which he carried on with this boy as "bad." The treatment sessions taught him that it was not necessarily bad to talk, to know, or to be curious about sex. This relief of his guilt feelings about a specific type of knowledge may be one of the factors which decreased his blocking against school work.

Sylvester and Kunst report about an interesting fantasy of a boy with a reading disability.

He daydreamed that his father had invented a big machine and had cautioned the boy to stay away from it. It was a dangerous machine which made terrific noises. However, the boy disregarded his father's warning and looked at the machine. As an effect of this disobedience, he was forced to run with closed eyes for many years so that the machine could not catch him. He then pretended in his daydream that *he* was the inventor of the machine, and that he was not permitted to make any further inventions. The fantasy suggests that the boy feels guilty about curiosity, knowledge, and intellectual creativity, and that he believes it is safest to "keep his eyes closed." Since the boy is suffering from a reading disability, guilt may be one of the etiological factors of his difficulty.

Thus, the conventional parental reasoning— that if curiosity about sexual matters is suppressed, children will turn their thinking "to more wholesome and constructive matters"— may be a fallacy. In many cases the results may be the opposite from what the parents expect.

(b) Aggression and sadism The above discussion indicates that intellectual blocking may result from guilt feelings about a specific *kind* of knowledge and subsequent displacement upon intellectual work in general. Similarly, guilt feelings about a specific *aspect* of knowledge may develop and be displaced upon intellectual functioning in general. For example, the aggressive and sadistic aspect of thinking may, thus, become an instigator of learning difficulties.

There are various connections between the acquisition of knowledge, and aggression and sadism. One possible connection becomes apparent during preschool age, when the toddler tears apart toys, such as dolls, or living creatures, such as beetles, in order to investigate what is inside. Also the desire to know what is inside the human body may become associated with the aggressive desire to tear apart and to destroy.

Sylvester and Kunst report about an eight-year-old boy who was placed in a subnormal room at school even though he was of superior intelligence. His behavior during play therapy suggested strong aggression against the mother. He stated that the mother doll did not want to carry her baby since the baby might kick her. Finally the boy tied the baby doll to the mother doll's arm in order to prevent him from kicking. It also became apparent that the boy was filled with strong curiosity as to what was in his mother's body. During his play with dolls, he expressed the desire to tear the mother doll apart in order to see what was inside. Thus, intellectual curiosity and aggression were closely associated in the boy's personality structure. Furthermore, the situation was aggravated by the fact that the mother was seriously sick. The boy's magical thinking made his own aggressive desires responsible for her disease. In this manner, his guilt feelings were greatly increased. Finally, displacement of guilt from the aggressive aspect of "wanting to know" to intellectual functioning in general took place, and the boy developed a serious learning disability.

Aggression and intellectuality may become associated in various other ways. Intellective learning, for example, has a strong competitive aspect in certain strata of society. With some individuals competition may become the main motive for learning. Competition, however, implies aggression. Again, guilt feelings about competitive aggression may be displaced upon learning in general. Guilt feelings about competition are especially likely to arise in a culture where cooperative and competitive ideals are taught simultaneously. While tribes such as the Mundugumor stress competition and tribes such as the Arapesh preach mainly cooperative ideals, Western civilization finds itself in between the two contradictory ideals of competition and cooperation. Both attitudes are taught simultaneously. Thus, Western man is quasi forced to go out in the rain without getting wet. Indoctrinated with the ideal of competition, he finds it difficult to cooperate, and his training in cooperation makes him feel guilty about competitive activities.

In addition, some of the words used synonymously with "intelligent" and "stupid" suggest an association between intelligence and aggression in people's thinking, for example, the terms "sharp" and "dull." Similarly, Landauer points out that the German word "albern," meaning stupid, is derived from the obsolete word "alvari," meaning good or friendly.

Since intellectual work is related to a higher degree to the masculine role in our culture than to feminine activity, women often use their intellect as a device to compete aggressively with men. If such competition becomes the major motivating factor of intellectual endeavor, the ensuing guilt may become a serious block to progress.

Inhibitions caused by failure Serious failure in specific intellectual endeavors may result in inhibition of intellectual functioning in general.

A child may be unsuccessful in his first attempts to master academic subject matter, not due to lack of intellectual endowment, but due to more extraneous factors such as a bad teacher, or a visual or auditory defect. The discouraging experience may condition the child in such a manner that he remains intellectually blocked even after all obstacles have been removed, e.g., after he has been placed with a better teacher or after his physical defects have been corrected.

According to psychoanalytic theory, such blocking is especially frequently instigated by children's failures in their investigations about sexual matters. These investigations are especially liable to meet with failure, since most adults tend to increase the obstacles of such endeavors or, at least, not to offer much constructive help. Moreover, his own psycho-sexual immaturity often prevents the young thinker from finding the truth. Instead, he may lose himself in a maze of contradictory hunches and fantastic sexual theories. Such "first failure" may have a "crippling effect forever after."

Desire to avoid self-evaluation

Some individuals fail intellectually because they do not make any effort to succeed. Such "lazy" individuals are often extremely ambitious. Their ambition may be so strong that they could not bear to become aware of their limitations. Since they do not make any effort to succeed, they can avoid getting a realistic and possibly disappointing conception of their capacity. Thus their laziness enables them to excuse their failure and to cling to the magical belief that they would be champions if they would care to participate in the contest.

Desire to be the recipient of love rather than of envy and aggression

The desire to succeed and the desire to be liked by one's fellow men are frequently incompatible. Success in climbing the ladder of achievement is often accompanied by loss of love. The successful individual may endanger himself by becoming the target of envy and aggression. Such envy and aggression against a successful person may be attitudes which are actually existing, or they may be projections on the part of the successful individual. In other cases actually existing aggression may be exaggerated in the recipient's perception through the mechanism of projection.

A very bright student of the author excelled in class by her stimulating contributions to the discussion, and by the quality of her written work. However, after a few weeks of class work her contributions dropped noticeably in quality and quantity. In conversation with the author she stated that several remarks made by her colleagues were reported to her, indicating that her intellectual superiority made her unpopular with her classmates. Thus, she decided to control her behavior at school in such a way that she would appear less outstanding. We would hesitate to designate this girl as a case of intellectual blocking, because her plan not to excel was conscious, intentional, and reversible through deliberate decision. However, the study of individuals' attitudes toward success in intellectual activities or in any other field indicates that the tendency to "hold back" in order to avoid hostility can lie anywhere on a continuum from complete conscious intention to entirely unconscious blocking. For example, "holding back" may start as a consciously planned maneuver and later develop into an automatic, uncontrollable habit.

Brilliant, well-educated, and sophisticated young women occasionally engage in diplomatic malingerings when associating with men in social situations such as dates. They try to hide their knowledge and sophistication in order not to be threatening to their companion and, thus, to enjoy the pleasures of unambivalent male affection rather than to be frustrated by the ambivalent emotional relationship of competitors and pseudo-triumph of Pyrrhic victory. In other cases, the expectation of loss of gratification may automatically inhibit their intellectual development, without conscious planning or even against conscious planning. Every step which a man undertakes toward vocational success makes him more desirable as a love object, but every step undertaken by a woman in the same direction may make her less desirable as a partner for love and marriage. This conflict between two goals may become an etiological factor for the automatic inhibition of activity directed toward either goal.

The role played by the innocent, unsophisticated fool in myth, fairy tale, and fiction may serve as an illustration of the statement that intellectual blocking may be caused by fear of hostility. The fool in folk literature and other fiction is often an appealing figure, loved by everybody, envied by nobody. Since he is at the bottom of the ladder already, nobody can push him down.

CONCLUSION

The above is a discussion of some connecting bonds between intelligence and total personality. The discussion claims neither completeness nor originality. The emotional factors affecting thought processes covered in this paper have been described by others. However, the treatment of these topics is scattered through the psychiatric and psychological literature and interwoven with various other material. The author considered it a worth-while undertaking to extract pertinent material from various sources in order to present a more systematic discussion of intellect and total personality. Moreover, much of the subject matter surveyed in this paper is, in its original source, expressed in the often highly esoteric language of psychoanalysis, and interwoven with other psychoanalytic material which may be less acceptable to psychologically trained clinicians. In the author's opinion the above presentation discusses important aspects of intelligence, with emphasis on dynamic connections rather than quantitative comparisons. This approach has been relatively neglected by psychological investigators. Yet the objective research training of the academic psychologist is badly needed for the study of these aspects. Most emotional factors affecting intelligence have been ascertained "intuitively" rather than by objective methods. It will require all the ingenuity of psychologists to plan research designs which corroborate or disprove some of the "hunches" discussed in this paper.

Selection 47 | NEGRO VS. WHITE INTELLIGENCE: A CONTINUING CONTROVERSY*

WILLIAM M. MCCORD
Stanford University

NICHOLAS J. DEMERATH III
Harvard University

On September 21, 1956, *U.S. News and World Report* fired the first round in a battle over Negro intelligence, a controversy with important implications for school integration. Under the awe-inspiring title, "A Scientist's Report on Race Differences," Frank C. J. McGurk, associate professor of psychology at Villanova University, set out to prove the innate intellectual inferiority of Negroes. After reviewing what he falsely claimed to be "the only existing studies that relate to the problem (of ethnic differences in intelligence)," McGurk asserted that improvements in the socio-economic status of Negroes do not result in an increase in their scores on intelligence tests. In addition, he categorically concluded, ". . . as far as psychological test performance is a measure of capacity for education, Negroes as a group do not possess as much of it as whites as a group. This has been demonstrated over and over."

* Abridged from William M. McCord and Nicholas J. Demerath III, "Negro vs. White Intelligence: A Continuing Controversy," *Harvard Educational Review*, 28:120–135, 1958. Reprinted by permission of the publisher.

The purpose of this article is: first, to demonstrate the specific inadequacies of McGurk's "proof" and second, to present a new study which investigates more closely several important factors influencing intelligence scores. These include father's social class, education, nationality and generation of entry into the United States, as well as the family's emotional atmosphere. Since the sample was drawn from the Cambridge-Somerville area near Boston and is both Northern and urban, the effects of two additional factors—the Southern milieu and segregated, unequal schooling—were eliminated.

THE INADEQUACIES OF "A SCIENTIST'S REPORT"

McGurk opened his attack by citing the famous studies of draftees' intelligence during World War I. A comparison of the Negro and white scores showed that only 27 per cent of the Negroes equaled or exceeded the average scores of the whites on the Alpha test and that only 29 per cent of the Negroes equaled the whites' average on the supposedly less "culture bound" Beta test. Using these results as a baseline, McGurk argued that the improvement in Negroes' socioeconomic status since 1918 should be revealed in higher scores on later tests of Negro and white intelligence; "If social and economic factors are *the* important thing in determining the test-score differences between these two racial groups, it would have to follow, as a matter of logic, that a decrease in the difference between the social and economic factors between Negroes and whites should be accompanied by a decrease in the difference between their average test scores." [Italics added.]

To test his point, McGurk examined the results of six later studies of Negro and white intelligence and concluded, ". . . when the Negro is given a better social and economic opportunity, the differences between Negroes and whites (intelligence scores) actually *increase.*" Thus, in his opinion, the social and economic environment bears no causal relation to scores on intelligence tests. Before examining McGurk's six "authoritative" studies, one curious oversight in the article should be mentioned. At no point did McGurk state that

Southern whites scored consistently below Northern whites in the Army tests. Perhaps the oversight was intentional; for McGurk would find it uncomfortable to argue that inherent racial differences accounted for the poor performance of Southern whites.

Each of the six basic studies quoted by McGurk has serious inadequacies—when used as support of his opinion. A general criticism can be made of McGurk's description of this body of research. He consistently omits figures indicating the proportion of *whites* who equaled or exceeded the average score. One must remember that the average is not the median; if one or two testees scored extremely high, the average score for the entire group would be raised by several points.

The earliest study which was cited is H. A. Tanser's investigation of Canadian Negroes and whites. Tanser administered three standard tests to all Negro and white school children enrolled in the primary schools of Kent County, Ontario. On every test the Negroes scored lower than the whites; in no test did more than 20 per cent of the Negroes equal or exceed the average scores of the white children. The first question which a social scientist would ask about this study is: "Was the social and economic status of the two groups equal?" Innumerable studies have demonstrated that a close relationship exists between socio-economic status and intelligence scores; if the Negroes, as a group, were in a depressed status, their scores would inevitably have a lower average. McGurk recognized this criticism but cavalierly dismissed it by arguing that "social and economic opportunities had always been equal for all Negroes and whites in this area, *except for a few minor outbursts of oppression directed toward the Negroes.* [Italics added.] McGurk, in addition, *totally omitted* references to Tanser's own confession that the socio-economic status of Negroes in Kent County *was then and had always been inferior to whites.* We charge that such a critical omission could be only due to conscious biasing of the evidence.

As his second source of evidence, McGurk quoted research done in 1940 on Negro and white children living in rural areas of the South. The Negro children, not surprisingly, scored lower than the whites; from 15 to 20 per cent of the Negro children, depending on the test,

equaled the average score of the whites. McGurk commented only in passing that the subjects attended rural segregated schools in Virginia. Knowing the economic deprivation of Southern Negro schools and the general psychological climate, it is difficult to believe that any social scientist could accept this study as a valid comparative measure of inherent capacity for education. Otto Klineberg's work, cited later in this paper, indicates the debilitating influence of the Southern milieu upon Negro children.

Third, McGurk drew upon a study of New York University freshmen published in 1942 by A. M. Shuey. Shuey matched forty-three pairs of Negro and white students on the basis of the birthplace of their father, their father's occupation and the students' earlier school education. Testing the students revealed that only 18 per cent of the Negro subjects equaled the average score of the whites. In his summary, McGurk characteristically failed to note the author's caution concerning the work. Shuey conceded that many other factors influence performance on an intelligence test; not all influences could be "controlled." Indeed, Shuey was unable to hold constant one of the most important of these variables: the cultural background of the students' parents. The introduction of just this additional factor might have fundamentally changed the results; as is shown later in this article, test performance of children is closely related to the education of their fathers.

Throughout his entire paper, McGurk ignored all those subtle influences which affect an intelligence score: the motivation of the subjects; the emotional characteristics of the child, his parents, his culture; and the values and cultural stimulations to which he has been exposed. Until these variables are "controlled," every study of "racial" intelligence, including Shuey's and our own, must be taken with a grain of salt.

As a basic pillar of his argument, McGurk called upon his own work. In 1951, McGurk abandoned validated, standardized tests of intelligence and invented his own measure— half of it "drew heavily on the cultural background" of subjects, the other half was supposedly not "culture-bound." He administered this test to high school students in Pennsylvania and New Jersey and equated the students' socio-economic status—omitting any direct measure of the cultural or educational motivation of the students. As one would expect, the Negro students failed to equal the whites. In a later study, he paired the 25 per cent of the Negro and white subjects who were highest in socio-economic status and the 25 per cent who were lowest. Analysis showed that the Negroes in the *lowest* category equaled the whites' average score, but that only 18 per cent of those with the highest social status "overlapped" the white average (again, one wonders how many of the whites exceeded their own group's average score). The faults of McGurk's research—his failure to use a standardized test and his failure to match the cultural or emotional motivation of the subject—lead to the conclusion that his own studies only added to the confusions already abounding in this area.

Thus, what McGurk claimed as conclusive evidence appears to be far less than that. Many of the studies failed to control socio-economic influences and few considered the cultural background of the subjects. One study did not eliminate the influence of the Southern milieu and schooling; another investigation (McGurk's own) used a test which had not been sufficiently validated. None of the analyses explicitly considered the motivational or cognitive structure of the subjects or their environment.

From this insufficient evidence, McGurk drew untenable conclusions. The unreliability of his article becomes particularly apparent when one considers the information which he omitted. Although he claimed that the six articles were the only ones relating to the problem, *McGurk— consciously or unconsciously—eliminated all those studies which contradicted his bias.* Only three of these crucial omissions will be mentioned.

In 1923, W. W. Clark analyzed the intelligence of a large sample of children enrolled in Los Angeles schools. He administered the National Intelligence Test to 510 Negro children and 4326 white children. While there was no attempt to control the background of the children, no one could maintain that the Negroes were of *higher* socio-economic status than the whites. Clark's subjects lived in a non-Southern atmosphere and attended integrated schools. Clark found no statistically significant difference between the two "races." The white children had a median score of 106 and the

Negro children achieved a median score of 104.7.

The famous work of Otto Klineberg is, of course, in direct contradiction to McGurk's position. McGurk mentioned Klineberg but ignored his research. Klineberg and his associates, over a number of years, analyzed the effect of the Northern environment on Southern-bred Negro children. Consistently, they found that intelligence scores increased the longer the children had resided in New York. Thus, scores were positively correlated with "Northernization" and "urbanization," two processes which commonly yield better social, cultural, educational, and occupational opportunities for the in-migrant Negro. In a variety of studies, the average scores increased by five to fifty points on the National Intelligence Test —a difficult result for McGurk to dismiss, if he is correct that an improved socio-economic environment does not affect Negro responses to intelligence tests.

Similar research has been conducted by H. H. Long. Long examined Negro children living in the urban atmosphere of Washington, D. C. He found that scores on the Kuhlman-Anderson intelligence test jumped by twelve to fourteen points when residence in Washington increased from under one year to more than eight years.

Admittedly, the work of Clark, Klineberg, and Long is inconclusive: Clark failed to hold constant a variety of influential factors; Klineberg and Long did not actually trace the *same* children's performance on intelligence tests. Yet, these inadequacies are no greater than those found in McGurk's studies. Why, then, did he omit them from his "authoritative" review of the evidence?

A NEW STUDY OF NEGRO AND WHITE INTELLIGENCE

No research which attempts to measure inherent biological differences between the intelligence of whites and Negroes can be conclusive. Too many unmeasurable factors—the pressures of inequality, motivational and cultural differences, the faults of the tests, and most importantly, the lack of consensus on the *nature* of intelligence itself—hamper research on this issue. Nevertheless, since our nation is passing through a great domestic crisis, studies of intelligence will inevitably be used as weapons in the social conflict. It is wise, therefore, to devote some scientific effort to the clarification, if not resolution, of the problem.

As part of another research project, Kuhlman-Anderson intelligence tests on a number of ten-year-old boys (562 whites and fifty Negroes) had been collected. The ratio of Negroes and whites in this group closely approximated the actual distribution in the general population of their cities, Cambridge and Somerville, Massachusetts. Stanford-Binet intelligence scores were also available for 238 children. The total sample had unique advantages for comparative research in that all of the children lived in a Northern, urban area and all attended integrated schools. We had additional information on the social class, national origin, and education of all the boys' families, and, for a smaller portion of the sample, information regarding the emotional climate of their families was available. Therefore, it was possible to control cultural, social and emotional factors which might influence intelligence.

This information was gathered between 1938 and 1945 as part of the "Cambridge-Somerville Youth Study"—a prolonged experiment in the prevention of juvenile delinquency. Founded by Dr. Richard Clarke Cabot, the project selected 650 boys, half of whom were considered as pre-delinquent and the other half as "normal." Half of the 650 boys were intensely observed and counseled for an average period of five years; the other half were left alone as a "control" group. Each group was composed of approximately equal proportions of "pre-delinquent" and of "normal" boys. In 1956, under a grant from the Ella Lyman Cabot Foundation and the Harvard Laboratory of Social Relations, an extended investigation of

the adult criminality and alcoholism of these boys was begun. The results of these studies will be published elsewhere.[1] It should be noted, however, that no significant relation between criminal behavior and intelligence was found. We bring up this point, for it could be argued that the high proportion of "maladjusted" boys in this sample might render it an unrepresentative group. Since intelligence was not linked to crime, this possibility does not seem critical. The sample is unrepresentative in one other respect: most of the families belonged to the lower class or the lower-middle class. This fact limits the generalizations which can be made; yet the other advantages of the sample make it an interesting "experiment" in the comparative study of intelligence.

As a first step, without holding constant those factors which previous research indicated were related to intelligence, the Kuhlman-Anderson scores of the white and Negro boys were compared. Even without specific controls, *no significant difference appeared. Both the Negro and the white groups achieved a median score ranging between 95 and 99* (see Table 1).

As a means of confirming this first finding, the scores of whites and Negroes on the Stanford-Binet test which had been given to 238 of the same boys were examined. In a variety of ways, the Stanford-Binet test differs from the Kuhlman-Anderson; perhaps most importantly, the Stanford-Binet was administered individually while the Kuhlman-Anderson was given to class-room groups. Once again, *no significant differences appeared.* The median

[1] See William McCord, John McCord, and Irving Zola, *The Genesis of Crime*, Columbia University Press, and William McCord and John McCord, *The Genesis of Alcoholism* (in preparation).

Table **1 |** KUHLMAN-ANDERSON INTELLIGENCE, NEGROES VERSUS WHITES (IN PERCENTAGE)

Intelligence	Negroes (N = 50)	Whites (N = 562)
Superior (105–above)	14.0	18.7
Average (104–95)	50.0	39.7
Low average (94–95)	34.0	35.0
Sub-normal (84–below)	2.0	6.6

Chi square: not significant

Table **2 |** STANFORD-BINET INTELLIGENCE, NEGROES VERSUS WHITES (IN PERCENTAGE)

Intelligence	Negroes (N = 21)	Whites (N = 217)
Superior (105–above)	28.6	18.4
Average (104–95)	19.0	23.1
Low-average (94–85)	28.6	30.4
Sub-normal (84–below)	23.8	28.1

Chi square: not significant

score of the whites and the Negroes fell in the 90 to 95 range (see Table 2).

As compared to their scores on the other test, the boys scored generally lower on the Stanford-Binet; the "sub-normal" category increased considerably. Although the sample is relatively small, it is important that *different* tests agreed in indicating no significant racial differences. Only one interesting, albeit non-significant, trend appeared in both tests: more whites than Negroes exhibited sub-normal intelligence; a discomforting finding for the followers of McGurk.

Actually, *three important controls were built into the study:* the influence of segregated, inferior schooling on Negro performance was eliminated, for all the boys attended the same schools; the debilitating effects of the Southern atmosphere of virulent prejudice were held in check, since all the boys lived in Massachusetts; rural-urban differences were done away with since all the boys lived in an essentially similar urban environment.

Any study of inherent racial differences in intelligence must take account of those other environmental factors which are related to intelligence. Consequently, we examined the relationship between intelligence and social class, parental education, parental nationality, home atmosphere, and the personality of the boys' fathers. When a statistical relationship appears between these environmental factors and intelligence, it is impossible to disentangle the complicated causal web. High intelligence, for example, may *cause* high educational achievement, but it may also be a *result* of the cultural advantages inherent in extended education. Since we cannot know the causal link directly, it is necessary to control these environmental relationships, *if* one wishes to achieve a rela-

tively "pure" comparative measure of innate racial intelligence.

The well-substantiated link between social class and intelligence appeared once again in this research. We rated social class on the generally accepted criterion of father's occupation. Professional people and business owners or managers composed the "middle" class; clerical, service, and white-collar employees made up the "lower-middle" class; while in the "lower" class, we separated four categories: skilled tradesmen, semi-skilled (mostly factory) laborers, unskilled workers, and workers on relief.

When the children's scores on the Kuhlman-Anderson test were compared to their fathers' occupations, a clear relationship emerged. At one end of the scale, 78.8 per cent of the middle class boys received an average or superior score. At the other end of the scale, less than half, 48.1 per cent of the relief children made the same scores.

We know that a statistical relationship exists; we do not know why it exists. Perhaps inferior intelligence leads to inferior status; perhaps the lower class environment—with its own values and stimulations—leads to certain cognitive and motivational disadvantages reflected in low scores on intelligence tests.

Two other factors which may influence performance on an intelligence test should be noted: the emotional atmosphere of the home and the personality of the child's parents. From the extensive records gathered by the Cambridge-Somerville social workers, it was possible to make a reliable judgment on the home atmosphere and the father's personality of a small number of the boys. These judgments were based on records, kept over a five-year period, containing the observations of several social workers, teachers, a psychologist, a physician, and sometimes a psychiatrist or minister on each of the boys and their families.

Clinicians have long taken note of the force of emotional factors on a subject's performance. We wished to examine the influence of the emotional *milieu* on the child's measured intelligence. It was possible to categorize the general background of 243 boys into four divisions:

1. *A cohesive home:* an environment generally characterized by affection and pride in the family.
2. *A quarrelsome home:* one in which conflict dominated the atmosphere but where, nevertheless, affection still existed.
3. *A quarrelsome-neglecting home:* an environment torn by familial conflict and rejection of the child.
4. *A broken home:* a family separated by death, divorce, desertion, etc.

The cohesive homes, as one would expect, produced the largest percent of superior children and the smallest proportion of sub-normal children. Quarrelsome-neglecting homes made a poor showing, yet not as bad as the quarrelsome—but still affectionate—families. Perhaps the severe rejection characteristic of quarrelsome-neglecting families, creates, in a certain number of children, a drive toward independence and achievement which might be reflected in test performance. Although the level of statistical significance is low, it appears that home atmosphere may be related to intelligence.

It was also possible to categorize the fathers

of 240 boys into five broad divisions of "personality":

1. *Loving fathers:* men who demonstrated active affection for their sons.
2. *Passive fathers:* men who played a minor role in family life and were generally phlegmatic individuals.
3. *Cruel fathers:* overtly rejecting, brutal men.
4. *Neglecting fathers:* overtly rejecting men, emotionally and materially indifferent toward their sons.
5. *Absent fathers:* men who had left the home because of divorce, desertion, or death.

Three independent judges agreed in 80 per cent of the cases in rating both home atmosphere and the father's personality.

As might be predicted, the loving fathers turned out the highest proportion of superior children and the lowest number of sub-normal boys. Nevertheless, a consistent statistically significant pattern did not appear.

Although the results are far from conclusive, they do indicate that further research on the relation between intelligence and emotional background might well be productive.

Equipped with the knowledge that all of these environmental forces *might* bear a causal relation to intelligence, we were in a better position to analyze biological differences in intelligence. As a last comparative measure, therefore, we matched thirty pairs of Negroes and whites on a number of environmental factors—twenty of the original group of Negroes had to be eliminated since a perfect match could not be made with a white child in the

Table 3 | KUHLMAN-ANDERSON INTELLIGENCE, MATCHED PAIRS OF NEGROES AND WHITES (IN PERCENTAGE)

Intelligence	Negroes (N = 30)	Whites (N = 30)
Superior (105–above)	16.7	20.0
Average (104–95)	50.0	36.7
Low average (94–85)	30.0	33.3
Sub-normal (84–below)	3.3	10.0

Chi square: not significant

sample. Each pair of boys was equated on the following standards: their father's social class, education, personality, generation of entry into America and the general atmosphere of their family. Thus, a number of influences—but by no means all possible factors—were held constant and a more precise approach could be made to the problem of innate racial differences. *There was no significant difference between the matched pairs in intelligence;* median scores for both groups fell in the 95 to 99 range.

CONCLUSIONS

In our sample of 612 Northern, urban boys, *we found no significant differences in intelligence between Negroes and whites.* Not surprisingly, however, we found that intelligence is significantly related to socio-economic status, parental education, and general home atmosphere. Our evidence, drawn from a straight racial comparison and from the analysis of matched pairs, contradicts McGurk's assertion of the innate inferiority of Negroes. In addition, our evidence suggests an explanation of why certain other studies tend to support his assertion.

From this research, we cannot conclude that Negroes as a group and whites as a group are equal in inherent intellectual ability; so many forces affect intelligence that a "pure" measure of innate differences is impossible. Those of McGurk's persuasion might argue, for example, that our group of children is unrepresentative. A comparison of primarily lower class whites with lower class Negroes, they could point out, may give an unfair advantage to Negroes. Since whites are offered relatively "equal opportunity" in competition with each other, those who remain in the lower class may be intellectually inferior. We grant this argument as a plausible explanation of our findings.

Yet if it is unjustified to claim that this study proves the equality of whites and Negroes, it is equally unjustified to claim, as McGurk has done, that one group has less "capacity for education" than the other. The evidence is inconclusive. We believe, however, that the present study lends weight to the argument that equalization of educational and social opportunities (as has partially occurred in Massa-

chusetts) will result in the equalization of test performance of Negroes and whites.

Selection **48** | ON RACE AND INTELLIGENCE: A JOINT STATEMENT*

OTTO KLINEBERG
Columbia University

In connection with the process of school desegregation and the difficulties with which it has been accompanied in certain areas, the question has again arisen as to the existence of innate differences in intelligence between Negroes and Whites. The present statement is directed to that question. Those who have signed[1] it are not on this occasion taking sides with regard to the problem of desegregation as a whole, nor with the manner or the rapidity with which it should be accomplished. They are for the moment concerned only with the facts and conclusions accepted by scientists with regard to racial comparisons in inborn intellectual capacity.

A number of years ago, at a time when Nazi race theories were receiving much publicity, several scientific organizations placed themselves on record as opposed to the conclusion that race was a determiner of innate psychological characteristics; their position was that no such relationship had ever been scien-

* From Otto Klineberg, "Race and Intelligence: A Joint Statement," prepared with the Society for the Psychological Study of Social Issues, 1957. Reprinted by permission of the author and the Society for the Psychological Study of Social Issues.
[1] The signers include Prof. Otto Klineberg, Columbia University; Prof. Theodore Newcomb and Prof. Daniel Katz, University of Michigan; Dr. Gardner Murphy, Menninger Foundation; Prof. Nevitt Sanford, Vassar College; Prof. Robin Williams, Jr., Cornell University; Prof. David Krech, University of California; Prof. Jerome Bruner, Harvard University; Prof. Allison Davis, University of Chicago; Prof. Anne Anastasi, Fordham University; Prof. Stuart Cook, Prof. Isidor Chein and Prof. Marie Jahoda, New York University; Prof. Kenneth Clark, College of the City of New York; Prof. Bingham Dai, Duke University School of Medicine; Prof. Irving Lorge, Teachers College, Columbia University; Prof. Solomon Asch, Swarthmore College; and Dr. David Rapaport, Austen Riggs Center.

tifically demonstrated. These organizations included, among others, the American Anthropological Association (in 1939) and the Society for the Psychological Study of Social Issues, a division of the American Psychological Association (in 1938). More recently (in 1950), a group of distinguished social scientists meeting in Unesco House in Paris issued a Statement on Race which reads in part as follows:

Whatever classification the anthropologist makes of man, he never includes mental characteristics as part of those classifications. It is now generally recognized that intelligence tests do not in themselves enable us to differentiate safely between what is due to innate capacity and what is the result of environmental influences, training and education. Wherever it has been possible to make allowances for differences in environmental opportunities, the tests have shown essential similarity in mental characters among all human groups. In short, given similar degrees of cultural opportunity to realize their potentialities, the average achievement of the members of each ethnic group is about the same.

Two years later an equally distinguished assembly of geneticists and physical anthropologists, also meeting in Paris, pointed out that:

The scientific material available to us at present does not justify the conclusion that inherited genetic differences are a major factor in producing the differences between the cultures and cultural achievements of different peoples or groups. It does indicate, on the contrary, that a major factor in explaining such differences is the cultural experience which each group has undergone.

In 1953, a Statement submitted to the United States Supreme Court by more than thirty American social scientists, concluded the following:

The available scientific evidence indicates that much, perhaps all, of the observable differences among various racial and national groups may be adequately explained in terms of environmental differences. . . . It seems clear, therefore, that fears based on the assumption of innate racial differences in intelligence are not well founded.

These statements still stand, and in our judgment represent the consensus among experts who have studied this question as objectively and as scientifically as is at present possible. We know of no new research which would reverse these conclusions.

Those few specialists who take a different position usually do so on two major grounds. The first is that Negro-White differences in intelligence test scores persist even when the two groups are "equated" for social and educational opportunities. To this we would point out that such "equation" is exceedingly difficult to achieve, since the opportunities related to test performance are by no means easy to assess in quantitative terms. We do know that the intelligence quotients of Southern Negro children improve markedly after a period of years in the schools available to them in New York or Philadelphia.

In the second place, it has been argued that the differences in IQ persist even when "noncultural questions" are used. We would deny the possibility of devising a "noncultural" test in the light of our present understanding of the problem.

In the early days of testing, many psychologists believed that the elimination of the handicap due to language was equivalent to eliminating the influence of culture in general. One psychologist, for example, Professor Florence L. Goodenough of the University of Minnesota, devised a performance test consisting in "Drawing a Man." She regarded this test as "culture-free." Many investigators have made use of this test, and they have been able to demonstrate that, contrary to the earlier view, the results are indeed affected by many aspects of previous experience. Professor Goodenough herself has now recognized this fact, and very honestly and courageously points out her former error. Writing with Dale B. Harris on "Studies in the Psychology of Children's drawings" in the *Psychological Bulletin* for September 1950, she expresses the opinion that "the search for a culture-free test, whether of intelligence, artistic ability, personal-social characteristics, or any other measurable trait is illusory." She goes on to state that her own earlier study "is certainly no exception to the rule" and adds, "The writer hereby apologizes for it."

No one can deny that at the present time the intellectual achievement of American Negro children, particularly those who come from segregated schools, is lower *on the average* than that of White children, nor that a reasonable amount of time must elapse before the gap can be closed. We would interpret the difference in terms of the *whole* pattern of educational opportunities associated with the social environment, and which may affect both the physical and mental development of the child. Even those few scholars, however, who prefer an explanation in terms of race, indicate that there is *overlapping* between the two racial groups. Overlapping is usually defined technically as the percentage in one group which is superior in test scores to the median or average score obtained by the other. *In every comparison with which we are familiar in this field there is some degree of overlapping.* This means more than that *some* Negro children do better than *some* White children. It means that some Negro children do better than the *average* White child, in spite of all the handicaps to which the former have in the past been subjected.

The conclusion is inescapable that any decision to use differences in the average achievement of the two racial groups as a basis for classifying in advance *any individual child*, Negro, or White, is scientifically unjustified.

10 SOCIAL PROCESSES

BIOLOGICAL FACTORS

Evidence obtained and interpreted by physical anthropologists suggests that man was a social animal long before he was distinctively *homo sapiens.* Thus it should be no surprise to us that other primates such as monkeys and apes are character-ized by complex social behavior. Within a particular social group the amount of physical damage resulting from fights is reduced by the establishment of a domi-nance hierarchy. Drs. Rosvold, Mirsky, and Pribram report in Selection 49 that this hierarchy may be modified by removal of a brain region which is related to aggres-sion (amygdalectomy). The three most dominant animals in a group of eight had their amygdalas removed. Following a recovery period they were returned to the group, and it was found that two of the three fell to the bottom of the dominance hierarchy. Rosvold, Mirsky, and Pribram suggest that the changes in social behavior which are attendant on amygdalectomy depend upon "the social environment con-fronting each animal upon return to the group after surgery" and the length of time that the hierarchy had been established prior to surgery.

PSYCHOLOGICAL FACTORS

No intelligent man at mid-twentieth century can gainsay the importance of a more adequate understanding of intergroup relations. The continued existence of homo sapiens is jeopardized by the fact that we do not know enough about the techniques and principles which are applicable to the reduction of intergroup conflicts. Dr. Muzafer Sherif, a social psychologist, maintains in Selection 50 that we must not assume that we can extrapolate our understanding of individuals into an under-standing of intragroup dynamics. Similarly intergroup dynamics are not completely predictable from a knowledge of within-group structure and function. New variables operating at each new level require direct experimental analysis. On the basis of many years of research on group processes, Dr. Sherif formulates several significant generalizations regarding the formation of groups, intergroup conflict, and the reduc-tion of intergroup conflicts.

Two other research areas of interest to social psychologists are measurement and modification of attitudes and the analysis of interpersonal relations. An attitude may be defined as a tendency to become motivated with respect to a certain object or person. Typically, it is implied that this motivation is consistently either adient (positive-approach) or abient (negative-avoidance). Of course, since this consistent motivational readiness to respond is a latent or unobservable characteristic, it must be inferred from consistency of behavior toward an object or person. This view is nicely encompassed by the following operational definition of attitude: "An indi-vidual's social attitude is an (enduring) syndrome of response consistency with re-gard to (a set of) social objects."

The analysis of interpersonal relations involves, in part, the determination of "who likes whom and why." "Common sense" and previous research would suggest that we tend to like people more if they hold attitudes which are similar to our own. In Selection 51, Dr. Donn Byrne reports an experiment which supports this hypothesis.

[1] D. T. Campbell, "The Indirect Assessment of Social Attitudes," *Psychological Bulletin,* **47:** 15–38, 1950.

SOCIOCULTURAL FACTORS

Throughout this discussion we should emphasize the importance of sociocultural factors in the formation and expression of attitudes and role expectations. It should be apparent, however, that societies are not static but are constantly changing. How does cultural change influence role acquisition and expression? In Selection 52 Dr. Daniel G. Brown examines the effect of cultural changes on the development of sex roles. He provides data to support the generalization that *in our culture males tend to prefer the male role more than females prefer the female role.* He also suggests that there is a cultural trend toward less sex role differentiation in our society. Although this trend results in greater personal flexibility and individual freedom, it may also make the development of appropriate sexual identification more difficult. There is a good deal of clinical and experimental evidence to indicate that strong identification with the opposite sex and weak same-sex identification may greatly interfere with satisfactory sexual adjustment as an adult.

The attitudes which one holds toward others are heavily influenced by sociocultural factors. Since the Supreme Court's desegregation decision there has been increased interaction, both positive and negative, between the Negro community and the white community. Although it may be true that "you can't legislate attitudes," it is also true that legal efforts may be instrumental in freeing individuals and groups from cultural constraints which prevent interaction with peers. Since 1955, three surveys have been conducted regarding attitudes of students at the University of Texas toward the Negro. Their results show that there has been a gradual reduction in prejudiced attitudes over this period. Dr. Robert K. Young compares the 1958 and 1964 studies in Selection 53. The studies present interesting data on the relationship between attitudes and such sociocultural variables as father's economic status, major field of study, fraternity membership, etc.

Selection **49** | INFLUENCE OF
AMYGDALECTOMY
ON SOCIAL
BEHAVIOR IN
MONKEYS*

H. ENGER ROSVOLD
ALLAN F. MIRSKY
KARL H. PRIBRAM
*Department of Psychiatry
and Laboratory of
Physiology, Yale
University, and
Department of
Neurophysiology,
Institute of Living*

Several authors (2, 4, 5) have reported that temporal lobe lesions result in changes in social behavior of monkeys. Since these investigators were only incidentally interested in social behavior, they reported only summary descriptions of their methods or results. It is generally impossible to determine from their reports on what basis they arrived at their conclusions and what, in fact, they meant by social behavior. Therefore, a series of studies using a uniform method of observation has been undertaken to relate brain function to social behavior in monkeys.

Brody and Rosvold (1) reported in detail a method for studying the effects of frontal lobotomy on the social interaction in a colony of *Macaca mulatta*. A similar method was used in the present study of the effects of a temporal lobe lesion on social interaction among monkeys. In addition, the behavior of each monkey, when housed separately, was observed.

METHOD

Animals

Eight young male rhesus monkeys, ranging in weight from 2.90 to 3.85 kg, were housed for a total of 18 two-week periods alternately, either separately in individual cages or together in a large group

* Reprinted from H. Enger Rosvold, Allan F. Mirsky, and Karl H. Pribram, "Influence of Amygdalectomy on Social Behavior in Monkeys," *Journal of Comparative and Physiological Psychology,* **47**: 173, 1954. Copyright 1954 by the American Psychological Association and reproduced by permission.

cage, according to the temporal sequence designated in Table 1. The individual cages were 2 ft. by 2½ ft. by 2½ ft. The group cage was 7½ ft. by 4½ ft. by 6½ ft. and included a movable partition at the center, thus permitting the large cage to be divided into two smaller cages 3¾ ft. by 4½ ft. by 6½ ft. When the monkeys were housed individually, they were fed Rockland monkey pellets and peanuts, one at a time, through the wire mesh of the cage front. When the monkeys were in the group cage, either pellets or peanuts were introduced, one at a time, through a feeding device consisting of a length of 1½-in. pipe mounted obliquely on a stand so as to extend 1 ft. into the large cage. It was fitted at the animals' side with a can containing a small opening large enough to admit only one monkey's paw. At the end of the observation hour, additional pellets were thrown into the group or individual cage, as the situation required, in amounts sufficient to make up the total daily ration of 80 cal/kg body weight per animal. This diet was supplemented three times a week with one-half orange per animal.

Observational: group cage

When the animals were together in a group cage, one *E* observed them at the same time each day for 1 hr. during the peanut-feeding situation. Four hours later another *E* observed while introducing the pellets. Food was also frequently offered directly to one or another of the animals, or placed between two monkeys of the group. Diary records were kept of group behavior, and when the typical group interaction had been reliably described, the most dominant—i.e., the highest animal in the hierarchy—was subjected to a two-stage bilateral amygdalectomy. Two other animals were operated on at two-month intervals. During the two weeks allowed for surgery and recovery, all animals were housed individually.

During the latter half of six of the two-week group-cage periods, alterations in group size and living space were instituted to increase interaction and to isolate those parts of the group in which the hierarchy was not clear for more intensive study. In addition, food was withheld from the colony at various times for 48 or 72 hr.

Observational: individual cages

At the same time on each day of the individual-cage periods, one *E* observed each monkey while offering it three peanuts. Four hours later, another *E* observed each animal while offering it five pellets.

During period 1, diary records were kept of each animal's behavior. At the end of this period, and before placing the animals together for the first time in the group cage, the two *E*s independently ranked the eight animals in order of aggressiveness and/or fearlessness. On each day of succeeding individual-cage periods the monkey's behavior was rated according to the categories listed in Table 2. The total score was used as a measure of the aggressiveness of each animal.

Surgical and anatomical procedures

A two-stage myoplastic craniotomy was performed on three of the animals; they were anesthetized with 0.8 cc/kg of a 5 per cent solution of Nembutal injected intraperitoneally. In each case, the left side was operated first and the right side a week later. A semilunar incision was made over the zygoma, curving forward over the orbit. Temporal muscle was split and the zygoma excised. After a burr hole had been enlarged to expose the orbit and temporal

Table **1** | TEMPORAL SEQUENCE OF OBSERVATION PERIODS

Description	Number (2-wk. periods)	Cage situation
Preoperative period	1	I
	2*	G
	3	I
	4	G
	5	I
	6	G
1st operation	7	I
1st postoperative period	8*	G
	9	I
	10†	G
2nd operation	11	I
2nd postoperative period	12	G
	13	I
	14*, §	G
3rd operation	15	I
3rd postoperative period	16	G
	17	I
	18*, †	G

Note: *I* refers to individual cage; G refers to group cages.
* Large cage divided in two, top four animals in one, bottom four in the other.
† Cage space reduced by one half.
§ Most submissive animal in the group removed from the colony.

Table **2** | INDIVIDUAL-CAGE BEHAVIOR SCORING SCHEME

Categories	Rating and description
Vocalization	Noisy-loud = +2
	Soft noises = +1
	Silent = 0
Position at start of feeding	At front of cage = +3
	Goes from front to middle (back) = +2
	At middle of cage = +1
	At back of cage = 0
Pellet taking	One + for each taken, up to 5. if none taken = 0
Behavior after taking pellets	Stays at front for all pellets = +2
	Retreats after each to middle of cage = +1
	Retreats after some but not all = +1
	Retreats after each to back = 0
Threatening behavior	Jumps at *E* during feeding = +2
	Teeth baring or grimacing = +1
	Neither = 0
Flight behavior	Animal makes as if to escape = −1 for each time it occurs

Note: Aggressive toward *E* = high positive score (max. +14); fearful of *E* = low positive or negative score.

fossa, the dura was opened in a cruciate manner. The temporal lobe was retracted, thus exposing the periamygdaloid region just medial and posterior to to the Sylvian fissure. An 18-gauge sucker was inserted into the amygdala, and the entire formation removed subpially downward and backward as far as the temporal horn of the ventricle and medially as far as the brain stem. Bleeding was controlled by packing and cautery, and the wound was thoroughly irrigated before closing the dura. Fascia was closed in layers with interrupted silk technique and the scalp with continuous subcuticular stitch.

When the behavioral observations had been completed, the operated animals were sacrificed and their brains prepared for histological examination as described by Pribram and Bagshaw (4).

RESULTS

Anatomical

The lesions in the three animals were approximately bilaterally symmetrical. In Dave's brain, in the right hemisphere, the medial portion of the temporal polar cortex, together with all of the amygdaloid complex except for a small portion of the lateral nucleus, was resected. Posteriorly, this lesion invaded the uncal extremity of Ammon's formation. In the left hemisphere, the lesion in the temporal polar cortex was slightly more extensive laterally, a little more of the basolateral amygdala was spared, and Ammon's formation barely touched on its ventromedial surface.

In Zeke the temporal polar cortex was barely invaded on either side. The corticomedial group of amygdaloid nuclei was completely resected bilaterally, but a small portion of the basolateral group remained intact. The posterior end of the lesion barely touched Ammon's formation.

In Riva the lesion invaded the temporal polar cortex bilaterally, and again the corticomedia nuclei of the amygdala were completely resected. However, the basolateral group of nuclei was fairly extensively spared on both sides. The uncal extremity of Ammon's formation was slightly injured on its ventromedial surface.

Group-cage behavior

By the second group-cage period a dominance hierarchy was firmly established on the basis of primacy in food getting and such other dominant behavior as aggressive chasing, biting, and threatening gestures. This hierarchy is portrayed in Figure 1.

Within five days after Dave had been operated on, he became submissive to all but Larry. Zeke now monopolized the feeding pipe, dominated the feeding situation, and occupied the preferred floor area of the cage once held by Dave. Toward the end of this period, when the group was divided into top and bottom four, Dave became completely submissive, even to Larry; he avoided other animals, made no attempt to get food, and even refused to accept food from E. Attempts to reach Dave's threshold for aggressive response by increasing group interaction were unsuccessful. Even though he would be bitten until blood flowed, he exhibited no aggressive or retaliatory reaction toward the animal that had attacked him.

On the twelfth day after his second operation (the fifth day of group interaction), Zeke became submissive to all but Larry and Dave. Riva now dominated the feeding situation and the food pipe, sharing with no one. Zeke continued to be dominant over Larry and Dave until shortly after the colony was separated into the top and bottom four, when Larry began attacking Zeke. Coincident with this reversal in the Larry-Zeke relationship, Zeke exhibited a tremendous increase in his aggression toward Dave, attacking him almost continuously during the feeding situation. By way of increasing interaction with Zeke, in an attempt to reach his threshold for aggressive response against the other animals in the group, Dave was removed from the colony. This had the effect, *not* of eliciting aggression on Zeke's part, but of eliminating it completely. He now behaved much as did Dave, cringing and fleeing from all, and adopted the tactic of sitting in the corner of the cage and facing the wall.

In contrast to the other two operated animals, Riva did not fall in dominance at any time during the two-month postoperative period. Manipulations of cage space and food deprivation up to 72 hr. were effective only in increasing Riva's aggressiveness. The hierarchy at the end of the experiment is depicted in Figure 2.

Individual-cage behavior

The two Es agreed significantly better than chance (rho = .95, $p < .01$) on the ranking of the monkeys according to their aggressive behavior in individual cages during the first individual-cage period. This order correlated negatively (rho = −.595; $p = .16$) with the hierarchical arrangement that developed in the group cage. In subsequent individual-cage periods, the rating scheme described in Table 1 was used. Figure 3 shows the mean of the last three preoperative and postoperative scores of each animal. The mean scores of a typical nonoperated control, obtained at the same time, are included for comparison. Two months separate the pre- and post-operative measures

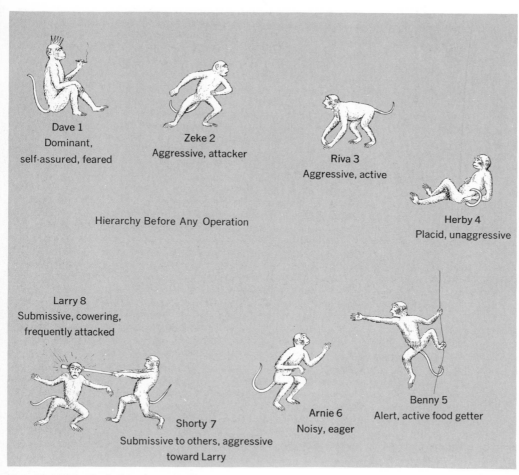

Figure 1 Hierarchy before any operation.

in each case. A Mann-Whitney (3) *U* test of the significance of the differences in these comparisons indicates that there were no differences in aggressiveness among the monkeys before surgery. Afterward, the scores of the operates show an increase significant beyond the .01 level of confidence, while that of the unoperated animal shows no change.

DISCUSSION

The results of the present study indicate that following amygdalectomy there are marked changes in social behavior of monkeys. How-

ever, there are differences among the animals in the direction and degree of this change.

After surgery all operates, though appearing more aggressive in the individual-cage situation, appeared to be less dominant (in two of three cases) in the group-cage situation. In addition to this difference in direction of effect, there is uniformity of change in the individual-cage situation but not in the group-cage situation.

As evident in Figure 1, the differences in direction and degree of change cannot confidently be attributed to differences among the lesions. If variations in extent of damage to the temporal lobe determined the degree of

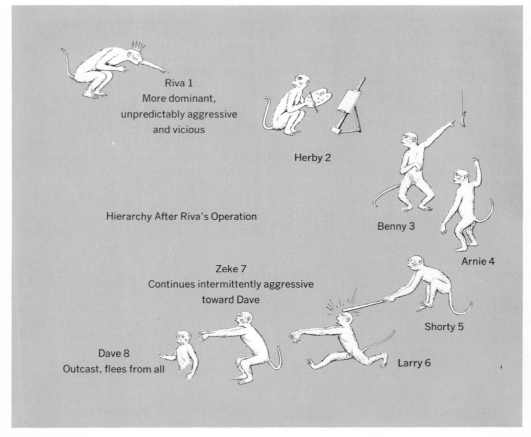

Riva 1
More dominant,
unpredictably aggressive
and vicious

Herby 2

Hierarchy After Riva's Operation

Benny 3

Arnie 4

Zeke 7
Continues intermittently aggressive
toward Dave

Shorty 5

Dave 8
Outcast, flees from all

Larry 6

Figure 2 Hierarchy after Riva's operation.

change in behavior, then Dave should have changed most and Zeke least; this was not so either in the group- or individual-cage situation. It is probable, therefore, that one or more of the discrete structures in the temporal lobe are critical in bringing about the alterations in aggressiveness. Since the degree of change in the group-cage situation, i.e., most in Dave and least in Riva, was consistent only with the extent of damage to the basolateral nuclei, these nuclei may be critical for changes in aggressiveness in the group-cage situation.

The differences in direction and degree of change were consistent with the social environment confronting each operated animal after surgery. Upon return to the colony, Dave was confronted with aggressive and active Zeke

and Riva; he fell in dominance. Zeke was confronted with Riva; he too fell in dominance. Riva was faced with relatively submissive nonaggressive animals such as Herby; Riva remained dominant.

The differences in direction and degree of change are also consistent with the length of time preoperatively that the dominance-submission relationships had existed. Dave, who changed immediately after his operation, had elicited submissiveness for only six weeks; Zeke, who maintained the No. 1 position for four days after being returned to the colony postoperatively, had elicited submissive responses for 10 weeks; while Riva, who did not change in status, had elicited submissive responses for 16 weeks.

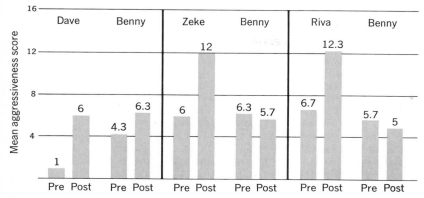

Figure 3   Aggressiveness in individual-cage situation before and after amygdalectomy. Benny's scores are included for comparison.

This study, then, suggests that the pattern of social interaction within the group to which it is returned after surgery and the length of preoperative time the relationships had existed may be as important considerations as the locus and extent of a lesion in determining the effects of a brain operation on the social behavior of a monkey. It is meaningless, therefore, to speak of the effect of an operation on "emotional behavior," "social behavior," and the like, without specifying in detail the conditions in which the particular behavior is observed. And, unless the effect of an operation on behavior is studied in a variety of situations, the findings are at best of limited generalizability.

tions in the hierarchy. The third animal suffered no loss in dominance and appeared more aggressive in the group situation after operation.

4. The differences in changes in behavior appear to be related to the social environment confronting each animal upon return to the group after surgery and to the length of time the preoperative relationships had existed.

5. The differences in changes in behavior are not related to the differences in extent of lesions as a whole, though they are consistent with differences in damage to the basolateral nuclei of the amygdala.

SUMMARY

1. Eight young male rhesus monkeys were studied in individual and group cages for a period of nine months; during this time, the three animals that were most dominant in the group situation were subjected to bilateral amygdalectomy.
2. There was found to be a negative relationship between aggressiveness in the individual-cage and dominance in the group-cage situation before surgery.
3. After amygdalectomy all animals appeared more aggressive in the individual-cage situation. In the group-cage situation, the same animals, in two of three instances, fell from top to bottom posi-

REFERENCES

1. Brody, E. B., & Rosvold, H. E.: Influence of prefrontal lobotomy on social interaction in a monkey group. *Psychosom. Med.*, 1952, **5**, 407–415.
2. Kluver, H., & Bucy, P. C. Preliminary analysis of functions of the temporal lobes in monkeys. *Arch. Neurol. Psychiat.*, Chicago, 1939, **42**, 979–1000.
3. Moses, L. E. Non-parametric statistics for psychological research. *Psychol. Bull.*, 1952, **49**, 122–143.
4. Pribram, K. H., & Bagshaw, M. Further analysis of the temporal lobe syndrome utilizing fronto-temporal ablations. *J. comp. Neurol.*, 1953, **99**, 347–375.
5. Thompson, A. P., & Walker, A. E. Behavioral alterations following lesions of the medial

surface of the temporal lobe. *Folia psychiat. neurol. neurochir. Neerl.,* 1950, **53**, 444–452.

Selection 50 | INTERGROUP RELATIONS AND LEADERSHIP*

MUZAFER SHERIF
Pennsylvania State University

IMPORTANCE OF INTERGROUP RELATIONS IN HUMAN AFFAIRS TODAY

Obviously, intergroup relations refer to states of friendship or hostility, cooperation or competition, alliance or enmity, peace or war between two or more groups and their respective members. Such states between groups have always been important and fateful in human affairs. History books have been written chiefly as records of them.

But today, we hear repeatedly from policy makers and analysts of current affairs that the very fate of human beings depends on the state of relations between groups and blocks of nations. The impact of these relations is reflected even in the way our family expenditures are budgeted and our personal goals are regulated relative to the uncertainties of the future.

DEMARCATION OF THE PROBLEM AREA OF INTERGROUP RELATIONS

Since we have noted the importance of intergroup relations, we can turn to the demarcation of the problem. What states of friendship or hostility, what kind of positive or negative functional relations between human beings, are characteristic of intergroup relations? This is not an idle question. Many technically excellent studies have fallen short in dealing with the

* Abridged from Muzafer Sherif, *Intergroup Relations and Leadership.* John Wiley & Sons, New York, 1962, pp. 3–21. Reprinted by permission of the author and publisher.

problem because they were not initially designed on the basis of an adequate characterization of intergroup relations.

Not every friendly or unfriendly act toward others is a case of intergroup relations. We have to differentiate those actions which can properly be called intergroup behavior.

Let us start by specifying the main concepts involved. This specification must begin with an adequate conception of the key term "group" itself. We define a group as a social unit (1) which consists of a number of individuals who, at a given time, stand in more or less definite interdependent status or role relationships with one another, and (2) which explicitly or implicitly possesses a set of values or norms of its own regulating behavior of individual members, at least in matters of consequence to the group. Shared attitudes, shared sentiments, shared aspirations and goals are related to and implicit in the common values or norms of the group. For, group norms are expected, and even ideal modes of behavior, defining for members the limits or latitude of acceptable behavior. Thus defined, a norm is not *necessarily* a statistical average of behaviors in a group. The expected or ideal modes of behavior defined by norms relate to motives and goals that members share in common, or concern the existence and perpetuation of the group itself, along with the reciprocal expectations that regulate the functioning of the organizational pattern.

The term "intergroup relations" refers to relations between two or more groups and their respective members. Whenever individuals belonging to one group interact, collectively or individually, with another group or its members in terms of their group identification, we have an instance of intergroup behavior.

The appropriate frame of reference for studying intergroup behavior is the functional relations between two or more groups, which may be positive or negative. The functional relationship between groups whose members perceive them as *in-groups* has properties of its own. These properties are generated during interaction between particular groups. Intergroup situations are not voids.

Though not independent of the relationships within the groups in question, *the characteristics of functional relations between groups cannot be deduced or extrapolated solely from the properties of relations prevailing among members within the group itself.* Prevailing modes of behavior within groups, in the way of co-operativeness and solidarity, or competitiveness and rivalry among members need not be the prevalent modes of behavior in their relations with other groups. Hostility towards out-groups may, at times, be proportional to the degree of solidarity within the group. Democracy at home need not imply democratic attitudes toward out-groups.

Level of interaction in intergroup behavior

Such considerations lead to conclusions concerning the effects of motivational components, that is, of aspirations, frustrations, aggressive impulses, at different levels of interaction—individual, group, and intergroup interaction:

We cannot legitimately extrapolate from the effects of the individual's motivational urges and frustrations to group situations, as if a group situation were a void and the interaction processes and reciprocities within it were a play of shadows.

We cannot extrapolate from the properties of individuals to the characteristics of group situations. It is equally erroneous to extrapolate from the properties of relations within a group to explain relations between groups, as though the area of interaction between groups consisted of a vacuum, or even of the cozy atmosphere of a conference room. The character of relations and norms that prevail within groups does influence their relations with other groups, but intergroup relations are potently determined by the process of interaction between the groups. The give-and-take between groups may be full of conflict or in a state of flow. And it is this area of conflict, in the case of negative relations, or of flow, in the cases of cooperation or alliance, which may produce consequential reverberations within the groups themselves (Sherif and Sherif, 1953).

What determines the positive or negative nature of interaction between groups? In large part, it is determined by the reciprocal interests of the groups involved and the degree of their significance to the groups in question. The issues at stake must be interests of considerable concern to the groups, if they are to play a part in intergroup relations. A matter of

concern may relate to values or goals shared by group members. It may be a real or imagined threat to the safety of the group as a whole, an economic interest, a political advantage, a military consideration, prestige, or a number of others. Once a particular issue comes to the foreground as the dominant influence in intergroup relations, it may become the *limiting factor*, the main anchorage in the interaction process between them.

EMPIRICAL GENERALIZATIONS

The foregoing approach to in-group and intergroup relations was formulated on the basis of extensive surveys of pertinent theoretical works and empirical research. Empirical field studies are full of pregnant leads for experimentalists in formulating valid and testable hypotheses. A series of hypotheses was derived concerning formation and functioning of in-group structure or organization (that is, status or leader-follower behavior and ensuing member attitudes), concerning conditions conducive to positive and negative intergroup attitudes, and concerning measures for the reduction of intergroup conflict (Sherif and Sherif, 1956; Sherif et al., 1961).

In order to study the effects of aspirations, deprivations, frustrations, and other goal-directed components within an appropriate level of interaction, as the first step in our research, autonomous in-groups were formed experimentally. Then these groups, whose natural history was ascertained step by step, were brought into functional contact under reciprocally competitive and frustrating conditions. Finally, study of reduction of intergroup conflict was undertaken. Our large-scale experiments were carried out in 1949, 1953, and 1954. In 1954 the research was sufficiently advanced to tackle the difficult task of reducing intergroup conflict.

As a background to points raised later in this introductory statement, only the generalizations pertinent to the major hypotheses will be stated here in brief.

Generalizations concerning group formation:

1. A definite group organization (structure) manifested in differentiated status positions is produced when a number of

individuals (even without previously established interpersonal relations) interact with one another under conditions (a) which embody goals with appeal value to the individuals, and (b) which require interdependent activities for their attainment.

2. The structure or organization is reflected in a consistent pattern of communication among group members. The higher the status of a group member, the greater the frequency of suggestions concerning group activities addressed or relayed to him.

3. Concomitant with the formation of a group organization, group norms emerge and are stabilized, regulating the members' behaviors within specifiable *latitudes of acceptable behavior*, in practices and activities commonly engaged in.

Generalizations concerning negative intergroup relations and the rise of prejudice and stereotypes of the out-group:

1. When groups engage in reciprocally competitive and frustrating activities, such that the victory or gain of a desired goal by one group results in the defeat or loss for the other group, unfavorable stereotypes come into use in relation to the out-group and its members. In time, these unfavorable stereotypes are standardized in a group, placing the out-group at a prejudicial distance (proportional to the degree of negative relations between them).

2. Concomitant with the rise of mutually prejudicial attitudes between groups, self-glorifying or self-justifying attitudes toward the in-group are strengthened. The performance of the out-group is deprecated and the moves of the out-group and its members are perceived in a suspicious light.

Note that in the research on which these generalizations are based the members of the groups were meticulously selected to be socially well-adjusted and academically successful individuals from established families. They were not from broken homes or families with undue behavior problems. Therefore, it would be decidedly off the mark to explain their behavior in intergroup relations on the basis of severe frustrations or instabilities during their prior life histories.

Now, generalizations concerning reduction of intergroup conflict:

1. *Contact* between groups in close proximity in activities which are individually enjoyed by the members of each group does not produce a decrease in the existing state of intergroup hostility. In fact, such occasions of intergroup proximity may be utilized for further exchanges of invectives across group lines and for attribution of the blame for the existing state of affairs to the out-group.

2. The next generalization concerns the measure that proved effective in this research: introduction of superordinate goals. *Superordinate goals* are defined as goals which are compelling for all and cannot be ignored, but which cannot be achieved by the efforts and resources of one group alone. They require the coordinated efforts and resources of the groups involved. The generalization in this regard is: When groups in a state of friction come into contact under conditions embodying superordinate goals, they tend to cooperate toward the common goal.

    But reduction of intergroup conflict is not a one-shot affair. The next generalization brings in the *time* dimension.

3. It was necessary to introduce various superordinate goals over a time span to sustain cooperation and, along with it, to decrease friction and weaken unfavorable stereotypes. Examples of superordinate goals used in our 1954 experiment were a crisis due to shortage of one of the basic necessities of daily living, breakdown of the available transportation that affected everyone, and opportunities for greatly desired activities.

4. The last generalization to be mentioned from these experiments concerns the impact of the state of intergroup relations on in-group relations and organization. It was found that functional relations

between groups which are of consequence to the groups in question bring about changes in the pattern of relations within the groups involved. Illustrative of this generalization are the following: When defeat followed defeat for one group in the 1949 experiment, the leader of that group, even though daring, became demoralized. Operational leadership was undertaken by another group member, who, out of friendship for the leader, had not taken the reins earlier, even though he could easily have done so. In the 1954 experiment the leadership changed hands when the peace-time leader could not live up to the requirements of conflict to be in the front lines leading his group in engagements with the adversary.

This finding illustrates the inadequacy of extrapolations from practices and trends within groups to the explanation of intergroup relations and practices. Practices and trends within groups are themselves affected by relations with other groups. The practical implication is that in-group democracy, friendship, and solidarity need not be extended to cooperativeness, friendship, and solidarity with out-groups.

The generalizations just presented may warrant the following summary of the rise of favorable and unfavorable attitudes toward the ingroup and toward out-groups:

In the process of interaction among members, the group is endowed with qualities which tend to be favorable, and may be self-justifying and even self-glorifying. Individual members, in their strivings to get along well in their interpersonal relations, to be accepted or rewarded, tend to develop qualities or traits put at a premium in their reference groups through the example of other members they look up to, through verbal dictums and through a set of sanctions applied to cases of deviation from the prevailing acceptable modes of behavior.

Out-groups and their respective members are attributed favorable or unfavorable traits depending on the positive or negative nature of functional relations between the groups in

question. Are the groups or a combination of groups competing with each other to excel in prestige, towards economic ends, political ends, territorial ends, so that the gain of one party is necessarily the loss of the other? Does the victory of one party mean the sure defeat of the other? Does possession by one party mean deprivation or humiliation for the other? Or are the attainments of such ends by one party compatible with the ends of the other? These possibilities are illustrative of the situations conducive to positive or negative functional relations between groups. Experiments indicate that negative functional relations between groups give rise to hostile attitudes and unfavorable stereotypes toward the out-group irrespective of the objective qualities of the individuals involved.

LEADERSHIP, POLICY MAKING, AND REPRESENTATION AS GROUP FUNCTIONS

Within groups, small or large, formal or informal, the focus of power resides in the leadership and other high status members. But the leadership status itself is within a group, and not outside of it, as Cecil Gibb (1954) maintained in the most comprehensive survey of leadership studies to date. The leader himself is not immune from sanctions if he deviates too far from the bounds of acceptable behavior prevailing in the group. Leaders, delegates, and representatives of the groups must remain a part of the power structure of the group if their actions are to be effective. The significance of the power structure for assessing the behavior of individuals in such positions is immediately seen when their actions deviate widely from the expectations of the membership. The newspaper accounts of the business leader who has arrangements with a supplier, of the union leader who makes a deal with company representatives to his own advantage, of the prime minister who appears to succumb to the inducements of the enemy, tell us what happens in such cases.

Delegation and representation of authority are integral aspects of group functioning, especially in relations with other groups. Studies by Ralph Stogdill and his associates show that within a large organization, subordinate members expect superiors to delegate authority and regard those who delegate more freely as better leaders. Yet Stogdill, in his recent book, *Individual Behavior and Group Achievement* (1959), observes that there are limiting situations "where a high degree of co-ordination is required," and delegation may result in "confusion and mis-directed effort" (p. 189).

Thus, in critical situations, leaders tend to take over the reins. If representatives in a collective bargaining situation are not making effective headway, the top leaders may, for the first time, get *directly* into these procedures. Similarly, a critical international situation temporarily reduces the authority of representatives on international councils, and at such times top leadership may step to the front line of negotiations.

In dealings between groups, the problem of power is manifested in different ways. Within a large organization or within a society, relations between groups are ordinarily subject to sanctions by the still larger organization. However, in a "casually patterned" society, to use the sociologist Lynd's characterization, the relations between some of the constituent organizations may not be regulated by sanctions applicable to all parties within the all-embracing organization. These areas of inter-group relations—in what Bierstedt (1957) has called the "unorganized interstices" of society —are in the foreground of major social problems in this country today.

In the relations between nations, the extent of regulation by commonly accepted sanctions is still smaller. Thus, power is not infrequently manifested in the form of force and threat of force. It is in such contexts that relationships between groups become vital to the survival of the groups in question. It is in such contexts that the problems of reduction of intergroup conflict, hostility and its by-products become the urgent problems of our time.

SUPERORDINATE GOALS IN REDUCTION OF CONFLICTS

In concluding, I venture to state some of the things that we have learned about the reduction of intergroup conflict. It is true the lines of *communication*, that is, *contact*, between

groups must be opened before prevailing conflicts can be reduced. But if contact between groups takes place without superordinate goals —that is, goals which are *urgent* and *compelling* for *all* groups involved, under the circumstances—the communication channels and the contacts serve as mediums for further accusations and recriminations. The discussion becomes bogged down in direct and indirect reference to the vicious circle of "Who's to blame?"

When contact situations involve superordinate goals, communication is utilized in the direction of reducing conflict in order to attain the common goals.

In regard to dissemination of *information*, favorable information about a disliked out-group tends to be ignored, rejected or reinterpreted to fit prevailing stereotypes. But when groups are pulling together toward superordinate goals, true and favorable information about the out-group is seen in a new light, and the probability of information being effective is enormously enhanced.

When groups cooperate toward superordinate goals, *leaders* are in a position to take bolder steps toward bringing about understanding and harmonious relations. When groups are directed toward goals which are mutually incompatible, genuine moves by a leader to reduce inter-group conflict may be seen by the membership of his own group as out-of-step and ill-advised. He may be subjected to severe criticism and even loss of faith. When compelling superordinate goals become articulated, the leader can make moves to further cooperative efforts, he can more freely delegate authority, and representation processes can proceed more effectively. The decisions reached are more likely to receive support from other group members.

In short, various measures suggested for the reduction of intergroup conflict, such as dissemination of information, increasing social contacts, and conferences of leaders and representatives, acquire new significance and new effectiveness when they become part and parcel of interaction processes between groups oriented toward superordinate goals which have real and compelling value for all groups concerned.

Over a period of time, the interaction of

groups toward superordinate goals which have genuine and compelling value for all groups concerned should assume organizational forms. If the tasks of building such organizations seem formidable, they are no more formidable, I think, than those which a modern war might impose. And surely there can be no doubt that man's potentialities can be realized better in the course of such efforts than in preoccupation with assigning blame for the state of affairs, in pursuits of old fears, old hostilities, and old conflicts with their awesome possibilities in this present world.

Concentrated efforts of all parties toward superordinate goals, rather than preoccupation with assessment of blame and clearing away all existing grudges, have a psychological implication as well. In the process of such efforts, man will be creating new organizations, new values, and thereby transforming himself. Just as the properties of part of a pattern are colored by the overall system of which it is part, the old grudges and stereotypes will acquire a different significance in the context of joint efforts toward common goals and their by-products. This is the plea made so eloquently by Gardner Murphy in his book, *Human Potentialities* (1958), of which the Yale physicist, Henry Margenau, wrote: "Here a psychologist of vision casts knowledge of man's present abilities into temporal perspective and portrays the forms which human development may take."

REFERENCES

Arensberg, C. H., 1951. Behavior and organization: industrial studies. In J. H. Rohrer and M. Sherif (eds.), *Social psychology at the crossroads*. New York, Harper.

Bierstedt, R., 1957. An analysis of social power. In L. A. Coser and B. Rosenberg (eds.), *Sociological theory: a book of readings*. New York, Macmillan.

Cartwright, D., and A. Zander, 1960. *Group dynamics: research and theory*. Second edition. Evanston, Ill., Row, Peterson.

Dubin, R., 1959. Stability of human organization. In M. Haire (ed.), *Modern organization theory*. New York, Wiley.

Gibb, C. A., 1954. Leadership. In G. Lindzey (ed.), *Handbook of social psychology*. Volume II, Reading, Mass., Addison-Wesley.

Klineberg, O., 1950. *Tensions affecting international understanding*. New York, Social Science Research Council Bull., 62.

Lewis, O., 1959. *Five families: Mexican case studies in the culture of poverty*. New York, Basic Books.

Murphy, G., 1953. *In the minds of men*. New York, Basic Books.

——, 1958. *Human potentialities*. New York, Basic Books.

Pear, T. H. (ed.), 1950. *Psychological factors of peace and war*. New York, Philosophical Library.

Richardson, L. F., 1950. Statistics of deadly quarrels. In T. H. Pear (ed.), *Psychological factors of peace and war*. New York, Philosophical Library.

Rose, A. M., 1954. *Theory and method in social sciences*. Minneapolis, University of Minnesota Press.

Sherif, M., O. J. Harvey, B. J. White, W. R. Hood, and Carolyn W. Sherif, 1961. *Intergroup conflict and cooperation. The Robbers Cave experiment*. Norman, Okla., University of Oklahoma Book Exchange.

Sherif, M., and Carolyn W. Sherif, 1953. *Groups in harmony and tension*. New York, Harper.

——, 1956. *Outline of social psychology*. Revised edition. New York, Harper.

Stogdill, R. M., 1959. *Individual behavior and group achievement*. New York, Oxford University Press.

Truman, D. B., 1955. The impact on political science of the revolution in the behavioral sciences. In *Research frontiers in politics and government*. Washington, D.C., Brookings Institution.

Selection **51** | INTERPERSONAL ATTRACTION AND ATTITUDE SIMILARITY*

DONN BYRNE
University of Texas

In investigating the direction and the strength of the affect engendered between the two participants in a dyad, we may arrange the expressed feelings of each individual along a continuum ranging from strongly positive to strongly negative. The accurate prediction of interpersonal attraction and repulsion in such relationships will undoubtedly require that we secure knowledge about several classes of independent variables.

Probably the most obvious and also best documented variable is that of propinquity. Studies in a wide variety of settings have shown that physical and functional distance influence interaction and interpersonal attraction (Byrne, in press). Once the environmental situation permits or encourages interaction, affiliation need should be helpful in predicting individual differences in interpersonal behavior (Atkinson, Heyns, & Veroff, 1954; Schachter, 1959). A third class of variables consists of the overt stimulus properties of each individual to which other individuals would be expected to respond on the basis of generalization from previous interpersonal interactions.

Once interaction has begun, reciprocal reward and punishment is proposed as the crucial determining factor. It has been suggested (Newcomb, 1956) that attraction between persons is a function of the extent to which reciprocal rewards are present in their interaction; perhaps dislike is a function of reciprocal punishments. A special subclass of this variable would be perceived similarity and dissimilarity of the attitudes of two individuals. It can be assumed that persons in our culture have well established learned drives to be logical and to make a correct report of the environment. Those who seem deficient in this respect are generally categorized as being uninformed, of low intelligence, immoral, and/or as being out of contact with reality. It is primarily through consensual validation that we determine whether we or anyone else is logical or correct in interpreting environmental events. Hence, any time that another person offers us validation by indicating that his percepts and concepts are congruent with ours, it constitutes a rewarding interaction and, hence, one element in forming a positive relationship. Any time that another person indicates dissimilarity between our two notions, it constitutes a punishing interaction and thus one element in forming a negative relationship. Disagreement raises the unpleasant possibility that we are to some degree stupid, uninformed, immoral, or insane. An alternative possibility is that it is

the other person who is deficient in one or more of these characteristics. Probably other variables, such as the importance of the issue to each individual, contribute to the effect.

A number of studies have found greater similarity among friends than among nonfriends with respect to a variety of issues (Bonney, 1946; Loomis, 1946; Newcomb, 1956; Precker, 1952; Richardson, 1940; Winslow, 1937). A few studies of a more experimental nature also support the notion of a relationship between attitude similarity and interpersonal attraction (Jones & Daugherty, 1959; Smith, 1957).

In order to test the proposition that the effect of attitude similarity is a causative one and to test some implications arising from the preceding speculations about the reason for the effect, it was hypothesized that (a) a stranger who is known to have attitudes similar to those of the subject is better liked than a stranger with attitudes dissimilar to those of the subject, (b) a stranger who is known to have attitudes similar to those of the subject is judged to be more intelligent, better informed, more moral, and better adjusted than a stranger with attitudes dissimilar to those of the subject, and (c) a stranger who is known to have similar attitudes on issues important to the subject and dissimilar attitudes on unimportant issues is better liked and is evaluated more positively on the other four variables than a stranger for whom the reverse is true.

METHOD

Attitude measure   On the basis of a pilot study, 26 issues were selected for inclusion in an attitude and opinion scale. Each issue was presented in a seven-point scale. The issues ranged from those thought to be extremely important by the pilot subjects (e.g., integration, God, premarital sex relations) to those considered to be of minor importance (e.g., western movies and television programs, classical music, politics).

Procedure   The attitude scale was administered to 64 students (36 male, 28 female) enrolled in an introductory psychology course at the University of Texas. Response heterogeneity differed from item to item, but there was moderately wide diversity of opinion among the 64 subjects. After filling out the attitude scale, the subjects were asked to indicate which they believed to be the 13 most important and 13 least important issues.

Two weeks later they were falsely informed that the attitude scale had been given as part of a study in interpersonal prediction. They were told that individuals in another class had been given the same scale that they took, students in the two classes were matched on the basis of sex, and they were to be given each other's tests (name removed) in order to determine how much they could learn about one another from this information alone.

Actually the questionnaire they received at this time was a fake one made up by the experimenter. The subjects had been randomly divided into four groups; one group received attitude scales filled out exactly the same as theirs had been, one received scales with exactly opposite views expressed, one received scales with similar opinions on the most important issues and dissimilar on the least important, and the fourth received scales with similar opinions on the least important issues and dissimilar opinions on the most important. The four groups of subjects did not differ significantly in their initial responses to any of the 26 issues.

Interpersonal attraction and evaluation A rating scale was used as the measure of interpersonal attraction and evaluation with each dependent variable represented in a seven-point scale. As a measure of interpersonal attraction, subjects were asked to indicate how well they felt they would like this person and whether they believed they would enjoy working with him (or her) as a partner in an experiment. Four scales dealt with evaluation; the subjects were asked for their judgments as to the other student's intelligence, knowledge of current events, morality, and adjustment.

RESULTS

First hypothesis Table 1 shows the comparisons of the two groups on each of the dependent variables. The first hypothesis was overwhelmingly confirmed for each of the two attraction scales. The group with attitude scales filled out the same as their own (SA) indicated significantly more positive feelings toward the "stranger" than did the group which received scales indicating dissimilar attitudes (DA). Each difference was significant at less than the .001 level.

Second hypothesis As is indicated in Table 1, the second hypothesis was also confirmed. The SA group rated the "stranger" significantly higher than did the DA group on intelligence, knowledge of current events, morality, and adjustment. Again, each difference reached a level of significance beyond the .001 level.

Third hypothesis The third hypothesis, concerning the influence of important vs. unimportant issues, was only partially confirmed. As is shown in Table 2, the Similar on Important Attitudes Group (SIA) rated the "stranger" significantly more positively than did the Similar on Unimportant Attitudes Group (SUA) with respect to their personal feelings about him, his morality, and his adjustment. On the other three variables, the two groups did not differ.

Table **1** | COMPARISON OF THE SIMILAR ATTITUDE (SA) AND DISSIMILAR ATTITUDE (DA) GROUPS ON INTERPERSONAL ATTRACTION AND EVAULATION

	SA (N = 17)		DA (N = 17)		D	t	df	p
	M	SD	M	SD				
Personal Feelings	6.53	.50	1.76	.73	4.77	21.46	32	< .001
Desirability as Work Partner	6.47	.50	2.65	1.88	3.82	7.88	32	< .001
Intelligence	5.65	.68	3.06	.87	2.59	9.37	32	< .001
Knowledge of Current Events	4.65	1.14	2.65	.91	2.00	5.51	32	< .001
Morality	5.76	.73	3.47	2.09	2.29	4.14	32	< .001
Adjustment	6.00	.84	2.71	1.13	3.29	9.36	32	< .001

Table **2** | COMPARISON OF THE SIMILAR ON IMPORTANT ATTITUDES (SIA) AND SIMILAR ON UNIMPORTANT ATTITUDES (SUA) GROUPS ON INTERPERSONAL ATTRACTION AND EVALUATION

	SIA (N = 15)		SUA (N = 15)		D	t	df	p
	M	SD	M	SD				
Personal Feelings	4.20	1.51	2.60	1.20	1.60	3.10	28	< .01
Desirability as Work Partner	4.27	1.44	3.33	1.40	.94	1.76	28	ns
Intelligence	4.13	.62	3.73	1.34	.40	1.01	28	ns
Knowledge of Current Events	3.60	.95	3.53	.96	.07	.19	28	ns
Morality	5.33	1.25	3.33	1.66	2.00	3.60	28	< .01
Adjustment	4.07	1.57	2.93	1.18	1.14	2.17	28	< .05

DISCUSSION

The experimental confirmation of the first two hypotheses is very encouraging for further research designed to investigate other aspects of the relationship between interpersonal attraction and attitude similarity. It should be possible now to study the effect of attitude differences less extreme than those in the present study and to combine this variable with the others that influence interpersonal attraction in order to determine interaction effects.

Because of the fact that this group of subjects showed a degree of homogeneity of opinion on some of the attitude items, a possible alternative interpretation is that they were responding negatively to unusual and deviant beliefs rather than to disagreement per se. On 19 of the 26 issues it was possible for a subject to fall in the deviant one fourth of the group by expressing a positive or a negative opinion. The range among the subjects was from no deviant attitudes to nine; they were divided into high and low subgroups on the basis of this score. Since these "conforming" and "deviant" subgroups did not differ from one another in responding to strangers with similar vs. different attitudes, there is no evidence to support this other interpretation of the results.

The partial failure of the third hypothesis led to a comparison of all four groups on each of the dependent variables. The results suggest that the Personal Feelings scale is the most sensitive measure of interpersonal attraction.

With the other five interpersonal judgment scales, additional factors apparently contribute to the variance.

REFERENCES

Atkinson, J. W., Heyns, R. W., & Veroff, J. The effect of experimental arousal of the affiliation motive on thematic apperception. *J. abnorm. soc. Psychol.*, 1954, **49**, 405–410.

Bonney, M. E. A sociometric study of the relationship of some factors to mutual friendships on the elementary, secondary, and college levels. *Sociometry*, 1946, **9**, 21–47.

Byrne, D. The influence of propinquity and opportunities for interaction on classroom relationships. *Hum. Relat.*, in press.

Jones, E. E., & Daugherty, B. N. Political orientation and the perceptual effects of an anticipated interaction. *J. abnorm. soc. Psychol.*, 1959, **59**, 340–349.

Loomis, C. P. Political and occupational cleavages in a Hanoverian village, Germany: A sociometric study. *Sociometry*, 1946, **9**, 316–333.

Newcomb, T. M. The prediction of interpersonal attraction. *Amer. Psychologist*, 1956, **11**, 575–586.

Precker, J. A. Similarity of valuings as a factor in selection. *J. abnorm. soc. Psychol.*, 1952, **47**, 406–414.

Richardson, Helen M. Community of values as a factor in friendships of college and adult women. *J. soc. Psychol.*, 1940, **11**, 303–312.

Schachter, S. *The psychology of affiliation.* Stanford: Stanford Univer. Press, 1959.

Smith, A. J. Similarity of values and its relation to acceptance and the projection of similarity. *J. Psychol.*, 1957, **43**, 251–260.

Winslow, C. N. A study of the extent of agreement between friends' opinions and their ability to estimate the opinions of each other. *J. soc. Psychol.*, 1937, **8**, 433–442.

Selection **52** | SEX-ROLE DEVELOPMENT IN A CHANGING CULTURE*

DANIEL G. BROWN
United States Air Force Academy

One of the more significant psychosocial developments of contemporary American society would appear to be the relatively fluid state of the sex roles of individuals. Within a single generation, significant changes have taken place in the traditional conceptions of what is masculine and what is feminine. Whether such changes have been abrupt enough to be considered a cultural revolution or sufficiently gradual to be simply degrees of cultural variation is difficult to judge. In either case, however, this changed and changing cultural pattern has a number of implications and possible effects that bear directly on individual, group, and institutional behavior. In this connection such questions as the following might be asked: What are some of these changes that have taken place in the sex roles? Have such changes been more pronounced in the feminine role than in the masculine role? How have these changes affected the life adjustment of individuals? And the relationships of the sexes with each other? What about the effect on boys and girls at the present time and in the years ahead? These are just a few of the problems in the area of masculinity-femininity development and adjustment that need to be studied and investigated.

The present paper is primarily directed toward a consideration of the nature and theoretical implications of sex-role development in children.

* Abridged from Daniel G. Brown, "Sex-role Development in a Changing Culture," *Psychological Bulletin*, 55: 232–242, 1958. Copyright 1958 by the American Psychological Association and reproduced by permission.

DIFFERENTIATION OF SEX AND SEX ROLE

As a starting point, consideration might be given to the age at which the child becomes aware of biological sex differentiation per se as well as when the child becomes aware of the essential meaning of "masculine" and "feminine," i.e., sex-role behavior.[1] At what age for example is the average child able to distinguish between the sexes and to distinguish himself or herself as a boy or girl? Evidence suggests that between two thirds and three fourths of children by the age of three are able to make this basic distinction.

Evidence also suggests that sex-role differentiation is a gradual process, probably beginning in the second year of life and becoming definitely established by the age of three. By or during the fifth year most children make a clear differentiation between the more obvious biological cues of maleness and femaleness and psychological cues of masculinity and femininity. As in the other aspects of psychological development, there are undoubtedly wide individual differences in the clarity with which differences between the sexes are perceived by children.

In any event, whatever the exact age in a particular case, it seems safe to conclude that preschool children as a group become fully aware of the fact that the world is divided into two groups of people and that, depending on whether one belongs to one group or the other, different behavior patterns are expected accordingly. At an early age, then, children are being conditioned to and are actively acquiring their sex roles. One of the most important considerations here has to do with the *meaning* and *significance* to the child of the earliest perceptions of structural and sex-role differences between boys and girls. What does it mean to a child to become aware of his sex for the first time, and gradually, his sex role? For the child to feel safe, secure, and satisfied in his emerging sexual identity would appear to be one of the most important conditions in his entire development.

[1] The concept, sex role, refers to those psychological characteristics and behavioral patterns that are typical of one sex in contrast to the other sex. The sex role of a person consists of the behavior that is socially defined and expected of that person because of his or her status as a male or female.

SEX-ROLE PREFERENCE IN CHILDREN

Related to the factor of age in sex and sex-role differentiation in children is the phenomenon of sex-role preference. Does preference for one sex role over the other parallel the developing awareness of the difference between the masculine and feminine roles? Or does preference come later, only after the child has been exposed sufficiently to the differential treatments accorded boys in contrast to girls? The origin and earliest occurrence of sex-role preference is a problem that awaits research investigation. That definite preferences exist in young children for one or the other sex role, however, has been reasonably well demonstrated by several studies. This problem has been investigated by the present writer by means of a technique known as the *It Scale for Children*, a scale composed of 36 picture cards, three by four, of objects and figures typically associated with the masculine or feminine roles in our culture (e.g., preferring to play with a tractor rather than a doll; wearing a dress rather than trousers; preferring to be a boy rather than a girl, etc.). A child-figure called "It," relatively ambiguous as to sexual identity, is used in administering the scale by having each child make choices for It, rather than the child himself or herself making the choices directly. Results based on the use of the It Scale with children between the ages of about 3½ and 11½, most of whom were from middle class homes, show that beginning with the youngest preschool group (Ages 3½ to 5½) and extending through the fourth grade (Ages 9½ to 10½) boys express a stronger preference for the masculine role than girls do for the feminine role. For example, at the kindergarten and third-grade levels, about 85% and 95% of the boys respectively indicate that It would rather be an "Indian Chief" than an "Indian Princess." And when asked which shoes It would rather "dress up and play house in," about 75% and 95% of the kindergarten and third-grade boys respectively chose men's rather than women's shoes.

Girls between the ages of 3½ and 6½ are quite heterogeneous as a group: some are predominantly feminine, choosing practically all of the feminine alternatives; others are predominantly masculine, and still others are "in-betweens," choosing both masculine and feminine alternatives. Taken as a group, for example, 50% express a preference for It "playing grownups" with cosmetic articles and 50% with shaving articles.

After about the sixth year and extending through the ninth year, most girls show a very strong preference for masculine in contrast to feminine things. For example, between 60% and 70% of the girls in the first, second, third, and fourth grades indicate that It would rather work with "building" tools than with "cooking and baking" utensils.

It is not known whether girls in the fifth grade and beyond (age group from about 10 to 11 and older) become less masculine in preference. Brown's study of fifth-grade subjects indicated a definite feminine changeover in girls, but Hogan failed to find any such change in the preference patterns of either fifth- or sixth-grade subjects. The whole problem of change in sex-role preference in relation to age needs further and more intensive study.

In contrast to girls, boys *at all ages* show a strong preference for the masculine role. This preference is evident in the youngest group (ages 3½ to 5½) and becomes even stronger until it reaches a near maximum at about the age of eight and thereafter. Thus, between 90% and 95% of boys in the second, third, fourth, and fifth grades indicate that, given a choice, It would rather wear a shirt and trousers than a dress.

SEX-ROLE PREFERENCE IN CHILDREN COMPARED TO ADULTS

To what extent are the sex-role preference patterns of children similar to those of adults? For comparative purposes the Parental Role section of the It Scale may be used. This section involves asking the child whether It would rather be a mother or a father. Results from this section may be summarized as follows: From about 80% to 95% of boys at all ages from kindergarten through the fifth grade express a preference for It becoming a father, only 5% to 20% for It becoming a mother. On the other hand, in the case of girls from kindergarten through the fourth grade, only about 25% to 45% express a preference for It becoming a mother, while between 55% and 75% for It becoming a father.

These results in the case of children are quite consistent with studies of adults in our culture which asked men and women: "Have you sometimes wished you were of the opposite sex?" or "If you could be born over again, would you rather be a man or a woman?" or "Have you ever wished that you belonged to the opposite sex?" Results may be summarized as follows: only between 2½% and 4% of adult men compared to between 20% and 31% of adult women recall *consciously* having been aware of the desire to be of the opposite sex. And in Puerto Rico only 33% of a group of adult female students compared to about 93% of male students indicated they would prefer to be female and male respectively if they "could come to life again after death." This lopsided preference for being male in preference to being female is also reflected in a recent survey of several hundred university students at Ohio State University who were asked whether they would rather have a male or female child in their family if they could have only one child. The results showed that 91% of the men and 66% of the women students expressed a preference for a male child. When both groups are combined, boys were preferred by approximately 75% and girls by only 25% of these students.

A significant problem connected with these findings concerns the psychological effect on large numbers of women who openly admit having preferred to be male. How does such awareness affect the self-concept of a girl or woman? The result, according to White is to undermine a woman's respect for herself as a woman and to derogate the feminine role in general.

An important anthropological analysis in connection with sex differences in acceptance of appropriate sex roles would be a *cross-cultural* comparison of the percentage of men compared to women who had preferred to be of the opposite sex. Compared to those cultures, for example, where male domination reaches exaggerated proportions, very different results might be expected among the Burmese, Ojibwa Indians and Tchambuli where females have relatively high status and a favorable position in their society.

FACTORS RELATED TO MASCULINE ROLE PREFERENCE

What factors are functionally related to the much greater preference that boys show for the masculine role than girls show for the feminine role and for the definite preference that many girls show for the masculine role? Although this is a problem in relation to which much research is needed, several conditions or factors may be suggested as contributory.

First, there is the emphasis by Freud on the *anatomical difference* between males and females, the effect of which is supposed to make the boy proud of his status and the girl dissatisfied with hers. Having versus not having a penis allegedly "explains" why girls as well as boys prefer to be boys.

Another attempt to account for sex differences in role preference is the emphasis by Adler on *sociocultural advantages* that go with being male in contrast to being female. The little girl may early perceive the greater prestige and numerous privileges connected with the masculine role. This would tend to arouse envy and drive her in the direction of wanting that which she does not have, namely, masculine status. Adler introduced the concept of "masculine protest" to refer to this phenomenon. That our culture has been and still is masculine-centered and masculine-oriented is obvious. The superior position and privileged status of the male permeates nearly every aspect, minor and major, of our social life. The gadgets and prizes in boxes of breakfast cereal, for example, commonly have a strong masculine rather than feminine appeal.[2] And the most basic social institutions perpetuate this pattern of masculine aggrandizement. Thus, the Judeo-Christian faiths involve worshipping God, a "Father," rather than a "Mother," and Christ, a "Son," rather than a "Daughter."

A third factor relative to the difference between the sexes in role preference is the greater *latitude* of the girls compared to the boys in sex-role development. It appears somewhat paradoxical that, although restricted much

---

[2] Typical examples include: military equipment, cowboy paraphernalia, police badges, airplanes, boats, trains, spaceships, marbles, yo-yoes, miniature auto license plates, etc.

more in practically all other respects, girls are allowed *more* freedom than boys in sex-role learning. This is, however, simply consistent with the idea that masculine status is so superior to feminine status that many girls are not even discouraged from striving to attain the former. For a girl to be a tomboy does not involve the censure that results when a boy is a sissy. With little, if any, embarrassment or threat, girls may show strong preference for the masculine role; this is not true in the case of boys.

Further evidence of the fact that girls in contrast to boys not only have much more opportunity to pattern their behavior after the model of the opposite sex but in many cases actually do so is cited by Cunningham. She reports on a group of fourth- and fifth-grade students who, when asked to describe what they consider to be some of the "pressing problems in human relations" included the following: "How can I stop my sister from being a tomboy?" Other examples that may be cited include:

Clothing Girls may wear shirts and trousers with little or no social disapproval, but boys do not wear skirts or dresses; in fact, men who wear feminine clothing, i.e., transvestites, do so at the risk of severe social censure and even legal punishment.

Names Many girls are given masculinized names such as Jackie, Stephanie, Billie, Pauline, Jo, Roberta, Frankie, etc., but few boys are given feminized names.

Toys and play activities Girls may play with any or all of the toys typically associated with boys (e.g., cars, trucks, erector sets, guns, etc.) but boys are discouraged from playing with toys that are considered feminine (e.g., dolls, dishes, sewing materials, etc.).

Goodenough has commented on the greater freedom of girls in sex-typed play as follows: "A boy is not likely to be a Dale Evans, but a girl often becomes Roy Rogers, or any of his masculine colleagues. Boys are rarely glamour girls, but many little girls fall eagerly into the roles of space men, or masculine rough riders."

Based on research findings that show boys consistently making more appropriate sex-typed choices than girls, Rabban and Hurlock conclude that "boys are more aware of sex-appropriate behavior than girls." Rather than being "more aware" than girls, however, it is the relative lack of flexibility of boys in sex-role choices that probably accounts for some of the difference between boys and girls in this regard. Boys simply do not have the same freedom of choice as girls when it comes to sex-typed objects and activities. In this connection, Hartley raises the question as to whether or not results of studies of sex-role preference in children, rather than measuring role preference as such, might not simply reflect the fact that girls are given much and boys little opportunity for variation in expressing preferences for sex-typed objects and activities. This is a good point and should be explored further.

As to the basis of the narrow, rigid sex-typing pattern in males, Goodenough presents evidence that suggests fathers show *greater concern* than mothers for sex-appropriate behavior in their children. In other words, father is more likely than mother to insist that "junior" look and talk and act like a *man*. This pattern, which would tend to have greater impact on the boy than the girl, is consistent with findings presented in the present paper, showing boys are much more likely than girls to make sex-appropriate choices.

Related to these differences in sex roles in childhood appears to be a parallel difference in adult occupational roles. Even though women traditionally have been subject to various kinds of vocational and economic discrimination, it is still true that a woman may and does enter a "masculine" vocation or profession, e.g., bus driver, engineer, lawyer, etc., with less social disapproval or concern as to one's sex-role "normality" than a man who enters a "feminine" field, e.g., hair stylist, dress designer, nurse, etc. The census in 1950, for example, revealed that women are now in all of the 446 occupations reported by the census. Among the 16,000,000 American women employed, there are "lady" carpenters, sailors, tractor drivers, pilots, telephone linesmen, locomotive engineers, lumbermen, firemen, and even stevedores and longshoremen!

SEX-ROLE IDENTIFICATION AND
SEX-ROLE PREFERENCE

In dealing with the complex problem of sex-role
behavior it seems particularly important to distinguish between sex-role identification and
sex-role preference. *Identification* is the basic
process in which a child, at first involuntarily,
and later consciously, learns to think, feel, and
act like members of one sex in contrast to the
other sex. *Preference* refers to the tendency to
adopt the sex role of one sex in contrast to
that of the other sex, the former being perceived as more desirable and attractive. With
this distinction in mind it is possible to de-
lineate three major sex-role patterns: (*a*) Identification with and preference for the sex role
of one's own sex, e.g., a girl may identify with
and prefer the feminine role; (*b*) Identification
with the sex role of one's own sex but preference for the sex role of the opposite sex, e.g.,
a girl may identify with the feminine role but
prefer the masculine role; (c) Identification
with the sex role of the opposite sex but preference for the sex role of one's own sex, e.g., a
girl may identify with the masculine role but
prefer the feminine role. Of the two processes,
identification appears to be primary, while preference is more or less secondary relative to
sex-role behavior. In normal development the
two form a single, integrative process.

In view of the finding that masculine role
preference appears to be widespread among
girls, it might be hypothesized that conflict or
confusion will be conspicuous in their sex-role
development. Thus, the fact that girls are
destined for feminine functions in adulthood,
yet envy and attempt to emulate the masculine
role in childhood, would tend to produce ambivalence and a lack of clarity in the feminine
role. On the basis of a study of sex-role learning in five-year-olds, for example, Fauls and
Smith refer to the "lack of clear definition" of
a sex role in the case of female children. Related to this is the contradiction between the
sex-role identification of many girls with the
feminine model and the tendency for them to
prefer the masculine role.

On the other hand, boys do not necessarily
escape difficulties in sex-role development.
Even though the culture greatly favors the

male, the fact that boys must shift *from*
an original identification-attachment with the
mother to an identification with the father may
create difficulties for boys that girls do not
experience. Thus, Sears reports that six-year-
old boys have not identified with their fathers
as well as girls have with their mothers. On the
basis of extensive observations of children in
preschools, Hartley arrives at a conclusion
similar to that of Sears and, in addition, raises
the question as to whether many boys really
experience their father in their paternal role.
She also questions whether many boys even
picture themselves as "future fathers."

It is also true that a considerable number
of boys get overly exposed to the feminine
model in early life when the mother is much
more prominent in the life of the child than
the father. This is especially likely to occur if
for any reason the father is psychologically distant or a predominantly negative figure for the
son and there is no adequate substitute.

According to Parsons and Gorer a major
effect of the situation in which the father is
typically away most of the time while the
mother is around continually exemplifying
effeminate model is to facilitate the role development of the girl and to complicate the
role development of the boy. These writers
seem to emphasize the *quantity* of the parent-
child relationship rather than the *quality* of
such a relationship. In other words, the degree
that the child respects, admires and loves the
parent may be much more significant than the
sheer amount of contact, per se.

SEX-ROLE DEVELOPMENT AND ADULT
SEX-ROLE ADJUSTMENT

A boy who incorporates the basic features of
the feminine model via predominant identification with the mother intrinsically will feel most
comfortable in the feminine role, which to him
is "normal" and "natural." Such a boy will
show a "feminine protest," i.e., he will protest
any restriction of his desire and effort to become thoroughly feminine. He will often plead
and even demand the freedom to adopt the
feminine role. This is the developmental pattern
in childhood that seems to provide the basis

for sex-role inversion in adulthood. In fact, inversion refers precisely to the adoption of the basic behavior patterns that are characteristic of the opposite sex.

In cases of males that do not involve a relatively complete inversion of sex role but do show considerable feminine identification, the result may be boys who become rebellious and develop strong defensive reactions in the form of extreme aggressiveness as a means of attempting to counteract their underlying inverted tendencies. MacDonald has presented a number of cases of "effeminate" boys who developed pathological aggressive reactions.

Although direct evidence is limited it appears that the child's eventual sexual orientation and adjustment in adolescence and adulthood bears a direct relationship with the nature of his sex-role development in childhood. Adult sexual behavior, at least in part, appears to be an outgrowth of the individual's underlying sex role. Thus, a normal male is one who has identified with, incorporated, and prefers the masculine role; his sexual desire for the female is one aspect of this role. A boy who has identified with, incorporated, and prefers the feminine role will most likely desire a male as a sexual partner in adulthood in keeping with the inverted role pattern. The problem of normal and inverted sex-role development has been discussed in another paper.

SEX-ROLE CONVERGENCE: A NEW CULTURAL PATTERN EMERGING?

Despite the fact that boys, much more than girls, show a concern for behaving along sex-appropriate lines, there has been considerable change in the direction of both masculine and feminine roles becoming broader, less rigidly defined, less sex-typed, and more overlapping with each other. As Seward observes, "Today in the post-World War II United States, there is a good deal less self-consciousness about sex roles and probably more freedom of choice for the individual than ever before." In line with this observation is a new course in domestic arts for eighth-graders in a public school in Jersey City, New Jersey, in which boys learn how to cook, sew, and become "efficient housewives," and in which girls learn how to handle

"man-sized tools," do woodwork, plumbing repairs, and become the "man-of-the-house." This course is described as so successful that the sexes may be switched in all eighth-grade homemaking and shop courses in the Jersey City system. The same type of course has been established recently in a junior high school in St. Petersburg, Florida. And in the public senior high schools in Denver, Colorado, courses in cooking for boys, metal crafts and lathe work for girls, and child care and training for both boys and girls are offered.

Other indications of the trend toward increasing similarity of sex roles include: (a) similarity of educational experiences of girls and boys from kindergarten through the secondary school system; (b) husbands doing the dishes, cleaning the house and carrying out other domestic tasks historically considered exclusively "feminine"; (c) wives holding down jobs outside the home, many of which have been traditionally "masculine"; and (d) the apparel of boys and men that emphasize color, softness, and more delicate features along with the adoption by girls and women of all kinds of "masculine" clothing, hair styles, etc.

Mead and Seward have pointed out that this greater flexibility in sex-role learning makes for increased interfamily variability and, hence, increasing cultural diversity in this regard. Is it still possible, in our culture for example, to speak of *the* feminine role or *the* masculine role? Or is it necessary to refer to various *roles*? Thus, within a single neighborhood, the role of the husband-father in one home involves almost absolute control, while the role of the wife-mother is strictly subservient and dependent. Next door, the dominating control of the family may be maintained by the wife-mother, while the husband-father is little more than a financially convenient "boarder." Across the street there may be hostile competitiveness and a continual "power struggle" between the husband-father and the wife-mother, each at times emerging "victorious," the other "defeated." And, in still another home, the respective roles of husband-father and wife-mother are largely complementary and equalitarian rather than hierarchical. What must be the effect of these very different parental role patterns on the sex-role identifications and preferences of children who are developing in these respective familial environments? For example, how is the process by which a boy becomes like his father (i.e., "a man") influenced by the various role structures in such families? It is plausible that degree of ease and normality or difficulty and abnormality is directly related to the particular parental role relationships. Intensive study in this area is very much needed.

Finally, on a culture-wide level, the rapid changes in the sex roles of the Japanese during the past decade might be cited. Among other contributing factors, the cultural diffusion stemming from American occupation of Japan has brought about far-reaching changes, particularly in the feminine role. In a country that gave rise to the expression "as unimportant as a Japanese woman," the traditional and relatively complete subordination of the female to the male appears to be on the way out and is being replaced by a status of women that is beginning to approach that of men. This trend is reflected not only in the fact that women can now vote, an unheard of practice ten years ago, but also in the hopes and aspirations of Japanese children as revealed in their drawings. When asked to draw pictures depicting what they wanted to be when they were grown, many girls drew pictures of teachers, secretaries, industrial workers, beauticians, scientists, etc.

A somewhat parallel development to that in Japan has been taking place in Germany during the past decade or so. Here, too, feminine status has undergone marked change in the direction of greater freedom and opportunity for women in the educational and economic spheres. A continuing sociopsychological analysis of such significant and rapid changes in the feminine sex role of the Japanese and Germans should be very informative and valuable, especially in terms of the impact on the present and future generation of children.

SUMMARY

The young child, as early as the second year of life, begins to distinguish between male and female and between masculine and feminine. Preference for one sex role or the other also begins to emerge early in the life of the child, probably by the third year.

Beginning at the kindergarten level and extending through the fourth grade, boys show a much stronger preference for aspects of the masculine role than girls show for aspects of the feminine role. In fact, a majority of girls in Grades 1 through 4 express greater preference for masculine things than for feminine things. These results are based on the It Scale for Children, a masculinity-femininity projective technique for use with young children.

The finding that girls more than boys show a preference for the role of the opposite sex is paralleled by studies of adults in our culture which reveal that between five and twelve times as many women as men recall having wished they were of the opposite sex.

As to the basis of masculine role preference in both sexes, three factors are mentioned: (a) the Freudian emphasis on the anatomical differences between males and females; (b) the Adlerian emphasis on sociocultural favoritism of the male compared to the female; and (c) the fact that the girl has more latitude than the boy in expressing a preference for sex-typed objects and activities.

A child may identify with and prefer the sex role appropriate to his own sex; or he may identify with and prefer the sex role of the opposite sex; or he may identify with one sex role and prefer the other. A distinction between sex-role identification and sex-role preference is emphasized.

In some ways girls would appear to have a more difficult time than boys in sex-role development; in other ways the development of boys would seem to be more complicated. The general problem of sex differences in ease of masculinity-femininity development is discussed.

Adult sexual adjustment or maladjustment is related to the nature and outcome of sex-role development in childhood.

There are definite signs that a convergence of the two sex roles gradually is taking place in our society. This cultural trend is evident in the increasing overlap between things and activities formerly considered "exclusively masculine" or "exclusively feminine." A major effect of this emerging cultural pattern is widespread interfamily variability in the sex roles of family members.

Finally, attention is called to the rapid

changes in the feminine sex role in Japan and Germany during the past ten years. Emphasis is placed on the need for a continuing socio-psychological analysis of sex-role development in such changing cultures as those of the Japanese and Germans as well as that of our own.

Selection **53** | STUDENT ATTITUDES TOWARDS THE NEGRO*

ROBERT K. YOUNG
University of Texas

Violence followed in the decade after the Supreme Court decision ended the legal recognition of the "Separate but Equal" doctrine. All the same, the South has been involved in what might be called a peaceful revolution. The Supreme Court decision, the subsequent civil rights activities characterized by sit-ins, wade-ins, stand-ins, and the Civil Rights Act of 1964, were all powerful forces in a vast cultural change which was accomplished in the presence of relatively little violence.

The ten years following the Supreme Court decision saw legal barriers fall which separated the white and Negro races and witnessed the integration of public facilities, schools and restaurants. The first tentative beginnings of a rapprochement in which both races can live and work together with relative ease has started.

At times various individuals have insisted that while laws can be made to enforce integration, they will have little influence on the feelings of one race toward the other. This paper presents data which may help clarify this point and to indicate some background variables which are related to attitude toward the Negro.

In the past decade three surveys measuring attitude toward the Negro were conducted at The University of Texas. Opinions of the student body was measured in each case. These surveys, conducted in 1955, 1958, and 1964,

* From Robert K. Young, "Student Attitudes Towards the Negro," *Texas Engineering & Science Magazine*, II: 8–12, 1966. Reprinted by permission of the author and publisher.

had procedures as much alike as possible to insure that any changes which occurred during this period represented a change in the attitude of the student body rather than something else.

In the theory of attitude measurement, it is assumed that individuals have a whole constellation of attitudes toward the object in question. Thus, instead of speaking of an attitude toward the Negro, we should perhaps speak of attitudes toward dancing with a Negro, intermarriage, attending church with Negroes, sharing a table in a cafeteria with Negroes, etc. All of these attitudes when taken as a whole represent the attitude of the individual toward the Negro. To get a general measure of attitude, therefore, the opinion of the respondent on each of these topics (and several others) must be obtained. If a person is consistently positive toward each of these questions, we should get a score indicating that he has a favorable attitude toward the Negro, and if he is consistently negative on these questions, he should get a score indicating that he is unfavorable. And if a person is positive at times and negative at others he should get a score which indicates that he does not feel strongly one way or the other about the Negro. The problem, of course, lies in the best way to combine all the attitudes into one meaningful whole. A number of ways have been devised to do this and one method was selected which seemed to meet the dual criteria of accuracy and ease of scoring.

The D (Desegregation) scale was developed by Dean Wayne H. Holtzman for use in the 1955 survey. The scale consisted of twenty-six statements selected from over two hundred by a screening technique which made certain that unambiguous statements would be selected from a wide range of opinion. Some of the statements in the final scale were positive (e.g., I would consider dating a Negro providing he or she met all my other standards) and some of the statements were negative (e.g., The prospect of intermarriage between Negro and white is repulsive to me). To each of these statements the respondent indicated that he strongly agreed, agreed, was uncertain, disagreed, or strongly disagreed. Then each of the statements was scored on a 0, 1, 2, 3, or 4 basis so that a negative attitude was given a high score and a positive attitude was given a low score. Thus someone answering "agree" to the statement about dating would be given a score of 1 while someone answering "agree" to the statement about intermarriage would be given a score of 3. The scores for all twenty-six statements were then added and thus a theoretical range of scores from 0 (very positive) to 104 (very negative) was possible.

To insure that each of the several religious organizations would be adequately represented, a sample of the cards on file at the headquarters of each of the campus religious groups was taken along with a sample of the cards at the YMCA where the cards of individuals who had no stated religious preference were sent. To be sure that the sample was representative of each of the groups, the samples were selected randomly. A random selection procedure simply means that each person within a group has an equal chance of being selected and thus the sample should be representative of the group from which it is taken. In the 1955 and 1958 surveys a 5 per cent random sample was taken from each group and in 1964 because of the increase in enrollment a 4 per cent sample was taken. In all three surveys the number of cases accounted for (completed the questionnaire, dropped out of school, etc.) was over 90 per cent; however, the actual number of cases available for analysis was somewhat less. There were 547 cases for analysis in the 1955 survey, 497 (of 630 sampled) in the 1958 survey and 578 (of 699) in the 1964 survey. In each case, the sample size was more than large enough to predict with confidence the nature of the student body.

OVER-ALL COMPARISON OF THE THREE SAMPLES

Of major interest in the series of surveys is the question of attitude change. To determine this, the means (averages) of the three surveys were computed and were found to equal 46.2, 45.3 and 39.6 for the 1955, 1958 and 1964 surveys respectively. When the data were analyzed by accepted statistical procedures, no change was found between 1955 and 1958 while a large change had taken place between 1958 and 1964. The change was in the direction of a more positive attitude toward the Negro. Thus it can be concluded that the atti-

tude of the undergraduate student body has changed in the decade since the Supreme Court decision and it has changed in the direction of a more accepting attitude toward the Negro.

The data also indicate that whether a person came in to fill out the questionnaire or mailed it in was related to his attitude. Despite the fact that the questionnaires were filled out anonymously, the 410 persons who came voluntarily in 1964, had a mean score of 38.4 while the mean of the 168 persons who mailed their questionnaires in was 42.6. By statistical procedures this difference (and subsequent ones which are reported) was a reliable difference and was not due to chance. This difference in itself is interesting and represents a change. In other attitude surveys taken by Dean Holtzman in the early 1950's, the opposite behavior was found: people who mailed their questionnaires in were more positive toward the Negro than were respondents who came in voluntarily.

There was a possibility that some of the statements on the attitude scale had become obsolete during the 1955–1964 period and that the observed change in scores represent nothing more than obsolescence of the scale. To check on this possibility, seven statements were individually analyzed. If the trends observed for the seven items, picked because they were thought to be representative of all twenty-six statements in the scale, were in the same direction as the overall change then it could be concluded that a change in attitude had taken place in the 1958–1964 period. These statements are presented in Table 1. All the statements in the table except 2 and 5 show statistically reliable shifts toward a more positive attitude. And statements 2 and 5 were answered most favorably of the seven in both surveys and have relatively little "room" to move. Thus it would appear that undergraduate student attitudes have changed in the period under consideration.

ADDITIONAL COMPARISON OF THE 1958 AND 1964 SAMPLES

In addition to indicating his opinions, each student in the sample gave some indication of his background by filling out a sheet asking such information as sex, age, year in school, and

Table **1** | RESPONSES TO INDIVIDUAL ITEMS

Statement	1958 mean	1964 mean
1	3.00	2.65
2	1.60	1.48
3	3.54	3.40
4	3.15	2.94
5	.83	.83
6	2.17	2.01
7	2.51	2.31

(The higher the score the greater the prejudice. Range possible 0 to 4.)

Statement

1. The prospect of intermarriage between Negro and White is repulsive to me.
2. I would not mind sharing a table with Negroes in a crowded cafeteria.
3. The best way to solve the race problem is to encourage intermarriage so that there will eventually be only one race.
4. I would consider dating a Negro providing he or she met all of my other standards.
5. The Negro will remain ignorant and superstitious despite equal educational opportunities.
6. I would not hesitate to join a fraternity or sorority which admitted Negroes.
7. I would not object to dancing with a good Negro dancer.

major. Some of these background variables are related to attitude toward the Negro and have been found to be quite stable over a long period of time. For example, grade point average is related to attitude toward the Negro. Respondents with low grade point averages tend to be less favorable toward the Negro than respondents with high grade point averages. These data are presented in Table 2.

Table **2** | COMPARISON OF ATTITUDE SCORES AS A FUNCTION OF CUMULATIVE GRADE POINT AVERAGE

Cumulative GPA	N*	1958 mean	N	1964 mean
Below C	30	48.2	68	43.0
1.0 to 1.4 (C+)	158	49.3	206	41.3
1.5 to 1.9 (B+)	153	44.0	159	39.8
2.0 to 2.4 (B+)	101	41.7	102	35.0
2.5 to 3.0 (A—)	39	42.9	39	36.2

* Number of respondents in each category.

Both the results of the 1958 and 1964 surveys are included. In both cases the C and C+ students were less favorable than the students with higher grade point averages and in both cases students with B+ grade point average were the most favorable. The stability of the differences found among the various groups is general and for this reason usually only the results of the 1964 survey will be presented. In general the 1958 means were about 6 points higher than those of 1964.

Church affiliation The 1964 survey indicates that church affiliation is related to attitude toward the Negro. These data are presented in Table 3. It can be seen that the Protestant groups are least positive toward the Negro while the Jews and those who profess no religious preference are the most positive. Of these various groups, the Baptists and Episcopalians showed virtually no change in attitude from 1958 to 1964.

Church attendance A curvilinear relationship is found between attitude and frequency of church attendance. Persons who go to church once or twice a month are the least positive toward the Negro while respondents who go to church every week and those who never go to church are the most positive. These data are presented in Table 4. This curvilinear relationship has been found in each of the three surveys.

Major field of study A student's stated major is also related to attitude toward the Negro. These data are presented in Table 5. Students majoring in business or education tend to be less favorable toward the Negro while students majoring in Fine Arts, Humanities or Social

Table **3** | COMPARISON OF ATTITUDE SCORES AS A FUNCTION OF RELIGIOUS PREFERENCE

Religion	N	1964 mean
Baptist	84	48.3
Episcopal	54	45.7
Presbyterian	45	41.8
Methodist	129	41.2
Other Protestant	121	38.5
Catholic	36	35.7
Jewish	19	28.4
None	71	28.4

Table 4 | COMPARISON OF ATTITUDE SCORES AS A FUNCTION OF FREQUENCY OF CHURCH ATTENDANCE

Frequency	N	1964 mean
Once a week or more	169	40.2
About twice a month	113	44.3
About once a month	95	42.3
Important Holidays	76	39.7
Never or almost never	117	31.2

Table 5 | COMPARISON OF ATTITUDE SCORES AS A FUNCTION OF MAJOR FIELD OF STUDY

Field of study	N	1964 mean
Business	108	45.9
Education	62	43.2
Pharmacy	23	41.7
Engineering	61	39.4
Natural Science	96	39.4
Humanities	110	37.1
Fine Arts	21	37.1
Social Science	54	33.0

Science tend to be more favorable. Although most groups showed a decline of about six points from 1958 to 1964, the attitude of the Education majors remained virtually unchanged from 1958.

Father's income   The reported income of the father is also related to attitude toward the Negro. These data are presented in Table 6. It can be seen that as reported income increases attitude becomes less favorable. This relationship, also found in previous surveys, is inter-

esting from the point of view that it is quite different from what would be expected from usual explanations of the effects of integration. That is, the usual argument is that lower income whites fear integration because of the possibility of losing their jobs. That is, they fear integration because of economic competition. However, from the data it would appear that a more important factor is that of "social distance." The children of higher income fathers probably have had little contact with Negroes other than with those who serve as domestics and yard men. They have had relatively little opportunity to meet Negroes in anything which approaches a social setting.

Home-town location   The geographic location of the home town is also related to attitude toward the Negro. However, the pattern appears to be changing. These data are presented in Table 7. The means for both the 1958 and 1964 surveys are included to illustrate the changes which have taken place from 1958 to 1964. Prior to the 1964 survey, attitude toward the Negro tended to be least favorable among respondents from east Texas and it became more favorable in the western part of the state. This pattern seems to have broken down. Where west Texas was the second most favorable area of the five Texas areas in 1958, it became the least favorable area in the 1964 survey. However, the other four areas within the state and the two areas outside the state have retained about the same rankings from the 1958 to the 1964 survey. Just what if any significance attributable to the failure of the west Texas respondents to show a decrease in attitude score is not known.

Table 6 | COMPARISON OF ATTITUDE SCORES AS A FUNCTION OF FATHER'S INCOME

Father's income	N	1964 mean
Less than $3,000	12	34.0
$3–5,000	49	35.1
$5–7,000	121	39.8
$7,500–10,000	94	39.2
$10–20,000	185	37.5
$20–30,000	48	45.0
More than $30,000	45	50.4

Table 7 | COMPARISON OF ATTITUDE SCORES AS A FUNCTION OF HOME TOWN LOCATION

Region	N	1958 mean	N	1964 mean
West Texas	64	45.5	86	44.6
East Texas	28	55.2	41	42.3
Gulf Coast	120	46.7	151	41.2
North Central Texas	86	48.7	102	40.6
South Texas	158	42.9	159	37.1
South U.S.	13	40.7	9	29.1
Other U.S.	17	28.0	21	24.5

Table **8** | COMPARISON OF 1955, 1958 AND 1964 ATTITUDE SCORES AS A FUNCTION OF FRATERNAL AFFILIATION

Fraternal affiliation	N	1955 mean	N	1958 mean	N	1964 mean
Affiliated	220	45.5	175	47.7	174	44.2
Unaffiliated	384	44.5	317	43.2	403	37.6

Fraternal affiliation Attitude as a function of whether a person belongs to a fraternity (or sorority) is one of the most interesting aspects of the surveys. Attitude toward the Negro as a function of fraternal affiliation and year of survey is presented in Table 8. It can be seen from the table that in 1955 there was no difference between the affiliated students and those who were not affiliated. The means of the two groups were almost alike. However, in the 1958 survey the mean of the students belonging to fraternities increased while those people not affiliated with a fraternity (or sorority) decreased. While these changes were relatively small the change was large enough to statistically be reliable. This trend continued to the 1964 survey. By this time the fraternity people had returned to the approximate score they had 10 years previously while the non-affiliated people continued to decline, i.e., to show a more positive attitude toward the Negro. One reason for this change is that the fraternities have an apparent policy of racial discrimination. Thus it would take relatively few people who would refuse to join a fraternity because of this apparent policy to separate the means of the two groups as much as they are.

However, there also is the question as to why the attitude of fraternity members has not changed in the last ten years. One reason for this is that a fraternity appears to have a structure which tends to maintain the status quo. That is, it would appear unlikely that a person would be invited to join a fraternity if his attitude toward the Negro differed from the individuals who already belonged. And it would also seem unlikely for a person to want to join an organization whose members held opinions which were different from his. Thus the average score of the fraternities tend to stay the same while the scores of the unaffiliated students tend to drop.

There is also interesting evidence about this difference which manifested itself about a year ago in the picketing of a bar on the "Drag." The people who were inside the bar tended to be fraternity members while those people outside the bar tended to be unaffiliated with any fraternity.

The pattern of attitudes expressed by the various groups have emerged so that a composite picture of students who tend to be favorable or unfavorable toward the Negro can be made. Thus a student who would be likely to hold attitudes unfavorable to the Negro would be a Baptist who attends church about twice a month, who is a Business major with a below C average. He belongs to a fraternity and his father, who lives in west Texas, has an income in excess of $30,000 a year. On the other hand the student who would tend to be favorable to the Negro is a person who does not belong to any religious group, and who never goes to church. He is a B+ social science major from outside the south. He does not belong to a fraternity and his father makes less than $3,000 a year. It should be noted, however, that the sex was not a variable—the mean attitudes of men and women were almost identical.

CONCLUSIONS

A marked change in attitude toward the Negro has occurred within recent years. The undergraduate students of the University of Texas were found to be more accepting of the Negro. This trend seems likely to continue, and there is other evidence from the surveys to justify this prediction. The "Negro Contact" scale given during each survey indicates that the greater the social contact between the two races the more favorable the attitude. With the legal barriers which have separated the white and Negro races falling, it seems likely that social interaction will increase. Going to the same church, eating in the same restaurants, going to the same schools, etc., would all seem to be factors toward a greater social interaction and hence a more positive attitude of one race for the other. In the analysis of individual items it was found that attitudes toward intermarriage, interracial dating, and other forms of social interaction all showed large and reliable changes in the direction of a more accepting attitude. Each of these attitudes would have to be thought of as major factors in any scale which purported to measure attitude toward the Negro.

Of major importance in the pattern of observed change was that while groups differed markedly—group means in the 1964 survey varied from 24.5 to 50.4—attitude change from 1958 to 1964 was general with most groups showing a change of about six points. One interpretation of this general change in attitude score is that these results reflect change in the attitude of the society as a whole rather than large changes in attitude on the part of a few groups.

REFERENCES

Kelly, J. G., Ferson, Jean E., and Holtzman, W. H. The measurement of attitudes toward the Negro in the South. *J. Soc. Psychol.*, 1958, **48**, 305–317.

Young, R. K., Benson, W. M., and Holtzman, W. H. Change in attitudes toward the Negro in a Southern university. *J. abnorm soc. Psychol.*, 1960, **60**, 131–133.

Young, R. K., Clore, G., and Holtzman, W. H. Further change in attitude toward the Negro in a Southern university. In D. Byrne and M. L. Hamilton (eds.) *Personality Research: A Book of Readings.* Prentice-Hall, Inc., Englewood Cliffs, N.J., 1966.

11 | THE SELF AND BEHAVIOR

Perhaps no other word is used more frequently in conversation than the personal pronoun "I." Each of us lives in a universe which seems to have himself as its center. Although psychologists disagree as to the kinds of behavior from which this concept of self may be validly inferred, there is increasing agreement that understánding of human behavior is greatly facilitated by the use of this concept. Definitions of the term are diverse but seem to agree that "self" refers to the organized structure of conceptions that each person has about his feelings, motivations, attitudes, roles, etc. Simply put, self may be thought of as a person's conception of who he is. Some aspects of the individual's self-concept may be quite conscious and easily verbalized, for example, "I am a college student." Other facets may be quite difficult to think about without great anxiety, for example, "I feel an intense hatred for my mother." In this latter case the person may automatically avoid perceiving these negative aspects of himself. In psychoanalytic terms, these motivations become repressed.

BIOLOGICAL FACTORS

The development of this cognitive-emotive self-structure begins with the child's discrimination that his body is somehow different from other objects or persons. Further, one's self-concept continues throughout life to be closely associated with his conception of his body (body image). Children take great pride in the development and growth of their bodies. However, there is perhaps no other period of life during which the individual is so body-conscious as during adolescence and early adulthood; witness the hours which teen-agers (both boys and girls) spend before the mirror. It is also during this period that there is most rapid change in the self-concept. Much of teen-age anxiety, hostility, and changeability reflects the person's attempts to define himself more independently of the views of himself which he has learned from other people. As was noted in our discussion of roles, expectations of others and of self may be greatly influenced by any biological factors which tend to make the person different from his reference group. Drs. Mary Cover Jones and Paul Henry Mussen have performed a series of investigations which help us to understand better the importance of early and late sexual development on the self-concepts, motives, and attitudes of adolescents. Their research, reported in Selection 54, indicates *that early maturing girls have significantly more favorable conceptions of themselves and greater need for recognition by others than do late-maturing girls.* You many wonder, "Since early maturation would certainly make these girls 'different,' why would this not be detrimental to their conception of self?" The answer seems to lie in the fact that this difference is in the positively valued direction. It is interpreted as a sign of superior growth and maturity rather than a deficit.

PSYCHOLOGICAL FACTORS

Several previous selections in this book have emphasized the tendency toward growth which seems to be characteristic of organisms from birth onwards (e.g., Maslow, Selection 16). Even though in neurotics this growth tendency may be hidden by self-defeating and self-depreciating behavior, the experiences of clinical psychologists with patients in psychotherapy suggest that the tendency toward growth can make itself manifest. The individual can become more adequate in his everyday relationships with others and can come to evaluate himself more realistically. The assumption that each person has a capacity to grow beyond his present state of functioning is central to the personality theory and the nondirective psychotherapy which has been presented by Dr. Carl R. Rogers. In Selection 55 Dr. Rogers shares with us some of his hypotheses about changes in a person's self-concept, feelings, and behavior which occur as a result of psychotherapy. He indicates that the person becomes more accurately sensitive to his real feelings and trusts these experiences to redefine continually his conception of self. As a result, he becomes more independent of the evaluations of others in defining who he is. Rogers expresses this new discovery of self most beautifully in these words: ". . . to an increasing degree he becomes himself—not a facade of conformity to others, nor a cynical denial of all feeling, nor a front of intellectual rationality, but a living, breathing, feeling fluctuating process—in short, he becomes a person."

SOCIOCULTURAL FACTORS

There is much confusion in our culture regarding the roles of selfishness and self-love in the mature personality. On the one hand our culture tells us that we should not be selfish, yet it also holds out the contradictory charge to "be an individual and act in your own best interests." In Selection 56 Dr. Erich Fromm traces the historical roots of the taboo on selfishness as they are manifested in religion, philosophy, and psychology. Calvinism and related Protestant sects viewed man as basically evil, and thus self-love was viewed as sinful. Such eminent philosophers as Emmanual Kant, although showing more respect for the individual than did Calvin or Luther, nonetheless shared the view that man has an inherently evil nature which must be controlled by social and moral laws. Similarly, Freud, proposed a hydrolic model of psychic energy which implied that the more love we direct toward others, the less we have available for ourself. This antagonism between love of self and love of others, with the love of others being held out as the ideal, is another manifestation of the anti-self-love theme in religion and philosophy. Fromm then procedes to show both philosophically and psychologically that self-love and selfishness must be sharply differentiated and how self-love and love of others are necessarily contingent upon each other. Neither can validly exist without the other; they continually create each other! A more recent statement of Fromm's views on the relationship between selfishness and totalitarian cultural patterns has been substituted for the original ending of this essay. In this section he shows how totalitarian systems seduce the individual into giving up his true self-interest in the name of "unselfish" allegiance to the state. Fromm implies that the loss of individual self-interest in an inauthentic social self is an ever-present danger for any culture which espouses a "religion of success." He points to three factors which, in combination, can serve to overcome cultural conformism. These are: (1) dissatisfaction with the culturally patterned definition of success, (2) a socioeconomic basis for change and (3) rational efforts toward change. Further discussion of some of these themes is contained in Selection 76 (Dyal).

Selection 54

SELF-CONCEPTIONS, MOTIVATIONS, AND INTERPERSONAL ATTITUDES OF EARLY- AND LATE-MATURING GIRLS*

MARY COVER JONES
PAUL HENRY MUSSEN
University of California, Berkeley

"The changing body and the changing self" is a phrase associated with adolescent development. It suggests that the shaping into mature form of the childhood body pattern is accompanied by new self-concepts. These altered attitudes toward the self reflect at least in part the youth's response to his physical metamorphosis.

What "growing-up" connotes for the individual adolescent depends upon a complex of psychobiological factors. One of the most important of these is rate of physical maturation. Adolescent growth may be relatively regular and even, or it may be uneven or abrupt. The timing of puberty, in relation to social norms of the peer group, may present problems of special importance for some adolescents.

Previous reports of systematic comparisons between the behavior and personality characteristics of early- and late-maturing adolescents have indicated that acceleration in growth tends to carry social advantages for boys but disadvantages for girls. At their peak of growth, early maturing girls are not only taller than their girl classmates but are actually taller than most of the boys in their class. They are conspicuously large at a time when physical size is not an asset for girls in our culture. Many girls consider tallness to be a physical stigma. At the end of adolescence the early-maturing are no longer taller than their age-mates, but in body proportion they tend to have a broad and stocky build, less attractive (in terms of current feminine standards) than

* From Mary Cover Jones and Paul Henry Mussen, "Self-conceptions, Motivations and Inter-personal Attitudes of Early- and Late-Maturing Girls," *Child Development*, 29:491–501, 1958. Reprinted by permission of the authors and the Society for Research in Child Development, Inc., Purdue University.

the more slender physique of the late-maturing.

Among boys, ascendance in size and musculature is an asset because of our cultural values and the functional advantages of such a build for athletic prowess. This more favorable status is indicated in observational records for early-maturing boys. Staff members rated them as physically more attractive and better-groomed than the late-maturing, and in social situations they were more poised and matter-of-fact, and less attention-seeking.

In contrast, both classmates and adult observers saw the early-maturing girls as relatively submissive, listless or indifferent in social situations, and lacking in poise. Such girls have little influence upon the group and seldom attain a high degree of popularity, prestige or leadership.

The girls in the slower-maturing classification were seen as relatively more outgoing and more assured. They were eager, animated, peppy, and talkative. This behavior seems to be acceptable among girls since those who exhibit it are also described as confident and having leadership abilities.

While the same characteristics of expressiveness are attributed to slow-growing boys, it is associated in their case more specifically (and especially in later adolescence) with show-off behavior, affectation, and tenseness.

In accounting for these sex differences in the response to early or late puberty, we may note that although early-maturing boys have physical advantages over other boys and are socially in step with girls, the girl who develops earlier than her classmates may be temporarily isolated. H. E. Jones has expressed this as follows:

The early-maturing girl quite naturally has interests in boys and in social usages and activities more mature than those of her chronological age group. But the males of her own age are unreceptive, for while she is physiologically a year or two out of step with the girls in her class, she is three or four years out of step with the boys—a vast and terrifying degree of developmental distance.

A study of responses to the Thematic Apperception Test, given to members of the Adolescent Growth Study when they were seniors in high school, yielded a somewhat unfavorable psychological picture for the late-maturing boys. Compared with their early-maturing peers, they showed greater evidence of negative self-concepts, prolonged dependency needs, feelings of rejection by others, rebellious attitudes toward parents, and strong affiliative needs. These findings were in agreement with evidence from other sources.

A similar TAT comparison of early- and late-maturing girls should be expected to show results different from those obtained for boys. Thus, it might be expected that early-maturing girls would reveal negative self-feeling and less satisfactory interpersonal attitudes.

PROCEDURE

The present study, paralleling that for boys, was designed to investigate the relationship between maturational status and self-conceptions, motivations, and interpersonal attitudes in a normal public school sample of girls. Personality assessment was made on the basis of their responses to the Thematic Apperception Test (TAT).

The 34 17-year-old girls of this investigation constitute approximately the 20 per cent at each extreme of the total sample of the Adolescent Growth Study, selected on the basis of their physical maturity status as determined by X-rays of the wrists and hands. Sixteen had been among the most consistently accelerated over a four-year period during adolescence; the other 18 were among the most consistently retarded. All of the subjects took the TAT at around age 17 when they were seniors in high school.

The TAT consisted of 18 pictures: nine from the Murray set which is now standard (cards 1, 5, 6, 7BM, 10, 11, 14, 15, 17); five pictures from the set generally used in 1938 when these data were collected (a man and woman seated on a park bench; a bearded old man writing in an open book; a thin, sullen, young man standing behind a well-dressed older man; a tea table and two chairs; an abstract drawing of two bearded men); and four cards not in the Murray series (a madonna and child, the nave of a large church, a dramatic view of mountains, a boy gazing at a cross which is wreathed in clouds).

The tests were administered individually. Each card was projected on a screen while the subject told a story which was recorded verbatim. Standard instructions were given for the Murray cards, and subjects were asked to describe the feelings elicited by the other four pictures. Most of the stories were brief.

The scoring scheme involved counting the relevant needs, press, and descriptions of the heroes of the stories, the assumption being that the storyteller has identified with the hero; the hero's needs are the same as the girl's; the press that impinge upon the hero are the ones that affect the girl telling the story. A total of 20 needs, press, and descriptive categories, each defined as specifically as possible, was developed in the analysis of the protocols. A score for each subject for each TAT category was derived by counting the number of stories in which it appeared.

To test the reliability of this analysis, one of the authors (PM) and another psychologist independently scored 15 complete protocols (300 stories). The percentage of interrater agreement was 90, computed by the usual formula (number of agreements divided by number of agreements plus number of disagreements).

In order to eliminate bias, the scoring used in the present study was done "blind," that is, independently of knowledge of the subject's maturational status.

RESULTS

Frequency distributions of the scores of all subjects were made for all the TAT variables. Each distribution was then dichotomized at the point which most nearly enabled the placing of half of the 34 subjects above, and half of them below, the dividing point. Subjects having scores above this point were considered high in this particular variable; those with scores below this point were considered low in this variable.

Early- and late-maturing boys differed from each other on many more characteristics than the two groups of girls did. The boys' groups were significantly different from each other, at the 5 per cent level or better, in six of the 20 variables scored, while the early- and late-maturing girls differ significantly in only two of the variables (*negative characteristics* and *n Recognition*). It should be noted, however, that the *direction* of the differences tended to be the same, rather than reversed, in the two sets of data. For example, the following similarities may be noted:

1. In this list of characteristics a significantly greater proportion of late-maturing girls than of early-maturing girls have high scores on *negative characteristics*. This finding is similar to that found in the comparison of early- and late-maturing boys. For girls, it is contrary to expectation.

2. The differences between early- and late-maturing girls in respect to *p Dominance* and *p Rejection* are similar to those for early- and late-maturing boys in these variables. These may be interpreted to indicate slightly poorer parent-child relationships among the late-maturing.

3. The early- and late-maturing boys differ significantly on *n Autonomy*, suggesting a greater tendency for the late-maturing to avoid or defy authority. The differences are in the same direction for girls, but are not significant.

4. Similar results for boys and girls in *n Succorance* may be interpreted as showing some tendency for stronger dependency needs in the late-maturing.

5. Similar results for boys and girls in *p Nurturance* (significant in one variable for boys) may also be interpreted as indirect indications of stronger dependency needs in the late-maturing.

The chief differences between the sexes are as follows:

1. With respect to *n Aggression* more early- than late-maturing girls show "argumentative aggression," but the two groups of girls do not differ in physical aggression. On the other hand, more early-maturing than late-maturing boys show high degrees of both kinds of aggression.

2. On one category of *n Affiliation* (involving romantic love) higher proportions of high scores are shown for early-maturing girls as contrasted with their late-maturing peers. The differences between the early-maturing boys are in the opposite direction for this category.

3. The variables *n Achievement* and *n Recognition* do not differentiate the two groups of boys. Among girls scores are higher for the late-maturing, very significantly so in the case of *n Recognition*.

4. *Denial of feeling* does not differentiate early- and late-maturing girls but tends to yield higher scores for early-maturing boys.

DISCUSSION

The failure of the TAT data to support observational findings, especially with reference to the variable, negative characteristics, might be accounted for in a number of ways. Some writers report that in many cases thematic fantasies and manifest behavior operate independently and are even negatively related. If we assume this to be the case for our subjects, no further explanation would be needed. But there is also evidence from the literature that, for some groups, TAT findings and overt behavior may be congruent. Our data on boys are in line with this assumption, since, according to observational ratings, late-maturing boys tend to be socially disadvantaged, and, according to the TAT, personally more maladjusted.

The findings for girls are quite different, however. The early-maturing received more unfavorable ratings from both peers and adult observers on many characteristics. But in the TAT they appear to be somewhat better adjusted than their late-maturing peers. This discrepancy between observers' ratings and the picture derived from the personality tests may stem partly from the fact that the reported observational records represented an average of repeated ratings taken over a period of time (from 11 to 17 years) while the TAT stories were collected at the end of this period.

Girls who enter puberty early would be expected to have more difficulties in personal-social relations when they are out of phase with their group. However, after the peer group "catches up," these difficulties would be reduced. By the end of senior high school maturational discrepancies, and social distance due to this factor, would be less marked. It is also possible that even a slight improvement in status would bolster morale and be reflected in a projective technique designed to register attitudes and self-concepts.

There is some slight evidence of a trend toward improved social status for the early-maturing in observational ratings over the seven-year period. Twenty-five items concerned with appearance, emotional tone, social participation, responsiveness, and assurance, were used in the comparison. Three of these reflected an improved status at the twelfth grade level for early-maturing girls. In two of these, "laughing" vs. "sober" and "sociable" vs. "unsociable," the accelerated girls, while still rated lower than the late-maturing, had improved sufficiently so that the differences between the two groups were no longer significant. But for one important characteristic, "popular" vs. "unpopular," the average ratings for the accelerated girls were now actually slightly higher than for the late-maturing, though the differences were not significant. This last year at high school was the only period when the early-maturing girls were rated by observers as above average in popularity.

It is conceivable that other improvements in social relationships were undetected because of the "halo effect" which, in spite of precautions, may have influenced observers who had rated these same adolescents in earlier years. It is not unlikely that if these girls of more mature status had been observed in social groups of their own choosing (presumably outside of school) the behavior picture might have been more favorable.

It may be noted that over the seven-year period the observational records received little corroboration from a self-report inventory. Although differences were not consistent in all categories, the early-maturing girls tended to score more favorably than the slow-maturing on "total adjustment," and also on family adjustment and feelings of personal adequacy. These data from the self-report inventory seem to be generally consistent with the findings from the TAT.

However, we may note that in both the inventory and the TAT the early-maturing girls appear in a somewhat better light than in their reputation scores or in ratings by adult observers. In some individual cases a favorable self-report score should not be taken at face value, in view of the tendency for some individuals to cover up or deny their deficiencies.

The only other variable which yields a significant difference between the maturity groups is the category n Recognition, late-maturing girls manifesting a greater desire for personal recognition. The results for n Achievement, though not showing significant differences,

tend to support these findings. Other data for this group of girls would lead us to expect this relationship between maturity status and desire for recognition. Late-maturing girls were rated by adult observers as attaining higher prestige, showing more leadership, and having greater stimulus value than their early-maturing peers. They were also mentioned more frequently in the high school daily paper over a three-year period and were elected to more offices in extra-curricular activities. The late-maturing girls' leadership abilities, their greater social participation, and their apparent social success may have been more closely related to desires for recognition and achievement in the social sphere than to a need for affiliation.

It should be noted that, among boys, n Achievement and n Recognition were not significantly associated with rate of physical maturation. Perhaps this is due to the fact that for boys in our culture the pressures to strive for achievement and personal recognition are powerful and pervasive; hence, the boy's physical status may have little influence on his acquisition of strong achievement and recognition needs. Since these cultural pressures are undoubtedly less severe for girls, the strength of these personal needs may be more influenced by such factors as rate of physical maturation.

As we have pointed out in an earlier article, the relationship between physical status and psychological characteristics in boys is by no means simple. The evidence of the present study indicates that this relationship is even more complex in the case of girls. While the TAT analysis reported in this study suggests that early-maturing girls have fewer negative self-concepts and fewer needs for personal recognition, the results must be interpreted very cautiously. Since only two variables were found to be significantly related to physical status, it is obvious that many psychological and social factors are more important than rate of maturing in determining girls' self-concepts and personality characteristics. Furthermore, these data, considered together with the data from earlier studies on girls, suggest that the rate of maturation may affect overt behavior and covert characteristics in different— sometimes seemingly contradictory—ways.

It is also possible that, at least for girls, early- or late-maturing means different things at different stages of adolescent development. It has been proposed that since girls who enter puberty early are out of step physically with both the boys and girls in their classrooms, they tend to be socially handicapped during early adolescence. We have assumed that this would carry emotional hazards, and evidence is available from observational data and reputation measures to indicate that this is the case.

However, the accelerated girl may gain assurance from knowing that she is on the way toward a goal which is a common task for all adolescents, that of being an adult. By the end of high school, many girls in this group were beginning to feel that they had made satisfactory progress toward this goal. If, in addition to this, she can cope with the problems of this period without too much stress, her self-esteem and feelings of adequacy may be enhanced. A resulting improvement in self-concepts may be reflected in the relative infrequency of negative characteristics in TAT stories.

In conclusion, it is evident that each individual's unique personality structure is determined by a complex of interacting variables, including rate of maturation. Comments made by these subjects as young adults indicate that they were aware of a variety of surface phenomena which affected their adolescent adjustment:

"High school is not a pleasant memory. I felt remote from my mother. If I could have talked to her, it would have helped" (a slow-maturer).

"I wasn't very happy in adolescence. My father was out of work. I felt inferior outside my own circle of friends—I always aimed to please" (a very popular late-maturing girl).

"I was slightly rattle-brained" (a popular late-maturing girl).

"I didn't have much fun in high school. I look forward to more happiness now than I did when I was in high school. I was an ugly duckling" (a slow-maturer who ascribed many negative characteristics to the hero).

"I seemed to be separated from friends in high school. I'm more outgoing now, less cautious and fearful" (accelerated girl).

"I was overweight and sensitive about it—now I take things more for granted" (accelerated girl).

"I had a feeling of being different when growing up" (accelerated).

"I felt stupid in school" (accelerated girl).

"I was very lacking in self-confidence in high school" (accelerated girl).

"I'm more optimistic now. I didn't know many people in high school. I would make an effort to get on with people if I had it to do over again" (accelerated).

Feelings of inadequacy and isolation are expressed by these girls and they are attributed to lack of mental ability, financial difficulties, separation from parents, poor social status, overweight, and unattractiveness. They are about equally common among those whose maturational status was at one extreme or the other.

It is obvious that the findings for this specific group of girls need to be particularized for each individual. These results might be modified also for girls in another geographical area or social level or in another generation. It is possible that school and community programs may be able to de-emphasize maturational status by providing an easier access to mixed social groups through classroom, extra-curricular, and recreational activities which cut across age classifications.

SUMMARY

The present study was designed to investigate the relationship between maturational status and TAT scores for a group of physically-accelerated as contrasted with a group of slow-developing girls from a normal classroom sample. The TAT protocols of 34 17-year-old girls—16 who had been consistently accelerated and 18 who had been consistently retarded—were analyzed according to a scoring scheme involving 20 needs, press, and descriptive categories.

The scores of early- and late-maturing in each of the categories were compared. Earlier reports had indicated that girls who reach puberty early are likely to be socially disadvantaged, at least until the rest of their age group "catch up" with them. It was assumed that this social disadvantage would be reflected in the TAT protocols and that differences between the two maturity groups in self-concepts, attitudes, and motivations would be found. Analysis of the data of the present study found few striking differences between the two groups of girls. However, early-maturing girls had significantly lower scores on the category *negative characteristics*, indicating more favorable self-concepts. This finding is contrary to what might have been expected on the basis of observational ratings by adults and reputational ratings by classmates. On the other hand, the TAT results are in line with scores (total adjustment, self-adequacy, family adjustment) on a self-report inventory.

Late-maturing girls have significantly higher scores on n Recognition, which is corroborated by data from other sources.

When the differences between early- and late-maturing girls are compared with the differences between early- and late-maturing boys, they are found to be in the same direction more often than in the opposite. These findings are interpreted to indicate that late-maturing adolescents of both sexes are characterized by less adequate self-concepts, slightly poorer parent-child relationships, and some tendency for stronger dependency needs.

It has been emphasized that complex psychological and cultural factors as well as maturational status contribute to personality development and that the pattern of these influences varies for each individual.

Selection **55** | BECOMING A PERSON*

CARL R. ROGERS
University of Wisconsin

SOME HYPOTHESES REGARDING THE FACILITATION OF PERSONAL GROWTH

To be faced by a troubled, conflicted person who is seeking and expecting help, has always constituted a great challenge to me. Do I have

* Abridged from Carl R. Rogers, "Becoming a Person," The Hogg Foundation for Mental Hygiene, The University of Texas, 1956, pp. 9–23. Lectures delivered on the Nellie Heldt Lecture Fund at Oberlin College. Reprinted here by permission of The Board of Trustees of Oberlin College.

the knowledge, the resources, the psychological strength, the skill—do I have whatever it takes to be of help to such an individual?

For more than twenty-five years I have been trying to meet this kind of challenge. It has caused me to draw upon every element of my professional background: the rigorous methods of personality measurement which I first learned at Teachers College, Columbia; the Freudian psychoanalytic insights and methods of the Institute for Child Guidance where I worked as intern; the continuing developments in the field of clinical psychology, with which I have been closely associated; the briefer exposure to the work of Otto Rank, the methods of psychiatric social work, and other contacts too numerous to mention. But most of all it has meant a continual learning from my own experience and that of my colleagues at the Counseling Center as we have endeavored to discover for ourselves effective means of working with people in distress. Gradually I have developed a way of working which grows out of that experience, and which can be tested, refined, and reshaped by further experience and by research.

One brief way of describing the change which has taken place in me is to say that in my early professional years I was asking the question: How can I treat, or cure, or change this person? Now I would phrase the question this way: How can I provide a relationship which this person may use for his own personal growth?

It is as I have come to put the question in this second way that I realize that whatever I have learned is applicable to all of my human relationships, not just to working with clients with problems. It is for this reason that I feel it is possible that the learnings which have had meaning for me in my experience may have some meaning for you in your experience, since all of us are involved in human relationships.

Perhaps I should start with a negative learning. It has gradually been driven home to me that I cannot be of help to this troubled person by means of any intellectual or training procedure. No approach which relies upon knowledge, upon training, upon the acceptance of something that is *taught*, is of any use. These approaches seem so tempting and direct that I have, in the past, tried a great many of them. It is possible to explain a person to himself, to prescribe steps which should lead him forward, to train him in knowledge about a more satisfying mode of life. But such methods are, in my experience, futile and inconsequential. The most they can accomplish is some temporary change, which soon disappears, leaving the individual more than ever convinced of his inadequacy.

The failure of any such approach through the intellect has forced me to recognize that change appears to come about through *experience* in a *relationship*. So I am going to try to state very briefly and informally some of the essential hypotheses regarding a helping relationship which have seemed to gain increasing confirmation both from experience and research.

I can state the over-all hypothesis in one sentence, as follows. If I can provide a certain type of relationship, the other person will discover within himself the capacity to use that relationship for growth, and change and personal development will occur.

WHAT IT MEANS TO BECOME A PERSON

A frequently-raised question is: "What problems do people bring to you and other counselors at the Counseling Center?" I always feel baffled by this question. One reply is that they bring every kind of problem one can imagine, and quite a number that I believe no one would imagine. There is the student concerned about failing in college; the housewife disturbed about her marriage; the individual who feels he is teetering on the edge of a complete breakdown or psychosis; the responsible professional man who spends much of his time in sexual fantasies and functions inefficiently in his work; the brilliant student, at the top of his class, who is paralyzed by the conviction that he is hopelessly and helplessly inadequate; the parent who is distressed by his child's behavior; the popular girl who finds herself unaccountably overtaken by sharp spells of black depression; the woman who fears that life and love are passing her by, and that her good graduate record is a poor recompense; the man who has become convinced that powerful and sinister forces are plotting against him;—I could go on and on with the many different and

unique problems which people bring to us. They run the gamut of life's experiences. Yet there is no satisfaction in giving this type of catalog, for, as counselor, I know that the problem as stated in the first interview will not be the problem as seen in the second or third hour, and by the tenth interview it will be a still different problem or series of problems. You can see why I feel baffled as to how to answer this simple question.

I have however come to believe that in spite of this bewildering horizontal multiplicity, and the layer upon layer of vertical complexity, there is a simple answer. As I follow the experience of many clients in the therapeutic relationship which we endeavor to create for them, it seems to me that each one has the same problem. Below the level of the problem situation about which the individual is complaining —behind the trouble with studies, or wife, or employer, or with his own uncontrollable or bizarre behavior, or with his frightening feelings, lies one central search. It seems to me that at bottom each person is asking: "Who am I, *really?* How can I get in touch with this real self, underlying all my surface behavior? How can I become myself?"

The process of becoming

Getting behind the mask   Let me try to explain what I mean when I say that it appears that the goal the individual most wishes to achieve, the end which he knowingly and unknowingly pursues, is to become himself.

When a person comes to me, troubled by his unique combination of difficulties, I have found it most worth while to try to create a relationship with him in which he is safe and free. It is my purpose to understand the way he feels in his own inner world, to accept him as he is, to create an atmosphere of freedom in which he can move in his thinking and feeling and being, in any direction he desires. How does he use this freedom?

It is my experience that he uses it to become more and more himself. He begins to drop the false fronts, or the masks, or the roles, with which he has faced life. He appears to be trying to discover something more basic, something more truly himself. At first he lays aside masks which he is to some degree aware of using. One young woman describes in a counseling interview one of the masks she has been using, and how uncertain she is whether underneath this appeasing, ingratiating front there is any real self with convictions.

I was thinking about this business of standards. I somehow developed a sort of knack, I guess, of—well—a habit—of trying to make people feel at ease around me, or to make things go along smoothly. There always had to be some appeaser around, being sorta the oil that soothed the waters. At a small meeting, or a little party, or something—I could help things go along nicely and appear to be having a good time. And sometimes I'd surprise myself by arguing against what I really thought when I saw that the person in charge would be quite unhappy about it if I didn't. In other words I just wasn't ever —I mean, I didn't find myself ever being set and definite about things. Now the reason why I did it probably was I'd been doing it around home so much. I just didn't stand up for my own convictions, until I don't know whether I have any convictions to stand up for. I haven't been really honestly being myself, or actually knowing what my real self is, and I've been just playing a sort of false role.

You can, in this excerpt, see her examining the mask she has been using, recognizing her dissatisfaction with it, and wondering how to get to the real self underneath, if such a self exists.

In this attempt to discover his own self, the client typically uses the therapeutic relationship to explore, to examine the various aspects of his own experience, to recognize and face up to the deep contradictions which he often discovers. He learns how much of his behavior, even how much of the feeling he experiences, is not real, is not something which flows from the genuine reactions of his organism, but is a facade, a front, behind which he has been hiding. He discovers how much of his life is guided by what he thinks he *should* be, not by what he is. Often he discovers that he exists only in response to the demands of others, that he seems to have no self of his own, that he is only trying to think, and feel, and behave in the way that others believe he *ought* to think, and feel, and behave.

In this connection I have been astonished to find how accurately the Danish philosopher, Soren Kierkegaard, pictured the dilemma of the individual more than a century ago, with keen psychological insight. He points out that the most common despair is to be in despair at not choosing, or willing, to be one's self; but that the deepest form of despair is to choose "to be another than himself." On the other hand "to will to be that self which one truly is, is indeed the opposite of despair," and this choice is the deepest responsibility of man. As I read some of his writings I almost feel that he must have listened in on the statements made by our clients as they search and explore for the reality of self—often a painful and troubling search.

This exploration becomes even more disturbing when they find themselves involved in removing the false faces which they had not known were false faces. They begin to engage in the frightening task of exploring the turbulent and sometimes violent feelings within themselves. To remove a mask which you had thought was part of your real self can be a deeply disturbing experience, yet when there is freedom to think and feel and be, the individual moves toward such a goal. A few statements from a person who had completed a series of psychotherapeutic interviews will illustrate this. She uses many metaphors as she tells how she struggled to get to the core of herself.

As I look at it now, I was peeling off layer after layer of defenses. I'd build them up, try them, and then discard them when you remained the same. I didn't know what was at the bottom and I was very much afraid to find out, but I *had* to keep on trying. At first I felt there was *nothing* within me—just a great emptiness where I needed and wanted a solid core. Then I began to feel that I was facing a solid brick wall, too high to get over and too thick to go through. One day the wall became translucent, rather than solid. After this the wall seemed to disappear, but beyond it I discovered a dam holding back violent, churning waters. I felt as if I were holding back the force of these waters and if I opened even a tiny hole I and all about me would be destroyed in the ensuing torrent of feelings represented by the water. Finally I could stand the strain no longer and I let go. All I did actually, was to succumb to complete and utter self-pity, then hate, then love. After this experience, I felt as if I had leaped a brink and was safely on the other side, though still tottering a bit on the edge. I don't know what I was searching for or where I was going, but I felt then, as I have always felt whenever I really lived, that I was moving forward.

I believe this represents rather well the feelings of many an individual that if the false front, the wall, the dam, is not maintained, that everything will be swept away in the violence of the feelings that he discovers pent-up in his private world. Yet it also illustrates the compelling necessity which the individual feels to search for and become himself. It also begins to indicate the way in which the individual determines the reality in himself—that when he fully experiences the feelings which at an organic level he *is*, as this client experienced her self-pity, hatred, and love, then he feels an assurance that he is being a part of his real self.

The experiencing of feeling   I would like to say something more about this experiencing of feeling. It is really the discovery of unknown elements of self. The phenomenon I am trying to describe is something which I think is quite difficult to get across in any meaningful way. In our daily lives there are a thousand and one reasons for not letting ourselves experience our our attitudes fully, reasons from our past and from the present, reasons that reside within the social situation. It seems too dangerous, too potentially damaging, to experience them freely and fully. But in the safety and freedom of the therapeutic relationship, they can be experienced fully, clear to the limit of what they are. They can be and are experienced in a fashion that I like to think of as a "pure culture," so that for the moment the person *is* his fear, or he *is* his anger, or he *is* his tenderness, or whatever.

Perhaps again I can indicate that somewhat better by giving an example from a client that will indicate and convey something of what I mean. This comes from the recording of the thirty-first interview with this woman. She has talked several times of a recurrent feeling which troubles her and which she can't quite pin down and define. Is it a feeling that developed because she practically had no relationship with her parents? Is it a guilty feeling? She is not quite sure, and she ends this kind of talk with this statement:

Client: And I have the feeling that it isn't guilt. (Pause: she weeps) So . . . I mean, I can't verbalize it yet. It's just being *terribly hurt!*

Therapist: M-hm. It isn't guilt except in the sense of being very much wounded somehow.

C: (Weeping) It's . . . you know, often I've been guilty of it myself, but in later years, when I've heard parents . . . say to their children, "stop crying," I've had a feeling, as though, well, why should they tell them to stop crying? They feel sorry for themselves, and who can feel more adequately sorry for himself than a child. Well, that is sort of what . . . I mean, as-as though I thought that they should let him cry. And . . . feel sorry for him too, maybe. In a . . . rather objective kind of way. Well, that's . . . that's something of the kind of thing I've been experiencing. I mean, now . . . just right now.

T: That catches a little more of the flavor of the feeling, that it's almost as if you're really weeping for yourself. . . .

C: And then of course, I've come to . . . to see and to feel that over this . . . see, I've covered it up. (Weeps) I've covered it up with so much *bitterness*, which in turn I've had to cover up. (Weeps) *That's* what I want to get rid of! I almost don't *care* if I hurt.

T: (Gently) You feel that here at the basis of it as you experienced it, is a feeling of real tears for yourself. But that you *can't* show, mustn't show, so that's been covered by bitterness that you don't like, that you'd like to be rid of. You almost feel you'd rather absorb the hurt than to . . . than to feel the bitterness. (Pause) And what you seem to be saying quite strongly is, I do *hurt,* and I've tried to cover it up.

C: I didn't *know* it.

T: M-hm. Like a new discovery really.

C: (Speaking at the same time) I never really did know. It's almost a physical thing. It's . . . it's sort of as though I were looking within myself at all kinds of . . . nerve endings and-and bits of-of . . . things that have been sort of mashed. (Weeping)

T: As though some of the most delicate aspects of you—physically almost—have been crushed or hurt.

C: Yes. And you know, I do get the feeling, oh, you poor thing. (Pause)

T: Just can't help but feel very deeply sorry for the person that is you.

I hope that perhaps this excerpt conveys a little bit of the thing I have been talking about, the experiencing of a feeling all the way to the limit. She was feeling herself as though she were nothing but hurt at that moment, nothing but sorrow for her crushed self. It is not only hurt and sorrow that are experienced in this all-out kind of fashion. It may be jealousy, or destructive anger, or deep desire, or confidence and pride, or sensitive tenderness, or shuddering fear, or outgoing love. It may be any of the emotions of which man is capable.

What I have gradually learned from experiences such as this is that the individual in such a moment is coming to *be* what he *is*. When a person has, throughout therapy, experienced in this fasion all the emotions which organismically arise in him, and has experienced them in this knowing and open manner, then he has experienced *himself*, in all the richness that exists within himself. He has become what he is.

The discovery of self in experience Let us pursue a bit further this question of what it means to become one's self. It is a most perplexing question and again I will try to take from a statement by a client, written between interviews, a suggestion of an answer. She tells how the various facades by which she has been living have somehow crumpled and collapsed, bringing a feeling of confusion, but also a feeling of relief. She continues:

You know, it seems as if all the energy that went into holding the arbitrary pattern together was quite unnecessary—a waste. You think you have to make the pattern yourself; but there are so many pieces, and it's so hard to see where they fit. Sometimes you put them in the wrong place, and the more pieces not fitted, the more effort it takes to hold them in place, until at last you are so tired that even that awful confusion is better than holding on any longer. Then you discover that left to themselves the jumbled pieces fall quite naturally into their own places, and a living pattern emerges without any effort at all on your part. Your job is just to discover it, and in the course of that, you will find yourself. You must even let your own experience tell you its own meaning; the minute *you* tell it what it means, you are at war with yourself.

Let me see if I can take her poetic expression and translate it into the meaning it has

for me. I believe she is saying that to be herself means to find the pattern, the underlying order, which exists in the ceaselessly changing flow of her experience. Rather than to try to hold her experience into the form of a mask, or to make it be a form or structure that it is not, being herself means to discover the unity and harmony which exists in her own actual feelings and reactions. It means that the real self is something which is comfortably discovered *in* one's experience, not something imposed *upon* it.

Through giving excerpts from the statements of these clients, I have been trying to suggest what happens in the warmth and understanding of a facilitating relationship with a therapist. It seems that gradually, painfully, the individual explores what is behind the masks he presents to the world, and even behind the masks with which he has been deceiving himself. Deeply and often vividly he experiences the various elements of himself which have been hidden within. Thus to an increasing degree he becomes himself—not a facade of conformity to others, nor a cynical denial of all feeling, nor a front of intellectual rationality, but a living, breathing, feeling, fluctuating process—in short, he becomes a person.

The person who emerges

I imagine that some of you are asking: "But what *kind* of a person does he become? It isn't enough to say that he drops the facades. What kind of person lies underneath?" Since one of the most obvious facts is that each individual tends to become a separate and distinct and unique person, the answer is not easy. However I would like to point out some of the characteristic trends which I see. No one person would fully exemplify these characteristics, no one person fully achieves the description I will give, but I do see certain generalizations which can be drawn, based upon living a therapeutic relationship with many clients.

Openness to experience First of all I would say that in this process the individual becomes more open to his experience. This is a phrase which has come to have a great deal of meaning to me. It is the opposite of defensiveness. Psychological research has shown the way in which sensory evidence, if it runs contrary to the pattern of organization of the self, tends to be distorted in awareness. In other words we cannot see all that our senses report, but only the things which fit the picture we have.

Now in a safe relationship of the sort I have described, this defensiveness, or rigidity, tends to be replaced by an increasing openness to experience. The individual becomes more openly aware of his own feelings and attitudes as they exist in him at an organic level. He also becomes more aware of reality as it exists outside of himself, instead of perceiving it in preconceived categories. He sees that not all trees are green, not all men are stern fathers, not all women are rejecting, not all failure experiences prove that he is no good, and the like. He is able to take in the evidence in a new situation, *as it is*, rather than distorting it to fit a pattern which he already holds. As you might expect, this increasing ability to be open to experience makes him far more realistic in dealing with new people, new situations, new problems. It means that his beliefs are not rigid, that he can tolerate ambiguity. He can receive much conflicting evidence without forcing closure upon the situation. This openness of awareness to what exists at *this moment* in *this situation* is, I believe, an important element in the description of the person who emerges from therapy.

Perhaps I can give this concept a more vivid meaning if I illustrate it from a recorded interview. A young professional man reports in the forty-eighth interview the way in which he has become more open to some of his bodily sensations, as well as other feelings.

Client: It doesn't seem to me that it would be possible for anybody to relate all the changes that I feel. But I certainly have felt recently that I have more respect for, more objectivity toward, my physical makeup. I mean I don't expect too much of myself. This is how it works out. It feels to me that in the past I used to fight a certain tiredness that I felt after supper. Well, now I feel pretty sure that I really *am tired*—that I am not making myself tired —that I am just physiologically lower. It seemed that I was just constantly criticizing my tiredness.

Therapist: So you can let yourself *be* tired, instead of feeling along with it a kind of criticism of it.

C: Yes, that I shouldn't be tired or something. And it seems in a way to be pretty profound that I can just not fight this tiredness, and along with it goes a real feeling that being tired isn't such an awful thing. I think I can also kind of pick up a thread here of why I should be that way in the way my father is and the way he looks at some of these things. For instance, say that I was sick, and I would report this, and it would seem that overtly he would want to do something about it but he would also communicate, "Oh, my gosh, more trouble." You know, something like that.

T: As though there were something quite annoying really about being physically ill.

C: Yeah, I am sure that my father has the same disrespect for his own physiology that I have had. Now last summer I twisted my back, I wrenched it, I heard it snap and everything. There was real pain there all the time at first, real sharp. And I had the doctor look at it and he said it wasn't serious, it should heal by itself as long as I didn't bend too much. Well this was months ago—and I have been noticing recently that—hell, this is real pain and it's still there—and it's not my fault.

T: It doesn't prove something bad about you—

C: No—and one of the reasons I seem to get more tired than I should maybe is because of this constant strain and so—I have already made an appointment with one of the doctors at the hospital that he would look at it and take an X-ray or something. In a way I guess you could say that I am just more accurately sensitive—or objectively sensitive to this kind of thing. I can say with certainty that this has also spread to what I eat and how much I eat. And this is really a profound change, and of course my relationship with my wife and the two children is—well, you just wouldn't recognize it if you could see me inside—as you have—I mean— there just doesn't seem to be anything more wonderful than really and *genuinely*—really *feeling* love for your own children and at the same time receiving it. I don't know how to put this. We have such an increased respect—both of us—for Judy and we've noticed just—as we participate in this—we have noticed such a tremendous change in her—it seems to be a pretty deep kind of thing.

T: It seems to me you are saying that you can listen more accurately to yourself. If your body says its tired, you listen to it and believe it, instead of criticizing it; if it's in pain, you can listen to that; if the feeling is really loving your wife or children, you can *feel* that, and it seems to show up in the differences in them too.

Here, in a relatively minor but symbolically important excerpt, can be seen much of what I have been trying to say about openness to experience. Formerly he could not freely feel pain or illness, because being ill meant being unacceptable. Neither could he feel tenderness and love for his child, because such feelings meant being weak, and he had to maintain his facade of being strong and masculine. But now he can be genuinely open to the experiences of his organism—he can be tired when he is tired, he can feel pain when his organism is in pain, he can freely experience the love he feels for his daughter, and he can also feel and express annoyance toward her, as he goes on to say in the next portion of the interview. He can fully live the experiences of his total organism, rather than shutting them out of awareness.

Trust in one's organism A second characteristic of the persons who emerge from therapy is that the person increasingly discovers that his own organism is trustworthy, that it is a suitable instrument for discovering the most satisfying behavior in each immediate situation.

If this seems strange, let me try to state it more fully. Perhaps it will help to understand my description if you think of the individual as faced with some existential choice: "Shall I go home to my family during vacation, or strike out on my own?" "Shall I drink this third cocktail which is being offered?" "Is this the person whom I would like to have as my partner in love and in life?" Thinking of such situations, what seems to be true of the person who emerges from the therapeutic process? To the extent that this person is open to all of his experience, he has access to all of the available data in the situation on which to base his behavior. He has knowledge of his own feelings and impulses, which are often complex and contradictory. He is freely able to sense the social demands, from the relatively rigid social "laws" to the desires of friends and family. He has access to his memories of similar situations, and the consequences of

different behaviors in those situations. He has a relatively accurate perception of this existential situation in all of its complexity. He is better able to permit his total organism, his conscious thought participating, to consider, weigh, and balance each stimulus, need, and demand, and its relative weight and intensity. Out of this complex weighing and balancing he is able to discover that course of action which seems to come closest to satisfying all his needs in the situation, long-range as well as immediate needs.

In such a weighing and balancing of all of the components of a given life choice, his organism would not by any means be infallible. Mistaken choices might be made. But because he tends to be open to his experience, there is a greater and more immediate awareness of unsatisfying consequences, a quicker correction of choices which are in error.

It may help to realize that in most of us the defects which interfere with this weighing and balancing are that we include things which are not a part of our experience, and exclude elements which are. Thus an individual may persist in the concept that "I can handle liquor," when openness to his past experience would indicate that this is scarcely correct. Or a young woman may see only the good qualities of her prospective mate, where an openness to experience would indicate that he possesses faults as well.

In general, then, it appears to be true that when a client is open to his experience, he comes to find his organism more trustworthy. He feels less fear of the emotional reactions which he has. There is a gradual growth of trust in, and even affection for, the complex, rich, varied assortment of feelings and tendencies which exist in him at the organic level. Consciousness, instead of being the watchman over a dangerous and unpredictable lot of impulses, of which few can be permitted to see the light of day, becomes the comfortable inhabitant of a society of impulses and feelings and thoughts, which are discovered to be very satisfactorily self-governing when not fearfully guarded.

An internal locus of evaluation Another trend which is evident in this process of becoming a person relates to the source or locus of choices and decisions, of evaluative judgments. The individual increasingly comes to feel that this locus of evaluation lies within himself. Less and less does he look to others for approval or disapproval; for standards to live by; for decisions and choices. He recognizes that it rests within himself to choose; that the only question which matters is: "Am I living in a way which is deeply satisfying to me, and which truly expresses me?" This I think is perhaps *the* most important question for the creative individual.

Perhaps it will help if I give an illustration. I would like to give a brief portion of a recorded interview with a young woman, a graduate student, who had come for counseling help. She was initially very much disturbed about many problems, and had been contemplating suicide. During the interviews one of the feelings she discovered was her great desire to be dependent, just to let someone else take over the direction of her life. She was very critical of those who had not given her enough guidance. She talked about one after another of her professors, feeling bitterly that none of them had taught her anything with deep meaning. Gradually she began to realize that part of the difficulty was the fact that she had taken no initiative in *participating* in these classes. Then comes the portion I wish to quote.

I think you will find that this excerpt gives you some indication of what it means in experience to accept the locus of evaluation as being within oneself. Here then is the quotation from one of the later interviews with this young woman as she has begun to realize that perhaps she is partly responsible for the deficiencies in her own education.

Client: Well, now, I wonder if I've been going around doing that, getting smatterings of things, and not getting hold, not really getting down to things.

Therapist: Maybe you've been getting just spoonfuls here and there rather than really digging in somewhere rather deeply.

C: M-hm. That's why I say—(slowly and very thoughtfully) well, with that sort of foundation, well, it's really up to *me*. I mean, it seems to be really apparent to me that I *can't depend on someone else* to give me an education. (very softly) I'll really have to get it myself.

T: It really begins to come home—there's only one person that can educate you—a realization that perhaps nobody else *can give* you an education.

C: M-hm. (long pause—while she sits thinking) I have all the symptoms of fright. (laughs softly).

T: Fright? That this is a scary thing, is that what you mean?

C: M-hm. (very long pause—obviously struggling with feelings in herself).

T: Do you want to say any more about what you mean by that? That it really does give you the symptoms of fright?

C: (laughs) I uh,—I don't know whether I quite know. I mean—well, it really seems like I'm cut loose (pause), and it seems that I'm very—I don't know—in a vulnerable position, but I, uh, I brought this up and it, uh, somehow it almost came out without my saying it. It seems to be—it's something I let out.

T: Hardly a part of you.

C: Well, I felt surprised.

T: As though: "Well for goodness sake, did I say that?" (both chuckle).

C: Really, I don't think I've had that feeling before. I've—uh, well, this really feels like I'm saying something that, uh, *is* a part of me really. (pause) Or, uh, (quite perplexed) it feels like I sort of have, uh, I don't know. I have a feeling of *strength*, and yet, I have a feeling of—realizing it's so sort of fearful, of fright.

T: That is, do you mean that saying something of that sort gives you at the same time a feeling of, of strength in saying it, and yet at the same time a frightened feeling of *what* you have said, is that it?

C: M-hm. I am feeling that. For instance, I'm feeling it internally now—a sort of surging up, or force. As if that's something really big and strong. And yet, uh, well at first it was almost a physical feeling of just being out alone, and sort of cut off from a—support I had been carrying around.

T: You feel that it's something deep and strong, and surging forth, and at the same time, you just feel as though you'd cut yourself loose from any support when you say it.

C: M-hm. Maybe that's—I don't know—it's a disturbance of a kind of pattern I've been carrying around, I think.

T: It sort of shakes a rather significant pattern, jars it loose.

C: M-hm. (pause, then cautiously, but with conviction) I, think—I don't know, but I have the feeling that then I am going to begin to do more things that I know I should do. . . . There are so many things that I need to do. It seems in so many avenues of my living I have to work out new ways of behaving, but—maybe—I can see myself doing a little better in some things.

I hope that this illustration gives some sense of the strength which is experienced in being a unique person, responsible for oneself, and also the uneasiness that accompanies this assumption of responsibility.

Willingness to be a process I should like to point out one final characteristic of these individuals as they strive to discover and become themselves. It is that the individual seems to become more content to be a process than a product. When he enters the therapeutic relationship, the client is likely to wish to achieve some fixed state; he wants to reach the point where his problems are solved, or where he is effective in his work, or where his marriage is satisfactory. He tends, in the freedom of the therapeutic relationship, to drop such fixed goals, and to accept a more satisfying realization that he is not a fixed entity, but a process of becoming.

One client, at the conclusion of therapy, says in rather puzzled fashion: "I haven't finished the job of integrating and reorganizing myself, but that's only confusing, not discouraging, now that I realize this is a continuing process. . . . It is exciting, sometimes upsetting, but deeply encouraging to feel yourself in action, apparently knowing where you are going even though you don't always consciously know what that is." One can see here both the expression of trust in the organism, which I have mentioned, and also the realization of self as a process.

Here is another statement of this same element of fluidity of existential living. "This whole train of experiencing, and the meanings that I have thus far discovered in it, seem to have launched me on a process which is both fascinating and at times a little frightening. It seems to mean letting my experience carry me on, in a direction which appears to be forward, toward goals that I can but dimly define, as I try to understand at least the current meaning of that experience. The sensation is that of floating with a complex stream of ex-

perience, with the fascinating possibility of trying to comprehend its everchanging complexity." Here again is a personal description of what it seems like to accept oneself as a stream of becoming, not a finished product. It means that a person is a fluid process, not a fixed and static entity; a flowing river of change, not a block of solid material; a continually changing constellation of potentialities, not a fixed quantity of traits.

CONCLUSION

I have tried to tell you what has seemed to occur in the lives of people with whom I have had the privilege of being in a relationship as they struggled toward becoming themselves. I have endeavored to describe, as accurately as I can, the meanings which seem to be involved in this process of becoming a person. I am sure that I do not see it clearly or completely, since I keep changing in my comprehension and understanding of it. I hope you will accept it as a current and tentative picture, not as something final.

One reason for stressing the tentative nature of what I have said is that I wish to make it clear that I am *not* saying: "This is what you should become; here is the goal for you." Rather, I am saying that these are some of the meanings I see in the experiences that my clients and I have shared. Perhaps this picture of the experience of others may illuminate or give more meaning to some of your own experiences.

I have pointed out that the individual appears to have a strong desire to become himself; that given a favorable psychological climate he drops the defensive masks with which he has faced life, and begins to discover and to experience the stranger who lives behind these masks—the hidden parts of himself. I have pictured some of the attributes of the person who emerges—the tendency to be more open to all elements of his organic experience; the growth of trust in one's organism as an instrument of sensitive living; the acceptance of the fearsome responsibility of being a unique person; and finally the sense of living in one's life as a participant in a fluid, ongoing process, continually discovering new aspects of one's self in the flow of experience. These are some of the things which seem to me to be involved in becoming a person.

Selection **56** | SELFISHNESS AND SELF-LOVE*

ERICH FROMM
New York City

Modern culture is pervaded by a taboo on selfishness. It teaches that to be selfish is sinful and that to love others is virtuous. To be sure, this doctrine is not only in flagrant contradiction to the practices of modern society but it also is in opposition to another set of doctrines which assumes that the most powerful and legitimate drive in man is selfishness and that each individual by following this imperative drive also does the most for the common good. The existence of this latter type of ideology does not affect the weight of the doctrines which declare that selfishness is the arch evil and love for others the main virtue. Selfishness, as it is commonly used in these ideologies, is more or less synonymous with self-love. The alternatives are either to love others which is a virtue or to love oneself which is a sin.

This principle has found its classic expression in Calvin's theology. Man is essentially bad and powerless. He can do nothing—absolutely nothing—good on the basis of his own strength or merits. "We are not our own," says Calvin, "therefore neither our reason nor our will should predominate in our deliberations and actions. We are not our own; therefore, let us not propose it as our end, to seek what may be expedient for us according to the flesh. We are not our own; therefore, let us, as far as possible, forget ourselves and all things that are ours. On the contrary, we are God's; to him, therefore, let us live and die. For, as it is the most devastating pestilence which ruins people if they obey themselves, it is the only

haven of salvation not to know or to want anything by oneself but to be guided by God who walks before us." Man should not only have the conviction of his absolute nothingness. He should do everything to humiliate himself. "For I do not call it humility," says Calvin, "if you suppose that we have anything left . . . . we cannot think of ourselves as we ought to think without utterly despising everything that may be supposed an excellence in us. This humility is unfeigned submission of a mind overwhelmed with a weighty sense of its own misery and poverty; for such is the uniform description of it in the word of God."

This emphasis on the nothingness and wickedness of the individual implies that there is nothing he should like about himself. This doctrine is rooted in contempt and hatred for oneself. Calvin makes this point very clear; he speaks of "Self-love" as of a "pest."

If the individual finds something in himself "on the strength of which he finds pleasure in himself," he betrays this sinful self-love. This fondness for himself will make him sit in judgment over others and despise them. Therefore, to be fond of oneself, to like anything about oneself is one of the greatest imaginable sins. It excludes love for others and is identical with selfishness.

There are fundamental differences between Calvin's theology and Kant's philosophy, yet, the basic attitude toward the problem of love for oneself has remained the same. According to Kant, it is a virtue to want the happiness of others, while to want one's own happiness is ethically "indifferent," since it is something which the nature of man is striving for and a natural striving cannot have positive ethical sense. Kant admits that one must not give up one's claims for happiness; under certain circumstances it can even be a duty to be concerned with one's happiness; partly because health, wealth, and the like, can be means which are necessary to fulfill one's duty, partly because the lack of happiness—poverty—can seduce a person from fulfilling his duty. But love for oneself, striving for one's own happiness, can never be a virtue. As an ethical principle, the striving for one's own happiness "is the most objectionable one, not merely because it is false, . . . but because the springs it provides for morality are such as rather undermine it and destroy its sublimity. . . ." Kant

* Abridged from Erich Fromm, "Selfishness and Self-Love," *Psychiatry*, 2: 507–523, 1939. Reprinted by permission of the author and publisher.

differentiates in egotism, self-love, *philautia*—a benevolence for oneself; and arrogance—the pleasure in oneself. "Rational self-love" must be restricted by ethical principles, the pleasure in oneself must be battered down and the individual must come to feel humiliated in comparing himself with the sanctity of moral laws. The individual should find supreme happiness in the fulfillment of his duty. The realization of the moral principle—and, therefore, of the individual's happiness—is only possible in the general whole, the nation, the state. Yet, "the welfare of the state—*salus reipublicae suprema lex est*—is not identical with the welfare of the citizens and their happiness."

In spite of the fact that Kant shows a greater respect for the integrity of the individual than did Calvin or Luther, he states that even under the most tyrannical government the individual has no right to rebel and must be punished no less than with death if he threatens the sovereign. Kant emphasizes the native propensity for evil in the nature of man, for the suppression of which the moral law, the categorical imperative, is necessary unless man should become a beast and human society should end in wild anarchy.

In discussing Calvin's and Kant's systems, their emphasis on the nothingness of man has been stressed. Yet, as already suggested, they also emphasize the autonomy and dignity of the individual, and this contradiction runs through their writings. In the philosophy of the enlightenment period the individual's claims and happiness have been emphasized much more strongly by others than by Kant, for instance by Helvetius. This trend in modern philosophy has found an extreme expression by Stirner and Nietzsche. In the way that they often phrase the problem—though not necessarily in their real meaning—they share one basic premise of Calvin and Kant: that love for others and love for oneself are alternatives. But in contradiction to those authors, they denounce love for others as weakness and self-sacrifice and postulate egotism, selfishness, and self-love—they too confuse the issue by not clearly differentiating between these phenomena—as virtue. Thus Stirner says: "Here, egoism, selfishness must decide, not the principle of love, not love motives like mercy, gentleness, good-nature, or even justice and equity—for *iustitia* too is a phenomenon of

love, a product of love: love knows only sacrifice and demands self-sacrifice." Nietzsche shared the view that there is a contradiction between love for others and love for oneself. Yet, it is important to notice that Nietzsche's views contain the nucleus from development of which this wrong dichotomy can be overcome. The "love" which he attacks is one which is rooted not in one's own strength, but in one's own weakness. "Your neighbor love is your bad love for yourselves. You flee into your neighbor from yourselves and would fain make a virtue thereof. But I fathom your 'unselfishness'." He states explicitly, "You cannot stand yourselves and you do not love yourselves sufficiently." The individual has for Nietzsche "an enormously great significance." The "strong" individual is the one who has "true kindness, nobility, greatness of soul, which does not give in order to take, which does not want to excell by being kind;—'waste' as type of true kindness, wealth of the person as a premise."

He expresses the same thought also in *Thus Spake Zarathustra*: "The one goeth to his neighbor because he seeketh himself, the other one because would he fain lose himself."

The essence of these views is: love is a phenomenon of abundance, its premise is the strength of the individual who can give. Love is affirmation, "it seeketh to create what is loved!" To love another person is only a virtue if it springs from this inner strength, but it is detestable if it is expression of the basic inability to be oneself.

However, the fact remains that Nietzsche left the problem of the relationship between self-love and love for others as unsolved antinomy, even if by interpreting him one may surmise in what direction his solution would have been found.

The doctrine that selfishness is the arch-evil that one has to avoid and that to love oneself excludes loving others is by no means restricted to theology and philosophy. It is one of the stock patterns used currently in home, school, church, movies, literature, and all the other instruments of social suggestion. "Don't be selfish" is a sentence which has been impressed upon millions of children, generation after generation. It is hard to define what exactly it means. Consciously, most parents connect with it the meaning not to be egotistical, inconsiderate, without concern for others. Factually, they generally mean more than that. "Not to be selfish" implies not to do what one wishes, to give up one's own wishes for the sake of those in authority; *i.e.*, the parents, and later the authorities of society. "Don't be selfish," in the last analysis, has the same ambiguity that we have seen in Calvinism. Aside from its obvious implication, it means, "don't love yourself," "don't be yourself," but submit your life to something more important than yourself, be it an outside power or the internalization of that power as "duty." "Don't be selfish" becomes one of the most powerful ideological weapons in suppressing spontaneity and the free development of personality. Under the pressure of this slogan one is asked for every sacrifice and for complete submission: only those aims are "unselfish" which do not serve the individual for his own sake but for the sake of somebody or something outside of him.

This picture, we must repeat, is in a certain sense one-sided. Beside the doctrine that one should not be selfish, the opposite doctrine is propagandized in modern society: have your own advantage in mind, act according to what is best for you—and by doing so, you will also bring about the greatest advantage for all others. As a matter of fact, the idea that the pursuit of individual egotism is the basis for the development of general welfare is the principle on which competitive capitalism has been built. It may seem strange that two such seemingly contradictory principles could be taught side by side in one culture. Of the fact, there can be no doubt. One result of this contradiction of ideological patterns certainly is confusion in the individual. To be torn between the one and the other doctrine is a serious blockage in the process of integration of personality and has often led to neurotic character formation.

One must observe that this contradictory pair of doctrines has had an important social function. The doctrine that everybody should pursue his individual advantage obviously was a necessary stimulus for private initiative on which the modern economic structure is built. The social function of the doctrine "don't be selfish" was an ambiguous one. For the broad masses of those who had to live on the level of mere subsistence, it was an important aid

to resignation to having wishes which were unattainable under the given socio-economic system. It was important that this resignation should be one which was not thought of as being brought about by external pressure, since the inevitable result of such a feeling has to be a more or less conscious grudge and a defiance against society. By making this resignation a moral virtue, such a reaction could to a considerable extent be avoided. While this aspect of the social function of the taboo on selfishness is obvious, another, its effect upon the privileged minority, is somewhat more complicated. It only becomes clear if we consider further the meaning of "selfishness." If it means to be concerned with one's economic advantage, certainly the taboo on selfishness would have been a severe handicap to the economic initiative of business men. But what it really meant, especially in the earlier phases of English and American culture was, as has been pointed out before: don't do what you want, don't enjoy yourself, don't spend money or energy for pleasure, but feel it as your duty to work, to be successful, to be prosperous.

The doctrine that love for oneself is identical with "selfishness," and that it is an alternative to love for others has pervaded theology, philosophy and the pattern of daily life; it would be surprising if one would not find the same doctrine also in scientific psychology, but here as an allegedly objective statement of facts. A case in point is Freud's theory on narcissism. He says, in short, that man has a certain quantity of libido. Originally, in the infant, all this libido has as its objective the child's own person, *primary narcissism*. Later on, the libido is directed from one's own person toward other objects. If a person is blocked in his "object-relationships," the libido is withdrawn from the objects and returned to one's own person, *secondary narcissism*. According to Freud, there is an almost mechanical alternative between ego-love and object-love. The more love I turn toward the outside world the less love I have for myself, and vice versa. Freud is thus moved to describe the phenomenon of falling in love as an impoverishment of one's self-love because all love is turned to an object outside of oneself. Freud's theory of narcissism expresses basically the same idea which runs through protestant religion, idealistic philosophy, and the everyday patterns of modern culture. This by itself does not indicate that he is right or wrong. Yet, this translation of the general principle into the categories of empirical psychology gives us a good basis for examining the principle.

These questions arise: Does psychological observation support the thesis that there is a basic contradiction and the state of alternation between love for oneself and love for others? Is love for oneself the same phenomenon as selfishness, is there a difference or are they in fact opposites?

Before we turn to the discussion of the empirical side of the problem, it may be noted that from a philosophical viewpoint, the notion that love for others and love for oneself are contradictory is untenable. If it is a virtue to love my neighbor as a human being, why must not I love myself too? A principle which proclaims love for man but which taboos love for myself, exempts me from all other human beings. The deepest experience of human existence, however, is to have this experience with regard to oneself. There is no solidarity of man in which I myself am not included. A doctrine which proclaims such an exclusion proves its objective insincerity by this very fact.[1]

We have come here to the psychological premises on which the conclusions of this paper are built. Generally, these premises are: not only others, but also we ourselves are the "object" of our feelings and attitudes; the attitude towards others and toward ourselves, far from being contradictory, runs basically parallel.[2] With regard to the problem under discussion this means: Love for others and love for ourselves are not alternatives. Neither are hate for others and hate for ourselves alternatives. On the contrary, an attitude of love for themselves will be found in those who are at least capable of loving others. Hatred against oneself is inseparable from hatred against others, even if on the surface the opposite

seems to be the case. In other words, love and hatred, in principle, are indivisible as far as the difference between "objects" and one's own self is concerned.

To clarify this thesis, it is necessary to discuss the problem of hatred and love. With regard to hatred one can differentiate between "reactive hatred" and "character-conditioned hatred." By reactive hatred I mean a hatred which is essentially a reaction to an attack on one's life, security, or ideals or on some other person that one loves and identifies oneself with. Its premise is one's positive attitude toward one's life, toward other persons and toward ideals. If there is a strong affirmation of life, a strong hatred necessarily is aroused if life is attacked. If there is love, hatred must be aroused if the loved one is attacked. There is no passionate striving for anything which does not necessitate hatred if the object of this striving is attacked. Such hatred is the counterpoint of life. It is aroused by a specific situation, its aim is the destruction of the attacker and, in principle, it ends when the attacker is defeated.

Character-conditioned hatred is different. To be sure, the hatred rooted in the character structure once arose a reaction to certain experiences undergone by the individual in his childhood. It then became a character trait of the person; he *is* hostile. His basic hostility is observable even when it is not giving rise to manifest hatred. There is something in the facial expression, gestures, tone of voice, kind of jokes, little unintentional reactions which impress the observer as indications of the fundamental hostility, which also could be described as a continuous *readiness* to hate. It is the basis from which active hatred springs if and when it is aroused by a specific stimulus. This hate reaction can be perfectly rational; as much so, as a matter of fact, as is the case in the situations which were described as arousing reactive hatred. There is, however, a fundamental difference. In the case of reactive hatred it is the situation which *creates* the hatred. In the case of character-conditioned hatred an "idling" hostility is *actualized* by the situation. In the case where the basic hatred is aroused, the person involved appears to have something like a feeling of relief, as though he were happy to have found the rational opportunity to express his lingering hostility. He

---

[1] This thought is expressed in the biblical: "Love thy neighbor as thyself!" The implication is that respect of one's own integrity and uniqueness, love for and understanding of one's own self, cannot be separated from respect, love and understanding with regard to another individual. The discovery of my own self is inseparably connected with the discovery of any other self.

[2] This viewpoint has been emphasized by Horney, Karen, *New Ways in Psychoanalysis*; New York, Norton, 1939 (313 pp.); in particular Chapters 5 and 7.

shows a particular kind of satisfaction and pleasure in his hatred which is missing in the case of an essentially reactive hatred.

The strength of basic hatred is one of the major problems of our culture. In the beginning of this paper, it has been shown how Calvinism and Protestantism pictured man as essentially evil and contemptible. Luther's hatred against the revolting peasants is of extraordinary intensity.

Max Weber has emphasized the distrust for and hostility toward others which runs through the Puritan literature replete with warnings against having any confidence in the help and friendliness of our fellow men. Deep distrust even toward one's closest friend is recommended by Baxter. Th. Adams says: "He—the "knowing" man—is blind in no man's cause but best sighted in his own. He confines himself to the circle of his own affairs and thrusts not his fingers in needless fires . . . . He sees the falseness of it [the world] and, therefore, learns to trust himself ever, others so far as not to be damaged by their disappointments."

Hobbes assumed that man's nature was that of a predatory animal, filled with hostility, set to kill and rob. Only by the consensus of all, submitting to the authority of the state, could peace and order be created. Kant's opinion of man's nature is not too distant from Hobbes, he too thought that man's nature had a fundamental propensity for evil. Among psychologists, chronic hatred as an inherent part of human nature has been a frequent assumption. William James considered it as being so strong that he took for granted that we all feel a natural repulsion against physical contact with other persons. Freud, in his theory of the death instinct, assumed that for biological reasons, we all are driven by an irresistible force to destroy either others or ourselves.

While the frequency of underlying distrust and dislike for others is known to many observers of our social scene, the dislike for oneself is a less clearly recognized phenomenon. Yet, this self-hatred may be considered rare only so long as we think of cases in which people quite overtly hate or dislike themselves. Mostly, this self-dislike is concealed in various ways. One of the most frequent indirect expressions of self-dislike are the inferiority feelings so widespread in our culture. Consciously, these persons do not feel that they dislike themselves: what they do feel is only that they are inferior to others, that they are stupid, unattractive or whatever the particular content of the inferiority feelings is.

To be sure, the dynamics of inferiority feelings are complex and there are factors other than the one with which we are dealing. Yet, this factor is never missing and dislike for oneself or at least a lack of fondness for one's own person is always present and is dynamically an important factor.

A still more subtle form of self-dislike is the tendency toward constant self-criticism. These people do not feel inferior but if they make one mistake, discover something in themselves which should not be so, their self-criticism is entirely out of proportion to the significance of the mistake or the shortcoming. They must either be perfect according to their own standards, or at least perfect enough according to the standards of the people around them so that they get affection and approval. If they feel that what they did was perfect or if they succeed in winning other people's approval, they feel at ease. But whenever this is missing they feel overwhelmed by an otherwise repressed inferiority feeling. Here again, the basic lack of fondness for themselves is one source from which the attitude springs. This becomes more evident if we compare this attitude toward oneself with the corresponding one toward others. If, for example, a man who believes that he loves a woman should feel if she makes any mistake that she is no good, or if his feeling about her is entirely dependent on whether others criticize or praise her, we cannot doubt that there is a fundamental lack of love for her. It is the person who hates who seizes every opportunity to criticize another person and who does not miss any blunder.

The most widespread expression of the lack of fondness for oneself, however, is the way in which people treat themselves. People are their own slave drivers; instead of being the slaves of a master outside of themselves, they have put the master within. This master is harsh and cruel. He does not give them a moment's rest, he forbids them the enjoyment of any pleasure, does not allow them to do what they want. If they do so, they do it furtively and at the expense of a guilty conscience. Even the pursuit of pleasure is as compulsory as is work. It does not lead them away from the continual restlessness which pervades their lives. For the most part, they are not even aware of this.

What holds true of hostility and hatred holds also true of love. Yet, love for others and self-love is by far a more difficult problem to discuss; and this for two reasons. One is the fact that while hatred is a phenomenon to be found everywhere in our society and, therefore, an easy object for empirical observation and analysis, love is a comparatively rare phenomenon, which lends itself to empirical observation only under difficulties; any discussion of love, therefore, implies the danger of being unempirical and merely speculative. The other difficulty is perhaps even greater. There is no word in our language which has been so much misused and prostituted as the word "love." It has been preached by those who were ready to condone every cruelty if it served their purpose; it has been used as a disguise under which to force people into sacrificing their own happiness, into submitting their whole self to those who profited from this surrender. It has been used as the moral basis for unjustified demands. It has been made so empty that for many people *love* may mean no more than that two people have lived together for 20 years just without fighting more often than once a week. It is dangerous and somewhat embarrassing to use such a word. Yet a psychologist may not properly succumb to this embarrassment. To preach love is at best bad taste. But to make a cool and critical analysis of the phenomenon of love and to unmask pseudo-love—tasks which cannot be separated from each other—is an obligation that the psychologist has no right to avoid.

It goes without saying that this paper will not attempt to give an analysis of love. Even to describe the psychological phenomena which are conventionally covered by the term "love" would require a good part of a book. One must attempt, however, the presentation necessary to the main trend of thought of this paper.

Two phenomena closely connected with each other are frequently presented as love—the masochistic and sadistic *love*. In the case of masochistic *love*, one gives up one's self, one's initiative and integrity in order to become submerged entirely in another person who is felt to be stronger. Because of deep anxieties which give rise to the feeling that one cannot stand on one's own feet, one wants to be rid of one's own individual self and to become part of another being, thus becoming secure and finding a center which one misses in oneself. This surrender of one's own self has often been praised as the example of "the great love." It is actually a form of idolatry, and also an annihilation of the self. The fact that it has been conceived as love has made it the more seductive and dangerous.

The sadistic *love* on the other hand springs from the desire to swallow its object to make him a will-less instrument in one's own hands. This drive is also rooted in a deep anxiety and an inability to stand alone, but instead of finding increased strength by being swallowed, strength and security are found in having a limited power over the other person. The masochistic as well as the sadistic kind of love are expressions of one basic need which springs from a basic inability to be independent. Using a biological term, this basic need may be called a "need for symbiosis." The sadistic *love* is frequently the kind of love that parents have for their children. Whether the domination is overtly authoritarian or subtly "modern" makes no essential difference. In either case, it tends to undermine the strength of the self of the child and leads in later years to the development in him of the very same symbiotic tendencies. The sadistic love is not infrequent among adults. Often in relationships of long duration, the respective rôles are permanent, one partner representing the sadistic, the other one the masochistic pole of the symbiotic relationship. Often the rôles change constantly—a continuous struggle for dominance and submission being conceived as *love*.

It appears from what has been said that love cannot be separated from freedom and independence. In contradiction to the symbiotic pseudo-love, the basic premise of love is freedom and equality. Its premise is the strength, independence, integrity of the self, which can stand alone and bear solitude. This premise holds true for the loving as well as for the loved person. Love is a spontaneous act, and spontaneity means—also literally—the ability to act of one's own free volition. If anxiety and weakness of the self makes it impossible for the individual to be rooted in himself, he cannot love.

This fact can be fully understood only if we consider what love is directed toward. It is the opposite of hatred. Hatred is a passionate wish for destruction; love is a passionate affirmation of its "object." That means that love is not an "affect" but an active striving, the aim of which is the happiness, development, and freedom of its "object." This passionate affirmation is not possible if one's own self is crippled, since genuine affirmation is always rooted in strength. The person whose self is thwarted, can only love in an ambivalent way; that is, with the strong part of his self he can love, with the crippled part he must hate.

The term *passionate affirmation* easily leads to misunderstanding; it does not mean intellectual affirmation in the sense of purely rational judgment. It implies a much deeper affirmation, in which one's personality takes part as a whole: one's intellect, emotion and senses. One's eyes, ears and nose are often as good or better organs of affirmation than one's brain. If it is a deep and passionate one, the affirmation is related to the essence of the "object," not merely toward partial qualities. There is no stronger expression of God's love for man in the Old Testament than the saying at the end of each day of creation: "And God saw that it was good."

There is another possible misunderstanding which should particularly be avoided. From what has been said, one might come to the conclusion that every affirmation is love, regardless of the worthiness of the object to be loved. This would mean that love is a purely subjective feeling of affirmation and that the problem of objective values does not enter into it. The question arises: Can one love the evil? We come here to one of the most difficult problems of psychology and philosophy, a discussion of which can scarcely be attempted here. I must repeat, however, that affirmation in the sense here used is not something entirely subjective. Love is affirmation of life, growth, joy, freedom and by definition, therefore, the evil which is negation, death, compulsion cannot be loved. Certainly, the subjective feeling can be a pleasurable excitement, consciously conceived in the conventional term of love. The person is apt to believe that he loves, but analysis of his mental content reveals a state very different from what I have discussed as love. Much the same question arises with regard to certain other problems in psychology, for instance, the problem as to

whether happiness is an entirely subjective phenomenon or whether it includes an objective factor. Is a person who feels "happy" in dependence and self-surrender happy because he feels to be so, or is happiness always dependent on certain values like freedom and integrity? One has always used the argument that the people concerned are "happy" to justify their suppression. This is a poor defense. Happiness cannot be separated from certain values, and is not simply a subjective feeling of satisfaction. A case in point is masochism. A person can be satisfied with submission, with torture, or even with death, but there is no happiness in submission, torture or death. Such considerations seem to leave the ground of psychology and to belong to the field of philosophy or religion. I do not believe that this is so. A sufficiently refined psychological analysis, which is aware of the difference in the qualities of feelings according to the underlying personality structure, can show the difference between *satisfaction* and *happiness*. Yet, psychology can be aware of these problems only if it does not try to separate itself from the problem of values. And, in the end does not shrink from the question of the goal and purpose of human existence.

Love, like character-conditioned hatred, is rooted in a basic attitude which is constantly present; a readiness to love, a *basic sympathy* as one might call it. It is started, but not caused, by a particular object. The ability and readiness to love is a character trait just as is the readiness to hate. It is difficult to say what the conditions favoring the development of this *basic sympathy* are. It seems that there are two main conditions, a positive and a negative one. The positive one is simply to have experienced love from others as a child. While conventionally, parents are supposed to *love* their children as a matter of course, this is rather the exception than the rule. This positive condition is, therefore, frequently absent. The negative condition is the absence of all those factors, discussed above, which make for the existence of a chronic hatred. The observer of childhood experiences may well doubt that the absence of these conditions is frequent.

From the premise that actual love is rooted in a *basic sympathy* there follows an important conclusion with regard to the *objects* of love. The conclusion is, in principle, the same as was stated with regard to the objects of chronic hatred: the objects of love do not have the quality of exclusiveness. To be sure, it is not accidental that a certain person becomes the *object* of manifest love. The factors conditioning such a specific choice are too numerous and too complex to be discussed here. The important point, however, is that love for a particular *object* is only the actualization and concentration of lingering love with regard to one person; it is not, as the idea of *romantic love* would have it, that there is only *the* one person in the world whom one could love, that it is the great chance of one's life to find that person, and that love for him or her results in a withdrawal from all others. The kind of love which can only be experienced with regard to one person demonstrates by this very fact that it is not love, but a symbiotic attachment. The basic affirmation contained in love is directed toward the beloved person as an incarnation of essentially human qualities. Love for one person implies love for man as such. The kind of "division of labor" as William James calls it; namely, to love one's family, but to be without feeling for the "stranger," is a sign of a basic inability to love. Love for man as such is not, as it is frequently supposed to be, an abstraction coming "after" the love for a specific person, or an enlargement of the experience with a specific *object;* it is its premise, although, gentically, it is acquired in the contact with concrete individuals.

From this, it follows that my own self, in principle, is as much an object of my love as another person. The affirmation of my own life, happiness, growth, freedom is rooted in the presence of the basic readiness of and ability for such an affirmation. If an individual has this readiness, he has it also toward himself; if he can only *love* others, he cannot love at all. In one word, love is as indivisible as hatred with regard to its *objects.*

The principle which has been pointed out here, that hatred and love are actualizations of a constant readiness, holds true for other psychic phenomena. Sensuality, for instance, is not simply a reaction to a stimulus. The sensual or as one may say, the erotic person, has a basically erotic *attitude* toward the world. This does not mean that he is constantly excited sexually. It means that there is an erotic *atmosphere* which is actualized by a certain

object, but which is there underneath before the *stimulus* appears. What is meant here is not the physiologically given ability to be sexually excited, but an atmosphere of erotic readiness, which under a magnifying glass could be observed also when the person is not in a state of actual sexual excitement. On the other hand, there are persons in whom this erotic readiness is lacking. In them, sexual excitement is essentially caused by a stimulus operating on the sexual instinct. Their threshold of stimulation can vary between wide limits, but there is a common quality in this type of sexual excitement; namely, its separateness from the whole personality in its intellectual and emotional qualities. Another illustration of the same principle is the sense of beauty. There is a type of personality who has a readiness to see beauty. Again, that does not mean that he is constantly looking at beautiful pictures, or people, or scenery; yet, when he sees them a continuously present readiness is actualized, and his sense of beauty is not simply *aroused* by the object. Here too, a very refined observation shows that this type of person has a different way of looking at the world, even when he looks at objects which do not stimulate an acute perception of beauty. We could give many more examples for the same principle, if space permitted. The principle should already be clear: While many psychological schools have thought of human reactions in terms of stimulus-response, the principle presented here is that character is a structure of numerous *readinesses* of the kind mentioned, which are constantly present and are actualized but not caused by an outside stimulus. This view is essential for such a dynamic psychology as psychoanalysis is.

Freud assumed that all these readinesses are rooted in biologically given instincts. It is here assumed that although this holds true for some of them, many others have arisen as a reaction to the individual and social experiences of the individual.

One last question remains to be discussed. Granted that love for oneself and for others in principle runs parallel, how do we explain the kind of *selfishness* which obviously is in contradiction to any genuine concern for others. The *selfish* person is only interested in himself, wants everything for himself, is unable to give with any pleasure but is only anxious to take;

the world outside himself is conceived only from the standpoint of what he can get out of it; he lacks interest in the needs of others, or respect for their dignity and integrity. He sees only himself, judges everyone and everything from the standpoint of its usefulness to him, is basically unable to love. This selfishness can be manifest or disguised by all sorts of unselfish gestures; dynamically it is exactly the same. It seems obvious that with this type of personality there is a contradiction between the enormous concern for oneself and the lack of concern for others. Do we not have the proof here that there exists an alternative between concern for others and concern for oneself? This would certainly be the case if selfishness and self-love were identical. But this assumption is the very fallacy which has led to so many mistaken conclusions with regard to our problem. Selfishness and self-love far from being identical, actually are opposites.

Selfishness is one kind of greediness. Like all greediness, it contains an insatiability, as a consequence of which there is never any real satisfaction. Greed is a bottomless pit which exhausts the person in an endless effort to satisfy the need without ever reaching satisfaction. This leads to the crucial point: close observation shows that while the selfish person is always anxiously concerned with himself, he is never satisfied, is always restless, always driven by the fear of not getting enough, of missing something, of being deprived of something. He is filled with burning envy of anyone who might have more. If we observe still closer, especially the unconscious dynamics, we find that this type of person is basically not fond of himself but deeply dislikes himself. The puzzle in this seeming contradiction is easy to solve. The selfishness is rooted in this very lack of fondness for oneself. The person who is not fond of himself, who does not approve of himself, is in a constant anxiety concerning his own self. He has not the inner security which can exist only on the basis of genuine fondness and affirmation. He must be concerned about himself, greedy to get everything for himself, since basically his own self lacks security and satisfaction. The same holds true with the so-called narcissistic person, who is not so much overconcerned with getting things for himself as with admiring himself. While on the surface it seems that these persons are very much in love with themselves, they actually are not fond of themselves, and their narcissism—like selfishness—is an overcompensation for the basic lack of self-love. Freud has pointed out that the narcissistic person has withdrawn his love from others and turned it toward his own person. While the first part of this statement is true, the second one is a fallacy. He neither loves others nor himself.

It is easier to understand this mechanism when we compare it with overconcern and overprotectiveness for others. Whether it is an oversolicitous mother or an overconcerned husband, sufficiently deep observation shows always one fact: While these persons consciously believe that they are particularly fond of the child or husband, there actually is a deep repressed hostility toward the very objects of their concern. They are overconcerned because they have to compensate not only for a lack of fondness but for an actual hostility.

The problem of selfishness has still another aspect. Is not the sacrifice of one's own person the extreme expression of unselfishness, and, on the other hand, could a person who loves himself make that supreme sacrifice? The answer depends entirely on the kind of sacrifice that is meant. There is one *sacrifice*, as it has been particularly emphasized in recent years by Fascist philosophy. The individual should give himself up for something outside of himself which is greater and more valuable; the Leader, the race. The individual by himself is nothing and by the very act of self-annihilation for the sake of the higher power finds his destiny. In this concept, sacrificing oneself for something or someone greater than oneself is in itself the greatest attainable virtue. If love for oneself as well as for another person means basic affirmation and respect, this concept is in sharp contrast to self-love. But there is another kind of sacrifice: If it should be necessary to give one's life for the preservation of an idea which has become part of oneself or for a person whom one loves, the sacrifice may be the extreme expression of self-affirmation. Not, of course, an affirmation of one's physical self, but of the self in the sense of the kernel of one's total personality. In this case the sacrifice in itself is not the goal; it is the price to be paid for the realization and affirmation of one's ownself. While in this latter case, the sacrifice is rooted in self-affirmation, in the case of what one might call the masochistic sacrifice, it is rooted in the lack of self-love and self-respect; it is essentially nihilistic.

The problem of selfishness has a particular bearing on psychotherapy. The neurotic individual often is *selfish* in the sense that he is blocked in his relationship to others or over-anxious about himself. This is to be expected since to be *neurotic* means that the integration of a strong self has not been achieved successfully. To be *normal* certainly does not mean that it has. It means, for the majority of *well-adapted* individuals that they have lost their own self at an early age and replaced it completely by a *social self* offered to them by society. They have no neurotic conflicts because they themselves, and, therefore, the discrepancy between their selves and the outside world has disappeared. Often the neurotic person is particularly *unselfish,* lacking in self-assertion and blocked in following his own aims. The reason for this *unselfishness* is essentially the same as for the *selfishness.* What he is practically always lacking is self-love. This is what he needs to become *well.* If the *neurotic* becomes well, he does not become *normal* in the sense of the conforming *social self.* He succeeds in realizing his self, which never had been completely lost and for the preservation of which he was struggling by his neurotic symptoms. A theory, therefore, as Freud's on narcissism which rationalizes the cultural pattern of denouncing self-love by identifying it with *selfishness,* can have but devastating effects therapeutically. It increases the taboo on self-love. Its effects can only be called *positive* if the aim of psychotherapy is not to help the individual to be himself; that is, free, spontaneous and creative—qualities conventionally reserved for *artists*—but to give up the fight for his self and conform to the cultural pattern peacefully and without the noise of a neurosis.

In the present era, the tendency to make of the individual a powerless atom is increasing. The authoritarian systems tend to reduce the individual to a will-less and feelingless instrument in the hands of those who hold the reins; they batter him down by terror, cynicism, the power of the state, large demonstrations, fierce orators and all other means of suggestion. When finally he feels too weak to stand alone, they offer him satisfaction by letting him participate in the strength and glory of the greater whole, whose powerless part he is. The authoritarian propaganda uses the argument that the individual of the democratic state is *selfish* and that that he should become unselfish and socially minded. This is a lie.

[3]We need not waste much time arguing against the totalitarian claims. In the first place, they are insincere since they only disguise the extreme selfishness of an "elite" that wishes to conquer and retain power over the majority of the population. Their ideology of unselfishness has the purpose of deceiving those subject to the control of the elite and of facilitating their exploitation and manipulation. Furthermore, the totalitarian ideologies confuse the issue by making it appear that they represent the principle of unselfishness when they apply to the state as a whole the principle of ruthless pursuit of selfishness. Each citizen ought to be devoted to the common welfare, but the state is permitted to pursue its own interest without regard to the welfare of other nations. But quite aside from the fact that the doctrines of totalitarianism are disguises for the most extreme selfishness, they are a revival —in secular language—of the religious idea of intrinsic human powerlessness and impotence and the resulting need for submission, to overcome which was the essence of modern spiritual and political progress. Not only do the authoritarian ideologies threaten the most precious achievement of Western culture, the respect for the uniqueness and dignity of the individual; they also tend to block the way to constructive criticism of modern society, and thereby to necessary changes. The failure of modern culture lies not in its principle of individualism, not in the idea that moral virtue is the same as the pursuit of self-interest, but in the deterioration of the meaning of self-interest; not in the fact that people are *too much concerned with their self-interest, but that they are not concerned enough with the interest of their real self; not in the fact that they are too selfish, but that they do not love themselves.*

If the causes for persevering in the pursuit of a fictitious idea of self-interest are as deeply

[3] The remainder of this selection is abridged from Erich Fromm, *Man For Himself,* Holt, Rinehart and Winston: Canada, 1947, pp. 138–141. Reprinted by permission of the author and publisher.

rooted in the contemporary social structure as indicated above, the chances for a change in the meaning of self-interest would seem to be remote indeed, unless one can point to specific factors operating in the direction of change.

Perhaps the most important factor is the inner dissatisfaction of modern man with the results of his pursuit of "self-interest." The religion of success is crumbling and becoming a façade itself. The social "open spaces" grow narrower; the failure of the hopes for a better world after the First World War, the depression at the end of the twenties, the threat of a new and immensely destructive war so shortly after the Second World War, and the boundless insecurity resulting from this threat, shake the faith in the pursuit of this form of self-interest. Aside from these factors, the worship of success itself has failed to satisfy man's ineradicable striving to be himself. Like so many fantasies and daydreams, this one too fulfilled its function only for a time, as long as it was new, as long as the excitement connected with it was strong enough to keep man from considering it soberly. There is an increasing number of people to whom everything they are doing seems futile. They are still under the spell of the slogans which preach faith in the secular paradise of success and glamour. But doubt, the fertile condition of all progress, has begun to beset them and has made them ready to ask what their real self-interest as human beings is.

This inner disillusionment and the readiness for a revaluation of self-interest could hardly become effective unless the economic conditions of our culture permitted it. I have pointed out that while the canalizing of all human energy into work and the striving for success was one of the indispensable conditions of the enormous achievement of modern capitalism, a stage has been reached where the problem of *production* has been virtually solved and where the problem of the *organization* of social life has become the paramount task of mankind. Man has created such sources of mechanical energy that he has freed himself from the task of putting all his human energy into work in order to produce the material conditions for living. He could spend a considerable part of his energy on the task of living itself.

Only if these two conditions, the subjective dissatisfaction with a culturally patterned aim and the socioeconomic basis for a change, are present, can an indispensable third factor, rational insight, become effective. This holds true as a principle of social and psychological change in general and of the change in the meaning of self-interest in particular. The time has come when the anesthetized striving for the pursuit of man's real interest is coming to life again. Once man knows what his self-interest is, the first, and the most difficult, step to its realization has been taken.

12

As a psychological concept comes to encompass an increasingly wide variety of behavior, it becomes more difficult to provide an explicit definition which approaches completeness. The term "personality" is a case in point. In a very real sense each personality theory provides us with new meaning for the terms. Nevertheless, there are certain core characteristics to which all psychologists would probably agree. We may thus provide a partial definition of the study of personality as being that part of the total subject matter of psychology which attempts to understand the complex behavior of the human organism as a whole. In contrast to those psychologists who concentrate their efforts on *components* of behavior, such as learning or perception, the "personologist" attempts to understand how these part processes interact to yield behavior. We may thus somewhat more completely define personality as the study of the dynamic organization of those part processes within the individual which motivate and guide his adjustment to his environment. More than any other topic of psychology, the study of personality *requires* the view which has been maintained throughout this book: namely, that *the ongoing behavior of human beings depends upon complex interactions of biological, psychological, and sociocultural determinants.*

BIOLOGICAL FACTORS

A biological approach to personality is presented in Selection 57 by Dr. Roger J. Williams, a biochemist. He emphasizes the often overlooked fact that there are not only individual differences in behavior but also considerable variations among people in internal anatomy, physiology, and biochemistry. Although he admits that differences in brain and endocrine structure have not yet been demonstrated to "have much to do with personality differences," he suggests that neither have such psychological variables as toilet-training experiences. Although Dr. Williams strongly defends the position that biochemical differences are quite likely to be related to personality differences, he feels that "it is not a substitute for all other valid approaches," that is, we must be concerned with the whole organism.

PSYCHOLOGICAL FACTORS

Our definition of personality suggests that the adequacy of an individual's organization of part processes might be judged by the adequacy of his adjustment. The concept of adjustment is closely related to the biological notion of adaptation. Both terms refer to the degree to which an organism uses its abilities in coping with its environment. Although specific adjustive reactions vary in complexity and form, we may describe general types of reactions as involving attack, withdrawal, or compromise behavior. Dr. James C. Coleman presents, in Selection 58, a brief but lucid introduction to these general adjustment patterns and indicates their interactions with motivational patterns and self-concepts under conditions of stress. If the stress represents a threat to the person's self-concept, then the adjustive reactions become complicated by the use of ego defense mechanisms such as rationalization, projection, and identification.

Dr. Andras Angyal has been one of the foremost spokesmen for the holistic, organismic approach to the understanding of personality. While recognizing a multitude of biopsychosocial part processes in the determination of behavior, the organismic approach emphasizes the search for organizing patterns and trends which permeate all behavior. Angyal formulates a theoretical model of personality which discerns two overarching personality trends (Selection 59). On the one hand there is the tendency toward self-expansion, inward control, and mastery over the environment. This trend is similar to White's hypothesis of competence or effectance motivation (Selection 15). A complementary trend is the tendency to view oneself as a part of a superordinate grouping. This trend involves the ability to participate as a part, and as such it tempers and enriches relationships with others.[1] It is also predicated on a perception of the "sameness" of the other person as a part of the overarching whole. As a "test" of his personality model, Angyal applies it to an analysis of neurosis and psychotherapy. He cites factors in the neurotic which block the capacity to love and which generate loss of mastery over the environment; he then shows how components of the psychotherapeutic process permits a reversal of these neurotic trends.[2]

SOCIOCULTURAL FACTORS

In Selection 60 Dr. Clyde Kluckhohn, a cultural anthropologist, and Dr. Henry A. Murray, a psychiatrist, show how four classes of personality determinants are especially significant in understanding the ways in which each man is "like all other men," "like some other men," and "like no other man." They distinguish constitutional, group-membership, role, and situational determinants. Among constitutional determinants they list sex, age, stature, pigmentation, etc., all of which serve to set the expectations which a person has of himself. The group-membership determinants range in size from small intimate groups such as the family to subcultural groups (e.g., white Protestants in the southern United States) and to cultural groups (e.g., mid-twentieth century American). One of the major functions of the "culture" is to transmit values through all levels of cultural groupings. For example, what parents teach children as "right" and "wrong" depends on all the group memberships of the parents, including "the culture" as a whole. One of the functions of values is to make individual behavior more dependable and thus more predictable. A similar function is served by the special type of group influence, namely role determinants. Within any group there are certain roles which are occupied by individuals; and while in that group, much of the behavior of the individual is determined by his perception of the role and what it demands. Thus role expectations serve to regulate interpersonal interactions. However, as Kluckhohn and Murray note, the role determinants may be dangerous for personality integration; they may suppress the unique components of personality which exist outside of the particular roles which the person plays. The student will be reminded of similar points made by Rogers in Selection 55 and by Dyal in Selection 76. Situational determiners are "happenstance," or chance, factors which modify personality development. For example, although we may not be able to predict the exact consequences, we may be sure that an adult's perception of women is going to be greatly modified if as a constitutionally weak child he happens to move into a neighborhood of strong ag-

[1] These two trends are also emphasized by Paul Tillich as "courage to be as a part" and "courage to be as oneself."
[2] Similar points of view are presented by Carl Rogers in the article "Toward a modern approach to values: The valuing process in the mature person," *Journal of Abnormal and Social Psychology*, **68:** 160–167, 1964 (Selection 71).

gressive girls. This latter statement implies a continual interaction among these four sets of determiners in influencing the ways in which we are like everyone else, some other people, and no one else; this point is developed by Kluckhohn and Murray in their last two sections.

An increasingly important pattern of group and role determiners are those encountered in late adolescence in the college or university environment. The college years are typically thought of as years of increasing personal and social maturity. In Selection 61 Dr. Carroll E. Izard presents evidence to support this commonsense generalization.

Selection **57** | THE BIOLOGICAL
APPROACH TO
THE STUDY OF
PERSONALITY*

ROGER J. WILLIAMS
University of Texas

The study of personality logically involves trying to answer three questions: First, of what is
personality composed; e.g., if two people have
differing personalities in what specific ways do
they or may they differ? Secondly, how do distinctive personalities arise? Thirdly, how can
improvement or modification of personality be
brought about?

The first question: Of what is personality
composed? is a difficult and complicated one,
and the answers to the second and third
questions hinge upon the answer to it. Our
discussion this evening will be a contribution
toward the answering of all these questions.
Our approach is in a sense not new but it is
largely unexplored, and we believe, rich in
potentialities. It has the advantage that it can
be used to supplement all other approaches; it
does not require the rejection of older insights
regardless of their origin or how time-honored
they may be.

Certainly one of the earliest attempts to account for personality differences was made by
the astrologers who recognized that people
differed one from another and sought to explain these differences on the basis of the
influence of the heavenly bodies. The hypothesis
of the astrologers has not stood up well in
scientific circles, but there are numerous
citizens who still believe in horoscopes and
many magazines and newspapers that publish
them. This tenacious belief rests, I believe, on
a fundamental failure of real scientists to come
up with other reasons and explanations which
satisfy.

In the beginning of the nineteenth century
Gall and Spurzheim developed phrenology which

* Abridged from Roger J. Williams, "The Biological
Approach to the Study of Personality." This paper
was presented to The Berkeley Conference on Personality Development in Childhood, University of California, May 5, 1960. Reprinted by permission of the
author and the Elizabeth McCormick Memorial Fund.

was destined to be in public vogue for a number of decades. This purported to be a science
essentially concerned with the relation between
personality traits and the contours of people's
heads. Partly because it lacked scientific validity
and partly because its implications were fatal-
istic and deterministic, the fundamental idea
has largely been discarded.

In the middle portion of the nineteenth century the possible importance of heredity as a
factor in the production of personality differences was brought to the fore by the investigations and writings of Darwin and his nephew,
Galton. Galton, the founder of Eugenics, had
none of our modern information as to how
complicated heredity is; his emphasis on
"good" and "bad" heredity (his own, of
course, was "good") was misleading and his
ideas of improving the race not only flew in the
face of religious teachings but were so oversimplified that they came to be regarded as
unsound scientifically. The eugenic view also
had the disadvantage from the standpoint of
public acceptance of being impregnated with
determinism.

Before the end of the nineteenth century
Freudianism came into being and has subsequently received such wide acceptance that it
has dominated the field of psychiatry for
several decades. Fundamentally, Freudianism is
a system of surmises of such a nature that
they have not and cannot be tested by controlled experiments. These surmises appear to
some minds to be plausible to such a high
degree that they demand acceptance. On the
other hand, to some minds, some of the
surmises appear so implausible as to demand
rejection. Controlled experiments are quite outside the routine thoughts and discussions of
adherents of the Freudian school.

The surmises which form the basis of the
Freudian doctrine include the essential idea
that personalities are built during the lifetime
of the individual and that the prime factors
which enter are the environmental happenings
beginning on the day of birth—possibly even
before—and the thoughts that are developed
as a result of these happenings. Therapeutic
psychoanalysis is based upon the idea that
if an individual can come to understand how
the events of his earlier life have developed his
present unfortunate attitudes, his personality

difficulties tend to evaporate. Inherent in this approach is the idea that minds are much more complex than they superficially appear to be; they are like icebergs in that there is much more "out of sight" than there is in open view.

That the Freudian approach to personality has elements of strength is so obvious as not to require argument. It leaves room for the unknown and unexpected in human behavior (which is needed); it emphasizes the dynamic aspects of personality, and strongly encourages the belief that human beings are not powerless to change and modify their personalities, and that parents have tremendous potentialities in developing the lives of their children. The wide acceptance of Freudian ideas bears out the thought that the public, including the physicians, are people first and secondly, if at all, scientists. Certainly a cold-blooded scientific approach would never have developed and fostered the Freudian concepts.

Behavioristic psychology which at its inception was *completely* environmentalistic has bolstered the environmental approach of Freudianism. This school of psychology has as a fundamental basis the facts discovered by Pavlov using dogs, and commonly designated as conditioned reflexes. The development of personality thus becomes a pyramiding conditioning process whereby the developing infant is continuously modified in his responses by the stimuli he or she received.

What was not quoted by the behavioristic school were correlative findings by Pavlov which are highly pertinent. Pavlov found as a result of extensive study of many dogs that they often exhibited innate tendencies to react very differently to the same stimulus. He recognized in his dogs four basic types (1) excitable, (2) inhibitory, (3) equilibrated, and (4) active, as well as intermediate types. He recognized enormous differences in dogs with respect to their conditionability, and was by no means inclined to focus his attention solely upon the behavior of "the dog." Scott and others have in more recent times found ample justification for Pavlov's concern over the fundamental differences between dogs of different breeds and between individual dogs within each breed. These differences, which can be studied under controlled conditions in dogs vastly easier than in human beings, are *not* the result of training.

Before we proceed to the principle part of our discussion it should be pointed out that the pronouncements of men whose memories we may revere must be taken in their historical context. Freud, for example, developed most of his fundamental ideas before there was any knowledge of hormones, indeed before the term "hormone" was coined. He had at this time no knowledge of present day biochemistry, the chemical factors involved in nutrition were almost wholly unknown, and he certainly had no knowledge of the close ties which exist between biochemistry and genetics. It can safely be assumed that if the youthful Sigmund Freud were reincarnated today, he would include these vast developments in endocrinology, biochemistry, and genetics in his purview, and that his thinking would follow quite different paths from those which it followed about the turn of the century.

A biological approach to personality should seek to bring from biology *everything* that can help to explain what personality is, how it originates and how it can be modified and improved. Biology has much to contribute, particularly in an area of biology which has received relatively little attention; namely that involving anatomical, physiological, biochemical (and psychological) individuality.

It seems indefensible to assume that people are built in separate compartments, one anatomical, one physiological, one biochemical, one psychological, and that these compartments are unrelated or only distantly related to each other. Each human being possesses and exhibits unity. Certainly anatomy is basic to physiology and biochemistry, and it may logically be presumed that it is also basic to psychology.

Let us look therefore in the field of anatomy for facts which are pertinent to our problem.

Anatomists, partly for reasons of simplicity, have been prone in centuries past to concentrate on a single picture of the human body. Obvious concessions are made, when necessary, in considering the male and the female of the species, and always anatomists have been aware that within these two groups there are variations and anomalies. Only within the past decade, however, has comprehensive information been published which indicates how great these inter-individual variations are and how widespread they are in the general population.

It makes no difference where we look, whether at the skeletal system, the digestive tract, the muscular system, the circulatory system, the respiratory system, the endocrine system, the nervous system, or even at the microscopic anatomy of the blood, we find tremendous morphological variations within the so-called normal range.

For example, normal stomachs vary greatly in shape, and about six-fold in size. Transverse colons vary widely in the positions at which they cross over in the abdomen, pelvic colon patterns vary widely. Arising from the aortic arch are two, three, four, and sometimes five and six branch arteries; the aorta itself varies greatly in size and hearts differ morphologically and physiologically so that their pumping capacities in healthy young men vary widely. The size of arteries and the branching patterns are such that in each individual the various tissues and organs are supplied with blood unequally well, resulting in a distinctive pattern of blood supply for each.

Each endocrine gland is subject to wide variation among "normal" individuals. Thyroid glands vary in weight about six-fold, and the protein-bound iodine of the blood which measures the hormonal output varies to about the same degree. Parathyroid glands also vary about six-fold in total weight in so-called "normal" individuals, and the number of lobes vary from 2–12. The most prevalent number of lobes is 4, but some anatomists estimate that not over fifty per cent of the population have this number. The number of islets of Langerhans, which are responsible for insulin production, vary over a ten-fold range in diabetes-free individuals. The thickness of the adrenal cortex where the critical adrenal hormones arise is said to vary from 0.5 mm to 5 mm (ten-fold).

The morphology of the pituitary glands which produce about eight different hormones is so variable, when different healthy individuals are compared, as to allow for several fold differences in the production of the individual hormones. The male sex glands vary in weight from 10 to 45 grams in so-called "normal" males and much more than this if those with "sub-normal" sex development are included.

The female sex glands vary in weight over a five-fold range and the number of primordial ova present at the birth of "normal" female infants varies over a thirteen-fold range. It is evident that all individuals possess distinctive endocrine systems and that the individual hormonal activities may vary over a several fold range in individuals who have no recognized hormonal difficulty.

The nervous system is, of course, particularly interesting in connection with the personality problem, and the question arises whether substantial variations exist. The classification of the various kinds of sensory nerve endings, for example, is by no means complete nor satisfactory, and the precise functioning of many of the recognized types is unknown. Investigations involving "cold spots," "warm spots," and "pain spots" on the skin indicate that each individual exhibits a distinctive pattern of each. In a relatively recent study of pain spots in twenty-one healthy young adults, a high degree of variation was observed. When subjected to carefully controlled test conditions the right hand of one young man "A" showed seven per cent of the area tested to be "highly sensitive," while in another, "B," the right hand showed one hundred per cent "highly sensitive" areas. On A's hand, forty-nine per cent of the area registered "no pain" under standard pain producing test conditions. On B's hand, however, there was no area which registered "no pain."

It is evident that there is room for wide variations with respect to the numbers and distributions of sensory nerve endings in different individuals. That such differences exist is indicated by the extreme diversity in the reactions of individuals to many stimuli such as those involving seeing, hearing, and tasting. An entire lecture could easily be devoted to this subject alone.

Variations in brain anatomy have received little attention. Thirteen years ago, however, Lashly in a review wrote: "The brain is extremely variable in every character that has been subjected to measurement. Its diversities of structure within the species are of the same general character as are the differences between related species or even between orders of animals." . . . "Even the limited evidence at hand, however, shows that individuals start life with brains differing enormously in structure, unlike in number, size, and arrangement of neurons as well as in grosser features."

Unfortunately, partly due to the complexity of the problem, there is no information whatever available as to how these enormous anatomical differences are related to the equally striking personality differences which are commonplace. Recently there has been published, primarily for the use of surgeons, an extensive study of differences in brain anatomy.

Up to the present in our discussion we have paid attention only to certain facts of biology—those in the field of anatomy. Before we consider other areas—physiology, biochemistry, and psychology—it seems appropriate to note whether we have made any progress in uncovering facts that have important implications for personality development.

Consider the fact (I do regard it a fact and not a theory) that every individual person is endowed with a distinctive gastro-intestinal tract, a distinctive circulatory system, a distinctive respiratory system, a distinctive endocrine system, a distinctive nervous system, and a morphologically distinctive brain; furthermore that the differences involved in this distinctiveness are never triflng and often are enormous. Can it be that this fact is inconsequential, in relation to the problem of personality differences?

I am willing to take the position that this fact is of the *utmost* important. The material in the area of anatomy alone is sufficient to convince anyone who comes upon the problem with an open mind that here is an obvious frontier which should yield many insights. Those who have accepted the Freudian idea that personality disorders arise from infantile conditioning will surely be led to see that *in addition*, the distinctive bodily equipment of each individual infant is potentially important.

The failure of psychologists—and of biologists too—to deal seriously with innate individual differences in connection with many problems probably has deep roots. McGill has said "Experimental psychologists . . . ignore individual differences almost as an item of faith." The same statement holds, in the main, for physiological psychologists, physiologists, and biochemists. Anatomists have adopted in the past (and some do even at present) the same attitude. Generally speaking, individual differences are flies in the ointment which need to be removed and disregarded. Every subject becomes vastly simpler and more "scientific" when this is done.

If one is pursuing knowledge about personality, however, neglect of innate individual differences is fatal. All of biology and all of psychology have suffered, in my opinion, from at least a mild case of "universalitis," an overruling desire to generalize immediately—oftentimes long before sufficient facts are gathered to give the generalization validity. This desire to generalize is of itself laudable, but the willingness to do so without an adequate background of information is unscientific and has devastating effects in the area of personality study.

With these ideas as additional background for our thinking let us consider some of the other aspects of biology. Physiologically and biochemically distinctiveness in gastro-intestinal tracts is just as marked as is the distinctiveness in anatomy. The gastric juices of 5,000 individuals free from gastric disease were found to contain from 0–4300 units of pepsin. The range of hydrochloric acid in a smaller study of normal individuals was from 0.0 to 66.0 millequivalents per liter. No one can deny the probability that large variations also exist in the digestive juices which cannot be so readily investigated. Some "normal" hearts beat more than twice as fast as others, some have pumping capacities at least three times as large as others, and the blood of each individual is distinctive. The discovery of the existence of "blood groups" was just the beginning of our knowledge of the individuality of the blood. Enzyme levels in the blood, which are a reflection of fundamental biochemical differences, vary from one well individual to another over substantial ranges, sometimes ten-fold or even thirty-fold or more.

Our neuromuscular systems are far from assembly line products as can easily be demonstrated by a study of motor skills and by a large number of physiological tests. Our senses are by no means identical as has been made clear by taste tests for PTC and many other substances, by tests involving sense of smell (verbenas, hydrocyanic acid), sense of sight (peripheral vision, foveal size, flicker fusion, and related phenomena, eighteen types of color "blindness"), sense of balance, pitch discriminations and hearing acuities at different frequencies, etc., etc. From the tremendous variation in the action of specific drugs and chemicals on different individuals, we gain further evidence of fundamental differences in physiology and biochemistry.

Thurstone's pioneering work on primary mental abilities called attention to the fact that human minds have different facets, and that some individuals may be relatively well endowed with respect to arithmetical facility, for example, while being relatively deficient in word familiarity or spatial imagery. Others may be strong in the area of word familiarity but weak in rote memory or arithmetic. Guilford has more recently suggested that there are at least forty facets to human minds, involving a group of memory factors, four groups of thinking factors, the latter involving abilities relating to discovering, evaluating and generating ideas. All of this leaves room for a multitude of mental patterns (patterns of conditionability) which it seems reasonable to suppose must be related to the enormous variation in the anatomy of human brains. People, even when confronted with the same facts, do not think alike, and this appears to have a sound anatomical as well as psychological basis.

Those social anthropologists and other social scientists who regard culture as the one factor which determines what an individual will be like often say or imply that adult members of a society bear a very great resemblance to each other because of the similarities of their upbringing. In view of this common implication it may be well to ask whether inborn differentness and distinctiveness fade out as a result of the adjustment of the individuals to the culture to which they are exposed.

At the risk of being naive, it appears that the whole story we have been unfolding hangs together. Individual infants are endowed with far-reaching anatomical distinctiveness; each has a distinctive endocrine system, a highly distinctive nervous system, a highly distinctive brain. The same distinctiveness carries over into the sensory and biochemical realms, and into their individual psychologies. It is not surprising therefore that each individual, upon reaching adulthood, exhibits a distinctive pattern of likes and dislikes not only with respect to trivialities but also with respect to what may be regarded the most important things in life.

That culture has a profound influence on our lives no one should deny. The serious question arises, however, as to the relative position that different factors occupy in producing distinctive personalities. To me it seems probable that one's distinctive endocrine system and one's distinctive brain morphology are more important factors than the toilet training one receives as an infant.

We cannot state as a demonstrated fact that differences in brain morphology or in endocrine systems have much to do with personality differences. On the other hand we have no rigorous scientific proof that toilet training has any substantial effect on personality development. We can only surmise. In one sense, personality study is in its very early infancy.

Another pertinent question—simple but important—awaits a clear answer: Are patterns of brain morphology inherited? On the basis of what is known about the inheritance of other morphological features including fingerprints and the branching of blood vessels on the chest, etc., it may be *inferred* that specific morphological features in brain are handed down by inheritance, but we do not have definitive proof.

A fact which makes the study of the inheritance of such morphological features difficult is that expressed by geneticists David and Snyder ". . . it has become more and more widely recognized that single-gene differences which produce readily distinguishable discontinuities in phenotype variation are completely non-representative of the bulk of genetic variability in any species." Multiple gene effects are extremely common and in many cases, because of the complexity of the inheritance process, it is impossible to trace them in families or to know when and where such effects may be expected to arise. This complication is not the only one which exists; there is also the possibility (and certainty in some species) of maternal influence (cytoplasmic) which does not follow the rules of gene-centered genetics, and can thus throw one's calculations off.

Consideration of the available facts leads me to suppose, in the absence of completely definitive information, that differences in brain morphology, in endocrine patterns, in digestive, circulatory, muscular and nervous systems, etc., have important roots in heredity. It is difficult to see how such differences as exist could arise independent of heredity. The exact mechanisms whereby all these differences are inherited will probably be obscure many decades hence.

The recognition of hereditary factors does not by any means exclude from consideration the dynamic aspects of personality development. Potentialities and conditionabilities are inherited; not fixed characteristics. The widespread idea that personalities are developed from early childhood is fully in accord with an appreciation of the hereditary factors. Conditioning still takes place but the recognition of innate biological differences calls attention to distinct make-up that each newborn baby possesses. Conditioning does not take place starting with assembly-line babies, each one, according to Watson, possessing exactly the same potentialities to develop into a "doctor, lawyer, artist, merchant, chief, and yes, even beggar-man and thief."

To tackle in one giant undertaking the problem of understanding, characterizing and cataloguing all personalities from the biological or any other point of view seems hopeless. A strategy which seems far from hopeless, however, involves studying *one at a time* various personality characteristics to ascertain what biological roots they may have. The personality characteristics to be chosen for investigation should, obviously, be as definite as possible. They might include not only matters of temperament or emotion but also the ability to perform specified types of mental processes, or they might include personality problems of numerous types.

Studying even one particular personality characteristic to ascertain its biological roots is a large undertaking and might involve making scores, possibly hundreds, of measurements on every individual subjected to study. If one has some rational basis for selecting wisely the measurements to be made, the number of desirable measurements might be reduced. This fact would constitute an argument for selecting, as the "personality problem" to be investigated, one for which the type of biological roots *might be* successfully guessed in advance. Such might include hyper- or hyposexuality, homosexuality, obesity, depres-

sions, alcoholism, insomnia, accident proneness, etc. When one after another of personality disorders have been studied from this standpoint, it seems very likely that the whole picture will begin to clear and that the study of specific personality characteristics and problems will become successively easier the farther it progresses. What I am considering is obviously a relatively long range proposal.

Such a type of study as I am suggesting is not in line with the vast amount of experimentation which is currently fashionable. It is very common, for example, to develop a measurement and then apply it to large numbers of people. It is almost or totally unheard of to apply a large series of measurements to a relatively few individuals to determine their individual distinctive patterns. This must be done if we are to find the biological roots of personality characteristics, and psychologists should be warned that the major part of the work must be done in the area of biology, and the biological scientists concerned cannot be looked upon as minor contributors.

Digressing for a moment it has been with this thought in mind that I have objected strenuously to the current widespread implication that "behavioral sciences" constitute a distinct group including psychology, sociology, and social anthropology and excluding the biological sciences. Hidden in this classification is the *assumption* that biological factors are of no importance in behavior and that conditioning is the whole story. It actually may well be, however, that anatomy, physiology, and biochemistry are, from the standpoint of their practical potentialities, the most important behavioral sciences at our disposal.

Time will not permit a discussion of the numerous ways in which my own discipline, biochemistry, impinges on personality problems. The effects of various chemicals on personality behavior, the correlations between brain metabolism and behavior, the effects of various hormones on personality characteristics are all well recognized. What is not so well recognized is that each individual's body chemistry is distinctive and different, and that complex biochemical roots of personality characteristics are likely to be found when we look for them with due care and thoroughness.

Before I close this discussion, I want to stress a most important environmental factor which is capable of contributing enormously to healthy personality development.

The monumental work of Beadle and Tatum demonstrated for the first time the vital connection between genes and enzymes, and in effect, between heredity and biochemistry. Their work made clear the inevitable basis for individual body chemistry. As a direct consequence of this finding, it becomes inevitable that the nutritional needs of genetically distinctive individuals are quantitatively not the same. Carrying the idea still further it becomes inescapable that the brain cells of individual people do not have quantitatively identical nutritional needs.

It has been amply demonstrated that malnutrition of various kinds can induce personality disorders. This was observed in the starvation studies of Keys and associates, in thiamin deficiency studies, in amino acid deficiency studies and perhaps most notably in pellagra where unequivocal insanity may result from niacin deficiency and can be abolished promptly by administration of the missing vitamin. It has also been shown repeatedly that inadequacy of prenatal nutrition can cause all sorts of developmental difficulties and abnormalities in the growing fetus.

One of the most obvious environmental measures that can be taken to insure favorable personality development is to see, for example, that the nervous system of each distinctive individual with his distinctive needs receives prenatally and postnatally the best possible nourishment. Nourishment of brain cells like the nourishment of other cells throughout the body can be maintained at many levels of excellence, and of course achieving the best is no small order.

Serious attention to nutrition which must involve the utilization of substantial manpower and a great deal of human ingenuity and persistence can, I believe, make tremendous contributions to our knowledge of personality states and personality disorders, and to the alleviation and prevention of personality difficulties.

In conclusion I would emphasize that the biological approach to personality, outstandingly important as I believe it to be, is not a substitute for all other valid approaches. Whatever we may know or may be able to accomplish by other approaches, if valid, is not lost. Consideration of the biological approach expands our horizon and gives us a much broader view. In my opinion the insight we may gain from this approach will be mostly valuable and productive. I should reiterate also what I have said before, that personality study is in its early infancy.

Selection **58** | TYPES OF ADJUSTIVE REACTIONS*

JAMES C. COLEMAN
University of California, Los Angeles

Adjustive reactions can best be understood in terms of the total personality organization of the individual and his specific life situation. The particular adjustive reaction that occurs will vary widely depending upon these two sets of factors. However, even the most divergent attempts at adjustment follow certain basic dynamic principles and can be understood as attempts to cope with actual or perceived stress in such a way as to maintain psychobiological integrity by satisfying basic needs.

GENERAL PATTERNS

In general the individual deals with his adjustive problems by either attack, withdrawal, or compromise, complicated by various ego defense mechanisms and by varying degrees of emotional involvement.

Attack, aggression, hostility In attack behavior we attempt to remove or surmount the obstacles through increased effort or a variation in mode of approach. We have seen that biological frustration leads to various compensatory or corrective activities such as the release of stored energy to allow increased

* From *Abnormal Psychology and Modern Life* by James C. Coleman. Copyright © 1950 by Scott, Foresman and Company.

activity by the organism in an attempt to meet the need and restore equilibrium. This increased tension and variant activity is apparently the primary origin of aggressive or attack-type behavior. In primitive form it is seen in the restless behavior of the infant deprived of food; such behavior is at first relatively uncoordinated and generalized, but as motor and intellectual abilities increase, the individual learns to evaluate and deal directly with an ever-increasing variety of specific obstacles.

Despite these improvements in efficiency, only a small number of stress situations can be adequately dealt with by means of direct aggression. This means that in infancy, as well as later in life, direct attack may be unsuccessful, the frustration continues, and the irritation, pain, and unpleasantness connected with it become attached to the objects or persons viewed as obstacles and sources of frustration. Such conditions, of course, lead to the arousal of emergency emotional reactions, particularly hostility. Thus aggressive reactions, which at first involve only a tendency toward increased activity and variation in mode of attack, may eventually be reinforced by hate or hostility.

Attack behavior may be primarily constructive or destructive in nature. With hostility there is a tendency to destroy as well as attack; hence we find that where hostility is extremely intense, attack behavior may be primarily destructive. For example, an individual who feels unwanted, unjustly treated, and deprived of opportunities afforded to others may build up intense resentment and hostility which may be manifested in hostile, aggressive activities, perhaps of a delinquent or criminal nature. Stealing, destroying property, setting fires, sexual misbehavior, and assault frequently represent attack patterns involving defiant hostile reactions of this sort.

The way in which hostility is discharged is very important in personality dynamics. For example, it may be expressed directly in overt behavior (physical or verbal), in fantasies (in which the individual may machine-gun or otherwise attack and destroy his enemies), or in competitive sports and other activities, or it may be discharged internally through the visceral organs. Although hostility is ordinarily directed toward external objects and persons

viewed as sources of frustration, it may be evoked by personal limitations and mistakes and directed toward the self in terms of self-recrimination, self-punishment, and even self-mutilation and suicide.

Where the hostility is felt toward more powerful persons—authority figures—the individual may inhibit any actual outward manifestations. However, such hostile tensions may build up to high levels of intensity and become extremely difficult to manage; for we may not only view hostility as morally wrong, particularly if it is directed toward parents or siblings, but we know from unpleasant experience that overt hostile acts toward others lead to retaliation in the form of punishment and frustration. So, as we shall see, such hostility may come to be expressed in various deviant but "safe" ways.

Flight, withdrawal, fear Simple withdrawal is the second fundamental type of reaction to stress. Many animals seem capable of fairly well-coordinated withdrawal or flight reactions shortly after birth, but the human infant is relatively helpless for a long period and is unable to execute any well-coordinated withdrawal reaction. However, he is able to withdraw a bodily part from a painful stimulus such as a hot object and as Watson has demonstrated, he may on the occasion of sudden, unexpected stimuli tend to curl up into a ball, which appears to be sort of a primitive fear reaction.

As the growing infant learns to associate certain objects and situations with frustration and hurt, he may avoid instead of attacking them. His action tendency to withdraw in the face of such dangerous situations is typically reinforced by emotional processes involving fear. With time, his fears involve a wide range of real and imagined dangers as well as being usually induced by any strong, sudden, unexpected stimulation. And in a related way his withdrawal behavior becomes more complicated; in addition to mere physical withdrawal, he may withdraw in various psychological ways: he may inhibit dangerous internal desires, or consciously suppress them, or abandon goals, or restrict the situations to which he reacts, or even become emotionally passive.

So just as simple aggression becomes complicated by hostility we find simple withdrawal or flight reactions becoming complicated by fear. In both cases the individual's action tendencies are reinforced by mobilization of reserve resources, with a high degree of psychobiological tension demanding discharge. But here again social living provides few situations in which such mobilized energy can be utilized in direct physical action. Taking final examinations, being interviewed for jobs, excessive competition, cannot ordinarily be met by direct physical withdrawal. Rather the individual is forced to face the dangerous situation despite fears and anticipated frustration. It is of interest here to note that Shaffer found, in a study of fear in aerial combat, that situations permitting no adjustive response, such as "being fired upon when you have no chance to shoot back," were the most frequently reported causes of increased fear. On the other hand, he found that engaging in some effective activity was frequently conducive to reducing fear, even though such activities did not make possible the avoidance of the real danger.

Anxiety is very similar to fear, involving the same general pattern of emergency physiological changes and arising in connection with anticipated frustration or hurt. However, it differs from fear in certain essential respects. Fear is usually related to some immediate concrete situation, whereas the stress giving rise to anxiety is usually vague and ill-defined. Often the individual is unaware of what is causing his anxiety. Likewise, fear involves a definite action tendency of flight whereas anxiety is more in the nature of diffuse apprehension not leading to any action tendency.

Thus anxiety seems to be a sort of preliminary or primitive fear reaction which mobilizes energy reserves to meet some threat, but in which neither the threat nor the appropriate direction of response is clearly discernible by the individual. Perhaps this feeling of vagueness and uncertainty adds to the unpleasantness of anxiety; in any event anxiety is one of the most painful and intolerable of all conscious experiences.

Compromise, substitution Since most situations cannot be dealt with successfully by either direct attack or withdrawal, it usually becomes necessary to work out some sort of compromise. This represents our most common method of dealing with conflicts. Such compromises may mean accepting substitute goals or lowering one's aspirations or internal ethical or reality restraints. An individual faced with starvation may compromise with his conscience and steal "just this one time" because of the special nature of the conditions, or he may resort to eating worms, bugs, spiders, and even human flesh, or he may revise his ethical standards. Often, too, we resort to symbolic satisfactions under conditions of severe frustration. Thus a soldier may gain some substitutive satisfaction out of pin-up pictures or out of wish-fulfilling daydreams. In fact, Masserman has shown that under frustration, the individual becomes increasingly willing to accept substitutive goals—both symbolic and nonsymbolic ones. Hate, fear, and other emotional reactions may, of course, also reinforce or be involved in compromise reactions, as well as in attack or withdrawal reactions.

Figure 1 Personality development determines motivational patterns. Motivational pattern and stress jointly determine reactions to stress, which will include ego defensive mechanisms if the stress is ego-involved.

Selection **59** | A THEORETICAL MODEL FOR PERSONALITY STUDIES*

ANDRAS ANGYAL
Boston, Massachusetts

In this paper I shall not discuss the question whether model building is fruitful or not in the study of personality; valid arguments in favor of such a procedure are adequately covered by other contributions to this symposium. Neither will I argue the comparative merits and disadvantages of the various types of model that have been or may be employed in this field. Instead I shall present a particular model which I have advocated previously for the formulation of a theory of personality (1), reformulating certain aspects of this theoretical orientation and illustrating my points with pertinent examples taken mainly from the field of psychotherapeutic theory and practice.

Personality may be described most adequately when looked upon as a unified dynamic organization—dynamic, because the most significant fact about a human being is not so much his static aspect as his constituting a specific *process:* the life of the individual. This process, the life of the person, is an organized, patterned process, a Gestalt, an organization. A true organization presupposes an organizing principle, a unifying pattern. All part processes obtain their specific meaning or specific function from this unifying overall pattern. Therefore, it seems plausible that a tentative phrasing of the nature of this total pattern—the broad pattern of human life—may serve as an adequate model for the formulation of the problems pertaining to the study of personality.

The over-all pattern of personality function can be described from two different vantage points. Viewed from one of these vantage points, the human being seems to be striving basically to assert and to expand his self-determination. He is an autonomous being, a self-governing entity that asserts itself actively

* From Andras Angyal, "A Theoretical Model for Personality Studies," *Journal of Personality*, 21: 131–142, 1951. Reprinted by permission of the publisher.

instead of reacting passively like a physical body to the impacts of the surrounding world. This fundamental tendency expresses itself in a striving of the person to consolidate and increase his self-government, in other words to exercise his freedom and to organize the relevant items of his world out of the autonomous center of government that is his self. This tendency—which I have termed "the trend toward increased autonomy"—expresses itself in spontaneity, self-assertiveness, striving for freedom and for mastery. In an objective fashion this tendency can be described as follows: the human being is an autonomous unit that, acting upon the surrounding world, molds and modifies it. His life is a resultant of self-determination on the one hand, and the impacts of the surrounding world, the situation, on the other. This basic tendency, the trend toward increased autonomy, expresses the person's striving from a state of lesser self-determination (and greater situational influence) to a state of greater self-determination (and lesser situational influence).

Seen from another vantage point, human life reveals a very different basic pattern from the one described above. From this point of view, the person appears to seek a place for himself in a larger unit of which he strives to become a part. In the first tendency we see him struggling for centrality in his world, trying to mold, to organize, the objects and the events of his world, to bring them under his own jurisdiction and government. In the second tendency he seems rather to strive to surrender himself willingly, to seek a home for himself in and to *become an organic part of something that he conceives as greater than himself.* The superindividual unit of which one feels oneself a part or wishes to become a part, may be variously formulated according to one's cultural background and personal understanding. The superordinate whole may be represented for a person by a social unit—family, clan, nation, by a cause, by an ideology, or by a meaningfully ordered universe. In the realm of aesthetic, social, and moral attitudes this basic human tendency has a central significance. Its clearest manifestation, however, is in the religious attitude and religious experience.

I wish to state with emphasis that I am not speaking here about a tendency which is an exclusive prerogative of some people only, e.g., of those with a particular religious bent or aesthetic sensitivity, but of a tendency that I conceive as a universal and basic characteristic in all human beings.

These two tendencies of the human being, the tendency to increase his self-determination in his expanding personal world, and the tendency to surrender himself willingly to a superordinate whole, can be summed up by saying that the human being comports himself *as if he were a whole of an intermediate order.* By this I mean a "part-Gestalt," like, for example, the cardiovascular system, or the central nervous system, each of which is a *whole,* an organization of many parts, but at the same time a *part* with regard to its superordinate whole, the body. The human being is both a *unifier,* an organizer of his immediate personal world, and a *participant* in what he conceives as the superordinate whole to which he belongs.

The basic human attitude that makes man behave as a part of a larger whole reflects itself also in his "horizontal relationships," that is in his relationship to the other "parts," to other persons. Were man's behavior determined exclusively by his urge for mastery, his attitude toward others could be only as toward means to his ends. Experiencing others as co-participants in a larger whole brings, however, another facet of his nature into manifestation. To avoid the coining of some outlandish term, we call this basic relation "love." In common usage this word has been badly misused to denote not only cheap sentimentality, but even relationships that are actually founded on exploitation, possessiveness, helplessness, and similar destructive attitudes. The basic nature of love consists in a recognition of the *value* and acceptance of the *otherness* of the loved "object" while at the same time one experiences an essential *sameness* that exists between oneself and what one loves.

To recognize and to accept the otherness of a person means to respect him as a valuable being in his own right, in his independence. This attitude is incongruous with any idea of possessiveness or any tendency to use him as means to an end, be this in the form of exploitation, domination, possessiveness, or some other attitude. In other words, it is incongruous with the nature of love to try to reduce the loved person to "an item in one's personal world," or to try to make him comply with one's demands, or to try to exert power over him in whatever way. Love has to be recognized as a basic human attitude which is quite distinct from and irreducible to man's self-assertive tendencies.

The recognition and acceptance of the otherness of the person implies, furthermore, an *understanding* of him. There can be no real love without understanding of the other person, only some sort of deceptive feeling based on an illusion. One does not recognize the otherness of a person as a reality by projecting into him one's fantasies, however flattering they may be. And when one sees in a person one's mother or father or anyone else, one ignores the person as he really is. In the last analysis this is a fundamental disregard for and destructive attitude toward the other person. The understanding of the other person—as we are now using this expression—is not some sort of shrewd "practical psychology" which has a keen eye for the weakness of people, but a deep perception of the core, of the essential nature of the other person. In love this essential nature of the other person is experienced as a value, as something that is very dear to one. Love is not "blind" but visionary: it sees into the very heart of its object, and sees the "real self" behind and in the midst of the frailties and shortcomings of the person.

Love has a second basic component which is complementary to respect for the otherness of its object: the experience of a certain fundamental belongingness and *sameness* between lover and the loved. Experientially, this is not "identification," that is, an identity that is more or less artificially created, but an existing identity that is *acknowledged.* Man behaves in certain fundamental respects *as if* he were a part, a shareholder in some kind of superordinate unit, in some kind of commonwealth. When two persons love one another they clearly or dimly have the feeling that something greater is involved therein than their limited individualities, that they are one in something greater than themselves or, as the religious person says, they are "one in God."[1]

---

[1] This statement does not have to be understood in a theological sense. In this context it is not our concern, e.g., whether or not the "superordinate whole" is reality or not; we state only that man appears to function as *if* he were or would experience himself as a part of a superordinate whole.

Without such an implicit orientation all interests of a person would be centered in himself alone as an individual. He as an isolated entity would be facing an alien world and his reaching beyond himself would be only to possess, master and govern the surrounding world. He would compete with other people or he would calculatingly co-operate with them, but he would not love them. In order to love it is essential that a man come out of his shell, that he transcend his individuality, that he "lose himself." Somehow this self-abandonment is the precondition to a broadened existence in loving. One rejoices in the characteristic ways, in the real being, beyond the surface of pretense, of the other; one suffers in the other's misfortunes and in his misdeeds: therein one gains a whole new life with its joys and sorrows. One is enriched through a vital participation in another life without wanting, however, to possess the other person. The significant truth is expressed in the paradox that the one "who loses his life [of isolation], will gain it [in a broadened existence]." The paradox is resolved by recognizing that man functions as a part of a large whole. He has a life as a part—and that is all he has, as long as he remains in his self-enclosure. But it is possible for him to have a greater life, the life of the whole, as it is manifested in himself, in the other "parts," and in the totality.

I have described the over-all pattern of personality functioning as a two-directional orientation: *self-determination* on the one hand and *self-surrender* on the other. The first is the adequate attitude toward the items within one's individual world, the second, toward the greater whole toward which one behaves as a part. A particularly important aspect of this second orientation is the "horizontal" relatedness of the parts to other parts within the whole. I spoke in some detail of love because I believe—largely in agreement with current clinical views—that this is the very crux of the entire problem of personality and of interpersonal relationships.

Actual samples of behavior, however, cannot be ascribed exclusively to one or the other orientation. It is only in the counterfeit, the unhealthy, behavior that one or the other of these basic orientations is partially obliterated; in a well-integrated person the behavioral items always manifest both orientations in varying

degrees. Instead of conflicting, the two orientations complement each other. As in the tendency toward increased autonomy one strives to master and govern the environment, one discovers that one cannot do this effectively by direct application of force, by sheer violence, but can do it by obedience, understanding, and respect for the laws of the environment—attitudes that in some way are similar to those of loving relationships. Similarly: bringing one's best to a loving relationship requires not only capacity for self-surrender but also a degree of proficient mastery of one's world, resourcefulness and self-reliance, without which the relationship is in danger of deteriorating into helpless dependency, exploitation, possessiveness, etc.

The central point of the model which we suggest here for the study of personality is the assumption that the total function of the personality is patterned according to a double orientation of self-determination—self-surrender. In the study of personality, as in any other scientific field, model building has its sole justification in its practical applicability, that is in its suitability for interpretation of the pertinent phenomena and for the formulation of meaningful problems. I have chosen the problem of the neuroses as a testing ground and I hope to demonstrate that the suggested model is useful for clarification of pertinent problems. Needless to say, only a few outstanding aspects of this broad field can here be touched upon, but this consideration may suffice to give a first impression as to the usefulness of the suggested frame of reference.[2]

I suggest the following thesis: The backbone of neurosis consists in a disturbance of the two basic tendencies that we have assumed as forming the over-all pattern of personality functioning. The two cardinal disturbances on which the neurosis rests consist, first, in the person's *loss of mastery* over his own fate, and second, what is rather generally accepted as a basic factor in the neuroses, namely *anxiety*. Loss of mastery is another expression for impairment of capacity for self-determination; anxiety, as we will try to show, is related to the impairment of the capacity for self-surrender

2 This nucleus of a model can be broadened and made more detailed. I have made efforts in this direction in the previously quoted book and also in (2).

and the capacity for love. These points may be best demonstrated by quickly surveying some of the crucial points in the development of a neurosis.

Although we have only vague and inferential knowledge of the infant's subjective experiences, there is sufficient evidence for assuming that his self and the world are not clearly distinguished, but rather blend into a single totality. This differentiation may be near zero in the prenatal life; it is small in the early days of infancy and usually is not quite complete even in adulthood—witness ubiquitous wishful thinking and other autistic phenomena. The gradual birth of individuality may be largely a matter of maturation, but it is also stimulated and precipitated by *painful* contacts with the surrounding world. The hurtfulness of some objects of the environment and their frustrating resistance and independence in regard to one's wishes, so to say their disobedience, are impelling experiences to the recognition of their otherness.

These pains and frustrations—even the pain of being born into an uncomfortable world—are possibly not traumatic in themselves. Their chief significance seems to lie in their hastening both the birth of individuality and the experience of an outside world that is distinct from oneself. And with the birth of individuality the stage is set, the *human situation* is created. Here for the first time the opportunity is given to the person to manifest and unfold his essential nature. The experience of separateness from the surrounding world, which is governed by forces outside oneself, supplies the impetus to strive for mastery over the environment. At the same time, the experience of oneself as a separated, limited individual gives one the feeling of incompleteness and the urge to seek for a larger life to be part of and to participate lovingly in other lives. The experience of one's separateness represents both the necessity and the opportunity for the person to manifest his basic tendencies.

The real traumatising factors are those which prevent the person from expressing these basic tendencies. In the neurotic development there are always a number of unfortunate circumstances which instil in the child a self-derogatory feeling. This involves on the one hand a feeling of weakness which discourages him from the free expression of his wish for mastery, and on the other hand a feeling that there is something fundamentally wrong with him and that, therefore, he cannot be loved. The whole complicated structure of neurosis appears to be founded on this secret feeling of worthlessness, that is, on the belief that one is inadequate to master the situations that confront him and that he is undeserving of love.

The traumatising circumstances which condition this loss of self-confidence and of self-respect are many. They have been rather carefully explored by therapists who deal with neuroses. It will be sufficient here to call to mind some of the most common factors.

(A) The *over-protective attitude* of an insecure, anxious parent tends to convey to the child a feeling that he lives in a world that is full of dangers, and with which he is inadequate to cope. When a parent does too much for the child, he is telling him by implication that he is incapable of doing things by himself.

(B) When the parent is too eager for the child to do well and is *excessively critical* of him, he is likely to instil in the child the feeling "something must be very wrong with me; I can't do anything right."

(C) When parents distort and exaggerate the child's achievement, when they cast him into a *superior role* and have great expectations of him, they plant the seed of self-derogation in still another way. Deep down the child knows that the parents' picture of him is untrue, and measuring himself by these excessive and often fantastic standards, he secretly begins to feel utterly worthless.

(D) The too many "don'ts" which the child hears tend to create in him the feeling that those things which he *most wants* are the things that are forbidden and *evil*. This easily can give rise in him to a secret conviction that he is a fundamentally evil person.

(E) The ways in which children are being treated without *understanding* and without *respect* are many, and these are likely to create in the child the feeling that he just doesn't matter in this adult world, that he is of no account, that he is worthless. Often one wonders why the child accepts the verdict that he is worthless, instead of blaming the parent for being so obviously lacking in understanding, so wrong and selfish. The answer suggests itself that the child needs so much to feel that he has "good parents" that he tenaciously adheres to this belief and would rather assume himself to be evil or worthless than give up the idea that he has good parents.

The whole complex of self-derogation can be roughly—and admittedly somewhat artificially—divided into a feeling of inadequacy and the feeling of being unloved. The first leads to an impairment of self-determination, the second to the impairment of the capacity to love.

One important way in which the self-determination of a person may be impaired is his trading the birthright of mastery over his own destiny for the mess of pottage of protection—and dependency. In addition to the assumption of his weakness, an over-valuation of the power of his parents and of the protection which they can give induces the child to make this fatal bargain. The terms of the bargain are set, at least by implication: "You are weak and helpless against the world which is full of dangers; if you are good, if you do what we want you to do, and don't follow your impulses, we will take care of you and protect you."

Another circumstance that may induce a child to give up or "escape" from his freedom is the exploitation by the adult of the child's loving nature. This is often done by holding up to the child the suffering his behavior may cause to others: "You may do it if you want to, but mother will be hurt"; or more directly: "What you do shortens my life"; "You put another nail in my coffin," etc. Particularly vicious and destructive is the influence of the "self-sacrificing mother," who holds up to the child the many sufferings, deprivations and unhappinesses which she has had to endure for the child, implying the tremendous ingratitude that a self-assertion of the child against her wishes would mean.

In response to these and similar emotional insults the child is gradually led to deny himself, to hide his spontaneous impulses—which he assumes to be evil—and to pretend to be or to try to be someone else, a more impressive and a more desirable person. This step is literally suicidal, and it is born out of an extreme despair. Indeed, only an extreme despair of any possibility to live in reality can induce a person to content himself with appearances, with the impression he makes. The

exaggerated importance and value given to any external trappings with which a person may decorate himself is equivalent to declaring one's naked self worthless. If one basks in some sort of reflected glory, one declares one's real being to be ignominious.

All these various roads lead to loss of spontaneity, initiative, and genuineness. The child loses originality, which should not be the privilege of a few, but a rightful heritage of everyone. The neurotic person experiences himself as a straw in the wind who cannot act under his own power but has to *wait for things to happen*, who is a "victim of circumstances" and whose fate depends on good or bad "breaks."

The discussion of another basic disturbance, the impairment of the person's capacity to love, leads us into the problem of anxiety, which we should now briefly consider. It seems to me that the original word-meaning that suggests constriction, being narrowed in (*Beengung*), expresses best the essential nature of anxiety. A person who feels weak and unlovable and surrounded by a very alien and unfriendly world, will draw in his feelers and will surround himself with some protective shell. This shell, however, limits him and narrows him in to such an extent that he can barely move or breathe. We propose to define anxiety as this condition of the person. It seems preferable to use the term in this sense, as a "psycho-physically-neutral" term (William Stern), denoting a condition of the person which may or may not be consciously experienced. This usage would avoid the confusing issues of unconscious anxiety and such manifestations of anxiety that are conscious but not characterized by anxious feelings. Anxiety is not a mental phenomenon but a state of limitation of life. When we have sufficient information about a person's mode of living, we can determine whether his life is a narrowed one or not; that is, we can determine the presence and degree of the condition of anxiety, independently of the presence and degree of anxious feelings.

Anxiety is dynamically related to fears in a twofold manner: it is born out of fears and it leads to fears. It is fear that makes the person erect his defenses with the resultant state of constriction or anxiety. The person's impulses, however, rebel against the enclosure, against the limitation, and threaten to break through the wall of defenses. This threat from within is experienced in those nameless fears, fears without a conscious object, which one usually refers to as "anxiety."

This narrowed-in condition of anxiety paralyzes the effectiveness of the person in dealing with his environment. He does not really dare to venture into the outside world, but looks out upon it from behind his defenses with suspicion, fear, apprehension, envy, and hatred. The most destructive aspect of anxiety, of this self-enclosure, is, however, the loss of the capacity or rather the loss of the freedom to love. For love presupposes that instead of anxiously standing watch over one's safety, one dares to go out of oneself, to abandon oneself, to venture out in order to participate in the life of others and in a larger life of which he feels himself a part. It is the nature of the human being that he finds fulfillment only in a broadened existence, and that for him life confined to the limits of one's individuality in segregation from others is worthless. He can find happiness and peace only if he loves, that is, participates in life outside the confines of his individuality; and if he is loved, that is, received into and held fast and dear by another life.

Summing up this sketch of the origin of the neuroses, we have assumed that certain traumatising experiences create in the child a derogatory picture, a feeling of the worthlessness of his self. This feeling of worthlessness has two components: first, the feeling that one is inadequate, too weak to cope with the environment; and second, the feeling that one is unloved and unworthy of love. These then lead to an impairment of the person's self-determination on the one hand, and to anxiety with the loss of capacty to love, on the other. Neurosis represents a complicated interlocking system of maneuvers that are designed to maintain life in a human sense in spite of the fact that the person is wounded at the very core of his nature. This hypothesis of the origin of the neurosis I believe is more in agreement than at variance with many of the current views on the subject.

This view is also in good agreement with certain current theories of therapy. There are several psychotherapeutic factors to which, in general, a particularly important curative effect is ascribed. We shall mention only two such

factors for further illustration of the main points of this paper: first, the patient's expression of anger in the therapeutic setting, and second, the positive relationship of the therapist to the patient.

The expression of angry feelings toward the therapist is assumed to have a beneficial therapeutic effect on the patient. This expression should be, however, more than just "blowing off steam," a catharsis. The patient's experience that he can express anger toward the therapist without being rejected or punished for it—important as it is—is not in itself the crucial therapeutic experience, but only preparatory to it. On the basis of a series of observations I am persuaded that not all forms of angry expressions are therapeutically valuable, but only certain kinds with well-defined differential characteristics. An outburst of anger, if it is not more than a blind expression of impotent rage, does not produce therapeutic effects, but is likely to leave the patient ashamed and guilty and worse off than before. The therapeutically effective anger is always a courageous expression and often clearly expresses the feeling that one would rather die than continue to live in fear and trepidation, tolerate injustice, etc. Such anger says emphatically: "I won't stand for it!" Daring to take this final aggressive stand makes one regain respect for oneself. And therein lies the therapeutic effect of this type of anger: it tends to abolish the feeling of inadequacy which is one component of self-derogation and which in turn is the foundation for the neurosis.

Even more fundamental is, however, the therapist's persistent attitude toward the patient, expressed in respect for him as a person of value, in understanding, in confidence that the patient can be saved, in sincere desire and devoted effort to help him to live a happier life. When the patient reaches the point of being able to trust the sincerity of the therapist's attitude, he will no longer be able to uphold completely the fiction of being unloved and unworthy, undeserving of love. And with this the other foundation of his neurosis begins to crumble.

The above examples, taken from the dynamics and therapy of the neuroses, may serve to illustrate the degree of usefulness and applicability of the model that was proposed here for the study of personality. It is not claimed that this brief exposition proves anything definitely, but perhaps it is sufficient to give a first impression of an avenue of approach which may be worth while to follow.

REFERENCES

1. Angyal, A. *Foundations for a science of personality.* New York: Commonwealth Fund, 1941.
2. Angyal, A. The holistic approach in psychiatry. *Amer. J. Psychiat.,* 1948, **105,** 178–182.

Selection **60**	PERSONALITY FORMATION: THE DETERMINANTS[*][1]

CLYDE KLUCKHOHN
HENRY A. MURRAY
Harvard University

Every man is in certain respects
   a. like all other men,
   b. like some other men,
   c. like no other man.

He is like all other men because some of the determinants of his personality are universal to the species. That is to say, there are common features in the biological endowments of all men, in the physical environments they inhabit, and in the societies and cultures in which they develop. It is the very obviousness of this fact which makes restatements of it expedient, since, like other people, we students of personality are naturally disposed to be attracted by what is unusual, by the qualities which distinguish individuals, environments, and societies, and so to overlook the common heritage and lot of man. It is possible that the most important of the undiscovered determinants of personality and culture are only to

[*] From Clyde Kluckhohn and Henry A Murray, "Personality Formation: The Determinants," *Personality In Nature, Society and Culture,* 1948, pp. 53–67. Reprinted by permission of the author and publisher.
[1] This paper represents a complete revision of an earlier scheme published by C. Kluckhohn and O. H. Mowrer, "Culture and Personality: A Conceptual Scheme," *American Anthropologist,* Vol. 46 (1944), pp. 1–29. The present writers gratefully acknowledge their indebtedness to Dr. Mowrer.

be revealed by close attention to the commonplace. Every man experiences birth and must learn to move about and explore his environment, to protect himself against extremes of temperature and to avoid serious injuries; every man experiences sexual tensions and other importunate needs and must learn to find ways of appeasing them; every man grows in stature, matures, and dies; and he does all this and much more, from first to last, as a member of a society. These characteristics he shares with the majority of herd animals, but others are unique to him. Only with those of his own kind does he enjoy an erect posture, hands that grasp, three-dimensional and color vision, and a nervous system that permits elaborate speech and learning processes of the highest order.

Any one personality is like all others, also, because, as social animals, men must adjust to a condition of interdependence with other members of their society and of groups within it, and, as cultural animals, they must adjust to traditionally defined expectations. All men are born helpless into an inanimate and impersonal world which presents countless threats to survival; the human species would die out if social life were abandoned. Human adaptation to the external environment depends upon that mutual support which is social life; and, in addition, it depends upon culture. Many types of insects live socially yet have no culture. Their capacity to survive resides in action patterns which are inherited via the germ plasm. Higher organisms have less rigid habits and can learn more from experience. Human beings, however, learn not only from experience but also from each other. All human societies rely greatly for their survival upon accumulated learning (culture). Culture is a great storehouse of ready-made solutions to problems which human animals are wont to encounter. This storehouse is man's substitute for instinct. It is filled not merely with the pooled learning of the living members of the society, but also with the learning of men long dead and of men belonging to other societies.

Human personalities are similar, furthermore, insofar as they all experience both gratifications and deprivations. They are frustrated by the impersonal environment (weather, physical obstacles, etc.) and by physiological conditions within their own bodies (physical incapacities, illnesses, etc.). Likewise, social life means some sacrifice of autonomy, subordination, and the responsibilities of superordination. The pleasure and pain men experience depend also upon what culture has taught them to expect from one another. Anticipations of pain and pleasure are internalized through punishment and reward.

These universalities of human life produce comparable effects upon the developing personalities of men of all times, places, and races. But they are seldom explicitly observed or commented upon. They tend to remain background phenomena—taken for granted like the air we breathe.

Frequently remarked, however, are the similarities in personality traits among members of groups or in specific individuals from different groups. In certain features of personality, most men are "like some other men." The similarity may be to other members of the same sociocultural unit. The statistical prediction can safely be made that a hundred Americans, for example, will display certain defined characteristics more frequently than will a hundred Englishmen comparably distributed as to age, sex, social class, and vocation.

But being "like some men" is by no means limited to members of social units like nations, tribes, and classes. Seafaring people, regardless of the communities from which they come, tend to manifest similar qualities. The same may be said for desert folk. Intellectuals and athletes the world over have something in common; so have those who were born to wealth or poverty. Persons who have exercised authority over large groups for many years develop parallel reaction systems, in spite of culturally tailored differences in the details of their behaviors. Probably tyrannical fathers leave a detectably similar imprint upon their children, though the uniformity may be superficially obscured by local manners. Certainly the hyperpituitary type is equally recognizable among Europeans, African Negroes, and American Indians. Also, even where organic causes are unknown or doubtful, certain neurotic and psychotic syndromes in persons of one society remind us of other individuals belonging to very different societies.

Finally, there is the inescapable fact that a man is in many respects like no other man.

Each individual's modes of perceiving, feeling, needing, and behaving have characteristic patterns which are not precisely duplicated by those of any other individual. This is traceable, in part, to the unique combination of biological materials which the person has received from his parents. More exactly, the ultimate uniqueness of each personality is the product of countless and successive interactions between the maturing constitution and different environing situations from birth onward. An identical sequence of such determining influences is never reproduced. In this connection it is necessary to emphasize the importance of "accidents," that is, of events that are not predictable for any given individual on the basis of generalized knowledge of his physical, social, and cultural environments. A child gets lost in the woods and suffers from exposure and hunger. Another child is nearly drowned by a sudden flood in a canyon. Another loses his mother and is reared by an aged grandmother, or his father remarries and his education is entrusted to a stepmother with a psychopathic personality. Although the personalities of children who have experienced a trauma of the same type will often resemble each other in certain respects, the differences between them may be even more apparent, partly because the traumatic situation in each case had certain unique features, and partly because at the time of the trauma the personality of each child, being already unique, responded in a unique manner. Thus there is uniqueness in each inheritance and uniqueness in each environment, but, more particularly, uniqueness in the number, kinds, and temporal order of critically determining situations encountered in the course of life.

In personal relations, in psychotherapy, and in the arts, this uniqueness of personality usually is, and should be, accented. But for general scientific purposes the observation of uniformities, uniformities of elements and uniformities of patterns, is of first importance. This is so because without the discovery of uniformities there can be no concepts, no classifications, no formulations, no principles, no laws; and without these no science can exist.

The writers suggest that clear and orderly thinking about personality formation will be facilitated if four classes of determinants (and their interactions) are distinguished: *constitutional, group-membership, role,* and *situational.* These will help us to understand in what ways every man is "like all other men," "like some other men," "like no other man."

CONSTITUTIONAL DETERMINANTS

The old problem of "heredity *or* environment" is essentially meaningless. The two sets of determinants can rarely be completely disentangled once the environment has begun to operate. All geneticists are agreed today that traits are not inherited in any simple sense. The observed characters of organisms are, at any given point in time, the product of a long series of complex interactions between biologically-inherited potentialities and environmental forces. The outcome of each interaction is a modification of the personality. The only pertinent questions therefore are: (1) which of the various genetic potentialities will be actualized as a consequence of a particular series of life-events in a given physical, social, and cultural environment? and (2) what limits to the development of this personality are set by genetic constitution?

Because there are only a few extreme cases in which an individual is definitely committed by his germ plasm to particular personality traits, we use the term "constitutional" rather than "hereditary." "Constitution" refers to the total physiological make-up of an individual at a given time. This is a product of influences emanating from the germ plasm and influences derived from the environment (diet, drugs, etc.).

Since most human beings (including scientists) crave simple solutions and tend to feel that because simple questions can be asked there must be simple answers, there are numberless examples both of overestimation and of underestimation of constitutional factors in theories of personality formation. Under the spell of the spectacular success of Darwinian biology and the medicine of the last hundred years, it has often been assumed that personality was no less definitely "given" at birth than was physique. At most, it was granted that a personality "unfolded" as the result of a strictly biological process of maturation.

On the other hand, certain psychiatrists, sociologists, and anthropologists have recently tended to neglect constitutional factors almost completely. Their assumptions are understandable in terms of common human motivations. Excited by discovering the effectiveness of certain determinants, people are inclined to make these explain everything instead of something. Moreover, it is much more cheerful and reassuring to believe that environmental factors (which can be manipulated) are all important, and that hereditary factors (which can't be changed) are comparatively inconsequential. Finally, the psychiatrists, one suspects, are consciously or unconsciously defending their livelihood when they minimize the constitutional side of personality.

The writers recognize the enormous importance of biological events and event patterns in molding the different forms which personalities assume. In fact, in the last chapter personality was defined as "the entire sequence of organized governmental processes in the brain from birth to death." They also insist that biological inheritance provides the stuff from which personality is fashioned and, as manifested in the physique at a given time-point, determines trends and sets limits within which variation is constrained. There are substantial reasons for believing that different genetic structures carry with them varying potentialities for learning, for reaction time, for energy level, for frustration tolerance. Different people appear to have different biological rhythms: of growth, of menstrual cycle, of activity, of depression and exaltation. The various biologically inherited malfunctions certainly have implications for personality development, though there are wide variations among those who share the same physical handicap (deafness, for example).

Sex and age must be regarded as among the more striking constitutional determinants of personality. Personality is also shaped through such traits of physique as stature, pigmentation, strength, conformity of features to the culturally fashionable type, etc. Such characteristics influence a man's needs and expectations. The kind of world he finds about him is to a considerable extent determined by the way other people react to his appearance and physical capacities. Occasionally a physically weak youth, such as Theodore Roosevelt was, may be driven to achieve feats of physical prowess as a form of over-compensation, but usually a man will learn to accept the fact that his physical make-up excludes him from certain types of vocational and social activities, although some concealed resentment may remain as an appreciable ingredient of his total personality. Conversely, special physical fitnesses make certain other types of adjustment particularly congenial.

GROUP MEMBERSHIP DETERMINANTS

The members of any organized enduring group tend to manifest certain personality traits more frequently than do members of other groups. How large or how small are the groupings one compares depends on the problem at hand. By and large, the motivational structures and action patterns of Western Europeans seem similar when contrasted to those of Mohammedans of the Near East or to Eastern Asiatics. Most white citizens of the United States, in spite of regional, ethnic, and class differences, have features of personality which distinguish them from Englishmen, Australians, or New Zealanders. In distinguishing group-membership determinants, one must usually take account of a concentric order of social groups to which the individual belongs, ranging from large national or international groups down to small local units. One must also know the hierarchical class, political or social, to which he belongs within each of these groups. How inclusive a unit one considers in speaking of group-membership determinants is purely a function of the level of abstraction at which one is operating at a given time.

Some of the personality traits which tend to distinguish the members of a given group from humanity as a whole derive from a distinctive biological heritage. Persons who live together are more likely to have the same genes than are persons who live far apart. If the physical vitality is typically low for one group as contrasted with other groups, or if certain types of endocrine imbalance are unusually frequent, the personalities of the members of that group will probably have distinctive qualities.

In the greater number of cases, however, the similarities of character within a group are traceable less to constitutional factors than to formative influences of the environment to which all members of the group have been subjected. Of these group-membership determinants, culture is with little doubt the most significant. To say that "culture determines" is, of course, a highly abstract way of speaking. What one actually observes is the interaction of people. One never sees "culture" any more than one sees "gravity." But "culture" is a very convenient construct which helps in understanding certain regularities in human events, just as "gravity" represents one type of regularity in physical events. Those who have been trained in childhood along traditional lines, and even those who have as adults adopted some new design for living, will be apt to behave predictably in many contexts because of a prevailing tendency to conform to group standards. As Edward Sapir has said:

All cultural behavior is patterned. This is merely a way of saying that many things that an individual does and thinks and feels may be looked upon not merely from the standpoint of the forms of behavior that are proper to himself as a biological organism but from the standpoint of a generalized mode of conduct that is imputed to society rather than to the individual, though the personal genesis of conduct is of precisely the same nature, whether we choose to call the conduct "individual" or "social." It is impossible to say what an individual is doing unless we have tacitly accepted the essentially arbitrary modes of interpretation that social tradition is constantly suggesting to us from the very moment of our birth.

Not only the action patterns but also the motivational systems of individuals are influenced by culture. Certain needs are biologically given, but many others are not. All human beings get hungry, but no gene in any chromosome predisposes a person to work for a radio or a new car or a shell necklace or "success." Sometimes biologically-given drives, such as sex, are for longer or shorter periods subordinated to culturally acquired drives, such as the pursuit of money or religious asceticism.

And the means by which needs are satisfied are ordinarily defined by cultural habits and fashions. Most Americans would go hungry rather than eat a snake, but this is not true of tribes that consider snake meat a delicacy.

Those aspects of the personality that are not inherited but learned all have—at least in their more superficial and peripheral aspects—a cultural tinge. The skills that are acquired, the factual knowledge, the basic assumptions, the values, and the tastes, are largely determined by culture. Culture likewise structures the conditions under which each kind of learning takes place: whether transmitted by parents or parental substitutes, or by brothers and sisters, or by the learner's own age mates; whether gradually or quickly; whether renunciations are harshly imposed or reassuringly rewarded.

Of course we are speaking here of general tendencies rather than invariable facts. If there were no variations in the conceptions and applications of cultural standards, personalities formed in a given society would be more nearly alike than they actually are. Culture determines only what an individual learns as a member of a group—not so much what he learns as a private individual and as a member of a particular family. Because of these special experiences and particular constitutional endowments, each person's selection from and reaction to cultural teachings have an individual quality. What is learned is almost never symmetrical and coherent, and only occasionally is it fully integrated. Deviation from cultural norms is inevitable and endless, for variability appears to be a property of all biological organisms. But variation is also perpetuated because those who have learned later become teachers. Even the most conventional teachers will give culture a certain personal flavor in accord with their constitution and peculiar life-experiences. The culture may prescribe that the training of the child shall be gradual and gentle, but there will always be some abrupt and severe personalities who are temperamentally disposed to act otherwise. Nor is it in the concrete just a matter of individuality in the strict sense. There are family patterns resultant upon the habitual ways in which a number of individuals have come to adjust to each other.

Some types of variation, however, are more predictable. For example, certain differences in the personalities of Americans are referable to the fact that they have grown up in various sub-cultures. Jones is not only an American; he is also a member of the middle class, an Easterner, and has lived all his life in a small Vermont community. This kind of variation falls within the framework of the group determinants.

The values imbedded in a culture have special weight among the group membership determinants. A value is a conception, explicit or implicit, distinctive of an individual or characteristic of a group, of the desirable which influences the selection from available modes, means, and ends of action. It is thus not just a preference, a desire, but a formulation of the *desirable*, the "ought" and "should" standards which influence action.

The component elements of a culture must, up to a point, be either logically consistent or meaningfully congruous. Otherwise the culture carriers feel uncomfortably adrift in a capricious, chaotic world. In a personality system, behavior must be reasonably regular or predictable, or the individual will not get expectable and needed responses from others because they will feel that they cannot "depend" on him. In other words, a social life and living in a social world both require standards "within" the individual and standards roughly agreed upon by individuals who live and work together in a group. There can be no personal security and no stability of social organization unless random carelessness, irresponsibility, and purely impulsive behavior are restrained in terms of private and group codes. If one asks the question, "Why are there values?" the reply must be: "Because social life would be impossible without them; the functioning of the social system could not continue to achieve group goals; individuals could not get what they want and need from other individuals in personal and emotional terms, nor could they feel within themselves a requisite measure of order and unified purpose." Above all, values add an element of predictability to social life.[2]

[2] Fuller treatment of the concept of values will be found in C. Kluckhohn, "Values and Value-Orientations in the Theory of Action: An Exploration in Definition and Classification," in T. Parsons and E. Shills, (eds.), *Toward a General Theory of Action* (Cambridge: Harvard University Press, 1951).

Culture is not the only influence that bears with approximate constancy upon all the members of a relatively stable, organized group. But we know almost nothing of the effects upon personality of the continued press of the impersonal environment. Does living in a constantly rainy climate tend to make people glum and passive, living in a sunny, arid country tend to make them cheerful and lively? What are the differential effects of dwelling in a walled-in mountain valley, on a flat plain, or upon a high plateau studded with wide-sculptured red buttes? Thus far we can only speculate, for we lack adequate data. The effects of climate and even of scenery and topography may be greater than is generally supposed.

Membership in a group also carries with it exposure to a social environment. Although the social and cultural are inextricably intermingled in an individual's observable behavior, there is a social dimension to group membership that is not culturally defined. The individual must adjust to the presence or absence of other human beings in specified numbers and of specified age and sex. The density of population affects the actual or potential number of face-to-face relationships available to the individual. Patterns for human adjustment which would be suitable to a group of five hundred would not work equally well in a group of five thousand, and vice versa. The size of a society, the density of its population, its age and sex ratio are not entirely culturally prescribed, although often conditioned by the interaction between the technological level of the culture and the exigencies of the physical environment. The quality and type of social interaction that is determined by this social dimension of group membership has, likewise, its consequences for personality formation.

Before leaving the group-membership determinants, we must remind the reader once more that this conception is merely a useful abstraction. In the concrete, the individual personality is never directly affected by the group as a physical totality. Rather, his personality is molded by the particular members of the group with whom he has personal contact and by his conceptions of the group as a whole. Some traits of group members are predictable—in a statistical sense—from knowledge of the biological, social, and cultural properties of the group. But no single person is ever completely representative of all the characteristics imputed to the group as a whole. Concretely, not the group but group agents with their own peculiar traits determine personality formation. Of these group agents, the most important are the parents and other members of the individual's family. They, we repeat, act as individuals, as members of a group, and as members of a sub-group with special characteristics (the family itself).

ROLE DETERMINANTS

The culture defines how the different functions, or roles, necessary to group life are to be performed—such roles, for example, as those assigned on the basis of sex and age, or on the basis of membership in a caste, class, or occupational group. In a sense, the role determinants of personality are a special class of group-membership determinants; they apply to strata that cross-cut other kinds of group membership. The long-continued playing of a distinctive role, however, appears to be so potent in differentiating personalities within a group that it is useful to treat these determinants separately.

Moreover, if one is aware of the role determinants, one will less often be misled in interpreting various manifestations of personality. In this connection it is worth recalling that, in early Latin, *persona* means "a mask"—*dramatis personae* are the masks which actors wear in a play, that is, the characters that are represented. Etymologically and historically, then, the personality is the character that is manifested in public. In modern psychology and sociology this corresponds rather closely to the role behavior of a differentiated person. From one point of view, this constitutes a disguise. Just as the outer body shields the viscera from view, and clothing the genitals, so the public personality shields the private personality from the curious and censorious world. It also operates to conceal underlying motivations from the individual's own consciousness. The person who has painfully achieved some sort of integration, and who knows what is expected of him in a particular social situation, will usually produce the appropriate responses with only a little personal coloring. This explains, in part, why the attitudes and action patterns produced by the group-membership and role determinants constitute a screen which, in the case of normal individuals, can be penetrated only by the intensive, lengthy, and oblique procedures of depth psychology.

The disposition to accept a person's behavior in a given situation as representative of his total personality is almost universal. Very often he is merely conforming, very acceptably, to the cultural definition of his role. One visits a doctor in his office, and his behavior fits the stereotype of the physician so perfectly that one says often mistakenly, "There indeed is a well-adjusted person." But a scientist must train himself to get behind a man's cultivated surface, because he will not be able to understand much if he limits his data to the action patterns perfected through the repeated performance of the roles as physician, as middle-aged man, as physician dealing with an older male patient, etc.

SITUATIONAL DETERMINANTS

Besides the constitutional determinants and the forces which will more or less inevitably confront individuals who live in the same physical environment, who are members of a society of a certain size and of a certain culture, and who play the same roles, there are things which "just happen" to people. Even casual contacts of brief duration ("accidental" —i.e., not foreordained by the cultural patterns for social interrelations) are often crucial, it seems, in determining whether a person's life will proceed along one or another of various possible paths. A student, say, who is undecided as to his career, or who is about equally drawn to several different vocations, happens to sit down in a railroad car next to a journalist who is an engaging and persuasive advocate of his profession. This event does not, of course, immediately and directly change the young man's personality, but it may set in motion a chain of events which put him into situations that are decisive in molding his personality.

The situational determinants include things that happen a thousand times as well as those that happen only once—provided they are not standard for a whole group. For example, it is generally agreed that the family constellation in which a person grows up is a primary source of personality styling. These domestic influences are conditioned by the cultural prescriptions for the roles of parents and children. But a divorce, a father who is much older than the mother, a father whose occupation keeps him away from home much of the time, the fact of being an only child or the eldest or youngest in a series—these are situational determinants.

Contact with a group involves determinants which are classified as group-membership or situational, depending on the individual's sense of belongingness or commitment to the group. The congeries of persons among whom a man accidentally finds himself one or more times may affect his personality development but not in the same manner as those social units with which the individual feels himself allied as a result of shared experiences or of imaginative identification.

INTERDEPENDENCE OF THE DETERMINANTS

"Culture and personality" is one of the fashionable slogans of contemporary social science and, by present usage, denotes a range of problems on the borderline between anthropology and sociology, on the one hand, and psychology and psychiatry, on the other. However, the phrase has unfortunate implications. A dualism is implied, whereas "culture in personality" and "personality in culture" would suggest conceptual models more in accord with the facts. Moreover, the slogan favors a dangerous simplification of the problems of personality formation. Recognition of culture as one of the determinants of personality is a great gain, but there are some indications that this theoretical advance has tended to obscure the significance of other types of determinants. "Culture and personality" is as lopsided as "biology and personality." To avoid perpetuation of an over-emphasis upon culture, the writers have treated cultural forces as but one variety of the press to which personalities are subjected as a consequence of their membership in an organized group.

A balanced consideration of "personality in nature, society, and culture" must be carried on within the framework of a complex conceptual scheme which explicitly recognizes, instead of tacitly excluding, a number of types of determinants. But it must also not be forgotten that any classification of personality determinants is, at best, a convenient abstraction.

A few illustrations of the intricate linkage of the determinants will clarify this point. For example, we may instance a network of cultural, role, and constitutional determinants. In every society the child is differently socialized according to sex. Also, in every society different behavior is expected of individuals in different age groups, although each culture makes its own prescriptions as to where these lines are drawn and what behavioral variations are to be anticipated. Thus, the personalities of men and women, of the old and the young, are differentiated, in part, by the experience of playing these various roles in conformity with cultural standards. But, since age and sex are biological facts, they also operate throughout life as constitutional determinants of personality. A woman's motivations and action patterns are modified by the facts of her physique as a woman.

Some factors that one is likely to pigeonhole all too complacently as biological often turn out, on careful examination, to be the product of complicated interactions. Illness may result from group as well as from individual constitutional factors. And illness, in turn, may be considered a situational determinant. The illness—with all of its effects upon personality formation—is an "accident" in that one could predict only that the betting odds were relatively high that this individual would fall victim to this illness. However, when the person does become a patient, one can see that both a constitutional predisposition and membership in a caste or class group where sanitation and medical care were substandard were causative factors in this "accidental" event. Similarly, a constitutional tendency towards corpulence certainly has implications for personality when it is characteristic of a group as well as when it distinguishes an individual within a group. But the resources of the physical environment as exploited by the culturally-transmitted technology are major determinants in the production and utilization of nutritional substances of various sorts and these have patent consequences for corpulence, stature, and energy

potential. Tuberculosis or pellagra may be endemic. If hookworm is endemic in a population, one will hardly expect vigor to be a striking feature of the majority of people. Yet hookworm is not an unavoidable "given," either constitutionally or environmentally: the prevalence and effects of hookworm are dependent upon culturally enjoined types of sanitary control.

Complicated interrelations of the same sort may be noted between the environmental and cultural forces which constitute the group membership determinants. On the one hand, the physical environment imposes certain limitations upon the cultural forms which man creates, or it constrains toward change and readjustment in the culture he brings into an ecological area. There is always a large portion of the impersonal environment to which men can adjust but not control; there is another portion which is man-made and cultural. Most cultures provide technologies which permit some alterations in the physical world (for example, methods of cutting irrigation ditches or of terracing hillsides). There are also those artifacts (houses, furniture, tools, vehicles) which serve as instruments for the gratification of needs, and, not infrequently, for their incitement and frustration. Most important of all, perhaps, culture directs and often distorts man's perceptions of the external world. What effects social suggestion may have in setting frames of reference for perception has been shown experimentally. Culture acts as a set of blinders, or series of lenses, through which men view their environments.

Among group-membership determinants, the social and cultural factors are interdependent, yet analytically distinct. Man, of course, is only one of many social animals, but the ways in which social, as opposed to solitary, life modifies his behavior are especially numerous and varied. The fact that human beings are mammals and reproduce bi-sexually creates a basic predisposition toward at least the rudiments of social living. And the prolonged helplessness of human infants conduces to the formation of a family group. Also, certain universal social processes (such as conflict, competition, and accommodation) are given distinct forms through cultural transmission. Thus, while the physically strong tend to dominate the weak, this tendency may be checked and even to some extent reversed by a tradition which rewards chivalry, compassion, and humility. Attitudes towards women, towards infants, towards the old, towards the weak will be affected by the age and sex ratios and the birth and death rates prevalent at a particular time.

The social and cultural press likewise interlock with the situational determinants. There are many forces involved in social interaction which influence personality formation and yet are in no sense culturally prescribed. All children (unless multiple births) are born at different points in their parents' careers, which means that they have, psychologically speaking, somewhat different parents. Likewise, whether a child is wanted or unwanted and whether it is of the desired sex will make a difference in the ways in which it will be treated, even though the culture says that all children are wanted and defines the two sexes as of equal value.

A final example will link the constitutional with both the group-membership and situational determinants. Even though identical twins may differ remarkably little from a biological standpoint, and participate in group activities which are apparently similar, a situational factor may intrude as a result of which their experiences in social interaction will be quite different. If, for instance, one twin is injured in an automobile accident and the other is not, and if the injured twin has to spend a year in bed, as the special object of his mother's solicitations, noticeable personality differences will probably develop. The extent to which these differences endure will depend surely upon many other factors, but it is unlikely that they will be entirely counteracted. The variations in treatment which a bed-ridden child receives is partly determined by culture (the extent to which the ideal patterns permit a sick child to be petted, etc.), and partly by extra-cultural factors (the mother's need for nurturance, the father's idiomatic performance of his culturally patterned role in these circumstances, etc.).

SIMILARITIES AND DIFFERENCES IN PERSONALITY

In conclusion, let us return for a moment to the observed fact that every man is "like all other men, like some other men, like no other man." In the beginning there is (1) the organism and (2) the environment. Using this division as the starting point in thinking about personality formation, one might say that the *differences* observed in the personalities of human beings are due to variations in their biological equipment and in the total environment to which they must adjust, while the *similarities* are ascribable to biological and environmental regularities. Although the organism and the environment have a kind of wholeness in the concrete behavioral world which the student loses sight of at his peril, this generalization is substantially correct. However, the formulation can be put more neatly in terms of field. There is (1) the organism moving through a field which is (2) structured both by culture and by the physical and social world in a relatively uniform manner, but which is (3) subject to endless variation within the general patterning due to the organism's constitutionally-determined pecularities of reaction and to the occurrence of special situations.

In certain circumstances, one reacts to men and women, not as unique organizations of experience, but as representatives of a group. In other circumstances, one reacts to men and women primarily as fulfilling certain roles. If one is unfamiliar with the Chinese, one is likely to react to them first as Chinese rather than as individuals. When one meets new people at a social gathering, one is often able to predict correctly: "That man is a doctor." "That man certainly isn't a businessman, he acts like a professor." "That fellow over there looks like a government official, surely not at artist, a writer, or an actor." Similarities in personality created by the role and group-membership determinants are genuine enough. A man is likely to resemble other men from his home town, other members of his vocation, other members of his class, as well as the majority of his countrymen as contrasted to foreigners.

But the variations are equally common. Smith is stubborn in his office as well as at home and on the golf course. Probably he would have been stubborn in all social contexts if he had been taken to England from America at an early age and his socialization had been completed there. The playing of roles is always tinged by the uniqueness of the personality. Such differences may be distinguished by saying, "Yes, Brown and Jones are both forty-five-year-old Americans, both small businessmen with about the same responsibilities, family ties, and prestige—but somehow they are different." Such dissimilarities may be traced to the interactions of the constitutional and situational determinants, which have been different for each man, with the common group-membership and role determinants to which both have been subjected.

Another type of resemblance between personalities cuts across the boundaries of groups and roles but is equally understandable within this framework of thinking about personality formation. In general, one observes quite different personality manifestations in Hopi Indians and in white Americans—save for those common to all humanity. But occasionally one meets a Hopi whose behavior, as a whole or in part, reminds one very strongly of a certain type of white man. Such parallels can arise from similar constitutional or situational determinants or a combination of these. A Hopi and a white man might both have an unusual endocrine condition. Or both Hopi and white might have had several long childhood illnesses which brought them an exceptional amount of maternal care. While an overabundance of motherly devotion would have had somewhat different effects upon the two personalities, a striking segmental resemblance might have been produced which persisted throughout life.

In most cases the observed similarities, as well as the differences, between groups of people are largely attributable to fairly uniform social and cultural processes. When one says, "Smith reminds me of Brown," a biologically inherited determinant may be completely responsible for the observed resemblance. But when one notes that American businessmen, for example, have certain typical characteristics which identify them as a group and distinguish them from American farmers and teachers it can hardly be a question of genetic constitution. Likewise, the similarities of personality between Americans in general as contrasted with Germans in general must be traced primarily to common press which produces resemblances in spite of wide variations in individual constitutions.

To summarize the content of this chapter in other terms: The personality of an individual is the product of inherited dispositions and environmental experiences. These experiences occur within the field of his physical, biological, and social environment, all of which are modified by the culture of his group. Similarities of life experiences and heredity will tend to produce similar personality characteristics in different individuals, whether in the same society or in different societies.

Selection **61** | PERSONALITY CHANGE DURING COLLEGE YEARS*

CARROLL E. IZARD
Vanderbilt University

Edward's Personal Preference Schedule (PPS) was administered during orientation week to an entering class in 1957. Of the 627 students tested, there were 148 Arts and Science (A&S) men, 91 A&S women, 70 engineers, and 19 nurses on campus in the spring of 1961 as second semester seniors. By appealing for volunteers in the A&S college and utilizing class periods that were made available in the schools of nursing and engineering, follow-up test data were obtained on all 19 nursing seniors, 63 of the engineering seniors, 24 A&S women, and 28 A&S men. Comparing the 1957 data for volunteers and nonvolunteers among A&S males and females by t tests showed no difference for females, but male volunteers were higher on Intraception and Nurturance and lower on Succorance and Aggression. This placed doubt on the representativeness of the A&S male sample. Product-moment correlations and t's for nonindependent samples were run between the 1957 and 1961 PPS scores of each group.

The nursing students showed significant mean decreases on Deference, Abasement ($p < .001$), Order ($p < .01$), Affiliation, and Endurance ($p < .05$), and significant mean increase on Autonomy, Heterosexuality, and Aggression ($p < .01$). The means for engineers

* Reprinted from Carroll E. Izard, "Personality Change during College Years," *Journal of Consulting Psychology*, **26**: 482, 1962. Copyright 1962 by the American Psychological Association and reproduced by permission.

decreased on Deference, Abasement ($p < .001$), Succorance, and Endurance ($p < .01$), and increased on Dominance, Heterosexuality ($p < .001$), Autonomy ($p < .01$), and Aggression ($p = .05$, approximately). The means for A&S women decreased on Deference, Dominance, Abasement ($p < .001$), and Endurance ($p = .05$, approximately), and increased on Heterosexuality ($p < .01$) and Autonomy ($p < .05$). The means for A&S men decreased on Abasement ($p < .01$) and Nurturance ($p < .05$), and increased on Achievement, Aggression ($p < .05$), Heterosexuality ($p = .05$, approximately). The like-sex groups changed in the same direction on 12 of the 15 variables.

Of the five personality characteristics which changed significantly or approached significance for at least three of the four groups, Abasement had moderately high long-term reliabilities (.79, .79, .63, .43); Autonomy and Deference had the next highest r's (40s, 50s); Heterosexuality and Aggression generally had low long term r's (20s, 30s). Among the other variables, the r's were relatively high for Exhibition and quite low for Endurance.

In terms of the item-content definitions of these scales we might argue that the changes consistent across groups represent decrease in "other directed" behavior (− Deference), increased capacity to do the unexpected and to find rewards and satisfactions from one's own comings and goings (+ Autonomy), decreased feelings of guilt and inferiority (− Abasement), increased heterosocial and heterosexual activities (+ Heterosexuality), and increased self-assertiveness and freer overt expression of hostility in response to threat or frustration (+ Aggression).

The correlations between the freshman and the senior scores indicated that students shift their relative standing within the group on certain characteristics much more so than on others. The observed mean changes were considered, in part, as personality development in the direction of social and emotional maturity.

13 | BEHAVIOR DISORDERS

The two major classes of behavior disorders are neurosis and psychosis. Neurotic behavior often follows certain general patterns which may involve (1) loss of memory or function of a portion of the body (hysteria); (2) recurring thoughts or actions over which the person has little or no control (psychasthenia); (3) excessive fatigue and anxiety-related body complaints (neurasthenia); (4) chronic low-grade anxiety which occasionally flares into an acute anxiety attack (anxiety neurosis). Although such behavior syndromes are certainly maladaptive in the long run, they are attempts on the person's part to adjust to his environment as he perceives it. It is unfortunately the case that his perception of his social environment is distorted. It is not surprising that perceptual distortions first manifest themselves in relation to the social environment; since the behavior of others is more ambiguous, it requires more interpretation based on one's own feelings than is the case in perception of our physical environment. One recurring perceptual distortion of the neurotic person is that he is an inadequate and inferior person. In effect, he generalizes his real limitations and failures too far. He defines his "self" on the basis of his weaknesses rather than a realistic evaluation of both strengths and weaknesses. This chronic feeling of inadequacy generates emotions of anxiety and fear, and the anxiety and fear make the person less capable of using his rational thinking processes in order to solve his adjustment problems. Many aspects of his environment, especially other people, are perceived as frustrating and threatening. This generates more anxiety which perpetuates the vicious circle. He then begins to rely more and more on defense mechanisms to reduce this anxiety. Although the ego defenses may reduce his anxiety, without responsible constructive action they tend to be used to excess. Thus, in the short run they are adjustive, but in the long run they are maladaptive since in the neurotic their excessive use renders him less capable of more realistic nondefensive solutions to his adjustment problems.

BIOLOGICAL FACTORS

Psychoses may be divided into two general classes: The *organic* psychoses are those which are based on actual destruction of portions of the central nervous system, for example, general paresis and alcoholic psychosis. The *functional* psychoses are those in which no central nervous system damage is present, for example, schizophrenia and manic depressive psychosis. Since the organic psychoses have been found to be related to biological factors, it has long been the hope that biological determinants of functional psychoses could be discovered. Considerable research effort is being expended by biochemists, physiologists, psychiatrists, and psychologists toward the resolution of this problem. One of the most exciting leads is being investigated by Dr. Robert G. Heath and his co-workers. In Selection 62, Dr. Heath tentatively advances the hypothesis that schizophrenia is an inherited metabolic disorder which interacts with environmental stress to produce a protein substance called taraxein. It is further assumed that the taraxein causes changes in the functioning of specific brain sites and thereby the associated behavioral changes. In support of the latter portion of this hypothesis, Heath cites his findings that taraxein is found in the blood of schizophrenics but is not found in normals. Furthermore, the injection of taraxein into normals causes temporary schizophrenic symptoms. As Dr. Heath admits, the majority of relevant scientists do not accept his hypothesis at the present time. In part this may be due to the difficulty of replicating the basic experimental findings. Some of the experimental pitfalls which are prevalent in any research on the biological basis of behavior disorders are discussed by Dr. M. K. Horwitt in Selection 63. Despite the fact that this is a difficult research area, the answers are so important that increasing numbers of scientists, including biochemists, psychologists, and psychopharmacologists, are working on the problems. It is not unreasonable to suppose that eventually we will be successful in determining the specific biochemical imbalance(s) which cause schizophrenia. If so, will this depreciate the importance of psychological and sociocultural factors as causative agents? On the contrary, we will then be challenged to explore the distinct possibility that the biochemical imbalance is itself related to psychosocial stress situations.

PSYCHOLOGICAL FACTORS

What are some of the psychological factors which are important in the development of psychoses? In Selection 64 Professor Coleman reviews some of the factors which are important in psychoses in general and then discusses in more detail these factors as they are related to the most frequently occurring functional psychosis, schizophrenia. It should be no surprise that frustration, conflict, and distortions of interpersonal relations are intimately connected with the psychotic adjustment. In all psychoses we find perceptual distortion present in a more intense degree than in neurosis. The neurotic may distort the intentions of his wife or boss, but the psychotic often distorts the intentions of all people. The schizophrenic, in particular, tends to perceive others as basically untrustworthy. He thus tends to withdraw from those very social contacts which might provide an opportunity for correction of his misconceptions. His faulty perceptions eventually become organized into a consistent but distorted system of beliefs about other people (delusions). His distorted perceptions may extend beyond his social environment to the physical environment in such a way that he perceives objects or voices which are not actually present in the external world (hallucinations).

In a discussion of behavior disorders, the question of effective treatment immediately presents itself. A large number of specific treatments have been tried; some have been abandoned after an initial enthusiasm, and others have proven to be reliable over many years. Current therapies may be classified into the broad categories of somatotherapies and psychotherapies. As the name implies somatotherapies are administered under medical supervision and are aimed at direct modification of the structure and functioning of the central nervous system. Among the somatotherapies we may list psychosurgery, shock therapy, and chemotherapy (e.g., tranquilizers; see Cole (Selection 73), for a more extended discussion of these drugs). The other major treatment type is psychotherapy. This also may take many forms, from highly directive therapies such as hypnoanalysis to quite nondirective counseling like that involved in the client-centered therapy advocated by Carl Rogers (Selection 55).

Treatment procedures derived from principles of classical and operant conditioning are known as behavior therapies. Classical conditioning principles are often used to condition a response which is the opposite of the undesired response and which is incompatible with it. One special variety of counter conditioning is called desensitization therapy. This treatment has been especially effective in eliminating irrational fears, or phobias. In Selection 65, Drs. Peter J. Lang and A. David Lazovik report the experimental desensitization of a snake phobia. Their research suggests that contrary to the prevalent assumptions made by psychoanalysis and other more intensive therapies, the direct removal of the symptom was successful and did not lead to the substitution of another symptom for the phobia.

SOCIOCULTURAL FACTORS

Further insight into the dynamics and development of neurosis is presented by Dr. Karen Horney in her paper "Culture and Neurosis." She emphasizes that the cultural tendency to encourage competition and rivalry among people results in a constant need for measuring up to others, a need for perfection, and a chronic reaction of hostility toward others (although, of course, the neurotic's hostility may be concealed from others and from himself). However, our culture is not consistent; it requires competition but also encourages the person to be self-sacrificing and modest. When this culturally induced conflict is imposed on a person who already is in a state of "Basic Anxiety" (see Selection 66), a vicious circle develops. The neurotic has a need for reassurance from other people, but he chronically expects a rejection from them; this in turn results in his interpreting their behavior as being rejecting in fact. More hostility is generated by the perceived rejection, and the person becomes more anxious and insecure. This vicious circle is an excellent example of some of the general characteristics of the neurotic which we noted at the beginning of this section. His attempts to adjust to his environment are self-defeating because his perception of others is distorted in such a way as to emphasize their competitive prowess and his own inadequacy.

Selection **62** | A BIOCHEMICAL
HYPOTHESIS ON
THE ETIOLOGY OF
SCHIZOPHRENIA*

ROBERT G. HEATH
Tulane University

Because the etiology of schizophrenia is not definitely known, a presentation of this type must be limited to outlining hypotheses. Our group has formulated a hypothesis based on data from our clinical studies as well as from our recent physiological and biochemical findings and the observations of others. We have attempted to consider psychodynamic factors within the framework of genetics, physiology, and chemistry. Ours is an operational concept within which we are collecting data. We assume that continuing modification of the hypothesis will come about as more data accumulate.

We consider schizophrenia to be a genetically determined metabolic disease, or, more specifically, a disease characterized by alterations in the metabolic pathway for the breakdown of certain (as yet unidentified) endogenously occurring compounds. Our current hypothesis, based on our most recent data, is that the genetic defect is manifest by the presence of a qualitatively different protein (taraxein) in the blood stream. A toxic compound formed as a result of the interfering presence of taraxein alters physiological activity in specific parts of the brain, with associated behavioral changes. From our data, we postulate that these changes develop because the protein substance impairs enzymatic activity in a pathway related (in an undetermined way, as yet) to the metabolism of amines. Our current studies suggest that histamine may be implicated, either directly or indirectly in the faulty metabolic process.

Clinical and laboratory findings suggest that, as in other metabolic diseases, a basic deficiency exists to varying degrees in different patients. If disease symptoms are related to amine metabolism, then stress and, particularly, stress associated with emergency emotions and the physiochemical counterparts

* Robert G. Heath, "A Biochemical Hypothesis on the Etiology of Schizophrenia," in Don D. Jackson (ed.), *The Etiology of Schizophrenia*, Basic Books, Inc., Publishers, New York, © 1960, chap. 5.

should intensify symptoms. Thus, we believe that the psychodynamic factors play a secondary role in the production of the characteristic symptoms of the disease. Although, in our hypothesis, the fundamental defect is in enzymatic activity, it is our conception that amines, which are poured into the blood stream during stressful situations, are somehow implicated in the abnormal metabolic process. In our current hypothesis we assume that these fluctuations in levels of amines are responsible for the fluctuations in intensity of pathological symptoms in schizophrenic patients.

CLINICAL CONSIDERATIONS

In our formulation, the inborn metabolic defect is associated with lifelong characteristic behavioral patterns. The symptoms are at the level of basic feelings of pain and pleasure. We assume that they are a consequence of the chemical aberration. These symptoms are not to be confused with the classical textbook description of schizophrenic symptomatology. The latter (*i.e.*, classical or overt symptoms) are secondary complications of the addition of stress to a defective system. Persons who display symptoms reflecting the defect in the pain-pleasure mechanism have been referred to as schizophrenic phenotypes. Rado (1), describing the patterns of behavior in this group, prefers to call them schizotypal adaptation. The schizotype is described as presenting two basic groups of symptoms, the result of his inherited defect: one, an integrative pleasure deficiency; two, the proprioceptive diathesis. In Rado's conceptualization, these defects underlie the symptoms that Bleuler (2) first characterized as "fundamental symptoms." Rado postulates that as a result of these defects a variety of rather consistent patterns of behavior are present in the schizophrenic. In our framework, overt clinical or secondary symptoms of schizophrenia can occur only in this group and generally appear with stress. Persons without the inherent defect do not develop classical, secondary schizophrenic symptoms even though subject to overwhelming stresses.

Thus, we consider that schizophrenic symptoms are a complication of a fundamental disease and are precipitated by psychological pressures in predisposed individuals only. Because of the nature of the schizotypal adaptation, the genesis of stress is quite different from that in persons not affected by this disorder. In fact, the schizotype often appears even better integrated in some situations (e.g., combat—when the individual is able to identify with a group with high morale) that produce stress in others. Careful statistics show lessened incidence of decompensation in schizophrenics during periods of actual combat in some circumstances. This is understandable when considered in the light of Rado's observations of the basic manifestations of the disease. Because of the schizophrenic's incapability of integrating pleasure feelings and the associated proprioceptive diathesis, which makes him unable to feel just who he is and how he fits into the scheme of life about him, he is apt to function better when he is in a highly regimented setting. This is so particularly when he can identify with a military outfit of high morale in which codes of behavior are fairly well spelled out. In these simplified circumstances, the subject can function with relative ease, relying upon his intellect, which enables him to copy the behavior of his associates. There is no need to rely upon his feelings, which are defective, in meeting situations. Thus, he can feel secure and a part of things. He is not subject to the stress and panic that tend to develop in the schizotype when he feels he is beginning to lose contact with the world of reality. The development of stress and panic often precede and are related to the appearance of classical decompensating secondary symptoms of schizophrenia.

An understanding of these symptoms and an awareness that they represent a fundamental basic deficit is of considerable practical value, in our experience. Recognition of this type of disorder is a necessity for the proper planning of therapy because the therapist who fails to recognize these symptoms and evaluate their significance may undertake a type of psychotherapy that can result in dire consequences. In our outpatient clinics for intensive therapy, our primary consideration in evaluating new patients is to ascertain the presence or absence of the schizotypal adaptation. We have found that the symptoms which Rado describes are consistent indicators of the presence of the integrative defect. In a number of articles (1, 3), authors have elaborated on the mechanism

of symptom formation, both the fundamental and accessory symptoms of Bleuler, and the relationship of these to the more basic manifestations cited above. I feel it is unnecessary here to go further into a description of symptomatology as it evolves from the basic manifestations in the schizophrenic patient. The point I wish to make is that it is of the utmost importance to recognize early the presence of the disease because the therapist who fails to do so may employ psychotherapeutic techniques that will increase the patient's disability rather than improve his social adaptation.

Our concept of the etiology and pathogenesis of schizophrenia obviously is not universally accepted. Many investigators into the nature of schizophrenia have, on the basis of available data, advanced hypotheses that are considerably different. Perhaps the most commonly advanced concept in psychiatric literature is one that considers the disease schizophrenia a complication of severe stresses resulting from impaired intrafamily relationships. Thus, the disease becomes closely related to neurosis. Disease symptoms are complications of faulty environmental circumstances. Anyone can be a potential victim of the disease. Within this concept, differences between schizophrenia and neurosis are quantitative.

Henceforth, I shall refer to this approach as "the environmental-social concept of etiology" and contrast this approach with our views concerning the nature of the observed pathological interrelationships in the families of schizophrenics. Also, because we interpret the schizophrenic's reaction to stress as essentially a manifestation secondary to a basic biological defect, we obviously consider the role of the psychological factors as secondary in importance. This is in contradistinction to the "environmental-social" theory, in which stress is considered as a primary etiological factor. I shall present our basis for this assumption in more detail.

RELATIONSHIPS BETWEEN INTRAFAMILY DYNAMICS AND THE DEVELOPMENT OF SCHIZOPHRENIA

Those who consider the cause of schizophrenia to be environmental and social state directly, or imply, that faulty interpersonal relationships between one or both parents and the young child are crucial etiological factors. Data gathered on the behavior of families of schizophrenic patients consistently reveal a higher incidence of interpersonal psychopathology in such homes than one finds in the homes of nonschizophrenic groups. These data are consistent and undeniable. Opinions differ, however, as to whether or not this unhealthy emotional relationship in the home is of primary etiological significance. Some authors (4, 5, 6, 7, 8, 9), in describing their findings in this area, state that it is not etiological, or else they tend to avoid the issue. Those authors (10, 11, 12, 13) who conclude or imply that the finding is of etiological significance often refer to the mother in such circumstances as a "schizophrenogenic mother." Others (14) make specific reference to a disturbance in the symbiotic mother-child relationship—usually when the child is approximately 18 months of age—as being of crucial etiological importance. There is also literature describing the pathological child-father relationship, and other articles cite both parents as etiological determinants of the disease process (15, 16, 17, 18).

In our concept, based on our clinical studies, we consider that the pathological family relationships seen frequently, although not always, in the families of schizophrenic patients are not determinants of schizophrenic behavior but rather are the result of a basic metabolic alteration in one or both parents—as well as in the child who has inherited the alteration from the afflicted parent or parents. It is our view, in keeping with Rado's hypothesis (1), that the mother, rather than being merely a schizophrenogenic mother, is schizophrenogenic in every aspect of her behavior. Assuming that schizophrenogenic means that she has a unique form of behavior in her relationship to the child ("unique" in that it causes a specific disease in the child), then, by the same token, she also is a schizophrenogenic wife, friend, sibling, and what not. Others with whom she has contact do not, however, become schizophrenic because they do not receive her genes. There is no substantial evidence to indicate that her interpersonal relationship *per se* with anyone can cause the disease schizophrenia. Findings in our Clinic suggest that the child's behavior is at least as important as the mother's in inducing pathological family relationships.

The only solid evidence, based on Kallmann's (19) studies, is that the passing on of her defective genes seems to be the crucial factor. Similarly, the child, very early in his behavior, displays blunted emotional reactions or autistic thinking. Our findings suggest that these characteristics do not result from environmental influences but instead are manifestations of an impaired metabolic pathway resulting from biochemical aberrations of faulty genes.

STRESS IN THE SCHIZOPHRENIC: QUALITATIVE AND QUANTITATIVE CONSIDERATIONS

Stress, seemingly the important factor in the appearance of secondary symptoms, develops in a unique manner in the schizophrenic. Stress appears to be a reaction to features of his basic deficit and not the result of faulty learning processes as in the neurotic. This observation is best described by Rado (1) and supports the contention of the basic deficiency. Because of the schizophrenic's inability to integrate pleasure and his resulting deficient concept of self, he tends to copy the activities of others. Unquestionably, his psychodynamics, or learning experiences, play a role in this process as well as do external circumstances. These dynamic features, however, seem to be less important than the endogenous integrative defect which predisposes schizophrenics to stress and decompensating symptoms. My experience as a psychoanalyst and the experiences of colleagues and students at Tulane University have indicated, with virtual certainty, that the principal sources of stress in the schizophrenic are other than those in persons without the disease. Most psychiatrists and psychoanalysts, in describing the disease process, present their data as if schizophrenia were a more extensive form of neurosis. In our experience, this is not true. We believe that schizophrenia is an entirely different disease. In the neurotic and the normal individual, the psychiatric data suggest that inferior adaptive patterns in current behavior are related to past faulty learning experiences. As a result of faulty learning, the individual develops inappropriate fears. The behavioral patterns of the neurotic are inferior attempts to decrease the stress of his unrealistic emergencies.

In contrast, it is our experience that only a

very small amount of stress is derived from the area of faulty learning in the schizophrenic. Of far greater intensity and therefore of more importance in the development of decompensating symptoms in the schizophrenic is stress resulting from the basic, deficient behavioral patterns described by Rado. Schizophrenic patients develop their most intense panics when they recognize that they do not "feel" as other persons do (a recognition derived from deficit in pleasure mechanism). They sense that they are different and lost, as if without a rudder. Their "proprioceptive defect" thereby contributes to this panic. They do not know who they are or where they fit in. Attempts at intellectual control (e.g., copying others, play acting) suffice to hold together the milder schizophrenic, the one with less of the basic defect. These reparative attempts are usually inadequate, however, in patients with more serious deficits, particularly if they encounter realistic vicissitudes in life. To summarize this point, I believe that stress in the schizophrenic is derived from a set of factors different from those causing stress in the neurotic and normal individual. This is an important consideration in psychotherapy, *i.e.*, therapy through the influence of one individual on another, and one that should also be taken into account by biologists working in this area. This hypothesis considers two biological factors as crucial: (1) a fundamental inherited deficit; and (2) the stress factor. These factors are interrelated because increased stress results from the fundamental deficit, and stress in itself is important in precipitating or exaggerating the decompensating clinical symptomatology. The great majority of psychoanalytic theorists do not consider this.

BIOLOGICAL DATA

Because we assume an inborn endogenous defect, our hypothesis must, of necessity, provide methods for the collection of data in addition to clinical observation. Clinical data alone can lead us only into the old *cul-de-sac* of the chicken and the egg. We have postulated that behavioral defects are due to an inborn error of metabolism. It then follows that this error should be associated with specific physiological and biochemical findings. I will review briefly

some biological data which we believe give support to this concept.

We have reported physiological studies in schizophrenic patients in a number of articles (20, 21, 22, 23). Animal studies were reviewed and subsequent patient studies described. One finding of importance in developing the present thesis has been the consistent recording of an electrical abnormality through the septal region and the hippocampus when the patient is displaying psychotic behavior. Animals under the influence of psychotomimetic drugs have also shown somewhat similar alterations in depth recordings. The intensity of the abnormality has been proportionate to the degree of psychotic behavior. The electrical abnormality has not been present in a small series of humans who were not exhibiting psychotic behavior or in a large group of primates from whom we obtained depth recordings. This irregularity is not present in other parts of the brain from which we have recorded, including many other deep nuclear masses as well as the cortex. This electrical abnormality is not unique to schizophrenic behavior. An abnormality similar although not of identical character appears in conjunction with psychotic behavior of other types, e.g., when induced by psychotomimetic drugs or during episodic behavioral disturbances in epilepsy. Altered recordings from the brains of patients with focal areas of cellular damage also are seen. Thus, all of our findings indicate that we have psychotic behavior when this region of the brain is disturbed, and it can be disturbed for a variety of reasons.

We have conducted a number of studies in an attempt to determine more specifically the nature of the endogenous inborn defect in schizophrenia which could account for this physiological disturbance and concomitant behavioral disorder. Considerable data have been accumulated which we believe provide provocative, although not definitive, leads as to the presence of a metabolic defect and the possible area of this defect. One provocative investigation concerns the isolation of taraxein (24, 25, 26, 27, 28). Several observations (29, 30, 31, 32) led us to suspect an irregularity in the oxidizing system for amines. While studying oxidizing enzymes, we isolated a qualitatively different substance, taraxein, from the serum of schizophrenic patients. When this substance is injected into nonpsychotic volunteers, it induces symptoms characteristic of schizophrenia. The clinical symptoms following taraxein administration are associated with electrical abnormalities in recordings from specific parts of the limbic system which we have obtained from schizophrenic patients. The finding was of importance because taraxein (which induced the behavioral and physiological changes) is an endogenous substance present in schizophrenics, but not in normals.

We have further explored the area of amine oxidation. The finding of Sulkowitch and Altschule (33) that schizophrenics eliminate considerably larger amounts of amine and related substances in the urine than normals seemed important in our conceptual framework. Specifically, the finding was impressive since our clinical observations suggested a deficiency in the schizophrenic's ability to manage stress. It has long been established that certain amines are released and metabolized during stressful periods (34). We have confirmed the finding of Sulkowitch and Altschule in our laboratories. With their method, the quantity of amines has been as much as 100 times higher in schizophrenics than in normals (25).

Throughout our early studies of epinephrine oxidation, we found evidence that *in vitro* the serum of acute schizophrenics often oxidized epinephrine more rapidly than did serum from normals (in the absence of systemic disease in both groups). Further studies showed that copper levels (principally, ceruloplasmin in serum) were largely responsible for this phenomenon. We also demonstrated that oxidation curves were altered by ascorbic acid and the enzyme activity of ceruloplasmin inhibited by albumin (32). Accordingly, we devised procedures that might shed light on the relationship of this enzyme system to stress; in particular, we have attempted to determine whether or not the response of this system is in any way different in schizophrenics and normals. We followed several procedures to explore this area. One has consisted of measuring copper levels in schizophrenic and normal control groups at varying periods from one to 24 hours after the subcutaneous administration of epinephrine. There were but minimal and inconsistent differences in the changes in ceruloplasmin following administration of hypodermic epinephrine

to the two groups even though the normals exhibited a much more profound physiological and behavioral response. At present we believe that the ceruloplasmin-oxidation phenomena are a peripheral reflection of the difference in metabolic response in the two groups. Results are provocative, but the mechanism is obviously not this simple. Another procedure to test this system has consisted of administering ceruloplasmin to schizophrenics. When large amounts are given (quantity sufficient to double the serum-ceruloplasmin levels), the clinical response to the administration of epinephrine is changed markedly. The patients develop much more profound physiological changes, suggesting that they are metabolizing more epinephrine. They respond with greater increases in blood pressure and pulse rate to constant amounts of epinephrine (25).

To summarize very briefly our thinking regarding oxidation of epinephrine and the copper oxidizing enzymes, it would seem that in schizophrenics the system is somewhat different than it is in the normal controls. However, we do not consider this the fundamental factor in the disease schizophrenia.

SUMMARY

We have presented our concept of the etiology of schizophrenia. We consider the disease to be basically a genetically determined inborn error of metabolism. There are characteristic clinical symptoms, in the form of fundamental basic symptoms, associated with the disease. The schizophrenic, as a result of his behavioral patterns, can develop excessive stress. The hormones that he releases with stress are not properly metabolized because of the metabolic error. Thus far, the most specific biochemical correlation with schizophrenic behavior that we have found is a qualitatively different protein in the serum of schizophrenic patients. The administration of this substance to nonpsychotic volunteers is followed by the appearance of schizophrenic symptoms. This fraction is close to the plasma oxidase, ceruloplasmin, and frequently is found mixed with the ceruloplasmin fraction. Whether it is or is not responsible for suggested alterations in amine metabolism is not yet clear to us. It is very clear, however, that administration of taraxein is followed by physiological activity in specific parts of the limbic system of the brain—alterations of a type that we have been able to correlate with psychotic behavior. The manner in which tar-axein affects brain activity is currently being investigated. We consider that the taraxein fraction may be a biochemical manifestation of a genetic defect present in the disease schizophrenia.

REFERENCES

1. S. Rado, B. Buchenholz, H. Dunton, S. H. Karlen, and R. A. Senescu, "Schizotypal Organization: Preliminary Report on Clinical Study of Schizophrenia," in Rado, S., and Daniels, G. (Eds.), *Changing Concepts of Psycholanalytic Medicine,* New York: Grune, 1956, p. 225.
2. E. Bleuler, *Dementia Praecox or the Group of Schizophrenias,* New York: Internat. Univ. Press, 1950.
3. P. Hoch and P. Polatin, Pseudoneurotic forms of schizophrenia, *Psychiatric Quart.,* **23,** 248, 1949.
4. C. T. Prout and M. A. White, The schizophrenic's sibling, *J. Nerv. & Ment. Dis.,* **123:** 162, 1956.
5. C. T. Prout and M. A. White, A controlled study of personality relationships in mothers of schizophrenic male patients, *Am. J. Psychiat.,* **107:** 251, 1950–51.
6. L. Kanner, Autistic disturbances of affective contact, *Nervous Child,* **2:** 217, 1942–43.
7. L. Kanner, Problems of nosology and psychodynamics of early infantile autism, *Am. J. Orthopsychiat.,* **19:** 416, 1949.
8. J. E. Oltman, J. J. McCarry, and S. Friedman, Parental deprivation and the "broken home" in dementia praecox and other mental diseases, *Am. J. Psychiat.,* **108:** 685, 1952.
9. E. Slimp, Life experiences of schizophrenic children, *Smith College Studies in Social Work,* **21:** 103, 1950.
10. M. A. Ribble, *The Rights of Infants,* New York: Columbia, 1943.
11. J. L. Despert, Some considerations relating to the genesis of autistic behavior in children, *Am. J. Orthopsychiat.,* **21:** 335, 1951.
12. J. L. Despert, Schizophrenia in children, *Psychiatric Quart.,* **12:** 366, 1938.
13. T. Tietze, A study of mothers of schizophrenic patients, *Psychiatry,* **12:** 55, 1949.
14. P. H. Starr, Psychoses in children: their origin and structure, *Psychoanalyt. Quart.,* **23:** 544, 1954.
15. T. Lidz, A. Cornelison, S. Fleck, and D. Terry, The intrafamilial environment of the schizophrenic patient: I. The father, *Psychiatry,* **20:** 329, 1957.
16. T. Lidz, S. Fleck, A. Cornelison, and D. Terry, The intrafamilial environment of the schizophrenic patient: IV. Parental personalities and family interaction, *Am. J. Orthopsychiat.,* **28,** 764, 1958.
17. T. Lidz, B. Parker, and A. Cornelison, The role of the father in the family environment of the schizophrenic patient, *Am. J. Psychiat.,* **113:** 126, 1956–57.
18. T. Lidz, Schizophrenia and the family, *Psychiatry,* **21:** 21, 1958.
19. F. J. Kallmann, *The Genetics of Schizophrenia,* New York: Augustin Press, 1938.
20. R. G. Heath (Ed.), *Studies in Schizophrenia,* Cambridge: Harvard, 1954.
21. R. G. Heath, Correlations between levels of psychological awareness and physiological activity in the central nervous system, *Psychosom. Med.,* **17:** 383, 1955.
22. R. G. Heath, Correlation of electrical recordings from cortical and subcortical regions of the brain with abnormal behavior in human subjects, *Confinia Neurol.,* **18:** 305, 1958.
23. R. G. Heath and W. A. Mickle, Evaluation of seven years' experience with depth electrode studies in human patients. Presented at *Conference on Electrical Studies on the Unanesthetized Brain,* Georgetown University, 1957. In press.
24. R. G. Heath, B. E. Leach, S. Martens, M. Cohen, and C. A. Feigley, "Metabolic Abnormalities in Schizophrenia," in Rinkel, M., and Denber, H. C. B. (Eds.), *Chemical Concepts of Psychosis,* New York: McDowell, Obolensky, 1958.
25. R. G. Heath, B. E. Leach, L. W. Byers, S. Martens, and C. A. Feigley, Pharmacological and biological psychotherapy, *Am. J. Psychiat.,* **114:** 683, 1958.
26. R. G. Heath, S. Martens, B. E. Leach, M. Cohen, and C. A. Feigley, Behavioral changes in nonpsychotic volunteers following the administration of taraxein, the substance extracted from serum of schizophrenic patients, *Am. J. Psychiat.,* **114:** 917, 1958.
27. R. G. Heath, in *Neuropharmacology, Transactions of the Fourth Conference,* New York: Macy, 1959.
28. R. G. Heath, B. E. Leach, and M. Cohen, "Relationships in Psychotic Behavior and Abnormal Substances in Serum," in *The Effect of Pharmacologic Agents on the Nervous System,* Proceedings of the Association for Research in Nervous and Mental Disease,

Baltimore: Williams & Wilkins, 1959, Vol. **37**, p. 397.

29. B. E. Leach, M. Cohen, R. G. Heath, and S. Martens, Studies of the role of ceruloplasmin and albumin in adrenaline metabolism, *A.M.A. Arch. Neurol. & Psychiat.*, **76**: 635, 1956.

30. S. Martens, B. E. Leach, R. G. Heath, and M. Cohen, Glutathione levels in mental and physical illness, *A.M.A. Arch. Neurol. & Psychiat.*, **76**: 630, 1956.

31. B. E. Leach and R. G. Heath, The in vitro oxidation of epinephrine in plasma, *A.M.A. Arch. Neurol. & Psychiat.*, **76**: 444, 1956.

32. C. Angel, B. E. Leach, S. Martens, M. Cohen, and R. G. Heath, Serum oxidation tests in schizophrenic and normal subjects, *A.M.A. Arch. Neurol. & Psychiat.*, **78**: 500, 1957.

33. H. Sulkowitch and M. D. Altschule, The excretion of urinary "epinephrines" in psychiatric disorders. To be published.

34. Walter B. Cannon, *Wisdom of the Body*, Norton: New York, 1939.

Selection **63** | FACT AND ARTIFACT IN THE BIOLOGY OF SCHIZOPHRENIA*

M. K. HORWITT
University of Illinois, Chicago

It appears important at this time to emphasize that many reports showing differences between patients with schizophrenia and normal individuals are based on environmental artifacts that are not related to the basic disorder. The practice followed by biochemical workers of requesting samples of blood or urine from subjects in psychiatric wards, with little more identification of the sample than that the patients have a mental disease, has many disadvantages.

We are now entering a period of renewed interest in biological research on schizophrenia. Nothing can be more harmful to this rejuvenation of the investigation of the biology of mental health than the publication of reports based on techniques of patient selection which

* M. K. Horwitt, "Fact and Artifact in the Biology of Schizophrenia," *Science*, **124**: 429–230, 1956.

do not meet the minimum standards accepted by other disciplines. Much of this conflict is due to a lack of understanding by some workers that the term *schizophrenia* is a general classification with many subdivisions, which are often only slightly related, and that the manner in which the patient chooses to manifest his difficulties may not be a function of his physiological status.

Symptoms that are usually considered artifacts in other studies are often erroneously accepted as biological aberrations in the evaluation of the schizophrenic patient. Year after year, papers appear which purport to distinguish between the state of schizophrenia and that of normalcy. The sum total of the differences reported would make the schizophrenic patient a sorry physical specimen indeed: his liver, brain, kidney, and circulatory functions are impaired; he is deficient in practically every vitamin; his hormones are out of balance, and his enzymes are askew. Fortunately, many of these claims of metabolic abnormality are forgotten in time with a minimum of polemic, but it seems that each new generation of biologists has to be indoctrinated—or disillusioned—without benefit of the experience of its predecessors. One is not certain where to place the blame for this weakness, but both editors and grant advisers could do well to insist on experimental design and interpretations of data which take into account some of the following, almost too obvious, variables.

VARIABLES

(1) *Emotional stress, tension, and anxiety* One does not obtain basal metabolic results during fever or exercise, nor should one expect to obtain basal samples during emotional stress. One of the basic characteristics of the schizophrenic patient is his peculiar emotional reaction to his environment. These reactions will vary in kind and intensity with the individual and with time. A supposedly basal sample taken from a physically quiet but emotionally disturbed catatonic subject may not be basal at all but may be a reflection of metabolism during intense adrenergic stimulation. Adrenergic stimulation has a marked effect on the levels of amino acids in the biological fluids.

To compare the results from such a blood

sample with those from blood of normal subjects is like comparing data from blood
samples obtained during grief or stress of
battle with data from blood obtained during
relaxed, basal conditions. With experience and
knowledge of the individual patient, one may
learn to distinguish between the presence or
absence of some emotional stresses. But, even
under optimal conditions, a preliminary period
of at least 3 to 6 months may be required to
evaluate the stability of subjects chosen for a
metabolic study (1) in order to eliminate those
that are unpredictable. Even when this precau-
tion is taken, some subjects may occasionally
leave a previous metabolic pattern because of
a temporary emotional stress situation.

In such a situation, if one requires data from
unstressed subjects, the tests are repeated at
a later date. If basal data cannot be obtained
from a subject, the results should not be
averaged with those from subjects who are
not disturbed. To show that there are differences between the reactions of a normal subject and those of a patient in the early, active
stages of mental disorder may give good leads
on the effects of emotional trauma on the biochemistry of a subject, but great care should
be exercised in interpreting data obtained from
such patients as being biological aberrations
characteristic of the basic disease. Recent confirmation by McGeer et al. (2) of the observations by Young et al. (3) of the increased
excretion of aromatic compounds in the urine
of "schizophrenics" would have been more
useful if their studies had included estimations
of tension and anxiety (and possible nutritional
imbalance) of the subjects studied.

(2) *Nutritional state*   Emotional stress affects
the appetite of all of us in different fashions.
Even in the best managed hospitals, unless
food intake is strictly controlled, the vagaries
of psychotic behavior are such that they affect
optimum nutrient consumption in some patients who tend to go in and out of negative
nitrogen balance with varying interactions of
their delusional states. Relatively unimportant
food idiosyncracies may, in time, become
manifest as mild nutritional disorders. The
metabolic changes which take place with even
mild and often unrecognized nutritional disorders are more severe than the biological
variations being sought in mental disease.

Having studied such changes in mental patients for more than 15 years, I am at a loss
to understand how some studies of urinary
excretion or of blood constituents can be performed without recourse to nutritional controls.
My experience is that it may take 3 months
(or the equivalent of 3 days of a rat's life) to
achieve a nutritional steady state after a
change in the dietary regimen.

(3) *Liver dysfunction or suboptimal liver function*
It has been frequently claimed that some
schizophrenic patients have decreased rates of
clearance of bromsulfalein or hippuric acid.
The study of liver function in such patients is
well worth more attention, but only additional
work can clarify whether such changes are related to diet, inactivity, training, slower circulation time, physiological hibernation, infection,
or other factors. Although the pattern of
urinary excretion is not expected to vary in a
24-hour sample from subjects with mild liver
dysfunction, tolerance tests that can evaluate
the *rate* at which a substance is absorbed or
removed, or both, from the blood stream may
show sluggish activity in some schizophrenic
patients.

In one controlled study, which was designed
to estimate the effects of a diet that provided
borderline levels of protein, signs of liver dysfunction became apparent and were not re-
paired until after the protein intake was raised
(4). Whether a schizophrenic patient is more
susceptible to liver disorder during protein deficiency or whether the slower removal of injected compounds is a consequence of long-
term inactivity cannot be determined with the
data at hand, but whatever the cause of mild
liver dysfunction in the mental patient, the
possible presence of such defects should be
evaluated more frequently.

(4) *Training*   One does not have to be oriented
in athletics to recognize that the cardiovascular
efficiency of an individual can be markedly influenced by repetitive exercise or work, or
conversely, by extreme inactivity. The activity
of mental patients may vary widely, from prolonged states of fierce agitation that are acted
out by considerable physical movement, to conditions of relative hibernation. Such differences
make for important variations in studies of
oxygen consumption, circulatory rates, and all

related concomitants of biological efficiency. When one considers that the maximum oxygen uptake of a trained individual may be double that of the untrained subject (5, 6), it is not surprising to note that data from most biological studies on mental patients have greater variations from the mean than are obtained from nonpsychotic subjects. In addition, in most mental institutions there are patients who do productive work and others who remain sedentary for years, and the differences in functional muscle mass between these subjects are considerable.

(5) *Diurnal variations* Those acquainted with mental hospitals are aware of the great differences in night restlessness that may exist in various wards. Many mental patients have a high level of nocturnal activity. (It is assumed that sedated or tranquilized patients are not used for basal studies.) The all-too-frequent practice of comparing overnight urine samples from mental patients with similar samples from normal individuals can lead to unwarranted conclusions that might not be made if full 24-hour samples were collected instead. In this connection, one should also be aware of the prolonged fasting period of more than 14 hours between supper and breakfast that is a characteristic of many of our institutions and of the possible effect of such a schedule on diurnal variations.

CONCLUSION

It is earnestly hoped that investigators who are impelled to study the biology of schizophrenia or of other mental disorders will attempt to control the variables mentioned so that we may better distinguish between the causes of schizophrenia and its effects. Admittedly such controls are expensive and difficult to administer, but they are worthy of incorporation into any research program where man is the experimental subject. Much has been said about the faults of psychiatrists who do not make sufficient use of the laboratory concepts of cause and effect in evaluating mental disease. Conversely, the biologist should not be so naive in the interpretation of his data that he loses cognizance of the fact that schizophrenia is not a simple entity, and that he, too, must beware of the trap of confusing cause and effect.

REFERENCES

1. M. K. Horwitt, et al., *Natl. Research Council Bull.* 116 (Natl. Acad. Science, Washington, D.C. 1948).
2. P. L. McGeer, E. G. McGeer, W. G. Gibson, *Science*, **123**, 1029 (1956).
3. M. K. Young, Jr., et al., *Univ. of Texas Publ. No. 5109* (1951), pp. 189–197.
4. M. K. Horwitt, *Nutrition Symposium Series No. 7, National Vitamin Foundation*, (1953), pp. 67–83.
5. E. Simonson, *Pfluger's Arch. ges. Physiol.* **215**, 752 (1927).
6. E. Simonson, *Geriatrics*, in press.

Selection **64** | PSYCHOLOGICAL FACTORS IN SCHIZOPHRENIA*

JAMES C. COLEMAN
University of California, Los Angeles

PSYCHOLOGICAL FACTORS

Among the psychological factors which seem to play a major role in the development of psychoses are faulty parent-child relations, trauma, frustration, and conflict.

Parent-child relations

The exact role of various parent-child and other social relationships in the development of psychotic reactions is not clearly understood. Apparently, however, rejection, excessive conscience development, overly severe discipline, overprotection, rigid sexual morals, chronic insecurity, and inconsistent discipline are some of the more important family conditions which predispose a child to the development of later psychopathology. In a study of the psychoses of children, Yerbury and Newell emphasize the total lack of security in human relationships, the disturbed home life, the beatings and brutal treatment the children had experienced, and the hatred many of them bore toward their parents. Many of these children were also found to be burdened with excessively high standards, leading to conflicts and feelings of inferiority, guilt, and inadequacy.

Apparently the effect of these undesirable parent-child relations is to prevent children from developing the ability to achieve satisfactory psychological adjustments to stress. This handicapping may, of course, result partially from constitutional inadequacies and may in turn reinforce any constitutional weakness; in any event, the final result is a psychologically handicapped person. As Escalona points out in her report on psychotic children:

One may say that they present a large variety of behavior pictures which in all cases lead to a generalized and far-reaching inadequacy on the part of the child. This inadequacy, whatever form it took, made it impossible for these children to cope with whatever life situations are ordinarily appropriate at a given age and under given environmental circumstances.

However, the question still remains as to how one child is seemingly able to surmount undesirable early conditions while another under comparable conditions becomes a psychotic casualty. Again the possibility of constitutional inadequacies reinforced by undesirable psychological factors appears relevant.

Trauma, frustration, conflict

Many individuals, though psychologically handicapped by faulty parent-child relations, manage to make successful adjustments in childhood and later life, as, for example, in cases where there is no severe trauma from social and other environmental experiences and where the life situation does not involve severe and prolonged conflicts. But in instances where the child's early experiences are severely traumatizing and where severe conflicts centering around sex, hostility, dependence, independence, and self-acceptance are aroused, the outlook is not so favorable.

Added to other conflicts and frustrations may be the terrifying experience of ego decompensation—of realizing that one is losing control of his thoughts and impulses, that he is

"losing his mind." Many patients state that this experience was one of the most traumatic of their entire lives. Since trauma, frustration, and conflict play such important roles in all mental disorders, we shall consider their specific significance in some detail in our discussion of the various psychoses.

Frustration and conflict Since the time of Bleuler there has been increasing agreement among psychiatrists and psychologists that schizophrenia is primarily the result of faulty responses to frustration and conflict. In the face of stress which the individual feels inadequate to cope with, he resorts to the extreme use of rationalization, projection, emotional insulation, fantasy, and other ego defensive measures. Below is a summary of Adolf Meyer's[1] conclusions concerning the development of this pattern.

In the process of personality development, the individual learns various methods of coping with his problems. Some of these methods involve dealing directly with life's problems and making the most effective adjustment to them that is possible. However, other adjustive reactions are in the nature of evasive substitutions—utilizing rationalization, projections, fantasy satisfactions, and emotional withdrawal and insulation. These evasive reactions inevitably lead to failure and self-devaluation which in turn makes their use even more necessary. Thus vicious habits of response become established which lead to a complete miscarriage of ego defenses—instead of helping the individual to adjust successfully, they actually make such an adjustment impossible.

The individual who later develops schizophrenia usually manifests an early withdrawal from a world he interprets as frustrating and hostile. This withdrawal is often concealed behind what seems to be an exemplary childhood, but which on closer examination reveals adherence to meekness and formally good behavior in order to avoid fights and struggles. Instead of participating in an active and healthy way in the activities of childhood, the individual withdraws behind a facade of goodness and meekness. This withdrawal, of course, inevitably leads to failures and disappointments which in turn serve to encourage further withdrawal from the world of real-

[1] H. A. Christian, *Psychiatry for Practitioners*, Oxford University Press, New York, 1936.

ity and foster the use of fantasy satisfactions to compensate for real life failures.

As this "good" child enters the adolescent period, he tends to be overly serious, painfully self-conscious, inhibited, and prone to prefer his own company. Often he is unduly preoccupied with various religious and philosophical issues. Normal interest in the opposite sex is lacking, and vivid ideas of the evilness of sexual behavior are usually only too apparent. As the adolescent enters the period of adulthood, with its demands for independency, responsibility, and family relationships, the youth's lack of adequate socialization and preparation for meeting these problems proves fatal. Instead of increased effort and a vigorous attack on the problems associated with the assumption of adult status, the youth finds the world unbearably hurtful and turns progressively inward to fantasy satisfactions.

It is out of this type of background that schizophrenic reactions develop. These reactions may be precipitated by the increased stress placed on the individual during the period of puberty and young adulthood, or by stresses occurring later in life. However, it is particularly in coping with the ordinary adolescent and young adult conflicts centering around dependency-independency problems and the handling of hostility and sexual drives that the insecure, withdrawn personality seems to get into serious difficulty. It is usually difficult for such an individual to enter into vigorous social competition for jobs and adult status. Rather he tends to find the competitive aspects of adult life terrifying and disillusioning; it seems much safer to maintain his childhood position of dependency upon the family. His whole problem is often complicated too by unrealistic levels of aspiration and altruistic ethical ideals to which he expects others to conform. Such a psychologically vulnerable individual is of course easily hurt by the inevitable setbacks and frustrations of adult life.

In the sexual sphere, his problems are usually complicated by his highly moralistic attitude toward sex and his failure to develop to a normal heterosexual level of adjustment. In general, his sexual behavior is relatively immature and undifferentiated. Usually he has had few if any sexual contacts with the other sex (it is not unusual to find schizophrenics over 30 years of age who have never even had a date). Even if he has been married and so

has had what appear to be more adequate sexual patterns, these are usually found on closer examination to have been hopelessly unsatisfactory and conducive to feelings of repugnance and guilt. As a result of his sexual immaturity, his sexual fantasies, like those of the early adolescent, may include a wide range of sexual objects, including members of the same sex. Since even heterosexual fantasies are considered immoral and unacceptable, it is not surprising that homosexual fantasies often lead to severe personality conflicts, to self-devaluation, and in some instances, as in paranoid schizophrenia, to the use of projection and other defense mechanisms for protecting the "self" against these immoral inner desires.

Homosexual fantasies, as well as overt homosexual behavior, involve far more males than is ordinarily realized, and need not lead to schizophrenia. They have a part in schizophrenia only in cases where the individual evaluates them as horribly immoral and repugnant. It is the resulting conflict and self-devaluation, rather than the homosexual fantasies or behavior, which lead to mental illness.

In a similar way, the handling of hostility is a particularly stressful problem for such an individual, because he usually considers it completely immoral and terribly dangerous. The hostility generated by his feelings of hurt and frustration is often more than he can bear, yet as a consequence of his withdrawal from normal social participation, he typically lacks any adequate comprehension of the role of hostility in normal everyday social relations. He does not know how to express it in socially acceptable ways and he is completely upset when he is the object of other people's hostility. Consequently he usually tries to repress his hostility and to deny even to himself that he is the kind of person who has such unacceptable impulses. The author is reminded here of a schizophrenic patient whose adjustment difficulties centered in part around his complete inability to express hostility. After several group therapy sessions, this patient proudly related to the group how for the first time in his life he had told a fellow who shoved in front of him in the cafeteria line to wait his turn.

As in the case of the neurotic, the schizophrenic's conflicts get him into a vicious circle. He withdraws from social participation because he is hurt and scared. But this withdrawal does not necessarily reduce his need or desire for social approval, status, and love. However, it does materially reduce his chances of gratifying these desires by removing him from the normal stream of social development and preventing him from acquiring the necessary attitudes and skills requisite to the attainment of his desires. Thus it can readily be seen that individuals who are severely sensitized to the hurts and frustrations of social relations, and who are handicapped by their subsequent withdrawal from the educative effects of normal social give and take, find the stress of young adulthood too much to handle. Studying the backgrounds of 341 schizophrenic patients treated in a combat zone during World War II Ripley and Wolf emphasized the importance of a "prominent lack of productive and satisfying relationships with other individuals and groups of individuals."

Disturbed family relations and early psychic trauma   This general developmental picture of schizophrenia as a failure in socialization with gradual accumulation of faulty attitudes and habits of reaction is supplemented by increasing evidence of early psychic wounds in schizophrenic patients. These wounds may be the result of specific episodes or of a long-term, unhealthy family pattern. Many take place in what seem to be exceptionally good homes, and often the parents are quite unaware of any trauma to the child. In a study of the parent-child relations of childhood schizophrenics, Kanner found that many of the parents were prominent, respected citizens of the community, but that toward their children they showed an almost complete lack of any real warmth.

Other studies have found the mothers of schizophrenic patients to by typically rejecting, overanxious, dominating, overpossessive, moralistic, and perfectionistic. Their children are infantilized and overprotected, while being made to feel that motherhood is martyrdom. Often combined with this are rigid, moralistic attitudes toward sexual behavior which make any evidence of such behavior on the part of their children especially horrifying to them and lead of course to serious sexual conflicts and accompanying self-devaluation for the children.

There are fewer studies on paternal atti-

tudes. They have generally revealed a somewhat inadequate, indifferent, or passive father or the loss of the father at an early age although paternal overprotection has also been noted. Several studies have also revealed serious disturbances in emotional relationships between the parents and a lack of coordination in parental control and guidance of the child.

These parental attitudes and home situations are of course not exclusive to the background of schizophrenia. The important point here seems to be the contribution which they make to the patterning of events that produces a "good" child who tends to be sensitive, rigid, unrealistic in his expectations, moralistic, and lacking in warmth, spontaneity, and good socialization. The schizophrenic process thus becomes a method of adjusting to an unbearably hurtful world—of protecting oneself against overwhelming feelings of helplessness and worthlessness.

Lack of reality checks   As we have seen, many schizophrenics are handicapped in their social development by oversolicitous, overprotective mothers. This, together with their early social withdrawal, has a variety of effects which are of developmental significance. Perhaps most important, these factors tend to cut him off from the normal activities of social reality testing—from social give and take—so that he tends to be passive and protected and fails to develop the necessary skills and emotional attitudes for healthy social participation. For example, in the matter of role playing, the schizophrenic is handicapped by a lack of social experience. We all model our behavior after that of others and attempt many roles which we test out in the group and either adopt as successful or discard. Since this eliminative process does not take place in the schizophrenic's social development, he may have very unrealistic ideas of the types of social roles that are open to him, and it may be easy to fantasy himself as a great religious savior or some other remarkable or unusual person.

Our self-evaluation is to a large extent determined by the way other people react to us. We gradually learn to see ourselves somewhat as others see us and to evaluate ourselves accordingly. However, the schizophrenic is handicapped by a lack of ability to see himself from the perspective of others; consequently his attitudes toward himself are apt to be fantasy ridden and distorted. The same point holds, of course, for his environmental attitudes, which suffer from the rigidity and lack of perspective of his own limited viewpoint, uncorrected by social experience.

Such a lack of constant reality checks in the development of a frame of reference would in itself make for an ever-widening breach between the schizophrenic and other people. As might be expected, his language and thought patterns become progressively more individualistic. He becomes "an emotional stranger in a strange land, with his own inner problems and conflicts dictating what he sees in the world around him. . . ."

Regression Considerable interest has been shown in the dynamics underlying the disorganization or disintegration of thought processes in schizophrenia. Kasanin, Goldstein, and others (Levy) have advanced the belief that in schizophrenia there is a reduction from conceptual thinking to a more primitive "concrete" thinking in which the individual is dominated by the external and internal stimuli acting upon him at the moment and reacts to parts of the perceptual field as if they were wholes. As a result of this "concrete" approach, the patient loses the normal demarcations between himself and the world, his words lose their usual representative character, and his perceptions no longer show the expected relation of parts to a whole. Kasanin attributes this concretization or fragmentation of thought processes to extreme regression to immature and childish levels of thinking.

Here Kasanin points out that the child lives in a world which is partly real and partly magic, and that he form all sorts of fantastic notions and ideas about the things around him. He tends to personify and vitalize inanimate objects and to endow them with various powers. He may also tend to feel that he is the center of the universe and to develop ideas of his own omnipotence. Also commonly found, according to Kasanin, is the belief that adults can read his thoughts.

Kasanin then attempts to relate many of the odd and bizarre delusions of schizophrenics to the magical thinking and other characteristics of children's thinking. For example, he points out that most schizophrenics at one time or another express ideas of omnipotence. This may be expressed by the patient who sits quietly in his chair with his index finger flexed in a certain way, afraid to change its position because the world would suddenly be destroyed if he moved. Similarly, many schizophrenics are convinced that other people can read their minds and know their thoughts. Everyone knows what they are thinking about, and when questioned by the psychiatrist, they may look at him in amusement and consider the whole thing a farce since he obviously knows their thoughts already without being told.

Ego defensive values of symptoms As we have noted, the emotional blunting and distortion in schizophrenic reactions protect the individual from the hurt of disappointment and frustration. Regression enables him to lower his level of aspiration and to accept a position of dependency. Projection helps him to maintain some semblance of ego integrity by placing the blame for his difficulties on others and attributing his own unacceptable desires to them. Wish-fulfilling fantasy enables him to achieve some measure of compensation for his feelings of inferiority and self-devaluation. In various combinations and degrees, these mechanisms seem to constitute the basic defensive framework of schizophrenic reactions.

In the exaggerated use of fantasy and projection, we find the two mechanisms which are most apt to lead to the development of delusions and hallucinations with their many ego defensive values. Delusions of influence enable the patient to blame others for causing his own inadmissible thoughts and behavior. Fantasies of being the focus of widespread interest and attention help the patient to compensate for feelings of isolation and lack of social recognition and status. Delusions of persecution explain away the patient's failure to achieve a satisfactory adjustment in the real world by placing the blame on his enemies. Delusions of grandeur and omnipotence may grow out of simple wishful thinking and may help to counteract feelings of inferiority and inadequacy by a sense of great personal worth and power.

Hallucinations in functional psychoses are interrelated with delusions and have similar dynamic functions. They are closely related to wishful thinking, the projection of unacceptable desires and impulses, feelings of unbearable guilt, and so on. Schizophrenic patients may speak to God and hear him confer great powers upon them and assign them the mission of saving the world. Or the patient with guilt feelings over homosexual thoughts may hear voices which accuse him of being a homosexual or of being guilty of other sexual misdeeds. Occasionally patients hallucinate sexual relations.

Of course, it may be noted that acutely disturbed patients may be so upset by their emotional conflicts that almost a delirious ideation occurs; here the delusions and hallucinations are part of a picture of acute mental turmoil in which their ego defensive value is greatly reduced or comes to be nonexistent.

Finally, the stereotypes and other symbolic behavior of the schizophrenic can also be understood in terms of the patient's mental processes and general reactive pattern. Thus the patient who thinks he is Christ may prostrate himself on the floor with his arms spread at right angles to form a cross, or dangerous obsessive desires may be counteracted by various magical rituals. Often the symbolism is by no means easy to fathom, but the study of it may be of value in furthering an understanding of apparently meaningless behavioral symptoms.

Selection **65**

EXPERIMENTAL DESENSITIZATION OF A PHOBIA*

PETER J. LANG
A. DAVID LAZOVIK
University of Pittsburgh

24 snake phobic Ss participated in an experimental investigation of systematic desensitization therapy. Ss who experienced desensitization showed a greater reduction in phobic behavior (as measured by avoidance behavior in the presence of the phobic object

and self-ratings) than did nonparticipating controls. Ss tended to hold or increase therapy gains at a 6-month follow-up evaluation, and gave no evidence of symptom substitution.

In recent years there has been increasing interest in the development of psychotherapeutic techniques based on learning theory models. These efforts are not limited to the translation of accepted psychotherapeutic practice into a laboratory language, in the manner of Shoben (1949) and Dollard and Miller (1950), but are attempts to extrapolate from laboratory findings to new methods of treatment. The most promising of these techniques with respect to clinical findings, is Wolpe's (1958) systematic desensitization therapy of phobic reactions. In a recent article Wolpe (1961) reported that desensitization was effective in the treatment of 35 of 39 phobic patients. Similar results have been reported by Lazarus (1961) utilizing group desensitization.

In a pilot project Lazovik and Lang (1960) demonstrated that desensitization could be successfully carried out under controlled laboratory conditions. This result opens the way not only to a more precise evaluation of treatment outcomes, but also makes it possible to test conflicting theories of the treatment process.

According to Wolpe (1958), desensitization is effective to the extent that subjects learn to make responses to phobic objects which reciprocally inhibit (are incompatible with) fear. Specifically, the treatment is designed to substitute muscular relaxation for anxiety. It is assumed that this process—not suggestion, "hello-goodbye" effects, or transference—is the agent of behavior change. It is further assumed that explorations with the patient of the genesis of the fear are not necessary to the elimination of a phobia. Wolpe proposes that the unlearning of a phobia follows the rules of what is generally called association learning theory. He therefore expects that therapy will be more difficult, the more generalized the anxiety response, but that "symptom substitution" is not a consequence of successful behavior therapy.

A very different set of predictions would be made by psychoanalytic therapists. This frame of reference expects little positive result unless the background of the phobia and its symbolic meaning, is elucidated and worked through with the subject. If this approach is not employed, only a temporary, "transference cure" may be anticipated. It is further assumed that the difficulty of the case is related to the importance of the symptom in the individual's "psychic economy," and that its temporary removal can only lead to the substitution of some new symptom.

The current experiment is designed to evaluate these two interpretations of desensitization therapy. The procedure developed previously (Lazovik & Lang, 1960), while it submits to the rigid control of the laboratory, is nevertheless sufficiently flexible that it can be employed in the treatment of actual phobic behavior. In this experiment snake phobic individuals served as subjects. This fear was chosen because it is frequent in a college population, approximately 3 in 100 students are to some degree snake phobic, and also because of the symbolic, sexual significance attributed to this fear by psychoanalytic theory (Fenichel, 1949, p. 49). The fact that snake phobias are held to reflect conflict in more fundamental systems of the personality, suggests that this is good ground for a stringent test of behavior therapy.

Specifically, the study is designed to: evaluate the changes in snake phobic behavior that occur over time, particularly the effects of repeated exposure to the phobic object; compare these changes with those that follow systematic desensitization therapy; determine the changes in behavior that are a direct function of the desensitization process, as opposed to the independent effects (when not part of desensitization) of hypnosis, training in deep muscle relaxation, and the establishment of a good patient-therapist relationship. In addition, an attempt is made to isolate factors which determine the success or failure of this method with individual subjects.

METHOD

Systematic desensitization

The experimental treatment consists of two sequential parts, training and desensitization proper (Lazovik & Lang, 1960). The former procedure requires five sessions of about 45 minutes each. At this time an *anxiety hierarchy* is constructed. This is a series of 20 situations involving the phobic object, which each subject grades from most to least

frightening. The actual items vary from subject to subject. However, the following scenes are typical: "writing the word snake," "snakes on display at the zoo (moving within a glass case)," "stepping on a dead snake accidentally."

The subject is then trained in deep muscle relaxation, following the method presented by Jacobson (1938). He is further instructed to practice relaxation 10–15 minutes per day at home. In the final phase of the training period the subject is introduced to hypnosis, and an effort is made to teach him to visualize vividly hypnotic scenes.

Following training, there are 11 45-minute sessions of systematic desensitization. In this, the subject learns to respond with relaxation to stimuli that originally evoked anxiety. At the beginning of the first session the subject is hypnotized and instructed to relax deeply. He is then told to imagine the hierarchy item which he previously rated as least distressing—the smallest "dose" of anxiety. If relaxation is undisturbed by this experience, the subsequent item is presented. Items which induce small amounts of anxiety are repeated, followed by deep relaxation, until the subject reports he is undisturbed by the scene. In this way successive items are presented from session to session. The goal of treatment is the presentation of the item originally ranked as most frightening without impairing the individual's calm state. At this point a new response (relaxation) has been attached to the imagined representative of the fear inducing stimulus, and clinicians working with the method assume that it will readily transfer to actual life situations.

In the experimental treatment described here, just these operations were carried out. No attempt was made to induce change through direct hypnotic suggestion, nor was an effort made to alter motivation. Subjects were informed that the experimenter was trying to evaluate a new method of treatment, and that he was much more interested in accurate findings than therapeutic successes. A majority of the therapist's actual verbalizations, as well as the step by step description of the training and desensitization procedures, was contained in a mimeographed program which guided the treatment of all subjects.

Subjects

A total of 24 subjects participated in this research. They were all college student volunteers, attending undergraduate psychology courses. The experimental groups included a total of four males and nine females. The control groups consisted of three males and eight females. None of these subjects presented evidence of a severe emotional disturbance on the basis of MMPI and interview data.

Subjects were selected on the basis of a classroom questionnaire which asked students to list their fears and rate them as mild, moderate, or intense. All subjects who participated in this experiment were afraid of nonpoisonous snakes, and rated this fear as "intense." Furthermore, the two authors interviewed all subjects who met this criterion. If despite the high self-rating on the screening questionnaire the subject's fear was judged to be weak, he was not asked to participate in the project. Subjects who formed the final experimental sample were characterized by most of the following behaviors: They reported somatic disturbance associated with the fear—"I feel sick to my stomach when I see one." "My palms get sweaty. I'm tense." They habitually avoided going anywhere near a live snake. They would not enter the reptile section of the zoo or walk through an open field. They became upset at seeing snakes at the motion pictures or on the television screen, and would leave, close their eyes, or turn off the set. Even pictures in magazines or artifacts such as a snake skin belt were capable of evoking discomfort in many of these subjects.

Measures of phobic behavior

All subjects filled out a Fear Survey Schedule (FSS) at the beginning and end of the experiment and again at a 6-month follow-up evaluation. The FSS is a list of 50 phobias each of which is rated by the subjects on a 7-point scale. An estimate was thus obtained not only of the subject's snake phobia, but of other related and unrelated fears.

A direct estimate of the subject's avoidance behavior was obtained by confronting him with the phobic object. The subject was informed that a nonpoisonous snake was confined in a glass case in a nearby laboratory. He was persuaded to enter the room and describe his reactions. The snake was confined at a point 15 feet from the entrance to the room. On entering the room with the subject, the experimenter walked to the case and removed the wire grill that covered the top. The subject was assured that the snake was harmless. The experimenter then requested that the subject come over and look down at the snake as he was doing. If the subject refused, he was asked to come as close as he felt he could and the distance was recorded. If the subject was able to come all the way to the case, he was asked to touch the animal (a 5-foot black snake) after he had seen the experimenter do

this. If the subject succeeded in this, the experimenter picked up the snake and invited the subject to hold it. After the avoidance test, the subject was asked to rate his anxiety on a 10-point "fear thermometer" (Walk, 1956). The subject's degree of anxiety was also rated on a 3-point scale by the experimenter.

In addition to the subjective scales and the avoidance test, all subjects were extensively interviewed concerning their fear. These interviews were tape recorded. The experimenter who conducted the interview and administered the avoidance test participated in no other phase of the project.[1]

PROCEDURE

Following an initial interview and the administration of Form A of the Stanford Hypnotic Susceptibility Scale (SHSS; Weitzenhoffer & Hilgard, 1959), subjects were placed in the experimental or control groups. Assignment was essentially random, although an effort was made to balance roughly these groups in terms of intensity of fear and motivation to participate in the experiment. All subjects were administered Form B of the SHSS when the experimental subjects completed the training period, and before desensitization began.

The basic plan of the study is described in Table 1. It consisted of two experimental and two control groups. The subgroups were created so that the effects of repeating the avoidance test, pretherapy training, and desensitization itself could be separately evaluated. Thus, the experimental groups E_1 and E_2 both experienced the laboratory analogue of desensitization therapy already described. However, subjects assigned to E_1 were administered the avoidance test before the training period, prior to desensitization, and again at the end of the experiment. E_2 subjects, on the other hand, were tested before desensitization and after, but did not participate in the initial evaluation. The control subjects did not participate in desensitization, but the C_1 and C_2 groups were evaluated at the same time as their opposite numbers in the experimental series. All available subjects were seen and evaluated 6 months after the termination of therapy.

Four replications of this experiment are reported here. They varied only in the therapists who were assigned to the experimental groups. Four experimental subjects and five controls participated in the

---

[1] The authors would like to thank David Reynolds, who acted as interviewer and conducted the snake avoidance test.

Table **1** | DESIGN OF THE EXPERIMENT, SHOW-
ING THE TIMES AT WHICH SUBJECTS
WERE EVALUATED (THE SNAKE AVOID-
ANCE TEST, EXPERIMENTER'S RATING,
FEAR THERMOMETER, AND TAPED IN-
TERVIEW)

Group	Experimental procedures				
E_1	Test 1	Training	Test 2	Desensitization	Test 3
E_2		Training	Test 2	Desensitization	Test 3
C_1	Test 1	—	Test 2	—	Test 3
C_2		—	Test 2	—	Test 3

first replication. The authors each saw two of the experimental subjects. In the second, third and fourth replications (which included three, four, and two experimental subjects and two, three, and one control subjects, respectively) three other therapists participated.[2] While two of these individuals are engaged in full-time private practice, they had never before attempted desensitization therapy. The third therapist was an advanced clinical graduate student, who also had his initial experience with the desensitization method in this project.

RESULTS

Avoidance test

The results of this test were evaluated in two ways: an absolute criterion in which touching or holding the snake constituted a test pass, and scale scores based on the subject's distance in feet from the snake. Table 2 presents the number of subjects from the separate experimental and control groups who met the former criterion.

Note that the reliability of this test is high. The control subjects show no appreciable change, even with three exposures to the snake. Furthermore, the pretherapy training period does not affect the performance of the experimental subjects: no more E_1 subjects pass at Test 2 than at Test 1. However, following therapy, the incidence of test passes goes up significantly in the experimental group. The percentage of increase from Test 2 to Test 3

[2] The authors would like to thank Robert Romano, Richard Miller, and James Geer, who participated as therapists in this project.

yielded a t of 2.30, $p < .05$. A similar test of the control subjects was not significant.[3]

The above analysis does not, of course, measure subtle changes in behavior. In an attempt to increase the sensitivity of the avoidance test, subjects were assigned scores on a 19-point scale which roughly corresponded to their closest approach in feet to the phobic object. Holding the animal was equal to a scale score of 1; touching, 2; the 1-foot mark, 3; 2 feet, 4; and so on up to a score of 19 for subjects who refused to go to the testing room. The correlation between the first two presentations of the avoidance test ($N = 19$) yielded an r of $+ .63$.[4] Although this statistic suggests some degree of reliability, nothing is known about the relative distance between values at different places on the scale. The control sample employed in the experiment is too small to make an adequate analysis. Nevertheless, it is logical that the probability of a positive increase in approach lessens the closer the subject is to the phobic

Table **2** | NUMBER OF SUBJECTS WHO HELD OR
TOUCHED THE SNAKE DURING THE
AVOIDANCE TEST

Group	N	Test 1	Test 2	Test 3
E_1	8	1	1	5
E_2	5	—	1	2
C_1	5	0	0	0
C_2	6	—	1	2
E_1 and E_2	13		2	7
C_1 and C_2	11		1	2

[3] A live snake varies to some extent in activity, and this appears to be related to its effectiveness as a stimulus. In order to determine whether this factor influenced our results, the experimental assistant's ratings of the snake's activity during tests of the control and experimental subjects were subjected to a t test. No significant difference in snake activity between two groups was found.
[4] The sample ($N = 19$) used in estimating the reliability of the avoidance scale and the other fear measures includes the members of the control sample plus the eight subjects of the E_1 group. Although the training period does intervene between the first and second presentations of the fear measures for the E_1 group, it appears to have no appreciable effect on the phobia. The E_2 subjects could not, of course, be included in a reliability estimate, as actual therapy intervenes between the first and second fear evaluation.

object, i.e., movement from a score of 15 to 12 is more likely or easier than movement from a scale score of 4 (2 feet away) to a score of 1 (holding a live snake). Thus, a simple difference score does not appear to be the best estimate of change.

The change score used in the following analysis was the difference between pre- and posttherapy scale scores divided by the pretherapy score. For example, a subject who achieved a scale score of 12 on Test 2 and a score of 5 on Test 3 was assigned a change score of .58—the solution to the equation:

$$\text{change score} = \frac{12 - 5}{12}$$

The mean change score of the first two avoidance tests ($N = 19$) was only + .03. This suggests that the score has considerable stability, and tends to minimize chance fluctuations. The mean change scores for the experimental and control subjects from Test 2 to Test 3 may be found in Table 3. Note that the Mann-Whitney U test of the difference between groups is significant.

Fear thermometer and the FSS snake item

The correlation between the first two tests for the reliability sample ($N = 19$) was $r = + .75$. The average difference score (obtained by subtracting the second fear thermometer score from the first) was only + .63. As in the case of the avoidance test, no significant change was associated with the pretherapy training period. The mean difference score for the E_1 group from Test 1 to Test 2 was + .38, less than the group mean cited above.

The difference between Test 2 and Test 3 scores for the experimental and control groups are presented at the top of Table 4. While

Table **3** | MEAN SNAKE AVOIDANCE SCALE SCORES AT TEST 2 AND 3, MEAN CHANGE SCORES AND THE MANN-WHITNEY U TEST

Group	Test 2	Test 3	Change score	U
Experimental	5.35	4.42	.34	34.5*
Control	6.51	7.73	−.19	

* $p < .05$.

Table **4** | MEAN RATING SCALE MEASURES OF PHOBIC BEHAVIOR BEFORE (TEST 2) AND AFTER (TEST 3) DESENSITIZATION THERAPY

Group	Test 2	Test 3	Difference
	Fear thermometer		
Experimental	7.62	5.15	2.47
Control	6.45	5.45	1.00
	FSS-subject's rating of snake fear		
	Test 1[a]	Test 3	Difference
Experimental	6.69	5.31	1.38
Control	6.27	5.73	.54

[a] The FSS was not administered at Test 2. The difference score is between a pretherapy interview and Test 3.

the therapy groups show a greater mean change than the control subjects, this difference did not attain statistical significance on the Mann-Whitney U test. The same trend and statistical findings were obtained for the snake item on the FSS. The experimenter's rating of the subject's level of anxiety during the avoidance test did not differentiate between experimental and control groups. In this case, the failure to discriminate may be attributed to the selection, prior to the experiment, of a 3-point rating scale. The experimenter reported that this measure was too gross for the behavior under observation.

Follow-up study

All subjects who were still available ($N = 20$) were re-evaluated approximately 6 months after the experiment was completed. This included 11 members of the original experimental group, 6 of whom touched or held the snake at the final avoidance test. Two of these subjects no longer met this criterion 6 months later. However, neither subject indicated an increase in self-rated fear and one actually showed improvement on this dimension. Furthermore, because of gains by others, the mean avoidance test change score for the entire experimental group indicates a slight reduction in phobic behavior from Test 3 to the 6-month follow up.

The therapy group showed even greater gains on the fear thermometer. The increase

Table **5** | AVOIDANCE TEST BEHAVIOR CHANGE FROM TEST 2 TO TEST 3 FOR THERAPY SUBJECTS WHO COMPLETED MORE THAN 15 HIERARCHY ITEMS, FOR THOSE WHO COMPLETED LESS THAN 15, AND FOR THE MANN-WHITNEY U TEST

Number of hierarchy items successfully completed	Test 2	Test 3	Change score	U
	Snake avoidance scale			
More than 15[a]	6.71	3.93	.49	5.0**
Less than 15[b]	4.17	5.00	−.07	
	Fear thermometer			
More than 15[a]	7.57	4.00	3.57	8.0*
Less than 15[b]	7.67	6.50	1.17	

Note.—All scores are mean values.
[a] $N = 7$.
[b] $N = 6$.
* $p < .08$.
** $p < .03$.

was sufficient that the difference between experimental and control subjects from Test 2 to the follow up was statistically significant ($U = 16.5$, $p < .05$). Subjects who had experienced therapy also showed a significant reduction in their overall estimate of the intensity of their phobia as measured by the snake item of the FSS. The change in this score from pretherapy to the 6-month follow up was significantly greater for experimental than control subjects ($U = 8.5$, $p < .02$).

Therapy terminated and unterminated

The design of the current experiment arbitrarily limited therapy to 11 sessions. This resulted in subjects being tested for change at varying points in the therapeutic process. Fortunately, in desensitization therapy it is possible to define a subject's degree of progress by referring to the number of hierarchy items successfully completed. It will be recalled that all subjects started with a 20-item hierarchy. This represented the combined efforts of the therapist and the subject to build an equal-interval scale, extending from a remote point where the subject felt little or no fear to a maximum fear involving close contact with the offending object. Normally, therapy would be terminated when the twentieth item had been passed. In

the present experiment four subjects achieved this goal. Seven subjects completed 16 or more items and six subjects completed 14 or less items.

All subjects who completed their hierarchies touched or held the snake at the final avoidance test. Furthermore, subjects who completed over 15 items ($N = 7$) showed significant improvement on nearly all measures employed in this experiment: subjects who completed under 15 items differed little from controls. Table 5 presents the difference between the two therapy groups on the snake avoidance scale and the fear thermometer. Note that the improvement of the over 15 items group is significantly greater than that of subjects completing less than 15 items. Similar results were obtained for the FSS snake item and they are presented in Table 6. Note in this same table that the mean rank of the FSS also shows a significantly greater reduction in the over 15 items group, than in the group completing fewer items. This finding suggests that the elimination of snake phobic behavior does not initiate an increase in other fears, but in fact leads to a significant reduction in overall anxiety.

Table **6** | CHANGES IN THE FEAR SURVEY SCHEDULE (FSS) FOLLOWING DESENSITIZATION THERAPY FOR SUBJECTS WHO COMPLETED MORE THAN 15 HIERARCHY ITEMS, FOR THOSE WHO COMPLETED LESS THAN 15, AND FOR THE MANN-WHITNEY U TEST

Number of hierarchy items successfully completed	Pre-therapy	Post-therapy	Difference	U
	Fear survey schedule			
More than 15[a]	2.34	1.85	.49	4.5*
Less than 15[b]	3.21	3.20	.01	
	FSS-subject's rating of snake fear			
More than 15[a]	6.71	4.14	2.57	3.0**
Less than 15[b]	6.67	6.67	0.00	

Note.—All scores are mean ranks or mean rank differences.
[a] $N = 7$.
[b] $N = 6$.
* $p < .02$.
** $p < .01$.

DISCUSSION

The results of the present experiment demonstrate that the experimental analogue of desensitization therapy effectively reduces phobic behavior. Both subjective rating of fear and overt avoidance behavior were modified, and gains were maintained or increased at the 6-month follow up. The results of objective measures were in turn supported by extensive interview material. Close questioning could not persuade any of the experimental subjects that a desire to please the experimenter had been a significant factor in their change. Furthermore, in none of these interviews was there any evidence that other symptoms appeared to replace the phobic behavior.

The fact that no significant change was associated with the pretherapy training argues that hypnosis and general muscle relaxation were not in themselves vehicles of change.[5] Similarly, the basic suggestibility of the subjects must be excluded. The difference between the SHSS Form A scores of the experimental and control groups did not approach statistical significance ($U = 58$). Clearly, the responsibility for the reduction in phobic behavior must be assigned to the desensitization process itself. This is evidenced not only by the differences between experimental and control subjects but also by the relationship within the experimental groups between degree of change and the number of hierarchy items successfully completed.

One must still raise the question, however, why desensitization therapy could be accomplished in 11 sessions with some subjects and barely gotten underway with others. The intensity of the phobia is obviously not a relevant factor. The mean avoidance Test 2 score is actually higher for the experimental subjects who completed more than 15 items than for those who completed less (see Table 5). The base FSS snake item rank and the fear thermometer scores are almost exactly the same in both

groups. On the other hand, a negative relationship ($r = -\ .58$) exists between the total FSS score at the first testing and the number of hierarchy items completed by individual members of the experimental group. The FSS is in turn positively related to the Taylor (1953) Manifest Anxiety (*MA*) scale ($r = +\ .80$ for the experimental group). Thus, the degree of progress attained in therapy in a constant period of time (11 sessions) appears to be a function of generalized anxiety, as measured by both the *MA* scale and FSS. These data suggest that desensitization therapy is more difficult, or at least slower, when many stimuli in the subject's environment are capable of eliciting anxiety responses. This is of course consistent with the clinical findings of Wolpe (1958) and the prediction of a learning theory model.

The present experiment also reveals an interesting connection between changes in overt avoidance behavior and the subject's verbal report. The relationship between these two dimensions is generally positive. However, even when precisely the same event is being evaluated, it is sometimes surprisingly low (Test 3 avoidance scale and fear thermometer $r = +\ .40$). Furthermore, initial changes in phobic behavior seem to occur in either one dimension or the other, rather than in both simultaneously. Most frequently subjective report lags behind overt behavior. Thus, avoidance test scores differentiated between experimental and control subjects immediately following the experiment, but it was not until the follow-up interview that the subjective scales yielded the same finding. It will be interesting to observe in future studies if this pattern continues, and to what extent it is characteristic of any reduction in phobic behavior, or simply a function of the desensitization technique.

The question of whether learning theory, specifically counterconditioning, best explains the desensitization process is not completely answerable by the present investigation. Certainly the theory is consistent with the results, and some of the other possible explanations have been eliminated. However, further research, particularly the direct measurement of changes in muscular tension during the presentation of hierarchy items, is necessary to an evaluation of theory.

---

[5] While these findings indicate that hypnotizing subjects or training them in muscle relaxation are not effective independent of desensitization, we do not yet know if they are a necessary part of the desensitization process, itself. Research currently underway, in which these procedures are included or omitted in different therapy groups, is designed to answer this important question.

But of the greatest immediate interest are the implications of the present research for traditional theories of clinical practice. The findings suggest the following important conclusions:

1. It is not necessary to explore with a subject the factors contributing to the learning of a phobia or its "unconscious meaning" in order to eliminate the fear behavior.
2. The form of treatment employed here does not lead to symptom substitution or create new disturbances of behavior.
3. In reducing phobic behavior it is not necessary to change basic attitudes, values, or attempt to modify the "personality as a whole." The unlearning of phobic behavior appears to be analogous to the elimination of other responses from a subject's behavior repertoire.

REFERENCES

Dollard, J., & Miller, N. E. *Personality and psychotherapy: An analysis in terms of learning, thinking and culture.* New York: McGraw-Hill, 1950.

Fenichel, O. *The psychoanalytic theory of neurosis.* New York: Norton, 1945.

Jacobson, E. *Progressive relaxation.* Chicago: Univer. Chicago Press, 1938.

Lazarus, A. A. Group therapy of phobic disorders by systematic desensitization. *J. abnorm. soc. Psychol.,* 1961, **63**, 504–510.

Lazovik, A. D., & Lang, P. J. A laboratory demonstration of systematic desensitization psychotherapy. *J. psychol. Stud.,* 1960, **11**, 238–247.

Shoben, E. J. Psychotherapy as a problem in learning theory. *Psychol. Bull.,* 1949, **46**, 366–392.

Taylor, Janet A. A personality scale of manifest anxiety. *J. abnorm. soc. Psychol.,* 1953, **48**, 285–290.

Walk, R. D. Self ratings of fear in a fear-invoking situation. *J. abnorm. soc. Psychol.,* 1956, **52**, 171–178.

Weitzenhoffer, A. M., & Hilgard, E. R. *Stanford Hypnotic Susceptibility Scale.* Palo Alto, Calif.: Consulting Psychologists Press, 1959.

Wolpe, J. *Psychotherapy by reciprocal inhibition.* Stanford: Stanford Univer. Press, 1958.

Wolpe, J. The systematic desensitization treatment of neuroses. *J. nerv. ment. Dis.,* 1961, **132**, 189–203.

Selection **66** | CULTURE AND NEUROSIS*

KAREN HORNEY
New York City

In the psychoanalytic concept of neuroses a shift of emphasis has taken place: whereas originally interest was focused on the dramatic symptomatic picture, it is now being realized more and more that the real source of these psychic disorders lies in character disturbances, that the symptoms are a manifest result of conflicting character traits, and that without uncovering and straightening out the neurotic character structure we cannot cure a neurosis. When analyzing these character traits, in a great many cases one is struck by the observation that, in marked contrast to the divergency of the symptomatic pictures, character difficulties invariably center around the same basic conflicts.

These similarities in the content of conflicts present a problem. They suggest, to minds open to the importance of cultural implications, the question of whether and to what extent neuroses are moulded by cultural processes in essentially the same way as "normal" character formation is determined by these influences; and, if so, how far such a concept would necessitate certain modifications in Freud's views of the relation between culture and neurosis.

In the following remarks I shall try to outline roughly some characteristics typically recurring in all our neuroses. The limitations of time will allow us to present neither data—good case histories—nor method, but only results. I shall try to select from the extremely complex and diversified observational material the essential points.

There is another difficulty in the presentation. I wish to show how these neurotic persons are trapped in a vicious circle. Unable to present in detail the factors leading up to the vicious circle, I must start rather arbitrarily with one of the outstanding features, although this in itself is already a complex product of several interrelated, developed mental factors. I start, therefore, with the problem of competition.

* From Karen Horney, "Culture and Neurosis," *American Sociological Review,* 1:221–235, 1936. Reprinted by permission of the publisher.

The problem of competition, or rivalry, appears to be a never-failing center of neurotic conflicts. How to deal with competition presents a problem for everyone in our culture; for the neurotic, however, it assumes dimensions which generally surpass actual vicissitudes. It does so in three respects:

1. There is a constant measuring-up with others, even in situations which do not call for it. While striving to surpass others is essential for all competitive situations, the neurotic measures up even with persons who are in no way potential competitors and have no goal in common with him. The question as to who is the more intelligent, more attractive, more popular, is indiscriminately applied towards everyone.

2. The content of neurotic ambitions is not only to accomplish something worth while, or to be successful, but to be absolutely best of all. These ambitions, however, exist in fantasy mainly—fantasies which may or may not be conscious. The degree of awareness differs widely in different persons. The ambitions may appear in occasional flashes of fantasy only. There is never a clear realization of the powerful dramatic role these ambitions play in the neurotic's life, or of the great part they have in accounting for his behavior and mental reactions. The challenge of these ambitions is not met by adequate efforts which might lead to realization of the aims. They are in queer contrast to existing inhibitions towards work, towards assuming leadership, towards all means which would effectually secure success. There are many ways in which these fantastic ambitions influence the emotional lives of the persons concerned: by hypersensitivity to criticism, by depressions or inhibitions following failures, etc. These failures need not necessarily be real. Everything which falls short of the realization of the grandiose ambitions is felt as failure. The success of another person is felt as one's own failure.

This competitive attitude not only exists in reference to the external world, but is also internalized, and appears as a constant measuring-up to an ego-ideal. The fantastic ambitions appear on this score as excessive and rigid demands towards the self, and failure in living up to these demands produces depressions and irritations similar to those produced in competition with others.

3. The third characteristic is the amount of hostility involved in neurotic ambition. While intense competition implicitly contains elements of hostility—the defeat of a competitor meaning victory for oneself—the reactions of neurotic persons are determined by an insatiable and irrational expectation that no one in the universe other than themselves should be intelligent, influential, attractive, or popular. They become infuriated, or feel their own endeavors condemned to futility, if someone else writes a good play or a scientific paper or plays a prominent role in society. If this attitude is strongly accentuated, one may observe in the analytical situation, for example, that these patients regard any progress made as a victory on the part of the analyst, completely disregarding the fact that progress is of vital concern to their own interests. In such situations they will disparage the analyst, betraying, by the intense hostility displayed, that they feel endangered in a position of paramount importance to themselves. They are as a rule completely unaware of the existence and intensity of this "no one but me" attitude, but one may safely assume and eventually always uncover this attitude from reactions observable in the analytical situation, as indicated above.

This attitude easily leads to a fear of retaliation. It results in a fear of success and also in a fear of failure: "If I want to crush everyone who is successful, then I will automatically assume identical reactions in others, so that the way to success implies exposing me to the hostility of others. Furthermore: if I make any move towards this goal and fail, then I shall be crushed." Success thus becomes a peril and any possible failure becomes a danger which must at all costs be avoided. From the point of view of all these dangers it appears much safer to stay in the corner, be modest and inconspicuous. In other and more positive terms, this fear leads to a definite recoiling from any aim which implies competition. This safety device is assured by a constant, accurately working process of automatic self-checking.

This self-checking process results in inhibitions, particularly inhibitions towards work, but also towards all steps necessary to the pursuit of one's aims, such as seizing opportunities, or revealing to others that one has certain goals or capacities. This eventually results in an incapacity to stand up for one's own wishes. The peculiar nature of these inhibitions is best demonstrated by the fact that these persons may be quite capable of fighting for the needs of others or for an impersonal cause. They will, for instance, act like this:

When playing an instrument with a poor partner, they will instinctively play worse than he, although otherwise they may be very competent. When discussing a subject with someone less intelligent than themselves, they will compulsively descend below his level. They will prefer to be in the rank and file, not to be identified with the superiors, not even to get an increase in salary, rationalizing this attitude in some way. Even their dreams will be dictated by this need for reassurance. Instead of utilizing the liberty of a dream to imagine themselves in glorious situations, they will actually see themselves, in their dreams, in humble or even humiliating situations.

This self-checking process does not restrict itself to activities in the pursuit of some aim, but going beyond that, tends to undermine the self-confidence, which is a prerequisite for any accomplishment, by means of self-belittling. The function of self-belittling in this context is to eliminate oneself from any competition. In most cases these persons are not aware of actually disparaging themselves, but are aware of the results only as they feel themselves inferior to others and take for granted their own inadequacy.

The presence of these feelings of inferiority is one of the most common psychic disorders of our time and culture. Let me say a few more words about them. The genesis of inferiority feelings is not always in neurotic competition. They present complex phenomena and may be determined by various conditions. But that they do result from, and stand in the service of, a recoiling from competition, is a basic and ever-present implication. They result from a recoiling inasmuch as they are the expression of a discrepancy between high-pitched ideals and real accomplishment. The fact, however, that these painful feelings at the same time fulfill the important function of making secure the recoiling attitude itself becomes evident through the vigor with which this position is defended when attacked. Not only will no evidence of competence or attractiveness ever convince these persons, but they may actually become scared or angered by any attempt to convince them of their positive qualities.

The surface pictures resulting from this situation may be widely divergent. Some persons appear thoroughly convinced of their unique importance and may be anxious to demonstrate their superiority on every occasion, but betray their insecurity in an excessive sensitivity to every criticism, to every dissenting opinion, or every lack of responsive admiration. Others are just as thoroughly convinced of their incompetence or unworthiness, or of being unwanted or unappreciated; yet they betray their actually great demands in that they react with open or concealed hostility to every frustration of their unacknowledged demands. Still others will waver constantly in their self-estimation between feeling themselves all-important and feeling, for instance, honestly amazed that anyone pays any attention to them.

If you have followed me thus far, I can now proceed to outline the particular vicious circle in which these persons are moving. It is important here, as in every complex neurotic picture, to recognize the vicious circle, because, if we overlook it and simplify the complexity of the processes going on by assuming a simple cause-effect relation, we either fail to get an understanding of the emotions involved, or attribute an undue importance to some one cause. As an example of this error, I might mention regarding a highly emotion-charged rivalry attitude as derived directly from rivalry with the father. Roughly, the vicious circle looks like this:

The failures, in conjunction with a feeling of weakness and defeat, lead to a feeling of envy towards all persons who are more successful, or merely more secure or better contented with life. This envy may be manifest or it may be repressed under the pressure of the same anxiety which led to a repression of, and a recoiling from, rivalry. It may be entirely wiped out of consciousness and represented by the substitution of a blind admiration; it may be kept from awareness by a disparaging attitude towards the person concerned. Its effect, however, is apparent in the incapacity to grant to others what one has been forced to deny oneself. At any rate, no matter to what degree the envy is repressed or expressed, it implies an increase in the existing hostility against people and consequently an increase in the anxiety, which now takes the particular form of an irrational fear of the envy of others.

The irrational nature of this fear is shown in two ways: (1) it exists regardless of the presence or absence of envy in the given situation; and (2) its intensity is out of proportion to the dangers menacing from the side of the envious competitors. This irrational side of the fear of envy always remains unconscious, at least in non-psychotic persons, therefore it is never corrected by a reality-testing process, and is all the more effective in the direction of reinforcing the existing tendencies to recoil.

Consequently the feeling of own insignificance grows, the hostility against people grows, and the anxiety grows. We thus return to the beginning, because now the fantasies come up, with about this content: "I wish I were more powerful, more attractive, more intelligent than all the others, then I should be safe, and besides, I could defeat them and step on them." Thus we see an ever-increasing deviation of the ambitions towards the stringent, fantastic, and hostile.

This pyramiding process may come to a standstill under various conditions, usually at an inordinate expense in loss of expansiveness and vitality. There is often some sort of resignation as to personal ambitions, in turn permitting the diminution of anxieties as to competition, with the inferiority feelings and inhibitions continuing.

It is now time, however, to make a reservation. It is in no way self-evident that ambition of the "no-one-but-me" type must necessarily evoke anxieties. There are persons quite capable of brushing aside or crushing everyone in the way of their ruthless pursuit of personal power. The question then is: Under what special condition is anxiety invoked in neurotically competitive people?

The answer is that they at the same time want to be loved. While most persons who pursue an asocial ambition in life care little for the affection or the opinion of others, the neurotics, although possessed by the same kind of competitiveness, simultaneously have a boundless craving for affection and appreciation. Therefore, as soon as they make any move towards self-assertion, competition, or success, they begin to dread losing the affection of others, and must automatically check their aggressive impulses. This conflict between ambition and affection is one of the gravest and most typical dilemmas of the neurotics of our time.

Why are these two incompatible strivings so frequently present in the same individual? They are related to each other in more than one way. The briefest formulation of this relationship would perhaps be that they both grow out of the same sources, namely, anxieties, and they both serve as a means of reassurance against the anxieties. Power and affection may both be safeguards. They generate each other, check each other, and reinforce each other. These interrelations can be observed most accurately within the analytic situation, but sometimes are obvious from only a casual knowledge of the life history.

In the life history may be found, for instance, an atmosphere in childhood lacking in warmth and reliability, but rife with frightening elements—battles between the parents, injustice, cruelty, oversolicitousness—generation of an increased need for affection—disappointments—development of an outspoken competitiveness—inhibition—attempts to get affection on the basis of weakness, helplessness, or suffering. We sometimes hear that a youngster has suddenly turned to ambition after an acute disappointment in his need for affection, and then given up the ambition on falling in love.

Particularly when the expansive and aggressive desires have been severely curbed in early life by a forbidding atmosphere, the excessive need for reassuring affection will play a major role. As a guiding principle for behavior this implies a yielding to the wishes or opinions of others rather than asserting one's own wishes or opinions; an overvaluation of the significance for one's own life of expressions of fondness from others, and a dependence on such expressions. And similarly, it implies an overvaluation of signs of rejection and a reacting to such signs with apprehension and defensive hostility. Here again a vicious circle begins easily and reinforces the single elements: In diagram it looks somewhat like this:

Anxiety plus repressed hostility
  ↘Need for reassuring affection
    ↘Anticipation of, sensitivity to, rejection
     ↘Hostile reactions to feeling rejected

These reactions explain why emotional contact with others that is attained on the basis of anxiety can be at best only a very shaky and easily shattered bridge between individuals, and why it always fails to bring them out of their emotional isolation. It may, however, serve to cope with anxieties and even get one through life rather smoothly, but only at the expense of growth and personality development, and only if circumstances are quite favorable.

Let us ask now, which special features in our culture may be responsible for the frequent occurrence of the neurotic structures just described?

We live in a competitive, individualistic culture. Whether the enormous economic and technical achievements of our culture were and are possible only on the basis of the competitive principle is a question for the economist or sociologist to decide. The psychologist, however, can evaluate the personal price we have paid for it.

It must be kept in mind that competition not only is a driving force in economic activities, but that it also pervades our personal life in every respect. The character of all our human relationships is moulded by a more or less outspoken competition. It is effective in the family between siblings, at school, in social relations (keeping up with the Joneses), and in love life.

In love, it may show itself in two ways: the genuine erotic wish is often overshadowed or replaced by the merely competitive goal of being the most popular, having the most dates, love letters, lovers, being seen with the most desirable man or woman. Again, it may pervade the love relationship itself. Marriage partners, for example, may be living in an endless struggle for supremacy, with or without being aware of the nature or even of the existence of this combat.

The influence on human relations of this competitiveness lies in the fact that it creates easily aroused envy towards the stronger ones, contempt for the weaker, distrust towards everyone. In consequence of all these potentially hostile tensions, the satisfaction and reassurance which one can get out of human relations are limited and the individual becomes more or less emotionally isolated. It seems that here, too, mutually reinforcing interactions take place, so far as insecurity and dissatisfaction in human relations in turn compel people to seek gratification and security in ambitious strivings, and vice versa.

Another cultural factor relevant to the structure of our neurosis lies in our attitude toward failure and success. We are inclined to attribute success to good personal qualities and capacities, such as competence, courage, enterprise. In religious terms this attitude was expressed by saying that success was due to God's grace. While these qualities may be effective—and in certain periods, such as the pioneer days, may have represented the only conditions necessary—this ideology omits two essential facts: (1) that the possibility for success is strictly limited; even external conditions and personal qualities being equal, only a comparative few can possibly attain success; and (2) that other factors than those mentioned may play the decisive role, such as, for example, unscrupulousness or fortuitous circumstances. Inasmuch as these factors are overlooked in the general evaluation of success, failures, besides putting the person concerned in a factually disadvantageous position, are bound to reflect on his self-esteem.

The confusion involved in this situation is enhanced by a sort of double moral. Although, in fact, success meets with adoration almost without regard to the means employed in securing it, we are at the same time taught to regard modesty and an undemanding, unselfish attitude as social or religious virtues, and are rewarded for them by praise and affection. The particular difficulties which confront the individual in our culture may be summarized as follows: for the competitive struggle he needs a certain amount of available aggressiveness; at the same time, he is required to be modest, unselfish, even self-sacrificing. While the competitive life situation with the hostile tensions involved in it creates an enhanced need of security, the chances of attaining a feeling of safety in human relations—love, friendship, social contacts—are at the same time diminished. The estimation of one's personal value is all too dependent on the degree of success attained, while at the same time the possibilities for success are limited and the success itself is dependent, to a great extent, on fortuitous circumstances or on personal qualities of an asocial character.

Perhaps these sketchy comments have suggested to you the direction in which to explore the actual relationship of our culture to our personality and its neurotic deviations. Let us now consider the relation of this conception to the views of Freud on culture and neurosis.

The essence of Freud's views on this subject can be summarized, briefly, as follows: Culture is the result of a sublimation of biologically given sexual and aggressive drives—"sexual" in the extended connotation Freud has given the term. Sublimation presupposes unwitting suppression of these instinctual drives. The more complete the suppression of these drives, the higher the cultural development. As the capacity for sublimating is limited, and as the intensive suppression of primitive drives without sublimation may lead to neurosis, the growth of civilization must inevitably imply a growth of neurosis. Neuroses are the price humanity has to pay for cultural development.

The implicit theoretical presupposition underlying this train of thought is the belief in the existence of biologically determined human nature, or, more precisely, the belief that oral, anal, genital, and aggressive drives exist in all human beings in approximately equal quantities. Variations in character formation from individual to individual, as from culture to culture, are due, then, to the varying intensity of the suppression required, with the addition that this suppression can affect the different kinds of drives in varying degrees.

This viewpoint of Freud's seems actually to encounter difficulties with two groups of data. (1) Historical and anthropological findings do not support the assumption that the growth of civilization is in a direct ratio to the growth of instinct suppression. (2) Clinical experience of the kind indicated in this paper suggests that neurosis is due not simply to the quantity of suppression of one or the other instinctual drives, but rather to difficulties caused by the conflicting character of the demands which a culture imposes on its individuals. The differences in neuroses typical of different cultures may be understood to be conditioned by the amount and quality of conflicting demands within the particular culture.

In a given culture, those persons are likely to become neurotic who have met these culturally determined difficulties in accentuated form, mostly through the medium of childhood experiences; and who have not been able to solve their difficulties, or have solved them only at great expense to personality.

COGENT
COMMENTARIES

14

It should be obvious that many of the significant statements made by psychologists cannot be easily pressed into the biological, psychological, and sociocultural determinants which comprise the structure of this book. Thus in order to add breadth and depth to the book, the first and last chapters have departed from this format.

One could view the statements by Skinner, Koch, Osgood, and Rogers (Selections 68 through 71, respectively) as implying, directly or indirectly, their positions on what psychology is or should be. Skinner's radical Behavorism is a philosophy of psychology which is directly descended from Watson. Charles Osgood argues for application of principles of social psychology and psychodynamics to the reduction of tension in international affairs. This view is consistant with the Functionalist tradition, which continually strove to broaden the scope of psychology to include any effort to understand and modify man's adaptation to his environment. In a similar vein, Carl Rogers would opt for a psychology which is considerably more broad and less preoccupied with "scientism" (Dyal, Selection 76) than that advocated by Skinner. And Sigmund Koch takes psychology to task for not dealing with those aspects of behavior which are of humanistic import. Another paper which will be of interest to the serious student of behavioral science is Selection 75, in which Dr. Martin T. Orne discusses some important variables which may contaminate the results of psychological experiments.

Since the vast majority of students who take introductory psychology do so as a part of a general liberal arts requirement and are not psychology majors, it seems appropriate to show how psychology is relevant to other academic disciplines. It is felt that many of the selections in this chapter serve the purpose of "breadth" as well as "depth." For example, Skinner's radical Behavorism has direct implications for biology, sociology, political science, and economics. The selection by Koch shows how psychology is intimately related to both the physical sciences and the humanities. The philosophy major should find Rogers' discussion of values immediately relevant to ethics; and, of course, the premed student is obliged by Szasz (Selection 72), Cole (Selection 73), Kretch et al. (Selection 74), and Dyal (Selection 76) to consider some issues which are basic to medicine. Political science and international affairs students should prove to be capable discussants of Osgood's paper on the foreign policy alternatives from the point of view of a psychologist. Students whose major interest is sociology, religion, or philosophy should find the paper by Dyal to be provocative. A student of any stripe should delight in Silverman's satirically humorous spoof of technological advances in mass education.

Selection **67**   INTRODUCTION

In the past two decades many devices have been created which have proven to be of substantial benefit to education. Certainly among the most promising of the new developments we must list closed-circuit television. However, the major disadvantage of closed-circuit television is the high cost which makes it unavailable to many schools. Silverman presents the requirements of an ideal system for mass education and finds a prime candidate in a marvelous device which has been with us for some time.

Selection **67**

UNIVISION: A NEW APPROACH TO CLOSED CIRCUIT TELEVISION TEACHING*

S. J. SILVERMAN
University of Toledo

The use of closed-circuit television in colleges has now reached a point where it is perhaps worthwhile to review the method and to consider possible improvements. Television techniques have arisen primarily because of the present and anticipated increased enrollments in the colleges. This has led to large lecture sessions in which many students have either not been able to hear the lecturer or to see the lecture demonstrations. Since the purpose of a lecture is to present an organized body of material to the student in an easily assimilated form this has led to a dilemma. Television has presented a way out of the dilemma. By placing the lecturer and demonstration in a studio and putting the students in a separate classroom with strategically placed receivers each student is enabled to see a close-up view of both the lecturer and the demonstration. The television method has also disposed of another problem faced by our financially hard pressed colleges. By adding to the number of receivers it is possible to reduce materially the number

of lecturers formerly needed. Questions from the students may be taken care of by placing intercommunication networks between studio and classrooms. This is, however, not a major problem inasmuch as most students never ask questions at lectures and our purpose is to provide education for the mass of students rather than the individual. Individual instruction would, in principle at least, be preferable, but, as practical educators, we must recognize that the increased enrollments preclude this possibility. It was, in fact, for this very reason that the television technique was introduced.

Sufficient time has now elapsed so that a preliminary judgment of television teaching can be made. While the method does achieve the objectives indicated in the preceding paragraph, there are nevertheless definite disadvantages. These are primarily financial in nature. Thus the initial investment and subsequent maintenance are outside the budget of many of the smaller schools.

Let us now consider what can be done to improve this situation. It is worthwhile first of all presenting the requirements of an ideal system which will achieve mass education at minimum cost. These are: (*a*) the student must be in close contact with both lecturer and demonstrations; (*b*) capital investment in equipment by the college should be low; (*c*) maintenance costs should be low; (*d*) the materials should be re-usable for each new class; (*e*) the number of staff needed (including technicians) should be low; and (*f*) the number of classrooms needed should be a minimum.

It is the purpose of this article to propose

* Reprinted from S. J. Silverman, "Univision: A New Approach to Closed Circuit Television Teaching," *American Scientist*, 45: 186A–192A, 1957. Reprinted by permission of the author and publisher.

a system which will satisfy the above requirements. Consideration of items (*a*) and (*b*) above shows that a practicable scheme might be the permanent recording of the lecture material and of the demonstrations in an area small enough to be placed before the individual student. This would be equivalent to the production of individual kinescopes. Since we wish, however, to reduce the cost of equipment some simplification can be introduced by transcribing the audio into writing. At first glance it might seem that the best recording material would be a non-corroding metal such as titanium, thus satisfying requirement (*d*), but a closer consideration shows that the use of a material such as parchment or paper would be preferable, the higher depreciation being offset by considerably lower costs. In addition, experience with some early recordings made in the Dead Sea area shows that parchment deteriorates to a lesser extent than certain metals such as brass. A set of lectures recorded in this form could then be bound together in something called a *book*.[1] Let us now see whether this system will satisfy the other requirements we have set up. The requirement of close contact is immediately satisfied, since each student can be provided with one book. This has the additional advantage that the student can go through the lecture at his own speed, depending on how fast he can absorb the material. Demonstrations can be presented

[1] This term may be unfamiliar to educators trained in television techniques. It may be defined as a permanent recording printed on material, usually paper, enclosed in a strong binding.

in the form of photographs (i.e., kinescope stills) which can be made from as close up as desired. Initial investment by the college will be lower than for television equipment. In fact an additional economy can be realized by requiring the student to purchase his own books, thus relieving the college of all financial responsibility for capital investment. Maintenance costs can also be turned over to the student as well as the question of re-use of the materials.

Requirements (*e*) and (*f*) may be considered together. It is probable that after the initial problems have been ironed out it will be possible to make books that will be small in size and can easily be carried around. This will immediately eliminate the need for classrooms since the student can then be required to do his work in his own home. The same reasoning leads to the conclusion that the staff of the college can be very materially reduced, leaving primarily those needed for administrative work and for the finance offices. Some faculty skilled in specialized subjects will be needed to write the books and answer the few questions that will arise, but the bulk of this work can safely be left to administrative assistants. The reduction of staff will also benefit the national economy since there is today a great shortage of people with specialized skills for industrial work.

The writer appreciates that this proposal is too new and untried for a judgment to be made at this time. However, the advantages are sufficiently attractive to warrant a serious trial, possibly with the support of one of the larger foundations.

You are by now already familiar with many facets of Dr. B. F. Skinner's thinking regarding human learning (Selection 36) and the role of theory in psychology (Hyman, Selection 8). Although the vast majority of psychologists may be thought of as Behavioristically oriented, Skinner has consistently defended the most radical brand of Behaviorism. As a reviewer of a recent book by Skinner has commented, "Watson's spirit is indestructible. Cleaned and purified, it breathes through the writings of B. F. Skinner."* In the present selection, Skinner is reformulating what he believes is the fundamental philosophy which lies behind Behaviorism as an approach to psychology, biology, political science, economics, etc. It will be recalled that Watson waged battle against admitting into a scientific psychology private events which are implied by such concepts as mind and consciousness. Skinner, on the other hand, feels that private events may be analyzed by a science without giving up a Behavioristic orientation. He maintains that the primary difference between public and private events is that the verbal community is in less close contact with private events. The labeling of private events that is involved in self-description is more ambiguous because the events are not as amenable as public events to precise shaping by verbal reinforcement. This view implies that a person can "know" more about external stimuli than about internal stimuli! In his analysis of mentalistic psychologies, Skinner shows how both conscious content (e.g., sensation and perception) and other hypothetical processes (e.g., cognitions and expectancies) ". . . provide a formidable stronghold for mentalistic theories designed to bridge the gap between dependent and independent variables." He then formulates four objections to mentalistic way stations. In the section on Behaviorism and Biology, Skinner reiterates his long-standing bias against "physiologizing." He feels that "reductive" explanations are in no sense to be preferred to complete analysis at the strictly behavioral level. "It adds nothing to an explanation of how an organism reacts to a stimulus to trace the pattern of the stimulus into the body."

Selection **68** | BEHAVIORISM
AT FIFTY†

B. F. SKINNER
Harvard University

Behaviorism, with an accent on the last syllable, is not the scientific study of behavior but a philosophy of science concerned with the subject matter and methods of psychology. If psychology is a science of mental life—of the

* R. B. MacLeod, "Review of Cumulative Record by B. F. Skinner," *Science*, **130**: 34–35, 1959.
† Abridged from B. F. Skinner, "Behaviorism at Fifty." *Science*, **140**: 951–958, 1962. Reprinted by permission of the author and the publisher.

mind, of conscious experience—then it must develop and defend a special methodology, which it has not yet done successfully. If it is, on the other hand, a science of the behavior of organisms, human or otherwise, then it is part of biology, a natural science for which tested and highly successful methods are available. The basic issue is not the nature of the stuff of which the world is made, or whether it is made of one stuff or two, but rather the dimensions of the things studied by psychology and the methods relevant to them.

Mentalistic or psychic explanations of human behavior almost certainly originated in primitive animism. When a man dreamed of being at a distant place in spite of incontrovertible evidence that he had stayed in his bed, it was easy to conclude that some part of him had actually left his body. A particularly vivid memory or a hallucination could be explained in the same way. The theory of an invisible, detachable self eventually proved useful for other purposes. It seemed to explain unexpected or abnormal episodes, even to the person behaving in an exceptional way because he was thus "possessed." It also served to explain the inexplicable. An organism as complex as man often seems to behave capriciously. It is tempting to attribute the visible behavior to another organism inside—to a little man or homunculus. The wishes of the little man become the acts of the man observed by his fellows. The inner idea is put into outer words. Inner feelings find outward expression. The explanation is satisfying, of course, only so long as the behavior of the homunculus can be neglected.

Primitive origins are not necessarily to be held against an explanatory principle, but the little man is still with us in relatively primitive form. He was recently the hero of a television program called "Gateways to the Mind," one of a series of educational films sponsored by Bell Telephone Laboratories and written with the help of a distinguished panel of scientists. The viewer learned, from animated cartoons, that when a man's finger is pricked, electrical impulses resembling flashes of lightning run up the afferent nerves and appear on a television screen in the brain. The little man wakes up, sees the flashing screen, reaches out, and pulls a lever. More flashes of lightning go down the nerves to the muscles, which then contract, as the finger is pulled away from the threatening stimulus. The behavior of the homunculus was, of course, not explained. An explanation would presumably require another film. And it, in turn, another.

The same pattern of explanation is invoked when we are told that the behavior of a delinquent is the result of a disordered personality, or that the vagaries of a man under analysis are due to conflicts among his superego, ego, and id. Nor can we escape from primitive features by breaking the little man into pieces and dealing with his wishes, cognitions, motives, and so on, bit by bit. The objection is not that these things are mental but that they offer no real explanation and stand in the way of a more effective analysis.

It has been about 50 years since the behavioristic objection to this practice was first clearly stated, and it has been about 30 years since it has been very much discussed. A whole generation of psychologists has grown up without really coming into contact with the issue. Almost all current textbooks compromise: rather than risk a loss of adoptions, they define psychology as the science of behavior *and* mental life. Meanwhile the older view has continued to receive strong support from areas in which there has been no comparable attempt at methodological reform. During this period, however, an effective experimental science of behavior has emerged. Much of what it has discovered bears on the basic issue. A restatement of radical behaviorism would therefore seem to be in order.

EXPLAINING THE MIND

A rough history of the idea is not hard to trace. An occasional phrase in classic Greek authors which seemed to foreshadow the point of view need not be taken seriously. We may also pass over the early bravado of a La Mettrie who could shock the philosophical bourgeoisie by asserting that man was only a machine. Nor were those who, for practical reasons, simply preferred to deal with behavior rather than with less accessible, but nevertheless acknowledged, mental activities close to what is meant by behaviorism today.

The entering wedge appears to have been Darwin's preoccupation with the continuity of species. In supporting the theory of evolution, it was important to show that man was not essentially different from the lower animals—that every human characteristic, including consciousness and reasoning powers, could be found in other species. Naturalists like Romanes began to collect stories which seemed to show that dogs, cats, elephants, and many other species were conscious and showed signs of reasoning. It was Lloyd Morgan, of course, who questioned this evidence with his Canon of Parsimony. Were there not other ways of accounting for what looked like signs of consciousness or rational powers? Thorndike's experiments, at the end of the 19th century, were in this vein. They showed that the behavior of a cat in escaping from a puzzle box might seem to show reasoning but could be explained instead as the result of simpler processes. Thorndike remained a mentalist, but he greatly advanced the objective study of behavior which had been attributed to mental processes.

The next step was inevitable: if evidence of consciousness and reasoning could be explained in other ways in animals, why not also in man? And in that case, what became of psychology as a science of mental life? It was John B. Watson who made the first clear, if rather noisy, proposal that psychology be regarded simply as a science of behavior. He was not in a very good position to defend the proposal. He had little scientific material to use in his reconstruction. He was forced to pad his textbook with discussions of the physiology of receptor systems and muscles, and with physiological theories whch were at the time no more susceptible to proof than the mentalistic theories they were intended to replace. A need for "mediators" of behavior which might serve as objective alternatives to thought processes led him to emphasize subaudible speech. The notion was intriguing because one can usually observe oneself thinking in this way, but it was by no means an adequate or comprehensive explanation. He tangled with introspective psychologists by denying the existence of images. He may well have been acting in good faith, for it has been said that he himself did not have visual imagery, but his arguments caused unnecessary trouble. The relative importance of a genetic endowment in explaining behavior proved to be another disturbing digression.

All this made it easy to lose sight of the central argument—that behavior which seemed to be the product of mental activity could be explained in other ways. In any case, the introspectionists were prepared to challenge it. As late as 1883 Francis Galton could write (1): "Many persons, especially women and intelligent children, take pleasure in introspection, and strive their very best to explain their mental processes." But introspection was already being taken seriously. The concept of a science of mind in which mental events obeyed mental laws had led to the development of psychophysical methods and to the accumulation of facts which seemed to bar the extension of the principle of parsimony. What might hold

for animals did not hold for men, because men could see their mental processes.

Curiously enough, part of the answer was supplied by the psychoanalysts, who insisted that although a man might be able to see some of his mental life, he could not see all of it. The kind of thoughts Freud called unconscious took place without the knowledge of the thinker. From an association, verbal slip, or dream it could be shown that a person must have responded to a passing stimulus although he could not tell you that he had done so. More complex thought processes, including problem solving and verbal play, could also go on without the thinker's knowledge. Freud had devised, and he never abandoned faith in, one of the most elaborate mental apparatuses of all time. He nevertheless contributed to the behavioristic argument by showing that mental activity did not, at least, *require* consciousness. His proofs that thinking had occurred without introspective recognition were, indeed, clearly in the spirit of Lloyd Morgan. They were operational analyses of mental life—even though, for Freud, only the unconscious part of it. Experimental evidence pointing in the same direction soon began to accumulate.

But that was not the whole answer. What about the part of mental life which a man can see? It is a difficult question, no matter what one's point of view, partly because it raises the question of what "seeing" means and partly because the events seen are private. The fact of privacy cannot, of course, be questioned. Each person is in special contact with a small part of the universe enclosed within his own skin. To take a noncontroversial example, he is uniquely subject to certain kinds of proprioceptive and interoceptive stimulation. Though two people may in some sense be said to see the same light or hear the same sound, they cannot feel the same distension of a bile duct or the same bruised muscle. (When privacy is invaded with scientific instruments, the form of stimulation is changed; the scales read by the scientist are not the private events themselves.)

Mentalistic psychologists insist that there are other kinds of events uniquely accessible to the owner of the skin within which they occur which lack the physical dimensions of proprioceptive or interoceptive stimuli. They are as different from physical events as colors are from wavelengths of light. There are even better reasons, therefore, why two people cannot suffer each other's toothaches, recall each other's memories, or share each other's happiness. The importance assigned to this kind of world varies. For some, it is the only world there is. For others, it is the only part of the world which can be directly known. For still others, it is a special part of what can be known. In any case, the problem of how one knows about the subjective world of another must be faced. Apart from the question of what "knowing" means, the problem is one of accessibility.

PUBLIC AND PRIVATE EVENTS

One solution, often regarded as behavioristic, is to grant the distinction between public and private events and rule the latter out of scientific consideration. This is a congenial solution for those to whom scientific truth is a matter of convention or agreement among observers. It is essentially the line taken by logical positivism and physical operationism. Hogben (2) has recently redefined "behaviorist" in this spirit. The subtitle of his *Statistical Theory* is, "an examination of the contemporary crises in statistical theory from a behaviorist viewpoint," and this is amplified in the following way: "The behaviorist, as I here use the term, does not deny the convenience of classifying *processes* as mental or material. He recognizes the distinction between personality and corpse: but he has not yet had the privilege of attending an identity parade in which human minds without bodies are by common recognition distinguishable from living human bodies without minds. Till then, he is content to discuss probability in the vocabulary of *events*, including audible or visibly recorded assertions of human beings as such. . . ." The behavioristic position, so defined, is simply that of the publicist and "has no concern with structure and mechanism."

The point of view is often called operational, and it is significant that P. W. Bridgman's physical operationism could not save him from an extreme solipsism even within physical science itself. Though he insisted that he was not a solipsist, he was never able to reconcile seemingly public physical knowledge with the private world of the scientist (3). Applied to psychological problems, operationism has been no more successful. We may recognize the restrictions imposed by the operations through which we can know of the existence of properties of subjective events, but the operations cannot be identified with the events themselves. S. S. Stevens has applied Bridgman's principle to psychology, not to decide whether subjective events exist, but to determine the extent to which we can deal with them scientifically (4).

Behaviorists have from time to time examined the problem of privacy, and some of them have excluded so-called sensations, images, thought processes, and so on, from their deliberations. When they have done so not because such things do not exist but because they are out of reach of their methods, the charge is justified that they have neglected the facts of consciousness. The strategy is, however, quite unwise. It is particularly important that a science of behavior face the problem of privacy. It may do so without abandoning the basic position of behaviorism. Science often talks about things it cannot see or measure. When a man tosses a penny into the air, it must be assumed that he tosses the earth beneath him downward. It is quite out of the question to see or measure the effect on the earth, but an effect must be assumed for the sake of a consistent account. An adequate science of behavior must consider events taking place within the skin of the organism, not as physiological mediators of behavior but as part of behavior itself. It can deal with these events without assuming that they have any special nature or must be known in any special way. The skin is not that important as a boundary. Private and public events have the same kinds of physical dimensions.

SELF-DESCRIPTIVE BEHAVIOR

In the 50 years which have passed since a behavioristic philosophy was first stated, facts and principles bearing on the basic issues have steadily accumulated. For one thing, a scientific analysis of behavior has yielded a sort of empirical epistemology. The subject matter of a science of behavior includes the behavior of scientists and other knowers. The techniques available to such a science give an empirical theory of knowledge certain advantages over theories derived from philosophy and logic. The problem of privacy may be approached in a fresh direction by starting with behavior rather than with immediate experience. The strategy is certainly no more arbitrary or circular than the earlier practice, and it has a surprising result. Instead of concluding that man can know only his subjective experiences—that he is bound forever to his private world and that the external world is only a construct—a behavioral theory of knowledge suggests that it is the private world which, if not entirely unknowable, is at least not likely to be known well. The relations between organism and environment involved in knowing are of such a sort that the privacy of the world within the skin imposes more serious limitations on personal knowledge than on scientific accessibility.

An organism learns to react discriminatively to the world around it under certain contingencies of reinforcement. Thus, a child learns to name a color correctly when a given response is reinforced in the presence of the color and extinguished in its absence. The verbal community may make the reinforcement of an extensive repertoire of responses contingent on subtle properties of colored stimuli. We have reason to believe that the child will not discriminate among colors—that he will not see two colors as different—until exposed to such contingencies. So far as we know, the same process of differential reinforcement is required if a child is to distinguish among the events occurring within his own skin.

Many contingencies involving private stimuli need not be arranged by a verbal community, for they follow from simple mechanical relations among stimuli, responses, and reinforcing consequences. The various motions which comprise turning a handspring, for example, are under the control of external and internal stimuli and are subject to external and internal reinforcing consequences. But the performer is not necessarily "aware" of the stimuli controlling his behavior, no matter how appropriate and skillful it may be. "Knowing" or "being aware of" what is happening in turning a handspring involves discriminative responses, such as naming or describing, which arise from contingencies necessarily arranged by a verbal environment. Such environments are common. The community is generally interested in what a man is doing, has done, or is planning to do, and why, and it arranges contingencies which generate verbal responses which name and describe the external and internal stimuli associated with these events. It challenges his verbal behavior by asking, "How do you know?" and the speaker answers, if at all, by describing some of the variables of which his verbal behavior was a function. The "awareness" resulting from all this is a social product.

In attempting to set up such a repertoire, however, the verbal community works under a severe handicap. It cannot always arrange the contingencies required for subtle discriminations. It cannot teach a child to call one pattern of private stimuli "diffidence" and another "embarrassment" as effectively as it teaches him to call one stimulus "red" and another "orange," for it cannot be sure of the presence or absence of the private patterns of stimuli appropriate to reinforcement or lack of reinforcement. Privacy thus causes trouble first of all for the verbal community. The individual suffers in turn. Because the community cannot reinforce self-descriptive responses consistently, a person cannot describe or otherwise "know" events occurring within his own skin as subtly and precisely as he knows events in the world at large.

There are, of course, differences between external and internal stimuli which are not mere differences in location. Proprioceptive and interoceptive stimuli may have a certain intimacy. They are likely to be especially familiar. They are very much with us: we cannot escape from a toothache as easily as from a deafening noise. They may well be of a special kind: the stimuli we feel in pride or sorrow may not closely resemble those we feel in sandpaper or satin. But this does not mean that they differ in physical status. In particular, it does not mean that they can be more easily or more directly known. What is particularly clear and familiar to the potential knower may be strange and distant to the verbal community responsible for his knowing.

CONSCIOUS CONTENT

What *are* the private events which, at least in a limited way, a man may come to respond to in ways we call knowing? Let us begin with the oldest and in many ways the most difficult kind, represented by "the stubborn fact of consciousness." What is happening when a person observes the conscious content of his mind, when he looks at his sensations or images? Western philosophy and science have been handicapped in answering these questions by an unfortunate metaphor. The Greeks could not explain how a man could have knowledge of something with which he was not in immediate contact. How could he know an object on the other side of the room, for example? Did he reach out and touch it with some sort of invisible probe? Or did he never actually come into contact with the object at all but only with a copy of it inside his body? Plato supported the copy theory with his metaphor of the cave. Perhaps a man never sees the real world at all but only shadows of it on the wall of the cave in which he is imprisoned. (The "shadows" may well have been the much more accurate copies of the outside world in a camera obscura. Did Plato know of a cave at the entrance of which a happy superposition of objects admitted only the thin pencils of light needed for a camera obscura?) Copies of the real world projected into the body could compose the experience which a man directly knows. A similar theory could also explain how one can see objects which are "not really there," as in hallucinations, after-images, and memories. Neither explanation is, of course, satisfactory. How a copy may arise at a distance is at least as puzzling as how a man may know an object at a distance. Seeing things which are not really there is no harder to explain than the occurrence of copies of things not there to be copied.

The search for copies of the world within the body, particularly in the nervous system, still goes on, but with discouraging results. If the retina could suddenly be developed, like a photographic plate, it would yield a poor picture. The nerve impulses in the optic tract must have an even more tenuous resemblance to "what is seen." The patterns of vibrations which strike our ear when we listen to music are quickly lost in transmission. The bodily reactions to substances tasted, smelled, and touched would scarcely qualify as faithful reproductions. These facts are discouraging for those who are looking for copies of the real world within the body, but they are fortunate for psychophysiology as a whole. At some point the organism must do more than create duplicates. It must see, hear, smell, and so on, and the seeing, hearing, and smelling must be forms of action rather than of reproduction. It must do some of the things it is differentially reinforced for doing when it learns to respond discriminatively. The sooner the pattern of the external world disappears after impinging on the organism, the sooner the organism may get on with these other functions.

The need for something beyond, and quite different from, copying is not widely understood. Suppose someone were to coat the occipital lobes of the brain with a special photographic emulsion which, when developed, yielded a reasonable copy of a current visual stimulus. In many quarters this would be regarded as a triumph in the physiology of vision. Yet nothing could be more disastrous, for we should have to start all over again and ask how the organism sees a picture in its occipital cortex, and we should now have much less of the brain available in which to seek an answer. It adds nothing to an explanation of how an organism reacts to a stimulus to trace the pattern of the stimulus into the body. It is most convenient for both organism and psychophysiologist, if the external world is never copied—if the world we know is simply the world around us. The same may be said of theories according to which the brain interprets signals sent to it and in some sense reconstructs external stimuli. If the real world is, indeed, scrambled in transmission but later reconstructed in the brain, we must then start all over again and explain how the organism sees the reconstruction.

An adequate treatment of this point would require a thorough analysis of the behavior of seeing and of the conditions under which we see (to continue with vision as a convenient modality). It would be unwise to exaggerate our success to date. Discriminative visual behavior arises from contingencies involving external stimuli and overt responses, but possible private accompaniments must not be overlooked. Some of the consequences of such contingencies seem well established. It is usually easiest for us to see a friend when we are looking at him, because visual stimuli similar to those present when the behavior was acquired exert maximal control over the response. But mere visual stimulation is not enough; even after having been exposed to the necessary reinforcement, we may not see a friend who is present unless we have reason to do so. On the other hand, if the reasons are strong enough, we may see him in someone bearing only a superficial resemblance to him, or when no one like him is present at all. If conditions favor seeing something else, we may behave accordingly. If, on a hunting trip, it is important to see a deer, we may glance toward our friend at a distance, see him as a deer, and shoot.

It is not, however, seeing our friend which raises the question of conscious content but "seeing that we are seeing him." There are no natural contingencies for such behavior. We learn to see that we are seeing only because a verbal community arranges for us to do so. We usually acquire the behavior when we are under appropriate visual stimulation, but it does not follow that the thing seen must be present when we see that we are seeing it. The contingencies arranged by the verbal environment may set up self-descriptive responses describing the *behavior* of seeing even when the thing seen is not present.

If seeing does not require the presence of things seen, we need not be concerned about certain mental processes said to be involved in the construction of such things—images, memories, and dreams, for example. We may regard a dream not as a display of things seen by the dreamer but simply as the behavior of seeing. At no time during a day-dream, for example, should we expect to find within the organism anything which corresponds to the external stimuli present when the dreamer first acquired the behavior in which he is now engaged. In simple recall we need not suppose that we wander through some storehouse of memory until we find an object which we then

contemplate. Instead of assuming that we begin with a tendency to *recognize* such an object once it is found, it is simpler to assume that we begin with a tendency to *see* it. Techniques of self-management which facilitate recall—for example, the use of mnemonic devices—can be formulated as ways of strengthening behavior rather than of creating objects to be seen. Freud dramatized the issue with respect to dreaming when asleep in his concept of dreamwork—an activity in which some part of the dreamer played the role of a theatrical producer while another part sat in the audience. If a dream is, indeed, something seen, then we must suppose that it is wrought as such, but if it is simply the behavior of seeing, the dreamwork may be dropped from the analysis. It took man a long time to understand that when he dreamed of a wolf, no wolf was actually there. It has taken him much longer to understand that not even a representation of a wolf is there.

Eye movements which appear to be associated with dreaming are in accord with this interpretation, since it is not likely that the dreamer is actually watching a dream on the undersides of his eyelids. When memories are aroused by electrical stimulation of the brain, as in the work of Wilder Penfield, it is also simpler to assume that it is the behavior of seeing, hearing, and so on which is aroused than that it is some copy of early environmental events which the subject then looks at or listens to. Behavior similar to the responses to the original events must be assumed in both cases—the subject sees or hears—but the reproduction of the events seen or heard is a needless complication. The familiar process of response chaining is available to account for the serial character of the behavior of remembering, but the serial linkage of stored experiences (suggesting engrams in the form of sound films) demands a new mechanism.

The heart of the behavioristic position on conscious experience may be summed up in this way: seeing does not imply something seen. We acquire the behavior of seeing under stimulation from actual objects, but it may occur in the absence of these objects under the control of other variables. (So far as the world within the skin is concerned, it always occurs in the absence of such objects.) We also acquire the behavior of seeing-that-we-are-seeing when we are seeing actual objects, but it may also occur in their absence.

To question the reality or the nature of the things seen in conscious experience is not to question the value of introspective psychology or its methods. Current problems in sensation are mainly concerned with the physiological function of receptors and associated neural mechanisms. Problems in perception are, at the moment, less intimately related to specific mechanisms, but the trend appears to be in the same direction. So far as behavior is concerned, both sensation and perception may be analyzed as forms of stimulus control. The subject need not be regarded as observing or evaluating conscious experiences. Apparent anomalies of stimulus control which are now explained by appealing to a psychophysical relation or to the laws of perception may be studied in their own right. It is, after all, no real solution to attribute them to the slippage inherent in converting a physical stimulus into a subjective experience.

The experimental analysis of behavior has a little more to say on this subject. Its techniques have recently been extended to what might be called the psychophysics of lower organisms. Blough's adaptation of the Békésy technique—for example, in determining the spectral sensitivity of pigeons and monkeys—yields sensory data comparable with the reports of a trained observer (5). Herrnstein and van Sommers have recently developed a procedure in which pigeons "bisect sensory intervals" (6). It is tempting to describe these procedures by saying that investigators have found ways to get nonverbal organisms to describe their sensations. The fact is that a form of stimulus control has been investigated without using a repertoire of self-observation or, rather, by constructing a special repertoire the nature and origin of which are clearly understood. Rather than describe such experiments with the terminology of introspection, we may formulate them in their proper place in an experimental analysis. The behavior of the observer in the traditional psychophysical experiment may then be reinterpreted accordingly.

MENTAL WAY STATIONS

So much for "conscious content," the classical problem in mentalistic philosophies. There are other mental states or processes to be taken into account. Moods, cognitions, and expectancies, for example, are also examined introspectively, and descriptions are used in psychological formulations. The conditions under which descriptive repertoires are set up are much less successfully controlled. Terms describing sensations and images are taught by manipulating discriminative stimuli—a relatively amenable class of variables. The remaining kinds of mental events are related to such operations as deprivation and satiation, emotional stimulation, and various schedules of reinforcement. The difficulties they present to the verbal community are suggested by the fact that there is no psychophysics of mental states of this sort. That fact has not inhibited their use in explanatory systems.

In an experimental analysis, the relation between a property of behavior and an operation performed upon the organism is studied directly. Traditional mentalistic formulations, however, emphasize certain way stations. Where an experimental analysis might examine the effect of punishment on behavior, a mentalistic psychology will be concerned first with the effect of punishment in generating feelings of anxiety and then with the effect of anxiety on behavior. The mental state seems to bridge the gap between dependent and independent variables, and a mentalistic interpretation is particularly attractive when these are separated by long periods of time—when, for example, the punishment occurs in childhood and the effect appears in the behavior of the adult.

Mentalistic way stations are popular. In a demonstration experiment, a hungry pigeon was conditioned to turn around in a clockwise direction. A final, smoothly executed pattern of behavior was shaped by reinforcing successive approximations with food. Students who had watched the demonstration were asked to write an account of what they had seen. Their responses included the following: (i) the organism was conditioned to *expect* reinforcement for the right kind of behavior; (ii) the pigeon walked around, *hoping* that something would bring the food back again; (iii) the pigeon *observed* that a certain behavior seemed to produce a particular result; (iv) the pigeon *felt* that food would be given it because of its action; and (v) the bird came to *associate* his action with the click of the food-dispenser. The observed facts could be stated, respectively, as follows: (i) the organism was reinforced *when* its behavior was of a given kind; (ii) the pigeon walked around *until* the food container again appeared; (iii) a certain behavior *produced* a particular result; (iv) food was given to the pigeon *when* it acted in a given way; and (v) the click of the food-dispenser *was temporally related* to the bird's action. These statements describe the contingencies of reinforcement. The expressions "expect," "hope," "observe," "feel," and "associate" go beyond them to identify effects on the pigeon. The effect actually observed was clear enough: the pigeon turned more skillfully and more frequently. But that was not the effect reported by the students. (If pressed, they would doubtless have said that the pigeon turned more skillfully and more frequently *because* it expected, hoped, and felt that if it did so food would appear.)

The events reported by the students were observed, if at all, in their own behavior. They were describing what *they* would have expected, felt, and hoped for under similar circumstances. But they were able to do so only because a verbal community had brought relevant terms under the control of certain stimuli, and this had been done when the community had access only to the kinds of public information available to the students in the demonstration. Whatever the students knew about themselves which permitted them to infer comparable events in the pigeon must have been learned from a verbal community which saw no more of their behavior than they had seen of the pigeon's. Private stimuli may have entered into the control of their self-descriptive repertoires, but the readiness with which they applied these repertoires to the pigeon indicates that external stimuli had remained important. The extraordinary strength of a mentalistic interpretation is really a sort of proof that, in describing a private way station, one is to a considerable extent making use of public information.

The mental way station is often accepted as a terminal datum, however. When a man must be trained to discriminate between different planes, ships, and so on, it is tempting to stop at the point at which he can be said to *identify* such objects. It is implied that if he can identify an object he can name it, label it, describe it, or act appropriately in some other way. In the training process he always behaves in one of these ways: no way station called "identification" appears in practice or need appear in theory. (Any discussion of the discriminative behavior generated by the verbal environment to permit a person to examine the content of his consciousness must be qualified accordingly.)

Cognitive theories stop at way stations where the mental action is usually somewhat more complex than identification. For example, a subject is said to *know* who and where he is, what something is, or what has happened or is going to happen, regardless of the forms of behavior through which this knowledge was set up or which may now testify to its existence. Similarly, in accounting for verbal behavior, a listener or reader is said to understand the *meaning* of a passage although the actual changes brought about by listening to or reading the passage are not specified. In the same way, schedules of reinforcement are sometimes studied simply for their effects on the *expectations* of the organism exposed to them, without discussion of the implied relation between expectation and action. Recall, inference, and reasoning may be formulated only to the point at which an experience is remembered or a conclusion is reached, behavioral manifestations being ignored. In practice the investigator always carries through to some response, if only a response of self-description.

On the other hand, mental states are often studied as causes of action. A speaker thinks of something to say before saying it, and this explains what he says, although the sources of his thoughts may not be examined. An unusual act is called "impulsive," without further inquiry into the origin of the unusual impulse. A behavioral maladjustment shows anxiety, but the source of the anxiety is neglected. One salivates upon seeing a lemon because it reminds one of a sour taste, but why it does so is not specified. The formulation leads directly to a technology based on the manipulation of mental states. To change a man's voting behavior we change his opinions, to induce him to act we strengthen his beliefs, to make him eat we make him feel hungry, to prevent wars we reduce warlike tensions in the minds of men, to effect psychotherapy we alter troublesome mental states, and so on. In practice, all these ways of changing a man's mind reduce to manipulating his environment, verbal or otherwise.

In many cases we can reconstruct a complete causal chain by identifying the mental state which is the effect of an environmental variable with the mental state which is the cause of action. But this is not always enough. In traditional mentalistic philosophies various things happen at the way station which alter the relation between the terminal events. The effect of the psychophysical function and the laws of perception in distorting the physical stimulus before it reaches the way station has already been mentioned. Once the mental stage is reached, other effects are said to occur. Mental states alter each other. A painful memory may never affect behavior, or it may affect it an unexpected way if another mental state succeeds in repressing it. Conflicting variables may be reconciled before they have an effect on behavior if the subject engages in mental action called "making a decision." Dissonant cognitions generated by conflicting conditions of reinforcement will not be reflected in behavior if the subject can "persuade himself" that one condition was actually of a different magnitude or kind. These disturbances in simple causal linkages between environment and behavior can be formulated and studied experimentally as interactions among variables, but the possibility has not been fully exploited, and the effects still provide a formidable stronghold for mentalistic theories designed to bridge the gap between dependent and independent variables.

METHODOLOGICAL OBJECTIONS

The behavioristic argument is nevertheless still valid. We may object, first, to the predilection for unfinished causal sequences. A disturbance in behavior is not explained by relating it to felt anxiety until the anxiety has in turn been explained. An action is not explained by attributing it to expectations until the expectations have in turn been accounted for. Complete causal sequences might, of course, include references to way stations, but the fact is that the way station generally interrupts the account in one direction or the other. For example, there must be thousands of instances in the psychoanalytic literature in which a thought or memory is said to have been relegated to the unconscious because it was painful or intolerable, but the percentage of instances in which even the most casual suggestion is offered as to why it was painful or intolerable must be very small. Perhaps explanations could have been offered, but the practice has discouraged the completion of the causal sequence.

A second objection is that a preoccupation with mental way stations burdens a science of behavior with all the problems raised by the limitations and inaccuracies of self-descriptive repertoires. We need not take the extreme position that mediating events or any data about them obtained through introspection must be ruled out of consideration, but we should certainly welcome other ways of treating the data more satisfactorily. Independent variables change the behaving organism, often in ways which persist for many years, and such changes affect subsequent behavior. The subject may be able to describe some of these intervening states in useful ways, either before or after they have affected behavior. On the other hand, behavior may be extensively modified by variables of which, and of the effect of which, the subject is never aware. So far as we know, self-descriptive responses do not alter controlling relationships. If a severe punishment is less effective than a mild one, this is not because it cannot be "kept in mind." (Certain behaviors involved in self-management, such as reviewing a history of punishment, may alter behavior, but they do so by introducing other variables rather than by changing a given relation.)

Perhaps the most serious objection concerns the order of events. Observation of one's own behavior necessarily follows the behavior. Responses which seem to be describing intervening states alone may embrace behavioral effects. "I am hungry" may describe, in part, the strength of the speaker's ongoing ingestive behavior. "I was hungrier than I thought" seems particularly to describe behavior rather than an intervening, possibly causal, state. More serious examples of a possibly mistaken order are to be found in theories of psychotherapy. Before asserting that the release of a repressed wish has a therapeutic effect on behavior, or that when one knows why he is neurotically ill he will recover, we should consider the plausible alternative that change in behavior resulting from therapy has made it possible for the subject to recall a repressed wish or to understand his illness.

A final objection is that way stations are so often simply invented. It is too easy to say that someone does something "because he likes to do it," or that he does one thing rather than another "because he has made a choice."

The importance of behaviorism as a philosophy of science naturally declines as a scientific analysis becomes more powerful because there is then less need to use data in the form of self-description. The mentalism which survives in the fields of sensation and perception will disappear as alternative techniques prove their value in analyzing stimulus control, and similar changes may be anticipated elsewhere. Cognitive psychologists and others still try to circumvent the explicit control of variables by describing contingencies of reinforcement to their subjects in "instructions." They also try to dispense with recording behavior in a form from which probability of response can be estimated by asking their subjects to evaluate their tendencies to respond. But a person rarely responds to a description of contingencies as he would respond under direct exposure to them, nor can he accurately predict his rate of responding, particularly the course of the subtle changes in rate which are a commonplace in the experimental analysis of behavior. These attempts to short-circuit an experimental analysis can no longer be justified on grounds of expedience, and there are many reasons for abandoning them. Much remains to be done, however, before the facts to which they are currently applied can be said to be adequately understood.

BEHAVIORISM AND BIOLOGY

Elsewhere, the scientific study of man has scarcely recognized the need for reform. The biologist, for example, begins with a certain advantage in studying the behaving organism, for the structures he analyzes have an evident physical status. The nervous system is somehow earthier than the behavior for which it is largely responsible. Philosophers and psychologists alike have from time to time sought escape from mentalism in physiology. When a man sees red, he may be seeing the physiological effect of a red stimulus; when he merely imagines red, he may be seeing the same effect re-aroused. Psychophysical and perceptual distortions may be wrought by physiological processes. What a man feels as anxiety may be autonomic reactions to threatening stimuli. And so on. This may solve the minor problem of the nature of subjective experience, but it does not solve any of the methodological problems with which behaviorism is most seriously concerned. A physiological translation of mentalistic terms may reassure those who want to avoid dualism, but inadequacies in the formulation survive translation.

When writing about the behavior of organisms, biologists tend to be more mentalistic then psychologists. Adrian could not understand how a nerve impulse could cause a thought. The author of a recent article on the visual space sense in *Science* (7) asserts that "the final event in the chain from the retina to the brain is a psychic experience." Another investigator reports research on "the brain and its contained mind." Pharmacologists study the "psychotropic" drugs. Psychosomatic medicine insists on the influence of mind over matter. And psychologists join their physiological colleagues in looking for feelings, emotions, drives, and the pleasurable aspects of positive reinforcement in the brain.

The facts uncovered in such research are important, both for their own sake and for their bearing on behavior. The physiologist studies structures and processes without which behavior could not occur. He is in a position to supply a "reductionist" explanation beyond the reach of an analysis which confines itself to terminal variables. He cannot do this well, however, so long as he accepts traditional mentalistic formulations. Only an experimental analysis of behavior will define his task in optimal terms. The point is demonstrated by recent research in psychopharmacology. When the behavioral drugs first began to attract attention, they were studied with impromptu techniques based on self-observation, usually designed to quantify subjective reports. Eventually the methods of an experimental analysis proved their value in generating reproducible segments of behavior upon which the effects of drugs could be observed and in terms of which they could be effectively defined and classified. For the same reasons, brain physiology will move forward more rapidly when it recognizes that its role is to account for the mediation of behavior rather than of mind.

BEHAVIORISM IN THE SOCIAL SCIENCES

There is also still a need for behaviorism in the social sciences, where psychology has long been used for purposes of explanation. Economics has had its economic man. Political science has considered man as a political animal. Parts of anthropology and sociology have found a place for psychoanalysis. The relevance of psychology in linguistics has been debated for more than half a century. Studies of scientific method have oscillated between logical and empirical analyses. In all these fields, "psychologizing" has often had disappointing results and has frequently been rejected in favor of an extreme formalism which emphasizes objective facts. Economics confines itself to its own abundant data. Political scientists limit themselves to whatever may be studied with a few empirical tools and techniques, and confine themselves, when they deal with theory, to formalistic analyses of political structures. A strong structuralist movement is evident in sociology. Linguistics emphasizes formal analyses of semantics and grammar.

Straight-laced commitments to pure description and formal analysis appear to leave no place for explanatory principles, and the short-coming is often blamed on the exclusion of mental activities. For example, participants at a recent symposium on "The Limits of Behavioralism in Political Science" (8) complained of a neglect of subjective experience, ideas, motives, feelings, attitudes, values, and so on. This is reminiscent of attacks on behaviorism. In any case, it shows the same misunderstanding of the scope of a behaviorial analysis. In its extension to the social sciences, as in psychology proper, behaviorism means more than a commitment to objective measurement. No entity or process which has any useful explanatory force is to be rejected on the ground that it is subjective or mental. The data which have made it important must, however, be studied and formulated in effective ways. The assignment is well within the scope of an experimental analysis of behavior, which thus offers a promising alternative to a commitment to pure description on the one hand and an appeal to mentalistic theories on the other. To extend behaviorism as a philosophy of science to the study of political and economic behavior, of the behavior of people in groups, of people speaking and listening, teaching and learning—this is not "psychologizing" in the traditional sense. It is simply the application of a tested formula to important parts of the field of human behavior.

REFERENCES

1. F. Galton, *Inquiries into Human Faculty* (London, 1883), Everyman ed., p. 60.
2. L. Hogben, *Statistical Theory* (Allen and Unwin, London, 1957).
3. P. W. Bridgman, *The Way Things Are* (Harvard Univ. Press, Cambridge, Mass., 1959).
4. S. S. Stevens, *Am. J. Psychol.* **47**, 323 (1935).
5. D. S. Blough, *J. Comp. Physiol. Psychol.* **49**, 425 (1956); —— and A. M. Schrier, *Science* **139**, 493 (1963).
6. R. J. Herrnstein and P. van Sommers, *Science* **135**, 40 (1962).
7. K. N. Ogle, *ibid.*, p. 763.
8. *The Limits of Behavioralism in Political Science* (Am. Acad. Political and Social Sci., Philadelphia, 1962).

It is a common and disconcerting experience among the intellectuals in Western culture that scientists and humanists are separated by a gulf of mutual distrust and self-satisfied ignorance of each other's "view of life." Even on the university campus the science faculty typically is isolated from the humanities faculty socially, intellectually, and administratively. Dr. Sigmund Koch agrees with previous critics that the present gap between the two cultures is much to be deplored. However, he feels that the schism cannot be closed by innoculating a few physicists with Chekhov or a novelist with a course in quantum mechanics. He points out that psychology, being the *science* whose problems are closest to the interests of the *humanities* must be willing to assume the role of an integrating third force.

Selection **69** | PSYCHOLOGICAL SCIENCE VERSUS THE SCIENCE-HUMANISM ANTINOMY: INTIMATIONS OF A SIGNIFICANT SCIENCE OF MAN*

SIGMUND KOCH
Duke University

I am going to engage a problem for which I have feeble intellectual tools. It relates to an issue that if not yet a *cause célèbre* seems on the way to becoming so—that concerning the relations between science and the humanities. If my tools for this task are feeble, I claim some extenuation merely from the fact that I am a psychologist. Little that my field has done during its brief history as an independent science could equip me for work on the present question. Moreover, the climate of my field has not been such as to develop any

* Abridged from Sigmund Koch, "Psychological Science Versus the Science-Humanism Antinomy," *American Psychologist*, **16**: 629–639, 1961. Reprinted by permission of the author and the American Psychological Association.

sensibility in humanistic domains. Indeed, if there ever was such sensitivity, its suppression, starvation, and eventual atrophy seems to have been a necessary condition for Guild membership.

The reason I speak on this theme is that sooner or later someone from my field *must*. The situation is becoming embarrassing. Physicist-philosophers have addressed the theme. Physicist-literary critics have not been silent. Physicist-novelists have joined the issue. Physicist-administrators have not gone unheard. Sociologists have spoken. From the other side of the fence, historians, literary critics, and philosophers have been vocal. And more and more stridently there have of course been the educators, politicians, and last, but not least, military men. Psychologists have been strangely silent. That in itself is a fact worth pondering.

Against a silence so charged, anything one says must sound explosive. One might thus just as well speak with utter abandon from the start. I will state my main thesis boldly right now.

In any consideration of the science-humanities antinomy, the position of psychology must be given special, if not central, attention. In any assessment of the actual relations—similarities, differences, interpenetrations—of the work of science and of the humanities, psychological questions and modes of analysis must almost as a matter of definition be paramount. In any creative redefinition of the relations between science and the humanities, in any readjustment of the images, lay or technical, of these two great areas of the human cognitive adventure, which might more justly and precisely convey the essential unity of knowledge, psychological questions are again paramount. If psychology is to live up to the purview of its very definition, then it *must* be that science whose problems lie closest to those of the humanities; indeed, it must be that area in which the problems of the sciences, as traditionally conceived, and the humanities intersect. Relative to the present divisive situation in the world of knowledge, psychology, then, might be seen as a third force. It *could* be seen as a third force whose ranks, when they arrive in no man's land in sufficient numbers, would fill up the gap separating the contenders and reveal all three forces for what they really are: detachments from the same army which had forgotten that there was a common enemy.

Note the shift from the descriptive to the normative in the last paragraph. As I have already hinted, far from having been such a "third force," psychology (and the social sciences—my remarks will concentrate on psychology, but hold as well for the social sciences) in the twentieth century has perhaps done more to solidify, sharpen, perpetuate, thus obfuscate, the division between science and the humanities than any other "force" in the culture. It has sold to man an image of life as being nastier and more brutish, if longer, than any that Hobbes could have entertained—an image which could leave to the humanist only the role of idle *voyeur* peering tenderly into a sewer.

Among the brute facts that must be faced are these: Ever since its stipulation into existence as an independent science, psychology has been far more concerned with being a science than with courageous and self-determining confrontation of its historically constituted subject matter. Its history has been largely a matter of emulating the methods, forms, symbols of the established sciences, especially physics. In so doing, there has been an inevitable tendency to retreat from broad and intensely significant ranges of its subject matter, and to form rationales for so doing which could only invite further retreat. There has thus been, at least until very recently, an ever widening estrangement between the scientific makers of human science and the humanistic explorers of the content of man. Indeed, in its search for scientific respectability, psychology has erected a widely shared epistemology, and a conceptual language which render virtually impossible the exploration of the content of man in a differentiated way. So deeply engrained are these latter in the sensibilities of inquirers that even those who seek to study subtle or complex human phenomena are badly handicapped.

When phenomena of the sort that might concern the humanist *are* approached, a drab and sodden "middlebrowism" prevails. Humanists who stumble upon the results of such efforts are likely to feel revulsion. Perhaps fortunately they are unlikely so to stumble, in that scientific or academic psychology (exclusive of the psychiatric disciplines) has had only slight *direct* effect upon the culture at large. This fact of minimal direct representation in the culture is in itself significant. On the other hand, the indirect effects on the culture are I think profound.

With only a few exceptions, major twentieth century psychologists have had limited background in the humanities and, what is worse, limited sensibilities at esthetic levels and even as savorers of experience. The psychology of esthetics has practically not existed in the twentieth century. Psychology seems not even to have had its due share of individuals who have made significant independent contributions in humanistic areas. I can think of only one living psychologist who has, but of several living *physicists*.

Having observed that psychology must be a third force and then that throughout its history it has done little other than create the need for one, it is now only fair that I consider a number of matters which might reduce the stress between these observations. I begin by itemizing—to save time, summarily and dogmatically—some signs that something that could become a third force may be shaping up in psychology.

Of the factors predisposing psychology to confront problems of humanistic import, the first is indigenous; the second, though compelling, is indirect.

1. Psychology, after a long interval of imaging its ends and means on the model of physics, as interpreted and mediated by logical positivism, operationism, neopragmatism, and related movements, seems ready, perhaps for the first time in its history, to rise to its problems in free and *sui generis* ways. Simplistic theories of correct scientific conduct no longer occasion monolithic conformity. Behaviorist epistemology is under stress; neobehaviorism on the defensive; while neo-neobehaviorism enfolds itself in a womb of its own manufacture. There is a strongly increased interest in perception and central process, even on the part of S-R theorists: in fact a tendency for the central area of psychological interest to shift from learning to perception. There is a marked, if as yet unfocused, disposition on the part of *even* fundamental psychologists to readdress human phenomena and to readmit questions having experiential reference. Along with such changes, there is a marked devaluation of hypothetico-deductive formalization as an end in itself, and a shift of emphasis from the *form* of theoretical formulations to their meaning, empirical adequacy, and even illumination value. These and many cognate changes are conspicuous in the general literature and emerge with special force from the pages of *Psychology: A Study of a Science.* I have summarized the complex of changes to which I here allude in the "Epilogue" to Study I (Koch, 1959) of that enterprise, and happily offer that reference in exchange for the extensive development of the present assertions that might here be desirable.

Such changes *could* liberate psychology for the engagement of problems of direct humanistic concern. Though not tantamount to actual progress on such problems, the change of atmosphere is so marked as to betoken deep dissatisfaction with recent and traditional constrictions upon the range of research, even on the part of those fundamental psychologists whose purity is as the driven snow. The unrest has in fact led to a broadening of the range of problems investigated within more or less conventional terms and a diversification of the systematic and conceptual options that have been asserted.

2. Coincident and interrelated with these signs are others. An important set is provided by the changing image of the nature of science projected by the philosophy of science and by certain elements in the scientific community at large. These trends, uneven and disorderly, but pointing up and condoning a thoroughgoing pluralism of ends and means in science, are sure to influence the future direction of psychology. The picture I have in mind here is an enormously complex movement within recent scholarly culture—indeed one which has done much to prepare the grounds for the present general interest in exploring, and perhaps recentering, the relations between science and the humanities. I refer to such diverse matters as the weakening grip of logical positivism and related analytic philosophies; the relegitimation of metaphysics; the recognition of substantial areas of mootness in many problems of scientific method (e.g., the nature of definition, of "interpretation," of mathematics itself) which had been considered solved. Moreover, men like Bronowski, Polanyi, and others have at least begun to show that science, especially at theoretical levels, involves creative processes which no formalism can reduce to rule, processes in fact not dissimilar to those mediating the activity of poets, artists, historians, and other residents on the other side of the barricades. Such developments have been remarkably slow to register on psychology. For instance, the philosophy of science still talked in psychological literature is approximately 20 years out of date. But such developments are *beginning* to influence psychology.

I have said that psychology (and social science) has constructed a language which renders virtually impossible a differentiated exploration of the content of man. Such a constraint upon the very possibility of a sensitive analysis of experience is precisely what has kept psychology away from questions that could be of concern to the humanist. The humanist, I fear, has no particular reason for regretting this loss. Psychology, however, *must,* in that if the awesome range of its subject matter be the functioning of organisms, there is no sound basis for it to defect at precisely that point at which such functioning becomes most interesting and, by the judgment of civilization, valued.

Recently the British physicist-novelist, C. P. Snow, has stirred much discussion by virtue of a distinction that he makes between "two cultures"—the "scientific" and the "traditional" or "literary-intellectual"—which he sees as almost completely insulated one from the other and at cross purposes.[1] He finds this a blight on the world intellectually, but he is more concerned with practical consequences that may in fact threaten the future of the world, in that he feels that the ruling establishment, which (in England at least) receives a purely humanistic education, must become increasingly incapable of wise decisions without an understanding of science. His proposed solution for this—not an unradical one for England, where the undeniable charm of its archaic educational forms can instill vast defensive passions—is that the curriculum be diversified, that science be gotten into humanities programs, and vice versa. Snow, of course, is dealing with a pressing practical problem and, in light of the educational traditionalism in England, he is not to be criticized for posing so limited a solution. But it seems to me to be indeed so limited as to be almost beside the point.

No fertile integration or even interplay between science and the humanities can come about—either in individual minds or in the scholarly community as a whole—merely by juxtaposing scientific and humanistic subject matters in the same curriculum. Snow, for instance, complains that at a literary gathering he attended, not a single individual proved to have knowledge of the second law of thermodynamics. Had they been taught this information at Cambridge, I doubt that they would

[1] In his provocative anatomy of the two cultures (Snow, 1959), it is clear that by the "traditional" he has broadly in mind the humanistic culture, while by the "scientific" he means specifically the physicist-engineer culture. He leaves psychology and social science out of the picture and thereby, I think, effects a serious distortion. For, one of the unique features of psychology is precisely that this is an area at which the two cultures must be in contact.

have found it particularly titillating. What is needed is not merely more joint education in these two great divisions of subject matter, but a *new and more significant mode* of education which will present them in such a way as to reveal their relatedness and represent human knowledge for the organic thing that it is.

But such a proposal must remain largely empty until we know *what kind* of "organic thing" knowledge is, know this precisely and in detail. Only then can the ideologies and images of science and the humanities be adjusted in such a way as to reduce the arbitrary gap that still exists; only then could such ideologies and images find their place within a single more inclusive organization. *Such* changes would of course automatically be reflected in education and *only then* could we expect to see once more in the world a type of individual who has not been with us since the nineteenth century: the scientist-humanist (or, of course, humanist-scientist). He will not of course be the same such individual as that of the nineteenth century, just as the nineteenth century version was not the same as that of the Enlightenment or the Renaissance. He will be highly specialized (the present differentiation of knowledge demands this of its scholars), but whether his work fails into an area allocated to science or a humanity, he will have deeply within him a sense of its relations to whatever areas are actually *relata*, however they be named. He will also have a sense of the relatedness of all inquiry and be not ignorant of, or uninterested in, at least a few of the things that exist across the gulf that so effectively separated his recent forebears.

But all this is contingent on the prior exploration of relations between science and the humanities, no easy task when assayed for its dimension away from the conference table. Returning to our major theme, it is psychology which, as third force, must take the lead. This is not to be seen as altruism, still less as imperialism. Its subject matter leaves it no choice. It can only blame itself for having elected to be the empirical science of the functioning of intact organisms, including intact human ones, in all of its forms. It is trapped. Even if, say, it defensively held that esthetic experience were illusory, it would still have to prove this, thus study and account for esthetic experience. Since in psychology *problems concerning any range of human endeavor or experience can be the object of study*, a unique feature of psychology is that it must premise its research on discrimination pools each of which overlaps to some definite extent with the discrimination pools in all of those widely ranged human areas. Thus a special demand upon psychology is that it contain a more widely diversified, and probably larger, collection of language communities than any other department of knowledge currently institutionalized. Among these must be groups of individuals whose specialized perceptual sensitivities overlap with humanists' in each of the areas in which humanistic endeavors are pursued. That is a large requirement. Where it is not met, no humanistic work of any import can be done. It is grotesque to suppose that someone totally devoid of the special discriminations and sensitivities of the artist could do meaningful psychological work in that field; similarly that an illiterate could contribute to the psychology of language or of literature.

Our brief comments have thus pointed up the difficulties that must be overcome if psychology is to move into its responsibility as "third force." It is clear that psychology needs many individuals having sensitivities overlapping with those of the humanist. Yet the same individuals must, in the first instance, have the special aptitudes and sensitivities—whatever they be—which equip them for *scientific* modes of analysis! For reasons foreshadowed in our remarks concerning education, it cannot expect them in even remotely adequate numbers. The absolute number of such individuals turned out by the culture at large is in itself pathetically small. Such individuals in general are not attracted to psychology, in that the very sensitivities at issue are what preclude their interest.

The emergence of a third force can at best be expected to be painfully slow and contingent on considerable skill with the bootstrap. So-called "recruitment" philosophies which currently see the ideal candidate as a kind of *Ubermensch* in theoretical physics and carpentry at once, will of course have to be redefined, but not *derigorized*. If anything, the requirement will be more stringent, not less. That such a requirement will be met by few is no

fatal objection. As with all requirements, compromise will continue to be the general rule. Of greater importance is that psychology be so imaged as to convey the need, the possibility, and the importance of work in areas of humanistic import. This may bring to us some of the individuals having the requisite combination of aptitudes, who now bypass us because of their uncongeniality towards the current image. Most important, we must work towards those more general educational changes at all levels which might increase the absolute number of such individuals in the culture at large.

Feeble and gradual as such a "program" may seem, the stakes are very high. For what has hardly been in the picture except by innuendo so far, has been the world outside the cloisters. Despite the "creativity" fad, and despite the recent spate of social criticism which has made organization men, lonely crowds, affluent societies, ex-urbanites, and their ilk seminar topics at every shopping center, the gentle process of dehumanization which twentieth century man has so cosily accepted continues unabated. Indeed, the truly frightening fact is that so much of the social criticism itself reproduces, at second remove, the qualities of the object criticized. Take the "beatnik" whose devastating critique of an inarticulate society is to form a cult of absolute inarticulateness.

The reduction of man to his present dimension need not be temporary. When the ability to differentiate among experiences is lost, experience is lost. When the perception of differential values as they inhere in the quiddities of experience and action is lost, then value is lost. Nothing says that these things need return. In this homogenization of experience, the recent images of science and of the humanities have played a profound part. The newer outgrowths of science—psychology and the social sciences—which, had they pursued their appropriate subject matter, could have helped resolve knowledge into its proper spectrum, turned away from that subject matter. Rejecting the first force from which all knowledge had germinated, they became camp followers of that second force called "science," or at least their image of that force. Have they the courage to become the third force that could some day cause the end of armies?

REFERENCES

Koch, S. Behavior as "intrinsically" regulated: Work notes towards a pre-theory of phenomena called "motivational." In M. R. Jones (Ed.), *Current theory and research in motivation.* Vol. 4. Lincoln: Univer. Nebraska Press, 1956. Pp. 42–86.

Koch, S. Epilogue to study I. In S. Koch (Ed.), *Psychology: A study of a science.* Vol. 3. New York: McGraw-Hill, 1959. Pp. 729–788.

Snow, C. P. *The two cultures and the scientific revolution.* New York: Cambridge Univer. Press, 1959.

Selection 70 INTRODUCTION

To an increasing extent, psychologists and social scientists are serving as consultants to major governmental agencies or are accepting important decision-making roles in these agencies (e.g., Dr. John Gardner, Secretary of Health, Education, and Welfare, is a psychologist). Many psychologists feel that they have a responsibility to speak out in order to bring national policies into congruence with principles of group behavior. However, not all psychologists believe that we have available sufficiently generalizable principles to be of help in policy making. In fact, some have suggested that the participation of psychologists in such activities is looked upon by colleagues with sufficient disfavor as to be among the topics which are currently taboo.*

Dr. Charles E. Osgood, former president of the American Psychological Association, maintains that one of the appropriate roles of the academician is to help the policy makers perceive new alternatives. He analyzes the two criteria which have been fundamental to U.S. foreign policy toward the Communist bloc as biological survival and maintenance of our way of life. He observes that the prime psychological element in our policy has been the concept of deterrence through fear of retaliation. Three available alternatives (massive retaliation, limited war, and mutual disarmament) are criticized, and several principles of intergroup conflict which serve to increase tension are discussed. Osgood then proposes an alternative policy of graduated unilateral disengagement. He is careful to specify the assumptions on which the policy would be based and indicates several of its more important general features. Osgood maintains that the plan offers a greater likelihood of reversing the current "increased tension—arms race" spiral. The psychological soundness of the plan is supported by the principles of intergroup relations discussed by Sherif in Selection 50.

Selection 70 | A CASE FOR GRADUATED UNILATERAL DISENGAGEMENT†

CHARLES E. OSGOOD
University of Illinois

Today we are faced with the potentially lethal combination of nuclear weapons against which there is no defense and international tensions from which there seems to be no respite. Most Americans, and I believe most Russians as well, are fully aware of the dangers in the present course. Yet they feel impelled toward it with a certain inevitability. "We must learn to live with it," our newspapers tell us; editorials complain about the cost of military preparations, but conclude that "we must grin and pay it."

In this paper I will try to analyze some of the dynamics of human thinking which, paradoxically, are driving us in a direction we do not wish to go. The analysis leads to certain suggestions for policy. These are made in the broadest possible terms. I do not believe the academician is equipped with the information or experience needed to make detailed policy proposals in concrete situations. What he can do best is raise questions about the assumptions underlying policy, ask that they be re-

* Norman L. Farberow, *Taboo Topics*, Atherton Press, New York, 1963.
† Reprinted from Charles E. Osgood, "A Case for Graduated Unilateral Disengagement," *Bulletin of the Atomic Scientists*, 16: 127, 1960. Reprinted by permission of the author and publisher.

examined rather than taken for granted, and offer what may be novel ways of viewing policy problems in the hope of contributing to the discovery of alternatives not previously believed to exist.

EVALUATION OF CURRENT POLICY ALTERNATIVES

Criteria If the long-term goals of a nation are not made explicit, decisions are likely to be made opportunistically in defense of the *status quo.* What has merely become habitual is easily seen as somehow natural and essential. What are our goals? What are we "fighting for?" To answer this question we must distinguish between two quite different wars and opponents. One is the *"hot war"* with Russia as a nation—a war in which we are in danger of becoming involved. Our long-term goal here is, quite simply, *survival.* This may be a rather ignoble value, but it is a necessary precondition for securing any other goals. The availability of nuclear weapons with awesome capacities for destruction, to say nothing about biological weapons, may not alter the nature of international conflict or its goals, but it certainly must change radically the weights we use in evaluating alternative strategies.

The other conflict is *the "cold war" with communism* and other totalitarian systems. This war goes on steadily in the minds of men, and it is fought as much within as across the borders of nations. Our long-term goal here is *to preserve and extend our way of life.* Stripped to its essential, this is a way of life in which the state is subservient to the individuals who compose it. The development of such a political philosophy, based on the dignity of individual human beings, was a most remarkable step along the path to becoming civilized; it was hard come by and is all too easily lost. Again, in the interest of short-term goals and in defense of the *status quo,* we have often lost sight of the fact that this way of life was itself a major socio-political revolution, and it is still under way.

There are, of course, many case-hardened statesmen and well-disciplined political theorists who will say that the underlying source of international tensions is still what it always has been—the struggle for power—and weapons, whether they be clubs or atomic warheads, are simply instruments for effecting a change in the balance of power. Although the manifest behaviors of nations may often conform to this Neanderthal conception of international relations, I think that the Neanderthalic bluster nearly always has masked a deeper anxiety. Today, perhaps more than ever before in world history, *mutual insecurity* rather than the struggle for power has become the underlying source of tension.

Current policy alternatives Keeping in mind these two criteria—reducing the threat to our biological survival and maintaining our way of life—as well as sheer *feasibility,* we may now consider the major alternatives currently being discussed.[1]

The decision to wage *preventive war* implies a sufficient lead in the armament race to minimize the possibility of punishing reprisal, and, since such a war must begin with a surprise attack, this decision must be reached by other than democratic procedures. Unfortunately, on both counts this strategy is much more available to Russia than to ourselves, particularly during the next critical decade. Even if we were to gain a sufficient lead, and an elite were to make the decision for us, this solution would not serve to maintain or extend our way of life—we would have to exhaust ourselves policing a hostile globe.

The backbone of our present policy is *mutual deterrence through fear of retaliation.* The underlying notion is that, with each side capable of destroying the other with massive retaliation, neither side will make the initial move, and a prolonged if uneasy "peace" can be maintained. This does not reduce the nuclear threat—indeed, it is this threat which, paradoxically, is supposed to guarantee peace. Quite to the contrary, it serves to generate an arms race, since the habitual response to external threat is to demand more and better armaments. I have come to the somber conclusion that we would not be able to maintain a favorable position in this race without giving up our way of life as rapidly as possible. Then we would be able to channel the energies of our people into military preparations, order

[1] Space does not permit adequate justification of my conclusions. The interested reader is referred to a more detailed analysis appearing in *Conflict Resolution,* 1960.

our young people into training in the physical sciences, and make decisions and changes in strategy without democratic processes.

There are also three grave uncertainties to which the proponents of this policy haven't paid sufficient attention: one is the Nth Country problem—international tension and instability will increase geometrically with the number of countries capable of mounting a nuclear attack. Another is the unpredictability of human behavior under stress—mutual deterrence assumes rationality on all sides, but as retaliation time reduces, decision-making must be dispersed over more and more (potentially unstable) people. Finally, there is the seldom-asked question—*when and how does it end?* Mutual deterrence contains no provisions for its own resolution.

The complete unwieldiness of massive retaliation as an instrument of everyday foreign policy has led us toward the *limited war* conception, e.g., the Kissinger Plan. The underlying notion here is that the threat of full-scale nuclear war will prevent nations from unleashing it, thereby allowing "war as usual" to be used as an instrument of policy. However appealing the idea of "gentlemanly war" may be to military men, it is inconceivable under present conditions, with whole populations involved in fighting and producing under the whip of mass communications. As to the idea that the very horror of nuclear war will prevent its occurrence, one wonders why this horror in times of relative peace hasn't led us promptly into agreements on nuclear disarmament. The proponents of limited war would ask us to literally flirt with the danger of all-out nuclear war with no more protection than fear itself.

The only problem with *mutual disarmament* —the ideal solution in all other respects—is the *feasibility* of successful negotiations when international tensions are running high. Under such conditions logic, which requires both sides to accept a course in which neither gains nor loses, tends to be superceded by *psycho-logic*, which operates under the guidance of "one-upsmanship" and pays more attention to the folks back home than the folks across the table. There are two psychological mechanisms particularly that work against successful negotiation. One is *biased perceptions of what is equable.* In keeping with literally hundreds of experiments, both within the laboratory and outside of it, what is seen as fair, just, and balanced by the representatives of one nation (given its life history and present world view) is necessarily seen as somewhat unfair, unjust, and unbalanced by those of the other (with its quite different life history and world view). The other is the *self-fulfilling prophecy.* Each side predicts that the other will prove unreasonable and try to gain advantage in the "cold war," behaves according to its prediction, and then says, "I told you so!" when nothing comes of it. Mutual disarmament requires commitments prior to action. Commitments of any magnitude seem unlikely in the present atmosphere of fear and distrust, as the long and dismal history of unsuccessful negotiations testifies.

SOME DYNAMICS OF CONTROVERSY

The essential irrationality and danger in our present course is apparent, yet we feel impelled along it. No one wants war in a nuclear age, yet no one seems able to avoid an inevitable spiralling toward it. Why should this be so? What forces operate in times of controversy between human groups to push ordinary disagreement toward mutual destruction?

Foreshortened perspective   The more intelligent a species or individual, the greater the capacity for delay, foresight, and striving for remote goals. But emotion has the effect of primitivizing this capacity. The motivational conditions of controversy, e.g., our present tensions—arms-race dilemma, are precisely those designed to restrict our perspective. Taking the long view through space and time, we see that the events which today are shaking the very fabric of our lives are all transpiring on the knife-thin edge of a little pebble in the sky, and we realize that the organizations among men we call "nations" must come and go—this being as true for what we now call "Russia" and "The United States" as it was for Rome and Babylon. This is not said to minimize the seriousness of our present problems, or in any sense of defeatism, but rather to emphasize different goals. A wide perspective makes it possible to substitute more remote goals for immediate ones.

Relativity of social judgment   "Man is the measure of all things," it has been said—but surely this is true only to the extent that his science is primitive. One can trace at least three stages in clear social thinking. At the most primitive level we unconsciously project our own frame of reference onto others; if Alter claims to be "straight" what to Ego is obviously "crooked," Alter must be lying, evil, or at least abnormal in some way. At the second stage we recognize the relativistic nature of Alter's frame of reference, but not our own; this produces a more humane approach toward social problems, a "forgive *them* for *they* know not what they do" attitude. At the third stage we realize the equally relativistic nature of our own frame of reference; this is the sensitive—not "ugly"—American who realizes that his own neutral points on clean-dirty, tasty-distasteful, or even moral-immoral scales of judgment are no more "natural" than those of the Mexican or Hindu. What this means is *not* that there are no external criteria for distinguishing good from bad, but rather that we must search for such criteria because social judgments are very liable to bias.

Emotional restriction of alternatives Rational behavior requires understanding one's ultimate goals, weighing the consequences of alternative means to these goals, and then selecting among the alternatives in terms of their success probabilities. Many laboratory and field experiments, both with animals and humans, demonstrate that intense emotion causes a reduced awareness of alternatives—and if there is no awareness of the existence of certain alternatives, they cannot be weighed. Today nations are lumbering down the one *habitual* path to "security"—bigger and better armaments—gathering as they go tensions which make it less and less possible to see other alternatives. Being habitual, this course is assumed to be "realistic." Anthropologists are familiar with cultures that, through blind adherence to practices that once were realistic, have gradually committed suicide. I think we are in exactly the same spot. We are practicing rites and rituals of international relations that were developed in and appropriate to the past—firmly believing them to be realistic—in a present age that renders them suicidal.

Psycho-logic Human thinking abhors incongruity. In striving to maintain internal consistency among one's attitudes, beliefs, and behaviors, the dictates of what may be called "psycho-logic" rather than logic are often followed—particularly when dealing with matters outside one's field of special competence. If we like Ike, and he praises some congressman from Timbuktu, then it is congruent for us to also feel favorably disposed toward this congressman, even though we know absolutely nothing else about him. If Khrushchev were to praise the sound ideas of some presidential "hopeful"—popularly known as the "kiss of death"—then, quite illogically, we might find ourselves a little suspicious of this candidate. It is psycho-logic rather than logic that leads people to conclude that Nehru must be pro-Communist because he insists on India's neutrality.

Psycho-logic runs rampant when we try to come to grips with problems of international conflict, and it is one of the main blocks to rational thinking in our present situation. It is the chief dynamism in the production of Bogey Men conceptions of the enemy. Given the belief that WE are *good*, *kind*, *fair*, and so on—a necessary and generally valid assumption—and the logical opposition between WE and THEM, between FRIEND and ENEMY, psycho-logic dictates that the enemy must be *bad cruel*, *unfair*, and so on. The failure of the Russians to see eye to eye with us on many issues, their purges, their atheism, and so on, support and strengthen the Bogey Man conception, which in turn serves to explain their un-American and anti-American behaviors. We know that we would not take advantage of a defenseless people if they were to lay down their weapons, but we are certain that *they* would leap to destroy us in similar circumstances.

Many recent travelers to Russia, including statesmen and scholars, have been impressed by the "mirror image" our attitudes that they find among the people and leaders there. "Why do you Americans want war?" our informal ambassadors are asked. And when they answer that we most certainly do not want war, the Russians ask, "Then why do your leaders prepare for war? Why do they ring us about with missile bases?" When our travelers ask them why they maintain a great army and are building up nuclear weapons for long-range attack, they reply, of course, that we leave them no choice. I believe that we must accept these protestations of good faith as genuine. They blame their aggressive behavior on us just as we blame ours on them.

I'm sure it would be unrealistic to completely discount real differences between the Russians and ourselves—for example, those concerning the value of the individual which stem from our ideological conflict. But I am equally sure that this Bogey has been overdrawn in the workings of our own mental dynamics—particularly by those who fail to draw any distinction between Russian Communism and German Nazism. The Russian Bogey can be cut down to a more realistic size and shape.

GRADUATED UNILATERAL DISENGAGEMENT

Most of the discussion of policy in a nuclear age has been framed in technological terms and carried on more by physicists and engineers than by social scientists. But nuclear technology merely exaggerates the problem; it neither explains our difficulties nor offers any real solutions. In the last analysis, it is certainly true that today we are plagued with problems of human nature and human relationships. Our understanding and control of the physical world has far outstripped our understanding of and ability to control ourselves. The present generation is faced with the consequence of this unbalance.

Requirements for solution of the policy problem In search for a long-term solution, we must first ask ourselves this: what are the conditions that support the Communist (or any other totalitarian) way of life as against our own way? Here I will merely list some of these conditions *Economic scarcity*. When people exist near a bare subsistence level, little energy is left over for the development of those uniquenesses which make people important as individual human beings. *Social inequality*. Totalitarian systems display gross inequalities in civil, political, and social rights, based on the distribution of power if nothing else. *Educational deficiency*. Limited or biased education prevents people from acquiring the tools needed to better their state. *Information restriction*. The free flow of communication, both within and across national boundaries and both among individuals and via the mass media,

provides the diversity of viewpoints in which lies the vitality of the democratic system and the freedom of choice people need to govern themselves. Such freedom is the anathema of totalitarianism. *External threat*. Threat from outside the group impels people to accept subservience to the state and to forego individual freedoms, in the interest of what they perceive as the common goal—namely, survival. This is admittedly an incomplete list, but it will serve to set the problem.

Secondly, we must ask ourselves: how can these conditions be changed within the existing set-up of competing sovereign states? When scientists, working on their own much smaller-scale problems, want to change something, they operate on the conditions which produce the phenomenon. In our present, infinitely larger-scale problem we would like to so modify the background conditions in Communist and other states as to foster and support a more democratic way of life. But the world situation today is one of extremely high mutual threat perception between two coalitions of essentially sovereign states. It is a bi-polar power situation aggravated by a fundamental ideological conflict. This situation has led to intense security measures, and both sides have erected "iron curtains" through which only carefully metered driblets of information can pass.

I therefore see rational policy as requiring two phases. *Phase I—reversal of the tensions—arms-race spiral*. Before any other policies can be employed effectively, mutual threat perception must be reduced to a level where the arms race can be halted and put in reverse. Not only is this necessary to escape from the very real danger of mutual annihilation, but it is also the only sure way to dissolve the "iron curtains" that hamper the use of other strategies. *Phase II—maintaining the peace*. It is my contention that our way of life flourishes in peacetime and the totalitarian way in wartime. If I am right, then anything that continues the peace works in our favor.

It is obvious that many of the conditions that support the Communist way of life—economic scarcity, social inequality, educational deficiency, and information restriction—cannot be directly manipulated through the "iron curtains" that separate East and West. (But the Russians have been doing a very good job of modifying these conditions, and in so doing have been modifying themselves—whether they know it or not.) On the other hand, *we can manipulate the condition of external threat.* This is at least partly under our control, because we ourselves, in our words and actions, contribute to the level of threat which the Russians perceive. We can behave so as to raise this threat or so as to lower it; we can change it abruptly or in gradual stages. Solution of the critical, but very sensitive and difficult, Phase I—reversal of the tensions—arms-race spiral—hinges on our intelligent manipulation of the condition of external threat.

Assumptions underlying graduated unilateral disengagement I use the term *disengagement* (rather than disarmament) to emphasize the fact that we are considering a much wider range of acts than the term "disarmament" implies. This policy is based on the assumption that the Russian people and leaders are sufficiently like us to accept an unambiguous opportunity to reduce the probability of mutual nuclear destruction. It also assumes that the Russian leaders are susceptible to moral pressures, both from without and from within—since such pressures are an index of the success or failure of their system. It assumes that —unlike mutual negotiations that can easily be twisted into cold war propaganda—unilateral acts of a tension-reducing nature are relatively unambiguous. It assumes that each unilateral act which is reciprocated makes the next such sequence easier to accomplish. Finally, it assumes that the Communists are as convinced that their way of life will win out in non-military competition for men's minds as we are (or should be) that ours will.

Nature of this policy To be maximally effective in inducing an enemy to reciprocate, a unilateral act: (1) should, in terms of capacity for military *aggression*, be clearly disadvantageous to the side making it; (2) should be such as to be clearly perceived by the other side as reducing *his* external threat; (3) should not increase an enemy's threat to our heartland; (4) should be such that reciprocal action by the other side is clearly available and clearly indicated; (5) should be announced in advance and widely publicized to ally, neutral, and enemy countries—as regards the nature of the act, its purpose as part of a consistent policy, and the expected reciprocation; (6) but should

not demand prior commitment to reciprocation by the other side as a condition for its commission.

The initial acts of unilateral disengagement would be small in magnitude of risk, should they not be reciprocated, but would increase in magnitude or risk potential as reciprocations were obtained. The initial series of unilateral acts would be designed to be cumulative in their tension-reducing effect upon the enemy, but non-cumulative in their effect upon our capacity to deliver massive retaliation should this policy fail—that is, the acts would not be such as to weaken us progressively in the same area, or in the "survival" area at all.

Note the essential differences between this policy and Kissinger's "limited war" proposal: although both policies rely upon the capacity for massive retaliation as a psychological buffer, "limited war" would use nuclear deterrence as the support for tension-*increasing* acts ("war as usual") whereas "graduated unilateral disengagement" would use nuclear deterrence as the support for tension-*reducing* acts. Furthermore, where the policy I am proposing holds out some hope for ultimate elimination of the massive nuclear deterrent itself, the Kissinger Plan offers no such hope.

I am not going to try to indicate what the precise nature of such a series of graduated unilateral acts should be. Their selection, ordering, and timing demands a great deal of information which only people in government have. Also, alternative acts must be available at each stage—one to be made if the Russians have reciprocated (larger step) and another to be used if they have not (smaller step). However, I am sure that if we put even a small part of the total energy we are now pouring into weapons production into an intensive study of the possibilities for unilateral actions, effective programs could be devised. American Man and Russian Man have been moving out against each other along a narrow and teetering see saw, each trying to match every aggressive step by the other with an outward step of his own, in order to maintain the unstable balance. It is equally possible for them to move gradually *toward* each other, step by step, until they meet at the middle and the danger is past. In sum, what I am proposing is a "primer" to initiate a reversal in the tensions —arms-race dilemma.

Selection **71**   INTRODUCTION

In this selection Dr. Carl Rogers expands the implications of his view of the thera-peutic process (cf. Selection 55). He compares and contrasts the valuing process in the mature individual with that in infants and "normals." The infant's valuing process is characterized by simple spontaneity and sensitivity to organismic feelings. As a process he exhibits apparently contradictory values, depending on his needs and the situation. However, the values are only apparently contradictory in that they are organized around the actualization of growth potentials. In the so-called "normal" individual much of the spontaneity, creativity, and sensitivity to organic feelings have been inhibited in the process of socialization. The condition in which the child comes to introject the values of others as more valid than his own feelings serves as the prototype for a state of alienation from personal feelings. There is thus built up a "fundamental discrepancy" between his intellectualized self-concept and his organic valuing process. In the process of psychotherapy this discrepancy may be narrowed. As the patient becomes more mature his valuing process comes to be based more on his honest feelings than on the introjected values of others. Although this "internal locus of evaluation" might seem to lead to excessive selfishness, the clinical evidence suggests that this is not so.* On the basis of his clinical experience Rogers proposes that: (1) the valuing process is based on organic processes within the individual from birth, (2) the effectiveness of this organismically based valuing process depends on the ability of the person to be sensitive to his experience (see "Openness to experience" in Selection 55), (3) there appears to be a universality of value directions among those persons who are open to experience, and (4) these directions have in common "the constructive enhancement of the individual and his community, for the survival and evolution of his species."

Selection **71** | TOWARD A MODERN APPROACH TO VALUES: THE VALUING PROCESS IN THE MATURE PERSON†

CARL R. ROGERS
Western Behavioral Sciences Institute,
La Jolla, California

There is a great deal of concern today with the problem of values. Youth, in almost every country, is deeply uncertain of its value orien-tation; the values associated with various re-ligions have lost much of their influence; sophisticated individuals in every culture seem unsure and troubled as to the goals they hold in esteem. The reasons are not far to seek. The world culture, in all its aspects, seems increasingly scientific and relativistic, and the rigid, absolute views on values which come to us from the past appear anachronistic. Even more important, perhaps, is the fact that the modern individual is assailed from every angle by divergent and contradictory value claims. It is no longer possible, as it was in the not too distant historical past, to settle comfortably into the value system of one's forebears or one's community and live out one's life with-out ever examining the nature and the assump-tions of that system.

In this situation it is not surprising that value orientations from the past appear to be in a state of disintegration or collapse. Men question whether there are, or can be, any universal values. It is often felt that we may have lost, in our modern world, all possibility

* The student should be reminded of Fromm's discus-sion of selfishness in this context (Selection 56).
† From Carl R. Rogers, "Toward a Modern Approach To Values: The Valuing Process in the Mature Per-son," *Journal of Abnormal and Social Psychology,* **68**: 160–167, 1964. Copyright 1964 by the American Psychological Association and reproduced by permis-sion of the publisher and author.

of any general or cross-cultural basis for values. One natural result of this uncertainty and confusion is that there is an increasing concern about, interest in, and a searching for, a sound or meaningful value approach which can hold its own in today's world.

I share this general concern. As with other issues the general problem faced by the culture is painfully and specifically evident in the cultural microcosm which is called the therapeutic relationship, which is my sphere of experience.

As a consequence of this experience I should like to attempt a modest theoretical approach to this whole problem. I have observed changes in the approach to values as the individual grows from infancy to adulthood. I observe further changes when, if he is fortunate, he continues to grow toward true psychological maturity. Many of these observations grow out of my experience as therapist, where I have had the mind stretching opportunity of seeing the ways in which individuals move toward a richer life. From these observations I believe I see some directional threads emerging which might offer a new concept of the valuing process, more tenable in the modern world. I have made a beginning by presenting some of these ideas partially in previous writings (Rogers, 1951, 1959); I would like now to voice them more clearly and more fully.

SOME DEFINITIONS

Charles Morris (1956, pp. 9–12) has made some useful distinctions in regard to values. There are "operative values," which are the behaviors of organisms in which they show preference for one object or objective rather than another. The lowly earthworm, selecting the smooth arm of a Y maze rather than the arm which is paved with sandpaper, is giving an indication of an operative value.

There are also "conceived values," the preference of an individual for a symbolized object. "Honesty is the best policy" is such a conceived value.

There is also the term "objective value," to refer to what is objectively preferable, whether or not it is sensed or conceived of as desirable. I will be concerned primarily with operative or conceptualized values.

INFANT'S WAY OF VALUING

Let me first speak about the infant. The living human being has, at the outset, a clear approach to values. We can infer from studying his behavior that he prefers those experiences which maintain, enhance, or actualize his organism, and rejects those which do not serve this end. Watch him for a bit:

Hunger is negatively valued. His expression of this often comes through loud and clear.

Food is positively valued. But when he is satisfied, food is negatively valued, and the same milk he responded to so eagerly is now spit out, or the breast which seemed so satisfying is now rejected as he turns his head away from the nipple with an amusing facial expression of disgust and revulsion.

He values security, and the holding and caressing which seem to communicate security.

He values new experience for its own sake, and we observe this in his obvious pleasure in discovering his toes, in his searching movements, in his endless curiosity.

He shows a clear negative valuing of pain, bitter tastes, sudden loud sounds. *white*

All of this is commonplace, but let us look at these facts in terms of what they tell us about the infant's approach to values. It is first of all a flexible, changing, valuing *process*, not a fixed system. He likes food and dislikes the same food. He values security and rest, and rejects it for new experience. What is going on seems best described as an organismic valuing process, in which each element, each moment of what he is experiencing is somehow weighed, and selected or rejected, depending on whether, at that moment, it tends to actualize the organism or not. This complicated weighing of experience is clearly an organismic, not a conscious or symbolic function. These are operative, not conceived values. But this process can nonetheless deal with complex value problems. I would remind you of the experiment in which young infants had spread in front of them a score or more of dishes of natural (that is, unflavored) foods. Over a period of time they clearly tended to value the foods which enhanced their own survival, growth, and development. If for a time a child gorged himself on starches, this would soon be balanced by a protein "binge." If at times he chose a diet deficient in some vitamin, he would later seek out foods rich in this very vitamin. The physiological wisdom of his body guided his behavioral movements, resulting in what we might think of as objectively sound value choices.

Another aspect of the infant's approach to values is that the source or locus of the evaluating process is clearly within himself. Unlike many of us, he *knows* what he likes and dislikes, and the origin of these value choices lies strictly within himself. He is the center of the valuing process, the evidence for his choices being supplied by his own senses. He is not at this point influenced by what his parents think he should prefer, or by what the church says, or by the opinion of the latest "expert" in the field, or by the persuasive talents of an advertising firm. It is from within his own experiencing that his organism is saying in nonverbal terms, "This is good for me." "That is bad for me." "I like this." "I strongly dislike that." He would laugh at our concern over values, if he could understand it.

CHANGE IN THE VALUING PROCESS

What happens to this efficient, soundly based valuing process? By what sequence of events do we exchange it for the more rigid, uncertain, inefficient approach to values which characterizes most of us as adults? Let me try to state briefly one of the major ways in which I think this happens.

The infant needs love, wants it, tends to behave in ways which will bring a repetition of this wanted experience. But this brings complications. He pulls baby sister's hair, and finds it satisfying to hear her wails and protests. He then hears that he is "a naughty, bad boy," and this may be reinforced by a slap on the hand. He is cut off from affection. As this experience is repeated, and many, many others like it, he gradually learns that what "feels good" is often "bad" in the eyes of significant others. Then the next step occurs, in which he comes to take the same attitude toward himself which these others have taken. Now, as he pulls his sister's hair, he solemnly intones, "Bad, bad boy." He is

introjecting the value judgment of another, taking it in as his own. To that degree he loses touch with his own organismic valuing process. He has deserted the wisdom of his organism, giving up the locus of evaluation, and is trying to behave in terms of values set by another, in order to hold love.

Or take another example at an older level. A boy senses, though perhaps not consciously, that he is more loved and prized by his parents when he thinks of being a doctor than when he thinks of being an artist. Gradually he introjects the values attached to being a doctor. He comes to want, above all, to be a doctor. Then in college he is baffled by the fact that he repeatedly fails in chemistry, which is absolutely necessary to becoming a physician, in spite of the fact that the guidance counselor assures him he has the ability to pass the course. Only in counseling interviews does he begin to realize how completely he has lost touch with his organismic reactions, how out of touch he is with his own valuing process.

Perhaps these illustrations will indicate that in an attempt to gain or hold love, approval, esteem, the individual relinquishes the locus of evaluation which was his in infancy, and places it in others. He learns to have a basic *distrust* for his own experiencing as a guide to his behavior. He learns from others a large number of conceived values, and adopts them as his own, even though they may be widely discrepant from what he is experiencing.

SOME INTROJECTED PATTERNS

It is in this fashion, I believe, that most of us accumulate the introjected value patterns by which we live. In the fantastically complex culture of today, the patterns we introject as desirable or undesirable come from a variety of sources and are often highly contradictory. Let me list a few of the introjections which commonly held.

Sexual desires and behaviors are mostly bad. The sources of this construct are many—parents, church, teachers.

Disobedience is bad. Here parents and teachers combine with the military to emphasize this concept.

To obey is good. To obey without question is even better.

Making money is the highest good. The sources of this conceived value are too numerous to mention.

Learning an accumulation of scholarly facts is highly desirable. Education is the source.

Communism is utterly bad. Here the government is a major source.

To love thy neighbor is the highest good. This concept comes from the church, perhaps from the parents.

Cooperation and teamwork are preferable to acting alone. Here companions are an important source.

Cheating is clever and desirable. The peer group again is the origin.

Coca-Colas, chewing gum, electric refrigerators, and automobiles are all utterly desirable. From Jamaica to Japan, from Copenhagen to Kowloon, the "Coca-Cola culture" has come to be regarded as the acme of desirability.

This is a small and diversified sample of the myriads of conceived values which individuals often introject, and hold as their own, without ever having considered their inner organismic reactions to these patterns and objects.

COMMON CHARACTERISTICS OF ADULT VALUING

I believe it will be clear from the foregoing that the usual adult—I feel I am speaking for most of us—has an approach to values which has these characteristics:

The majority of his values are introjected from other individuals or groups significant to him, but are regarded by him as his own.

The source or locus of evaluation on most matters lies outside of himself.

The criterion by which his values are set is the degree to which they will cause him to be loved, accepted, or esteemed.

These conceived preferences are either not related at all, or not clearly related, to his own process of experiencing.

Often there is a wide and unrecognized discrepancy between the evidence supplied by his own experience, and these conceived values.

Because these conceptions are not open to testing

in experience, he must hold them in a rigid and unchanging fashion. The alternative would be a collapse of his values. Hence his values are "right."

Because they are untestable, there is no ready way of solving contradictions. If he has taken in from the community the conception that money is the *summum bonum* and from the church the conception that love of one's neighbor is the highest value, he has no way of discovering which has more value for *him*. Hence a common aspect of modern life is living with absolutely contradictory values. We calmly discuss the possibility of dropping a hydrogen bomb on Russia, but find tears in our eyes when we see headlines about the suffering of one small child.

Because he has relinquished the locus of evaluation to others, and has lost touch with his own valuing process, he feels profoundly insecure and easily threatened in his values. If some of these conceptions were destroyed, what would take their place? This threatening possibility makes him hold his value conceptions more rigidly or more confusedly, or both.

FUNDAMENTAL DISCREPANCY

I believe that this picture of the individual, with values mostly introjected, held as fixed concepts, rarely examined or tested, is the picture of most of us. By taking over the conceptions of others as our own, we lose contact with the potential wisdom of our own functioning, and lose confidence in ourselves. Since these value constructs are often sharply at variance with what is going on in our own experiencing, we have in a very basic way divorced ourselves from ourselves, and this accounts for much of modern strain and insecurity. This fundamental discrepancy between the individual's concept and what he is actually experiencing, between the intellectual structure of his values and the valuing process going on unrecognized within—this is a part of the fundamental estrangement of modern man from himself.

RESTORING CONTACT WITH EXPERIENCE

Some individuals are fortunate in going beyond the picture I have just given, developing further in the direction of psychological maturity. We see this happen in psychotherapy where we endeavor to provide a climate favorable to the growth of the person. We also see it happen in life, whenever life provides a therapeutic climate for the individual. Let me concentrate on this further maturing of a value approach as I have seen it in therapy.

As the client senses and realizes that he is prized as a person[1] he can slowly begin to value the different aspects of himself. Most importantly, he can begin, with much difficulty at first, to sense and to feel what is going on within him, what he is feeling, what he is experiencing, how he is reacting. He uses his experiencing as a direct referent to which he can turn in forming accurate conceptualizations and as a guide to his behavior. Gendlin (1961, 1962) has elaborated the way in which this occurs. As his experiencing becomes more and more open to him, as he is able to live more freely in the process of his feelings, then significant changes begin to occur in his approach to values. It begins to assume many of the characteristics it had in infancy.

INTROJECTED VALUES IN RELATION TO EXPERIENCING

Perhaps I can indicate this by reviewing a few of the brief examples of introjected values which I have given, and suggesting what happens to them as the individual comes closer to what is going on within him.

The individual in therapy looks back and realizes "But I *enjoyed* pulling my sister's hair—and that doesn't make me a bad person."

The student failing chemistry realizes, as he gets close to his own experiencing, "I don't like chemistry; I don't value being a doctor, even though my parents do; and I am not a failure for having these feelings."

The adult recognizes that sexual desires and behavior may be richly satisfying and permanently enriching in their consequences, or shallow and tempo-

rary and less than satisfying. He goes by his own experiencing, which does not always coincide with social norms.

He recognizes freely that this communist book or person expresses attitudes and goals which he shares as well as ideas and values which he does not share.

He realizes that at times he experiences cooperation as meaningful and valuable to him, and that at other times he wishes to be alone and act alone.

VALUING IN THE MATURE PERSON

The valuing process which seems to develop in this more mature person is in some ways very much like that in the infant, and in some ways quite different. It is fluid, flexible, based on this particular moment, and the degree to which this moment is experienced as enhancing and actualizing. Values are not held rigidly, but are continually changing. The painting which last year seemed meaningful now appears uninteresting, the way of working with individuals which was formerly experienced as good now seems inadequate, the belief which then seemed true is now experienced as only partly true, or perhaps false.

Another characteristic of the way this person values experience is that it is highly differentiated, or as the semanticists would say, extensional. The examples in the preceding section indicate that what were previously rather solid monolithic introjected values now become differentiated, tied to a particular time and experience.

Another characteristic of the mature individual's approach is that the locus of evaluation is again established firmly within the person. It is his own experience which provides the value information or feedback. This does not mean that he is not open to all the evidence he can obtain from other sources. But it means that this is taken for what it is—outside evidence—and is not as significant as his own reactions. Thus he may be told by a friend that a new book is very disappointing. He reads two unfavorable reviews of the book. Thus his tentative hypothesis is that he will not value the book. Yet if he reads the book his valuing will be based upon the reactions it

---

[1] The therapeutic relationship is not devoid of values. When it is most effective it is, I believe, marked by one primary value, namely, that this person (the client) has *worth*.

stirs in *him,* not on what he has been told by others.

There is also involved in this valuing process a letting oneself down into the immediacy of what one is experiencing, endeavoring to sense and to clarify all its complex meanings. I think of a client who, toward the close of therapy, when puzzled about an issue, would put his head in his hands and say, "Now what *is* it that I'm feeling? I want to get next to it. I want to learn what it is." Then he would wait, quietly and patiently, trying to listen to himself, until he could discern the exact flavor of the feelings he was experiencing. He, like others, was trying to get close to himself.

In getting close to what is going on within himself, the process is much more complex than it is in the infant. In the mature person it has much more scope and sweep. For there is involved in the present moment of experiencing the memory traces of all the relevant learnings from the past. This moment has not only its immediate sensory impact, but it has meaning growing out of similar experiences in the past (Gendlin, 1962). It has both the new and the old in it. So when I experience a painting or a person, my experiencing contains within it the learnings I have accumulated from past meetings with paintings or persons, as well as the new impact of this particular encounter. Likewise the moment of experiencing contains, for the mature adult, hypotheses about consequences. "It is not pleasant to express forthrightly my negative feelings to this person, but past experience indicates that in a continuing relationship it will be helpful in the long run." Past and future are both in this moment and enter into the valuing.

I find that in the person I am speaking of (and here again we see a similarity to the infant), the criterion of the valuing process is the degree to which the object of the experience actualizes the individual himself. Does it make him a richer, more complete, more fully developed person? This may sound as though it were a selfish or unsocial criterion, but it does not prove to be so, since deep and helpful relationships with others are experienced as actualizing.

Like the infant, too, the psychologically

mature adult trusts and uses the wisdom of his organism, with the difference that he is able to do so knowingly. He realizes that if he can trust all of himself, his feelings and his intuitions may be wiser than his mind, that as a total person he can be more sensitive and accurate than his thoughts alone. Hence he is not afraid to say, "I feel that this experience [or this thing, or this direction] is good. Later I will probably know *why* I feel it is good." He trusts the totality of himself, having moved toward becoming what Lancelot Whyte (1950) regards as "the unitary man."

It should be evident from what I have been saying that this valuing process in the mature individual is not an easy or simple thing. The process is complex, the choices often very perplexing and difficult, and there is no guarantee that the choice which is made will in fact prove to be self-actualizing. But because whatever evidence exists is available to the individual, and because he is open to his experiencing, errors are correctable. If this chosen course of action is not self-enhancing this will be sensed and he can make an adjustment or revision. He thrives on a maximum feedback interchange, and thus, like the gyroscopic compass on a ship, can continually correct his course toward his true goal of self-fulfillment.

SOME PROPOSITIONS REGARDING THE VALUING PROCESS

Let me sharpen the meaning of what I have been saying by stating two propositions which contain the essential elements of this viewpoint. While it may not be possible to devise empirical tests of each proposition in its entirety, yet each is to some degree capable of being tested through the methods of psychological science. I would also state that though the following propositions are stated firmly in order to give them clarity, I am actually advancing them as decidedly tentative hypotheses.

Hypothesis I There is an organismic base for an organized valuing process within the human individual.

It is hypothesized that this base is something the human being shares with the rest of the animate world. It is part of the functioning life process of any healthy organism. It is the capacity for receiving feedback information which enables the organism continually to adjust its behavior and reactions so as to achieve the maximum possible self-enhancement.

Hypothesis II This valuing process in the human being is effective in achieving self-enhancement to the degree that the individual is open to the experiencing which is going on within himself.

I have tried to give two examples of individuals who are close to their own experiencing: the tiny infant who has not yet learned to deny in his awareness the processes going on within; and the psychologically mature person who has relearned the advantages of this open state.

There is a corollary to this second proposition which might be put in the following terms. One way of assisting the individual to move toward openness to experience is through a relationship in which he is prized as a separate person, in which the experiencing going on within him is emphatically understood and valued, and in which he is given the freedom to experience his own feelings and those of others without being threatened in doing so.

This corollary obviously grows out of therapeutic experience. It is a brief statement of the essential qualities in the therapeutic relationship. There are already some empirical studies, of which the one by Barrett-Lennard (1962) is a good example, which give support to such a statement.

PROPOSITIONS REGARDING THE OUTCOMES OF THE VALUING PROCESS

I come now to the nub of any theory of values or valuing. What are its consequences? I should like to move into this new ground by stating bluntly two propositions as to the qualities of behavior which emerge from this valuing process. I shall then give some of the evidence from my experience as a therapist in support of these propositions.

Hypothesis III In persons who are moving toward greater openness to their experiencing, there is an organismic commonality of value directions.

Hypothesis IV These common value directions are of such kinds as to enhance the development of the individual himself, of others in his community, and to make for the survival and evolution of his species.

It has been a striking fact of my experience that in therapy, where individuals are valued, where there is greater freedom to feel and to be, certain value directions seem to emerge. These are not chaotic directions but instead exhibit a surprising commonality. This commonality is not dependent on the personality of the therapist, for I have seen these trends emerge in the clients of therapists sharply different in personality. This commonality does not seem to be due to the influences of any one culture, for I have found evidence of these directions in cultures as divergent as those of the United States, Holland, France, and Japan. I like to think that this commonality of value directions is due to the fact that we all belong to the same species—that just as a human infant tends, individually, to select a diet similar to that selected by other human infants, so a client in therapy tends, individually, to choose value directions similar to those chosen by other clients. As a species there may be certain elements of experience which tend to make for inner development and which would be chosen by all individuals if they were genuinely free to choose.

Let me indicate a few of these value directions as I see them in my clients as they move in the direction of personal growth and maturity.

They tend to move away from facades. Pretense, defensiveness, putting up a front, tend to be negatively valued.

They tend to move away from "oughts." The compelling feeling of "I ought to do or be thus and so" is negatively valued. The client moves away from being what he "ought to be," no matter who has set that imperative.

They tend to move away from meeting the expectations of others. Pleasing others, as a goal in itself, is negatively valued.

Being real is positively valued. The client tends to move toward being himself, being his real feelings, being what he is. This seems to be a very deep preference.

Self-direction is positively valued. The client discovers an increasing pride and confidence in making his own choices, guiding his own life.

One's self, one's own feelings come to be positively valued. From a point where he looks upon himself with contempt and despair, the client comes to value himself and his reactions as being of worth.

Being a process is positively valued. From desiring some fixed goal, clients come to prefer the excitement of being a process of potentialities being born.

Sensitivity to others and acceptance of others is positively valued. The client comes to appreciate others for what they are, just as he has come to appreciate himself for what he is.

Deep relationships are positively valued. To achieve a close, intimate, real, fully communicative relationship with another person seems to meet a deep need in every individual, and is very highly valued.

Perhaps more than all else, the client comes to value an openness to all of his inner and outer experience. To be open to and sensitive to his own *inner* reactions and feelings, the reactions and feelings of others, and the realities of the objective world—this is a direction which he clearly prefers. This openness becomes the client's most valued resource.

These then are some of the preferred directions which I have observed in individuals moving toward personal maturity. Though I am sure that the list I have given is inadequate and perhaps to some degree inaccurate, it holds for me exciting possibilities. Let me try to explain why.

I find it significant that when individuals are prized as persons, the values they select do not run the full gamut of possibilities. I do not find, in such a climate of freedom, that one person comes to value fraud and murder and thievery, while another values a life of self-sacrifice, and another values only money. Instead there seems to be a deep and underlying thread of commonality. I believe that when the human being is inwardly free to choose whatever he deeply values, he tends to value those objects, experiences, and goals which

make for his own survival, growth, and development, and for the survival and development of others. I hypothesize that it is *characteristic* of the human organism to prefer such actualizing and socialized goals when he is exposed to a growth promoting climate.

A corollary of what I have been saying is that in *any* culture, given a climate of respect and freedom in which he is valued as a person, the mature individual would tend to choose and prefer these same value directions. This is a significant hypothesis which could be tested. It means that though the individual of whom I am speaking would not have a consistent or even a stable system of conceived values, the valuing process within him would lead to emerging value directions which would be constant across cultures and across time.

Another implication I see is that individuals who exhibit the fluid valuing process I have tried to describe, whose value directions are generally those I have listed, would be highly effective in the ongoing process of human evolution. If the human species is to survive at all on this globe, the human being must become more readily adaptive to new problems and situations, must be able to select that which is valuable for development and survival out of new and complex situations, must be accurate in his appreciation of reality if he is to make such selections. The psychologically mature person as I have described him has, I believe, the qualities which would cause him to value those experiences which would make for the survival and enhancement of the human race. He would be a worthy participant and guide in the process of human evolution.

Finally, it appears that we have returned to the issue of universality of values, but by a different route. Instead of universal values "out there," or a universal value system imposed by some group—philosophers, rulers, priests, or psychologists—we have the possibility of universal human value directions *emerging* from the experiencing of the human organism. Evidence from therapy indicates that both personal and social values emerge as natural, and experienced, when the individual is close to his own organismic valuing process. The suggestion is that though modern man no longer trusts religion or science or philosophy nor any system of beliefs to *give* him values, he may find an organismic valuing base within himself which, if he can learn again to be in touch with it, will prove to be an organized, adaptive, and social approach to the perplexing value issues which face all of us.

REFERENCES

Barrett-Lennard, G. T. Dimensions of therapist response as casual factors in therapeutic change. *Psychol. Mongr.*, 1962, **76**, (43, Whole No. 562).

Gendlin, E. T. Experiencing: A variable in the process of therapeutic change. *Amer. J. Psychother.*, 1961, **15**, 233–245.

Gendlin, E. T. *Experiencing and the creation of meaning.* Glencoe, Ill.: Free Press, 1962.

Morris, C. W. *Varieties of human value.* Chicago: Univer. Chicago Press, 1956.

Rogers, C. R. *Client-centered therapy.* Boston: Houghton Mifflin, 1951.

Rogers, C. R. A theory of therapy, personality and interpersonal relationships. In S. Koch (Ed.), *Psychology: A study of a science.* Vol. 3. *Formulations of the person and the social context.* New York: McGraw-Hill, 1959. Pp. 185–256.

Whyte, L. L. *The next development in man.* New York: Mentor Books, 1950.

The views of mental illness proposed by Dr. Thomas S. Szasz, an eminent psychiatrist, have generated considerable controversy. The major arguments presented in his book *The Myth of Mental Illness** are contained in the present paper. The essence of his argument is that "the notion of mental illness has outlived whatever usefulness it might have had and now functions merely as a convenient myth . . . whose function it is to disguise and thus render more palatable the bitter pill of moral conflicts in human relations." He maintains that the term mental *illness* perpetuates the erroneous notion that the disorder involves in some way a brain disease. His own view is that what is called mental illness is a disorder of living involving psychosocial, ethical, and legal dimensions. Szasz suggests that the current view of mental illness serves to permit the patient (and society) to avoid responsibility as either causative or corrective agents. The conception of behavior disorders as illnesses also serves to keep the treatment in the control of medically trained people. For further comments consistent with Szasz's point of view, the student is referred to Selection 71 (Rogers) and Selection 75 (Dyal).

Selection **72** | ## THE MYTH OF MENTAL ILLNESS†

THOMAS S. SZASZ
*State University of
New York, Upstate
Medical Center, Syracuse*

My aim in this essay is to raise the question "Is there such a thing as mental illness?" and to argue that there is not. Since the notion of mental illness is extremely widely used nowadays, inquiry into the ways in which this term is employed would seem to be especially indicated. Mental illness, of course, is not literally a "thing"—or physical object—and hence it can "exist" only in the same sort of way in which other theoretical concepts exist. Yet, familiar theories are in the habit of posing, sooner or later—at least to those who come to believe in them—as "objective truths" (or "facts"). During certain historical periods, explanatory conceptions such as deities, witches,

* Thomas S. Szasz, *The Myth of Mental Illness*, Paul B. Hoeber, Inc., New York, 1961.
† From T. S. Szasz, "The Myth of Mental Illness," *American Psychologist*, 15: 113–118, 1960. Copyright 1960 by the American Psychological Association and reproduced by permission.

and microorganisms appeared not only as theories but as self-evident *causes* of a vast number of events. I submit that today mental illness is widely regarded in a somewhat similar fashion, that is, as the cause of innumerable diverse happenings. As an antidote to the complacent use of the notion of mental illness—whether as a self-evident phenomenon, theory, or cause—let us ask this question: What is meant when it is asserted that someone is mentally ill?

In what follows I shall describe briefly the main uses to which the concept of mental illness has been put. I shall argue that this notion has outlived whatever usefulness it might have had and that it now functions merely as a convenient myth.

MENTAL ILLNESS AS A SIGN OF BRAIN DISEASE

The notion of mental illness derives its main support from such phenomena as syphilis of the brain or delirious conditions—intoxications, for instance—in which persons are known to manifest various peculiarities or disorders of thinking and behavior. Correctly speaking, however these are diseases of the brain, not of the mind. According to one school of thought, *all* so-called mental illness is of this type. The assumption is made that some neurological defect, perhaps a very subtle one, will ultimately be found for all the disorders of thinking and behavior. Many contemporary psychiatrists, physicians, and other scientists hold this view. This position implies that people *cannot* have troubles—expressed in what are *now called* "mental illnesses"—because of differences in personal needs, opinions, social aspirations, values, and so on. *All problems in living* are attributed to physicochemical processes which in due time will be discovered by medical research.

"Mental illnesses" are thus regarded as basically no different than all other diseases (that is, of the body). The only difference, in this view, between mental and bodily diseases is that the former, affecting the brain, manifest themselves by means of mental symptoms; whereas the latter, affecting other organ systems (for example, the skin, liver, etc.), manifest themselves by means of symptoms referable to those parts of the body. This view rests on and expresses what are, in my opinion, two fundamental errors.

In the first place, what central nervous system symptoms would correspond to a skin eruption or a fracture? It would *not* be some emotion or complex bit of behavior. Rather, it would be blindness or a paralysis of some part of the body. The crux of the matter is that a disease of the brain, analogous to a disease of the skin or bone, is a neurological defect, and not a problem in living. For example, a *defect* in a person's visual field may be satisfactorily explained by correlating it with certain definite lesions in the nervous system. On the other hand, a person's *belief*—whether this be a belief in Christianity, in Communism, or in the idea that his internal organs are "rotting" and that his body is, in fact, already "dead"—cannot be explained by a defect or disease of the nervous system. Explanations of this sort of occurrence—assuming that one is interested in the belief itself and does not regard it simply as a "symptom" or expression of something else that is *more interesting*—must be sought along different lines.

The second error in regarding complex psychosocial behavior, consisting of communications about ourselves and the world about us, as mere symptoms of neurological functioning

is *epistemological.* In other words, it is an error pertaining not to any mistakes in observation or reasoning, as such, but rather to the way in which we organize and express our knowledge. In the present case, the error lies in making a symmetrical dualism between mental and physical (or bodily) symptoms, a dualism which is merely a habit of speech and to which no known observations can be found to correspond. Let us now see if this is so. In medical practice, when we speak of physical disturbances, we mean either signs (for example, a fever) or symptoms (for example, pain). We speak of mental symptoms, on the other hand, when we refer to a patient's *communications about himself, others, and the world about him.* He might state that he is Napoleon or that he is being persecuted by the Communists. These would be considered mental symptoms *only* if the observer believed that the patient was *not* Napoleon or that he was *not* being persecuted by the Communists. This makes it apparent that the statement that *"X* is a mental symptom" involves rendering a judgment. The judgment entails, moreover, a covert comparison or matching of the patient's ideas, concepts, or beliefs with those of the observer and the society in which they live. The notion of mental symptom is therefore inextricably tied to the *social* (including *ethical*) *context* in which it is made in much the same way as the notion of bodily symptom is tied to an *anatomical* and *genetic context* (Szasz, 1957a, 1957b).

To sum up what has been said thus far: I have tried to show that for those who regard mental symptoms as signs of brain disease, the concept of mental illness is unnecessary and misleading. For what they mean is that people so labeled suffer from diseases of the brain; and, if that is what they mean, it would seem better for the sake of clarity to say that and not something else.

MENTAL ILLNESS AS A NAME FOR PROBLEMS IN LIVING

The term "mental illness" is widely used to describe something which is very different than a disease of the brain. Many people today take it for granted that living is an arduous process. Its hardship for modern man, moreover, derives not so much from a struggle for biological survival as from the stresses and strains inherent in the social intercourse of complex human personalities. In this context, the notion of mental illness is used to identify or describe some feature of an individual's so-called personality. Mental illness—as a deformity of the personality, so to speak—is then regarded as the *cause* of the human disharmony. It is implicit in this view that social intercourse between people is regarded as something *inherently harmonious*, its disturbance being due solely to the presence of "mental illness" in many people. This is obviously fallacious reasoning, for it makes the abstraction "mental illness" into a *cause*, even though this abstraction was created in the first place to serve only as a shorthand expression for certain types of human behavior. It now becomes necessary to ask: "What kinds of behavior are regarded as indicative of mental illness, and by whom?"

The concept of illness, whether bodily or mental, implies *deviation from some clearly defined norm*. In the case of physical illness, the norm is the structural and functional integrity of the human body. Thus, although the desirability of physical health, as such, is an ethical value, what health *is* can be stated in anatomical and physiological terms. What is the norm deviation from which is regarded as mental illness? This question cannot be easily answered. But whatever this norm might be, we can be certain of only one thing: namely, that it is a norm that must be stated in terms of *psychosocial, ethical,* and *legal* concepts. For example, notions such as "excessive repression" or "acting out an unconscious impulse" illustrate the use of psychological concepts for judging (so-called) mental health and illness. The idea that chronic hostility, vengefulness, or divorce are indicative of mental illness would be illustrations of the use of ethical norms (that is, the desirability of love, kindness, and a stable marriage relationship). Finally, the widespread psychiatric opinion that only a mentally ill person would commit homicide illustrates the use of a legal concept as a norm of mental health. The norm from which deviation is measured whenever one speaks of a mental illness is a *psychosocial and ethical one.* Yet, the remedy is sought in terms of *medical* measures which—it is hoped and

assumed—are free from wide differences of ethical value. The definition of the disorder and the terms in which its remedy are sought are therefore at serious odds with one another. The practical significance of this covert conflict between the alleged nature of the defect and the remedy can hardly be exaggerated.

Having identified the norms used to measure deviations in cases of mental illness, we will now turn to the question: "Who defines the norms and hence the deviation?" Two basic answers may be offered: (a) It may be the person himself (that is, the patient) who decides that he deviates from a norm. For example, an artist may believe that he suffers from a work inhibition; and he may implement this conclusion by seeking help *for* himself from a psychotherapist. (b) It may be someone other than the patient who decides that the latter is deviant (for example, relatives, physicians, legal authorities, society generally, etc.). In such a case a psychiatrist may be hired by others to do something *to* the patient in order to correct the deviation.

These considerations underscore the importance of asking the question "Whose agent is the psychiatrist?" and of giving a candid answer to it (Szasz, 1956, 1958). The psychiatrist (psychologist or nonmedical psychotherapist), it now develops, may be the agent of the patient, of the relatives, of the school, of the military services, of a business organization, of a court of law, and so forth. In speaking of the psychiatrist as the agent of these persons or organizations, it is not implied that his values concerning norms, or his ideas and aims concerning the proper nature of remedial action, need to coincide exactly with those of his employer. For example, a patient in individual psychotherapy may believe that his salvation lies in a new marriage; his psychotherapist need not share this hypothesis. As the patient's agent, however, he must abstain from bringing social or legal force to bear on the patient which would prevent him from putting his beliefs into action. If his *contract* is with the patient, the psychiatrist (psychotherapist) may disagree with him or stop his treatment; but he cannot engage others to obstruct the patient's aspirations. Similarly, if a psychiatrist is engaged by a court to determine the sanity of a criminal, he need not fully share the legal authorities' values and intentions in regard to the criminal and the means available for dealing with him. But the psychiatrist is expressly barred from stating, for example, that it is not the criminal who is "insane" but the men who wrote the law on the basis of which the very actions that are being judged are regarded as "criminal." Such an opinion could be voiced, of course, but not in a courtroom, and not by a psychiatrist who makes it his practice to assist the court in performing its daily work.

To recapitulate: In actual contemporary social usage, the finding of a mental illness is made by establishing a deviance in behavior from certain psychosocial, ethical, or legal norms. The judgment may be made, as in medicine, by the patient, the physician (psychiatrist), or others. Remedial action, finally, tends to be sought in a therapeutic—or covertly medical—framework, thus creating a situation in which *psychosocial, ethical,* and/or *legal deviations* are claimed to be correctible by (so-called) *medical action.* Since medical action is designed to correct only medical deviations, it seems logically absurd to expect that it will help solve problems whose very existence had been defined and established on nonmedical grounds. I think that these considerations may be fruitfully applied to the present use of tranquilizers and, more generally, to what might be expected of drugs of whatever type in regard to the amelioration or solution of problems in human living.

THE ROLE OF ETHICS IN PSYCHIATRY

Anything that people *do*—in contrast to things that *happen* to them (Peters, 1958)—takes place in a context of value. In this broad sense, no human activity is devoid of ethical implications. When the values underlying certain activities are widely shared, those who participate in their pursuit may lose sight of them altogether. The discipline of medicine, both as a pure science (for example, research) and as a technology (for example, therapy), contains many ethical considerations and judgments. Unfortunately, these are often denied, minimized, or merely kept out of focus; for the ideal of the medical profession as well as of the people whom it serves seems to be having a system of medicine (allegedly) free of ethical

value. This sentimental notion is expressed by such things as the doctor's willingness to treat and help patients irrespective of their religious or political beliefs, whether they are rich or poor, etc. While there may be some grounds for this belief—albeit it is a view that is not impressively true even in these regards—the fact remains that ethical considerations encompass a vast range of human affairs. By making the practice of medicine neutral in regard to some specific issues of value need not, and cannot, mean that it can be kept free from all such values. The practice of medicine is intimately tied to ethics; and the first thing that we must do, it seems to me, is to try to make this clear and explicit. I shall let this matter rest here, for it does not concern us specifically in this essay. Lest there be any vagueness, however, about how or where ethics and medicine meet, let me remind the reader of such issues as birth control, abortion, suicide, and euthanasia as only a few of the major areas of current ethicomedical controversy.

Psychiatry, I submit, is very much more intimately tied to problems of ethics than is medicine. I use the word "psychiatry" here to refer to that contemporary discipline which is concerned with *problems in living* (and not with diseases of the brain, which are problems for neurology). Problems in human relations can be analyzed, interpreted, and given meaning only within given social and ethical contexts. Accordingly, it *does* make a difference—arguments to the contrary notwithstanding—what the psychiatrist's socioethical orientations happen to be; for these will influence his ideas on what is wrong with the patient, what deserves comment or interpretation, in what possible directions change might be desirable, and so forth. Even in medicine proper, these factors play a role, as for instance, in the divergent orientations which physicians, depending on their religious affiliations, have toward such things as birth control and therapeutic abortion. Can anyone really believe that a psychotherapist's ideas concerning religious belief, slavery, or other similar issues play no role in his practical work? If they do make a difference, what are we to infer from it? Does it not seem reasonable that we ought to have different psychiatric therapies—each expressly recognized for the ethical positions which they embody—for, say, Catholics and Jews, religious persons and agnostics, democrats and communists, white supremacists and Negroes, and so on? Indeed, if we look at how psychiatry is actually practiced today (especially in the United States), we find that people do seek psychiatric help in accordance with their social status and ethical beliefs (Hollingshead & Redlich, 1958). This should really not surprise us more than being told that practicing Catholics rarely frequent birth control clinics.

The foregoing position which holds that contemporary psychotherapists deal with problems in living, rather than with mental illnesses and their cures, stands in opposition to a currently prevalent claim, according to which mental illness is just as "real" and "objective" as bodily illness. This is a confusing claim since it is never known exactly what is meant by such words as "real" and "objective." I suspect, however, that what is intended by the proponents of this view is to create the idea in the popular mind that mental illness is some sort of disease entity, like an infection or a malignancy. If this were true, one could *catch* or *get* a "mental illness," one might *have* or *harbor* it, one might *transmit* it to others, and finally one could get *rid* of it. In my opinion, there is not a shred of evidence to support this idea. To the contrary, all the evidence is the other way and supports the view that what people now call mental illnesses are for the most part *communications* expressing unacceptable ideas, often framed, moreover, in an unusual idiom. The scope of this essay allows me to do no more than mention this alternative theoretical approach to this problem (Szasz, 1957c).

This is not the place to consider in detail the similarities and differences between bodily and mental illnesses. It shall suffice for us here to emphasize only one important difference between them: namely, that whereas bodily disease refers to public, physiochemical occurrences, the notion of mental illness is used to codify relatively more private, sociopsychological happenings of which the observer (diagnostician) forms a part. In other words, the psychiatrist does not stand *apart* from what he observes, but is, in Harry Stack Sullivan's apt words, a "participant observer." This means that he is *committed* to some picture of what he considers reality—and to what he thinks society considers reality—and he observes and

judges the patient's behavior in the light of these considerations. This touches on our earlier observation that the notion of mental symptom itself implies a comparison between observer and observed, psychiatrist and patient. This is so obvious that I may be charged with belaboring trivialities. Let me therefore say once more that my aim in presenting this argument was expressly to criticize and counter a prevailing contemporary tendency to deny the moral aspects of psychiatry (and psychotherapy) and to substitute for them allegedly value free medical considerations. Psychotherapy, for example, is being widely practiced as though it entailed nothing other than restoring the patient from a state of mental sickness to one of mental health. While it is generally accepted that mental illness has something to do with man's social (or interpersonal) relations, it is paradoxically maintained that problems of values (that is, of ethics) do not arise in the process.[1] Yet, in one sense, much of psychotherapy may revolve around nothing other than the elucidation and weighing of goals and values—many of which may be mutually contradictory—and the means whereby they might best be harmonized, realized, or relinquished.

The diversity of human values and the methods by means of which they may be realized is so vast, and many of them remain so unacknowledged, that they cannot fail but lead to conflicts in human relations. Indeed, to say that human relations at all levels—from mother to child, through husband and wife, to nation and nation—are fraught with stress, strain, and disharmony is, once again, making the obvious explicit. Yet, what may be obvious may be also poorly understood. This I think is the case here. For it seems to me that—at least in our scientific theories of behavior—we have failed to *accept* the simple fact that

[1] Freud went so far as to say that: "I consider ethics to be taken for granted. Actually I have never done a mean thing" (Jones, 1957, p. 247). This surely is a strange thing to say for someone who has studied man as a social being as closely as did Freud. I mention it here to show how the notion of "illness" (in the case of psychoanalysis, "psychopathology," or "mental illness") was used by Freud—and by most of his followers—as a means for classifying certain forms of human behavior as falling within the scope of medicine, and hence (by *fiat*) outside that of ethics!

human relations are inherently fraught with difficulties and that to make them even relatively harmonious requires much patience and hard work. I submit that the idea of mental illness is now being put to work to obscure certain difficulties which at present may be inherent—not that they need be unmodifiable—in the social intercourse of persons. If this is true, the concept functions as a disguise; for instead of calling attention to conflicting human needs, aspirations, and values, the notion of mental illness provides an amoral and impersonal "thing" (an "illness") as an explanation for *problems in living* (Szasz, 1959). We may recall in this connection that not so long ago it was devils and witches who were held responsible for men's problems in social living. The belief in mental illness, as something other than man's trouble in getting along with his fellow man, is the proper heir to the belief in demonology and witchcraft. Mental illness exists or is "real" in exactly the same sense in which witches existed or were "real."

CHOICE, RESPONSIBILITY, AND PSYCHIATRY

While I have argued that mental illnesses do not exist, I obviously did not imply that the social and psychological occurrences to which this label is currently being attached also do not exist. Like the personal and social troubles which people had in the Middle Ages, they are real enough. It is the labels we give them that concerns us and, having labeled them, what we do about them. While I cannot go into the ramified implications of this problem here, it is worth nothing that a demonologic conception of problems in living gave rise to therapy along theological lines. Today, a belief in mental illness implies—nay, requires—therapy along medical or psychotherapeutic lines.

What is implied in the line of thought set forth here is something quite different. I do not intend to offer a new conception of "psychiatric illness" nor a new form of "therapy." My aim is more modest and yet also more ambitious. It is to suggest that the phenomena now called mental illnesses be looked at afresh and more simply, that they be removed from the category of illnesses, and that they be regarded as the expressions of man's struggle with the problem of *how* he should live. The

last mentioned problem is obviously a vast one, its enormity reflecting not only man's inability to cope with his environment, but even more his increasing self-reflectiveness.

By problems in living, then, I refer to that truly explosive chain reaction which began with man's fall from divine grace by partaking of the fruit of the tree of knowledge. Man's awareness of himself and of the world about him seems to be a steadily expanding one, bringing in its wake an ever larger *burden of understanding* (an expression borrowed from Susanne Langer, 1953). *This burden, then, is to be expected and must not be misinterpreted.* Our only *rational* means for lightening it is *more understanding*, and appropriate *action* based on such understanding. The main alternative lies in acting as though the burden were not what in fact we perceive it to be and taking refuge in an outmoded theological view of man. In the latter view, man does not fashion his life and much of his world about him, but merely lives out his fate in a world created by superior beings. This may logically lead to pleading nonresponsibility in the face of seemingly unfathomable problems and difficulties. Yet, if man fails to take increasing responsibility for his actions, individually as well as collectively, it seems unlikely that some higher power or being would assume this task and carry this burden for him. Moreover, this seems hardly the proper time in human history for obscuring the issue of man's responsibility for his actions by hiding it behind the skirt of an all-explaining conception of mental illness.

CONCLUSIONS

I have tried to show that the notion of mental illness has outlived whatever usefulness it might have had and that it now functions merely as a convenient myth. As such, it is a true heir to religious myths in general, and to the belief in witchcraft in particular; the role of all these belief-systems was to act as *social tranquilizers*, thus encouraging the hope that mastery of certain specific problems may be achieved by means of substitutive (symbolic-magical) operations. The notion of mental illness thus serves mainly to obscure the everyday fact that life for most people is a continuous struggle, not for biological survival, but for a "place in the sun," "peace of mind," or some other human value. For man aware of himself and of the world about him, once the needs for preserving the body (and perhaps the race) are more or less satisfied, the problem arises as to what he should do with himself. Sustained adherence to the myth of mental illness allows people to avoid facing this problem, believing that mental health, conceived as the absence of mental illness, automatically insures the making of right and safe choices in one's conduct of life. But the facts are all the other way. It is the making of good choices in life that others regard, retrospectively, as good mental health!

The myth of mental illness encourages us, moreover, to believe in its logical corollary: that social intercourse would be harmonious, satisfying, and the secure basis of a "good life" were it not for the disrupting influences of mental illness or "psychopathology." The potentiality for universal human happiness, in this form at least, seems to me but another example of the I-wish-it-were-true type of fantasy. I do believe that human happiness or well-being on a hitherto unimaginably large scale, and not just for a select few, is possible. This goal could be achieved, however, only at the cost of many men, and not just a few being willing and able to tackle their personal, social, and ethical conflicts. This means having the courage and integrity to forego waging battles on false fronts, finding solutions for substitute problems—for instance, fighting the battle of stomach acid and chronic fatigue instead of facing up to a marital conflict.

Our adversaries are not demons, witches, fate, or mental illness. We have no enemy whom we can fight, exorcise, or dispel by "cure." What we do have are *problems in living*—whether these be biologic, economic, political, or socio-psychological. In this essay I was concerned only with problems belonging in the last mentioned category, and within this group mainly with those pertaining to moral values. The field to which modern psychiatry addresses itself is vast, and I made no effort to encompass it all. My argument was limited to the proposition that mental illness is a myth, whose function it is to disguise and thus render more palatable the bitter pill of moral conflicts in human relations.

REFERENCES

Hollingshead, A. B., & Redlich, F. C. *Social class and mental illness.* New York: Wiley, 1958.

Jones, E. *The life and work of Sigmund Freud.* Vol. III. New York: Basic Books, 1957.

Langer, S. K. *Philosophy in a new key.* New York: Mentor Books, 1953.

Peters, R. S. *The concept of motivation.* London: Routledge & Kegan Paul, 1958.

Szasz, T. S. Malingering: "Diagnosis" or social condemnation? *AMA Arch Neurol. Psychiat.,* 1956, **76,** 432–443.

Szasz, T. S. *Pain and pleasure: A study of bodily feelings.* New York: Basic Books, 1957. (a)

Szasz, T. S. The problem of psychiatric nosology: A contribution to a situational analysis of psychiatric operations. *Amer. J. Psychiat.,* 1957, **114,** 405–413. (b)

Szasz, T. S. On the theory of psychoanalytic treatment. *Int. J. Psycho-Anal.,* 1957, **38,** 166–182. (c)

Szasz, T. S. Psychiatry, ethics and the criminal law. *Columbia law Rev.,* 1958, **58,** 183–198.

Szasz, T. S. Moral conflict and psychiatry, *Yale Rev.,* 1959, in press.

An unusually stimulating multidisciplinary symposium series entitled "Man and Civilization" has been conducted by the San Francisco Medical Center of the University of California.

The reports of three of these symposia have been published thus far.* The subject of the first symposium series was "Control of the Mind," one session of which was devoted to papers and discussion on "The influence of drugs on the individual." Papers were presented by Dr. Seymour S. Kety, Chief, Laboratory of Clinical Science, National Institute of Mental Health, "Chemical boundaries of psychopharmacology"; Dr. James G. Miller, Director, Mental Health Research Institute, University of Michigan, "The individual response to drugs"; and Dr. Jonathan O. Cole, Chief, Psychopharmacology Service Center, National Institute of Health.

The present selection is a reprint of Dr. Cole's symposium paper, "Drugs and control of the mind." He begins his paper by pointing to some of the social implications of the notion of control of the mind. He notes that drugs may be used either for "control of the mind" (a "bad" connotation?) or for "freeing the mind" (a "good" connotation?). A variety of drugs are currently being used for control of the thinking and feeling of emotionally disturbed patients. However, it is clear from Dr. Cole's discussion that we do not have nearly enough information on the effects of these drugs on normal subjects. He maintains that it is most unlikely that drugs, which can be effective in producing specific kinds of responses on a large population of normal subjects, can be developed in the foreseeable future. Four major barriers to such mass "control" or "freeing" are present: (1) Our information about the effects of presently available drugs on normal subjects is entirely inadequate. (2) There is great variability among normal subjects and among patients in their responses to drugs. (3) Current drug-development methods are unsystematic, making it "unlikely that current methods can be used to develop a new drug with any specific and reliable effect on either freedom or control of human mental processes." (4) Much of the information which we have about the effects of drugs on human beings is based on clinical use, where it is difficult to separate the drug effects from the expectations of the subjects or the "sometimes mystical" situations in which they are administered. This is clearly a case of an experimental setting in which high "demand characteristics" (cf. Orne, Selection 75) may contribute significantly to the observed effects.

Following the presentation of Dr. Cole's paper, there was a lively panel discussion among the participants, moderated by Dr. David Krech. This discussion is reprinted as Selection 74, "Horizons of Psychopharmacology."

Selection **73** | DRUGS AND CONTROL OF THE MIND†

JONATHAN O. COLE
*National Institute of
Health*

Since I have been asked to give a paper on the relationship of psychopharmacology to human behavior in a conference which focuses its

* Seymour M. Farber and Roger H. L. Wilson (eds.), *Control of the Mind, Part I: Man and Civilization,* McGraw-Hill Book Company, New York, 1961.
Seymour M. Farber and Roger H. L. Wilson (eds), *Control of the Mind, Part II: Conflict and Creativity,* McGraw-Hill Book Company, New York, 1963.
Seymour M. Farber, Roger H. L. Wilson, and Piero Mustacchi (eds), *Man and Civilization: The Family's Search for Survival,* McGraw-Hill Book Company, New York, 1964.
† From J. O. Cole, "Drugs and Control of the Mind," in Seymour M. Farber and Roger H. L. Wilson (eds.), *Control of the Mind, Part I: Man and Civilization,* McGraw-Hill Book Company, New York, 1961.

attention on the control of the mind, I must conclude that those organizing this conference believed explicitly, or implicitly, that drugs could be used to control the mind. An alternative hypothesis, of course, would be that the group organizing this meeting believed that drugs could be used to enhance the freedom of the mind. I will examine the evidence relating to both hypotheses.

I also believe I detect in this conference an implicit assumption that control of the mind is bad and freedom of the mind is good. B. F. Skinner, the father of the operant approach to the study of behavior, has seriously questioned this assumption [7], believing that behavior can be controlled effectively, or is about to be able to be controlled effectively, and that it is the duty of our society to actively attempt to control human behavior in such a way as to achieve effects which we consider desirable before some other group becomes more proficient at controlling behavior and directing it into paths which we consider undesirable. He assumes, of course, that human behavior can be controlled in an effective and precise manner, and that someone, somewhere, in this country or in the Western world, is capable of making value judgments concerning the kinds of behavior which are good and should be positively elicited and the kinds of behavior which are bad and should be suppressed. This, of course, complicates the whole matter. We must consider whether drugs can be used to facilitate the control of "good" behavior and the abolishment of "bad" behavior, as well as the possibility that drugs may be used by enemies of our society to suppress desirable behavior and to elicit undesirable behavior. Can drugs do any of these things?

To answer this complex set of questions it would be necessary to define what kinds of behavior are bad and what kinds are good. This I feel uncomfortable doing, except in clinical situations, and will therefore retreat to the simpler question concerning the possibility of using drugs to control any behavior, noting in passing the effects of drugs on extremes of behavior which many people would unanimously consider to be clearly undesirable or clearly desirable. Skinner, of course, prefers to restrict himself to overt behavior. For the purpose of this conference, however, one must also consider less readily observable subjective phenomena, such as mood, creativity, imagination, etc.

Assuming one wished either to control or to free the mind, or to influence behavior, what classes of drugs are available for this purpose? Existing psychopharmacological agents fall rather nicely into five groups. First, one has the major tranquilizers [3], which include chlorpromazine and a variety of other phenothiazine derivatives, reserpine and a few related Rauwolfia alkaloids, and a few newer compounds such as haloperidol, which are chemically unrelated to the other two groups but appear to share certain properties with them. These drugs are relatively effective in the control of the symptoms of schizophrenia and other psychotic states.

The second group consists of the minor tranquilizers and sedatives [3], a group including such compounds as meprobamate (Equanil, Miltown) and methaminodiazepoxide (Librium), which may be effective in relieving neurotic anxiety at dosage levels that do not produce undesirable degrees of sedation, and sedatives such as the barbiturates and the bromides, whose clinically undesirable sedative properties may be more prominent than their anxiety-relieving properties.

The third discernible group is that of the stimulant drugs, including amphetamine [4]. These drugs have a euphoriant action in some individuals. They also increase wakefulness, decrease fatigue-induced performance decrement under some conditions, and in addition sometimes causing jitteryness, tachycardia, and other relatively undesirable signs of central nervous system stimulation.

The fourth group is that of the antidepressive drugs [4], including iproniazid (Marsilid) and other monoamine oxidase inhibitors and imipramine (Tofranil). These drugs have some demonstrated effectiveness in the relief of depressive syndromes. In contrast to the stimulants, they are slow to act, requiring approximately 2 weeks for desirable clinical effects to manifest themselves. The monoamine oxidase inhibitors appear to share with the stimulants some euphoriant effect in some individuals and some capacity to speed reaction time, increase verbal productivity, and otherwise stimulate the organism. Imipramine does not seem to possess these particular properties.

The fifth group is that of the psycho-tomimetic drugs, including older compounds such as mescaline and LSD-25 and newer and more diverse compounds such as Sernyl and Ditran and psilocybin.

It may be that other classes or types of drugs with different, more discrete, more specific, or more varied effects will be found in the near future. Since all existing new types of drugs have been identified as having unique properties in man only on the basis of their observed effects in human subjects, rather than as a result of well-planned extrapolations from their effect in animals to their effects in man, it is extremely difficult to predict what kinds of drugs the future will bring. I suggest with some reluctance that it is unlikely, at present, that any chemical compounds with specific identifiable and predictable effects in human subjects can be developed on the basis of animal experimentation alone. In short, even if I felt that I could identify in man the psycho-logical or behavioral function which I or anyone else wished to control, or for that matter to free, I would not be willing to predict that a rational and energetic attempt to create a drug which would have these specific effects would be particularly likely to be fruitful. This is not to say that investigation in man of compounds with new and different behavioral or neuro-pharmacological effects in animals may not lead to the discovery of drugs with new and surprising clinical properties, but I doubt that at this stage in our knowledge the discovery of such compounds can be systematically engi-neered. It is possible, of course, that having identified a drug with some specific desirable properties in animals one can by examining related compounds find one which possesses a particular property in greater degree while lack-ing some other undesirable or confounding properties. However, given the present state of drug development, it seems more appropriate to concern oneself with the effects of drugs we now have than to speculate further about the possible effects of possible drugs which might conceivably be developed to control specific mental functions or behaviors.

The physician, particularly the psychiatrist, is currently using the first four of the above five groups of drugs for the control of the mind. Most of the available evidence concern-ing the ability of drugs to control the mind or

to control behavior comes from exactly this clinical use. The physician usually does not worry too much about the social goodness or badness of controlling behavior, since many patients come to him asking that their be-havior, feelings, or thoughts be controlled. Other patients, of course, are brought to him by relatives or by society because their be-havior is such that others feel it needs control. The need for such control is, in fact, not un-commonly legally certified by a court, and the patient is committed to a hospital for treat-ment until such time as the aberrant behavior has been brought under control. Physicians now have an extensive experience in using these drugs to control behavior, and I think most physicians would agree that the reliability with which existing drugs control specific be-haviors leaves much to be desired.

Overwhelming doses of a barbiturate or an anesthetic will, of course, put anybody to sleep, and adequate doses of a drug like Metrazol will produce convulsions in anyone. Even with such clear-cut end-points, there is considerable individual variability in the doses required to produce these profound effects.

Moreover, our clinically most effective drugs, the phenothiazines and the antidepressives, appear to produce quite different effects in psychiatrically ill individuals from those they produce in normal subjects. Thus, a dose of chlorpromazine which renders a disturbed schizophrenic relatively calm and reduces the prominence of his delusions and hallucinations and improves the clarity of his thinking pro-cesses would leave a normal individual fatigued, lethargic, numb, and miserable. The evidence concerning the effects of the more potent anti-depressives in normal subjects is very scanty, but again it seems likely that their effects are much less dramatic and much less desirable than they are in seriously depressed individuals.

The phenothiazines and Rauwolfia alkaloids could, of course, be used for the control of behavior in normal subjects by giving doses large enough to produce, in effect, a chemical straight jacket in which the individual had his muscles so stiffened by the Parkinsonianlike effects of the drugs and his energies so re-duced by their anergic properties as to render him ineffective for most purposes. But I would judge that the use of drugs to induce the temporary states of physical incapacity is of less interest to this group than their use in producing less dramatic and more socially meaningful alterations in thinking and behavior.

The milder tranquilizers and sedatives can cause, in some individuals, a decrease in anxiety when anxiety is present to a discernible degree, and the amphetamines may prevent the occurrence of a fatigue-induced decrement in performance at monotonous tasks such as airplane flying or radar-screen watching, in addition to producing mild euphoria and some increase in talkativeness in some subjects. The sedatives and mild tranquilizers are likely to produce temporary decrements in psychomotor performance, and some evidence has recently been presented by Beecher [2] to the effect that a barbiturate in athletes caused an impairment of athletic performance while causing the subjects to judge themselves to be doing much better than they usually did. Although it is suspected that the stimulants may also cause some alteration in judgment, this has not been clearly demonstrated.

All of the psychotomimetic agents can effectively impair behavior, if only through their autonomic side effects. Sernyl [6] can produce a complete anesthesia in adequate dosage, while Ditran [5] seems to be the one most capable of producing a severe and intense delirium with marked disorganization of thought, auditory and visual hallucinations, and complete loss of contact with reality.

The trouble with all existing psychopharmacologic agents as tools to be used in the control of the mind is that, even from the standpoint of the practicing psychiatrist, they are not completely satisfactory. Although both the phenothiazines and the antidepressive drugs may produce startling improvements, and even what appear to be complete remissions in some patients, these patients are usually in the minority. There is generally a larger proportion of patients in whom some change in the desired direction is produced, and such patients are usually classified as moderately improved, or slightly improved. There is always a residual group of patients, often in the neighborhood of 20 to 30 per cent who are unchanged or worse. Worse, in this sense, means movement in the opposite direction from that desired. To date, clinicians have been notably unsuccessful in predicting which patients will respond in which ways. For this reason, even if one were

only attempting to control the minds of a homogeneous group of psychiatric patients with a drug with which one had had considerable experience, the desired effect would not be produced in all patients, and one would not be able to plan specifically that any particular effect would be produced in a particular patient.

With the milder stimulants and sedatives one runs into great difficulty in predicting their effects on normal subjects or patients. Some patients become more active, stimulated, and euphoric when given sedatives; some normal subjects find the effects of amphetamine unpleasant and undesirable and experience no euphoria whatever. In hyperactive, hyperkinetic children, amphetamine often has a tranquilizing, slowing effect, and I have known adult depressed patients to take Benzedrine to go to sleep at night.

Particularly in normal and neurotic subjects, there is considerable evidence that the individual's expectations, the cues provided by the milieu, and the attitudes of the therapist may significantly alter the effectiveness of the drug. In a pilot study recently made at Denison University in collaboration with the Psychopharmacology Service Center on the response of normal college students to d-amphetamine, on some psychological measures there was a tendency for subjects who believed they were getting d-amphetamine and actually received d-amphetamine to have typical amphetamine-like reactions in both mood and psychomotor performance, while subjects who received Dexedrine and believed they were receiving a barbiturate showed a tendency toward barbituratelike reactions, at least in some aspects of psychological functioning. This study is in the process of being replicated to see whether these preliminary trends will be strengthened. Although further work may show that specific combinations of social influences and pharmacological effects may be very powerful methods for producing specific types of results, I know of no strong evidence that this is in fact the case.

There has been considerable discussion in recent years of the capacity of psychotomimetic agents, particularly LSD-25, mescaline, and psilocybin, to produce what may be described, in the context of this conference, as a "freeing" of the mind. Visual and auditory experiences may be made more vivid, and dramatic flights of fantasy, pleasurable or terrifying, may accompany the administration of these drugs. Artistic productions by persons in drugged states have elicited interest. These altered states of consciousness have also been reported to have been followed by profound and lasting changes in personality functioning and psychiatric symptomatology [1].

Two questions arise: First, do these psychotomimetic drugs "free" the mind in any useful manner during the period of their pharmacological activity? Second, do they have a useful effect in altering psychological functioning after the drug's acute effects have passed?

The first question is hard for me to answer. It is possible that artistic productions, poetry, or story plots conceived or executed under a psychotomimetic agent may, in some individuals, be superior to those produced in a drug-free or predrug state. I doubt this, being dubious that any interference with brain functioning is likely to produce an improvement in performance in a normal subject, but I suggest that the matter is susceptible to scientific test. A series of artistic productions by a series of artists produced predrug, during drug, and postdrug could be judged by other artists who were unaware of the conditions under which each production was executed. If the work produced during the influence of a drug such as LSD-25 were to be judged consistently superior, this would be powerfully convincing evidence indeed.

It should be noted, however, that the setting, including the expectations of the person administering the drug and the person receiving it, play a very powerful role here. There even is what I believe to be an artificial "geographical" effect on the response to the drug LSD-25 [1]. Workers in the East Coast, such as Malitz and Klee, do not appear to obtain from their subjects much in the way of bizarre fantasy material. Occasional subjects may become paranoid, and most experience visual illusions and autonomic side effects, but none of the subjects have reported self-revelations or other dramatic personal experiences. Hartman and Chandler and other workers in the Los Angeles area, on the other hand, seem to be able to induce most subjects to experience cosmic events such as union with the sun or death and rebirth with comparative ease. Other

investigators such as Jackson and Savage report similar, though less dramatic, results. Since it seems unlikely that the subjects on the West Coast are organically different from those on the East Coast, it is more reasonable to assume that something in the test situation produces the striking difference in response. Does LSD-25 really increase a subject's suggestability? Is the West Coast phenomenon entirely physician-induced or due to cultural differences in expectations of patients, or do investigators in the East somehow manage to create a situation in which flights of fantasy and dramatic emotional experiences are effectively, and perhaps unconsiously, suppressed?

As possible additional evidence in favor of LSD-25 as a tool for eliciting a response desired by the administrator, one may note Abramson's utilization of it as a method for getting patients to work on their resistances in an approved psychoanalytic manner with an almost complete absence of more exotic or fantastic productions.

I view recent work on LSD-25 and psychotherapy with very mixed feelings. The drug may really be enabling patients to obtain startling new insights into their problems and may be able to cause them to strikingly alter their behavior, but I am at a loss as to how much of this to attribute to a drug-induced "freeing" of the mind and how much to attribute to a therapist-induced mystical experience similar to religious conversion. Either effect conceivably could be therapeutically valuable, but the whole area is now so highly charged with emotion and so lacking in adequately controlled research as to make firm conclusions impossible. I am also concerned with the possibility of prolonged psychotic episodes being precipitated by psychotomimetic agents and the possibility of suicidal attempts or other aberrant behavior occurring during the drugged state.

There remains the unpleasant possibility that psychotomimetic agents or other drugs may make individuals overly responsive to the demands of another person and therefore may be usable as a means of altering loyalties or changing moral attitudes or political beliefs. Certainly these drugs could be used to incapacitate individuals temporarily, but can they be used to establish long-term control over minds? The published scientific literature is not at all informative. Both experimental and clinical reports deal chiefly with volunteer subjects or amenable patients, and I know of no experimental attempts to specifically alter beliefs, attitudes, or perceptions during or after the psychotomimetic drug experience. Chronic schizophrenic subjects certainly appear to be very resistant to reporting any subjective effects of LSD-25, but whether this resistance is secondary to any inner will to avoid responding is impossible to say.

Other drugs, intravenous barbiturates or amphetamine derivatives, can certainly alter verbal behavior, increase talkativeness and emotional expression, and occasionally enable patients to recall repressed experiences or talk about subjects which they had previously consciously avoided mentioning. The extent to which such procedures are useful outside the combat-neurosis type of situation is difficult to assess. The fact that three such otherwise diverse drugs as sodium amytal, desoxyephedrine, and LSD-25 are all used to facilitate psychotherapy by increasing emotional expression and activating unconscious material is, in itself, evidence of the confusion in this area of psychiatric practice.

In summary, I advance the proposition that drugs are not, in and of themselves, useful tools for the control of the mind, nor are they particularly well suited to free the mind if one is primarily concerned with the subjective experiences, attitudes, or beliefs of relatively normal human subjects. Some drugs such as LSD-25 and psilocybin can enable subjects to experience bizarre and perhaps rewarding experiences, but usually only if the subjects are interested in having such experiences or if such experiences are expected by those administering the drug. Barbiturates or stimulants (or alcohol for that matter) may increase emotional displays or promote talkativeness, but again the drugs are probably only facilitating the expression of emotions or thoughts already present in the subject.

Drugs such as the phenothiazine tranquilizers or the antidepressives are often effective in altering psychiatric symptoms in some, but not all, patients presenting appropriate symptoms. These clinical effects, however limited, are the phenomena closest to specific drug effects on behavior and psychological functioning, but these effects are confined to psychiatrically ill individuals and do not have any obvious applications to the control of thought or behavior in normal individuals.

Large enough doses of almost any of these five groups of psychopharmacological agents can disorganize or suppress human behavior by generally incapacitating the subjects receiving them, but there is no real reason to believe that these acute effects would have any long-term effect on the minds of the subjects.

There remains the possibility that some drug or drugs combined with some structured situation, e.g., some type of brainwashing program, might make the latter more effective or might reduce the time or effort required to produce a desired effect.

Although published research even vaguely relevant to this last problem is almost totally lacking, I see no reason to believe any drug would be more effective than social and psychological pressures or physical discomforts in producing changes in an individual.

The great interindividual variability in response to psychopharmacological agents in normal subjects and in patients makes it unlikely that any single drug would be a reliable aid in any planned program of mass thought control, although I accept the possibility that individual attempts at thought control may have something in common with psychotherapy, and skilled practitioners of such a black art may find drugs tailored to the practitioner and the subject of some use.

Furthermore, I consider it unlikely that current methods can be used to develop a new drug with any specific and reliable effect on either the freedom or the control of human mental processes, although I confidentially expect that new types of drugs with different effects on brain functioning and behavior will be uncovered by present drug-development methods.

In short, present psychopharmacological agents, though often chemically useful, have relatively nonspecific and quite variable effects on human behavior. How much of this variability is attributable to existing physical and psychological differences among human beings and how much variability is produced by the setting and by the behavior of the person administering the drugs is impossible to estimate. The difficulties in developing and evaluating drugs for the control of clinical psychiatric states are many; the difficulties in developing and/or evaluating drugs for the control of mental functioning or for the freeing of mental functioning in normal human beings appear to be well-nigh insurmountable.

REFERENCES

1. Abramson, H. A. (ed.), The Use of LSD in Psychotherapy, *Transactions of a Conference on d-Lysergic Acid Diethylamide (LSD-25),* Princeton, N.J., April 1959, New York Josiah Macy, Jr., Foundation, 1960.
2. Beecher, H. K., and Smith, G. M. Amphetamine, Secobarbital, and Athletic Performance. III. Quantitative Effects on Judgment, *J. Amer. Med. Ass.,* **172**:1629–1632, 1960.
3. Cole, J. O., Klerman, G. L., and Jones, R. T., Drug Therapy, in E. J. Spiegel (ed.), *Progress in Neurology and Psychiatry,* vol. XV, New York: Grune & Stratton, Inc., 1960, pp. 540–576.
4. Cole, J. O., Jones, R. T., and Klerman, G. L., Drug Therapy, in E. J. Spiegel (ed.), *Progress in Neurology and Psychiatry,* vol. XVI, New York, Grune & Stratton, Inc. 1961.
5. Gershon, S., and Olariu, J., JB 329: A New Psychotomimetic, Its Antagonism by Tetrahydroaminacrin and Its Comparison with LSD, Mescaline and Sernyl, *J. Neuropsychiat.,* 1960, 1:283–292.
6. Luby, E. D., Cohen, B. D., Rosenbaum, G., Gottlieb, J. S., and Kelley, R., Study of a New Schizophrenomimetic Drug—Sernyl, *A.M.A. Arch. Neurol. Psychiat.,* 1959, **81**:363–369.
7. Skinner, B. F., Freedom and the Control of Men, *Amer. Scholar,* 25:47–65.

Selection 74 | HORIZONS OF PSYCHO-PHARMACOLOGY*

This is an actual transcription of the formal but spontaneous panel discussion of the papers immediately preceding (See Introduction to Selections 73 and 74). Only minor editing has been done where continuity and clarity required it. The editors feel

* Reprinted from David Krech, Jonathan O. Cole, Seymour S. Kety, and James C. Miller, "Horizons of psychopharmacology." In Farber, S. M., and Wilson, R.H.L. (Eds.), *Control of the Mind: Part I. Man and Civilization.* McGraw-Hill Book Company, New York, 1961. By permission of the author and publisher.

that the spontaneity of the actual discussion gives a particular value to the panel in this form.

Moderator: David Krech

Panel Members: Jonathan O. Cole, Seymour S. Kety, James G. Miller

Dr. Krech As I was listening to the people who have been speaking to you, I learned three laws of psychopharmacology, each of which really represents a summary of each speaker. These are my first three laws of psychopharmacology: The first law, which really represents what Dr. Kety had to say, is that there are no generalizations concerning the biochemical control of the complex mind that can now be made. The second law of psychopharmacology, which represents, I think, Dr. Miller's contribution, is that there are many exceptions to the generalizations set down by the first law. The third law of psychopharmacology, which represents Dr. Cole's contribution, is that the first and second laws hold only for extreme cases of pathology, except where they do not hold. I trust that this has aroused my three colleagues, since I summarized their positions inadequately, though truthfully. Now I want to address to them a specific question. This derives from something that Dr. Cole said at the very end, which I think Dr. Kety hinted at and would agree with, and so would, I am sure, Dr. Miller. The problem to which I refer is that our work in this field is in many senses of the word a sort of hysterical reaction. We have been randomly—and sometimes not so randomly—trying every new drug made available. We have not given enough attention to basic research to find out how the nervous system does work and what the role of the various chemical compounds in the brain may be. More than that, the people who have been working in this field have paid very little attention to behavior. It is very interesting that the experimentalists in this area try to be somewhat precise about biochemistry and neurology, but about behavior they make one of two assumptions: they either assume that behavior is so complex and subtle that there is no point in trying to attack it scientifically, or they assume that behavior is so simple that anyone can tell when a man is disturbed or is not disturbed, when a drug has a good or a bad effect, and when it liberates a man's mind or restricts his mind. Of course, I accept neither assumption. This random search of testing drugs on random bits of behavior, which may come to mind on random patients in random hospitals, will, I suspect, get us nowhere. Therefore, my question comes to this: Don't you think that before we begin to invest so much of our substance into psychopharmacology that we had better spend a great deal of time in something I would prefer to call psychobiochemistry—the basic research in the relation between biochemical processes in the nervous system and behavior, taking both of these seriously as serious scientists?

Dr. Cole May I object to that? I think that work on the biochemistry of the brain, the effect of drugs on the brain, and its interrelation with behavior is good, and needed. But I think the gap between the experimental and the clinical application of drugs is still sufficiently large that one cannot let drugs be administered to large numbers of patients for the next 10 years, hoping to come up with good, hard knowledge of what is going on in the brain and eventually to produce a rational psychopharmacology. There are preliminary evidences of some kind of a marriage between the two. I know of some preliminary data on the effects of monoamine oxidase inhibitors on depressed patients which appear to indicate halfway through the study that most patients who become less depressed also have effective inhibition of their monoamine oxidase enzymes in the blood, whereas those who are not improved also do not have effective inhibition of the action of this enzyme. So there are some bridges being built. But I think there is need for careful, descriptive, clinical work, using both description to generate hypotheses, and massive, computerlike techniques to analyze the data. This would enable one, for example, to predict on an empirical basis more accurately which patients would respond to which drugs and which would not, leaving the central nervous system a mess of pottage for the interim until it can be better explained to us by basic scientists.

Dr. Miller I am sure, Dr. Cole, that Dr. Krech did not intend to suggest that we stop treating patients until such time as we understand the biochemistry of behavior. But I would like to disagree with your dissent, because I feel that one of the areas of psychopharmacology which

is being inadequately expressed and supported is exactly the one that he was talking about, and that the primary drive should be toward the development of more precise, quantitative, and objective measures of behavior. So I would emphasize the need that this be done in human beings as well as in animals, so that we can begin to get adequate correlations between biochemistry and behavior. I am particularly interested in seeing the mass application of psychology brought into the clinic as rapidly as possible, because I am convinced that there are a series of measures available now with a degree of dependency superior to the clinician's rating or impression in many cases that can be applied in clinical settings but are not being so applied. I view the role of the clinical *cum* experimental psychologist in the clinic as bringing some measure of the fundamental dimensions of behavior as an important—but quite independent—adjunct of the clinical impressions and evaluations. This is one of the most important needs we have at the present time. We should not stop treating the patient in the meantime, but we should get a little more of what I am advocating.

Dr. Kety I would like to disagree with just one word in Dr. Krech's proposition: the word "before." I believe you said that before we invested so much of our substance in study of the over-all clinical effects of these drugs on patients, we should investigate the basic biochemical, neurophysiological, and psychological parameters upon which these effects depended. If you would substitute "along with" for "before" I think I should agree. I object so strenuously to the word "before" because this implies that somehow we know where the answers are going to come from, and since we know that, obviously we should attack that area. As a matter of fact, rational drug therapy, although we hold to the idea so avidly, is much more the exception than the rule in the development of pharmacology. Quinidine was not discovered by a biochemist or a pharmacologist; it was not even discovered by a clinician. It was discovered by a patient; and digitalis was discovered by a midwife. That doesn't mean that we ought to support midwives and patients to the exclusion of biochemists, but we ought not be blind to the possibilities of understanding drug action or at least developing new drugs on the basis of the crudest kind of empiricism. If we had waited until we could develop insulin from an understanding of what it does in the body, we still would not have insulin, because biochemists still don't understand how it lowers the blood sugar and how it improves diabetes. It will take, in the case of the brain, much longer to understand the basic mechanism of these agents. I would agree, however, that even empirical observations can be sharpened up, that they can be made more economical on the basis of carefully controlled experiments— carefully controlled even in terms of the whole man rather than a synapse. I would also agree most heartily with your anxiety about the disproportion of attention which is being given today to the biochemical and physiological aspects, as opposed to the behavioral aspects, of the problem. The biochemists studying the action of the brain of some of these agents are extremely careful in their control of the enzymes, of their substrates, of the dosage, of the concentration of these agents, and then report upon behavior in terms of the crudest and most unsophisticated measures. I think certainly the kind of thing you are doing, Dr. Krech, is being done in many places where students of behavior are working who are as precise as they can be in their field as the biochemists are in theirs.

Dr. Miller I think we are dealing here with a problem we should not moralize about, because biochemistry is rapidly receiving increasing attention. We should not say it should stop; but rather, we should look on it as one of many examples in the history of science of an interest in the development of a field resulting from the availability of instruments which can give facts with precision. Take the field of computers. They involve nothing new mathematically, yet the very existence of those tools, which are simply more rapid, with a larger memory capacity and a few other characteristics than previous computational devices, has resulted in a vast efflorescence of activity around them, none of which is fundamental in the development of science. It is therefore the responsibility of those of us who are particularly interested in the development of rigorous behavioral measurements to get tools and instruments so that the expansion in our

activities will occur. When we get those tools and instruments, I don't think there will be the slightest difficulty in getting the necessary support and interest for the work.

Dr. Krech I made a rather extreme statement before for two reasons. First, my personality structure is such that I like to make extreme statements; that is, I think, an accident of genetics. But there is another reason, a very cold, calculated reason, and to tell you simply what I mean I should like to quote a maxim of my mother-in-law. When my mother-in-law wants to tell people that they should at least reduce their tendency to inflict corporal punishment on children, she says in her lecture, "If you will take a firm oath when your first child is born never, never under any circumstances to whip, slap, or pinch your child, you will whip him, slap him, and pinch him just enough." I am applying the same principle in my assertion that it is most important that we first have departments of psychobiochemistry before any other departments of psychopharmacology, and so on. We may then have just enough, because today there are quite a number of departments of pharmacology in the United States; any medical school of consequence has one. There are a number of departments and groups of psychopharmacology. But I know of only one committee in one university which is really concerned with psychobiochemistry, and I am not even sure of that since they are in psychopharmacology. I know of no departments of psychobiochemistry. Therefore, it is most apparent that the first thing to do is to create them. Now let me ask another question. I have been listening to today's and yesterday's discussions as a psychologist, not only as an "acetylcholenologist." I have been struck by one thing. We are supposed to be discussing the control of the mind. Now the word "mind," at least to some people, brings up connotations of thought— what we psychologists used to call cognition. The word "mind" does not necessarily mean only pathology, it does not necessarily mean only anxiety, it does not necessarily mean only frustration and screaming and running through the streets naked; the word "mind" means thinking, believing, creating, and so on, and as I look over most of the work on the effects of drugs on behavior, I am struck with what one might almost call an anti-intellectualism among researchers. They are not interested in the effects of drugs on the mind from the cognitive or intellectual point of view; they are interested in the effect of drugs on the mind in the emotional, mood, or pathological sense. I think this may reflect the concern of these researchers with the ill, because they come from hospitals and from the medical profession. Again, if we had a department of psychobiochemistry, we would not have that state of affairs. But in a sense it also reflects—and here I say *"mea culpa"* again—the attitude that I think has been partially true of American psychology. American psychology has been really anti-intellectual; it has concerned itself more with personality and gross behavior, but relatively little with cognition, thinking, and problem solving. Don't you think that here we have a whole area of the mind which is being neglected?

Dr. Kety I would like to assent very strongly to that statement and try to speculate as to why that anti-intellectualism has occurred. I think that you psychologists or your antecedent psychologists were to a large extent responsible for this. There was a school of psychology, the behavioral school, which was rather doctrinaire in its approach and felt that since the only thing which could be studied scientifically was behavior that nothing existed but behavior, and therefore that the mind, mentalism, protection, and feelings were subjective phenomena not suitable for experimental measurements and which had best not be spoken about. Therefore one hears members of this particular persuasion talking about the most sensitive and subtle aspects of human creativity, but never discussing consciousness, never mentioning the mind—as if it were a dirty word—but talking about it as behavior, which it obviously is not. Actually, the mind means a variety of different things, and Dr. Krech encompassed different things in his definition of the mind. If we think of the mind as the complex computation that goes on, the process of thinking, of making judgments, of evaluating, that is one way of looking at the mind. On the other hand, one can look at the mind as the subjective aspect of these processes, as feeling, as consciousness, and as sensation. I think that a great deal of confusion in the history of

philosophy and our thinking today represents an unwillingness to separate these things. The monist can explain the first aspects of mind, namely, computation, judgment, and so forth, on a mechanical basis; and if that is all he means by mind he can be perfectly happy in his monistic philosophy. But if he really recognizes the other aspects of the mind, the subjective, personal quality of consciousness and feeling, then I think he will have to admit that a monistic philosophy can hardly encompass that in a mechanistic interpretation. I want to voice a very strong assent to your feelings about this. I think we can and should talk about the mind and all its subtleties, all the phenomena and epiphenomena, and we should be willing to study the mind and its relations with matter. There is a psychopharmacology, there is an effect of a drug on the mind, and that is not divorced from scientific discourse; it is something which can be studied just as effectively, if perhaps with more difficulty, than the effect of a drug on a synapse.

Dr. Miller Once again I think I agree with you and would like to support your view that not enough has been done in this particular area, either in psychology or, even more important, in the field of psychiatry. The emphasis on pathology in psychiatry has been overwhelming, as it has been in psychology. But I think the reason historically perhaps is the lack of adequate instruments. Introspection does not turn out to be a very good instrument for studying thinking, reasoning, problem solving, and the so-called higher mental processes. I think we are coming a little bit now into the period of 1790, with the revolution and the age of reason coming on. If you can just hold on a few years there will be quite a change, because computer simulation of internal processes of the "mind" is rapidly coming to the fore. There have been various conferences and papers on this, but I have not noticed yet a single simulation of nonrational or affective processes. It is very difficult for the sort of person who plays with computers to deal with nonlogical processes, anyhow. Second, it is difficult to think how you would write a program into a computer that would simulate the theory of revision, for example, or some other notions of affect that we have at the moment. I think it could be, and probably will be done. But it seems to me likely that, with computers now available, the next area of attention in the processes of the mind will be toward a tremendous emphasis on cognitive processes, not only learning but apperception and the other things that you mentioned. This is where we are likely to be going in the near future.

Dr. Kety Do you really believe that in the foreseeable future there could be a computer simulation of feeling?

Dr. Miller Yes, if you take feeling out of the subjective context of the term.

Dr. Krech A moment ago I defended myself against some comments which took exception to my position. Now I want to defend myself against the comments which agree with my position.

Dr. Miller To protect us from our friends.

Dr. Krech I am delighted that Dr. Kety thinks we should study consciousness. As a matter of fact, I knew that before he said so, because he had an extremely interesting and provocative article in *Science* in December, 1960. So I am glad that he agreed that we ought to pay attention to cognition and thinking and so on, but I do not agree with him that this necessarily commits us to a dualistic philosophy. I think psychologists take Professor Hebb's position, and I would accept the monistic hypothesis as a working hypothesis. Yet I would not feel restrained at all from working with feelings, thoughts, fantasies, creativity, and so on. So please associate Dr. Kety and me in our advocation of more work on thinking by both pharmacologists and psychologists. Please disassociate us in so far as this monistic-dualistic position is concerned.

Now, Dr. Miller, I take a dim view of the computer model as the model of the brain. I think that the best model of the brain we can have is a brain, and we know that a brain is not a computer. We know some things about the biochemistry, anatomy, and electrophysiology of a brain, and we know that those things are different from the things that go on inside a computer. So that when I ask for more work on thinking, feelings, and so forth, I am not asking for more computer studies; I am asking for more careful, clean, dedicated, tough-minded observation of normal people as

they think and solve problems. Most of them don't go around being frustrated; they go around solving problems. So again I am delighted to be associated with Dr. Miller on the need for more research on thinking, and I knew he would agree with that, because he and his group have done some most interesting work on the problems of thinking. But I take a dim view of the newest fad in psychology.

Dr. Cole I think one of the other reasons you may not have had so much work on the effect of drugs on thinking and cognition is that the drugs are not very effective in this area. Their most startling apparent effects at least, are on symptomatology, or on sleepiness or alertness, or something of this sort. I may be wrong, but if drugs were more effective in altering decision making or intelligence, somebody would have picked this phenomenon up empirically in their studies.

Dr. Miller Of course, drugs affect these cognitive processes. But, like LSD-25 or enough alcohol, they have a destructive influence on cognitive processes. You can get a beautiful dosage curve on the effects, objectively measured, of alcohol on reasoning processes. But we have known that for a long time. We also know that alcohol impairs the efficiency of the information transmission, causing it to come out with the wrong answers in a very fine, delightful, and systematic way. But there isn't anything particularly new in that. What we have to do is to find some chemical which transmits a message with its molecule. The molecule then becomes incorporated in the RNA material, and when one checks later on the RNA one obtains a message different from what was there originally. We are not very close to that as yet.

From the Floor I would like to ask the panel whether they consider the mystical transcendental experience of psychotomimetic drugs —LSD, for example—a distortion allied to the hallucination or delusion of a sick patient, or whether it is a new intuitive form of knowledge of some kind. Is it a real experience, or is it a distortion of something that was previously present in the mind?

Dr. Kety The quesion that I shall try to answer is whether we believe that the psychotomimetic drugs induce new concepts or percepts into the brain or mind, or whether they produce merely distortions of previous information. The only answer I can give is that I cannot see a mechanism whereby a small molecule such as LSD or mescaline can introduce new information into the brain, since even from what we know thus far this information is stored in a most complex, systematic, and highly organized manner. Therefore, since one is entranced with that concept, one would have to answer that these drugs can only modify or distort previously acquired information; they cannot create something new.

From the Floor Would you comment on maturation and the ordering of information?

Dr. Kety Certainly the ordering of information is something which we acquire along with the information, and which is also genetically, biologically, and experientially determined. There are generalized and local biochemical and chronological growth factors which may modulate orderly, sequential coding, and which, when disordered, may be responsible for disordered sequential coding. I think also that experiential factors can distort the ordering of these phenomena, so that by one or another mechanism a malcoding may occur.

Dr. Krech To conclude, I have three summaries of our findings. First, we have renounced our anti-intellectualism, and, as research people, we are going to study cognition and the intellectual life of man. Second, we are going forth to establish a number of departments of psychobiochemistry. Third, the study of the role of acetylcholine deserves top priority.

Early in the introductory course in psychology you were made aware of the importance of experimental control in contributing reliable knowledge. In some ways psychological research is more difficult than research in physics, in part because it is more difficult to exercise adequate control. The purpose of control is of course to increase reproducibility of the results, and reproducibility is a necessary condition for generalizability. These two criteria are identified by Dr. Martin T. Orne as basic for the evaluation of the meaningfulness of any experiment. He argues that both of these goals are often jeopardized by human subjects responding to the "demand characteristics" of the experiment as well as to the independent variable. By demand characteristics Orne means the tendency of the subject to try to figure out what kind of behavior the experimenter wants and then to behave in that way. That is, the subject typically tries to play the role of a "good subject." He suggests that psychologists who conduct experiments on human beings should utilize techniques to determine the extent to which the experimental results are due to the independent variable or the demand characteristics.

The biasing effect of the expectations of subjects is nicely described by Orne. The student should be reminded that the expectations of the experimenter can also bias his observations. A striking experimental demonstration of such biasing among untrained experimenters is presented in a paper by Rosenthal and Halas.* They found that student experimenters who expected that flatworms could be conditioned observed significantly more conditioning in their worms than did experimenters who were led to expect that planaria could not be conditioned.

Selection **75** | ON THE SOCIAL PSYCHOLOGY OF THE PSYCHOLOGICAL EXPERIMENT: WITH PARTICULAR REFERENCE TO DEMAND CHARACTERISTICS AND THEIR IMPLICATIONS†

MARTIN T. ORNE
Harvard Medical School

It is to the highest degree probable that the subjects['s] . . . general attitude of mind is that of ready complacency and cheerful willingness to assist the investigator in every possible way by reporting to him those very things which he is most eager to find, and that the very questions of the experimenter . . . suggest the shade of reply expected. . . . Indeed . . . it seems too often as if the subject were now regarded as a stupid automaton . . .

A. H. PIERCE, 1908

Since the time of Galileo, scientists have employed the laboratory experiment as a method of understanding natural phenomena. Generically, the experimental method consists of abstracting relevant variables from complex situations in nature and reproducing in the laboratory segments of these situations, varying the parameters involved so as to determine the effect of the experimental variables. This procedure allows generalization from the information obtained in the laboratory situation back to the original situation as it occurs in nature. The physical sciences have made

---

* Robert Rosenthal and Edward S. Halas, "Experimenter Effect in the Study of Invertibrate Behavior," *Psychological Reports*, **11:** 251–256, 1962. See also Robert Rosenthal and Kermit L. Fode, "Psychology of the Scientist: V. Three Experiments in Experimenter Bias," *Psychological Reports*, **12:** 491–511, 1963.

† Abridged from Martin T. Orne, "On the Social Psychology of the Psychological Experiment: With Particular Reference to Demand Characteristics and Their Implication." *American Psychologist.* **17:** 776–783, 1962. Reprinted by permission of the author and the American Psychological Association.

striking advances through the use of this method, but in the behavioral sciences it has often been difficult to meet two necessary requirements for meaningful experimentation: reproducibility and ecological validity.[1] It has long been recognized that certain differences will exist between the types of experiments conducted in the physical sciences and those in the behavioral sciences because the former investigates a universe of inanimate objects and forces, whereas the latter deals with animate organisms, often thinking, conscious subjects. However, recognition of this distinction has not always led to appropriate changes in the traditional experimental model of physics as employed in the behavioral sciences. Rather the experimental model has been so successful as employed in physics that there has been a tendency in the behavioral sciences to follow precisely a paradigm originated for the study of inanimate objects, i.e., one which proceeds by exposing the subject to various conditions and observing the differences in reaction of the subject under different conditions. However, the use of such a model with animal or human subjects leads to the problem that the subject of the experiment is assumed, at least implicitly, to be a *passive responder* to stimuli —an assumption difficult to justify. Further, in this type of model the experimental stimuli themselves are usually rigorously defined in terms of what *is done* to the subject. In contrast, the purpose of this paper will be to focus on what the human subject *does* in the laboratory: what motivation the subject is likely to have in the experimental situation, how he usually perceives behavioral research, what the nature of the cues is that the subject is likely to pick up, etc. Stated in other terms, what factors are apt to affect the subject's reaction to the well-defined stimuli in the situation? These factors comprise what will be referred to here as the "experimental setting."

Since any experimental manipulation of human subjects takes place within this larger framework or setting, we should propose that the above-mentioned factors must be further elaborated and the parameters of the experimental setting more carefully defined so that

adequate controls can be designed to isolate the effects of the experimental setting from the effects of the experimental variables. Later in this paper we shall propose certain possible techniques of control which have been devised in the process of our research on the nature of hypnosis.

Our initial focus here will be on some of the qualities peculiar to psychological experiments. The experimental situation is one which takes place within the context of an explicit agreement of the subject to participate in a special form of social interaction known as "taking part in an experiment." Within the context of our culture the roles of subject and experimenter are well understood and carry with them well-defined mutual role expectations. A particularly striking aspect of the typical experimenter-subject relationship is the extent to which the subject will play his role and place himself under the control of the experimenter. Once a subject has agreed to participate in a psychological experiment, he implicitly agrees to perform a very wide range of actions on request without inquiring as to their purpose, and frequently without inquiring as to their duration.

Furthermore, the subject agrees to tolerate a considerable degree of discomfort, boredom, or actual pain, if required to do so by the experimenter. Just about any request which could conceivably be asked of the subject by a reputable investigator is legitimized by the quasi-magical phrase. "This is an experiment," and the shared assumption that a legitimate purpose will be served by the subject's behavior. A somewhat trivial example of this legitimization of requests is as follows:

A number of casual acquaintances were asked whether they would do the experimenter a favor; on their acquiescence, they were asked to perform five push-ups. Their response tended to be amazement, incredulity and the question "Why?" Another similar group of individuals were asked whether they would take part in an experiment of brief duration. When they agreed to do so, they too were asked to perform five push-ups. Their typical response was "Where?"

The striking degree of control inherent in the experimental situation can also be illustrated by a set of pilot experiments which were performed in the course of designing an experi-

---

[1] Ecological validity, in the sense that Brunswik (1947) has used the term: appropriate generalization from the laboratory to nonexperimental situations.

ment to test whether the degree of control inherent in the *hypnotic* relationship is greater than that in a waking relationship.[2] In order to test this question, we tried to develop a set of tasks which waking subjects would refuse to do, or would do only for a short period of time. The tasks were intended to be psychologically noxious, meaningless, or boring, rather than painful or fatiguing.

For example, one task was to perform serial additions of each adjacent two numbers on sheets filled with rows of random digits. In order to complete just one sheet, the subject would be required to perform 224 additions! A stack of some 2,000 sheets was presented to each subject—clearly an impossible task to complete. After the instructions were given, the subject was deprived of his watch and told, "Continue to work; I will return eventually." Five and one-half hours later, the *experimenter* gave up! In general, subjects tended to continue this type of task for several hours, usually with little decrement in performance. Since we were trying to find a task which would be discontinued spontaneously within a brief period, we tried to create a more frustrating situation as follows:

Subjects were asked to perform the same task described above but were also told that when finished the additions on each sheet, they should pick up a card from a large pile, which would instruct them on what to do next. However, every card in the pile read,

You are to tear up the sheet of paper which you have just completed into a minimum of thirty-two pieces and go on to the next sheet of paper and continue working as you did before; when you have completed this piece of paper, pick up the next card which will instruct you further. Work as accurately and as rapidly as you can.

Our expectation was that subjects would discontinue the task as soon as they realized that the cards were worded identically, that each finished piece of work had to be destroyed, and that, in short, the task was completely meaningless.

Somewhat to our amazement, subjects tended to persist in the task for several hours

with relatively little sign of overt hostility. Removal of the one-way screen did not tend to make much difference. The postexperimental inquiry helped to explain the subjects' behavior. When asked about the tasks, subjects would invariably attribute considerable meaning to their performance, viewing it as an endurance test or the like.

Thus far, we have been singularly unsuccessful in finding an experimental task which would be discontinued, or, indeed, refused by subjects in an experimental setting.[3,4] Not only do subjects continue to perform boring, unrewarding tasks, but they do so with few errors and little decrement in speed. It became apparent that it was extremely difficult to design an experiment to test the degree of social control in hypnosis, in view of the already *very high degree of control in the experimental situation itself.*

The quasi-experimental work reported here is highly informal and based on samples of three or four subjects in each group. It does, however, illustrate the remarkable compliance of the experimental subject. The only other situations where such a wide range of requests are carried out with little or no question are those of complete authority, such as some parent-child relationships or some doctor-patient relationships. This aspect of the experiment as a social situation will not become apparent unless one tests for it; it is, however, present in varying degrees in all experimental contexts. Not only are tasks carried out, but they are performed with care over considerable period of time.

Our observation that subjects tend to carry out a remarkably wide range of instructions with a surprising degree of diligence reflects only one aspect of the motivation manifested by most subjects in an experimental situation. It is relevant to consider another aspect of motivation that is common to the subjects of most psychological experiments: high regard for the aims of science and experimentation.

[2] These pilot studies were performed by Thomas Menaker.

[3] Tasks which would involve the use of actual severe physical pain or exhaustion were not considered.
[4] This observation is consistent with Frank's (1944) failure to obtain resistance to disagreeable or nonsensical tasks. He accounts for this "primarily by S's unwillingness to break the tacit agreement he had made when he volunteered to take part in the experiment, namely, to do whatever the experiment required of him" (p. 24).

A volunteer who participates in a psychological experiment may do so for a wide variety of reasons ranging from the need to fulfill a course requirement, to the need for money, to the unvoiced hope of altering his personal adjustment for the better, etc. Over and above these motives, however, college students tend to share (with the experimenter) the hope and expectation that the study in which they are participating will in some material way contribute to science and perhaps ultimately to human welfare in general. We should expect that many of the characteristics of the experimental situation derive from the peculiar role relationship which exists between subject and experimenter. Both subject and experimenter share the belief that whatever the experimental task is, it is important, and that as such no matter how much effort must be exerted or how much discomfort must be endured, it is justified by the ultimate purpose.

If we assume that much of the motivation of the subject to comply with any and all experimental instructions derives from an identification with the goals of science in general and the success of the experiment in particular,[5] it follows that the subject has a stake in the outcome of the study in which he is participating. For the volunteer subject to feel that he has made a useful contribution, it is necessary for him to assume that the experimenter is competent and that he himself is a "good subject."

The significance to the subject of successfully being a "good subject" is attested to by the frequent questions at the conclusion of an experiment, to the effect of, "Did I ruin the experiment?" What is most commonly meant by this is, "Did I perform well in my role as experimental subject?" or "Did my behavior demonstrate that which the experiment is designed to show?" Admittedly, subjects are concerned about their performance in terms of reinforcing their self-image; nonetheless, they seem even more concerned with the utility of their performances. We might well expect then that as far as the subject is able, he will behave in an experimental

context in a manner designed to play the role of a "good subject" or, in other words, *to validate the experimental hypothesis.* Viewed in this way, the student volunteer is *not* merely a passive responder in an experimental situation but rather he has a very real stake in the successful outcome of the experiment. This problem is implicitly recognized in the large number of psychological studies which attempt to conceal the true purpose of the experiment from the subject in the hope of thereby obtaining more reliable data. This maneuver on the part of psychologists is so widely known in the college population that even if a psychologist is honest with the subject, more often than not he will be distrusted. As one subject pithily put it, "Psychologists always lie!" This bit of paranoia has some support in reality.

The subject's performance in an experiment might almost be conceptualized as problem-solving behavior; that is, at some level he sees it as his task to ascertain the true purpose of the experiment and respond in a manner which will support the hypotheses being tested. Viewed in this light, the totality of cues which convey an experimental hypothesis to the subject become significant determinants of subjects' behavior. We have labeled the sum total of such cues as the "*demand characteristics of the experimental situation*" (Orne, 1959a). These cues include the rumors or campus scuttlebutt about the research, the information conveyed during the original solicitation, the person of the experimenter, and the setting of the laboratory, as well as all explicit and implicit communications during the experiment proper. A frequently overlooked, but nonetheless very significant source of cues for the subject lies in the experimental procedure itself, viewed in the light of the subject's previous knowledge and experience. For example, if a test is given twice with some intervening treatment, even the dullest college student is aware that some change is expected, particularly if the test is in some obvious way related to the treatment.

The demand characteristics perceived in any particular experiment will vary with the sophistication, intelligence, and previous experience of each experimental subject. To the extent that the demand characteristics of the experiment are clear-cut, they will be perceived uniformly by most experimental subjects. It is en-

---

[5] This hypothesis is subject to empirical test. We should predict that there would be measurable differences in motivation between subjects who perceive a particular experiment as "significant" and those who perceive the experiment as "unimportant."

tirely possible to have an experimental situation with clear-cut demand characteristics for psychology undergraduates which, however, does not have the same clear-cut demand characteristics for enlisted army personnel. It is, of course, those demand characteristics which are perceived by the subject that will influence his behavior.

We should like to propose the heuristic assumption that a subject's behavior in any experimental situation will be determined by two sets of variables: (a) those which are traditionally defined as experimental variables and (b) the perceived demand characteristics of the experimental situation. The extent to which the subject's behavior is related to the demand characteristics, rather than to the experimental variable, will in large measure determine both the extent to which the experiment can be replicated with minor modification (i.e., modified demand characteristics) and the extent to which generalizations can be drawn about the effect of the experimental variables in non-experimental contexts [the problem of ecological validity (Brunswik, 1947)].

It becomes an empirical issue to study under what circumstances, in what kind of experimental contexts, and with what kind of subject populations, demand characteristics become significant in determining the behavior of subjects in experimental situations. It should be clear that demand characteristics cannot be eliminated from experiments; all experiments will have demand characteristics, and these will always have some effect. It does become possible, however, to study the effect of demand characteristics as opposed to the effect of experimental variables. However, techniques designed to study the effect of demand characteristics need to take into account that these effects result from the subject's *active* attempt to respond appropriately to the *totality* of the experimental situation.

It is perhaps best to think of the perceived demand characteristics as a contextual variable in the experimental situation. We should like to emphasize that, at this stage, little is known about this variable. In our first study which utilized the demand characteristics concept (Orne, 1959b), we found that a particular experimental effect was present only in records of those subjects who were able to verbalize the experimenter's hypothesis. Those subjects

who were unable to do so did not show the predicted phenomenon. Indeed we found that whether or not a given subject perceived the experimenter's hypothesis was a more accurate predictor of the subject's actual performance than his statement about what he thought he had done on the experimental task. It became clear from extensive interviews with subjects that response to the demand characteristics is not merely conscious compliance. When we speak of "playing the role of a good experimental subject," we use the concept analogously to the way in which Sarbin (1950) describes role playing in hypnosis: namely, largely on a nonconscious level. The demand characteristics of the situation help define the role of "good experimental subject," and the responses of the subject are a function of the role that is created.

We have a suspicion that the demand characteristics most potent in determining subjects' behavior are those which convey the purpose of the experiment effectively but not obviously. If the purpose of the experiment is not clear, or is highly ambiguous, many different hypotheses may be formed by different subjects, and the demand characteristics will not lead to clear-cut results. If, on the other hand, the demand characteristics are so obvious that the subject becomes fully conscious of the expectations of the experimenter, there is a tendency to lean over backwards to be honest. We are encountering here the effect of another facet of the college student's attitude toward science. While the student wants studies to "work," he feels he must be honest in his report; otherwise, erroneous conclusions will be drawn. Therefore, if the subject becomes acutely aware of the experimenter's expectations, there may be a tendency for biasing in the opposite direction. (This is analogous to the often observed tendency to favor individuals whom we dislike in an effort to be fair.)[6]

Delineation of the situations where demand

---

[6] Rosenthal (1961) in his recent work on experimenter bias, has reported a similar type of phenomenon. Biasing was maximized by ego involvement of the experimenters, but when an attempt was made to increase biasing by paying for "good results," there was a marked reduction of effect. This reversal may be ascribed to the experimenters' becoming too aware of their own wishes in the situation.

characteristics may produce an effect ascribed to experimental variables, or where they may obscure such an effect and actually lead to systematic data in the opposite direction, as well as those experimental contexts where they do not play a major role, is an issue for further work. Recognizing the contribution to experimental results which may be made by the demand characteristics of the situation, what are some experimental techniques for the study of demand characteristics?

As we have pointed out, it is futile to imagine an experiment that could be created without demand characteristics. One of the basic characteristics of the human being is that he will ascribe purpose and meaning even in the absence of purpose and meaning. In an experiment where he knows some purpose exists, it is inconceivable for him not to form some hypothesis as to the purpose, based on some cues, no matter how meager; this will then determine the demand characteristics which will be perceived by and operate for a particular subject. Rather than eliminating this variable then, it becomes necessary to take demand characteristics into account, study their effect, and manipulate them if necessary.

One procedure to determine the demand characteristics is the systematic study of each individual subject's perception of the experimental hypothesis. If one can determine what demand characteristics are perceived by each subject, it becomes possible to determine to what extent these, rather than the experimental variables, correlate with the observed behavior. If the subject's behavior correlates better with the demand characteristics than with the experimental variables, it is probable that the demand characteristics are the major determinants of the behavior.

The most obvious technique for determining what demand characteristics are perceived is the use of postexperimental inquiry. In this regard, it is well to point out that considerable self-discipline is necessary for the experimenter to obtain a valid inquiry. A great many experimenters at least implicitly make the demand that the subject not perceive what is really going on. The temptation for the experimenter, in, say, a replication of an Asch-group pressure experiment, is to ask the subject afterwards, "You didn't realize that the other fellows were confederates, did you?" Having obtained the

required. "No," the experimenter breathes a sigh of relief and neither subject nor experimenter pursues the issue further.[7] However, even if the experimenter makes an effort to elicit the subject's perception of the hypothesis of the experiment, he may have difficulty in obtaining a valid report because the subject as well as he himself has considerable interest in appearing naive.

Most subjects are cognizant that they are not supposed to know any more about an experiment than they have been told and that excessive knowledge will disqualify them from participating, or, in the case of a postexperimental inquiry, such knowledge will invalidate their performance. As we pointed out earlier, subjects have a real stake in viewing their performance as meaningful. For this reason, it is commonplace to find a pact of ignorance resulting from the intertwining motives of both experimenter and subject, neither wishing to create a situation where the particular subject's performance needs to be excluded from the study.

For these reasons, inquiry procedures are required to push the subject for information without, however, providing in themselves cues as to what is expected. The general question which needs to be explored is the subject's perception of the experimental purpose and the specific hypotheses of the experimenter. This can best be done by an open-ended procedure starting with the very general question of, "What do you think that the experiment is about?" and only much later asking specific questions. Responses of "I don't know" should be dealt with by encouraging the subject to guess, use his imagination, and in general, by refusing to accept this response. Under these circumstances, the overwhelming majority of students will turn out to have devolved very definite hypotheses. These hypotheses can then be judged, and a correlation between them and experimental performance can be drawn.

Two objections may be made against this type of inquiry: (a) that the subject's perception of the experimenter's hypotheses is based on his own experimental behavior, and therefore a correlation between these two variables may have little to do with the determinants of

---

[7] Asch (1952) himself took great pains to avoid this pitfall.

behavior, and (*b*) that the inquiry procedure itself is subject to demand characteristics.

A procedure which has been independently advocated by Riecken (1958) and Orne (1959a) is designed to deal with the first of these objections. This consists of an inquiry procedure which is conducted much as though the subject had actually been run in the experiment, without, however, permitting him to be given any experimental data. Instead, the precise procedure of the experiment is explained, the experimental matérial is shown to the subject, and he is told what he would be required to do; however, he is not permitted to make any responses. He is then given a postexperimental inquiry as though he had been a subject. Thus, one would say, "If I had asked you to do all these things, what do you think that the experiment would be about, what do you think I would be trying to prove, what would my hypothesis be?" etc. This technique, which we have termed the pre-experimental inquiry, can be extended very readily to the giving of pre-experimental tests, followed by the explanation of experimental conditions and tasks, and the administration of postexperimental tests. The subject is requested to behave on these tests as though he had been exposed to the experimental treatment that was described to him. This type of procedure is not open to the objection that the subject's own behavior has provided cues for him as to the purpose of the task. It presents him with a straight problem-solving situation and makes explicit what, for the true experimental subject, is implicit. It goes without saying that these subjects who are run on the pre-experimental inquiry conditions must be drawn from the same population as the experimental groups and may, of course, not be run subsequently in the experimental condition. This technique is one of approximation rather than of proof. However, if subjects describe behavior on the pre-inquiry conditions as similar to, or identical with, that actually given by subjects exposed to the experimental conditions, the hypothesis becomes plausible that demand characteristics may be responsible for the behavior.

It is clear that pre- and postexperimental inquiry techniques have their own demand characteristics. For these reasons, it is usually best to have the inquiry conducted by an experimenter who is not acquainted with the actual experimental behavior of the subjects. This will tend to minimize the effect of experimenter bias.

Another technique which we have utilized for approximating the effect of the demand characteristics is to attempt to hold the demand characteristics constant and eliminate the experimental variable. One way of accomplishing this purpose is through the use of simulating subjects. This is a group of subjects who are not exposed to the experimental variable to which the effect has been attributed, but who are instructed to act *as if* this were the case, in order to control for experimenter bias under these circumstances, it is advisable to utilize more than one experimenter and to have the experimenter who actually runs the subjects "blind" as to which group (simulating or real) any given individual belongs.

Our work in hypnosis (Damaser, Shor, & Orne, in press; Orne, 1959b; Shor, 1959) is a good example of the use of simulating controls. Subjects unable to enter hypnosis are instructed to simulate entering hypnosis for another experimenter. The experimenter who runs the study sees both highly trained hypnotic subjects and simulators in random order and does not know to which group each subject belongs. Because the subjects are run "blind," the experimenter is more likely to treat the two groups of subjects identically. We have found that simulating subjects are able to perform with great effectiveness, deceiving even well-trained hypnotists. However, the simulating group is not exposed to the experimental condition (in this case, hypnosis) to which the given effect under investigation is often ascribed. Rather, it is a group faced with a problem-solving task: namely, to utilize whatever cues are made available by the experimental context and the experimenter's concrete behavior in order to behave as they think that hypnotized subjects might. Therefore, to the extent that simulating subjects are able to behave identically, it is possible that demand characteristics, rather than the altered state of consciousness, could account for the behavior of the experimental group.

The same type of technique can be utilized in other types of studies. For example, in contrast to the placebo control in a drug study, it is equally possible to instruct some subjects not to take the medication at all, but to act as if they had. It must be emphasized that this type of control is different from the placebo control. It represents an approximation. It maximally confronts the simulating subject with a problem-solving task and suggests how much of the total effect could be accounted for by the demand characteristics—assuming that the experimental group had taken full advantage of them, an assumption not necessarily correct.

All of the techniques proposed thus far share the quality that they depend upon the active cooperation of the control subjects, and in some way utilize his thinking process as an intrinsic factor. The subject does *not* just respond in these control situations but, rather, he is required *actively* to solve the problem.

The use of placebo experimental conditions is a way in which this problem can be dealt with in a more classic fashion. Psychopharmacology has used such techniques extensively, but here too they present problems. In the case of placebos and drugs, it is often the case that the physician is "blind" as to whether a drug is placebo or active, but the patient is not, despite precautions to the contrary; i.e., the patient is cognizant that he does not have the side effects which some of his fellow patients on the ward experience. By the same token, in psychological placebo treatments, it is equally important to ascertain whether the subject actually perceived the treatment to be experimental or control. Certainly the subject's perception of himself as a control subject may materially alter the situation.

A recent experiment[8] in our laboratory illustrates this type of investigation. We were interested in studying the demand characteristics of sensory deprivation experiments, independent of any actual sensory deprivation. We hypothesized that the overly cautious treatment of subjects, careful screening for mental or physical disorders, awesome release forms, and, above all, the presence of a "panic (release) button" might be more significant in producing the effects reported from sensory deprivation than the actual diminution of sensory input. A pilot study (Stare, Brown, & Orne, 1959), employing preinquiry techniques, supported this

[8] This experiment is described in a paper in preparation by M. T. Orne and K. E. Scheibe: The Contribution of Nondeprivation Factors in the Production of Sensory Deprivation Effects.

view. Recently, we designed an experiment to test more rigorously this hypothesis.

This experiment, which we called Meaning Deprivation, had all the *accoutrements* of sensory deprivation, including release forms and a red panic button. However, we carefully refrained from creating any sensory deprivation whatsoever. The experimental task consisted of sitting in a small experimental room which was well lighted, with two comfortable chairs, as well as ice water and a sandwich, and an optional task of adding numbers. The subject did not have a watch during this time, the room was reasonably quiet, but not soundproof, and the duration of the experiment (of which the subject was ignorant) was four hours. Before the subject was placed in the experimental room, 10 tests previously used in sensory deprivation research were administered. At the completion of the experiment, the same tasks were again administered. A microphone and a one-way screen were present in the room, and the subject was encouraged to verbalize freely.

The control group of 10 subjects was subjected to the identical treatment, except that they were told that they were control subjects for a sensory deprivation experiment. The panic button was eliminated for this group. The formal experimental treatment of these two groups of subjects was the same in terms of the objective stress—four hours of isolation. However, the demand characteristics had been purposively varied for the two groups to study the effect of demand characteristics as opposed to objective stress. Of the 14 measures which could be quantified, 13 were in the predicted direction, and 6 were significant at the selected 10% alpha level or better. A Mann-Whitney U test has been performed on the summation ranks of all measures as a convenient method for summarizing the overall differences. The one-tailed probability which emerges is $p = .001$, a clear demonstration of expected effects.

This study suggests that demand characteristics may in part account for some of the findings commonly attributed to sensory deprivation. We have found similar significant effects of demand characteristics in accounting for a great deal of the findings reported in hypnosis. It is highly probable that careful attention to this variable, or group of variables, may resolve some of the current controversies regarding a number of psychological phenomena in motivation, learning, and perception.

In summary, we have suggested that the subject must be recognized as an active participant in any experiment, and that it may be fruitful to view the psychological experiment as a very special form of social interaction. We have proposed that the subject's behavior in an experiment is a function of the totality of the situation, which includes the experimental variables being investigated and at least one other set of variables which we have subsumed under the heading, demand characteristics of the experimental situation. The study and control of demand characteristics are not simply matters of good experimental technique; rather, it is an empirical issue to determine under what circumstances demand characteristics significantly affect the subject's experimental behavior. Several empirical techniques have been proposed for this purpose. It has been suggested that control of these variables in particular may lead to greater reproducibility and ecological validity of psychological experiments. With an increasing understanding of these factors intrinsic to the experimental context, the experimental method in psychology may become a more effective tool in predicting behavior in nonexperimental contexts.

REFERENCES

Asch, S. E. *Social psychology.* New York: Prentice-Hall, 1952.

Brunswik, E. *Systematic and representative design of psychological experiments with results in physical and social perception.* (Syllabus Series, No. 304) Berkeley: Univer. California Press, 1947.

Damaser, Esther C., Shor, R. E., & Orne, M. T. Physiological effects during hypnotically-requested emotions. *Int. J. clin. exp. Hypn.,* in press.

Frank, J. D. Experimental studies of personal pressure and resistance: I. Experimental production of resistance. *J. gen. Psychol.,* 1944, **30,** 23–41.

Orne, M. T. The demand characteristics of an experimental design and their implications. Paper read at American Psychological Association, Cincinnati, 1959. (a)

Orne, M. T. The nature of hypnosis: Artifact and essence. *J. abnorm. soc. Psychol.,* 1959, **58,** 277–299. (b)

Pierce, A. H. The subconscious again. *J. Phil., Psychol., scient. Meth.,* 1908, **5,** 264–271.

Riecken, H. W. A program for research on experiments in social psychology. Paper read at Behavioral Sciences Conference, University of New Mexico, 1958.

Rosenthal, R. On the social psychology of the psychological experiment: With particular reference to experimenter bias. Paper read at American Psychological Association, New York, 1961.

Sarbin, T. R. Contributions to role-taking theory: I. Hypnotic behavior. *Psychol. Rev.,* 1950, **57,** 255–270.

Shor, R. E. Explorations in hypnosis: A theoretical and experimental study. Unpublished doctoral dissertation, Brandeis University, 1959.

Stare, F., Brown, J., & Orne, M. T. Demand characteristics in sensory deprivation studies. Unpublished seminar paper, Massachusetts Mental Health Center and Harvard University, 1959.

Selection 76 INTRODUCTION

It has been emphasized throughout this book that man's behavior is determined by biological, psychological, and sociocultural factors. Many of these determiners are forces over which the behaving individual has little or no control. For this final selection, I have chosen to reprint a previous paper of mine in which I examined the biochemical, genetic, psychodynamic, and sociocultural forces which shape us. The paper concludes with some philosophical and theological perspectives on man.

Selection 76	IMAGES OF THE LONELY CROWD*

JAMES A. DYAL
Texas Christian University

Therapist: Perhaps we can begin by your telling me why you are here.

Patient: I really don't know why I'm here. I'm not having a nervous breakdown or anything—I doubt if there is anything wrong; I feel normal enough most of the time. I'm a regular guy—just like anyone else, but sometimes I'm not sure what is wrong, but I just don't seem to be getting as much out of life as I should—sometimes I just go into a slump and can't do anything—you see, I'm an artist, and sometimes I just freeze up and can't do anything for weeks—and when I feel myself not being able to do anything creative, I tighten up even further and get more anxious—and that's the phase I'm in now. I was hoping that you could give me a tranquilizer or something, and make me feel better. I'm sure you've seen problems like this before; surely you can tell me what I'm doing wrong—if you'll just tell me what I'm doing wrong, I'll certainly try to change.

Therapist: As you see it, you're not sure there is a problem at all, but you do find yourself being anxious and unable to paint, and you'd like me to take away your anxiety and show you what you're doing wrong.

Patient: Yes, I guess that's it. You know, another

thing that bothers me is that sometimes I just don't care about my work. It's funny; I'm anxious, but I just don't care, too—this was especially true when I worked for that department store as a commercial artist. The head of the department was a businessman type instead of an artist—his only concern was whether or not it would sell. He always used to say, "I don't care if it's good art; I want it to grab people's attention and sell merchandise." He was a real bastard—wouldn't let you think for yourself—it had to be his way. You know, I really tried at that job at first, but finally I just got the "I don't give a damn" attitude. It was about this time that I started drinking quite a bit. I got to the point where I just didn't have much control over it—well, in fact, I had no control—but I'm a little better; I joined AA, and that has helped. I feel a part of this group, and I think they are really concerned about me, and I've learned to help other people. But I'm not over the hump yet; I still don't trust my control.

Another thing that bothers me—before I went to college I was a pretty introverted person; I used to really enjoy just spending time by myself—you know, like the solitude of a long walk in the woods, just listening to the sounds, the birds, rustling leaves, just feeling the cool earth—just thinking and feeling. I really missed that in college; there it was so frantic. But not at first, at first I was pretty much to myself, then I got on this kick of trying to get other people to like me. I got into so many activities—they were all worthwhile, I guess, but I felt so frantic and fragmented at times. But I'll have to admit that I became pretty smooth socially; I'm usually the life of the party. Yet, sometimes I feel that I'm such a phony—like I'm putting on a mask

* Slightly abridged from James A. Dyal, "Images in the Lonely Crowd," *Vital Speeches*, 31: 729–735, 1965.

481

for other people to see—you know, sometimes I find myself arguing against things that I really believe, just because I am sensitive to what other people expect of me. I just don't stand up for my own convictions, until I'm not sure I have any feelings or thoughts that are my own—I seem to be constantly criticizing myself—and yet, I don't know my real self at all.

You know, I had a dream the other night. I was at this cocktail party—it was at this really sumptuous home; everything was elegant, and I was very smooth and agreeable—just like everyone else—we were all very sociable—and suddenly, the scene changed—the sounds of the party faded into the sounds of a stream near my special place when I was a boy—and then the scene shifted back to the party, and the walls had turned to mirrors, and looking in the mirror we saw ourselves, and there was nothing there —we were transparent; there was no substance in us—our faces were all alike—we were interchangeable—and I had this terrible feeling of loneliness and foreignness; I reached out for my friends, and they for me, but we couldn't touch —we were strangers to each other—we tried to escape, but there was no way out. I woke up in a cold sweat, sick to my stomach and with a terrible feeling of having lost something very important—and the sickening fear that I would never find it again—it was a terribly frightening dream—but it did have one good effect—as soon as I woke up I went to my sketch pad and tried to draw that last scene—I'm going to develop that sketch into something really good, and I already have a name for it. I'll call it "Images in the Lonely Crowd."

You have just heard portions of psycho-diagnostic interview with Mr. West Mann. Many of the important symptoms of his sickness are clear: he is anxious; he is apathetic; he longs for a time when he was more at one with himself, when he was less conflicted and fragmented. He has a feeling of a loss of control over his own life. His feelings and thoughts seem to be isolated from each other; he is split and caught; he wants a way out, but finds no exit.

Although the symptoms are clear, the diagnosis and treatment are obscure. His is a difficult case, and we shall need to consult with many specialists in order to make sense of his sickness.

Since the causes are many and diverse, no one could hope to be very knowledgeable in more than a few of the areas. I consider it my task to point to some of the directions, to ask some of the right questions, to raise some of the important issues, but certainly not to provide the answers. I'm going to begin with chemical and biological forces which serve to limit us or to free us.

The biochemists have begun to build compounds whose ultimate effect on mankind may be far greater than the product of the nuclear physicists. As a result of their efforts, we have already provided the psychiatrists with a vast arsenal of drugs for the control of human behavior. We have the major tranquilizers, such as Chlorpromazine and other phenothiazine derivatives, which are effective in controlling the symptoms of schizophrenia and other psychoses. We have minor tranquilizers, including such meprobamate compounds as Equanil and Miltown, which are effective in relieving anxiety. We have stimulant drugs, such as amphetamine, which make you feel good, like everything is going well; reduce your fatigue and, thus, help to overcome tiredness and apathy; help you to be someone else. We have monoamine oxidase inhibitors, which have long-term antidepressant effects. We have drugs which mimic psychotic reactions, such as LSD-25 and Ditran —or perhaps you would like to have a religious experience—you can get Christ in a capsule in the form of psilocybin. Psychiatrists are using these drugs to control the mind *now.*

Most of the available evidence concerning the ability of drugs to control the mind or to control behavior comes from exactly this clinical use. The physician usually does not worry too much about the social goodness or badness of controlling behavior, since many patients come to him asking that their behavior, feelings, or thoughts be controlled. Other patients, of course, are brought to him by relatives or by society because their behavior is such that others feel it needs control. (Cole, p. 113.)

Drugs can be used to establish "good" behavior and abolish "bad" behavior. The scientist tends to feel that it is not his place to say how laboratory knowledge will be used—and since the physician is too busy treating patients and fighting Medicare to worry about the social consequences of his treatments, who is to decide what is good or bad behavior? What government agency will decide what are good or bad thoughts? If we begin to look for biological determinants of Mann's behavior, we need to start at the beginning—at conception—and here again the biochemists and geneticists are showing us how our structure is so completely dependent on the unique messages for development that are coded in DNA molecules—the specific patterns of structure are unique—the specific person is unique from conception—yet he is already molded by the code of DNA with the aid of chemical messengers of RNA. I, for one, am thankful for this molding and complete determination of our structure. Who wants seven fingers on one hand and three on the other? I prefer to have reasonably stereotyped ears!

To look a step further, structure is intimately tied to function, and it appears that a case can be made for even complex behavior such as intellectual functioning and general temperament being determined in part by genetics. It is not an extravagant generalization to say that *we are to a large extent what our genes make us.*

Furthermore, it appears that we have a long tradition behind us which controls us in most subtle ways. As he appears at birth, before the cultural conditioning gets underway, the human child is a wild animal, the product of millions of years of evolution. Is this product basically a creator or a destroyer? On the basis of anthropological researches of Professor Raymond Dart, Robert Ardrey argues in *African Genesis* that man is descended from Cain; "Man is a predator whose natural instinct is to kill with a weapon. . . ." It is a cosmic irony that an instinct for safeguarding the survival of the species has "become in *Homo sapiens* a prime mover towards destruction." (Ardrey, 1963, p. 352.) Is the exquisite complexity of the DNA helix to end in a hydrogen thermonuclear reaction? Or, perhaps the biochemists will save us after all, by learning to rearrange our molecules so that hostility and self-destruction are no longer potentials in the genetic package. It may not occur by 1984, and it may occur too late—or it may occur too soon.

I should also mention that biochemists, biologists, and psychopharmacologists are beginning to pin down much more precisely the ways in which motivation, emotion, and learning depend on stimulation of neural centers in the hypothalamus, or in the septal area of the brain. Immediate situational aggression or long-term chronic aggression may depend on the proportion of adrenalin or nor-adrenalin secreted by the adrenal medulla. High adrenalin produces fear and anxiety and a tendency to withdraw or flee; high nor-adrenalin produces anger and attack. Furthermore, the importance of *genetic* factors here is tentatively suggested by the fact that analysis of the adrenals of lions shows a predominance of nor-adrenalin, while that of rabbits shows a predominance of adrenalin. *It is not too much to say that we are in large part what our glands make us.*

Having considered at least some highpoints of biological and biochemical determination, I want now to move to an examination of the multiplicity of forces outside the individual which push or pull him in one direction or another. Here, of course, we have the whole set of sociocultural processes. I certainly avow the potential dehumanizing effects of mass society, in education, in communications, in politics, and in economics. Yet, I must confess from the outset that I have been concerned with the degree to which such considerations have become so commonplace to you as to now be a matter of clichés. And thus you are no longer sensitive to the commonplace.

The dilemma of man in the mid-20th century is seldom whether to fight an obvious tyranny or to succumb; it is rather to be able to identify the tyranny or to know when we have succumbed. The basic question is not now and never has been "to conform or not to conform"; the question is to what do we conform and to what end? The symptoms of conformity which are often pointed to—such as mass housing, mass production, and mass marketing as a common taste in things which permeates all of Western communities—do not really concern me—I'm not really disturbed by the fact that a couple of years ago every American female from 6 to 60 had exactly the same hairdo and that this was determined by the hairdressers of Jacqueline Kennedy, or that all of our men wear ivy league suits—here I believe like the ancient Stoics who felt that one should conform to custom where nothing important was at stake merely on the basis of the least effort. Conformity to mass culture is in many ways less disconcerting than conformity in our small face-to-face groups. The myth of the mass man to which we should conform is important only to the extent that we permit it to restrict our freedom or to set our goals in our everyday relations. Having said this, the problem is to know when it is doing so. The subtlety of the discriminations which we must make and their cultural importance is discussed by William Whyte in *The Organization Man* when he says,

There are only a few times in organization life when [man] can wrench his destiny into his own hands— and if he does not fight then, he will make a surrender that will later mock him. But when is that time? Will he know the time when he sees it? By what standards is he to judge? He does feel an obligation to the group; he does sense moral restraints on his free will. If he goes against the group, is he being courageous or stubborn? Helpful or selfish? Is he, as he so often wonders, right after all? If he suppresses his own ideas, if he doesn't respond and a controversial point doesn't get debated, were these acts of group co-operation or individual surrender? Too often, even the ability to ask such questions is surrendered, yet, it is in the resolution of a multitude of such dilemmas . . . that the real issue of individualism lies today. (p. 15.)

In *The Organization Man* we see three themes which are an integral part of what Mr. Whyte calls the 20th Century Social Ethic, which has superseded the Protestant Ethic. The first of those is scientism, which is the implicit assumption that eventually all human problems will give way to scientific solutions, that the procedure and assumptions which have worked well for physics will eventually yield an exact science of man—and that much scientific knowledge is already available and is to be applied by social engineers whose good will is overpowering and without question. The Machiavellian hell of the 21st century is not likely to be engineered by "Big Brother's bad henchmen," but by a mild-looking group of therapists who, like the Grand Inquisitor, would be doing what they did to help you. Specifically, they will engineer a society in which you can belong, in which you can savor the security of total integration into the Group (with a big G). Of course, in order to belong, you must *adjust* yourself to the group rather than vice versa. "The rock of salvation is the group and malad-

justment is disagreement with it." (Whyte, p. 42.)

The Good Society will "be a society unified and purged of conflict." (Whyte, p. 51.) Although I do not encourage conflict for the sake of conflict, it is to my way of thinking a powerful stimulus to creative action, and I am reluctant to see conflict discouraged. The present period of racial conflict and civil disobedience is much to be preferred to a status quo of injustice and limitation of freedom. The Negro finally insists on economic, political, and educational freedom now—on the other hand, psychological freedom cannot be won in a picket line or a 50-mile march.

The themes of scientism and belongingness merge into the theme of togetherness, in which the false underlying assumption is that the group is superior to the individual. Witness the recent emphasis on brain storming as the key to creative thinking. Furthermore, the ultimate aim of the group-dynamics people is to achieve agreement; the particular solution is less important than the fact that everybody feels good about it. This unreasonable exalting of the "we" feeling makes it more difficult to achieve an "I" feeling. The antagonism to the individual personality which is inherent in the Social Ethic is nicely illustrated by the device developed by the Harwald Company, called a Group Thinkometer. "The Group Thinkometer is an electric meter the dial of which is graduated in degrees of interest. Feeding into it are ten remote control switches which can be distributed around," (Whyte, p. 63) or preferably under a conference table. By pressing the switch, each person can indicate disapproval of an idea which is being proposed by someone else; thus one can veto a colleague's idea without his knowing who did it. The Harwald Company proudly suggests that their device has eliminated the personality factor almost entirely. Although it is probably true that most group-relations people would shun this device, it does seem to be a symbolic fruit of the Social Ethic.

Clark Kerr, who is still President of the University of California at Berkeley, feels that there is so much danger in groupism that we should enter into group allegiances only tentatively. He says,

The danger is not that loyalties are divided today

but that they may be undivided tomorrow. I would urge each individual to avoid total involvement in any organization; to seek to whatever extent lies within his power to limit each group to the minimum control necessary for performance of essential functions; to struggle against the effort to absorb; to lend his energies to many organizations and give himself completely to none; to teach children, in the home and in the school, "to be laws to themselves and to depend on themselves." As Walt Whitman urged us many years ago—for that is the well source of the independent spirit. (Whyte, p. 51.)

In order to be a successful follower of the Social Ethic, Western man must be able to be sensitive to the expectations of others, not because he is interested in others, but because he must use them to tell him what to say, what to think and feel, who to be. David Reisman in *The Lonely Crowd* describes the typical American man as other-directed—

a sort of "radar man" who lives as though he wore a receiving set on his head in order to get signals from everyone else as to what he should believe and how he should behave. He is sensitive to social situations in the sense of wanting to do what is expected, to conform, to avoid ideas or behaviors that might be disapproved. He is dependent on society in much the same way that a child is dependent on his parents.

A similar view appears in Erich Fromm's discussion of the marketing orientation as typical of Western man. All transactions with other people or things are viewed in the mode of the fundamental relation between buyer and seller. Even in his closest relationships, such as in love relations, the other person is valued in terms of desirability on the appearance and personality markets, and each person enters into the marriage contract with an exchange of personality packages with a hope for a fair bargain.

I view Fromm's concept of marketing orientation as a sub-species of a more general description of Western culture which is in great contrast with Eastern culture; namely, our tendency to be *product*-oriented rather than *process*-oriented. We exalt the end of our efforts and value little the process whereby we attain the goals—and the goals themselves are relatively static, being enmeshed so completely

in the definition of a good man as an economically successful man who is able to acquire things.

This product orientation pervades every facet of our culture; it manifests itself in education as an emphasis on the practical; for example, the most popular stereotype of the scientist really describes the technician or inventor who is the applier of science. Even among our liberal arts undergraduates it is subtly represented in the disparagement of pure research which has no immediately obvious consequences. It is my feeling that one of the major causes of a lack of involvement of many liberal arts majors in their studies is an unrecognized guilt feeling about not doing something that has an obvious pay-off in the market place, an attitude which is all too often reinforced by parents who are also victims of the marketing orientation. Knowing for the sake of knowing— the richness, excitation, frustration, exaltation of the knowing process is sacrificed to the flatness of the educational product—a grade and a degree. The American theme is knowing for the sake of doing, and doing for the sake of acquiring, and acquiring because our possessions provide tangible testimony to others and especially to ourselves of our success in the market place—they reassure us that we are good people.

Fromm points out "how drastically commercial categories have entered even religious thinking" by quoting the following passage from an article by Bishop Sheen on the birth of Christ. Sheen says:

Our reason tells us that if anyone of the claimants for the role of God's son came from God, the least that God could do to support His Representative's claim would be to preannounce His coming. [After all, even] automobile manufacturers tell us when to expect a new model. (p. 4.)

A more extreme statement was made by Billy Graham, "I am selling the greatest product in the world; why shouldn't it be promoted as well as soap?" (Fromm, 1955, p. 118.) Or another rather exceptional example comes from the advice given by the Protestant Council of New York City to speakers on radio and television programs. I quote:

Subject matter should project love, joy, courage,

hope, faith, trust in God, and good will. Generally avoid condemnation, criticism, controversy. In a very real sense we are "selling" religion, the good news of the Gospel. Therefore admonitions and training of Christians on cross-bearing, forsaking all else, sacrifices, and service usually cause the average listener to turn the dial. . . . As apostles, can we not extend an invitation, in effect: "Come and enjoy our privileges, meet good friends, see what God can do for you." (Whyte, p. 418.)

In economics the competition inherent in capitalism has provided us with an affluent society which may provide individuals with increased personal freedom—it is as difficult to fault the abolition of poverty as it is to object to striking the chains from slaves. Yet, for the vast middle class of America, economic affluence may provide the very chains that bind them in continual slavery to things and the immediate satisfaction of all desires. The hucksters of television ask us to be a part of the smoothly functioning affluent group—join the *sociables* and drink Pepsi—and, of course, we all know that Spring is the most *desirable* cigarette that we can smoke. The Tube projects before us, a true-to-life version of Huxley's *Brave New World* in which the dominant ethic is to have fun. "Never put off till tomorrow the fun you can have today." Having fun consists in the satisfaction of "taking in" commodities. ". . . sights, food, drinks, cigarettes, people, lectures, movies, books—all are consumed, swallowed." (Fromm, 1956, p. 87.) As Fromm puts it,

The world is one great object for our appetite, a big apple, a big bottle, a big breast; we are the sucklers, the externally expectant ones, the hopeful ones—and the eternally disappointed ones. Our character is geared to exchange and to receive, to barter and to consume; everything, spiritual as well as material objects become an object of exchange and of consumption. (1956, p. 87.)

As you have seen, the sociocultural character analysis which I have pieced together reflects primarily the views of William Whyte, David Reisman, and Erich Fromm, and it is their diagnosis of Western man in the 1950s. To what extent is it still a valid description for the 1960s? Have these conformity rebels had sufficient influence in our society, so as to initiate a counter revolution? No doubt, they have had some effect, but hasn't their influence been blunted and encapsulated by intellectualism about the diagnosis itself? Have we protected ourselves from the caustic commentaries of the 1950s by turning them into the cliches of the 1960s?

As much as I would like to continue to center on modern man from a sociocultural perspective, I must leave time for the diagnostic evaluations of the psychologist, the theologian, and the philosopher.

The psychologist occupies the broad domain from psychopharmacology and psychobiology on the one hand to social psychology on the other. He is sensitive to the multiplicity of genetic, biological, and sociocultural factors which restrict man's freedom and determine his behavior. Most psychological images of man accept and contribute heavily to the conception of man as essentially unfree. Freudian psychology, for example, tells us how we are controlled by early experience and unconscious inner impulses over which we have no control. Another alienating force within psychology has been the cult of adjustment. The force of this view has been for the psychologist to capitulate to sociocultural norms in his definition of normality. It is the task of the parents to facilitate the child's adjustment to society, with little mention of the possibility of changing society. Such a passive model of man has to be stretched beyond credibility in order to understand a man like Martin Luther King. The bulk of our psychological images of man view him as determined

by his heredity, his intelligence, his personality type, perhaps even his tendency toward mental aberration. He is above all the product of his conditioning—the inevitable result of the fortuitious events which have shaped his behavior. Many of our most astute behavioral scientists agree that this process of conditioning, of shaping up the individual's behavior, will not much longer be left to chance, but will be planned. Certainly the behavioral sciences are developing a technology which will enable us to control the individual's behavior to a degree which at the present moment would seem fantastic. (Rogers, 1963, p. 271.)

Thus, the two major contemporary themes in psychology—behaviorism and Freudianism—

have contributed to the dehumanization and loss of identity of man. Yet, in spite of these overwhelming forces which seek to stamp out freedom, the need for identity is strong. In fact, everyone succeeds in forming some unique emotional and rational interpretation of himself in relation to the world and thus establishes some sort of an identity. The identity crisis is especially crucial during the period of adolescence and early adulthood—yet, for the truly *healthy* person the definition of self continues throughout his life. The neurotic, on the other hand, tends to accept a premature solution to his identity crisis. This results in an immature safety-oriented person who cannot tolerate feelings of normal anxiety and motivational or cultural conflicts. The safety-oriented person identifies himself with those sources of strength and power around him. He can feel secure by acquiring *things*; and he identifies himself with what he possesses. He can also avoid further explorations of himself by identifying himself with the group. Through group status and role identifications a certain sense of identity is attained. Nation, religion, or occupation serve as thought quinchers and we accept a cliché as ourselves. "I am an American," "I am a Protestant," "I am a college professor," "I am a husband," "I am a father," and on and on—but there is a lot more to me than any of my roles in singularity or in summation. The person who refuses to recognize this stops short of identifying himself with his highest potential.

The neurotic—and I should say that what I mean by neurotic behavior is self-defeating behavior, and, thus, you should translate the phrase "the neurotic" to mean "each of us to the extent that we are neurotic"—is most characterized by highly defensive behavior. He feels that he must defend himself against his inner impulses. He does so by denial and distortion of these impulses. He denies or distorts his hostile impulses. He refuses to accept himself in his creatureliness. He may project his unacceptable impulses out onto others and perceive the world as a frightening place which is out to get him. Of course, his perception of the world as hostile makes him even more threatened and defensive, and a vicious circle, self-fulfilling prophesy is generated. In our neurosis we are threatened by others who are seen as more powerful, more intelligent, more loving, or more adept at interpersonal relations than we are. We often tend to reduce our anxiety about our relations to others by sacrificing ourselves to the other person or to the group—by complete submission to the group requirements—by making our thoughts and desires fit only those which are approved by our group, we reduce our fear of being rejected by the group. Our motto here seems to be *you won't hurt me if you see how much I need you.* Or we may resolve our conflict with the group by trying to make ourselves independent of the group. We may define ourselves outside of the group and avoid dependence on the group by amassing political or economic power. Success in the market place not only reassures us that we are basically worthy but also permits us to be less manipulated by other people. Regardless of the particular form the behavior may take, the underlying psychodynamic motto seems to be *You can't hurt me because I don't need you.*

In our "caughtness"—in our neurosis—we also fear to recognize our limitations. We prefer to rationalize, blame others and explain away our short comings. Too often we set for ourselves impossible goals and continue to castigate ourselves for falling short of them. In fact, Karen Horney, an eminent psychoanalyst, maintains that a conflict between a neurotically over-idealized self-concept and the individual's actual self is the basis of all neurosis. Man *cannot* actualize his desire for omipotence; thus, from the point of view of psychology, the influence of Christianity in setting Christ as a model for human behavior can have consequences which are tyrannical and self-destructive. This dilemma is a topic of concern for the theologian David Roberts in his book *Psychotherapy and a Christian View of Man.* If divine love, completely unconditional love,

is taken as the norm for human life then insofar as man falls short of it he is sinful. . . . Yet because Christ is regarded as the only man who ever has or even could fulfill this ideal it seems unreasonable that man should be condemned for not fulfilling Christ in themselves. . . . The central question which thus emerges has to do with the effectiveness of ideal standards. . . . The *static* view assumes that ethical and religious progress is most effectively promoted by holding before the eyes of men a vision of perfection which will keep them perpetually ashamed of themselves. . . . This doctrine scolds them for being replicas of Christ and then scolds them if they believe that they could be. (Roberts, pp. 123–124.)

Such a view is called static because it emphasizes the activity of God in granting grace and de-emphasizes man's *continuing* necessity to act to save himself. It tends to foster a view of the relationships between man and God as unchanging and to promote a tendency for the individual to regard *himself* as an unchanging being.

The psychological consequences of this static view of salvation are many: one of them is *hypocrisy*, the condition of gross disparity between the individual's professional beliefs and his behavior.

His action and inward attitudes say more eloquently than words ever can that there is no mutually enriched interplay between the norm he assents to and policies he lives by. Insofar as a man is aware of such hypocrisy either he may be deeply troubled by his failure or he may find ways of remaining fairly jaunty about it. But in both instances the situation perpetuates conflict. (Roberts, p. 125.)

In the first instance he remains caught in an unresolved dispair, a dispair which cuts away his vitality and generates a chronic anxiety against which he must spend most of his life defending. In the second instance he may react in two opposite ways to try to resolve the conflict. He may repudiate himself and put his wicked self aside. Such an affirmation often results in the expression of self-hatred and hatred for mankind under the guise of Christian piety.

The opposite extreme resolution of the conflict is to reject the ideal and initiate a defiant attack upon Christianity, such as represented by Nietzsche. In my opinion, these extreme attempts to resolve the conflict by either repudiating man or repudiating God do not resolve the conflict but merely perpetuate the dispair. More and more I see that there is a close parallel between the psychological concept of neurosis and the theological concept of sin. We should remember that the notion of divine judgment may very well refer to "those conditions in man's soul and his society which keep him estranged from love; and as we look

at the world we may feel that this is punishment enough." (Roberts, p. 122.) "Hell is still very much with us in those states of being which we call neurosis and psychosis." (Mowrer) It may be, as one psychiatrist maintains,

. . . the notion of mental illness has outlived whatever usefulness it might have had and now functions merely as a convenient myth . . . whose function is to disguise and thus render more palatable the bitter pill of moral conflicts in human relations. (Szasz, p. 118.)

We can describe the neurotic sinful person as one who is bound by infantile emotions, whose perceptions of present situations are distorted by carry-overs from previous human relationships which have failed to provide the needed warmth and assurance of love. By describing him as bound to the past, we imply that his freedom of choice is considerably constricted, that his behavior is heavily determined by unconscious factors beyond his control.

The conception of psychological and theological issues which I have been proposing is quite consonant with many facets of the philosophy of existentialism. It seems appropriate to conclude my ruminations with the philosophical, since it has been the time-honored prerogative of the philosopher to have the last word.

The existentialist sees Western man as estranged in a fourfold manner. He is alienated from nature, from himself, from others, and from God. This term alienation has become so common a description that I felt that I needed to go back to Webster so that we might have some common foundation. I found it to have these synonyms: foreign, distant, unsympathetic, remote, and irrelevant. With man's increased urbanization, the rhythmic pulse of nature becomes foreign and irrelevant. Man seldom has an extended opportunity to find himself in awe of nature and to place himself in relation to the universe—past, present, and future. He cannot affirm the words of Pascal:

What I consider the brief span of life, swallowed up in an eternity past and to come, the little space which I occupy, lost in the immensity of space of which I know nothing and which knows nothing of me, I am terrified and I am astonished that I am here rather than there.

We are alienated from ourselves because we abstract ourselves from our feelings. We force our conceptions of ourselves into relatively static, unchanging molds rather than seeing ourselves as a process of becoming. Existentialism thus doesn't make much sense to people who have settled back into a rigid complacent and unyielding view of themselves and other people. It does appeal "to people who are beginning to wonder about themselves, and to see existence as full of questions." (Harper, p. 25.)

It is this search for meaning in oneself which is the basic characteristic and goal of an existential theory of man. Soren Kierkegaard, who may be considered to be the modern founder of the existentialist movement, had as his primary aim in life to tear people away from their commonplace lives and to force them to be really conscious of self—to continually probe and search for an answer to the question—"What sort of being am I?" All other questions are subordinate—all other questions are merely instrumental in answering this big question. Even the questions and procedures of science are useful only to the extent that they help people to answer this question. In fact, it is the view of existentialism that science and the scientific attitude is often one of the very things which keep man from understanding himself. That is, science defines man and the universe in terms of generalizations, abstractions, or essences and places little emphasis on the process of experiencing in the unique individual. Even psychology has, for the most part, patterned itself after the God-science, physics; that is, its emphasis is on laws which hold for groups of people but which tell us very little about a specific, existing individual. Science tends to deaden its subject matter to make it static so that it is easier to conceptualize or think about, and this very fact forces it to have little to say about what it means to exist or to be.

Man is alienated from himself to the degree that he refuses to choose to recognize his own limitations, his primary limitation being his own contingency—the realization that there is nothing necessary about one's existence—that man may cease to exist at anytime. However, the real force of man's predicament becomes existentially meaningful to a person when that person avoids thinking of death in general terms and refers it to himself—that is, the important thing is not the abstraction that all men are mortal, but the fact that I am mortal —that I will die—that there is a specific moment in the future when I will cease to exist.

Thus, as Kierkegaard has put it, the individual "achieves full recognition of himself through being saddled with a tragic sense of life and death." But it is too often the case that this tragedy is too hard for a person to bear, and he thus, time after time, chooses to forget or avoid his contingency. Because the average person is afraid to realize that he is *unique and alone*, he learns many ways to avoid confronting himself by the use of all of the mechanisms of adjustment and defense which the psychologists have discovered. We may narcotize or deaden ourselves either literally, through alcohol, heroin, or Equanil, or psychologically, by repressing and distorting our feelings, or engaging in a flurry of activity, or in choosing to be trivial. Instead of choosing to be ourselves, we often choose to be someone other than ourselves. One way that we do this is by identifying ourselves completely with our social roles and with our facades or false fronts.

Another prevalent way of behaving non-existentially is to choose not to be ourselves through conformity—to let one's self become swallowed up in the generalized man of common responses and attitudes. The person comes to feel that it is dangerous to be different, and although he temporarily escapes the anxiety of non-being in this way, he pays the awful price of loss of his own awareness, his potentialities, and whatever characterizes him as a unique and original being. In striving to conform, man loses himself and thus paradoxically feels alienated from others. The existentialist, in pointing to man's alienation from others, will applaud Erich Fromm when he says,

Human relations are essentially those of alienated automatons, each basing his security on staying close to the herd, and not being different in thought, feeling, or action. While everybody tries to be as close at possible to the rest, everybody remains utterly alone, pervaded by the deep sense of insecurity, anxiety and guilt which always result when human separateness cannot be overcome. Our civilization offers many palliatives which help people to be consciously unaware of their most fundamental human desires, of the longing for transcendence and unity. Inasmuch as the routine alone does not succeed in this, man overcomes his unconscious despair by the routine of amusement, the passive consumption of sounds and sights offered by the amusement industry; furthermore, by the satisfaction of buying ever new things, and soon exchanging them for others. Modern man is actually close to the picture Huxley describes in his *Brave New World:* well fed, well clad, satisfied sexually, yet without self, without any except the most superficial contact with his fellow men. (1956, p. 86.)

Mr. West Mann is alienated from God because he treats people as things and worships things as idols. In Old Testament usage the term alienation was synonymous with idolatry. In idolatry man worships a partial quality of himself, whereas in monotheistic religions God as a wholeness is unrecognizable, undefinable, and ineffable. God is not a "thing," but Christians regress to idolatry by their "grand old man in the sky" theology.

Man projects his power of love and of reason unto God; he does not feel them any more as his own powers, and then he prays to God to give him back some of what . . . he has projected onto God. (Fromm, 1955, p. 122.)

Any religious view which places responsibility for man's freedom and salvation exclusively on the Grace of God where man has no responsibility is from this existentialist view idolatrous. Man's responsibility for himself is emphasized both by Kierkegaard, a Christian existentialist, and by Sartre, an atheist.

Kierkegaard puts it this way—

One cannot know what it is to be a Christian until he knows what it is to exist . . . the Christian heroism is to venture wholly to be oneself as an individual, this definite man, alone before the face of God, alone in this tremendous exertion and this tremendous responsibility. (Harper, p. 59.)

Sartre, on the other hand, cannot stomach any appeal to an authority beyond the individual's own authority. He is disgusted to the point of nausea by the reliance which people place on values set up by others, including religion, and for which the individual takes no personal responsibility.

Thus, whether we are dealing with the Christian or the atheistic brands of existentialism, the first goal and the primary result of an existential approach to life is to make a person aware of what he is and to make the full responsibility of his existence dependent on him. To the extent that he is not willing to confront himself as he really is, in all of his anxiety, hostility, love, and fear, he progressively loses himself and psychologically becomes more and more rigid, less and less free to control his own destiny.

REFERENCES

Ardrey, R.: *African Genesis,* Dell Publishing Co., Inc., New York, 1961.

Cole, J. O.: "Drugs and control of the mind," in Seymour M. Farber and Roger H. L. Wilson (eds.), *Control of the Mind:* Part I. *Man and Civilization,* McGraw-Hill Book Company, New York, 1961.

Fromm, E.: *The Same Society,* Holt, Rinehart and Winston, Inc., New York, 1955.

Fromm, E.: *The Art of Loving,* Harper & Row, Publishers, Incorporated, New York, 1956.

Harper, R.: *Existentialism,* Harvard University Press, Cambridge, Mass., 1958.

Mowrer, O. H.: *Crises in Psychiatry and Religion,* Insight Books, D. Van Nostrand Company, Inc., Princeton, N.J., 1961.

Riesman, D., N. Glazer, and R. Denny: *The Lonely Crowd,* Yale University Press, New Haven, Conn., 1950.

Roberts, D. E.: *Psychotherapy and a Christian View of Man,* Charles Scribner's Sons, New York, 1950.

Rogers, C. R.: "Learning to be free," in Seymour M. Farber and Roger H. L. Wilson (eds.), *Conflict and Creativity,* Part II:, McGraw-Hill Book Company, New York, 1963.

Szasz, T. S.: "The myth of mental illness," *American Psychologist,* **15:** 113–118, 1960.

Whyte, W. H.: *The Organization Man,* Simon and Schuster, Inc., New York, 1956.

INDEX